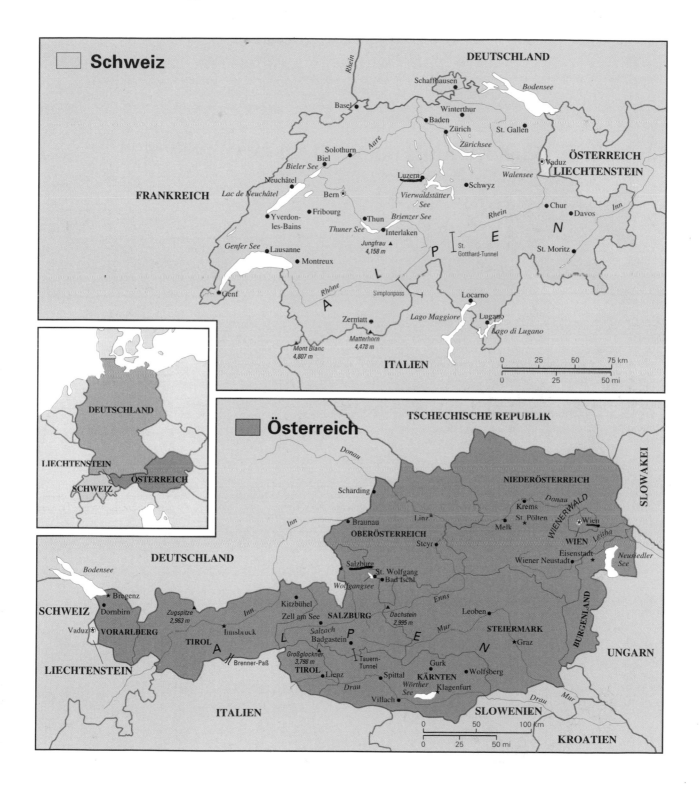

Schweiz

DEUTSCHLAND

Rhein

Schaffhausen

Bodensee

Basel

Winterthur

Baden

Zürich

St. Gallen

Aare

Solothurn

Biel

Bieler See

Luzern

Zürichsee

Walensee

ÖSTERREICH

★ Vaduz

LIECHTENSTEIN

Neuchâtel

FRANKREICH

Lac de Neuchâtel

Bern ✴

Schwyz

Vierwaldstätter See

Rhein

Chur

Davos

Fribourg

Yverdon-les-Bains

Thun

Brienzer See

A   L   P   E   N

Thuner See

Interlaken

Genfer See

Lausanne

Jungfrau
4,158 m ▲

St. Gotthard-Tunnel

St. Moritz

Montreux

Rhône

Simplonpass

Locarno

Zermatt

Matterhorn
4,478 m

Lago Maggiore

Lugano

Lago di Lugano

Mont Blanc
4,807 m

ITALIEN

0   25   50   75 km

0   25   50 mi

DEUTSCHLAND

LIECHTENSTEIN

SCHWEIZ

ÖSTERREICH

Österreich

TSCHECHISCHE REPUBLIK

Donau

SLOWAKEI

Scharding

NIEDERÖSTERREICH

Krems

Donau

Inn

Braunau

Linz ★

St. Pölten

Melk

WIENERWALD

Wien ✴

OBERÖSTERREICH

Steyr

WIEN

Leitha

Salzburg

St. Wolfgang

Bad Ischl

Eisenstadt

Wiener Neustadt ★

Neusiedler See

Bodensee

Wolfgangsee

Enns

Bregenz ★

Kitzbühel

Leoben

SCHWEIZ

Dornbirn

Zugspitze
2,963 m

Inn

Zell am See

SALZBURG

Dachstein
2,995 m

Mur

STEIERMARK

Vaduz ✴

VORARLBERG

Innsbruck ★

Salzach

Badgastein

A   L   P   E   N

Graz ★

UNGARN

TIROL

A

Großglockner
3,798 m

Tauern-Tunnel

Gurk

LIECHTENSTEIN

Brenner-Paß

TIROL

Lienz

Spittal

Wolfsberg

KÄRNTEN

Drau

Wörther See

Klagenfurt

ITALIEN

Villach

Drau

Mur

SLOWENIEN

0   50   100 km

0   25   50 mi

KROATIEN

Deutsch heute

INTRODUCTORY GERMAN

8TH EDITION

Jack Moeller
Oakland University

Winnifred R. Adolph
Florida State University

Gisela Hoecherl-Alden
University of Maine

Simone Berger
Rösrath, Germany

John F. Lalande II
State University of New York at Oswego

Houghton Mifflin Company

Boston   New York

Publisher: Rolando Hernández
Sponsoring Editor: Van Strength
Development Manager: Sharla Zwirek
Development Editor: Peggy Potter
Editorial Assistant: Patricia Osborne
Project Editor: Harriet C. Dishman/Stacy Drew, Elm Street Publications
Senior Production/Design Coordinator: Carol Merrigan
Senior Manufacturing Coordinator: Priscilla J. Bailey
Senior Marketing Manager: Tina Crowley Desprez
Associate Marketing Manager: Claudia Martínez

Cover image: Gerhard Richter, German, born 1932, *Vase,* 1984, oil on canvas, 224.8 cm × 200 cm (88 ½ × 78 ¾ inches), Museum of Fine Arts, Boston/Juliana Cheney Edwards Collection, 1985.229, © Museum of Fine Arts, Boston

Printed in the U.S.A.

Library of Congress Control Number: 2002117262

Student Text ISBN: 0-618-33829-2
Instructor's Annotated Edition ISBN: 0-618-33830-6

56789-DOW-10 09 08 07

Contents

EINFÜHRUNG

Wie heißt du?   1

KAPITEL 1

Guten Tag! Wie geht's?   23

An Overview of Your Textbook's Main Features

By maintaining a focus on building your listening, speaking, reading, and writing skills, **Deutsch heute** has become a classic among introductory German texts. You learn grammar in a clear and concise format while being introduced to contemporary life and culture in German-speaking countries through a cast of recurring characters. This cast appears in the *Bausteine* and in some readings and exercises, as well as in the *Arbeitsheft* and tests. Familiar characters and the integration of all program components—workbook, video, and function-based activities—foster language learning and skill development.

The **Deutsch heute** text consists of an introductory chapter (*Einführung*) plus 12 regular chapters (*Kapitel*).

Chapter Opener

Each chapter opens with a photo, which sets the scene and introduces the chapter's cultural theme.

The *Lernziele* objectives establish clear learning goals in five basic areas: communication, reading, culture, grammar, and vocabulary.

Recurring Cast of Characters Engages Learners

Throughout the **Deutsch heute** program, you are engaged in the learning process as you follow events in the lives of a group of university students who appear in chapter-opening dialogues, some readings, and many exercises, as well as in the workbook and tests. The cast is introduced on pages xix–xxi.

Bausteine für Gespräche

Wie ist das Wetter?

Im Sommer

FRAU KLUGE: Schönes Wetter, nicht wahr, Professor Lange? Zu schön für die Bibliothek!
PROFESSOR LANGE: Ja, aber es ist zu heiß und zu sonnig. Heute Abend arbeite ich mal im Garten. Da ist alles ganz trocken.
FRAU KLUGE: Vielleicht regnet es morgen ja.
PROFESSOR LANGE: Na, hoffentlich!

Richtig oder falsch?

1. Frau Kluge findet das Wetter nicht schön.
2. Professor Lange findet das Wetter toll.
3. Er arbeitet am Wochenende im Garten.
4. Der Garten ist trocken.
5. Vielleicht schneit es morgen.

Brauchbares

1. In German an adjective that precedes a noun has an ending, e.g., **schönes Wetter.** If the adjective does not precede a noun it has no ending (e.g., **Es ist schön**).
2. The use of little words like **mal, ja,** and **na** is common in colloquial German; they are called flavoring particles. When Professor Lange says **Heute Abend arbeite ich mal im Garten,** he is leaving the exact time vague. In Frau Kluge's statement **Vielleicht regnet es morgen ja,** the **ja** conveys the meaning of *after all.* Professor Lange replies: **Na, hoffentlich!** The word **na** is equivalent to English *well.* Flavoring particles will be discussed further in *Kapitel 3.*

Accessible, Contextualized Language Provides a Focus for Learning

Bausteine für Gespräche   New idiomatic and colloquial phrases are presented in the context of realistic dialogues, which follow the cast of characters through a variety of events in their daily lives. Activities that follow each dialogue provide oral practice (*Fragen, Richtig oder Falsch*) and vocabulary development and expansion (*Erweiterung des Wortschatzes*).

Dialogues are often accompanied by a section called *Brauchbares,* which highlights, explains, or amplifies linguistic features and cultural information.

Erweiterung des Wortschatzes

1. Die Monate +

Der Mai war schön, nicht?   May was nice, wasn't it?

All the names of the months are **der**-words.

Januar	Februar	März
April	**Mai**	**Juni**
Juli	**August**	**September**
Oktober	**November**	**Dezember**

2. Die Jahreszeiten +

der **Frühling**

der **Sommer**

der **Herbst**

der **Winter**

1. Was für ein Monat ist … ? Choose a month and ask your partner what kind of month it is: **Frühlingsmonat, Sommermonat, Herbstmonat,** or **Wintermonat.**

S1: Was für ein Monat ist der Juni?
S2: Der Juni ist ein Sommermonat.

Vokabeln 1

Nouns whose plural forms are commonly used are listed with their plural forms: **die Jahreszeit, -en = die Jahreszeiten.**

Substantive

der **Frühling** spring
der **Geburtstag** birthday
der **Grad** degree *(temperature only)*
der **Herbst** autumn, fall
die **Jahreszeit, -en** season
der **Monat, -e** month
der **Regen** rain

der **Schnee** snow
der **Sommer** summer
die **Sonne** sun
das **Wetter** weather
der **Wind** wind
der **Winter** winter
For the months see page 60.

Verben

bleiben to remain, stay
finden to find; to think
regnen to rain; **es regnet** it's raining

scheinen to shine
schneien to snow; **es schneit** it's snowing
war was *(past tense of* **sein***)*

This section concludes with *Vokabeln 1,* a grouping of some of the chapter's active vocabulary.

Reading Skill Development Fosters Understanding of Culture and Written German

The goal of the *Lesestücke* (Readings) and *Leserunde* (Reading Session) sections is to help you become a more proficient reader. Chapter reading selections in *Lesestücke* introduce you to contemporary life and culture in the three primary German-speaking countries: Germany, Austria, and Switzerland. Pre-reading exercises (*Vorbereitung auf das Lesen*) activate background knowledge and provide direction for accessing the selections. *Beim Lesen* (While Reading) provides questions, tasks, and words or phrases to look for to aid the reading process.

Vorbereitung auf das Lesen

■ Vor dem Lesen

1. Look at the advertisement on the next page and answer the following questions.
   a. What does the advertisement imply about the winter weather in Germany?
   b. What is the weather like in Florida?
   c. How much does a ticket from Frankfurt to Miami cost? Do you find the price expensive (**teuer**), reasonable (**günstig**), or cheap (**billig**)?

■ Beim Lesen

1. In the reading you will find data on the number of inhabitants of Germany, Germany's size, and distances within the country. As you are reading, make notes on the relevant facts about Germany.
2. Which words or concepts in the text would you consider to be relative, depending on a person's experience?
3. Circle or make a list of the cognates.

Like most American exchange students, David takes classes in the German language. One of his assignments is to write a short paper on differences between the United States and Germany. David chooses to concentrate on the weather and geography.

Each reading section concludes with post-reading practice (*Nach dem Lesen*) including written and oral exercises, comprehension questions, pair and group work, vocabulary expansion, and a second grouping of active vocabulary (*Vokabeln 2*).

Recorded on the Student Audio CD, poems in *Leserunde* are introduced by a brief note about the author and the poem.

Ich komme aus Washington D.C. und bin seit° drei Wochen in Tübingen. Ich finde Tübingen sehr schön und auch interessant, aber sehr klein. Am Wochenende war ich in Berlin. Berlin ist toll und sehr groß. Ich denke,
5 Washington ist nicht so groß, aber wie in Washington liegt dort alles weit auseinander°.

Was ist anders in Deutschland? Ganz einfach – Amerika ist groß, Deutschland ist klein. Amerika hat zweihundertachtundsiebzig Millionen Einwohner, Deutschland hat nur dreiundachtzig Millionen. Und Deutschland ist nur etwa halb so groß wie Texas (oder Alberta).
10 Für die Menschen hier sind Distanzen anders. Meine Freunde sagen: „Berlin ist weit weg von Tübingen. Fast 700 km." 700 km finde ich nicht weit. Von Seattle im Nordwesten der USA nach Miami im Südosten sind es fast 5500 km. Das finde ich weit! Aber von Tübingen nach Berlin ist ja nur eine Tagesreise°. Das ist schön in Deutschland. Interessante Städte
15 liegen oft nicht weit auseinander.

Das Wetter ist hier anders. Generell sind die Temperaturen in Deutschland nicht so extrem wie sie manchmal in Nordamerika sind. Hier beeinflusst nämlich° der Ozean das Klima und er beeinflusst es mehr im Norden als im Süden und mehr im Westen als im Osten. Mein Freund Michael kommt aus
20 Hamburg im Norden. Dort ist der Sommer relativ kühl und der Winter ist mild. Aber in München im Süden von Deutschland ist der Winter ziemlich kalt und es schneit oft.

Aber alles ist relativ. Auch Temperaturen! Im Sommer ist es hier nicht so heiß wie in Washington. Washington liegt ja auch circa° 1200 km weiter
25 südlich als Tübingen. Meine Freunde hier finden 33 Grad im Sommer sehr heiß und sagen: „Oh, es ist furchtbar heiß". In Washington ist das ganz normal. Ich glaube, viele Leute hier finden das Wetter sehr wichtig. Sie sagen oft: „Oh je, es regnet" und „Oh je, es ist zu kalt!" oder „Oh, es ist zu heiß". Ich rede nicht so viel über° das Wetter. Das finde ich zu uninteressant. Außer-
30 dem° finde ich Schnee und auch Regen sehr schön. Hoffentlich schneit es viel im Winter. Dann gehe ich in die Schweiz zum Snowboarden.

Brauchbares

1. **km (kilometer):** German-speaking countries use kilometers to measure distance. One kilometer equals .62 mile.
2. Note the phrase in l. 13: **sind es fast 5500 Kilometer** (*it is almost 5500 kilometers*). In German **es** is only a "dummy" subject; the real subject, **5500 Kilometer**, is plural; therefore the verb is plural, i.e., **sind**. With a singular subject the verb would be **ist: Es ist nur ein Kilometer** (*It is only one kilometer*). The equivalent English phrase, *it is*, never changes, whether the real subject is singular or plural.

Nach dem Lesen

1. Ergänzen Sie. Using your notes on the reading, complete the following sentences.

1. Deutschland hat _____ Einwohner.
2. Deutschland ist etwa halb so groß wie _____ .

Leserunde

Rudolf Otto Wiemer (1905–1998) was both a teacher and a writer. His poems, stories, and books made him known to a wide public. Many of his poems contain surprises and twists, not unlike those in the poem "empfindungswörter." This poem contains other elements common to concrete poetry: everyday words, lists, repetition, and variation, all of which cause the listener or reader to see words in a new light.

words of emotion

empfindungswörter°

aha die deutschen
ei die deutschen
hurra die deutschen
pfui die deutschen
5 ach die deutschen
nanu die deutschen
oho die deutschen
hm die deutschen
nein die deutschen
10 ja ja die deutschen

Rudolf Otto Wiemer

Offers a Firm Foundation in the Basic Elements of German Language

Grammatik und Übungen (Grammar and Exercises) present grammatical concepts, explained in English, with illustrative examples, marginal glosses of German grammatical terms, and often with translations and linguistic comparisons to English. The grammar presentations are accompanied by a variety of supporting practice, including listening comprehension, pair work, and illustration- and realia-based activities.

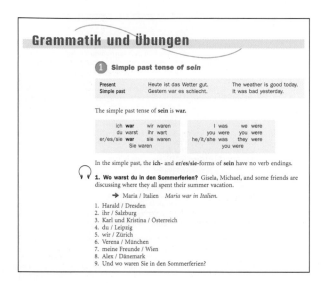

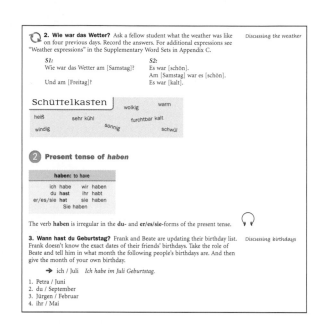

New and recycled vocabulary and grammar concepts and thematic content are reinforced in the *Wiederholung* (Review) section through a variety of practice activities, including situational role-plays.

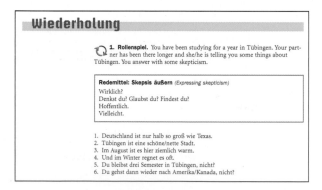

To help you review or prepare for quizzes and exams, *Grammatik: Zusammenfassung* (Grammar: Summary) offers tables, and where useful, brief concept summaries.

Emphasis on The German-Speaking World Develops Cultural Awareness

Land und Leute (The Country and Its People) culture readings in English offer in-depth information on a range of aspects of the German-speaking countries. Illustrative photos, realia, and supporting practice encourage you to think critically about German culture and often require you to make cross-cultural comparisons to your own culture. Icons direct you to the ***Deutsch heute*** website for further investigation into the cultural topic.

Land und Leute

Berlin: Deutschlands „neue" Hauptstadt

www Go to the *Deutsch heute* website at http://college.hmco.com.

The origins of Berlin lie in the twelfth century. In its long history Berlin has served as the capital city of many German states and forms of government, including the monarchy of the Hohenzollerns, the Third Reich, and the German Democratic Republic. In 1990 Berlin became the capital of a newly united Germany. History, geography, and politics have all contributed to make Berlin a cultural center of Europe.

Berlin is a **Stadtstaat** (city state) and Germany's largest city in population (3.39 million). Berlin's population is diverse, with almost 13% consisting of foreigners from 185 countries, the largest group from Turkey. Historically, Berlin was a center of education, commerce, culture, and science. This tradition is still alive today. Berlin has more than 250 state and private centers for scientific research, including fourteen colleges and universities, as well as 150 theaters that offer programs ranging from the classics to the newest artistic forms. It is also the home of 179 museums. With five major museums, the **Museumsinsel** is one of the most important museum complexes in the world. Separate from the **Museumsinsel** are other well-known museums such as the Egyptian Museum (**das Ägyptische Museum**), with the famous bust of Queen Nefertiti, and the new Jewish museum (**das Jüdische Museum**), opened in 2001. Each year Berlin hosts the international film festival, the **Berlinale,** founded in 1951. A more recent annual event is the **Loveparade.** More than a half million people attend this festival for techno and international electronic music that promotes music as a way to international understanding. A visitor to Berlin is struck by the wide variety of architectural styles ranging from the palaces to the remnants of the socialist architecture of East Germany to the modern office buildings erected after unification. Perhaps surprisingly, Berlin also offers a wide choice of outdoor activities, because approximately one-fourth of Berlin's 888 square kilometers consists of green space and one-tenth is covered by lakes and rivers.

Hier ist **BerlinOnline**
www.BerlinOnline.de
🅱 Berlin*Online*
BERLIN AUF EINEN KLICK!

Diskussion

If you visited Berlin, which aspect of the city would you most want to explore—its history, its museums, its parks? Explain your choice.

Engaging Activities Strengthen Listening and Speaking Skills

 The Student Audio CD also contains two in-class activities called *Hören Sie zu* (Listen) in each chapter. Formats include conversations, interviews, a radio report, a commercial, a weather report, and a letter.

---

10. Hören Sie zu.
A. Erstes Hören. Listen to the description of David's room. Indicate how many of the listed objects he has in his room.

_____ Tisch	_____ Lampen	_____ Bilder
_____ Bett	_____ Computer	_____ Poster
_____ Pflanze	_____ Bücherregal	_____ Telefon
_____ Stühle	_____ Bücher	_____ Fenster

B. Zweites Hören. Now listen to the description again. This time complete the description of the objects according to what you have heard. Be sure to provide the correct definite articles.

1. _____ Tisch ist _____.

2. _____ Pflanze ist auch _____.

3. _____ Stühle sind _____.

4. _____ Computer ist _____.

5. _____ Telefon ist _____.

6. _____ Fenster sind _____.

A variety of interactive practice ranging from guided pair work and information gap activities (*Frage-Ecke*) to more open-ended situational activites encourages you to use German creatively to discuss your personal opinions, attitudes, and experiences. New vocabulary (marked by⁺) and Supplementary Expressions in Appendix D help support self-expression in German.

---

7. Frage-Ecke. Find out how old the following people are, when their birthdays are, and what the typical weather in that month is. Obtain the missing information from your partner. **S1**'s information is below; the information for **S2** is in Appendix B.

S1: Wie alt ist Manfred?
S2: Manfred ist 21 Jahre alt. Wann hat er Geburtstag?
S1: Im Januar. Wie ist das Wetter im Januar?
S2: Es ist kalt.

S1:

	Wie alt?	Geburtstag	das Wetter
Manfred		Januar	
Stefanie	30		kühl
Herr Hofer		Juli	heiß und trocken
Frau Vogel	39		
ich			
Partnerin/Partner			

Program Components

Arbeitsheft

The *Arbeitsheft (Workbook/Lab Manual/Video Workbook)* consists of four sections: (1) a workbook with writing exercises coordinated with each chapter of the text; (2) a lab manual that requires you to react orally or in writing to material on the recordings; (3) a video workbook that offers a number of pre- and post-viewing activities for the *Unterwegs!* video; and (4) self-tests with an answer key for correction.

Quia Online Activities Manual

An online version of the *Arbeitsheft* contains the same content as the print version in an interactive environment that provides immediate feedback on many activities.

Audio CD Program

The audio program provides the best possible models of German speech. Using a cast of native Germans, it provides material from the *Bausteine,* the *Lesestücke,* exercises from the *Grammatik und Übungen,* and the short stories that follow *Kapitel 12* of the textbook. In addition, exercises called *Variation* practice the same grammatical features as their corresponding numbers in the text, but appear only in the recordings. The audio program is available in your language lab or for purchase so that you can listen to the recordings at any time.

Student Audio CD

Packaged with your textbook, this audio CD contains the in-class listening activities called *Hören Sie zu* and the *Leserunde* poems that appear in each chapter.

Deutsch heute Multimedia CD-ROM

The dual platform multimedia CD-ROM also packaged with the textbook contains materials that supplement each chapter of *Deutsch heute.* It provides additional interactive practice on various language components: vocabulary, grammar, application, video, and games such as crosswords and timed word searches. Your knowledge in these areas is tested by varied question types, such as fill-in exercises, true or false statements, and multiple-choice activities.

Video Program

A video program entitled *Unterwegs!* reinforces topics and vocabulary found in *Deutsch heute.* The video was shot on location in the university town of Tübingen. It includes twelve five- to seven-minute episodes, featuring a continuing story line about three young people: two university students, Julian and Sabine, and Sabine's cousin Lisa. Pre-viewing and post-viewing activities in the Video Workbook section of the *Arbeitsheft* guide your viewing of the video material so that you may get the most out of the experience.

Deutsch heute Website

The *Deutsch heute* website at **college.hmco.com/ students** relates specifically to *Deutsch heute* and offers an opportunity for you to test yourself on the grammar and vocabulary from each *Kapitel.* You will also be able to work in a culturally authentic context by completing the Web search activities at the *Deutsch heute* website. The site also lists Web addresses for additional information about the cultural topics in *Land und Leute.*

German Web Resources

The website, **college.hmco.com/students,** provides links to existing German sites, maps of the German-speaking world, and transparencies of a general nature that can be downloaded.

Classroom Expressions

Below is a list of common classroom expressions in German (with English equivalents) that the instructor may use in class. Also provided are common expressions you can use to make comments or requests and ask questions.

Terms of Praise and Disapproval

Gut. Das ist (sehr) gut.   Good. That is (very) good.

Schön. Das ist (sehr) schön.   Nice. That is (very) nice.

Ausgezeichnet.   Excellent.

Wunderbar.   Wonderful.

Das ist schon besser.   That's better.

Viel besser.   Much better.

Nicht schlecht.   Not bad.

Richtig.   Right.

Natürlich.   Of course.

Genau.   Exactly.

Sind Sie/Bist du sicher?   Are you sure?

Nein, das ist nicht (ganz) richtig.   No, that's not (quite) right.

Ein Wort ist nicht richtig.   One word isn't right.

Nein, das ist falsch.   No, that's wrong.

Sie haben/Du hast mich nicht verstanden. Ich sage es noch einmal.   You didn't understand me. I'll say it again.

Sie haben/Du hast den Satz (das Wort) nicht verstanden.   You didn't understand the sentence (the word).

Sagen Sie/Sag (Versuchen Sie/Versuch) es noch einmal bitte.   Say (Try) it again please.

General Instructions

Nicht so laut bitte.   Not so loud please.

Würden Sie/Würdet ihr bitte genau zuhören.   Would you please listen carefully.

Stehen Sie/Steht bitte auf.   Stand up please.

Bilden Sie/Bildet einen Kreis.   Form a circle.

Arbeiten Sie/Arbeitet einen Moment mit Partnern.   Work for a minute with partners.

Bringen Sie/Bringt (Bilder) von zu Hause mit.   Bring (pictures) along from home.

(Morgen) haben wir eine Klausur.   (Tomorrow) we're having a test.

Schreiben Sie/Schreibt jetzt bitte.   Please write now.

Lesen Sie/Lest jetzt bitte.   Please read now.

Ich fange (Wir fangen) jetzt an.   I'll (We'll) begin now.

Fangen Sie/Fangt jetzt an.   Begin now.

Hören Sie/Hört bitte auf zu schreiben (lesen).   Please stop writing (reading).

Könnte ich bitte Ihre/eure Aufsätze (Klassenarbeiten, Tests, Übungsarbeiten, Hausaufgaben) haben?   Could I please have your essays (tests, tests, exercises, homework)?

Jeder verbessert seine eigene Arbeit.   Everyone should correct her or his own work (paper).

Verbessern Sie Ihre/Verbessere deine Arbeit bitte.   Please correct your work (paper).

Tauschen Sie mit Ihrem/Tausch mit deinem Nachbarn.   Exchange with your neighbor.

Machen Sie/Macht die Bücher auf (zu).   Open (Shut) your books.

Schlagen Sie/Schlagt Seite (11) in Ihrem/eurem Buch auf.   Turn to page (11) in your book.

Schauen Sie/Schaut beim Sprechen nicht ins Buch.   Don't look at your book while speaking.

Wiederholen Sie/Wiederholt den Satz (den Ausdruck).   Repeat the sentence (the expression).

Noch einmal bitte.   Once again please.

(Etwas) Lauter. (Deutlicher./Langsamer./Schneller.)   (Somewhat) Louder. (Clearer./Slower./Faster.)

Sprechen Sie/Sprich bitte deutlicher.   Please speak more distinctly.

(Jan), Sie/du allein.   (Jan), you alone.

Alle zusammen.   All (everybody) together.

Sprechen Sie/Sprecht mir nach.   Repeat after me.

(Nicht) Nachsprechen bitte.   (Don't) Repeat after me.

Hören Sie/Hört nur zu. Nur zuhören bitte.   Just listen.

Hören Sie/Hört gut zu.   Listen carefully.

Lesen Sie/Lies den Satz (den Absatz) vor.   Read the sentence (the paragraph) aloud.

Jeder liest einen Satz.   Everyone should read one sentence.

Student Responses and Questions

Fangen Sie/Fang mit Zeile (17) an.   Begin with line (17).

Nicht auf Seite (19), auf Seite (20).   Not on page (19), on page (20).

Gehen Sie/Geh an die Tafel.   Go to the board.

(Jan), gehen Sie/gehst du bitte an die Tafel? (Jan), will you please go to the board?

Wer geht an die Tafel?   Who will go to the board?

Schreiben Sie/Schreib den Satz (das Wort) an die Tafel.   Write the sentence (the word) on the board.

Schreiben Sie/Schreibt ab, was an der Tafel steht.   Copy what is on the board.

Wer weiß es (die Antwort)?   Who knows it (the answer)?

Wie sagt man das auf Deutsch (auf Englisch)?   How do you say that in German (in English)?

Auf Deutsch bitte.   In German please.

Verstehen Sie/Verstehst du die Frage (den Satz)?   Do you understand the question (the sentence)?

Ist es (zu) schwer (leicht)?   Is it (too) difficult (easy)?

Sind Sie/Seid ihr fertig?   Are you finished?

Kommen Sie/Komm (morgen) nach der Stunde zu mir.   Come see me (tomorrow) after class.

Jetzt machen wir weiter.   Now let's go on.

Jetzt machen wir was anderes.   Now let's do something different.

Jetzt beginnen wir was Neues.   Now let's begin something new.

Das ist genug für heute.   That's enough for today.

Hat jemand Fragen?   Does anyone have a question?

Haben Sie/Habt ihr Fragen?   Do you have any questions?

Das verstehe ich nicht.   I don't understand that.

Das habe ich nicht verstanden.   I didn't understand that.

Ah, ich verstehe.   Oh, I understand.

Ich weiß es nicht.   I don't know (that).

Wie bitte? *(Said when you don't catch what someone said.)*   Pardon./Excuse me?/I'm sorry.

Wie sagt man ... auf Deutsch (auf Englisch)?   How do you say . . . in German (in English)?

Können Sie den Satz noch einmal sagen bitte?   Can you repeat that please?

Kann sie/er den Satz wiederholen bitte?   Can she/he repeat the sentence please?

Ich habe kein Papier (Buch).   I don't have any paper (a book).

Ich habe keinen Bleistift (Kuli).   I don't have a pencil (a pen).

Auf welcher Seite sind wir? Welche Zeile?   Which page are we on? Which line?

Wo steht das?   Where is that?

Ich habe eine Frage.   I have a question.

Was haben wir für morgen (Montag) auf?   What do we have due for tomorrow (Monday)?

Sollen wir das schriftlich oder mündlich machen?   Should we do that in writing or orally?

Wann schreiben wir die nächste Arbeit?   When do we have the next paper (written work)?

Wann schreiben wir den nächsten Test?   When do we have the next test?

Für wann (sollen wir das machen)?   For when (are we supposed to do that)?

Ist das so richtig?   Is that right this way?

(Wann) Können Sie mir helfen?   (When) Can you help me?

(Wann) Kann ich mit Ihnen sprechen?   (When) Can I see you?

Acknowledgments

The authors and publisher of **Deutsch heute, Eighth Edition** would like to thank the following instructors for their thorough and thoughtful reviews of the Seventh Edition of **Deutsch heute.** Their comments and suggestions were invaluable during the development of the Eighth Edition.

Gabriele W. Bosley, Bellarmine University, KY
Christine Geffers Browne, Brandeis University, MA
Iris Busch, University of Delaware, DE
George A. Everett, University of Mississippi, MS
Ruth V. Gross, University of Texas, Arlington, TX
David Pankratz, Loyola University, IL
Carmen Taleghani-Nikazm, University of Kansas, KS
Gerlinde Thompson, University of Oklahoma, OK

The authors wish to give a special thanks to Elizabeth Thibault, University of Delaware at Newark, for her helpful comments and suggestions. They also express their appreciation to Annina Luck of the Swiss Embassy for providing the list of useful Swiss addresses that appear in the Instructor's Annotated Edition and for suggesting and providing the material on the band *ZüriWest.*

The authors would also like to express their appreciation to the following Houghton Mifflin editorial, art, and design staff and freelancers for their technical and creative contributions to the text: Sharla Zwirek, Development Manager, for organizing the work on this revision and overseeing with efficiency and tact the development of the project to its conclusion; Linda Hadley, Art Editor, for her efforts in finding the appropriate art; Harriet C. Dishman and Stacy Drew of Elm Street Publications who once again managed the production process expertly, efficiently, and with creative contributions; and Marie Deer and Susanne van Eyl, proofreaders, who checked the final text for accuracy and authenticity.

We would like to express special thanks to Peggy Potter, Developmental Editor, and Karen Hohner, Copyeditor, for their invaluable contributions to this new edition of **Deutsch heute**. The final form of the text reflects Peggy's editorial expertise, critical judgment, and keen insights. As an editor of a variety of foreign language texts and teacher of ESL, Peggy has been able to offer many suggestions that have enhanced the usefulness of this text for learning German. Working with Peggy has been an authors' dream for she is ever patient, understanding, and always in good humor. Karen Hohner has been copyeditor of several editions of **Deutsch heute** and of the intermediate text **Kaleidoskop.** For this edition, as for all the previous ones, we are grateful for her careful reading and expert marking of the manuscript, as well as for her additional perceptive and useful suggestions.

Personen

(CAST OF CHARACTERS)

The following fictional characters appear regularly in the dialogues, some of the readings, many of the exercises and also in the workbook and tests. The characters are all students at either the *Universität Tübingen* or the *Freie Universität Berlin (FU Berlin)*.

Gisela Riedholdt (1): First-semester English major with minors in German and art history at the *Universität Tübingen*. Becomes a good friend of Alex. Lives in the same dormitory as Michael. Her home is in Mainz.

Alex Kaiser (2): Third-semester law student. Interested in art. Becomes a good friend of Gisela. Roommate of Uwe. Home is in Hamburg.

David Carpenter (3): American exchange student at the *Universität Tübingen*. Knows Gisela and her friends.

Uwe Ohrdorf (4): Seventh-semester computer major. Alex and Uwe are roommates. Is a good friend of Claudia.

Claudia Arnold (5): Seventh-semester medical student. Is a good friend of Uwe.

Melanie Beck (6): Fourth-semester German major (previously history). Is a good friend of Michael.

Michael Kroll (7): Third-semester English major. Lives in the same dormitory as Gisela. Plays guitar in a band. Is a good friend of Melanie. Home is in Hamburg.

Monika Berger (8): Attends the *FU Berlin (Freie Universität Berlin)*. Sister of Stefan and friend of Gisela from school days in Mainz.

Stefan Berger (9): Attends the *FU Berlin*. Brother of Monika and friend of Gisela.

Peter Clason (10): American exchange student at the *FU Berlin*. Friends with Monika and Stefan. He knew Monika when she was a German exchange student in the U.S.

Diane (11) and Joan White (12): Two Americans who visit Monika and Stefan Berger in Berlin.

Deutsch heute

Wie heißt du?

(Introduction)

Studenten an der Universität Trier

LERNZIELE *(Goals)*

Sprechintentionen *(Functions)*

Asking for and giving personal
  information: name, age, address,
  telephone number
Introducing oneself
Spelling
Working with numbers
Asking what day it is
Asking about colors

Land und Leute
(The Country and Its People)

Writing German addresses
The German language today
The telephone system in the
  Federal Republic of Germany
Making and receiving telephone
  calls

Vokabeln *(Vocabulary)*

The alphabet
Numbers
Days of the week
Objects in a student's room
Colors

Grammatik *(Grammar)*

Gender of nouns
Indefinite article
Pronouns
Noun-pronoun relationship

1

Bausteine für Gespräche *(Building Blocks for Conversation)*

The dialogues in this section will help you acquire a stock of idiomatic phrases that will enable you to participate in conversations on everyday topics.

 This symbol indicates printed material in the text that can be listened to and practiced outside of class using the audio program recordings. These recordings are available for student purchase on audio CDs.

Wie heißt du?

While at the art department to sign up for an excursion to Florence with her art history class, Gisela runs into Alex, who is in the same class but whom she has never really met. After chatting briefly, Gisela and Alex decide to meet before the trip. Then Gisela goes into the office to sign up for the trip to Florence.

Vorm schwarzen Brett

ALEX: Hallo! Ich heiße Alex. Und du?
GISELA: Grüß dich. Ich heiße Gisela.
ALEX: Willst du auch nach Florenz?
GISELA: Ja.
ALEX: Toll! Du, hier ist meine Telefonnummer: 35 67 81. (Drei, fünf, sechs, sieben, acht, eins.)
GISELA: Danke – und meine Telefonnummer ist 79 23 09. (Sieben, neun, zwei, drei, null, neun.)
ALEX: Wie bitte?
GISELA: 79 23 09.
ALEX: Okay. Also dann, bis bald!
GISELA: Tschüs.

Richtig oder falsch? *(True or false?)*   If the statement agrees with what is in the dialogue, say **richtig.** If not, say **falsch.**

1. Gisela will nach Rom.
2. Alex will nach Florenz.
3. Alex' Telefonnummer ist 79 23 09.

Wie heißen Sie?

Gisela is next in line. She goes into the office to sign up for the excursion to Florence.

Im Büro

FRAU KLUGE: Bitte? Wie heißen Sie?
GISELA: Gisela Riedholt.
FRAU KLUGE: Wie schreibt man das?
GISELA: R-i-e-d-h-o-l-t.
FRAU KLUGE: Und Ihre Adresse?
GISELA: Meine Semesteradresse oder meine Heimatadresse?
FRAU KLUGE: Ihre Semesteradresse, bitte.

GISELA: Pfleghofstraße 2 (zwei), Zimmer 15 (fünfzehn), 72070 (sieben, zwei, null, sieben, null) Tübingen.

FRAU KLUGE: Danke, Frau Riedholt.

GISELA: Bitte.

Richtig oder falsch?   If the statement agrees with what is in the dialogue, say **richtig.** If not, say **falsch.**

1. Gisela heißt auch Kluge, Gisela Kluge.
2. Giselas Semesteradresse ist Pfleghofstraße 14.
3. Giselas Zimmer hat die Nummer 15.

Brauchbares   *(Something useful)*

1. Note that when Alex gives Gisela his telephone number, he begins his sentence with **du (Du, hier ist meine Telefonnummer).** Germans often get the attention of people or introduce a thought by using **du.** In English one might well say *hey.*

2. How does the address (i.e., the position of the house number, the street name, and the postal code) in Germany differ from where you live?

3. Alex and Gisela give their telephone numbers in single digits. Many Germans give their numbers in double digits, so that Alex's number would be stated as **fünfunddreißig, siebenundsechzig, einundachtzig.** The numbers in the postal code can also be stated variously, either in double or single digits or in some other combination.

4. **Bitte** has several English equivalents. Can you name three?

5. **Cognates:** Words in different languages that are related in spelling and meaning and are derived from the same source language are called *cognates.* The words are often pronounced differently. There are hundreds of German-English cognates because the two languages have common roots. Name three cognates in the dialogues.

6. **False cognates:** Some words that look the same in German and English may not have the same meaning. These words are "false" cognates. Note that when Alex says: **"Okay. Also dann, bis bald!" also** means *well.* Other meanings of **also** are *therefore, thus, so.* The German word to express the English meaning *also* is **auch.**

Activities preceded by this symbol give you the opportunity to speak with fellow students about your personal feelings and experiences and to learn how to exchange ideas and negotiate in German, either one on one or as a group. The sentences and expressions to be used by one of the partners or members of a group are in the left column; the responses to be used by the other partner or members of a different group are in the right column. Substitute your own words for those in brackets.

New vocabulary is indicated by a raised plus sign ($^{+}$). The definitions of these words are found in the vocabulary lists in the sections called **Vokabeln.** In this chapter the **Vokabeln** section is on pages 18–20. Beginning with *Kapitel 2* the chapters have two **Vokabeln** sections—one in the **Bausteine für Gespräche** section and one in the reading section.

When you say or write something, you have a purpose in mind. In this sense there is a certain linguistic function or intention you are stating or performing, such as exchanging information (e.g., identifying or asking for information), evaluating (e.g., praising, criticizing), expressing emotions (e.g., pleasure, dissatisfaction), getting something done (e.g., asking for help, giving permission), using social conventions (e.g., greeting, excusing oneself). To help you know when to use the words, phrases, or sentences you are learning, the purpose or function is given in the margin.

Getting acquainted

 1. Wie heißt du? Get acquainted with members of your class. Introduce yourself to your fellow students and ask what their names are.

Student/Studentin 1 (S1):
Ich heiße [Dieter]. Wie heißt du?

Student/Studentin 2 (S2):
Ich heiße [Barbara].

Confirming information

2. Heißt du Sarah? See how well you remember the names of at least four fellow students. If you're wrong they will correct you.

Student/Studentin 1 (S1):
Heißt du [Mark Schmidt]?
Heißt du [Monika]?

Student/Studentin 2 (S2):
Ja[+].
Nein[+]. Ich heiße [Karin].

Asking someone's name

3. Wie heißen Sie? Ask your instructor for her/his name.

Student/Studentin:
Wie heißen Sie?

Herr[+]/Frau Professor[+]:
Ich heiße [Lange].

Erweiterung des Wortschatzes

(Vocabulary Expansion)

This vocabulary expansion section contains commonly used words and phrases that supplement those found in the dialogues (**Bausteine für Gespräche**) and in the readings beginning in *Kapitel 1.* You are expected to learn these words so that you will understand them in new contexts and be able to use them to express your own thoughts. The new words and phrases in the **Erweiterung des Wortschatzes** are included in the lists of words that appear in the vocabulary sections (**Vokabeln**).

1. The subject pronouns *du* and *Sie*

Wie heißt **du?**   What is your name? (What are *you* called?)
Wie ist **deine** Telefonnummer?   What is *your* telephone number?

Du is equivalent to *you* and is used when addressing a relative, close friend, or person under approximately 15 years of age. In the tenth grade some teachers start to address pupils with **Sie.** Members of groups such as students, athletes, laborers, and soldiers also usually address each other as **du.** It is used when talking to one person and is referred to as the familiar form. The word for *you* used to address more than one friend, relative, etc., will be explained in *Kapitel 1.*

Dein(e) is equivalent to *your.* It is used with a person to whom you say **du.**

Wie heißen **Sie?**   What is your name? (What are *you* called?)
Wie ist **Ihre** Adresse?   What is *your* address?

Sie is also equivalent to *you* but is a more formal form of address, and is used when addressing a stranger or adult with whom the speaker is not on intimate terms. **Sie** is used when speaking to one person or to more than one person.

Ihr(e) is equivalent to *your* and is used with a person to whom you say **Sie.** In writing, **Sie** and **Ihr(e)** are capitalized.

Dein and **Ihr** modify masculine and neuter nouns. **Deine** and **Ihre** modify feminine nouns. See the section on Gender of nouns on pages 13–14 of this chapter.

Postleitzahlen

In Germany postal codes (**Postleitzahlen**) have five digits and in Austria and Switzerland four. Large cities have several postal codes, each one designating a specific district of that city. German postal codes reveal the geographic location of a town or city. For example, a postal code beginning with 2 indicates a location in northern Germany, e.g., **27765 Hamburg.** A postal code that begins with 8 indicates a location in southern Germany, e.g., **80802 München.**

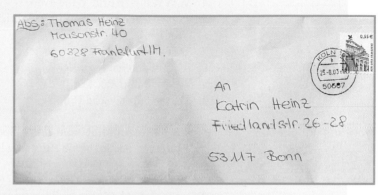

Die Postleitzahlen von Bonn beginnen alle mit 5–.

Diskussion

Look at the letter in the picture. What, if any, are the differences between the way the address is written and the form in your country? These differences are true for Austria and Switzerland, as well as Germany.

www Go to the *Deutsch heute* website at http://college.hmco.com.

2. Das Alphabet

The German alphabet has 26 regular letters and 4 special letters. They are pronounced as follows:

a	ah	**g**	geh	**l**	ell	**q**	kuh	**v**	fau	**ä**	äh (a-Umlaut)
b	beh	**h**	hah	**m**	emm	**r**	err	**w**	weh	**ö**	öh (o-Umlaut)
c	tseh	**i**	ih	**n**	enn	**s**	ess	**x**	iks	**ü**	üh (u-Umlaut)
d	deh	**j**	jot	**o**	oh	**t**	teh	**y**	üppsilon	**ß**	ess-tsett
e	eh	**k**	kah	**p**	peh	**u**	uh	**z**	tsett		
f	eff										

Capital letters are indicated by **groß: großes B, großes W.** Lowercase letters are indicated by **klein: kleines b, kleines w.**

Asking for information

 1. Wie schreibt man das? Ask your instructor or a fellow student for her/his name. Then ask how to spell it. (Use the **Sie**-form in speaking with your instructor: **Wie heißen Sie?**)

→ Wie heißt du?   *Mark Fischer.*
→ Wie schreibt man das?   *Emm-ah-err-kah. Eff-ih-ess-tseh-hah-eh-err.*

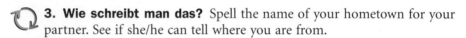 **2. Abkürzungen.** *(Abbreviations.)* Pronounce the following abbreviations and have your partner write them down.

1. CD (= CD)
2. VW (= Volkswagen)
3. BMW (= Bayerische Motorenwerke)
4. WWW (= World Wide Web)
5. PC (= Personal Computer/Political Correctness)
6. USA (= U.S.A.)
7. TV (= Television)
8. ICE (= Intercityexpress)
9. PR (= Public Relations)
10. EU (= Europäische Union)

Providing information

 3. Wie schreibt man das? Spell the name of your hometown for your partner. See if she/he can tell where you are from.

4. Schreiben Sie das. *(Write that.)* Spell several German words to a partner who will write them down. Then reverse roles. You may use the words listed or choose your own.

tschüs
danke
bitte
Adresse
Telefonnummer
Kindergarten
Gummibärchen
Mercedes
Europa

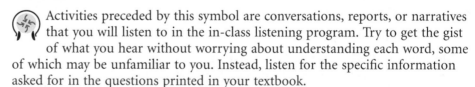 Activities preceded by this symbol are conversations, reports, or narratives that you will listen to in the in-class listening program. Try to get the gist of what you hear without worrying about understanding each word, some of which may be unfamiliar to you. Instead, listen for the specific information asked for in the questions printed in your textbook.

5. Hören Sie zu. Gisela has a summer job working at the information desk of Karstadt, a large department store. This is her first day, so she doesn't know many of the employees' names yet. She has to ask the callers to spell the names. Write down the names you hear on a piece of paper. Three important new words are: **der Nachname** *(surname)*, **der Vorname** *(first name)*, **buchstabieren** *(to spell)*.

Aischa ＿＿. 7 93 23 61–14
Kevin ＿＿. 7 93 23 61–23
＿＿ Losso. 7 93 23 61–07

3. Die Zahlen von 1 bis 1.000

0 = null	10 = zehn	20 = zwanzig	30 = dreißig
1 = eins	11 = elf	21 = einundzwanzig	40 = vierzig
2 = zwei	12 = zwölf	22 = zweiundzwanzig	50 = fünfzig
3 = drei	13 = dreizehn	23 = dreiundzwanzig	60 = sechzig
4 = vier	14 = vierzehn	24 = vierundzwanzig	70 = siebzig
5 = fünf	15 = fünfzehn	25 = fünfundzwanzig	80 = achtzig
6 = sechs	16 = sechzehn	26 = sechsundzwanzig	90 = neunzig
7 = sieben	17 = siebzehn	27 = siebenundzwanzig	100 = hundert
8 = acht	18 = achtzehn	28 = achtundzwanzig	101 = hunderteins
9 = neun	19 = neunzehn	29 = neunundzwanzig	1.000 = tausend

Note the following irregularities:

1. **Eins** *(one)* becomes **ein** when it combines with the twenties, thirties, and so on: **einundzwanzig, einunddreißig.**
2. **Dreißig** *(thirty)* ends in **-ßig** instead of the usual **-zig.**
3. **Vier** *(four)* is pronounced with long [ī], but **vierzehn** *(fourteen)* and **vierzig** *(forty)* are pronounced with short [i].
4. **Sechs** *(six)* is pronounced [ṣeks], but **sechzehn** *(sixteen)* and **sechzig** *(sixty)* are pronounced [ṣeç-].
5. **Sieben** *(seven)* ends in **-en,** but the **-en** is dropped in **siebzehn** *(seventeen)* and **siebzig** *(seventy).*
6. **Acht** *(eight)* is pronounced [axt], but the final **t** fuses with initial [ts] in **achtzehn** *(eighteen)* and **achtzig** *(eighty).*

Note also:

7. Numbers in the twenties, thirties, and so on follow the pattern of the nursery rhyme "four-and-twenty blackbirds":

   24 = **vierundzwanzig** *(four-and-twenty)*
   32 = **zweiunddreißig** *(two-and-thirty)*

8. German uses a period instead of a comma in numbers over 999. German uses a comma instead of a period to indicate decimals.

German	English
1.000 g (Gramm)	1,000 g
4,57 m (Meter)	4.57 m

9. Simple arithmetic:

   Addition (**+** [**und**]): **Fünf und drei ist acht.**
   Subtraction (**−** [**minus**]): **Fünf minus drei ist zwei.**
   Multiplication (**×** or **·** [**mal**]): **Fünf mal drei ist fünfzehn.**
   Division (**÷** [**(geteilt) durch**]): **Fünfzehn durch drei ist fünf.**

6. Rechnen. *(Doing arithmetic.)* Find a partner. On a piece of paper each of you writes out five simple mathematical problems. Read your five problems to your partner and let her/him solve them; then solve your partner's five problems.

Using numbers

S1:
Wie viel[+] ist drei und zwei [3 + 2]?
Wie viel ist zehn minus acht [10 − 8]?

S2:
Drei und zwei ist fünf.
Zehn minus acht ist zwei.

Land und Leute

Die deutsche Sprache heute

German is spoken by more than 200 million people worldwide. It is the first language of 24% of the residents of the European Union—more than any other language. German is the mother tongue of most residents of Germany, Austria, and many regions of Switzerland, as well as Luxembourg, Liechtenstein, and parts of northern Italy, eastern Belgium, and eastern France. The 1990 census of the United States reported that 1.5 million residents speak German at home. Many people associate German with its great poets and thinkers (**Dichter und Denker**) of the past, and it is true that German speakers still play an important role in literature, the arts, and the sciences. However,

German is also an important language for the global economy. Germany is often called the powerhouse of Europe and people who speak German have an important skill for the world economy. German is also an important language for international communications. After English, German is the most widely used language on the Internet and **Deutsche Telekom** is Europe's largest communications company. German speakers love to travel. In many places in the United States, German tourists comprise the largest group of non-English-speaking visitors. For these reasons and many more, approximately 20 million people around the world are learning German as a second language.

Most of them are in central and eastern Europe, but also 68% of Japanese students learn German. You should remember that when you learn German you are not only learning a commercial skill, you are also learning how culture, world view, and language are intertwined.

(top) Teamprojekt an der Technischen Universität Darmstadt; *(bottom left)* Deutsche Touristen in der Mongolei; *(bottom right)* Johann Wolfgang von Goethe (1749–1832), großer deutscher Dichter

Diskussion

www Go to the *Deutsch heute* website at http://college.hmco.com.

1. Discuss in class what you expect of the language-learning process. Which aspects do you think will be interesting or fun? Which aspects do you expect to be difficult? It might be helpful to interview a person who learned English as a second language.
2. Which German companies are you familiar with? Do you use any products produced by German companies?

Frage-Ecke *(Question corner)* activities, such as the one below, contain two charts, each one showing information that the other one lacks. The chart for **Student 1/Studentin 1 (S1)** is printed on the chapter page and the other chart, for **Student 2/Studentin 2 (S2),** is located in Appendix B. Each student looks at one chart to answer questions asked by her/his partner.

7. Frage-Ecke. The charts in this **Frage-Ecke** activity show the postal codes of particular sections of cities in Germany, Austria, and Switzerland. Take turns with a partner and find out the postal codes that are missing in your chart. **S1**'s chart is below; the chart for **S2** is in Appendix B.

S1: Wie ist eine Postleitzahl von Zürich?
S2: Eine Postleitzahl von Zürich ist 8000. Wie ist eine Postleitzahl von Berlin?

S1:

10585 Berlin
_____ Zürich
20095 Hamburg
_____ München
60311 Frankfurt
_____ Wien
5010 Salzburg

Each chapter in **Deutsch heute** contains a number of advertisements, cartoons, and other visual material from magazines, newspapers, or the Internet. Printed with some of the images are questions that ask you to find a particular bit of information. Try to find the information asked for without worrying about understanding every single word in the image. In this case, see if you can find the addresses, telephone numbers, and fax numbers in these ads and read them aloud.

Wie ist die Adresse von La donna?

Wie viel kostet ein Bild bei Foto Beer?

Land und Leute

I. Das Telefon

A s in all countries, the telecommunications system in Germany has changed dramatically in the last ten years. **Deutsche Telekom AG** is the largest service provider in Germany for telephone and Internet services. However, there is a competitive telecommunications market. The billing system for phone calls in Germany operates on a message-unit system. For example, a unit may cost 6 eurocents, but the length of the unit can vary according to the time of day and the type of call—local (**Ortsgespräch**) or long distance (**Ferngespräch**). There are extra charges for local calls when they exceed the number of units included in the basic rate. Calls outside the immediate area require an area code (**Vorwahl**) and incur additional charges.

Most public telephones in Germany are card-operated and can be easily spotted because they display the bright pink **Telekom** logo. Plastic debit cards (**Telefonkarten**) can be purchased at the post office and in many stores. They allow customers a specific pre-paid amount in telephone charges.

The cell phone (**das Handy**) is very popular in German-speaking countries and in Europe generally. In 2001, 75% of the citizens of the EU had cell phones, while in the U.S.A. only 41% of people had them. One reason for this difference is the fact that regular telephone service in Europe is more expensive than in the U.S.A. Despite the popularity of cell phones in Europe, it is illegal in Germany, Austria, and Switzerland to use a hand-held cell phone while driving.

In Deutschland sind die Telefonzellen pink.

Eine Telefonkarte für 5 Euro.

 Go to the *Deutsch heute* website at
http://college.hmco.com.

The fines for using a hand-held cell phone while driving are 40 euros in Germany, up to 21 euros in Austria, 65 francs in Switzerland, and 138 euros in the Netherlands.

Diskussion

1. Do you think that using a hand-held telephone while driving is a good idea? Should it be legal? Why or why not?
2. Compare the major characteristics of the German phone system with your own.
3. Phone numbers in Germany can vary in length. Compare the number of digits in the ads for **La donna** and **Foto Beer** on page 9.

11

EINFÜHRUNG

8. Dein Name? Deine Adresse? Deine Telefonnummer? Ask three of your fellow students for their names, addresses, and phone numbers. Then get the same information from your instructor. Remember to use **Sie** and **Ihre** with your instructor; also be sure to say thank you.

Asking for personal information

S1:
—Wie heißt du?
—Wie ist deine Adresse?
—Wie ist deine Postleitzahl?
—Wie ist deine Telefonnummer?
—Danke.

S2:
—[Julia Meier].
—[17 Wilson Street, Brewer, Maine].
—[04412]
—[989–2913]
—Bitte.

9. Hören Sie zu. You will hear three requests for addresses. As you listen, choose the correct street numbers and the correct postal codes from the list and write them on a sheet of paper.

→ Gisela Riedholts Adresse ist Pfleghofstraße ___2___ , Zimmer 15, __72070__ Tübingen.

2 ▪ 5 ▪ 13 ▪ 32 ▪ 72070 ▪ 72072 ▪ 82211 ▪ 87569

1. Die Adresse von Professor Lange ist Hölderlinallee _____ , _____ Tübingen.
2. Die Adresse von Siggis Snowboardschule ist Walserstraße _____ , _____ Mittelberg.
3. Die Adresse von Autohaus Kärcher ist Panoramastraße _____ , _____ Herrsching am Ammersee.

10. Gespräche (*Conversations*)

A. Wie alt bist du?[+] Find out the ages of four fellow students. Be sure you know their names. Write down the information.

Asking someone's age

S1:
Wie alt bist du?

S2:
Ich bin [19] Jahre alt.

B. Ich heiße … Introduce yourself to the class by giving the information mentioned in the model.

→ Ich heiße _____ . Ich bin _____ Jahre alt. Meine[+] Adresse ist _____ . Meine Telefonnummer ist _____ .

4. Die Wochentage

Welcher Tag ist heute?	What day is it today?
Heute ist Montag.	Today is Monday.
Dienstag	Tuesday
Mittwoch	Wednesday
Donnerstag	Thursday
Freitag	Friday
Samstag (*in southern Germany*)	Saturday
Sonnabend (*in northern Germany*)	
Sonntag	Sunday

Monday (**Montag**) is considered the first day of the week in German-speaking countries. As a result, calendars begin with **Montag** rather than **Sonntag**. **Sonnabend** is a regional variant for Saturday, especially in northern Germany.

11. Welcher Tag ist heute? Ask a fellow student what day it is today.

→ Welcher Tag ist heute? *Heute ist [Mittwoch].*

12. Frage-Ecke. You and a partner are talking about Rebecca, Dennis, Sara, and Kevin. Take turns finding out which subjects they study on which days. Note that Germans use the word **am** with days of the week: **am Montag.** **S1**'s information is below; the information for **S2** is in Appendix B.

S1: Was hat Dennis am Dienstag und Donnerstag?
S2: Mathe. Was hat Dennis am Montag, Mittwoch und Freitag?
S1: Deutsch. Was hat...

S1:

	Montag	Dienstag	Mittwoch	Donnerstag	Freitag
Dennis	Deutsch		Deutsch		Deutsch
Rebecca		Biologie		Biologie	
Sara		Musik		Musik	
Kevin	Psychologie		Psychologie		Psychologie

II. Ein Telefongespräch

Telephone customs vary from culture to culture. Read through the following informal telephone conversation and see if you can identify any differences between your telephone manners and this conversation. How can you change the English version to make it more idiomatic and appropriate in English?

—Ingrid Breimann.
—Hallo Ingrid. Hier ist Tanja. Kann ich bitte mit Thomas sprechen?
—Hallo Tanja. Thomas ist nicht zu Hause. Er spielt heute Fußball.
—Ach ja, richtig. Hmmmmm. Dann rufe ich am Montag wieder an. Bis dann, Ingrid. Tschüs.
—Tschüs, Tanja.

—*Ingrid Breimann.*
—*Hello Ingrid. Tanja here. May I please speak to Thomas?*
—*Hello Tanja. Thomas isn't at home. He's playing soccer today.*
—*Oh, that's right. Hmm. Then I'll call back on Monday. Till later, Ingrid. Bye.*
—*Bye, Tanja.*

Many Germans identify themselves at once when they answer the phone. Others simply say **hallo.**

Junge Leute sagen fast
immer „du" zueinander.
(Universität Frankfurt)

13

EINFÜHRUNG

5. Gender of nouns°

das Substantiv

Masculine	Neuter	Feminine
the man ← he	the baby ← it the computer ← it the radio ← it the lamp ← it	the woman ← she

Every English noun belongs to one of three genders: masculine, neuter, or feminine. The gender of a singular English noun shows up in the choice of the pronoun that is used to refer back to it.

The English type of gender system is one of natural gender. Nouns referring to male beings are masculine. Nouns referring to female beings are feminine. Nouns referring to young beings (if thought of as still undifferentiated as to sex) are neuter, and all nouns referring to inanimate objects are also neuter. (*Neuter* is the Latin word for *neither,* i.e., neither masculine nor feminine.)

Like English, German generally uses a system of natural gender for nouns that refer to living beings. Unlike English, however, German also makes gender distinctions in nouns that do not refer to living beings. This type of gender system is one of grammatical gender.

Masculine	Neuter	Feminine
der Mann[+] ← er der Computer ← er	das Kind[+] ← es das Radio[+] ← es	die Frau ← sie die Lampe ← sie

In German there are three groups of nouns: masculine (**der**-nouns), neuter (**das**-nouns), and feminine (**die**-nouns). The definite articles **der, das,** and **die** function like the English definite article *the.* Most nouns referring to males are **der**-nouns (**der Mann** = *man*), most nouns referring to females are **die**-nouns (**die Frau** = *woman*), and nouns referring to young beings are **das**-nouns (**das Kind** = *child*). Note that **der Junge**+ (= *boy*) is a **der**-noun, but **das Mädchen**+ (= *girl*) is a **das**-noun because all words ending in -**chen** are **das**-nouns. Other nouns belong to any one of the three groups: **der Computer, das Radio, die Lampe.**

■ Signals of Gender

Like English, German signals the gender of a noun in the choice of the pronoun that is used to refer back to it: **er** is masculine, **es** is neuter, and **sie** is feminine. Unlike English, however, German also signals gender in the choice of the definite article that precedes a noun: **der** is masculine, **das** is neuter, and **die** is feminine.

The article is the most powerful signal of gender. You should always learn a German noun together with its definite article, because there is no simple way of predicting the gender of a particular noun.

6. Ein Studentenzimmer   *(A student's room)*

Learn the following nouns:

1. der **Bleistift**	10. das **Bett**	22. die **Gitarre**
2. der **CD-Player**	11. das **Bild**	23. die **Lampe**
(der **CD-Spieler**)	12. das **Buch**	24. die **Pflanze**
3. der **Computer**	13. das **Bücherregal**	25. die **Tür**
4. der **DVD-Player**	14. das **Fenster**	26. die **Uhr**
(der **DVD-Spieler**)	15. das **Heft**	27. die **Wand**
5. der **Fernseher**	16. das **Kassettendeck**	
6. der **Kugelschreiber**	17. das **Papier**	
(der **Kuli**)	18. das **Poster**	
7. der **Rucksack**	19. das **Radio**	
8. der **Stuhl**	20. das **Handy**	
9. der **Tisch**	21. das **Zimmer**	

13. Rollenspiel (role-play): **Groß oder klein?** Gisela is moving to a new room and Alex plans to help arrange the furniture. He asks whether certain items are large (**groß**) or small (**klein**). Role-play with a partner.

→ Ist das Zimmer groß oder klein? *Das Zimmer ist [groß].*

1. Ist das Fenster groß oder klein?
2. Ist das Bett groß oder klein?
3. Ist der Fernseher groß oder klein?
4. Wie ist der Stuhl?
5. Ist die Pflanze groß oder klein?
6. Wie ist die Uhr?
7. Und die Lampe?
8. Und der Tisch?
9. Und das Bücherregal?
10. Wie ist der Rucksack?

14. Alt oder neu? Tell your partner whether various things in your room are new (**neu**), old (**alt**), large, or small.

Describing things

→ Computer *Der Computer ist [neu].*

1. Fernseher
2. Bett
3. Lampe
4. CD-Player
5. Radio
6. Rucksack
7. Buch
8. Kugelschreiber
9. Bild
10. Poster
11. Videorecorder (*m.*)
12. DVD-Player

7. The indefinite article *ein*

Im Zimmer ist **ein Tisch** und **eine Lampe.**   In the room there is a table and a lamp.

The German indefinite article **ein** is equivalent to English *a* or *an*.

Masculine	Neuter	Feminine
ein Tisch	ein Bett	eine Lampe

In German the indefinite article has two forms: **ein** for masculine and neuter and **eine** for feminine.

15. Was ist im Zimmer? Tell your partner five things that are in the **Studentenzimmer** on page 14.

→ *Im Zimmer sind ein Stuhl, eine Pflanze, ...*

16. In meinem° Zimmer. Now tell your partner five things that are in your room.

→ *In meinem Zimmer sind ein Bett, ein Computer, ...*

das Pronomen

8. Pronouns°

Wie alt ist **Alex?**	How old is Alex?
Er ist zweiundzwanzig.	He is twenty-two.
Wie alt ist **Gisela?**	How old is Gisela?
Sie ist zwanzig.	She is twenty.

A **pronoun** is a part of speech that designates a person, place, thing, or concept. It functions as a noun does. A pronoun can be used in place of a noun or a noun phrase.

9. Noun-pronoun relationship

Der Mann ist groß.	**Er** ist groß.	He is tall.
Der Stuhl ist groß.	**Er** ist groß.	It is large.
Das Kind ist klein.	**Es** ist klein.	She/He is small.
Das Zimmer ist klein.	**Es** ist klein.	It is small.
Die Frau ist groß.	**Sie** ist groß.	She is tall.
Die Lampe ist groß.	**Sie** ist groß.	It is large.

In German the pronouns **er, es,** and **sie** may refer to persons or things. In English the singular pronoun referring to things *(it)* is different from those referring to persons *(she, he)*.

Note that in referring to people, **groß** means *tall* and **klein** means *short* or *small*. In referring to things, **groß** means *large* or *big* and **klein** means *small* or *little*.

reading session

Leserunde°

The image below is a well-known example of *concrete poetry* (**Konkrete Poesie**). Concrete poetry is a movement that developed in the mid-1950s to focus on the characteristics of language itself as a literary medium. Authors use everyday language and play with it, using such techniques as repetition, syllables, or even arrangement of words to form a picture. Reinhard Döhl (b. 1934), the creator of the apple poem, is a professor of literature and media studies in Stuttgart. In addition to many scholarly papers, his works include poems, prose, and plays; he is also an artist. Döhl is especially known for creating experimental literature on the Internet, and he has been publishing his work there since 1996.

Reinhard Döhl

17. Wie ist das Zimmer? Tanja is seeing your room for the first time since you made some changes. She's trying to sort out which things are new and which are old. Respond, using a pronoun instead of the noun.

→ Ist der Tisch neu? *Ja, er ist neu.*

1. Ist der Stuhl alt?
2. Ist die Uhr neu?
3. Ist das Radio alt?
4. Ist die Pflanze neu?
5. Ist die Lampe alt?
6. Ist der DVD-Player neu?
7. Ist das Poster neu?
8. Ist der Computer neu?
9. Ist der Rucksack alt?
10. Ist das Kassettendeck neu?

18. Groß, klein, alt. With your partner look at the pictures of people and try to decide whether they are tall, short, or old. To get each other's opinions ask the questions below.

S1: Ist die Frau alt?
S2: Nein, sie ist nicht[+] alt.

S1:
1. Ist das Kind groß?
2. Ist der Mann alt?
3. Ist das Mädchen klein?

S2:
4. Ist der Junge groß?
5. Ist die Frau groß?
6. Ist das Kind klein?

10. Die Farben   *(Colors)*

The following sentences should help you remember the colors.

Der Ozean ist **blau.**   Das Gras ist **grün.**   Die Schokolade ist **braun.**   Die Tomate ist **rot.**

Die Banane ist **gelb.**   Der Asphalt ist **schwarz.**   Die Maus ist **grau.**   Das Papier ist **weiß.**

19. Welche⁺ Farbe? *(What color?)* Ask your partner the colors of five items in the student's room on page 14. Your partner will then ask you the color of five items.

To ask what color something is one asks:

→ Welche Farbe hat [der Stuhl]? *What color is [the chair]?*

To answer the question one says:

→ [Der Stuhl] ist [grau]. *[The chair] is [gray].*

Describing things

20. Welche Farbe hat das Land? Germany has sixteen states (**Länder**). With a partner, look at the map of Germany on the inside front cover and ask each other questions about the **Länder.**

S1: Welche Farbe hat [Bayern]?
S2: Bayern ist blau.

Vokabeln   *(Vocabulary)*

The vocabulary sections in each chapter contain the words and phrases that you are expected to learn actively. You should be able to understand them in many contexts and use them to express your own thoughts.

In English, proper nouns like *Monday* or *America* are capitalized, but not common nouns like *address* or *street*. In German, all nouns are capitalized: proper nouns like **Montag** or **Amerika** as well as common nouns like **Adresse** and **Straße.** Unlike English, German does not capitalize proper adjectives.

Compare the following: **amerikanisch**   American
                        englisch   English
                        deutsch   German

The German pronoun **Sie** (you *formal*) and the possessive adjective **Ihr** (your *formal*) are capitalized in writing. The pronoun **ich** (I) is not capitalized.

Substantive   *(Nouns)*

die **Adresse**   address
das **Bett**   bed
das **Bild**   picture; photo
der **Bleistift**   pencil
das **Buch**   book
das **Bücherregal**   bookcase
der **CD-Player** (der **CD-Spieler**) CD player
der **Computer**   computer
(das) **Deutsch**   German; German class
der **Dienstag**   Tuesday
der **Donnerstag**   Thursday
der **DVD-Player** (der **DVD-Spieler**) DVD Player
die **Farbe**   color
das **Fenster**   window
der **Fernseher**   television set

die **Frau**   woman; **Frau**   Mrs., Ms. *(term of address for adult women)*
der **Freitag**   Friday
der **Garten**   garden
die **Gitarre**   guitar
das **Handy**   cell phone
das **Heft**   notebook
die **Heimatadresse**   home address
der **Herr**   gentleman; **Herr**   Mr. *(term of address)*
das **Jahr**   year
der **Junge**   boy
das **Kassettendeck**   cassette deck
das **Kind**   child
der **Kugelschreiber** (der **Kuli**, *colloquial*)   ballpoint pen
die **Lampe**   lamp
das **Mädchen**   girl

der **Mann**   man
der **Mittwoch**   Wednesday
der **Montag**   Monday
die **Nummer**   number
das **Papier**   paper
die **Pflanze**   plant
das (*or* der) **Poster**   poster
der **Professor** (*m.*)/die **Professorin** (*f.*)
  professor
das **Radio**   radio
der **Rucksack**   backpack
der **Samstag** (*in southern Germany*)
  Saturday
die **Semesteradresse**   school
  address
der **Sonnabend** (*in northern
  Germany*) Saturday

der **Sonntag**   Sunday
die **Straße**   street
der **Student** (*m.*)/die **Studentin** (*f.*)
  student
der **Stuhl**   chair
der **Tag**   day
das **Telefon**   telephone
die **Telefonnummer**   telephone
  number
der **Tisch**   table
die **Tür**   door
die **Uhr**   clock, watch
der **Videorecorder**   VCR
die **Wand**   wall
die **Woche**   week
die **Zahl**   number, numeral
das **Zimmer**   room

Verben   *(Verbs)*

bin / bist / ist / sind   am / are / is /
  are
habe / hast / hat / haben   have / have /
  has / have

heißen   to be named, to be called
schreiben   to write

Andere Wörter   *(Other words)*

ach   oh
also   well
alt   old
auch   also
bitte   please; you're welcome (*after*
  danke)
blau   blue
braun   brown
da   there
danke   thanks; **danke schön**   thanks
  very much
dann   then
das   that; the (*neuter*)
dein(e)   your (*familiar*)
der   the (*masculine*)
die   the (*feminine*)
du   you (*familiar*)
ein(e)   a, an
er   he, it
es   it
falsch   false, wrong
gelb   yellow
(geteilt) durch   divided by (*in
  division*)
grau   gray
groß   large, big; tall (*people*)
grün   green
heute   today

ich   I
Ihr(e)   your (*formal*)
ja   yes
klein   small; short (*people*)
mal   times (*in multiplication*)
man   one, people
mein(e)   my
minus   minus (*in subtraction*)
nein   no
neu   new
nicht   not
richtig   correct, right
rot   red
schwarz   black
sie   she, it
Sie   you (*formal*)
so   so; this way
toll   great, fantastic, terrific
tschüs   so long, good-bye (*informal*)
und   and; plus (*in addition*)
von   of
wann   when
weiß   white
welch (-er, -es, -e)   which
wie   how
wie viel   how much; **wie viele**   how
  many
For the numbers 1–1,000, see page 7.

Besondere Ausdrücke   (Special Expressions)

am [Freitag]   on [Friday]

Bis bald!   See you soon.

Bitte?   May I help you?

Du, ...   Hey, . . . (used to get someone's attention)

Grüß dich.   Hello! Hi.

Hallo!   Hello! Hi.

Ich bin 19 Jahre alt.   I'm 19 years old.

Ich heiße ...   My name is . . .

Okay   okay, O.K.

Welche Farbe hat ... ?   What color is . . . ?

Welcher Tag ist heute?   What day is today?

(Wie) bitte?   (I beg your) pardon.

Wie alt bist du (sind Sie)?   How old are you?

Wie alt ist ... ?   How old is . . . ?

Wie heißt du (heißen Sie)?   What's your name?

Wie ist deine (Ihre) Adresse?   What's your address?

Wie ist deine (Ihre) Telefonnummer?   What is your telephone number?

Wie ist die Telefonnummer von [Clemens Neumann]?   What is [Clemens Neumann's] telephone number?

Wie schreibt man das?   How do you spell that? (literally: How does one write that?)

Willst du nach [Florenz]?   Are you planning to go to [Florence]?

Wiederholung   (Review)

The **Wiederholung** is a review section in which you will have the opportunity to work again with the content, vocabulary, and structures of the current chapter and earlier chapters.

1. Die Galerie. Tell what you know about the Galerie by completing the following sentences.

1. Die Galerie ist ein _____ , eine Bar und ein _____ .

every   2. Der Superbrunch ist jeden°_____ .

3. Die Musik ist _____ .

4. Die Adresse ist _____ .

5. Die Telefonnummer ist _____ .

2. Studentenzimmer. Students needing rooms in Tübingen can consult the bulletin board of a popular student café. Below are three of the ads. Read them and answer the questions that follow. You don't have to understand every word in order to get the information you need.

Ich (19 Jahre alt, Englischstudentin im 1. Semester) suche[1] ZIMMER IN WG[2] (im Zentrum maximal 250 €') Sabine Albrecht Schwabstraße 128 70193 Stuttgart Tel.: 0711/600953

Zimmer in WG frei[3]! groß, neu, in 2-Personen WG (Medizinstudent, 23 Jahre alt), kleiner Garten und Balkon, zum Superpreis von 300€. Sebastian Klein Schleifmühleweg 123 72070 Tübingen Tel.: 792238

Studentenzimmer zu vermieten[4]! Kleines Zimmer, großes Fenster: fünf Minuten zur Universität. Bett, Tisch, zwei Stühle, Bücherregal. 260€ im Monat. Kurt Riedl Mühlstraße 12 72074 Tübingen Tel.: 81 82 76

[1]*am looking for*   [2]**WG** = **Wohngemeinschaft:** *people sharing an apartment*   [3]*vacant, available*   [4]*to rent*

Ad 1
1. Wie heißt die Studentin?
2. Wie alt ist sie?
3. Wie ist die Adresse?
4. Wie ist die Telefonnummer?

Ad 2
1. Ist das Zimmer groß oder klein?
2. Ist es neu oder alt?
3. Wie alt ist der Medizinstudent?
4. Wie ist der Garten? Groß oder klein?
5. Wie ist die Adresse?
6. Wie ist die Telefonnummer?

Ad 3
1. Ist das Zimmer groß oder klein?
2. Wie ist das Fenster? Groß oder klein?
3. Im Zimmer sind ein _____ , ein _____ , ein _____ und zwei _____ .
4. Wie heißt der Vermieter°?   landlord
5. Wie ist die Adresse?
6. Wie ist die Telefonnummer?

3. Geburtstage! Read the birth announcement and answer the questions. You do not need to understand all the words to get the information required.

1. Wie heißt das Baby?
2. Wie alt ist Emanuel heute?
3. Wie ist Emanuels Adresse?
4. Wie ist seine Telefonnummer?
5. Wie heißen Emanuels Mutter° und Vater°?
6. Wer ist Franziska?

mother / father

Unser Sohn heißt

Emanuel Gerhard

und ist am 14. Juli 2004 um 20.13 Uhr auf die Welt gekommen.
Gewicht: 3000g
Größe: 50cm

Cornelia und Gerhard Mühlhäuser
sind die überglücklichen Eltern,
Franziska ist die überglückliche Schwester.

Schönbichlstraße 14
82211 Herrsching am Ammersee
Telefon: 08152-1538

Getting acquainted

4. Gespräche *(Conversations)*

1. Talk to people whose names you remember. Ask for their telephone numbers and addresses.
2. Introduce yourself to people you don't know.
3. Ask some of the people how to spell their names and be prepared to spell your own for someone else.

5. Zum Schreiben *(To be written)*

1. **Mein Zimmer.**   Identify fifteen items in your room. List them by gender. Then describe five of the items using full sentences.

   ➜   der Stuhl   *Der Stuhl ist braun. Er ist nicht groß.*

2. **Fragen.** *(Questions.)* While a student at the university in Hamburg in Germany, you are involved in a minor automobile accident. You need to get the name, address, telephone number, and age of the driver of the other vehicle. Write down the questions you would ask to obtain this information.

Guten Tag! Wie geht's?

Sagen diese Frauen „du" zueinander?

LERNZIELE

Sprechintentionen

Greeting people formally
Greeting friends
Saying good-bye
Asking people how they are
Expressing likes and dislikes
Asking about personal plans
Asking what kind of person
  someone is
Expressing agreement and
  disagreement
Describing people
Telling time
Making plans
Giving positive or negative
  responses

Lesestück   *(Reading)*

Eine Studentin in Tübingen

Land und Leute

Regional greetings and farewells
Staying in shape
The university town of Tübingen
Appropriate use of *du* and *Sie*
The role of sports in German-
  speaking countries

Vokabeln

Sports
Descriptive adjectives
Telling time

Grammatik

Pronouns and nouns as subjects
Three forms for *you: du, ihr, Sie*
The verb *sein*
Regular verbs
Expressing likes and dislikes with *gern*
Negation with *nicht*
Expressing future time with the
  present tense
Asking informational and yes/no
  questions
Tag questions

Bausteine für Gespräche

Wie geht's?

In der Bibliothek

PROFESSOR LANGE: Guten Morgen, Frau Riedholt. Wie geht es Ihnen?
GISELA: Guten Morgen, Professor Lange. Gut, danke. Und Ihnen?
PROFESSOR LANGE: Danke, ganz gut.

Im Hörsaal

ALEX: Hallo, Gisela.
GISELA: Grüß dich, Alex. Wie geht's?
ALEX: Ach, nicht so gut.
GISELA: Was ist los? Bist du krank?
ALEX: Nein, ich bin nur furchtbar müde.

Richtig oder falsch? Say whether the statements below agree with what is in the dialogue. For a correct statement say **richtig,** for an incorrect statement say **falsch.**

1. Gisela und Alex sind im Hörsaal.
2. Es geht Alex nicht so gut.
3. Alex ist sehr[+] krank.

Brauchbares

1. **Frau Riedholt:** Adult German women, married and unmarried, are addressed as **Frau.** It is equivalent to English *Ms.* or *Mrs.* Unmarried women under 18 are usually addressed as **Fräulein.**

2. In the *Einführung* you learned that the German words for *you* are **Sie** or **du.** In the phrases **Wie geht es Ihnen?** and **Und dir?, Ihnen** and **dir** are again different forms of *you.*

Greeting someone

 1. Guten Tag. Greet different people in the class. Choose a time of day and greet your partner, who responds appropriately.

S1:	*S2:*
Guten Morgen.	Morgen.
Guten Tag.[+]	Tag.
Guten Abend.[+]	Abend.
	Hallo.
	Grüß dich.

Asking people how they are

2. Wie geht's? Find a partner and role-play a scene between you and a friend or a professor. Assume you haven't seen your friend or the professor for several days and you run into her/him in the cafeteria (**die Mensa**). Say hello and ask how she/he is. **S2** should use expressions from the **Schüttelkasten** box on page 25.

S1:	*S2:*
Hallo, [Tanja]. Wie geht's?	Gut, danke. (Und dir?[+]/Und
Guten Tag, Herr/Frau Professor,	Ihnen?[+])
wie geht es Ihnen?	

Schüttelkasten

Danke, ganz gut.

Ich bin müde.

Es geht.⁺

Nicht so gut.   Schlecht⁺.   Ich bin krank.

Land und Leute

Guten Tag

www Go to the *Deutsch heute* website at
http://college.hmco.com.

Adults in German-speaking countries often greet each other with a handshake.
When one is first introduced or in a formal situation, a handshake is expected.
Greetings vary depending on the region and the speakers.

Expressions for greeting each other:

Guten Morgen/Morgen (*informal*)
Guten Tag/Tag (*informal*)
Hallo (*informal*)
Hi (*popular among young people*)
Grüß Gott (*common in southern Germany, Austria*)
Grüezi (*Switzerland*)
Grüß dich (*informal; common in southern Germany, Austria*)
Salut (*informal; Switzerland*)
Servus (*used only between good acquaintances; southern Germany, Austria*)
Guten Abend/n'Abend (*informal*)
Moin, moin (*northern German greeting gaining popularity throughout Germany*)

„Auf Wiedersehen!" (Frankfurter
Hauptbahnhof)

Expressions for saying good-bye:

(Auf) Wiedersehen
(Auf) Wiederschauen
Tschüs (*informal*)
Adieu
Ciao (*informal*)
Ade (*informal; southern Germany, Austria*)
Servus (*used only between good
acquaintances; southern Germany,
Austria*)
Salut (*informal; Switzerland*)
Gute Nacht (*at bedtime*)
Bis bald
Bis dann
Mach's gut

Diskussion

How do you greet people in English? Make a list
of several variations and say when you use them.

[1]*guess*

 Was machst du heute Abend?

Michael lives in the same dormitory as Gisela.

MICHAEL: Was machst du heute Abend?
GISELA: Nichts Besonderes. Musik hören oder so. Vielleicht gehe ich ins Kino.
MICHAEL: Hmm. Du spielst gern Schach, nicht?
GISELA: Schach? Ja. Aber nicht so gut.
MICHAEL: Ach komm, wir spielen
zusammen, ja?
GISELA: Na gut! Wann?
MICHAEL: Um sieben?
GISELA: Okay. Bis dann.

Richtig oder falsch?

1. Michael hört heute Abend Musik.
2. Gisela geht vielleicht ins Kino.
3. Michael spielt gern Schach.
4. Gisela spielt gut Schach.
5. Gisela und Michael spielen heute Abend Schach.

Erweiterung des Wortschatzes

1. Was machst du gern?

das Aerobic;
Aerobic machen

der Fußball;
Fußball spielen

das Schach;
Schach spielen

das Tennis;
Tennis spielen

die Karten;
Karten spielen

das Tischtennis;
Tischtennis spielen

der Basketball;
Basketball spielen

das Computerspiel; – e
ein Computerspiel spielen

das Inlineskating;
inlineskaten gehen

der Volleyball;
Volleyball spielen

das Gewichtheben;
Gewichte heben — *to lift*

das Golf;
Golf spielen

das Fitnesstraining;
Fitnesstraining machen

das Videospiel; – e
ein Videospiel spielen

das Jogging;
joggen gehen

1. Das mache ich gern. Verbs used with activities vary according to the activity. Say you do the activities by selecting the proper verb from the **Schüttelkasten.**

Expressing likes and dislikes

1. Ich _____ gern Fußball.

2. Ich _____ gern Computerspiele.

3. Ich _____ viel⁺ Fitnesstraining.

4. Ich _____ gern Schach.

5. Ich _____ oft⁺ Aerobic.

6. Ich _____ oft Gewichte.

7. Ich _____ gern inlineskaten.

8. Ich _____ auch oft joggen.

Schüttelkasten

spiele   hebe

    mache   gehe

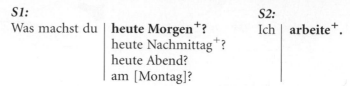

2. Was machst du? Think about what you are going to do today. Ask a few classmates what they are going to do in their free time. They will ask you in turn. **S2** should use expressions from the **Schüttelkasten**.

S1:
Was machst du | **heute Morgen[+]?**
heute Nachmittag[+]?
heute Abend?
am [Montag]?

S2:
Ich | **arbeite[+].**

Schüttelkasten

gehe spazieren[+] *go for a walk*

spiele Tennis

gehe tanzen[+]

gehe ins Kino

gehe schwimmen[+]

gehe wandern[+]

gehe inlineskaten

mache Fitnesstraining

mache Deutsch

höre Musik

gehe joggen

Reporting

3. Ich mache das. Report to the class four things you do or don't do. Use **gern, viel, oft, nicht gern, nicht viel, nicht oft.**

➡ *Ich spiele [nicht] viel Schach.*

2. Was für ein Mensch sind Sie?

The following adjectives can be used to characterize people. Some of them have English cognates and can be guessed easily.

fleißig	industrious	**egoistisch**	egocentric
faul	lazy	**ernst**	serious
		froh	happy
glücklich	happy	**intelligent**	intelligent
traurig	sad	**kreativ**	creative
		kritisch	critical
freundlich	friendly	**laut**	loud, noisy
unfreundlich	unfriendly	**lustig**	cheerful
		nett	nice
sympathisch	likeable, agreeable	**praktisch**	practical
unsympathisch	unpleasant, unappealing	**ruhig**	quiet, calm
		sportlich	athletic
musikalisch	musical	**tolerant**	tolerant
unmusikalisch	unmusical		

Asking what kind of person someone is and describing someone

4. Frage-Ecke. You and your partner are talking about the characteristics of certain people. Take turns finding out the information that is missing in your own chart. **S1's** information is on page 29; the information for **S2** is in Appendix B.

S1: Was für ein Mensch ist Alex?
S2: Er ist ruhig und freundlich. Was für ein Mensch ist Gisela?

S1:

Gisela	fleißig	nett
Alex		
Melanie	tolerant	sympathisch
Claudia		
Michael	ernst	musikalisch
Stefan		

5. Eine Freundin/Ein Freund. Ask three students what characteristics they look for in a friend. Then report on your findings. For additional traits, refer to "Personal qualities and characteristics" in the Supplementary Word Sets in Appendix C.

Asking and reporting

> *S1:* Wie sollte eine Freundin oder ein Freund sein°?
> *S2:* [lustig und intelligent]

sollte... sein: should a friend be

6. Wie ist diese Person? Characterize each of the persons pictured below, using the adjectives on page 28. See if your partner agrees.

Expressing agreement and disagreement

Stefan   Dirk   Bettina

Peter   Claudia   Oliver

> *S1:* [Bettina] ist sehr ernst, nicht?/Ist [Bettina] sehr ernst?
> *S2:* Ja, sehr.
> *S3:* Nein, ich glaube⁺ nicht. Sie ist sehr lustig.

Land und Leute

Fit bleiben

www Go to the *Deutsch heute* website at http://college.hmco.com.

People in German-speaking countries can avail themselves of a wide variety of sports ranging from the traditional biking (**Rad fahren**) to the most recent like in-line skating (**Inlineskating**). Historically, people in German-speaking countries are known for their love of hiking (**wandern**) and walking (**spazieren gehen**). There are well-maintained trails throughout German-speaking countries. Some are simple paths through parks or local scenic spots, while others are part of a vast complex of trails.

Swimming is also a popular activity. In addition to seashore and lakeside beaches, town pools — both indoors and outdoors — provide ample opportunity for swimming. An outdoor pool (**Freibad**), with a nominal admission fee, is generally located on the outskirts of a city. It is often large and surrounded by grassy areas. People come with food and blankets to spend the day picnicking, swimming, and playing volleyball or badminton. In many cities, public indoor pools (**Hallenbäder**) have developed into public spas, offering saunas, hot tubs, massages, swimming lessons, snack bars, hair salons, and exercise machines besides several large swimming and diving pools.

One can find health clubs (**Fitnesscenter**) in most cities. There one can play squash (**Squash**) or work out (**Fitnesstraining**), which includes weightlifting (**Gewichte heben**) and aerobics (**Aerobic**).

Radfahren als Fitnesstraining

Diskussion

How do you stay fit? Using the vocabulary in **Land und Leute,** the Supplementary Word Set "Sports and games" in Appendix C, or another source, describe your fitness routine.

 7. Hören Sie zu. You will hear Gisela and Alex talking about their plans for the afternoon. Indicate whether the statements below are **richtig** or **falsch** according to the conversation you have heard. Two new words are **Karten** *(tickets)*; **warum** *(why)*.

1. Gisela ist nicht sportlich.
2. Alex und David gehen inlineskaten.
3. Gisela geht mit Alex und David inlineskaten.
4. Gisela, Alex und David spielen Tennis.
5. Heute Abend hören sie Musik.

3. Telling time

The following methods are used to express clock time.

Wie viel Uhr ist es?[+]
Wie spät ist es?[+] } What time is it?

	Method 1	Method 2
1.00 Uhr	Es ist eins.	Es ist eins.
	Es ist ein Uhr.	Es ist ein Uhr.
1.05 Uhr	Es ist fünf (Minuten) nach eins.	Es ist ein Uhr fünf.
1.15 Uhr	Es ist Viertel nach eins.	Es ist ein Uhr fünfzehn.
1.25 Uhr	Es ist fünf (Minuten) vor halb zwei.	Es ist ein Uhr fünfundzwanzig.
1.30 Uhr	Es ist halb zwei.	Es ist ein Uhr dreißig.
1.35 Uhr	Es ist fünf nach halb zwei.	Es ist ein Uhr fünfunddreißig.
1.45 Uhr	Es ist Viertel vor zwei.	Es ist ein Uhr fünfundvierzig.
1.55 Uhr	Es ist fünf (Minuten) vor zwei.	Es ist ein Uhr fünfundfünfzig.
2.00 Uhr	Es ist zwei Uhr.	Es ist zwei Uhr.

Note that German uses a period instead of a colon in time expressions.

German has two ways to indicate clock time. With a few exceptions, they parallel the two ways English indicates clock time.

| *Method 1* | Es ist Viertel nach acht. | It's a quarter past eight. |
| *Method 2* | Es ist acht Uhr fünfzehn. | It's eight-fifteen. |

In conversational German, method 1 is used to indicate time. Notice that the **-s** of **eins** is dropped before the word **Uhr.** The expression with **halb** indicates the hour to come, not the preceding hour: **halb zwei = 1.30 Uhr.**

Mein Zug fährt um **7.30 Uhr [7 Uhr 30].**   My train leaves at 7:30 A.M.
Das Konzert beginnt um **19.30 Uhr [19**   The concert begins
Uhr 30].   at 7:30 P.M.

In official time, such as train and plane schedules and concerts, method 2 is used. Official time is indicated on a 24-hour basis.

Um wie viel Uhr spielen wir Tennis?   (At) what time are we
                                            playing tennis?
Um halb neun.   At 8:30.

German uses **um** + a time expression to ask or speak about the specific hour at which something will or did take place.

Wann spielen wir Tennis?   *When* are we playing tennis?
Morgen. Um 8.30 Uhr.   Tomorrow. At 8:30.

The question word **wann** (*when*) can imply a request for a specific time (e.g., **um 8.30 Uhr**) or a general time (e.g., **morgen**).

Bei Sport4You sind die Öffnungszeiten am Samstag von *(from)* 9.30 Uhr bis *(until)* 16 Uhr. Wie sind die Öffnungszeiten bei Sport4You am Dienstag? Wie ist die Adresse? Und die Telefonnummer?

Wie sind die Öffnungszeiten bei CybeRyder am Sonntag? Wie ist die Faxnummer?

Telling time

8. Frage-Ecke. Some of the clocks in this activity show particular times. Others are blank. Take turns with a partner and find out the times that are missing on your clocks. **S1**'s clocks are below; the clocks for **S2** are in Appendix B.

> *S1:* Nummer 1. Wie viel Uhr ist es?
> *S2:* Es ist Viertel nach neun. (Es ist neun Uhr fünfzehn.) Und Nummer 2? Wie spät ist es?
> *S1:* Es ist ...

S1:

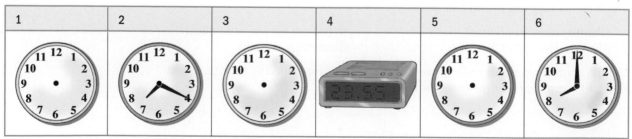

1	2	3	4	5	6

9. Giselas Terminkalender. *(Appointment calendar.)* Tell what Gisela's plans are by consulting her calendar and answering the questions.

1. Welcher Tag ist heute?
2. Wann hat Gisela Deutsch?
3. Um wie viel Uhr ist Gisela in der Bibliothek?
4. Wann spielen Gisela und Alex Tennis?
5. Geht Gisela um 1 Uhr schwimmen?
6. Arbeitet sie um 5 Uhr?
7. Wann geht Gisela ins Kino?

10. Hören Sie zu. You are calling to find out what time it is. Listen to the times and indicate the time you hear.

1. a. 8.45
   b. 4.58
   c. 18.45

2. a. 17.32
   b. 7.23
   c. 7.32

3. a. 1.15
   b. 15.01
   c. 5.01

4. a. 2.21
   b. 21.02
   c. 20.21

5. a. 5.36
   b. 6.53
   c. 3.56

September
9 Donnerstag
7 Uhr
8⁰⁰ 8.¹⁰ Deutsch
9⁰⁰
10⁰⁰ Bibliothek
11⁰⁰ Bibliothek
12⁰⁰ Tennis mit Alex
13⁰⁰
14⁰⁰ 14.⁴⁵ schwimmen
15⁰⁰
16⁰⁰ arbeiten
17⁰⁰ arbeiten
18⁰⁰ arbeiten
19⁰⁰
20⁰⁰ 20.¹⁵ Kino mit Martin, Alex und Ute

11. Hören Sie zu. Alex was gone for a week and his friends left messages on his answering machine to remind him of meeting times. Indicate which statements are correct. You will hear the new word **vergiss** (*forget*).

1. Gisela und Alex spielen am Montag _____ Tennis.
   a. um 8.15 Uhr
   b. um 18.15 Uhr
   c. um 15.08 Uhr
2. David und Alex gehen am Dienstag _____ ins Kino.
   a. um 7.45 Uhr
   b. um 8.15 Uhr
   c. um 8.45 Uhr
3. Alex und Uwe sehen Professor Lange am Freitag _____.
   a. um 5.06 Uhr
   b. um 6.05 Uhr
   c. um 16.05 Uhr
4. David und Alex spielen am Samstag _____ mit Uwe und Gisela Fußball.
   a. um 9.30 Uhr
   b. um 8.30 Uhr
   c. um 18.30 Uhr

Eine Studentin in Tübingen

Vorbereitung auf das Lesen *(Preparation for reading)*

Each chapter of *Deutsch heute* contains a reading section. The readings are designed to broaden your knowledge and familiarity with the culture, customs, history, and current life in Germany, Austria, and Switzerland.

Each reading is accompanied by pre-reading and post-reading activities. In the first pre-reading activity, called **Vor dem Lesen** *(Before reading),* you will be asked to think about what you already know about the reading topic or about what information and vocabulary you would expect to encounter in a reading on the topic at hand. **Vor dem Lesen** may also include a visual (e.g., an ad or photo) for you to interpret as a way to stimulate your thinking about the upcoming reading. In the second pre-reading activity, called **Beim Lesen** *(While reading),* you will find suggestions for things to look for as you work through the text. In the post-reading section, called **Nach dem Lesen** *(After reading),* activities such as **Fragen zum Lesestück** *(Questions about the reading)* help you check your comprehension and express your own views on the reading topic.

In the **Vor dem Lesen, Beim Lesen,** and **Nach dem Lesen** exercises, German words that are new and that you should learn and be able to use are followed by a raised plus sign[+]. These words and their definitions are listed in the **Vokabeln** section following the reading. Other unfamiliar words are defined in the margin.

The reading in this chapter is a letter Gisela has written to her friends, Monika and Stefan, who are students at the Freie Universität Berlin.

Studenten in ihrer Freizeit auf dem Neckar vor dem Hölderlinturm (Tübingen)

■ **Vor dem Lesen**

1. What would you write about your college or university and your living arrangements in your first letter to friends?
2. Glance at the form of the letter and compare it to that of a personal letter you might write. What is in the first line of the letter? What is the English equivalent of **Liebe .../Lieber ...** ?

■ **Beim Lesen**

1. Circle or make a list of the cognates in the letter.
2. Underline or make a list of the numbers in the letter.

Gisela's telephone number (l. 4):
The area code (**die Vorwahl**) is
0 70 71 and her local number
is 79 23 09.

Tübingen, den 21. Oktober°

den 21. Oktober: read as **den einundzwanzigsten Oktober**

Liebe Monika, lieber Stefan,
wie geht's? Wie ist Berlin? Und wie ist die Uni? Meine neue Adresse hier in Tübingen ist Pfleghofstraße 2, Zimmer 15, 72070 Tübingen und meine Telefonnummer ist 07071/79 23 09. Mein Zimmer ist nicht schlecht, vielleicht ein
5 bisschen klein, aber praktisch. Nur zehn Minuten bis zur° Uni. Tübingen ist klein und idyllisch, aber die Universität ist relativ groß und hat viele Studenten.

bis zur: to the

Mein Nachbar heißt Michael und kommt aus° Hamburg. Er studiert auch Englisch hier an der Uni. Am Wochenende spielt er oft Gitarre in einer Blues-
10 band. Sein Freund heißt Alex und studiert Jura. Beide treiben gern Sport. Alex ist sehr freundlich, lustig und fleißig und ich glaube, er ist auch sehr intelligent und tolerant. Jedenfalls° ist er furchtbar nett. Michael ist auch sehr sympathisch, aber etwas ernst und ruhig. Vielleicht ist er auch nur etwas schüchtern°. Heute ist Samstag und Alex und Michael arbeiten bis Viertel
15 nach zwei. Ich mache nichts Besonderes, aber heute Nachmittag gehen wir alle drei zusammen schwimmen und später tanzen.

from

at any rate

shy

Viele Grüße
eure° Gisela

yours

Nach dem Lesen   *(After reading)*

1. Fragen zum Lesestück. *(Questions about the reading.)* Answer the following questions about the reading.

1. Wie ist Giselas Adresse? Wie ist die Postleitzahl?
2. Wie ist Giselas Telefonnummer? Wie ist die Vorwahl° von Tübingen?
3. Wie ist Giselas Zimmer?
4. Wie ist die Universität?
5. Was macht Michael oft am Wochenende?
6. Was machen Gisela und Michael heute?
7. Was für ein Mensch ist Michael?

area code

2. Ergänzen Sie. *(Complete.)* Complete the following sentences using information from the text.

1. Giselas Zimmer ist ein bisschen klein, aber _____ .
2. Gisela glaubt, Michael ist _____ .
3. Heute Abend gehen Gisela und Michael _____ .
4. Die Universität ist _____ .
5. Gisela und Michael studieren _____ .

3. Erzählen Sie. *(Tell.)*

1. Using vocabulary from the letter, write down words or phrases that you can use when talking about the following topics in German.
   a. mein Zimmer
   b. meine Universität
   c. ein Freund oder eine Freundin
2. Using the words and phrases that you wrote down in 1, have a conversation with another student about the topics. Begin by writing two questions that you can ask your partner.

Vokabeln

Substantive

der **Abend**   evening
das **Aerobic**   aerobics
der **Basketball**   basketball
die **Bibliothek**   library
das **Computerspiel**   computer game
(das) **Deutsch**   German language
(das) **Englisch**   English language (academic subject)
das **Fitnesstraining**   fitness training; **Fitnesstraining machen**   to work out
die **Frage**   question
der **Freund**/die **Freundin**   friend; boyfriend/girlfriend
der **Fußball**   soccer
das **Gewichtheben**   weightlifting; **Gewichte heben**   to lift weights
das **Golf**   golf
das **Inlineskating**   in-line skating; **inlineskaten gehen**   to go in-line skating
das **Jogging**   jogging; **joggen gehen**   to go jogging
die **Karte**   card; postcard; ticket; die

Karten *(pl.)*   (playing) cards
das **Kino**   movie theater
der **Mensch**   person, human being
die **Minute**, die **Minuten** *(pl.)*   minute
der **Morgen**   morning
die **Musik**   music
der **Nachbar** *(m.)*/die **Nachbarin** *(f.)*   neighbor
der **Nachmittag**   afternoon
die **Nacht**   night
das **Schach**   chess
das **Spiel**   game
der **Sport**   sport; **Sport treiben** to engage in sports
das **Tennis**   tennis
das **Tischtennis**   table tennis, Ping-Pong
die **Universität**, die **Uni** *(colloquial)*   university
das **Videospiel**   video game
das **Viertel**   quarter
der **Volleyball**   volleyball
das **Wochenende**   weekend

Verben

arbeiten   to work; to study
gehen   to go
glauben   to believe

hören   to hear; to listen to
inlineskaten   to in-line skate
joggen   to jog

kommen to come
machen to do; to make
schwimmen to swim
sein to be
spazieren gehen to go for a walk

spielen to play
studieren to study; to attend college
tanzen to dance
wandern to hike; to go walking

Andere Wörter

aber but, however
alle all
beide both
bis until, till
bisschen: ein bisschen a little
egoistisch egocentric
ernst serious
etwas some, somewhat; something
faul lazy
fleißig industrious, hard-working
freundlich friendly
froh happy
furchtbar terrible; very
ganz complete, whole; very; **ganz
  gut** not bad, O.K.
gern gladly, willingly; *used with
  verbs to indicate liking, as in* **Ich
  spiele** *gern* **Tennis.**
glücklich happy
gut good, well; fine
halb half
heute Abend this evening
heute Morgen this morning
heute Nachmittag this afternoon
ihr you *(familiar pl.)*
intelligent smart, intelligent
interessant interesting
krank sick, ill
kreativ creative
kritisch critical
laut loud, noisy
lieb- (-er, -e) dear
lustig merry, cheerful
müde tired
musikalisch musical

nach after
natürlich natural
nett nice
nichts nothing
nur only
oder or
oft often
praktisch practical
relativ relatively
ruhig calm, easy-going, quiet
schlecht bad, badly
sehr very (much)
sein his, its
sie she, they
spät late; **später** later
sportlich athletic
sympathisch likeable, agreeable
tolerant tolerant
traurig sad
um at; **um zehn Uhr** at ten o'clock
unfreundlich unfriendly
unglücklich unhappy
unmusikalisch unmusical
unsympathisch unpleasant,
  unappealing
viel much
viele many
vielleicht maybe, perhaps
vor before
warum why
was what
was für (ein) what kind of (a)
wer who
wir we
zusammen together

Besondere Ausdrücke

am Wochenende on the weekend
Auf Wiedersehen good-bye
Bis dann. See you then.
Es geht. O.K.; Not bad.; All right.
Gute Nacht good night
Guten Abend/n'Abend good evening
Guten Morgen/Morgen good
  morning
Guten Tag / Tag. Hello.

halb half; **halb zwei** one-thirty
Ich glaube ja. I think so.
Ich glaube nicht. I don't think so.
Ich mache Deutsch. I'm doing
  German homework.
in der Bibliothek in the library
ins Kino to the movies
Mach's gut. Take it easy.
Musik hören listening to music

Na gut!   All right.
nicht (wahr)? *(tag question)*   don't you? isn't he? isn't that so?, etc.; **Du spielst Schach, nicht?**   You play chess, don't you?
nichts Besonderes   nothing special
um [sieben] Uhr   at [seven] o'clock
Um wie viel Uhr?   At what time?
Und dir?   And you? (How about you?) *(familiar)*
Und Ihnen?   And you? (How about you?) *(formal)*

Viele Grüße *(closing in a letter)*   regards
Viertel nach   quarter after
Viertel vor   quarter of, quarter to
Was ist los?   What's wrong?, What's the matter?; What's going on?, What's up?
Wie geht es Ihnen?   How are you?
Wie geht's?   How are you? *(literally: How's it going?)*
Wie spät ist es?   What time is it?
Wie viel Uhr ist es?   What time is it?

Land und Leute

Tübingen

Go to the *Deutsch heute* website at http://college.hmco.com.

Tübingen is a small city located on the Neckar River in the southwest part of Germany on the northern edge of the Black Forest **(Schwarzwald)**. It is about 30 km southwest of Stuttgart, the capital of the federal state Baden-Württemberg. Tübingen has a scenic medieval city center **(die Altstadt),** with parts of the old city wall still standing. Other tourist attractions are the Hölderlinturm, where the poet

Friedrich Hölderlin (1770–1843) lived, the Renaissance castle **Schloss Hohentübingen,** the fifteenth-century **Stiftskirche** (Collegiate Church of St. George), and the famous 800-year-old Cistercian cloister **Bebenhausen** outside of the city. But Tübingen is best known for its excellent university, which was founded in 1477. The 26,000 students make up almost one-third of the 84,000 inhabitants of Tübingen. The university and the small city are very much a unit. The older university buildings are spread throughout the city, although the new university buildings, particularly in the field of the sciences, are located on the outskirts of Tübingen. Studying in Tübingen means a large selection of academic activities and cultural events within a small city atmosphere. There is an abundance of outdoor cafés, restaurants, bars, theaters, movie theaters, and museums. The old saying **"Tübingen hat keine Universität, Tübingen ist eine Universität"** is still valid today, for the students and their lifestyle contribute to the charm and the relaxed atmosphere that characterize Tübingen.

Diskussion

In his mid-thirties, Friedrich Hölderlin was diagnosed with schizophrenia. He was taken in and cared for by the Zimmer family, and lived the last 36 years of his life in the tower attached to their house. He never saw the publication of much of his work.

Compare the integration of university and town to your school/town situation. What would appeal or not appeal to you about attending the University of Tübingen?

Grammatik und Übungen *(Grammar and Exercises)*

1 Subject° pronouns

das Subjekt

Singular *(sg.)*	Plural *(pl.)*
1. **ich** I	**wir** we
2. **du** you	**Ihr** you
(familiar sg.)	*(familiar pl.)*
3. { **er** he, it	
es it	**sie** they
sie she, it	
Sie you *(formal, sg. and pl.)*	

A personal pronoun is said to have "person," which indicates the identity of the subject.

1. First person refers to the one(s) speaking *(I, we)*.
2. Second person refers to the one(s) spoken to *(you)*.
3. Third person refers to the one(s) or thing(s) spoken about *(he/it/she, they)*.

2 The subject pronouns *du, ihr, Sie*

Tag, Julia. ... Was machst **du?**
Tag, Lisa. Tag, Gerd! ... Was macht **ihr?**

In the *Einführung* (p. 4) you learned when to use the familiar form **du. Du** is used to address one person. The familiar form used to address more than one person is **ihr.**

Tag, Herr Wagner. ... Was machen **Sie?**
Tag, Frau Braun. Tag, Fräulein Schneider! ... Was machen **Sie?**

In the *Einführung* (p. 4) you learned when to use the formal form **Sie.** Like the English *you,* **Sie** can be used to address one person or more than one.

3 The meanings and use of *sie* and *Sie*

Glaubt **sie** das?	Does *she* believe that?
Glauben **sie** das?	Do *they* believe that?
Glauben **Sie** das?	Do *you* believe that?

In spoken German, the meanings of **sie** *(she)*, **sie** *(they)*, and **Sie** *(you)* can be distinguished by the corresponding verb forms and by context. In written German, **Sie** *(you)* is always capitalized.

sie + singular verb form = *she*
sie + plural verb form = *they*
Sie + plural verb form = *you* (formal)

1. Ich, du, er. Give the subject pronouns you would use in the following situations.

→ You're talking about a female friend. *sie*
→ You're talking to a female friend. *du*

1. You're talking about a male friend.
2. You're talking to a male friend.
3. You're talking about yourself.
4. You're talking about yourself and a friend.
5. You're talking to your parents.
6. You're talking to a clerk in a store.
7. You're talking about your father.
8. You're talking about your sister.
9. You're talking about a child.
10. You're talking to your professor.
11. You're talking about your friends.

4 **Present tense of *sein***

sein			to be		
ich **bin**	wir **sind**		I am	we are	
du **bist**	ihr **seid**		you are	you are	
er/es/sie **ist**	sie **sind**		he/it/she is	they are	
	Sie **sind**			you are	

The verb **sein**, like its English equivalent *to be*, is irregular in the present tense.

Ich bin fit!

SPORTFABRIK
Der Fitness-Treff!
Auguststr. 32-36, Bonn-Beuel
Telefon 02 28/46 60 08

Wie bist du?

Land und Leute

Du vs. Sie

www Go to the *Deutsch heute* website at
http://college.hmco.com.

Historically speaking, **sie sind** *(they are)* and **Sie sind** *(you are)* are the same form. It was considered polite to address someone in the third-person plural and to capitalize the pronoun in writing.

The development of formal pronouns to address a person was a phenomenon common to most European languages. English used to distinguish singular *thou/thee* from plural *ye/you; thou/thee* was restricted to informal usage, and *ye/you* was used both as informal plural and formal singular and plural. Today only *you* survives as our all-purpose pronoun. In German (as well as in other European languages such as French, Spanish, and Italian) there are still distinctions between the formal and informal pronouns for *you.*

The formal pronoun **Sie** is used for everyday communication outside the realm of family and friends. Even neighbors and co-workers address each other as **Sie** (**siezen**). **Du** (along with its plural form **ihr**) is traditionally a form of address used among relatives or close friends. An older person usually decides on the appropriateness of this form in speaking to someone younger. Most young people address each other with **du** (**duzen**) nowadays. A step somewhere between **du** and **Sie** is to use a first name and **Sie**. It is often used by an older person with a person who is much younger, for example, when parents meet the friends of their children who are in their late teens or early twenties. The parents usually address them with **Sie**, but use their first names. The friends, of course, say **Herr/Frau ...** and use **Sie**.

Sagen diese Studenten „du" oder „Sie" zueinander? (Universität Frankfurt)

Diskussion

Imagine that you are in a German-speaking country. What form of address (**du, Sie,** or **ihr**) would you use when speaking to these people in these situations?

You run into some friends in a shopping mall.

You are introduced to a new business associate in a restaurant.

You are angry at a police officer who is writing out a speeding ticket for you.

You congratulate your best friend on winning the Nobel Prize.

You are asking your parents for money.

2. Was für ein Mensch? At a party you are discussing various people. Describe them by choosing the adjectives from the **Schüttelkasten** box.

→ Melanie   *Melanie ist intelligent.*

1. Gerd
2. du
3. Monika und Lars
4. Professor Schneider
5. ich
6. wir
7. ihr
8. Ihr Nachbar/Ihre Nachbarin
9. Ihr Partner/Ihre Partnerin
10. Und Sie? Wie sind Sie?

Schüttelkasten

lustig   sehr ruhig
                fleißig
laut
            sehr musikalisch

sympathisch   nett

Surmising

 3. So ist sie/er. Your partner will point to a person in one of the photos below and ask you what adjectives you would apply to that person.

S1: Was für ein Mensch ist die Frau?
S2: Sie ist intelligent, aber faul.

1.

2.

3.

4.

 **Infinitive°**   der Infinitiv

Infinitive	Stem + ending	English equivalents
glauben	glaub + en	*to believe*
heißen	heiß + en	*to be named*
arbeiten	arbeit + en	*to work; to study*
wandern	wander + n	*to hike; to go walking*

The basic form of a verb (the form listed in dictionaries and vocabularies) is the infinitive. German infinitives consist of a stem and the ending **-en** or **-n.**

6   **The finite verb°**   das Verb

Andrea **arbeitet** viel.	Andrea *works* a lot.
Arbeitest du viel?	*Do* you *work* a lot?

The term "finite verb" indicates the form of the verb that agrees with the subject.

7   **Present tense° of regular verbs**   das Präsens

glauben	
ich glaube	wir glauben
du glaub**st**	ihr glaubt
er/es/sie glaubt	sie glauben
Sie glauben	

to believe	
I believe	we believe
you believe	you believe
he/it/she believes	they believe
you believe	

In the present tense, most English verbs have two different forms; most German verbs have four different forms.

The present tense of regular German verbs is formed by adding the endings **-e, -st, -t,** and **-en** to the infinitive stem. The verb endings change according to the subject. (Note that a few verbs like **wandern** add only **-n** instead of **-en: wir wandern.**) In informal spoken German, the ending **-e** is sometimes dropped from the **ich**-form: **Ich glaub' das nicht.**

> Gisela **spielt** gut Tennis.
> Frank und Alex **spielen** gut Basketball.

With a singular noun subject (**Gisela**) the verb ending is **-t.** With a plural noun subject (**Frank und Alex**) the verb ending is **-en.**

arbeiten: to work; to study	
ich arbeite	wir arbeiten
du arbeit**est**	ihr arbeit**et**
er/es/sie arbeit**et**	sie arbeiten
Sie arbeiten	

In regular English verbs, the third-person singular ending is usually *-s: she works.* After certain verb stems, however, this ending expands to *-es: she teaches.*

German also has verb stems that require an expansion of the ending. If a verb stem ends in **-d** or **-t,** the endings **-st** and **-t** expand to **-est** and **-et.** The other endings are regular.

heißen: to be called, named	
ich heiße	wir heißen
du heißt	ihr heißt
er/es/sie heißt	sie heißen
Sie heißen	

If a verb stem ends in a sibilant (**s, ss, ß, z**), the **-st** ending contracts to a **-t: du heißt, du tanzt.** The other endings are regular.

Leserunde

"Konjugation," by Rudolf Steinmetz, is another example of concrete poetry (see **Leserunde,** page 16). In "Konjugation," Steinmetz starts with the conjugation of a verb but ends the poem with a sudden, surprising twist, a device that is also characteristic of much of concrete poetry.

Konjugation

Ich gehe
du gehst
er geht
sie geht
es geht

Geht es?

Danke – es geht.

Rudolf Steinmetz

4. Heute ist Samstag. Complete the following dialogues by filling in the missing verb endings.

1. Monika und Stefan sind Tinas Freunde. Stefan arbeit_____ in dem Café
   an der Uni. Monika arbeit_____ auch dort°. Samstags arbeit_____ Monika
   und Stefan nicht.

   MONIKA: Geh_____ du heute joggen?

   STEFAN: Nein, ich spiel_____ heute Morgen mit Kevin Tennis. Später
   geh_____ wir mit Tina und Peter schwimmen. Und du? Was mach_____
   du heute?

   MONIKA: Ich glaub_____ , ich geh_____ joggen. Später lern°_____ ich ein
   bisschen Englisch. Ich schreib_____ nämlich° am Montag eine Klausur°.
   Aber heute Abend geh_____ wir tanzen, nicht wahr?

   STEFAN: Ja, Kevin komm_____ um acht.

there

study

after all / test

2. Gisela und Professor Lange sind in der Bibliothek.

GISELA: Guten Tag, Professor Lange. Wie geh_____ es Ihnen?

PROFESSOR LANGE: Gut, danke, Frau Riedholt. Was mach_____ Sie denn am Samstagmorgen in der Bibliothek?

GISELA: Ich schreib_____ die Seminararbeit für Sie, Herr Professor!

PROFESSOR LANGE: Arbeit_____ Sie nicht zu viel, Frau Riedholt! Schönes Wochenende!

GISELA: Danke, und auf Wiedersehen, Professor Lange.

8 The construction verb + *gern*

Ich spiele **gern** Tennis.	I like to play tennis.
Ich spiele **nicht gern** Golf.	I don't like to play golf.

The most common way of saying in German that you like doing something is to use the appropriate verb + **gern.** To say that you don't like doing something, use **nicht gern.**

 5. Was für Musik hörst du gern? Ask four fellow students what kind of music they like.

Stating preferences

S1: Was für Musik hörst du gern?
S2: Ich höre gern [Jazz].

| **Jazz** | **Rock** | **Pop** | **Country und Western** | **Techno** | **Rap** | **Reggae** | **klassische Musik** |

6. Was machst du? State what various people are doing by using the cues in the columns below. Answer in complete sentences.

→ Jürgen   *Jürgen macht viel Sport. Er geht gern ins Kino.*

1	2	3	4
ich	hören	gern	Sport
Linda und ich (wir)	machen	oft	Volleyball
Christin (sie)	spielen	viel	Musik
du	gehen	gut	ins Kino
Gisela und Alex (sie)			inlineskaten
ihr			
Jürgen (er)			

9 Position of *nicht*

The position of **nicht** is determined by various elements in the sentence. Below are a few general guidelines. Additional guidelines are found in later chapters.

1. **Nicht** always follows
   a. the finite verb

Gisela *arbeitet* **nicht.**	Gisela is not working.

   b. specific adverbs of time (e.g., **heute**)

Alex kommt *heute* **nicht.**	Alex is not coming today.

2. **Nicht** precedes most other elements
   a. predicate adjectives (e.g., **gut, lustig**)

   Alex ist **nicht** *faul.*   Alex isn't lazy.

   b. most adverbs (exceptions are specific time adverbs, e.g., **heute**)

   David spielt **nicht** *gut* Tennis.   David doesn't play tennis well.

   c. dependent infinitives (e.g., **schwimmen, inlineskaten**)

   Michael geht **nicht** *inlineskaten.*   Michael is not going in-line skating.

7. Wir nicht. Jutta, a new acquaintance, has some questions for you and Hans-Dieter. Answer in the negative.

➡ Macht ihr viel Sport?   *Nein. Wir machen nicht viel Sport.*

1. Spielt ihr viel Basketball?
2. Spielt ihr oft Tennis?
3. Schwimmt ihr gern?
4. Hört ihr gern Musik?
5. Geht ihr oft ins Kino?
6. Seid ihr sportlich?
7. Tanzt ihr gern?

Finding common likes and dislikes

8. Was machst du gern oder nicht gern? With a partner, try to find two activities you both enjoy doing and two you both dislike doing.

S1: Ich schwimme gern. Schwimmst du auch gern?
S2: Ja, ich schwimme gern./Nein, ich schwimme nicht gern.
     Ich spiele gern Tennis. Spielst du gern Tennis?

Schüttelkasten

Basketball   joggen   tanzen   arbeiten

inlineskaten gehen   Musik hören

ins Kino gehen   Fitnesstraining machen

10 Present-tense meanings

Linda **arbeitet** gut. = {
Linda *works* well. (plain)
Linda *does work* well. (emphatic)
Linda *is working* well. (progressive)
}

German uses a single verb form to express ideas or actions that may require one of three different forms in English.

Du **gehst** heute Nachmittag   You*'re going* swimming this afternoon,
   schwimmen, nicht?   aren't you?
Ich **mache** das morgen.   I*'ll do* that tomorrow.

German, like English, may use the present tense to express action intended or planned for the future.

Land und Leute

Sportvereine

www Go to the *Deutsch heute* website at http://college.hmco.com.

In Germany, Austria, and Switzerland people of all ages engage in sports. For more than 100 years sports clubs (**Sportvereine**) have been an important part of life in German-speaking countries. People who want to participate in competitive sports (**Hochleistungssport**) join a **Sportverein.** School sports are intramural rather than intermural. Athletes are not recruited by schools, and athletic scholarships are uncommon. In Germany alone there are approximately 87,000 **Sportvereine** with 27 million registered members. Approximately 2.5 million people work as volunteers in these organizations. The **Sportvereine** sponsor sports for almost every possible athletic interest. Clubs exist for sports as varied as badminton (**Badminton),** track and field (**Leichtathletik**) or water-skiing (**Wasserskilaufen**) and, of course, the world's most popular sport, soccer (**Fußball**). In recent years American football has made inroads in Europe and is represented in the German Sport Association (**Deutscher Sportbund**). The **Deutscher Sportbund** is the umbrella organiza-

Zwei Fußballvereine spielen gegeneinander.
(Weimar)

tion of individual clubs and sponsors national campaigns that encourage fitness and participation in sports. There are special activities and clubs for disabled athletes. Most of the **Sportvereine** and sports facilities are subsidized by the 16 federal states and local governments as well as private firms. Even the smallest village has its own **Verein,** which also plays an important part in the social life of the town.

Millions of people participate in running (**Laufen**), swimming (**Schwimmen**), tennis (**Tennis**), and skiing (**Skilaufen**) competitions every year on the local, national, or international level. Those who win or finish are awarded badges of merit as a sign of personal accomplishment. However, for most people who play sports, the primary purpose is not to win games but to be physically active and to be with people in a social setting.

Fußball is the most popular sport in the German-speaking countries. The German Football Association (**Deutscher Fußball-Bund**) has more than 5.5 million members. More than 75,000 women play soccer. Germany has separate professional soccer leagues (**Bundesligen**) for men and women.

Diskussion

People in German-speaking countries who want to become professional athletes would probably begin their careers by joining a local **Sportverein.** How does this compare to the career path for a professional athlete in your country?

9. Wie sagt man das? *(How do you say that?)* Give the German equivalents of the following sentences.

➜ Frank does not work well.   *Frank arbeitet nicht gut.*

1. Karla does work a lot.
2. I do believe that.
3. Stefan does play soccer well.
4. You're working tonight, Beatrix.
5. You do that well, Tina.
6. I'm playing tennis today.
7. We're playing basketball today.
8. I believe so.
9. Detlev is going to the movies.
10. I'm going dancing.

11 Informational questions

Wann gehst du schwimmen? ∧   *When* are you going swimming?
Wer arbeitet heute Nachmittag? ∧   *Who* is working this afternoon?

A question that asks for a particular bit of information is called an informational question. It begins with an interrogative expression such as **wann** *(when)* or **wer** *(who)*. The interrogative is followed by the verb. In an informational question in German, the finite verb is used. In English, a form of the auxiliary verb *to be* or *to do* is often used with a form of the main verb. In German, the voice normally falls at the end of an informational question, just as it does in English.

Some common interrogatives are:

wann *(when)*	**was für (ein)** *(what kind of)*	**wie** *(how)*
warum *(why)*	**welch(-er, -es, -e)** *(which)*	**wie viel** *(how much)*
was *(what)*	**wer** *(who)*	**wie viele** *(how many)*

10. Wer bist du? Complete the questions with a suitable interrogative. Then ask your partner the questions.

1. —— heißt du?
2. —— ist deine Adresse?
3. —— alt bist du?
4. —— ein Mensch bist du?
5. —— machst du gern?
6. —— arbeitest du heute?
7. —— Uhr ist es?
8. —— bist du so müde?

Asking informational questions

11. Wer? Was? Wann? Your partner has a list showing when various people are playing particular games. Ask your partner three questions, one beginning with **wer** *(who)*, one with **was,** and one with **wann.**

S1:
Wer spielt heute Squash?
Wann spielt ihr Volleyball?
Was spielt Professor Krause?

S2:
Barbara spielt heute Squash.
Wir spielen **um halb sechs** Volleyball.
Er spielt **Golf.**

Wer?	Wann?	Was?
Barbara	heute	Squash
Anne und Kevin	um drei	Schach
ich	um acht	Fußball
Professor Krause	heute Abend	Golf
wir	um halb sechs	Volleyball

⑫ Yes/No questions

Gehst du heute schwimmen? ↘	*Are* you *going* swimming today?
Treiben Sie gern Sport? ↘	*Do* you *like to play* sports?

A question that can be answered with yes or no begins with the verb. A yes/no question in German uses the finite verb, whereas English often requires a form of the auxiliary verb *to do* or *to be* plus a form of the main verb. In German, the voice normally rises at the end of a yes/no question, just as it does in English.

12. Ja oder nein? Ask your partner three questions based on the cues. Your partner will then ask you the three questions.

Confirming or denying

arbeiten: heute Abend

> **S1:** Arbeitest du heute Abend?
> **S2:** Ja, ich arbeite heute Abend.
>   Nein, ich arbeite heute Abend nicht.

1. schwimmen: gern, oft, gut
2. spielen: gern, gut, oft / Basketball, Golf, Videospiele, Karten
3. schreiben: gern, viel, gut
4. gehen: heute Abend, gern, oft / ins Kino, in die Bibliothek
5. gehen: gern, oft, heute Abend / joggen, inlineskaten, tanzen
6. hören: oft, gern / Musik, Rock, Rap, klassische Musik
7. heben: oft, gern / Gewichte
8. machen: oft, gern, heute / Fitnesstraining, Aerobic

⑬ Tag questions

Du hörst gern Musik, **nicht wahr?**	You like to listen to music, *don't you?*
Mark geht heute Abend ins Kino, **nicht?**	Mark is going to the movies tonight, *isn't he?*

A tag question is literally "tagged on" to the end of a statement. In English the tag equivalent to **nicht wahr?** or **nicht?** depends on the subject of the sentence: *don't you?, aren't you?, isn't he?,* and *doesn't she?,* etc.

13. Nicht? In a conversation with a friend, ask for confirmation that what you think is correct. Use the tag question **nicht?** or **nicht wahr?**

> → Frau Meier ist sehr nett. *Frau Meier ist sehr nett, nicht?*
>   *Frau Meier ist sehr nett, nicht wahr?*

1. Professor Wagner arbeitet viel.
2. Sie und ihr Mann wandern gern.
3. Jürgen ist oft müde.
4. Rita macht viel Sport.
5. Sie schwimmt gut.
6. Sie ist auch sehr intelligent.

14. Wie sagt man das? You overhear someone on the phone talking with Ina. Translate the questions for Dieter, your German friend.

> → Ina, how are you? *Ina, wie geht's?*

1. What are you doing, Ina?
2. Are you working?

3. Are you going swimming today?
4. When are you playing tennis, Ina?
5. Does Rudi play well?
6. What kind of person is Rudi?
7. Do you like to play chess?
8. Rudi likes to play, too, doesn't he?
9. You're coming at seven, aren't you?

15. Ein Interview. You are looking for a new roommate. Write five questions you want to ask the person about her/his likes, dislikes, and activities. Then find a partner and conduct an interview.

Wiederholung

1. Rollenspiel. You and your partner meet on the street. Your partner asks how you are and what you intend to do. Give affirmative or negative answers.

speech patterns

Redemittel°: Positiv oder negativ beantworten (Giving positive or negative responses)			
Ich glaube ja.	Natürlich (nicht).	Ja, gern.	Es geht.
Ich glaube nicht.	Vielleicht (nicht).	Na gut.	

1. Wie geht es dir heute?
2. Bist du denn krank?
3. Arbeitest du heute Nachmittag?
4. Gehst du heute Abend ins Fitness-Studio?
5. Machst du gern Sport/Fitnesstraining?
6. Kommst du am Wochenende auch zum Basketballspiel/Hockeyspiel/Fußballspiel?

2. Ja, Veronika. Confirm Veronika's information about you and your friends. Use a pronoun in your answer.

→ Gabi arbeitet in Basel, nicht wahr?   *Ja, sie arbeitet in Basel.*

1. Du arbeitest in Zürich, nicht?
2. Wolf hört gern Musik, nicht wahr?
3. Renate und Paula spielen gut Rockmusik, nicht?
4. Wir spielen gut Basketball, nicht?
5. Trudi macht viel Sport, nicht wahr?
6. Du und Regina, ihr spielt gern Tennis, nicht?

3. Was machen sie? Somebody you know slightly is asking about your friends. Construct sentences using the following cues.

→ wie / heißen / der Junge / ?   *Wie heißt der Junge?*

1. er / heißen / Konrad
2. er / studieren / in Berlin / ?

3. nein / er / studieren / in München
4. wie / arbeiten / er / ?
5. er / sein / fleißig
6. was / machen / Martha und er / heute Abend / ?
7. sie / gehen / ins Kino
8. wann / sie / gehen / ins Kino / ?
9. wer / treiben / gern / Sport / ?
10. Martha / spielen / gut / Fußball

4. Ergänzen Sie. Complete the following exchanges with appropriate words.

1. PROFESSOR: _____ heißen Sie?

   STUDENT: Ich _____ Alex Fischer.

2. HERR WAGNER: Guten Tag, Frau Schneider. Wie _____ es Ihnen?

   FRAU SCHNEIDER: Danke. Es _____ .

3. MARIA: Arbeitest _____ heute nicht?

   VOLKER: Nein, ich _____ heute Tennis.

   MARIA: _____ du viel Sport?

   VOLKER: Ja, _____ spiele gern Volleyball.

4. ALEX: _____ gehst du ins Kino?

   GISELA: _____ 7 Uhr.

Was finden diese jungen Leute so lustig? (Universität Mannheim)

5. Wie sagt man das? Give the German equivalent of the questions you ask Cornelia.

1. Cornelia, how are you?
2. What are you doing?
3. Are you working?
4. Are you going swimming today?
5. Is Michael going also?

6. When are you playing tennis?
7. Does Michael play well?
8. What kind of person is Michael?
9. He likes to play chess, doesn't he?

6. Wer ist das? Choose one of the persons in the picture on page 51 and invent some facts about the person.

Wie heißt sie/er? Was für ein Mensch ist sie/er? Was macht sie/er gern? Wo studiert sie/er? ???

7. Frage-Ecke. You and your partner are talking about the activities of certain people. Ask each other questions to find out who does what and at what times. Then fill in the **ich** column of your schedule with your own information and ask your partner about her/his activities. **S1**'s information is below; the information for **S2** is in Appendix B.

S1: Was macht Peter heute Morgen?
S2: Er macht heute Morgen Deutsch. Was machen Alex und Gisela am Samstag?
S1: Sie spielen am Samstag Schach.

S1:

	heute Morgen	heute Abend	Samstag	Sonntag
Monika	Deutsch machen		ins Kino gehen	
Peter		Musik hören	in die Bibliothek gehen	
Alex und Gisela		tanzen	Schach spielen	
ich				
Partnerin/ Partner				

Meeting and greeting people

8. Gespräche. You meet a fellow classmate on campus. Work out the following dialogue with a partner.

1. Greet her/him.
2. Ask how she/he is.
3. Ask what she/he is doing this afternoon.
4. Tell what you are doing.
5. Ask whether she/he likes to play tennis.
6. Arrange a time to play together tomorrow.

9. Zum Schreiben

1. Think ahead to the weekend and, using complete sentences, write down at least three things you will do and three things you will not do. Use a separate sentence for each thing.

2. Using Gisela's letter to Monika and Stefan (see page 35) as a model, write a letter to a friend about your room, your school, and one friend. Before you write the letter, reread Gisela's letter and notice how she uses the words **und, aber, auch, furchtbar,** and **jedenfalls.** Try to use some of these words in your letter. You may also want to review the vocabulary for the names of things in your room that were presented in the *Einführung.*

Grammatik: Zusammenfassung *(Grammar: Summary)*

Subject pronouns

Singular		Plural	
1.	**ich** I	**wir** we	
2.	**du** you *(familiar)*	**ihr** you *(familiar)*	
	er he, it		
3.	**es** it	**sie** they	
	sie she, it		
		Sie you *(formal)*	

Present tense of *sein*

sein: to be	
ich **bin**	wir **sind**
du **bist**	ihr **seid**
er/es/sie **ist**	sie **sind**
Sie **sind**	

The verb **sein,** like its English equivalent *to be,* is irregular in the present tense.

Infinitive and infinitive stem

Infinitive	Stem + ending
glauben	glaub + en
wandern	wander + n

The basic form of a verb is the infinitive. Most German infinitives end in **-en;** a few end in **-n,** such as **wandern.** In vocabularies and dictionaries, verbs are listed in their infinitive form.

Present tense of regular verbs

	glauben	arbeiten	heißen
ich	glaube	arbeite	heiße
du	glaubst	arbeitest	heißt
er/es/sie	glaubt	arbeitet	heißt
wir	glauben	arbeiten	heißen
ihr	glaubt	arbeitet	heißt
sie	glauben	arbeiten	heißen
Sie	glauben	arbeiten	heißen

1. German verb endings change, depending on what the subject of the verb is. The verb endings are added to the infinitive stem. There are four basic endings in the present tense of most regular verbs: **-e, -st, -t, en.**
2. If a verb stem ends in **-d** or **-t,** the endings **-st** and **-t** expand to **-est** and **-et.**
3. If a verb stem ends in a sibilant (**s, ss, ß, z**), the **-st** ending contracts to **-t.**

Position of *nicht*

The position of **nicht** is determined by the various elements in the sentence. Because of the great flexibility of **nicht,** its use is best learned by observing its position in sentences you hear and read. Here are several guidelines:

1. **Nicht** always follows:

   a. the finite verb:

   Bernd *arbeitet* **nicht.**   Bernd is not working.

   b. specific adverbs of time

   Sara spielt *heute* **nicht.**   Sara is not playing today.

2. **Nicht** precedes most other elements:

   a. predicate adjectives

   Sebastian ist **nicht** *nett.*   Sebastian isn't nice.

   b. most adverbs (exceptions are specific adverbs of time)

   Er spielt **nicht** *gut* Tennis.   He doesn't play tennis well.

   c. adverbs of general time

   Er spielt **nicht** *oft* Tennis.   He doesn't play tennis often.

   d. dependent infinitives

   Tanya geht **nicht** *schwimmen.*   Tanya is not going swimming.

3. If several of the elements occur in a sentence, **nicht** usually precedes the first one.

   Ich gehe **nicht** *oft ins Kino.*   I don't often go to the movies.

Informational questions

1	2	3	
Wann	gehen	Sie?	When are you going?
Was	machst	du heute?	What are you doing today?

In an informational question in German, an interrogative is in first position and the finite verb in second position. Some common interrogatives are **wann, was, welch(-er, -es, -e), wer, wie, was für ein, warum,** and **wie viel/viele.**

Yes/No questions

1	2	3	
Bist	du	müde?	Are you tired?
Spielt	Andrea	gut?	Does Andrea play well?
Arbeitest	du	heute?	Are you working today?

In a yes/no question in German, the finite verb is in first position.

KAPITEL 2

Alles ist relativ

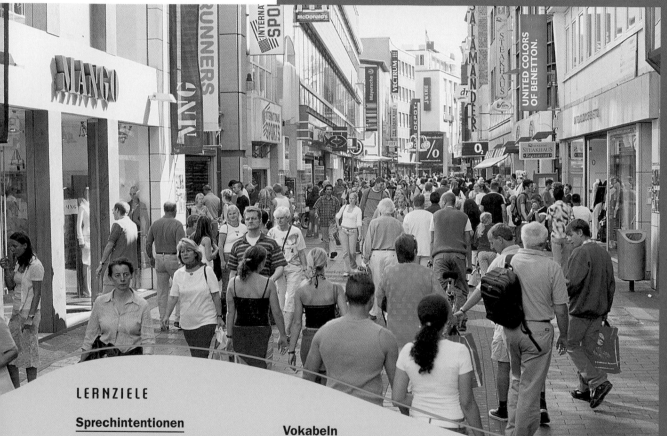

Viele Menschen auf der Hohestraße in Köln – ein typisch deutsches Straßenbild

LERNZIELE

Sprechintentionen

Talking about the weather
Inquiring about someone's birthday
Summarizing information
Stating one's nationality
Expressing skepticism

Lesestück

Groß oder klein? Alles ist relativ!

Land und Leute

Berlin
Birthday customs and greetings
Development of the standard
  German language

Vokabeln

Weather expressions
Months and seasons
Suffixes *-er* and *-in*
Names of countries and
  nationalities
The question word *woher*

Grammatik

Simple past tense of *sein*
Present tense of *haben*
Position of the finite verb in
  statements
Nominative case
Plural of nouns

Indefinite article *ein*
Expressing negation by *kein* and
  nicht
Possession with proper names
Possessive adjectives
Demonstrative pronouns *der, das,
  die*

56

Bausteine für Gespräche

Wie ist das Wetter?

Im Sommer

FRAU KLUGE: Schönes Wetter, nicht wahr, Professor Lange? Zu schön für die
Bibliothek!

PROFESSOR LANGE: Ja, aber es ist zu heiß und zu sonnig. Heute Abend arbeite ich
mal im Garten. Da ist alles ganz trocken.

FRAU KLUGE: Vielleicht regnet es morgen ja.

PROFESSOR LANGE: Na, hoffentlich!

Richtig oder falsch?

1. Frau Kluge findet das Wetter nicht schön.
2. Professor Lange findet das Wetter toll.
3. Er arbeitet am Wochenende im Garten.
4. Der Garten ist trocken.
5. Vielleicht schneit es morgen.

Im Herbst

GISELA: Was für ein Wetter! Der Wind ist furchtbar kalt! Und alles ist so grau. Ich
glaube, es regnet heute noch.

MICHAEL: Für Regen ist es fast zu kalt. Es ist nur ein Grad. Vielleicht schneit es ja.
Am Wochenende gehe ich wandern. Hoffentlich ist es da trocken und nicht so
kalt. Und vielleicht scheint ja die Sonne.

GISELA: Ja, bestimmt! Wer geht mit?

MICHAEL: Mein Freund Klaus aus Hamburg.

GISELA: Wie nett! Ich bleibe leider hier und arbeite für die Uni.

Richtig oder falsch?

1. Heute ist es sonnig.
2. Der Wind ist sehr kalt.
3. Es sind elf Grad.
4. Es regnet.
5. Es schneit auch.
6. Michael geht am Wochenende wandern.
7. Klaus ist Giselas Freund aus Hamburg.
8. Gisela bleibt am Wochenende in Tübingen und arbeitet für die Uni.

Brauchbares

1. In German an adjective that precedes a noun has an ending, e.g., **schön*es*
   Wetter.** If the adjective does not precede a noun it has no ending (e.g., **Es ist
   schön**).

2. The use of little words like **mal, ja,** and **na** is common in colloquial German;
   they are called flavoring particles. When Professor Lange says **Heute Abend
   arbeite ich mal im Garten,** he is leaving the exact time vague. In Frau Kluge's
   statement **Vielleicht regnet es morgen ja,** the **ja** conveys the meaning of *after
   all.* Professor Lange replies: **Na, hoffentlich!** The word **na** is equivalent to English *well.* Flavoring particles will be discussed further in *Kapitel 3.*

3. Note that in German when the subject (e.g., **es**) does not begin the sentence it follows the verb (e.g., **Vielleicht regnet es morgen ja**).
4. **Was für ein.** Compare the exclamation **Was für ein [Wetter]!**—*What (a) [weather]!*—to the question **Was für ein [Mensch ist er]?**—*What kind of (person is he)?*
5. German-speaking countries use the Celsius thermometer. Twenty degrees Celsius = 68 degrees Fahrenheit.

1. Das Wetter in Amerika. David Carpenter is an American exchange student in Tübingen. He is surfing the Web to find out what the weather is like in various cities in the United States where his family and friends live. He is telling Gisela and Alex what he has found. Change the Fahrenheit temperatures into Celsius by using the thermometer shown here.

1. In Phoenix sind es 102 Grad.
2. In Seattle sind es 68 Grad.
3. In Chicago ist es warm, 80 Grad.
4. In Bangor im Staat Maine sind es 71 Grad.
5. In Barrow in Alaska sind es nur 45 Grad.

Discussing the weather

 2. Schönes Wetter, nicht? A fellow student comments on the weather. Agree with her/him.

S2:		*S1:*	
Schönes	Wetter, hm?	Ja, es ist wirklich	**schön.**
Schlechtes			schlecht.

Schüttelkasten

schlecht gut nass⁺ furchtbar heiß kühl⁺ schön sonnig schwül⁺ windig⁺ warm⁺ wolkig⁺

 3. Was sagen Sie? Make each of the comments below to a partner. After each comment, your partner will respond with an appropriate expression from the list. Your partner should avoid using the same expression each time.

Na, hoffentlich. ■ Leider. ■ Vielleicht. ■ Jetzt⁺ bleibt es so. ■ Ja, sehr. ■ Vielleicht schneit es bald⁺. ■ Vielleicht regnet es ja. ■ Nein, noch nicht⁺.

1. Heute ist es ja warm.
2. Heute ist es wirklich heiß.
3. Es ist zu trocken.
4. Was für ein Wetter!
5. Der Wind ist furchtbar kalt.
6. Schneit es?
7. Jetzt bleibt es bestimmt kalt.
8. Vielleicht scheint die Sonne morgen.

4. Was für ein Wetter! A fellow student is unhappy with today's weather. Respond by commenting on the weather yesterday.

Stating displeasure about the weather

S2:		*S1:*	
Was für ein	**Wetter!**	Ja, und gestern war es	**noch schön warm.**
	Wind!		auch schlecht.
	Regen⁺!		auch kalt.
	Schnee⁺!		noch trocken.

5. Hören Sie zu. Listen to the following short weather report on the radio. Then indicate whether the statements made below are **richtig** or **falsch**. You will hear one new word: **Höchsttemperatur** *(highest temperature)*.

1. In Hamburg ist es heiß und schwül.
2. In Köln sind es 15 Grad und es regnet.
3. In Stuttgart ist es trocken und es sind 24 Grad.
4. In München ist es windig und kühl.
5. In Berlin ist es nass und es sind 16 Grad.

Sie sind in Köln. Was für Sport machen Sie hier im Sommer? Und im Winter?

Erweiterung des Wortschatzes

1. Die Monate+

Der Mai war schön, nicht?   May was nice, wasn't it?

All the names of the months are **der**-words.

Januar	Februar	März
April	**Mai**	**Juni**
Juli	August	September
Oktober	November	Dezember

2. Die Jahreszeiten+

der **Frühling**

der **Sommer**

der **Herbst**

der **Winter**

1. Was für ein Monat ist ... ? Choose a month and ask your partner what kind of month it is: **Frühlingsmonat, Sommermonat, Herbstmonat,** or **Wintermonat.**

> *S1:* Was für ein Monat ist der Juni?
> *S2:* Der Juni ist ein Sommermonat.

2. Wann ist es ... ? Tell in what months the following weather conditions occur where you live. Notice that with months the German word for *in* is **im.**

➔ Wann ist es oft kalt?   *Im Januar und im Februar.*

1. Wann regnet es viel?
2. Wann schneit es viel?
3. Wann ist es oft heiß / schwül / windig?

4. Wann scheint die Sonne nicht viel?
5. Wann ist es schön warm?
6. Wann ist es sehr trocken?
7. Wann ist der Wind kalt? warm? heiß?
8. Wann ist das Wetter gut – nicht heiß und nicht kalt?

 3. Wie ist das Wetter in ... ? Ask your partner about the weather in one of the four cities below. Your partner will then ask you about the weather in one of the other cities. The dates are spoken as **der zehnte Mai, der vierte Januar, der elfte Juli, der zweite Oktober.** Below are forms of the questions and answers you can use.

1. Wie ist das Wetter heute in [Berlin]?
   a. Das Wetter ist heute [schön / schlecht / gut].
   b. Es ist [warm / heiß / kalt / kühl / nass / trocken / sonnig / windig].
   c. Es [regnet / schneit].
   d. Die Sonne scheint heute.
2. Wie viel Grad sind es?
   Es sind [18 Grad]. / Es sind [minus zwei Grad].
3. Welche Jahreszeit ist es [in Berlin]?
4. Wie ist das Wetter [hier / in Vermont] im [Winter / Sommer / Herbst / Frühling]?

Hamburg: 10°C/50°F	Zürich: -15°C/5°F	München°: 36°C/97°F	Wien°: 21°C/70°F
10. Mai	4. Januar	11. Juli	2. Oktober

Munich / Vienna

 4. Wann hast du Geburtstag⁺? Interview four students to find out the months of their birthdays.

Discussing birthdays

S1: Wann hast du Geburtstag?
S2: Ich habe im [Mai] Geburtstag.

Vokabeln 1

Nouns whose plural forms are commonly used are listed with their plural forms:
die Jahreszeit, -en = die Jahreszeiten.

Substantive

der **Frühling** spring
der **Geburtstag** birthday
der **Grad** degree *(temperature only)*
der **Herbst** autumn, fall
die **Jahreszeit, -en** season
der **Monat, -e** month
der **Regen** rain

der **Schnee** snow
der **Sommer** summer
die **Sonne** sun
das **Wetter** weather
der **Wind** wind
der **Winter** winter
For the months see page 60.

Verben

bleiben   to remain, stay
finden   to find; to think
regnen   to rain; **es regnet**   it's
   raining

scheinen   to shine
schneien   to snow; **es schneit**   it's
   snowing
war   was (*past tense of* **sein**)

Andere Wörter

alles   everything; all
aus   (to come) from (city or country);
   aus Hamburg   from Hamburg
bald   soon
bestimmt   certain(ly), for sure
fast   almost
für   for
gestern   yesterday
heiß   hot
hier   here
hm   hm
hoffentlich   I hope so
jetzt   now
kalt   cold
kühl   cool
leider   unfortunately

morgen   tomorrow
na   well
nass   wet
noch   still; in addition; **noch nicht**
   not yet
schön   nice, beautiful
schwül   humid
sonnig   sunny
trocken   dry
warm   warm; **schön warm**
   nice and warm
windig   windy
wirklich   really
wolkig   cloudy
zu   too

Besondere Ausdrücke

Es sind [minus] [10] Grad.   It's
   [minus] [10] degrees.
Ich habe im [Mai] Geburtstag.   My
   birthday is in [May].
im [Herbst]   in the [fall]; **im [Mai]**
   in [May]
schönes Wetter   nice weather
Wann hast du Geburtstag?   When is
   your birthday?

Was für ein Wetter!   What weather!
Wer geht mit?   Who's coming along?
Wie ist das Wetter?   How's the
   weather?
Wie viel Grad sind es?   What's the
   temperature?

Groß oder klein? Alles ist relativ!

Vorbereitung auf das Lesen

▧ Vor dem Lesen

1. Look at the advertisement on the next page and answer the following
   questions.
   a. What does the advertisement imply about the winter weather in Germany?
   b. What is the weather like in Florida?
   c. How much does a ticket from Frankfurt to Miami cost? Do you find the
      price expensive (**teuer**), reasonable (**günstig**), or cheap (**billig**)?

3: Berlin lies approximately on the 52nd parallel, roughly on the same latitude as James Bay, Canada, or Edmonton, the capital of Alberta, Canada. No major population centers in Canada or the continental U.S. extend as far north as Berlin. For example, Winnipeg lies below the 51st parallel, Boston below the 42nd.

2. Do you think the concept of cold means the same thing to inhabitants of Florida as to those of Toronto, Canada? What temperature do you personally think is cold on a winter day?
3. On a map of the world locate Berlin, the capital of Germany, and Washington, D.C. Which city is farther north?
4. Where do you think winters are coldest: Minnesota (U.S.A.), Ontario (Canada), or northern Germany? Why?
5. Where do you think winters are colder: in northern Germany (Hamburg) or in southern Germany (Munich)?
6. In area, Germany is the third largest country of the European Union, after France and Spain. How large do you think Germany is compared to your state or province?
7. Using the map in the front of the book, locate the following cities: Tübingen, Berlin, Hamburg, and Munich.

▧ Beim Lesen

1. In the reading you will find data on the number of inhabitants of Germany, Germany's size, and distances within the country. As you are reading, make notes on the relevant facts about Germany.
2. Which words or concepts in the text would you consider to be relative, depending on a person's experience?
3. Circle or make a list of the cognates.

Like most American exchange students, David takes classes in the German language. One of his assignments is to write a short paper on differences between the United States and Germany. David chooses to concentrate on the weather and geography.

bin seit: have been for

apart

day's trip (by car)

after all

approximately

about

Besides

Ich komme aus Washington D.C. und bin seit° drei Wochen in Tübingen. Ich finde Tübingen sehr schön und auch interessant, aber sehr klein. Am Wochenende war ich in Berlin. Berlin ist toll und sehr groß. Ich denke, Washington ist nicht so groß, aber wie in Washington liegt dort alles weit 5 auseinander°.

Was ist anders in Deutschland? Ganz einfach – Amerika ist groß, Deutschland ist klein. Amerika hat zweihundertachtundsiebzig Millionen Einwohner, Deutschland hat nur dreiundachtzig Millionen. Und Deutschland ist nur etwa halb so groß wie Texas (oder Alberta).

10 Für die Menschen hier sind Distanzen anders. Meine Freunde sagen: „Berlin ist weit weg von Tübingen. Fast 700 km." 700 km finde ich nicht weit. Von Seattle im Nordwesten der USA nach Miami im Südosten sind es fast 5500 km. Das finde ich weit! Aber von Tübingen nach Berlin ist ja nur eine Tagesreise°. Das ist schön in Deutschland. Interessante Städte 15 liegen oft nicht weit auseinander.

Das Wetter ist hier anders. Generell sind die Temperaturen in Deutschland nicht so extrem wie sie manchmal in Nordamerika sind. Hier beeinflusst nämlich° der Ozean das Klima und er beeinflusst es mehr im Norden als im Süden und mehr im Westen als im Osten. Mein Freund Michael kommt aus 20 Hamburg im Norden. Dort ist der Sommer relativ kühl und der Winter ist mild. Aber in München im Süden von Deutschland ist der Winter ziemlich kalt und es schneit oft.

Aber alles ist relativ. Auch Temperaturen! Im Sommer ist es hier nicht so heiß wie in Washington. Washington liegt ja auch circa° 1200 km weiter 25 südlich als Tübingen. Meine Freunde hier finden 33 Grad im Sommer sehr heiß und sagen: „Oh, es ist furchtbar heiß." In Washington ist das ganz normal. Ich glaube, viele Leute hier finden das Wetter sehr wichtig. Sie sagen oft: „Oh je, es regnet" und „Oh je, es ist zu kalt!" oder „Oh, es ist zu heiß". Ich rede nicht so viel über° das Wetter. Das finde ich zu uninteressant. Außer- 30 dem° finde ich Schnee und auch Regen sehr schön. Hoffentlich schneit es viel im Winter. Dann gehe ich in die Schweiz zum Snowboarden.

Brauchbares

1. **km (kilometer):** German-speaking countries use kilometers to measure distance. One kilometer equals .62 mile.
2. Note the phrase in l. 13: **sind es fast 5500 Kilometer** (*it is almost 5500 kilometers*). In German **es** is only a "dummy" subject; the real subject, **5500 Kilometer,** is plural; therefore the verb is plural, i.e., **sind.** With a singular subject the verb would be **ist: Es ist nur ein Kilometer** (*It is only one kilometer*). The equivalent English phrase, *it is,* never changes, whether the real subject is singular or plural.

Nach dem Lesen

1. Ergänzen Sie. Using your notes on the reading, complete the following sentences.

1. Deutschland hat _____ Einwohner.
2. Deutschland ist etwa halb so groß wie _____ .

3. Von Tübingen nach Berlin sind es etwa _____ Kilometer.

4. In Deutschland ist das Klima mild, denn der _____ beeinflusst das Klima.

5. In Hamburg ist der Winter ziemlich _____ .

2. Fragen zum Lesestück

1. Wie lange ist David schon in Tübingen?
2. Welche Stadt liegt weiter nördlich – Washington oder Tübingen?
3. Findet David die Distanz zwischen° Tübingen und Berlin groß?   between
4. Wie viele Kilometer sind für Sie eine Tagesreise?
5. Was findet David schön in Deutschland?
6. Wie ist der Winter in München?
7. Welche Temperatur finden Davids Freunde heiß? Was sagen sie?
8. Finden Sie das Wetter wichtig? Sprechen Sie gern über das Wetter?

3. Erzählen wir. (Let's talk about it.)

1. Before you can talk about a topic you need to have the appropriate vocabulary. Go back to the text and write down several words in addition to the one provided that you could use when you talk about Germany.

   Klima: Sommer, _____ , _____

   Größe°: Kilometer, _____ , _____   size

2. Talk briefly about one of the following topics.

   Das Wetter in Deutschland.
   Deutschland ist klein.
   Das Wetter in meiner Stadt.

4. Deutschland und seine° Nachbarn. Germany is situated in the center of   its
Europe, and it has many neighboring countries. Using the map of Europe on the
inside back cover of your book, fill in the missing country names in the para-
graph below. Note: Certain names of countries in German are always used with a   Summarizing information
definite article. Some of these countries are: **die Schweiz** (Switzerland), **die
Niederlande** (The Netherlands), and **die Tschechische Republik** (Czech
Republic).

   Deutschland liegt im Zentrum° Europas. Es hat neun Nachbarn: Das   center

   Nachbarland im Norden ist _____ ; die Nachbarländer im Süden

   sind _____ und die _____ ; im Osten liegen _____ und

   die _____ ; im Westen _____ , _____ , _____ und

   die _____ .

**Auf der Autobahn sind es nur 72 Kilometer
von Augsburg nach Ulm. Wie weit ist es von
Karlsruhe bis nach Ulm? Bis nach Augsburg?**

[1]*part-time help* [2]*wanted*

Wer arbeitet im Restaurant?

Wie heißt das Restaurant?

[1]*taxi driver*

**Wie viele Euro verdient
(*earns*) ein Taxifahrer oder
eine Taxifahrerin?**

**Wie ist die Telefonnummer
von Taxi Schneider?**

Erweiterung des Wortschatzes

1. The suffix *-in*

Masculine	der Nachbar
Feminine	die Nachbar**in**
Feminine plural	die Nachbar**innen**

The suffix **-in** added to the singular masculine noun gives the feminine equivalent. The plural of a noun with the suffix **-in** ends in **-nen**.

1. Mann oder Frau? Give the other form—feminine or masculine—of the words listed below.

➡ die Professorin   *der Professor*

1. die Freundin
2. der Student
3. die Amerikanerin
4. der Einwohner
5. die Ingenieurin
6. der Journalist
7. die Musikerin
8. der Physiotherapeut

2. Names of countries

Wie groß ist **Deutschland?**	How large is Germany?
Existiert **das romantische Deutschland** noch?	Does romantic Germany still exist?

The names of most countries are neuter; for example (**das**) **Deutschland** and (**das**) **Österreich.** Articles are not used with names of countries that are neuter, unless the name is preceded by an adjective.

Die Schweiz ist schön.	Switzerland is beautiful.
Die USA sind groß.	The United States is large.

The names of a few countries are feminine (e.g., **die Schweiz**); some names are used only in the plural (e.g., **die USA**). Articles are always used with names of countries that are feminine or plural.

2. Andere Länder. Try to guess the English names for the countries listed below.

1. Italien
2. Spanien
3. Griechenland
4. Russland
5. Brasilien
6. Frankreich
7. Norwegen
8. Liechtenstein
9. die Türkei
10. die Niederlande

Land und Leute

Berlin: Deutschlands „neue" Hauptstadt

www Go to the *Deutsch heute* website at http://college.hmco.com.

The origins of Berlin lie in the twelfth century. In its long history Berlin has served as the capital city of many German states and forms of government, including the monarchy of the Hohenzollerns, the Third Reich, and the German Democratic Republic. In 1990 Berlin became the capital of a newly united Germany. History, geography, and politics have all contributed to make Berlin a cultural center of Europe.

Berlin is a **Stadtstaat** (city state) and Germany's largest city in population (3.39 million). Berlin's population is diverse, with almost 13% consisting of foreigners from 185 countries, the largest group from Turkey. Historically, Berlin was a center of education, commerce, culture, and science. This tradition is still alive today. Berlin has more than 250 state and private centers for scientific research, including fourteen colleges and universities, as well as 150 theaters that offer programs ranging from the classics to the newest artistic forms. It is also the home of 179 museums. With five major museums, the **Museumsinsel** is one of the most important museum complexes in the world. Separate from the **Museumsinsel** are other well-known museums such as the Egyptian Museum (**das Ägyptische Museum**), with the famous bust of Queen Nefertiti, and the new Jewish museum (**das Jüdische Museum**), opened in 2001. Each year Berlin hosts the international film festival, the **Berlinale**, founded in 1951. A more recent annual event is the **Loveparade.** More than a half million people attend this festival for techno and international electronic music that promotes music as a way to international understanding. A visitor to Berlin is struck by the wide variety of architectural styles ranging from the palaces to the remnants of the socialist architecture of East Germany to the modern office buildings erected after unification. Perhaps surprisingly, Berlin also offers a wide choice of outdoor activities, because approximately one-fourth of Berlin's 888 square kilometers consists of green space and one-tenth is covered by lakes and rivers.

Diskussion

If you visited Berlin, which aspect of the city would you most want to explore—its history, its museums, its parks? Explain your choice.

3. Nouns indicating citizenship and nationality

Berlin	der Berliner	die Berlinerin
Österreich	der Österreicher	die Österreicherin
die Schweiz	der Schweizer	die Schweizerin
Amerika	der Amerikaner	die Amerikanerin
Kanada	der Kanadier	die Kanadierin
Deutschland	der Deutsche (ein Deutscher)	die Deutsche

Nouns indicating an inhabitant of a city or a citizen of a country follow several patterns. While you won't be able to predict the exact form, you will always be able to recognize it.

The noun suffix **-er** is added to the name of many cities, states, or countries to indicate a male citizen or inhabitant (**Berliner**). Some nouns take an umlaut (**Engländer**). To indicate a female citizen or inhabitant the additional suffix **-in** is added to the **-er** suffix (**Berlinerin, Engländerin**).

In some instances the **-er/-erin** is added to a modified form of the country (**Kanadier/Kanadierin**). Other countries have still other forms to indicate the citizen or inhabitant (**Deutscher/Deutsche**).

Mark ist **Deutscher.**	Mark is (a) *German.*
Anna ist **Deutsche.**	Anna is (a) *German.*

Note that to state a person's nationality, German uses the noun directly after a form of **sein.** The indefinite article **ein** is not used, whereas in English nouns of nationality may be preceded by an indefinite article.

Leserunde

Rudolf Otto Wiemer (1905–1998) was both a teacher and a writer. His poems, stories, and books made him known to a wide public. Many of his poems contain surprises and twists, not unlike those in the poem "empfindungswörter." This poem contains other elements common to concrete poetry: everyday words, lists, repetition, and variation, all of which cause the listener or reader to see words in a new light.

words of emotion

empfindungswörter°

aha die deutschen
ei die deutschen
hurra die deutschen
pfui die deutschen
5 ach die deutschen
nanu die deutschen
oho die deutschen
hm die deutschen
nein die deutschen
10 ja ja die deutschen

Rudolf Otto Wiemer

4. The question word *woher*

Woher kommst du?	Where are you from?
Ich **komme aus** [Frankfurt/ der Schweiz/den USA].	I am from [Frankfurt/ Switzerland/the U.S.A.].

To ask in German where someone is from, use the interrogative **woher** and a form of the verb **kommen.** To answer such a question, use a form of the verb **kommen** and the preposition **aus.**

3. Frage-Ecke. Find out where the following people are from and where they live now. Obtain the missing information by asking your partner. **S1**'s information is on page 69; the information for **S2** is in Appendix B.

S1: Woher kommt Anton?
S2: Er kommt aus Deutschland. Was ist Anton?
S1: Er ist Deutscher. Wo wohnt[+] Anton?
S2: Er wohnt in Hamburg.

S1: Und woher kommst du?
S2: Ich komme aus ...

S1:

	Woher kommt ...?	Was ist ...?	Wo wohnt ... ?
Anton		Deutscher	
Anne		Liechtensteinerin	Vaduz
Kristina	Deutschland		
Herr Heller	Österreich		Wien
ich			
Partnerin/Partner			

4. Woher kommst du? Ask five classmates where they are from. Make notes so you can tell others where they are from.

Stating one's nationality

Vokabeln 2

Substantive

(das) **Amerika**   America
der **Amerikaner, -**/die
  Amerikanerin, -nen   American
  person
der **Deutsche** *(m.)*/die **Deutsche**
  (f.)/die **Deutschen** *(pl.)*   German
  person
ein **Deutscher** *(m.)*/eine **Deutsche** *(f.)*
  a German person
(das) **Deutschland**   Germany
der **Einwohner, -**/die **Einwohnerin,**
  -nen   inhabitant
(das) **Europa**   Europe
die **Hauptstadt, ⸚e**   capital
(das) **Kanada**   Canada
der **Kanadier,-**/die **Kanadierin,**
  -nen   Canadian person
der **Kilometer, -**   kilometer (= .62
  mile; abbrev. km)
das **Klima**   climate
das **Land, ⸚er**   country, land

die **Leute** *(pl.)*   people
die **Million, -en**   million
das **Nachbarland, ⸚er**   neighboring
  country
der **Norden**   north
der **Osten**   east
(das) **Österreich**   Austria
der **Österreicher, -**/die
  Österreicherin, -nen   Austrian
  person
der **Ozean**   ocean
die **Schweiz**   Switzerland
der **Schweizer, -**/die **Schweizerin,**
  -nen   Swiss person
die **Stadt, ⸚e**   city
der **Süden**   south
die **Temperatur, -en**   temperature
die **USA** *(pl.)*   U.S.A.
der **Westen**   west
das **Wort, ⸚er**   word

Verben

beeinflussen   to influence
denken   to think
haben   to have
liegen   to lie; to be situated, be located

reden   to talk, speak
sagen   to say; to tell
wohnen   to live, reside

Andere Wörter

als than
andere other
anders different(ly)
deutsch German (*adj.*)
dort there
einfach simply
etwa approximately, about
halb half; **halb so groß** half as
  large
in in
manchmal sometimes
mehr more
nach to (*with cities and neuter
  countries, e.g.,* **nach Berlin; nach
  Deutschland**)

nördlich to the north
relativ relative
so ... wie as . . . as
südlich to the south
von from; of
weg away, off, gone
weit far
weiter farther, further
wichtig important
wie as
wo where
woher where from
ziemlich quite, rather, fairly;
  ziemlich klein rather small

Besondere Ausdrücke

Ich bin [Schweizer/Amerikanerin].
  I am [Swiss/American].
Ich komme aus ...
  I come/am from . . .
nicht so [kalt/viel] not as
  [cold/much]

oh je oh dear
Woher kommst du? Where are you
  from?

Grammatik und Übungen

1 Simple past tense of *sein*

Present	Heute ist das Wetter gut.	The weather is good today.
Simple past	Gestern war es schlecht.	It was bad yesterday.

The simple past tense of **sein** is **war**.

ich **war**	wir waren	
du warst	ihr wart	
er/es/sie **war**	sie waren	
	Sie waren	

I was	we were	
you were	you were	
he/it/she was	they were	
	you were	

In the simple past, the **ich-** and **er/es/sie**-forms of **sein** have no verb endings.

 1. Wo warst du in den Sommerferien? Gisela, Michael, and some friends are discussing where they all spent their summer vacation.

➔ Maria / Italien *Maria war in Italien.*

1. Harald / Dresden
2. ihr / Salzburg
3. Karl und Kristina / Österreich
4. du / Leipzig
5. wir / Zürich
6. Verena / München
7. meine Freunde / Wien
8. Alex / Dänemark
9. Und wo waren Sie in den Sommerferien?

2. Wie war das Wetter? Ask a fellow student what the weather was like on four previous days. Record the answers. For additional expressions see "Weather expressions" in the Supplementary Word Sets in Appendix C.

Discussing the weather

S1:
Wie war das Wetter am [Samstag]?

Und am [Freitag]?

S2:
Es war [schön].
Am [Samstag] war es [schön].
Es war [kalt].

Schüttelkasten

wolkig   warm

heiß   sehr kühl   furchtbar kalt

windig   sonnig   schwül

2 Present tense of *haben*

haben: to have	
ich habe	wir haben
du **hast**	ihr habt
er/es/sie **hat**	sie haben
	Sie haben

The verb **haben** is irregular in the **du-** and **er/es/sie**-forms of the present tense.

3. Wann hast du Geburtstag? Frank and Beate are updating their birthday list. Frank doesn't know the exact dates of their friends' birthdays. Take the role of Beate and tell him in what month the following people's birthdays are. And then give the month of your own birthday.

Discussing birthdays

→ ich / Juli   *Ich habe im Juli Geburtstag.*

1. Petra / Juni
2. du / September
3. Jürgen / Februar
4. ihr / Mai
5. Ulrike und Heinz / Oktober
6. wir / April
7. Und wann haben Sie Geburtstag?

Hurra, unser Bruder ist da!

Julian Lucca

23.4.03, 4050 g, 57 cm

Es freuen sich[1] sehr Annika, Nadine und ihre Eltern
Anja und Thomas Eschenbach.
Beienburger Straße 42, St. Augustin

[1]**freuen sich:** *are happy*

Wann hat Julian Lucca Geburtstag?

Wo wohnt Julian Lucca?

Liebe Oma[1]
Herzlichen Glückwunsch[2]
zu deinem 80. Geburtstag!

Bleib weiter *so* gesund[3] und fit und optimistisch.
Alles Gute
deine Enkel[4] Hanna, Lea, Fabian,
David und Christina.

[1]*grandma* [2]**Herzlichen Glückwunsch:** *warmest wishes* [3]*healthy*
[4]**deine Enkel:** *your grandchildren*

Wie alt ist die Oma?

Wie ist die Oma?

Land und Leute

Geburtstage

www Go to the *Deutsch heute* website at
http://college.hmco.com.

Birthdays are very important to people in German-speaking countries. They seldom forget the birthday of a family member or friend—they write, call, give flowers and/or other gifts. Birthdays are celebrated in different ways. The "birthday child" (**Geburtstagskind**) may have an afternoon coffee party (**Geburtstagskaffee**) with family members and friends or a more extensive birthday party in the evening. At the **Geburtstagskaffee** candles are placed around the edge of a birthday cake (**Geburtstagskuchen**) and blown out by the person whose birthday it is. Although the **Geburtstagskind** is often taken out by family members or friends, he or she usually gives a party or brings a cake to work. Besides giving presents (**Geburtstagsgeschenke**), it is common to send a birthday card or make a phone call. Common greetings are: **Herzlichen Glückwunsch zum Geburtstag!** *(Happy Birthday!)* or **Alles Gute zum Geburtstag!** *(All the best on your birthday!).* Often friends or family place ads in newspapers (**Geburtstagsanzeigen**), in which the **Geburtstagskind** is congratulated on her/his birthday.

In Austria and the predominantly Catholic regions of Germany, name days (**Namenstage**) may be celebrated with as much excitement as a birthday. **Namenstage** commemorate the feast day of one's patron saint. Florist shops in these areas typically remind people whose name day is being celebrated.

Herzlichen Glückwunsch zum Geburtstag!

Diskussion

How does the typical celebration of birthdays in German-speaking countries differ from the way you celebrate birthdays, at home or at work?

3 Position of the finite verb in statements

1	2	3	4
Der Sommer	ist	in Deutschland	anders.
In Deutschland	ist	**der Sommer**	anders.

In a German statement, the finite verb is always in second position, even when an element other than the subject (for example, an adverb or a prepositional phrase) is in first position. When an element other than the subject is in first position, the subject follows the verb.

4. Hoffentlich ist es schön. You and Sonja are discussing the weather, hoping it will be nice for an outdoor activity. Agree with her by restating her comments, beginning with the word in parentheses. Follow the model.

➡ Es ist heute schön, nicht? (heute) *Ja. Heute ist es schön.*

1. Es bleibt hoffentlich warm. (hoffentlich)
2. Das Wetter war gestern schlecht, nicht? (gestern)
3. Das Wetter war aber am Mittwoch gut, nicht? (am Mittwoch)
4. Das Wetter bleibt jetzt bestimmt gut, nicht? (jetzt)
5. Die Sonne scheint hoffentlich. (hoffentlich)

5. Wer? Was? Wann? You and Sabrina have been talking to your friends to find out when they are free for a get-together. By consulting your list you are able to tell Sabrina when your various friends are busy and what they are doing. Begin with the time element.

➡ *Morgen Abend spielt Ramon Basketball.*

Wer?	Was?	Wann?
Ramon	Basketball spielen	morgen Abend
Michael und Hans	Tennis spielen	am Montag
Anna	ins Kino gehen	heute
Carla	Geburtstag haben	am Sonntag
David und Greta	Volleyball spielen	heute Abend
ich	nicht arbeiten	morgen

Describing the weather in a particular season

6. So ist das Wetter. Tell when your birthday is and what the weather is usually like at that time of year. Make a brief report to a group of four or to the whole class.

➡ *Ich habe im Februar Geburtstag. Im Februar ist es kalt. Es schneit oft und die Sonne scheint nicht viel.*

7. Frage-Ecke. Find out how old the following people are, when their birthdays are, and what the typical weather in that month is. Obtain the missing information from your partner. **S1**'s information is below; the information for **S2** is in Appendix B.

S1: Wie alt ist Manfred?
S2: Manfred ist 21 Jahre alt. Wann hat er Geburtstag?
S1: Im Januar. Wie ist das Wetter im Januar?
S2: Es ist kalt.

S1:

	Wie alt?	Geburtstag	das Wetter
Manfred		Januar	
Stefanie	30		kühl
Herr Hofer		Juli	heiß und trocken
Frau Vogel	39		
ich			
Partnerin/Partner			

4 **The nominative° case**　　　　　　　　　　　　　　　　der Nominativ

That woman plays tennis well.
She doesn't play volleyball very well.

English uses word order to signal different grammatical functions (e.g., subject) of nouns or pronouns. In a statement in English the subject precedes the verb.

Die Frau spielt gut Tennis.
Volleyball spielt **sie** aber nicht sehr gut.

German uses a different type of signal to indicate the grammatical function of nouns and pronouns. German uses a signal called *case*. When a noun or pronoun is used as the subject of a sentence, it is in the nominative case.

Masculine	Neuter	Feminine
der	das	die

In the nominative case, the German definite article has three forms. They are all equivalent to "the" in English.

Subject	Predicate noun
Herr Lange ist **Professor.**	
Das Mädchen heißt **Gabi Fischer.**	
Das ist nicht **der Junge.**	

Subject	Predicate noun
Mr. Lange is a *professor.*	
The girl's name is *Gabi Fischer.*	
That is not *the boy.*	

The nominative case is also used for a *predicate noun.* A predicate noun designates a person, concept, or thing that is equated with the subject. A predicate noun completes the meaning of linking verbs such as **sein** and **heißen.** In a negative sentence **nicht** precedes the predicate noun.

8. Wie war das Wetter? Look at the pictures and words below. Using the adjectives in the list, decide what the weather was like on each day. Be sure to use the correct article with the noun under the picture.

kalt ■ heiß ■ kühl ■ nass ■ stark° ■ schön ■ schlecht ■ warm　　　　heavy

➔ Am Samstag war der Regen stark.

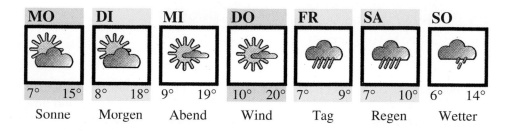

MO	DI	MI	DO	FR	SA	SO
7° 15°	8° 18°	9° 19°	10° 20°	7° 9°	7° 10°	6° 14°
Sonne	Morgen	Abend	Wind	Tag	Regen	Wetter

9. Was kostet ... ? Your partner is moving and wants to sell a few things. Ask how much each item costs. Your partner gives a price. Use a pronoun in your answer.

> *S1:* Was kostet [die Uhr]?
> *S2:* [Sie] kostet 15 Euro.

der Plural

5 Plural° forms of German nouns

A thousand years ago English had a variety of ways to signal the plural of nouns. With some nouns it used stem changes: *mann—menn (man, men); fōt— fēt (foot, feet);* with other nouns it used endings: *stān—stānas (stone, stones); oxa—oxan (ox, oxen);* and with still other nouns it used no signal at all: *scēap— scēap (sheep, sheep).* Over the centuries the ending *-as* gradually replaced most other plural endings, and its modern development *-(e)s* is now the almost universal signal for the plural of English nouns.

Type	Plural signal	Singular	Plural
1	-	das Fenster	die Fenster
	¨	der Garten	die Gärten
2	-e	der Tisch	die Tische
	¨e	der Stuhl	die Stühle
3	-er	das Kind	die Kinder
	¨er	das Buch	die Bücher
4	-en	die Frau	die Frauen
	-n	die Lampe	die Lampen
	-nen	die Studentin	die Studentinnen
5	-s	das Radio	die Radios

German uses five basic types of signals to mark the plural of nouns: no ending or the endings **-e, -er, -(e)n,** and **-s.** Some of the nouns of types 1, 2, and 3 add umlaut in the plural. Nouns of type 4 that end in **-in** add **-nen** in the plural. German makes no gender distinctions in the plural article; the definite article **die** is used with all plural nouns. The indefinite article has no plural form.

When you learn a German noun, you must also learn its plural form because there is no sure way of predicting to which plural-type the noun belongs. You will, however, gradually discover that there is a kind of system to the various types. This "system" depends partly on whether the noun is a **der-, das-,** or **die-**noun, and partly on how many syllables it has.

das Zimmer, - indicates that there is no change in the plural form of the noun: **das Zimmer, die Zimmer**

die Stadt, ̈e indicates that an **-e** is added in the plural, and an umlaut is added to the appropriate vowel: **die Stadt, die Städte**

In the vocabularies of this book, the plural of most nouns is indicated after the singular forms.

Die Kinder sind nett. **Sie** sind nett.
Die Lampen sind alt. **Sie** sind alt.

The personal pronoun **sie** *(they)* may refer to persons or things.

10. Hören Sie zu.

A. Erstes Hören. Listen to the description of David's room. Indicate how many of the listed objects he has in his room.

__1__ Tisch *groß*	__2__ Lampen	__4__ Bilder
__1__ Bett	__1__ Computer *neu*	__1__ Poster
__1__ Pflanze *große*	__1__ Bücherregal	__1__ Telefon *rot*
__2__ Stühle *weiße*	__50__ Bücher	__2__ Fenster *große*

B. Zweites Hören. Now listen to the description again. This time complete the description of the objects according to what you have heard. Be sure to provide the correct definite articles.

1. _____ Tisch ist _____.

2. _____ Pflanze ist auch _____.

3. _____ Stuhle sind _____.

4. _____ Computer ist _____.

5. _____ Telefon ist _____.

6. _____ Fenster sind _____.

11. Was ist hier los? *(What's going on here?)* Talk about the people and things in a small town in Germany. Use the plural.

➡ Haus / sein / alt   *Die Häuser sind alt.*

1. Garten / sein / klein
2. Straße / sein / alt
3. Nachbar / sein / nett
4. Kind / spielen / gern
5. Frau / arbeiten / viel
6. Mann / arbeiten / auch viel
7. Junge / spielen / gern / Fußball

Land und Leute

341 million people speak English as their native language; 200 million speak German, 358 million speak Spanish, and 874 million Mandarin.

Die deutsche Sprache

www   Go to the *Deutsch heute* website at http://college.hmco.com.

A thousand years ago there was no standard form of the German language. The large central European area from the North Sea and the Baltic Sea to the Alps in the south was inhabited by Germans who lived in many different societies and who spoke variations of the German language.

Martin Luther (1483–1546) played an important role in the development of German. For his Bible translation and other works, Luther used a form of the language spoken in east central Germany; eventually, it became the spoken and written standard for all of Germany as well as Austria and Switzerland. This single standard language is called **Hochdeutsch.** It is used in all domains of public life, including newspapers, radio, TV, and film. This way German speakers are linguistically unified despite the fact that local dialects are often incomprehensible to people from different regions within the German-speaking countries. Complete words, intonation, and pronunciation can vary dramatically. Different ways to say **sprechen,** for example, include **schwätzen** and **schnacken.** Fears in the beginning of the twentieth century that mass media and other developments might cause dialects to die out have not materialized. At the end of the twentieth century, dialects were gaining in prestige and were used to some extent in every German-speaking country. Realizing that they are an important part of popular culture, many writers and singers use their local dialects to express themselves artistically and to promote the use of dialects.

In 1996 representatives from German-speaking countries and areas (Austria, Germany, Liechtenstein, Switzerland, Italy, Belgium, Romania, and Hungary) agreed to the first revision of German orthography and punctuation (**Rechtschreibreform**) since 1901. These new spelling rules are intended to modernize and simplify German writing. In older texts and in the interim, you may encounter two different spellings for the same word, for example **Sinfonie** or **dass** (new spelling) and **Symphonie** or **daß** (old spelling). The new rules caused a great deal of controversy and raised legal issues about the right of the state to mandate changes in language as well as questions about the evolution of language.

Seit Martin Luther gibt es eine deutsche Sprache.

Diskussion

Starting in the mid-1870s there was a movement in Britain and the United States to simplify English spelling. George Bernard Shaw, Mark Twain, and President Theodore Roosevelt are three prominent persons who promoted a more phonetic spelling. Some of the changes never caught on, e.g., *ruf* instead of *rough.* However some alternate spellings are not unfamiliar today, e.g. *nite* for *night.* What other words are often spelled in simplified form? Do you think English spelling should be reformed? Why or why not?

6 The indefinite article° ein

der unbestimmte Artikel

Ist das **ein** Radio oder **eine** Uhr?   Is that *a* radio or *a* clock?

The German indefinite article **ein** is equivalent to English *a* or *an*.

Masculine	Neuter	Feminine
ein Mann	ein Kind	eine Frau

In the nominative case the German indefinite article has two forms: **ein** for masculine and neuter, and **eine** for feminine.

12. Was ist das? Help your partner learn German. Point to a picture and she/he will tell what it is in German.

S1: Was ist das?
S2: Das ist ein Buch.

7 The negative *kein*

Ist das **ein** Radio?
Nein, das ist **kein** Radio.

Is that *a* radio?
No, that's *not a* radio.

Sind die Studenten Amerikaner?
Nein, sie sind **keine** Amerikaner.

Are the students Americans?
No, they are *not* Americans.

The negative form of **ein** is **kein.** It is equivalent to English *not a, not any,* or *no*. It negates a noun that in the positive would be preceded by a form of **ein** (e.g., **ein Radio**) or no article at all (e.g., **Amerikaner**).

Masculine	Neuter	Feminine	Plural
kein Tisch	**kein** Radio	**keine** Uhr	**keine** Radios

In the nominative case **kein** has two forms: **kein** for masculine and neuter, and **keine** for feminine and plural.

13. Das ist es nicht. You are taking your first art course and are showing Jan what you have drawn. He tries to guess what your attempts portray. Tell him his guesses are wrong. Use a form of **kein** in your responses.

➔ Ist das **eine** Frau?   *Nein, das ist **keine** Frau.*

1. Ist das ein Kind?   2. Ist das eine Lampe?   3. Ist das ein Bücherregal?

4. Ist das ein Telefon?   5. Ist das ein Computer?   6. Ist das eine Gitarre?

8 *Kein* vs. *nicht*

Ist das **eine** Uhr?	Nein, das ist **keine** Uhr.
Sind sie Amerikaner?	Nein, sie sind **keine** Amerikaner.
Ist das **die** Uhr?	Nein, das ist **nicht die** Uhr.
Ist das Frau Müller?	Nein, das ist **nicht** Frau Müller.

Kein is used to negate a noun that in an affirmative sentence would be preceded by **ein** or no article at all. **Nicht** is used when negating a noun preceded by a definite article. It is also used before the name of a person.

14. Nicht oder kein? Gisela is showing Monika and Stefan pictures she took in Tübingen. They are not always sure what they are seeing. Take the role of Gisela and say they are mistaken. Use **nicht** or **kein** before the predicate noun, as appropriate.

➔ Ist das Michael?   *Nein, das ist nicht Michael.*
➔ Ist das ein Student?   *Nein, das ist kein Student.*

1. Ist das Professor Lange?   5. Ist das ein Amerikaner?
2. Ist das ein Nachbar?   6. Ist das die Bibliothek?
3. Ist das die Pfleghofstraße?   7. Ist das Frau Kluge?
4. Ist das eine Studentin?

¹nonsense   ²**weit ... :** *far and wide*

»Keine Angst¹, ich bin ein Jäger², kein Bandit!«

¹fear   ²hunter

9 Showing possession with a proper name

Das ist **Giselas** Buch.	That is *Gisela's* book.
Das ist **Jens'** Kuli.	That is *Jens's* ballpoint pen.

A proper name is a word that designates a specific individual or place (e.g., Laura, Berlin). In German as in English, possession and other close relationships are expressed by adding **-s** to the proper names. If the name already ends in a sibilant*, no **-s** is added. An apostrophe is used in written German only when no **-s** is added (e.g., **Jens' Kuli**). Note that if a name ends in **-s**, a construction using **von** is preferred (e.g., **der Kuli von Jens**).

15. Ist das Gerds Buch? After a club meeting you and a friend are straightening up. Tell your friend to whom the various things belong. Use the possessive form of the proper name.

→ Gerd / Buch   *Das ist Gerds Buch.*

1. Beate / Kuli
2. Bruno / Lampe
3. Franz / Radio
4. Regina / Heft
5. Thomas / Rucksack
6. Sylvia / Uhr

das Possessivpronomen

10 Possessive adjectives°

Mein Zimmer ist groß.	*My* room is large.
Ist **dein** Zimmer groß?	Is *your* room large?
Ist **sein** Zimmer groß?	Is *his* room large?
Ist **ihr** Zimmer groß?	Is *her* room large?
Unser Zimmer ist groß.	*Our* room is large.
Ist **euer** Zimmer groß?	Is *your* room large?
Ist **ihr** Zimmer groß?	Is *their* room large?
Ist **Ihr** Zimmer groß?	Is *your* room large?

German possessive adjectives are equivalent in meaning to the English possessive adjectives, such as *my, his,* and *her.* Context usually makes clear whether **ihr** is the subject pronoun *you,* the adjective *her* or *their,* or the adjective *your.* Note that **Ihr** *(your)* is capitalized, just as the corresponding subject pronoun **Sie** *(you)* is.

der Bleistift	Wo ist ein Bleistift?
	Wo ist **mein** Bleistift?
das Heft	Wo ist ein Heft?
	Wo ist **mein** Heft?
die Uhr	Wo ist eine Uhr?
	Wo ist **meine** Uhr?
die Bücher	Wo sind **meine** Bücher?

Since possessive adjectives have the same forms as **ein,** they are frequently called **ein**-words.

Wo ist **euer** Radio? Wo sind **eure** Bücher?

When **euer** has an ending, the **-e-** preceding the **-r-** is usually omitted.

Lieber Schatz¹!
Alles Liebe zum Valentinstag
wünscht dir
deine Dani

¹sweetheart

Wann ist Valentinstag?

---

*See *Kapitel 1,* p. 44.

■ *Negating nouns preceded by possessive adjectives*

Ist das dein Heft?   Nein, das ist **nicht** mein Heft.

Nicht is used to negate a noun that is preceded by a possessive adjective.

16. Wie sagt man das? Complete the sentences with the German equivalents of the cued words.

→ _____ Mann arbeitet nicht. *(her)*   *Ihr Mann arbeitet nicht.*

1. _____ Kind heißt Dieter. *(their)*

2. _____ Frau ist lustig. *(his)*

3. Barbara, Frank, was für ein Mensch ist _____ Nachbar? *(your)*

4. Wo sind _____ Kinder, Frau Neumann? *(your)*

5. Ich glaube, das ist _____ Kuli. *(my)*

6. Ist das _____ Uhr, Gisela? *(your)*

17. Ein Brief° von Gisela. Complete Gisela's letter to her grandmother by fill-   letter
ing in the appropriate possessive adjectives.

Liebe Oma,

ich studiere jetzt in Tübingen. _____ Adresse ist Pfleghofstraße 2 und

_____ Telefonnummer ist 79 23 09. _____ Zimmer ist klein, aber komfor-

tabel. _____ Nachbar heißt Michael und _____ Freund heißt Alex. Alex ist

auch _____ Freund. Geht _____ Freundin Frau Holz noch oft ins Café?

Wie sind _____ Samstage zusammen? Also, Oma, ich gehe jetzt joggen und

schreibe morgen mehr.

deine Gisela

⑪ **Demonstrative pronouns** *der, das, die*

Ist Andrea zu Hause?	Is Andrea at home?
Nein, **die** ist nicht zu Hause.	No, *she*'s not at home.
Ist der Computer wirklich neu?	Is the computer really new?
Ja, **der** ist wirklich neu.	Yes, *it*'s really new.
Ist das Bild neu oder alt?	Is the picture new or old?
Ach, **das** ist ziemlich alt.	Oh, *it*'s rather old.
Sind die Berliner freundlich?	Are the Berliners friendly?
Ja, **die** sind freundlich.	Yes, *they*'re friendly.

Der, das, and **die** are often used as demonstrative pronouns to replace nouns. A demonstrative pronoun is used instead of a personal pronoun (**er, es, sie**) when the pronoun is to be emphasized. Demonstrative pronouns usually occur at or near the beginning of a sentence. The English equivalent is usually a personal pronoun (*he, it, she, they*).

18. Ja, das stimmt. *(Yes, that's right.)* Look at the pictures of the objects on page 79. Make a statement about four of the objects. Your partner will agree or disagree, using a demonstrative pronoun in her/his answer.

> *S1:* Das Bücherregal ist klein, nicht wahr?
> *S2:* Ja, das ist wirklich klein. / Nein, das ist nicht klein.

Wiederholung

1. Rollenspiel. You have been studying for a year in Tübingen. Your partner has been there longer and she/he is telling you some things about Tübingen. You answer with some skepticism.

> **Redemittel: Skepsis äußern** *(Expressing skepticism)*
>
> Wirklich?
> Denkst du? Glaubst du? Findest du?
> Hoffentlich.
> Vielleicht.

1. Deutschland ist nur halb so groß wie Texas.
2. Tübingen ist eine schöne/nette Stadt.
3. Im August ist es hier ziemlich warm.
4. Und im Winter regnet es oft.
5. Du bleibst drei Semester in Tübingen, nicht?
6. Du gehst dann wieder nach Amerika/Kanada, nicht?

2. Am Telefon. Gisela and Alex are talking on the phone. Complete their conversation from the notes below. The word order may need to change.

> → GISELA: was / du / machen / jetzt / ? *Was machst du jetzt?*

1. ALEX: ich / hören / Musik
2. GISELA: ihr (du und Michael) / spielen / heute / wieder / Tennis / ?
3. ALEX: nein / Michael / kommen / heute Abend / nicht
4. GISELA: ah / er / arbeiten / wieder
5. ALEX: vielleicht / wir / spielen / morgen
6. GISELA: hoffentlich / es / regnen / morgen / nicht
7. ALEX: ich / glauben / das / nicht
8. GISELA: vielleicht / die Sonne / scheinen

3. Viele Fragen. Ask your partner questions using the words **Wann, Was, Was für, Warum, Wer, Wie, Wie alt, Wo,** and **Woher.** You can ask about your partner's family and friends, courses, leisure activities, the weather, and so on.

> *S1:* Wie ist das Wetter heute?
> *S2:* Es ist schön.
> *S1:* Woher kommst du?
> *S2:* Ich komme aus Minnesota.

4. Und auf Deutsch? Karoline, your guest from Germany, doesn't understand the conversation of your two American friends. Translate for her.

1. ED: We're playing tennis today, right?
2. KATIE: No, it's too cold. We'll play tomorrow. OK?
3. ED: But it's so nice (out)! The sun's shining and tomorrow it'll rain for sure.
4. KATIE: I don't think so. (Use **das**.)
5. ED: By the way°, what time are we going to the movies tonight?
6. KATIE: At six-thirty. George is coming, too.
7. ED: Really? Isn't he working this evening?
8. KATIE: No, he works on Monday and Tuesday.

Übrigens

5. Gespräche

Discussing the weather

1. You are talking to a travel agent. You can't decide where you want to spend your next vacation. Ask about the weather in various places.
2. You are talking to a German friend. She/He wants to know about your first weeks at school. Tell her/him about
   a. a friend or classmate, where she/he is from.
   b. what activities you like to do.
   c. your room and its contents (size, color).

6. Zum Schreiben

1. Imagine you have just arrived in Germany. Write a short paragraph (4–5 sentences) in German about Germany. Before you begin writing, look again at the reading on page 64 to review vocabulary, and at the section on word order on page 73. Then make a list (in German) of the things you want to mention in your paragraph, e.g., weather, size, and population. Organize your comments in a paragraph. After you've written your paragraph, review each sentence to be sure that each one has a subject and a verb and that the verb agrees with the subject. Finally, check the word order of each sentence.
2. Prepare a weather forecast that will tell your fellow students what the weather will be like for the next three days. Two or three sentences per forecast are sufficient. Watch your word order.

→ *Am Montag scheint die Sonne. Es bleibt schön.*
Am Dienstag kommt der Wind aus dem Osten. Vielleicht regnet es.
Am Mittwoch ist es sehr kalt. Es sind zwei Grad.

Grammatik: Zusammenfassung

Simple past tense of *sein*

sein: to be			
ich	**war**	wir	waren
du	warst	ihr	wart
er/es/sie	**war**	sie	waren
	Sie	waren	

Present tense of *haben*

haben: to have			
ich	habe	wir	haben
du	**hast**	ihr	habt
er/es/sie	**hat**	sie	haben
	Sie	haben	

Position of the finite verb in statements

1	2	3	4
Subject	*Verb*	*Adverb*	*Adjective*
Der Sommer	ist	in Deutschland	anders.
Adverb	*Verb*	*Subject*	*Adjective*
In Deutschland	ist	**der Sommer**	anders.

In a German statement, the verb is always in second position. In so-called normal word order, the subject is in first position. In so-called inverted word order, something other than the subject (for example, an adverb, an adjective, or indirect object) is in first position, and the subject follows the verb. Note that both "normal" and "inverted" word order are common in German.

Plural of nouns

Type	Plural signal	Singular	Plural
1	- *(no change)*	das Zimmer	die Zimmer
	¨	der Garten	die Gärten
2	-e	das Heft	die Hefte
	¨e	die Stadt	die Städte
3	-er	das Kind	die Kinder
	¨er	der Mann	die Männer
4	-en	die Tür	die Türen
	-n	die Lampe	die Lampen
	-nen	die Studentin	die Studentinnen
5	-s	das Radio	die Radios

Nominative case of definite articles, indefinite articles, and *kein*

	Masculine	Neuter	Feminine	Plural
Definite article	der	das	die	die
Indefinite article	ein } Stuhl	ein } Radio	eine } Lampe	— } Bücher
KEIN	kein	kein	keine	keine

Kein vs. nicht

Ist das **eine** Uhr?	Nein, das ist **keine** Uhr.
Ist das **die** Uhr?	Nein, das ist **nicht** die Uhr.
Ist das **deine** Uhr?	Nein, das ist **nicht meine** Uhr.

Kein is used to negate a noun that would be preceded by **ein** or no article at all in an affirmative sentence. **Nicht** is used in a negative sentence when the noun is preceded by a definite article (**die**) or a possessive adjective (**meine**). (For positions of **nicht,** see Appendix F.)

Possessive adjectives

■ *Forms and meanings*

Singular		Plural	
ich: **mein**	my	wir: **unser**	our
du: **dein**	your	ihr: **euer**	your
er: **sein**	his, its		
es: **sein**	its	sie: **ihr**	their
sie: **ihr**	her, its		
Sie: **ihr**	your		

■ *Nominative of possessive adjectives*

Masculine		Neuter		Feminine		Plural	
ein		ein		eine		—	
mein	Tisch	**mein**	Radio	**meine**	Uhr	**meine**	Bücher
unser		**unser**		**unsere**		**unsere**	

Demonstrative pronouns and personal pronouns

	Masculine	Neuter	Feminine	Plural
Personal Pronouns	er	es	sie	sie
Demonstrative Pronouns	der	das	die	die

Was brauchst du?

In einer Bäckerei in Wien. Die Leute kaufen frische Backwaren.

LERNZIELE

Sprechintentionen

Talking about shopping and buying
  groceries
Expressing and inquiring about
  needs
Discussing meals
Inquiring about personal habits
Giving directives
Expressing likes and dislikes
Responding to offers and requests

Lesestück

Einkaufen am Wochenende

Land und Leute

Types of bread
Specialty stores vs. supermarkets
Outdoor markets
Typical German breakfast
The euro
Shopping hours

Vokabeln

Flavoring particles: *mal, denn,*
  and *doch*
Common foods
Noun compounds
Days of the week and parts of days
  as adverbs

Units of weight, capacity,
  measurement, and quantity

Grammatik

Verbs with stem-vowel change *e > i*
Word order: time and place
  expressions
Imperatives
Direct objects
Accusative case
Es gibt

Bausteine für Gespräche

Gehst du heute einkaufen?

MONIKA: Stefan, gehst du heute nicht
   einkaufen?
STEFAN: Doch. Was brauchst du denn?
MONIKA: Wir haben keinen Kaffee mehr.
STEFAN: Ein Pfund ist genug, nicht? Möchtest
   du sonst noch etwas?
MONIKA: Ja, bitte ein Brot. Kauf das doch bei
   Reinhardt. Da ist es besser.
STEFAN: Brot haben wir noch genug. Und am
   Wochenende sind wir doch bei Gisela in
   Tübingen.
MONIKA: Ach ja, stimmt!

Richtig oder falsch?

1. Stefan geht heute nicht einkaufen.
2. Monika braucht Kaffee.
3. Stefan kauft ein Pfund Kaffee.
4. Monika findet das Brot bei Reinhardt nicht so gut.
5. Am Wochenende sind Monika und Stefan in Tübingen.
6. Dort besuchen+ sie ihren Freund Carsten.

Wo gibt es eine Apotheke?

DAVID: Sag mal, Gisela, wo ist hier eine Apotheke?
GISELA: Warum? Was brauchst du denn?
DAVID: Ich brauche etwas gegen Kopfschmerzen.
GISELA: Ich habe immer Aspirin im Rucksack. Hier, nimm eins.

Richtig oder falsch?

1. David sucht eine Apotheke.
2. Gisela sagt David, wo eine Apotheke ist.
3. David braucht etwas gegen Kopfschmerzen.
4. Gisela gibt David Geld+ für das Aspirin.
5. David kauft dann Aspirin.

Brauchbares

1. The words **denn** in "**Was brauchst du denn?**," **doch** in "**Kauf das doch bei Reinhardt**," and **mal** in "**Sag mal**" are called *flavoring particles*. They express a speaker's attitude about an utterance and do not have exact English equivalents. See pages 91–92.

2. Stefan says: **Möchtest du sonst noch etwas?** The verb **möchte** does not have the characteristic ending **-t** in the **er/es/sie**-form: **er möchte** (*he would like*).

Inquiring about shopping possibilities

1. Was suchen Sie? Think of three things you need to buy. A fellow student or your instructor asks what kind of store you're looking for. Respond. For names of specialty shops, refer to the Supplementary Word Sets in Appendix C.

S2:	S1:			
Was suchst⁺ du?	Ich brauche	**Brot.**	Gibt es hier	**eine Bäckerei⁺?**
Was suchen Sie?		Aspirin.		eine Apotheke?
		Wurst⁺.		eine Metzgerei⁺?
		Spaghetti⁺.		einen Supermarkt⁺?
		einen Kamm⁺.		eine Drogerie⁺?

Gesundheit aus der Apotheke

Expressing needs

2. Geh doch. Your friend needs some things. Tell her/him to go to the store that sells them.

S2:		S1:
Ich brauche	**etwas gegen Kopfschmerzen.**	**Geh doch⁺ in die Apotheke.**
	Brot für morgen.	
	Wurst für heute Abend.	
	Spaghetti.	
	ein Heft.	
	ein Buch über⁺ Schach.	

Schüttelkasten

zum Bäcker   in den Supermarkt
ins Kaufhaus⁺   zum Metzger
in die Buchhandlung⁺

Inquiring about needs

3. Sonst noch etwas? You've been telling a friend what you need, but there's something you've forgotten. What is it? When she/he asks whether there's anything else you need, say what it is.

S2:	S1:
Brauchst du sonst noch etwas?	Ja, wir haben **kein Brot mehr.**

Schüttelkasten

keine Spaghetti
keinen Kaffee   kein Bier⁺
keine Butter⁺

4. Frage-Ecke. Find out why various people, including your partner, are going to certain places of business. **S1**'s information is below; information for **S2** is in Appendix B.

> *S1:* Warum geht Herr Sommer ins Kaufhaus?
> *S2:* Er braucht ein Radio. Warum gehst du ins Kaufhaus?
> *S1:* Ich brauche ein Heft./Ich gehe doch nicht ins Kaufhaus. Ich brauche nichts.

S1:

	ins Kaufhaus	in die Drogerie	in die Metzgerei	in die Bäckerei	in den Supermarkt
Jochen	ein Heft		Wurst		Brötchen
Monika und Stefan		eine Kassette			
Herr Sommer		einen Kamm		Kuchen	200 Gramm Butter
Partnerin/Partner					

Erweiterung des Wortschatzes

1. Flavoring particles

"Flavoring" particles are little words used to express a speaker's attitude about an utterance. They often relate the utterance to something the speaker or the listener has said or thought. Depending on the choice of the flavoring particle and sometimes on the tone of voice, the speaker expresses interest, surprise, impatience, denial, and so on. Because a particle has various shades of meaning that depend on the context, a dictionary can give only the approximate English meaning. With experience you will gain a "feel" for the meaning and use of these words, which are very characteristic of colloquial German. Some of the meanings of the particles are given in the following examples; other meanings will be pointed out later.

◼ *Flavoring particle* mal

DAVID: Sag **mal**, Gisela, wo ist hier eine Apotheke?
Tell me, Gisela, where is there a pharmacy (around) here?

GISELA: Frag **mal** Alex.
Ask Alex.

Mal is frequently used with imperatives. It softens the tone of the command.

◼ *Flavoring particle* denn

STEFAN: Was brauchst du **denn**?
Tell me, what do you need?

MONIKA: Kaffee.
Coffee.

Denn is used frequently in questions to show the personal interest of the speaker. It softens the speaker's question and makes it less abrupt.

■ *Flavoring particle* doch

MONIKA: Kauf das Brot **doch** bei
Reinhardt. Geh **doch** nicht in
den Supermarkt.

Be sure and buy the bread at
Reinhardt's. Definitely don't go to
the supermarket.

The speaker uses **doch** to persuade the listener to do something.

2. *Doch* as a positive response to a negative question

MONIKA: Gehst du heute nicht
einkaufen?

Aren't you going shopping today?

STEFAN: **Doch.**

Yes, I am.

Doch may be used as a positive response to a negative question.

1. Viele Fragen. Your house guest wants to know a lot of things. Respond in
the positive, using **ja** or **doch** as appropriate.

➡ Gehst du heute nicht in die Bibliothek? *Doch.*
➡ Gehst du um sieben? *Ja.*

1. Gibt es hier eine Apotheke?
2. Hast du kein Aspirin?
3. Gehst du nicht in den Supermarkt?
4. Kaufst du Wurst?
5. Ist die Wurst da gut?
6. Machen wir heute Abend das Essen[+] nicht zusammen?
7. Brauchen wir Brot?
8. Trinkst[+] du heute keinen Kaffee?

You need not understand all the words to know what
this advertisement is about. If you know that the
meaning of **probieren** is *to try*, you can get quite a
lot. What are the flavoring particles telling the
reader? What is *Die Zeit?* Is it a serious
publication? Where can you order a subscription for
Die Zeit if you are in the United States or Mexico?
What about if you are in Canada?

3. Lebensmittel

das **Getränk, -e**
1. der **Apfelsaft**
2. der **Orangensaft** } der **Saft, ⁼e**
3. der **Kaffee**
4. der **Tee**
5. der **Weißwein, -e** } der **Wein, -e**
6. der **Rotwein, -e**
7. das **Bier, -e**
8. die **Milch**
9. das **Mineralwasser**
10. das **Wasser**

das **Gemüse**
11. die **Gurke, -n**
12. die **Karotte, -n**
13. die **Kartoffel, -n**
14. der **Salat, -e**
15. die **Tomate, -n**

das **Obst**
16. der **Apfel, ⁼**
17. die **Banane, -n**
18. die **Orange, -n**
19. die **Traube, -n**

das **Fleisch**
20. der **Rinderbraten, -**
21. der **Schinken, -**
22. die **Wurst, ⁼e**
23. das **Würstchen, -**

andere Lebensmittel
24. das **Brot, -e**
25. das **Brötchen, -**
26. das **Ei, -er**
27. der **Käse**
28. die **Nudeln** *(pl.)*
29. der **Fisch, -e**

30. das **Hähnchen, -**
31. die **Butter**
32. die **Margarine**
33. der **Kuchen, -**
34. die **Torte, -n**

2. Was isst du? Interview fellow students to learn what they eat at various meals.

S1:			S2:
Was	isst du	**zum Frühstück[+]?**	Ich esse [zwei Brötchen].
	trinkst du	zum Mittagessen[+]?	Ich trinke [Orangensaft].
		zum Abendessen[+]?	

Land und Leute

Das Brot

www Go to the *Deutsch heute* website at
http://college.hmco.com.

Bread plays a significant part in the daily nutrition of people in the German-speaking countries. Approximately 200 types of bread are baked in Germany alone. Names, shapes, and recipes vary from region to region. The most popular breads are baked fresh daily in one of the many bakeries (**Bäckereien**) and have a tasty crust. They also tend to have a firmer and often coarser texture than American breads.

In dieser Tübinger Bäckerei gibt es über zehn verschiedene Brotsorten.

A typical breakfast would not be complete without a crisp **Brötchen** or **Semmel,** as rolls are called in many areas. Open-faced sandwiches (**belegte Brote**) are popular for the evening meal and as a light lunch, and are often eaten with a knife and fork. Bread is made from a wide variety of grains, including rye (**Roggen**) and wheat (**Weizen**). Many types of bread are made from several kinds of grain—**Dreikornbrot, Vierkornbrot. Vollkornbrot** is made of unrefined, crushed grain. Bread with sunflower seeds (**Sonnenblumenbrot**) is also very popular. There are bread museums in Ulm, Mollenfelde, and Detmold which often feature **Gebildbrote** (picture breads) in the shape of animals, wreaths, even violins.

Other baked goods are also popular. There are 1200 kinds of **Kleingebäck** (a term used for baked goods like rolls, soft pretzels, bread sticks, etc.). A bakery or pastry shop (**Konditorei**) always has a large selection of cookies (**Kekse**), pastries (**Gebäck**), and cakes (**Kuchen** and **Torten**).

Diskussion

1. People from German-speaking countries often say that the food they miss the most when they visit the United States is bread. Why do you think that this is the case?
2. How important is bread in your diet? Do you eat a variety of breads?
3. Role-play. With a partner, act out a scene in which you buy products in a **Bäckerei**.

3. Hören Sie zu. Gisela and Alex meet at the university and discuss their lunch plans. Listen to their exchange and indicate the statement below that corresponds most closely to what you hear. You will hear several new words: **Hunger haben** (*to be hungry*); **die Mensa** (*university cafeteria*); **nee** (*nope, no*); **natürlich** (*naturally*); **schnell** (*quickly*).

1. Alex und Gisela
   a. essen in der Mensa.
   b. machen ein Picknick im Park.
   c. essen in der Metzgerei.

2. Alex
   a. hat ein Käsebrot und kauft eine Cola.
   b. kauft ein Käsebrot und hat eine Cola.
   c. kauft ein Käsebrot und Schokolade.

3. Giselas
   a. Lieblingsessen ist Wurstbrot.
   b. Lieblingsgetränk ist Cola.
   c. Lieblingsessen ist Schokolade.

4. Essen und Trinken. Complete the chart for yourself by listing your favorite drinks and foods and a food you do not like. Then ask your partner for the same information. Note that to express a favorite something, German uses the word **Lieblings-**.

Wer?	Lieblingsgetränke	Lieblingsobst	Lieblingsgemüse	Lieblingsfleisch	isst nicht gern
Ich					
Partner/in					

Vokabeln 1

Starting in *Kapitel 3*, vowel changes in the present tense will be noted in parentheses following the infinitive of the verb, e.g., **essen (isst)**.

Substantive

das **Abendessen, -** evening meal; supper
die **Apotheke, -n** pharmacy
das **Aspirin** aspirin
der **Bäcker, -** baker
die **Bäckerei, -en** bakery
das **Bier, -e** beer
das **Brot, -e** bread
die **Buchhandlung, -en** bookstore

die **Butter** butter
die **Drogerie, -n** drugstore
das **Essen, -** meal; prepared food
das **Frühstück** breakfast
das **Geld** money
der **Kaffee** coffee
der **Kamm, ⸚e** comb
das **Kaufhaus, ⸚er** department store
die **Kopfschmerzen** (*pl.*) headache

Wurst: There are over 1500 kinds of German Wurst—again, with many local names and variations. The basic types include: those made of uncooked and uncured meat such as Bratwurst, which is normally heated before eating; those made of cured and smoked meat such as Mettwurst; and those made of cooked meat such as Leberwurst. The latter two types can be eaten as cold cuts or sandwich spread.

die **Lebensmittel** *(pl.)* food; groceries
der **Liebling, -e** favorite
  das **Lieblingsgetränk, -e** favorite drink
der **Metzger, -** butcher
die **Metzgerei, -en** butcher shop, meat market

das **Mittagessen** midday meal
das **Pfund, -e** pound (= 1.1 U.S. pounds; *abbrev.* **Pfd.**)
der **Salat, -e** lettuce; salad
die **Spaghetti** *(pl.)* spaghetti
der **Supermarkt, ⸚e** supermarket
die **Wurst, ⸚e** sausage, lunch meat
For additional foods, see p. 93.

Verben

besuchen to visit
brauchen to need
einkaufen to shop; **einkaufen gehen** to go shopping
essen (isst) to eat
fragen to ask
kaufen to buy

möchte (ich möchte, du möchtest, er/sie/es möchte) would like
nehmen (nimmt) to take
stimmen to be correct
suchen to look for
trinken to drink

Andere Wörter

bei at; at a place of business (**beim [Metzger]**); at the home of (**bei [Gisela]**)
besser better
denn *flavoring particle added to question*
doch *(after a negative question or statement)* yes [I] am, [I] do; *(flavoring particle)* really; after all

etwas something
gegen against
genug enough
kein not a, not any
mal *flavoring particle added to an imperative;* **sag mal** tell me
offen open
sonst otherwise
über about; above

Besondere Ausdrücke

beim Bäcker at the baker's (bakery)
beim Metzger at the butcher's (butcher shop)
das stimmt that's right
es gibt there is; there are
geh doch well, then go
in die Apotheke to the pharmacy
in den Supermarkt to the supermarket
kein ... mehr no more . . . ; not . . . any more
Sonst noch etwas? Anything else?

Was gibt's zum [Abendessen]? What's for [dinner/supper]?
zum Abendessen for the evening meal, for dinner
zum Bäcker to the baker's (bakery)
zum Frühstück for breakfast
zum Metzger to the butcher's (butcher shop)
zum Mittagessen for the midday meal, for lunch

Vorbereitung auf das Lesen

■ **Vor dem Lesen**

Handwritten margin notes:
Einkaufstasche(-n)
die Umwelt - the environment
das Dorf - town

ACHTUNG!

SIE KÖNNEN JETZT STRESSFREIER EINKAUFEN

Ab heute neue Öffnungszeiten

KRONE

Ihr Supermarkt seit 45 Jahren!

Montags bis freitags sind wir von 8 bis 20 Uhr für Sie da,
und jeden Samstag von 8 bis 16 Uhr.

Look at the advertisement for **Krone** and answer the following questions.

1. Was ist Krone?
2. Wann ist Krone offen?
3. Wann ist Krone nicht offen?
4. Wie alt ist Krone?
5. Was kann man bei Krone kaufen? Machen Sie eine Liste von möglichen Dingen°.   things
6. Wo kaufen Sie Lebensmittel?
7. Wann ist Ihr Supermarkt offen?
8. Was ist Ihr Lieblingsgeschäft? Was kaufen Sie da?
9. Wo ist Einkaufen stressfreier – in Deutschland oder in Amerika/Kanada? Was denken Sie?

■ **Beim Lesen**

In the reading passage, you will learn about shopping habits in Germany. As you read, fill out the following table.

Wer	Geschäft	Was
Monika		
	im türkischen Lebensmittelgeschäft	
		Fisch
Stefan		
		Wurst
	Drogerie Kaiser	

Es ist Samstag und Gisela hat Besuch von Monika und Stefan aus Berlin. Die kennen Tübingen noch nicht, also gehen sie zusammen einkaufen. Gisela nimmt Einkaufstasche und Geld und die drei gehen in die Stadt. Gisela braucht Kaffee, Butter, Marmelade und Apfelsaft. Die kauft sie im Supermarkt,

5 doch den Käse kauft sie im türkischen Lebensmittelgeschäft. Dort ist es interessant. Es gibt so viele exotische Produkte. Der türkische Laden ist klein und dort ist es nicht so unpersönlich wie im Supermarkt. Hier kennt man Gisela und Herr Özmir sagt: »Guten Morgen, Frau Riedholt. Was bekommen Sie denn heute?«

cheese made from sheep's milk 10 »Ich brauche Schafskäse° und Oliven. Haben Sie heute den tollen Käse aus der Türkei?«

»Ja, natürlich. Wie viel brauchen Sie denn?«

»Hmmm, ich glaube ein Pfund. Ich habe Besuch aus Berlin und die essen gern und viel. Dann noch bitte 200 Gramm Oliven. Die da finde ich immer so

15 gut.«

»Ja, die sind fantastisch. Haben Sie sonst noch einen Wunsch?«

»Nein, danke, Herr Özmir. Das ist alles für heute.«

Gisela bezahlt und sie gehen auf den Markt. Sie kaufen Karotten und ein Kilo Kartoffeln fürs Abendessen. Der Fischmann ist auch da. Hier kaufen sie

20 frischen Fisch. Den essen sie auch zum Abendessen. Dann gehen sie noch zu einem Blumenstand. Es gibt Rosen – die findet Gisela so schön.

»Gisela, die Rosen bezahle ich aber«, sagt Monika.

Die drei gehen jetzt zur Bäckerei Lieb. Gisela ruft: »Oh je, es ist ja schon fast ein Uhr. Bald schließen die Geschäfte. Stefan, geh du bitte in die Bäckerei

across from here 25 und kauf zehn Brötchen. Wir gehen zur Metzgerei Zeeb gegenüber°. Hier Stefan, nimm die Tasche!«

In der Metzgerei kaufen Gisela und Monika noch Fleisch und Wurst. Dort
meet treffen° sie David aus Washington. Er findet die deutsche Wurst so gut und

Einkaufen in Braubach am Rhein

kauft ziemlich viel. David fragt Gisela: »Sag mal, wo bekomme ich in
30 Tübingen eigentlich Vitamintabletten? In der Apotheke sind die ja furchtbar
teuer!«

»Geh zur Drogerie Kaiser. Dort sind sie billig. Ach, ich brauche ja auch
Vitamintabletten. Ich habe keine mehr.«

»Warum nimmst du denn Vitamintabletten?« fragt Monika. »Bist du
35 krank?«*

»Oh nein, ich nehme schon lange Vitamintabletten und jetzt bin ich nicht
mehr so oft krank!«

Vor der° Metzgerei steht Stefan mit den Brötchen. »Hmmm, die riechen
gut! Jetzt aber schnell nach Hause. Ich habe einen Riesenhunger° und Durst!«

vor der: in front of the

Ich ... Riesenhunger: I'm very
hungry

Brauchbares

1. **Doch** has several meanings. In the dialogue on page 89, **doch** is used as a flavoring particle. Monika says: **Kauf das (Brot) doch bei Reinhardt.** In line 5 of
the reading, **doch** is equivalent to *however:* **doch den Käse kauft sie im
türkischen Lebensmittelgeschäft.**

2. Gisela notes that it is almost one o'clock and the stores will close soon
(ll. 23–24). In German-speaking countries, many small stores close early on
Saturday.

3. In line 24, Gisela says: **Stefan, geh du bitte in die Bäckerei. Geh** is a command
or imperative form (see pages 109–110) as in the English *Go to the bakery,
please.* The addition of the pronoun **du** adds emphasis or clarification.

4. **Apotheke vs. Drogerie.** Gisela tells David to buy the vitamin tablets in the
Drogerie, rather than in the **Apotheke.** An **Apotheke** sells both prescription
and nonprescription drugs. A **Drogerie** sells a wide variety of products: toi-
letries, herbal and homeopathic remedies, toys, film, and vitamins, much as do
American drugstores. A **Drogeriemarkt** is a larger self-service drugstore.
There are generally fewer over-the-counter drugs in German-speaking countries than in the United States and Canada. For instance, in Germany and
Austria aspirin can be bought only in an **Apotheke,** although in Switzerland
aspirin can also be bought in a **Drogerie.**

5. In the two utterances **Oh je, es ist ja schon fast ein Uhr** (ll. 23–24) and **In der
Apotheke sind die ja furchtbar teuer!** (ll. 30–31), **ja** is a flavoring particle. As
a flavoring particle, **ja** may be used to express the belief that an utterance is
related to a condition that both the speaker and the listener are aware of, or
should be aware of.

Nach dem Lesen

1. Fragen zum Lesestück

1. Warum gehen die drei zusammen einkaufen?
2. Was nimmt Gisela mit°?
3. Warum kauft Gisela gern im türkischen Lebensmittelgeschäft ein°?
4. Was gibt es zum Abendessen bei Gisela?
5. Wer bezahlt die Rosen?

nimmt mit: takes along
kauft ein: shops

---

*l. 34: Although Germans are also concerned about health, vitamin pills as a diet supplement do not play
the role they do in the United States. Vitamins are regarded more as a natural ingredient of any food.

6. Warum kauft David ziemlich viel Wurst?
7. Für wen sind die Vitamintabletten?
8. Wo sind Vitamintabletten teuer?
9. Welche Geschäfte besuchen die drei? Was kaufen sie in jedem° Geschäft?
10. Wo kaufen Sie ein? Kaufen Sie alles im Supermarkt oder gehen Sie in viele Geschäfte?

every

2. Vokabeln. Find the sentences you can use in the following situations.

1. Tell a friend you have guests from Berlin.
2. Say that something is fantastic.
3. Offer to pay for some flowers.
4. Tell a friend to buy ten rolls.
5. Ask a friend why she/he takes vitamin tablets.
6. Say that something smells good.
7. Say you are really hungry.

3. Erzählen wir. How do Gisela's shopping habits differ from your own? Be prepared to say a few sentences in class. Use the following topics to get you started.

Bäckerei ▪ Metzgerei ▪ Einkaufstasche ▪ Oliven

• Wo kaufen Sie ein? Wo kauft Gisela ein?

• Was kaufen Sie? Was kauft Gisela?

• Was ist anders?

Erweiterung des Wortschatzes

1. Noun compounds

die **Blumen** + der **Markt** = der **Blumenmarkt**
flowers + market = flower market

kaufen + das **Haus** = das **Kaufhaus**
to buy + building = department store

A characteristic of German is its ability to form noun compounds easily. Where German uses compounds, English often uses separate words. Your vocabulary will increase rapidly if you learn to analyze the component parts of compounds.

der Kopf + **die** Schmerzen = **die** Kopfschmerzen
der Fisch + **der** Mann = **der** Fischmann
die Lebensmittel + **das** Geschäft = **das** Lebensmittelgeschäft

The last element of a compound determines its gender.

1. Was bedeutet das? *(What does that mean?)* The compounds listed below are made up of cognates and familiar nouns. Give the English equivalent of each.

1. der Sportartikel
2. das Computerspiel
3. das Käsebrötchen
4. der Eiskaffee
5. das Schokoladeneis
6. die Kaffeemaschine
7. die Schreibtischlampe
8. die Zimmertür
9. der Sonnenschein

Einkaufen

www Go to the *Deutsch heute* website at
http://college.hmco.com.

There was a time when most Germans did their routine shopping at the mom-and-pop store on the corner (**Tante-Emma-Laden**). Now, however, these small stores have almost vanished and have been replaced by supermarkets which tend to be smaller than American ones and are often located within walking distance of residential areas. Although the supermarkets are self-service stores, fresh foods such as cheeses, meats, cold cuts, bread, and vegetables may be sold by shop assistants at separate counters. Many neighborhoods still have an individual bakery (**Bäckerei**) or a butcher shop (**Metzgerei**). A wide variety of foreign foods is available because many immigrants have opened small stores that specialize in the foods of their homelands, for example Turkey or Greece. Many of the larger department stores (**Kaufhäuser**) also have complete grocery departments (**Lebensmittelabteilungen**). There are also large discount stores (**Einkaufszentren**) on the outskirts of cities which sell not only groceries but a wide variety of items ranging from clothing to electronic equipment, even prefabricated houses.

**Viele Leute kaufen im Supermarkt ein.
(Seewalchen, Österreich)**

Customers bring their own bags (**Einkaufstaschen**) to the supermarket or buy plastic bags (**Plastiktüten**) or canvas bags at the check-out counter. Customers pack their own groceries and generally pay for their purchases with cash (**Bargeld**), although the use of credit cards (**Kreditkarten**) is becoming more common at larger stores and for on-line shopping.

Einige Leute kaufen immer noch gern in kleinen Lebensmittelgeschäften ein. (Hannover)

Diskussion

1. Many people in German-speaking countries do their routine shopping at stores within walking distance. How does this compare with the situation in many mid-sized cities in the United States and Canada, where people must drive to a store? What impact does it have on personal habits, on the design of cities?
2. Why do you think that neighborhood stores are becoming a thing of the past in Germany and other industrialized countries?

Lebensmittelabteilungen: The largest is on the sixth floor in the **Kaufhaus des Westens (KaDeWe)** in Berlin. It offers a great variety of international foods. Altogether it has more than 500 kinds of bread, 1,000 kinds of cheese, and 1,500 kinds of sausages and cold cuts.

2. Days of the week and parts of days as adverbs

Noun	Adverb	English equivalent
Montag	**montags**	Mondays
Samstag	**samstags**	Saturdays
Morgen	**morgens**	mornings
Abend	**abends**	evenings

A noun that names a day of the week or a part of a day may be used as an adverb to indicate repetition or habitual action. An **-s** is added to the noun. In German, adverbs are not capitalized.

Inquiring about personal habits

 2. Ein Interview. Interview a partner. Record her/his responses.

Wann isst du mehr – mittags oder abends?
Wann bist du sehr müde – morgens oder abends?
Wann arbeitest du mehr – samstags oder sonntags?
Wann gehst du einkaufen – freitags, samstags oder wann?
Gehst du morgens oder abends einkaufen?

3. Units of weight and capacity

Most Germans use a small scale for weighing dry ingredients like flour and sugar, rather than measuring cups and spoons.

```
1 Kilo(gramm) (kg)  = 1000 Gramm
1 Pfund (Pfd.)      = 500 Gramm
1 Liter (l)
```

In the United States a system of weight is used in which a pound consists of 16 ounces. In German-speaking countries, as in other industrialized countries, the metric system is used: the basic unit of weight is the **Gramm,** and a thousand grams are a **Kilo(gramm).** German speakers also use the older term **Pfund** for half a **Kilo(gramm),** or **500 (fünfhundert) Gramm.** The American *pound* equals **454 Gramm.** The basic unit of capacity in the German-speaking countries is **der Liter.** A liter equals 1.056 quarts.

4. Units of measurement and quantity

Geben Sie mir zwei **Pfund** Kaffee.	Give me two pounds of coffee.
Ich nehme zwei **Glas** Milch.	I'll take two glasses of milk.
Er kauft zwei **Liter** Milch.	He's buying two liters of milk.
Zwei **Stück** Kuchen bitte.	Two pieces of cake, please.

In German, masculine and neuter nouns expressing measure, weight, or number are in the singular. Note that feminine nouns are in the plural: **Sie trinkt zwei Tassen Kaffee.** *(She drinks two cups of coffee.)*

3. Wie viel brauchen Sie? You're going grocery shopping for an elderly neighbor and are finding out how much of each item she wants you to buy.

➡ Wie viel Kaffee brauchen Sie? (1 Pfd.)   *Ich brauche ein Pfund Kaffee.*

1. Wie viel Kartoffeln brauchen Sie? (5 kg)
2. Und wie viel Käse? (200 g)
3. Wie viel Milch brauchen Sie? (2 l)
4. Wie viel Fisch? (2 Pfd.)
5. Und Tee? (100g)
6. Und wie viel Bananen brauchen Sie? (1 kg)
7. Wie viel Wurst? (150g)

Land und Leute

Der Markt

www Go to the *Deutsch heute* website at
http://college.hmco.com.

**Auf dem Markt gibt es immer
frisches Obst und Gemüse.**

Many people in the German-speaking countries prefer to buy their groceries at an outdoor market (**Markt**) because of its larger selection of fresh vegetables, fruit, and flowers grown by local farmers. There may also be stands (**Stände**) with bread, fish, sausages, eggs, herbs, and teas. Some markets are held daily, others once or twice a week; still others, like the famous **Viktualienmarkt** in Munich, have become permanent and are open the same hours as regular stores. Smaller cities, like Freiburg, often have a market right in their medieval centers, thus presenting a picturesque image of the past. Large cities, like Berlin or Vienna, offer a more cosmopolitan ambiance with their Turkish, Italian, or Eastern European markets. Hamburg's famous **Fischmarkt** in the St. Pauli harbor district opens very early on Sunday mornings and sells not only fish but a great variety of products that have just arrived from all over the world.

Diskussion

1. Make a list in German of items that one can buy at an outdoor market.
2. Imagine that you are in Germany. You need to go shopping for the weekend. It's a beautiful Saturday morning and the outdoor market is open. Make a short shopping list and a list of the places where you would buy the items.

4. Einkaufen: Sie haben Besuch aus Berlin. You and a partner are having company from Berlin and need to shop for the weekend. You are on a tight budget and plan to buy only the items advertised at Eurospar. You have 15 euros to spend. Discuss with your partner the items you need, how much of each item you need, and what the cost of each item is. Make up a shopping list with the items and the cost of each.

Buying groceries

S1: Wir brauchen Kaffee, nicht?
S2: Ja. Wie viel?
S1: 1 Pfund.
S2: Gut. Wie viel kostet er?
S1: 2,99€.

S2: Wir brauchen Bananen, nicht?
S1: Ja. Wie viel?
S2: 2 Kilo.
S1: Gut. Wie viel macht das?
S2: 3,18€.

Vokabeln 2

Substantive

1 kilogram = 2.2 U.S. pounds

der **Besuch, -e**   visit; **wir haben Besuch**   we have company

die **Blume, -n**   flower; der **Blumenstand**   flower stand

der **Durst**   thirst; **Durst haben**   to be thirsty

die **Einkaufstasche, -n**   shopping bag

das **Eis**   ice; ice cream; das **Schokoladeneis**   chocolate ice cream

das **Geschäft, -e**   store, business

das **Glas, ⁼er**   glass

das **Gramm**   gram (*abbrev.* **g**)

das **Haus, ⁼er**   house

der **Hunger**   hunger; **Hunger haben**   to be hungry; **Riesenhunger haben**   to be very hungry

das **Kilo(gramm)**   kilogram (*abbrev.* **kg**)

der **Laden, ⁼**   store

die **Limonade**   soft drink; lemonade

der **Liter, -**   liter (*abbrev.* **l** = 1.056 U.S. quarts)

der **Markt, ⁼e**   market

die **Marmelade, -n**   marmalade, jam

die **Party, -s**   party

das **Stück, -e**   piece

die **Tablette, -n**   tablet, pill

die **Tasche, -n**   bag; pocket

die **Tasse, -n**   cup

der **Wunsch, ⁼e**   wish

Verben

bekommen   to receive

bezahlen   to pay (for); **sie bezahlt das Essen**   she pays for the meal

finden   to find; **Er findet die Wurst gut.**   He likes the lunch meat.

geben (gibt)   to give; **es gibt**   there is, there are

kennen   to know, be acquainted with

riechen   to smell

rufen   to call, cry out

schließen   to close

stehen   to stand

Andere Wörter

also therefore, so	**morgens** mornings, every morning
billig cheap; **billiger** cheaper	**natürlich** naturally
denn (*conj.*) for (because)	**noch ein(e)** another; still, in
doch (*conj.*) however; nevertheless;	addition
still	**persönlich** personal
dort there	**samstags** (on) Saturdays
eigentlich really, actually	**schnell** fast, quick(ly)
fantastisch fantastic, great	**schon** already
frisch fresh	**teuer** expensive
immer always	**unpersönlich** impersonal
interessant interesting	**viele** many
lange (*adv.*) for a long time	**zu** to
mit with	

Besondere Ausdrücke

auf den Markt to the market	**noch nicht** not yet
Besuch haben to have company	**Sonst noch einen**
nach Hause (to go) home	**Wunsch?** Anything else?
nicht mehr no longer, not anymore	

Grammatik und Übungen

1 Verbs with stem-vowel change e > i

essen: to eat		
ich esse	wir essen	
du **isst**	ihr esst	
er/es/sie **isst**	sie essen	
Sie essen		

geben: to give		
ich gebe	wir geben	
du **gibst**	ihr gebt	
er/es/sie **gibt**	sie geben	
Sie geben		

nehmen: to take		
ich nehme	wir nehmen	
du **nimmst**	ihr nehmt	
er/es/sie **nimmt**	sie nehmen	
Sie nehmen		

English has only two verbs with stem-vowel changes in the third-person singular, present tense: *say > says (sezz)*, and *do > does (duzz)*.

German, on the other hand, has a considerable number of verbs with a stem-vowel change in the **du-** and **er/es/sie**-forms. Some verbs with stem vowel **e** change **e** to **i.** The verbs of this type that you know so far are **essen, geben,** and **nehmen.** The stem of **essen** ends in a sibilant; the ending **-st** therefore contracts to a **-t = du isst** (see *Kapitel 1, Grammatik und Übungen,* section 7). **Nehmen** has an additional spelling change: **du nimmst, er/es/sie nimmt.** In the chapter vocabularies in this book, stem-vowel changes are indicated in parentheses: **geben (gibt).**

1. Was geben wir Christin? Christin needs things for her room at the university. Tell what various friends are giving her. Use the proper form of **geben**.

→ Jürgen / zwei alte Stühle
Jürgen gibt Christin zwei alte Stühle.

1. Claudia / zwei Hefte
2. Maria und Volker / ein Radio
3. wir / eine Lampe
4. ihr / eine Uhr
5. Frau Hauff / eine Tasche
6. du / ein Buch über Musik
7. ich / zwei Kugelschreiber

Land und Leute

Das Frühstück

Zu einem gemütlichen Frühstück gehören Brötchen, Marmelade, Käse, Eier und Kaffee.

Ein gutes Frühstück ist die wichtigste Mahlzeit am Tag (*A good breakfast is the most important meal of the day*) is a popular saying in the German-speaking countries. A German breakfast (**Frühstück**) can be quite extensive, especially on weekends or holidays. Usually it consists of a hot beverage, fresh rolls (**Brötchen**) or bread, butter and jam; often there are cold cuts, an egg, cheese or perhaps yogurt, whole grain granola (**Müsli**), and juice or fruit. Pancakes are not a common breakfast food. Eggs for breakfast are usually soft-boiled (**weich gekocht**). Scrambled eggs (**Rühreier**) and fried eggs (**Spiegeleier**) are more often served for a light meal either for lunch or in the evening. Traditionally, the main warm meal of the day was eaten at noon (**Mittagessen**). Recently, however, more and more people prefer to eat their warm meal in the evening (**Abendessen**).

www Go to the *Deutsch heute* website at http://college.hmco.com.

Diskussion

Have a short conversation with a classmate in German in which you plan a meal for a German visitor. Decide which meal you will prepare for the visitor, whether you will serve a German meal or not, and what you will serve.

2. Im Café. Complete the conversation among three friends in a café by supplying the appropriate form of the verbs in parentheses.

CLAUDIA: Du, Lars, was _____ du? (nehmen)

LARS: Ich _____ ein Stück Kuchen. (nehmen) Du auch?

CLAUDIA: Nein, aber Ina _____ ein Stück, nicht wahr? (nehmen)

INA: Nein. Kuchen _____ ich nicht so gern. (essen)

CLAUDIA: Was _____ du denn gern? (essen)

INA: Eis. Es _____ hier sehr gutes Eis. (geben)

LARS: Und zu trinken? Was _____ ihr beide? Kaffee oder Tee? (nehmen)

3. Gern oder nicht gern? Your partner wants to know what you like to eat and drink.

Answering questions about eating habits

Expressing likes and dislikes

S2:   *S1:*
Isst du | **viel** | **Brot?**   Ja, | **viel.**
      | gern | | gern.

                   Nein, | **nicht viel.**
                       | nicht so gern.

Schüttelkasten

	Käse	Fisch		Fleisch
Kuchen				
	Obst	Gemüse		Wurst

Trinkst du | **viel** | **Milch?**   Ja, | **viel.**
        | gern | | gern.

                    Nein, | **nicht viel.**
                      | nicht so gern.

Schüttelkasten

	Bier		Tee
Wein		Kaffee	
	Saft	Limonade	
			Mineralwasser

② Word order with expressions of time and place

	Time	Place
Sie geht	heute	in die Buchhandlung.

	Place	Time
She's going	to the bookstore	today.

When a German sentence contains both a time expression and a place expression, the time expression precedes the place expression. Note that the sequence of time and place in English is reversed.

Land und Leute

Der Euro

www Go to the *Deutsch heute* website at http://college.hmco.com.

Customers in German-speaking countries almost always pay cash in stores and restaurants. Only recently have credit cards become popular; checks are used infrequently. Regularly occurring bills, such as rent and utilities, are usually paid by bank transfers.

The euro zone consists of the twelve member nations of the European Union who began using the bills (**Scheine**) and coins (**Münzen**) of the international currency, the euro (**der Euro**), in 2002. Among these twelve nations are three German-speaking countries: Germany, Austria, and Luxembourg. The euro (€) is divided into 100 cents (**Cents**). Switzerland does not use the euro. It continues to use its national currency, the **Franken (SFr)**, which is divided into 100 **Rappen (Rp)**. Swiss currency is also used in Liechtenstein.

In order to make identification of the different denominations clearer, the euro bills are printed in various colors and their size increases with their value. For instance, the yellow 200 euro note is larger than the blue 20 euro bill. The design on the back of the banknotes consists of bridges that represent the connections among the members of the European Union and between Europe and the rest of the world. The windows and gateways on the front symbolize the cooperation and openness in the European Union. The banknotes have a uniform design throughout Europe, but the coins are uniform only on their faces. There are 8 euro coins denominated in 2 and 1 euros, then 50, 20, 10, 5, 2, and 1 euro cents. Every euro coin carries a common European face that represents a map of the European Union against a background of transverse lines to which are attached the stars of the European flag. The 1, 2, and 5 cent coins put emphasis on Europe's place in the world, while the 10, 20, and 50 cent coins present the Union as a gathering of nations. The 1 and 2 euro coins depict Europe without frontiers. The obverse side of the coins is printed with national motifs of the individual countries. The Austrian 2 euro coin, for example, depicts Bertha von Suttner, the 1905 winner of the Nobel peace prize, while the German 2 euro coin depicts the German eagle surrounded by stars representing the other European states. No matter which national motif they show, however, the coins, like the bills, are legal tender in all participating nations.

Diskussion

1. Find the exchange rate for your currency and the euro and **Franken** in your local newspaper or on the Internet. Using prices from an advertisement in your local paper, calculate how much several items (for example, a stereo, a computer) would cost in euros or **Franken.**

2. What emotional, economic, and political benefits or disadvantages can you see to a common currency in Europe? In North America?

4. Wann gehst du? Your friend is trying to guess when you're going to do various errands. Confirm the guesses.

→ Wann gehst du in die Stadt? Heute Morgen?
Ja, ich gehe heute Morgen in die Stadt.

1. Wann gehst du in den Supermarkt? Um neun?
2. Wann gehst du in die Buchhandlung? Morgen?
3. Wann gehst du zum Bäcker? Später?
4. Wann gehst du in die Apotheke? Heute Morgen?
5. Wann gehst du ins Kaufhaus? Jetzt?

③ Imperatives°

der Imperativ

The imperative forms are used to express commands, offer suggestions and encouragement, give instructions, and try to persuade people. In both German and English, the verb is in the first position.

Infinitive	Imperative		
	du-Form	*ihr-Form*	*Sie-Form*
fragen	frag(e)	fragt	fragen Sie
arbeiten	arbeite	arbeitet	arbeiten Sie
essen	iss	esst	essen Sie
geben	gib	gebt	geben Sie
nehmen	nimm	nehmt	nehmen Sie
sein	sei	seid	seien Sie

■ du-*imperative*

Nadja. { **Frag(e)** Frau List.
Arbeite jetzt, bitte.
Gib mir bitte das Brot.
Nimm doch zwei Aspirin.

Nadja. { *Ask* Mrs. List.
Work now, please.
Give me the bread, please.
Why don't you *take* two aspirin.

The **du**-imperative consists of the stem of a verb plus **-e,** but the **-e** is often dropped in informal usage: **frage** > **frag.** If the stem of the verb ends in **-d** or **-t,** the **-e** may not be omitted in written German: **arbeite.** If the stem vowel of a verb changes from **e** to **i,** the imperative has this vowel change and never has final **-e: geben** > **gib, essen** > **iss, nehmen** > **nimm.**

■ ihr-*imperative*

Carsten. Peter. { **Fragt** Frau List.
Gebt mir bitte das Brot.

Carsten. Peter. { *Ask* Mrs. List.
Give me the bread, please.

The **ihr**-imperative is identical with the **ihr**-form of the present tense.

■ Sie-*imperative*

Herr Hahn. { **Fragen Sie** Frau List.
Geben Sie mir bitte das Brot.

Mr. Hahn. { *Ask* Mrs. List.
Give me the bread, please.

The **Sie**-imperative is identical with the **Sie**-form of the present tense. The pronoun **Sie** is always stated and follows the verb directly. In speech, one differentiates a command from a yes/no question by the inflection of the voice. As in English, the voice rises at the end of a yes/no question and falls at the end of a command.

Gehen Sie online – so einfach installieren Sie AOL!

Gisela und Michael fragen Uwe: „Wie gehen wir online?"
Uwe hat AOL. Was sagt er?
TIPP: Er sagt es im Imperativ.

■ *Imperative of* **sein**

Fabian, **sei** nicht so nervös!	Fabian, don't *be* so nervous!
Kinder, **seid** jetzt ruhig!	Children, *be* quiet now!
Frau Weibl, **seien Sie** bitte so gut und ...	Mrs. Weibl, please *be* so kind and . . .

Note that the **du**-imperative (**sei**) and **Sie**-imperative (**seien Sie**) are different from the present-tense forms: **du bist, Sie sind.**

Giving directives

5. Auf einer Party: Frau Berg und Julia. The Bergs have guests. Below are some things Frau Berg says to Sarah and Martin, two people she knows well. She also knows Julia well. How would she say the same things to her?

➜ Sarah und Martin, nehmt noch etwas Käse.
Julia, nimm noch etwas Käse.

1. Trinkt doch noch ein Glas Wein.
2. Sagt mal, wie findet ihr die Musik?
3. Seid so nett und spielt etwas Gitarre.
4. Esst noch etwas.
5. Kommt, hier sind unsere Fotos von Berlin.
6. Bleibt noch ein bisschen hier.

6. Auf einer Party: Frau Berg und Herr Fromme. Herr Fromme is an acquaintance but not a personal friend of Frau Berg. Frau Berg uses **Sie** when speaking with him. How would she say the same things to him that she said to Sarah and Martin in exercise 5?

7. Noch eine Party. At a very large party you hear snatches of conversation. Translate for your German friend who finds it all confusing. Use the **du**- or **ihr**-imperative as appropriate with first names and the **Sie**-imperative with last names.

➜ Stay here, Jennifer.   *Bleib hier, Jennifer.*
➜ Don't ask, Mr. Lang.   *Fragen Sie nicht, Herr Lang.*

1. Don't work too much, Julia. *Arbeite nicht zu viel, Julia*
2. Say something, Max.
3. Tina and Ute, have another glass of mineral water. (Use **trinken.**)
4. Don't believe that, Mark and Tom. *Glaubt das nicht*
5. Don't eat so much, Peter. *Iss nicht so viele*
6. Take aspirin, Michael. *Nimm*
7. Be so kind, Mrs. Schulz, and stay here. *Seien Sie bitte so gut und bleiben Sie hier*
8. Michael, be quiet. *Sei ruhig*
9. Please have some cake, Mrs. Klein. (Use **nehmen.**)

4 Direct object°

das direkte Objekt

Ich höre **Andrea** nebenan.	I hear *Andrea* next door.
Ich schließe die **Tür.**	I shut the *door.*

The direct object is the noun or pronoun that receives or is affected by the action of the verb. The direct object answers the question whom (**Andrea**) or what (**Tür**).

5 Accusative° of the definite articles *der, das, die*

der Akkusativ

	Nominative	Accusative
Masculine	**Der** Kaffee ist billig.	Nehmen Sie **den** Kaffee.
Neuter	**Das** Brot ist frisch.	Nehmen Sie **das** Brot.
Feminine	**Die** Marmelade ist gut.	Nehmen Sie **die** Marmelade.
Plural	**Die** Blumen sind schön.	Nehmen Sie **die** Blumen.

The direct object of a verb is in the accusative case. In the accusative case, the definite article **der** changes to **den.** The articles **das** and **die** (*sg.* and *pl.*) do not show case change in the accusative.

8. Einkaufen gehen. You and your roommate are shopping for things for your room. She/He starts to say something and you interrupt to ask how she/he likes the things. The things are direct objects in your questions.

billig ■ groß ■ klein ■ lustig ■ modern ■ schön ■ teuer

→ Die Lampe ist ... *Findest du die Lampe lustig?*

1. Das Radio ist ...	3. Der Tisch ist ...	5. Die Uhr ist ...
2. Der Stuhl ist ...	4. Das Bett ist ...	6. Die Pflanze ist ...

6 Word order and case as signals of meaning

Subject	Verb	Direct object
The man	visits	the professor.
The professor	visits	the man.

English usually uses word order to signal the difference between a subject and a direct object. The usual word-order pattern in statements is *subject, verb,* and *direct object.* The two sentences above have very different meanings.

Subject (nom.)	Verb	Direct object (acc.)
Der Mann	besucht	den Professor.

Direct object (acc.)	Verb	Subject (nom.)
Den Professor	besucht	der Mann.

German generally uses case to signal the difference between a subject and a direct object. The different case forms of the definite article (e.g., **der, den**) signal the grammatical function of the noun. **Der,** in the example above, indicates that the noun **Mann** is in the nominative case and functions as the subject. **Den** indicates that the noun **Professor** is in the accusative case and functions as the direct object. The word-order pattern in statements may be *subject, verb, direct object,* or *direct object, verb, subject.* The two sentences above have the same meaning.

Since German uses cases to signal grammatical function, it can use word order for another purpose: to present information from different perspectives. A speaker may use so-called "normal" word order (*subject, verb, direct object*) or "inverted" word order (*direct object, verb, subject*). The English equivalents vary, depending on context and the meaning the speaker wishes to convey. The sentence **Der Mann besucht den Professor** is equivalent to *The man visits the professor.* The sentence **Den Professor besucht der Mann** is equivalent to saying something like *It's **the professor** the man is visiting.*

Der Professor fragt **die** Studentin etwas.	The professor asks the student something.

When only one noun or noun phrase shows case, it may be difficult at first to distinguish meaning. In the example above, **der Professor** has to be the subject, since the definite article **der** clearly shows nominative case. By the process of elimination, therefore, **die Studentin** has to be the direct object. If **die Studentin** were the subject, the article before **Professor** would be **den.**

Die Frau fragt **das** Mädchen etwas.

Sometimes neither noun contains a signal for case. In an example like the one above, one would usually assume normal word order: *The woman asks the girl something.* Depending on context, however, it is possible to interpret it as inverted word order: *It's **the woman** the girl is asking something.*

 9. Hören Sie zu. Two Americans, Diane and Joan White, are visiting their friend Monika in Berlin. At breakfast they tell Monika what they like about Germany in general and Berlin in particular. Listen carefully and indicate the things that Diane and Joan like. You will hear two new words: **vergiss** (*forget*) and **stark** (*strong*).

likes

	Diane mag°	*Joan mag*
Berlin	☐	☐
die Museen	☐	☐
die Restaurants und Cafés	☐	☐
den Kuchen	☐	☐
das Brot	☐	☐
die Wurst	☐	☐
den Kaffee	☐	☐

Land und Leute

Geschäftszeiten

Business hours for stores are regulated by law in German-speaking countries. In Germany stores may be open from 6:00 A.M. to 8:00 P.M. on weekdays and Saturdays. Most stores open between 8:30 and 9:30 in the morning, although bakeries and other small stores may open earlier to allow customers to buy fresh **Brötchen** for breakfast or make purchases on the way to work. Many small neighborhood stores close during the early afternoon (**Mittagspause**) for one or two hours from about 1:00 P.M. to 3:00 P.M. Stores are closed on Sundays and holidays.

There are some exceptions to these regulations for businesses in resort areas, for leisure activities, and for the traveling public. If you need to make a late purchase or shop on Sundays, it is often necessary to go to the train station (**Bahnhof**) or find an open gas station (**Tankstelle**). However, even on Sundays you can usually buy fresh flowers for a few hours at a flower shop (**Blumenladen**) and buy a pastry at a pastry shop (**Konditorei**).

ÖFFNUNGSZEITEN
MONTAG - FREITAG
10.00 UHR - 19.00 UHR
SAMSTAG
10.00 UHR - 18.00 UHR

Dieses Geschäft in Köln ist samstags bis 18.00 Uhr geöffnet.

Diskussion

Discuss the advantages and disadvantages of a strict shop closing law, and compare the regulations in your community to those in Germany.

www Go to the *Deutsch heute* website at http://college.hmco.com.

In Switzerland, business hours are determined by each canton. Hours vary greatly. In Austria, stores close at 7:30 P.M. on weekdays and at 5:00 P.M. on Saturdays.

10. Monika fragt ihre Freundinnen. Monika asks Diane and Joan what they like. Using the cues, give their answers. Make sure you answer with the subject.

→ Joan, wie findest du den Kaffee hier? (gut)   *Der Kaffee ist gut.*

1. Wie findet ihr das Brot? (super)
2. Diane, wie findest du den Rotwein in der Pizzeria Giovanni? (teuer)
3. Wie findet ihr das Uni Café? (billig)
4. Joan, wie findest du den Schokoladenkuchen? (sehr gut)
5. Wie findet ihr den Deutschprofessor? (interessant)
6. Wie findet ihr die Nachbarin? (arrogant)
7. Wie findet ihr die Studenten an der Uni? (nett)

7 Direct object vs. predicate noun°

Predicate noun	Dieter Müller ist **mein Freund.**	Dieter Müller is *my friend*.
Direct object	Kennst du **meinen Freund?**	Do you know *my friend*?

The predicate noun (e.g., **mein Freund**) designates a person, concept, or thing that is equated with the subject (e.g., **Dieter Müller**). A predicate noun completes the meaning of linking verbs such as **sein** and **heißen** and is in the nominative case.

The direct object (e.g., **meinen Freund**) is the noun or pronoun that receives or is related to the action of the verb. The direct-object noun or pronoun is in the accusative case.

Predicate noun	Das ist **nicht** Sabine Meier.
Direct object	Ich kenne Sabine Meier **nicht.**

Nicht precedes a predicate noun and usually follows a noun or pronoun used as a direct object.

11. Ein kleines Interview. Here are some questions Peter was asked about his German class. Identify the direct object or predicate noun.

1. Sind das alle Studenten?
2. Kennst du die Studenten gut?
3. Ist dein Professor eine Frau oder ein Mann?
4. Ist das dein Deutschbuch?
5. Brauchst du ein Buch aus Deutschland?
6. Hast du Freunde in Deutschland oder Österreich?

 12. Was kaufst du? You're studying in Germany and want to travel around Europe during the summer. In order to finance your trip, you're selling things in your room or apartment. Your partner will decide which items she/he wants, and asks the price. After you name the price, she/he decides whether to buy the article.

cost

S2: Was kostet° [der Stuhl]?
S1: [Zehn] Euro.
S2: Gut, ich kaufe/nehme [den Stuhl]./ Das ist zu viel. Ich kaufe/nehme [den Stuhl] nicht.

8 Demonstrative pronouns in the accusative case

Wie findest du **den** Kaffee?	How do you like the coffee?
Den finde ich gut.	This is (really) good!
Wie findest du **das** Fleisch?	How do you like the meat?
Das finde ich gut.	That's (really) good!
Wie findest du **die** Torte?	How do you like the cake?
Die finde ich gut.	That is (really) good!
Wie findest du **die** Eier?	How do you like the eggs?
Die finde ich gut.	Those are (really) good!

The accusative forms of the demonstrative pronouns are identical to the accusative forms of the definite articles.

13. Nein, das finde ich nicht. You and Gabi are shopping in a department store. Disagree with all of her opinions.

> ➡ Ich finde das Musikheft billig. Du auch?
> *Nein, das finde ich nicht billig.*

1. Ich finde das Buch über Schach schlecht. Du auch?
2. Ich finde den Fernseher zu klein. Du auch?
3. Ich finde den Kugelschreiber billig. Du auch?
4. Ich finde die Lampe schön. Du auch?
5. Ich finde das Radio gut. Du auch?
6. Ich finde den Tisch zu groß für das Zimmer. Du auch?
7. Ich finde die Stühle furchtbar. Du auch?
8. Ich finde die Uhr zu groß. Du auch?

9 Accusative of *ein* and *kein*

	Nominative	Accusative
Masculine	Wo ist **ein** Bleistift?	Haben Sie **einen** Bleistift?
	Da ist **kein** Bleistift.	Ich habe **keinen** Bleistift.
Neuter	Wo ist **ein** Heft?	Haben Sie **ein** Heft?
	Da ist **kein** Heft.	Ich habe **kein** Heft.
Feminine	Wo ist **eine** Uhr?	Haben Sie **eine** Uhr?
	Da ist **keine** Uhr.	Ich habe **keine** Uhr.
Plural	Sind das Kulis?	Haben Sie Kulis?
	Das sind **keine** Kulis.	Ich habe **keine** Kulis.

The indefinite article **ein** and the negative **kein** change to **einen** and **keinen** before masculine nouns in the accusative singular. The neuter and feminine indefinite articles and their corresponding negatives do not show case changes in the accusative singular. **Ein** has no plural forms. **Kein,** however, does have a plural form: **keine.**

14. Wer braucht was? There are a number of new people in your dorm and their rooms are not completely furnished. Tell what each person needs, using the pictures as cues.

→ Peter   *Peter braucht einen Tisch.*

Anja

Karin

Caroline

Peter

Robin

Lisa

Florian

15. Ich brauche [keinen Tisch]. Ask your partner if she/he needs the things in exercise 14. She/He will reply in the negative.

S1: Brauchst du [einen Tisch]?
S2: Nein, ich brauche [keinen Tisch].

10 Accusative of possessive adjectives

	Nominative	Accusative
Masculine	Ist das **mein** Bleistift?	Ja, ich habe **deinen** Bleistift.
Neuter	Ist das **mein** Heft?	Ja, ich habe **dein** Heft.
Feminine	Ist das **meine** Uhr?	Ja, ich habe **deine** Uhr.
Plural	Sind das **meine** Kulis?	Ja, ich habe **deine** Kulis.

The possessive adjectives (**mein, dein, sein, ihr, unser, euer, Ihr**) have the same endings as the indefinite article **ein** in both the nominative and accusative cases.

16. Unsere Freunde. You're in a café having cake and coffee with Jochen. You talk about your friends. Complete the conversation by supplying appropriate endings to the possessive adjectives.

JOCHEN: Sag' mal, du und Martin, ihr arbeitet jetzt bei BMW, nicht?

SIE: Ja, and unser_____ Freund Martin findet sein_____ Arbeit furchtbar.

Aber ich finde mein_____ Arbeit interessant. Freitags bekomme ich

mein_____ Geld.

JOCHEN: Du, warum gibt Frank Andrea sein_____ Computer?

SIE: Ich glaube, Andrea gibt Frank ihr_____ Kassettendeck.

JOCHEN: Ach, so. Brauchen wir heute unser_____ Bücher?

SIE: Nein. Du, Jochen, brauchst du dein_____ Kuli?

JOCHEN: Nein. Möchtest du ihn haben? Aber warum isst du dein_____ Kuchen nicht?

SIE: Die Äpfel sind so sauer! Mein_____ Kuchen ist nicht besonders° gut.　　　　　　　especially

17. Was suchst du? Coming back from a field trip, a number of students are missing items. Tell who is looking for what by completing the sentences with the appropriate possessive adjective.

> ➜ Gerd sucht _____ Bleistift. *Gerd sucht seinen Bleistift.*

1. Monika sucht _ihr_ Handy.
2. Wir suchen _unsere_ Kulis.
3. Katja sucht _ihr_ Radio.
4. Jakob und Dario suchen _ihren_ Bleistift.
5. Sarah sucht _ihre_ Zeitung.
6. Ich suche _mein_ Deutschbuch.
7. Florian und Julia suchen _ihre_ Bücher.

11 Accusative of *wer* and *was*

Nominative	Accusative
Wer fragt?	**Wen** fragt sie?
Was ist los?	**Was** fragst du?

The accusative case form of the interrogative pronoun **wer?** *(who?)* is **wen?** *(whom?)*. The accusative and nominative form of **was?** *(what?)* are the same.

18. Wen? Was? The party is loud and you keep missing the end of your partner's comments. Ask what or whom she/he is talking about. Replace the direct object with **wen?** or **was?** to pose your questions.

> ➜ Ich frage Michael morgen. *Wen fragst du morgen?*
> ➜ Ich brauche einen neuen Computer. *Was brauchst du?*

1. Ich kenne Beatrix gut.
2. Ich spiele morgen Golf.
3. Morgen kaufe ich einen neuen Computer.
4. Die Musik finde ich gut.
5. Ich finde Mark lustig.

12 Impersonal expression *es gibt*

Gibt es hier einen Supermarkt?	Is there a supermarket here?
Es gibt heute Butterkuchen.	There's [We're having] butter cake today.

Es gibt is equivalent to English *there is* or *there are*. It is followed by the accusative case.

19. Was gibt es heute zum Abendessen? Tell what is planned for dinner tonight, and what is not.

→ Fisch – Käse *Es gibt Fisch, aber keinen Käse.*

1. Brötchen – Kartoffeln
2. Milch – Saft
3. Butter – Margarine
4. Gemüse – Obst
5. Tee – Kaffee
6. Mineralwasser – Wein

die Präposition

13 Prepositions°

Margot kauft die Uhr **für ihren Freund.**	Margot is buying the watch for her friend.
Margot kauft die Uhr **für ihn.**	Margot is buying the watch for him.

A preposition (e.g., **für**—*for*) is used to show the relation of a noun (e.g., **Freund**—*friend*) or pronoun (e.g., **ihn**—*him*) to some other word in the sentence (e.g., **kauft**—*buying*). The noun or pronoun following the preposition is called the object of the preposition.

Margot geht heute nicht **ins Kino.**	Margot is not going to the movies today.

Nicht precedes a prepositional phrase.

14 Accusative prepositions

durch	through	Sie geht **durch** die Buchhandlung.
für	for	Sie kauft es **für** das Haus.
gegen	against	Sie hat nichts **gegen** den Mann.
ohne	without	Sie geht **ohne** das Kind.
um	around	Sie geht **um** den Tisch.

The objects of the prepositions **durch, für, gegen, ohne,** and **um** are always in the accusative case.

Er geht **durchs** Zimmer.	durch das = **durchs**
Er braucht eine Batterie **fürs** Auto.	für das = **fürs**
Er geht **ums** Haus.	um das = **ums**

[1]health

Für wen ist die Apotheke in Paffrath da?

The prepositions **durch, für,** and **um** often contract with the definite article **das** to form **durchs, fürs,** and **ums.** These contractions are common in colloquial German, but are not required.

20. Was machen Anja und David? Complete the information about Anja and David by filling in the appropriate preposition and adding the correct form of the article or possessive adjective. The gender of unfamiliar nouns is provided in parentheses.

durch ▪ für ▪ gegen ▪ ohne ▪ um

Anja und David gehen heute <u>durch</u> d<u>en</u> Park (*m.*). Sie gehen <u>um</u>

lake

d<u>en</u> See° (*m.*) und sprechen über die Universität. David mag seinen

Deutschkurs nicht und sagt etwas <u>gegen</u> sein<u>en</u> Deutschprofessor. Anja

geht in die Buchhandlung. Sie kauft ein Buch _für_ ihr_en_ Englisch-
kurs (*m.*). Stefan ist auch da. Er fragt Anja und David: „Kommt ihr mit° ins   Kommt mit: come along
Kino?" Anja und David kommen nicht mit. Sie arbeiten heute Abend. Stefan
geht _ohne_ sein_e_ Freunde ins Kino.

15 Accusative of masculine *N*-nouns

Nominative	Accusative
Der Herr sagt etwas.	Hören Sie **den** Herrn?
Der Student sagt etwas.	Hören Sie **den** Studenten?

German has a class of masculine nouns that have signals for case. Not only the
article, but the noun itself ends in **-n** or **-en** in the accusative. This class of nouns
may be referred to as masculine **N**-nouns or "weak nouns." In the vocabularies of
this book, masculine **N**-nouns will be followed by two endings: **der Herr, -n, -en.**
The first ending is the singular accusative and the second is the plural ending.
The masculine **N**-nouns you know so far are **der Herr, der Junge, der Mensch,
der Nachbar,** and **der Student.**

21. Wie sagt man das? Give the German equivalents of the conversational
exchanges below.

1. Do you know the gentleman there, Mrs. Kluge?
   — Yes. He's a neighbor.
2. Why is your neighbor going around the house?
   — Ask Mr. Heidemann.

3. Why is Mr. Leber coming without the children?
   — He's buying books for the children.
4. I have nothing against Mr. Knecht.
   — Who's Mr. Knecht?

Wo ist mein Traummann[1]? Ich, blond,
1,70 m, 17 Jahre alt, cool, suche dich,
18 oder 19, sportlich und auch cool!
Bist du mein Valentin?
Deine Susi Tel. 23478

[1]*dream man*

Wen sucht Susi?
Wie soll (*should*) er sein?
Wie ist Susi?

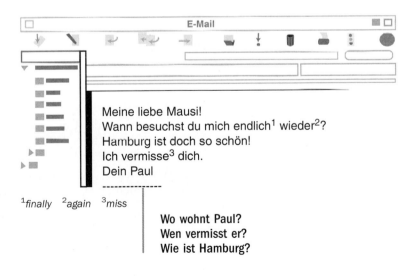

Meine liebe Mausi!
Wann besuchst du mich endlich[1] wieder[2]?
Hamburg ist doch so schön!
Ich vermisse[3] dich.
Dein Paul

----
[1]*finally* [2]*again* [3]*miss*

Wo wohnt Paul?
Wen vermisst er?
Wie ist Hamburg?

Lieber Alexander, lieber Daniel!
Alles Gute zum Valentinstag!
Seid nicht böse[1] – ich liebe[2] euch
doch beide! Eure Anne

[1]*angry* [2]*love*

Wer sind Alexander und Daniel?
Wen liebt Anne?

16 Accusative of personal pronouns

Nominative		Accusative	
Subject	*Object*	*Subject*	*Object*
Er braucht	**mich.**	*He* needs	*me.*
Ich arbeite für	**ihn.**	*I* work for	*him.*

Pronouns used as direct objects or objects of accusative prepositions are in the accusative case.

Subject pronouns	I	you	he	she	it	we	you	they
Object pronouns	me	you	him	her	it	us	you	them

Some English pronouns have different forms when used as subject or as object.

Nominative	ich	du	er	sie	es	wir	ihr	sie	Sie
Accusative	mich	dich	ihn	sie	es	uns	euch	sie	Sie

Some German pronouns also have different forms in the nominative and accusative.

22. Wie findest du das? With a partner, write five questions about your lives as students using the cues below. Use a personal pronoun in your answer as in the model.

> *S1:* Wie findest du Professor Smith?
> *S2:* Ich finde ihn nicht sehr interessant. Und du?
> *S1:* Ich finde ihn konservativ.

dein Computer	klein
das Deutschbuch	groß
dein Kugelschreiber	interessant
Professor _____	nett
dein DVD-Player	teuer
dein Rucksack	billig
die Studenten an der Uni	arrogant
das Essen an der Uni	progressiv
dein Zimmer	konservativ
das Wetter heute	furchtbar
dein Studentenjob (*m.*)	gut/schlecht

23. Wie sagt man das? Give the German equivalents of the conversational exchanges below.

1. Who is working for us?
   —We're working for you.
2. Are you asking me?
   —Yes, I'm asking you.

3. What do you have against me?
   —I have nothing against you, Mr. Meyer.
4. Do you know Uwe and Barbara?
   —No. I don't know them.

Leserunde

Pierre Aziz's poem "Liebe" is another example of concrete poetry (see **Leserunde,** p. 16). Aziz uses the physical placement of words to highlight and even to change the meaning of the words and phrases. This manipulation of language brings more meaning to the words themselves as the poem progresses from the beginning to the end.

liebe

es	gibt	keinen	platz[1]	für	dich	in	meinem	traum[2]
es	gibt	keinen	platz	für	dich	in	meinem	raum[3]
es	gibt	keinen	platz	für	dich			
es	gibt	kaum[4]	platz	für	dich			

es	gibt	einen	platz	für	dich
es	gibt	nur	platz	für	dich
es	gibt	nur			dich
es	gibt				dich
	gib[5]				dich

Pierre Aziz

[1]*room* [2]*dream* [3]*space* (here: *life*) [4]*hardly* [5]*give in*

Wiederholung

1. Rollenspiel. Your partner and her/his roommate (Sabine/Mark) are having you over for breakfast. Your partner offers you items and makes other requests. Respond to her/his offers and requests.

> **Redemittel: Fragen oder Aufforderungen beantworten** *(Responding to offers and requests)*
>
> Doch. ▪ Bitte. ▪ Das geht leider nicht. ▪ Gern. ▪ Machen wir. ▪ Natürlich. ▪ Vielleicht.

1. Möchtest du noch einen Kaffee?
2. Nimmst du keinen Zucker°?   sugar
3. Iss doch noch ein Brötchen!
4. Gib Sabine/Mark bitte die Butter!
5. Komm doch auch heute Abend!

2. Essen und Trinken. While having wine and cheese, Claudia and Uwe talk about eating and drinking. Form sentences, using the cues on pp. 121–122.

> ➔ CLAUDIA: wie / du / finden / der Wein / ?   *Wie findest du den Wein?*

1. UWE: gut // was für Wein / das / sein / ?
2. CLAUDIA: Wein / kommen / aus Kalifornien
3. UWE: du / kaufen / der Käse / im Supermarkt / ?
4. CLAUDIA: nein, / ich / kaufen / alles / auf dem Markt

5. CLAUDIA: zum Abendessen / es / geben / Fisch
6. CLAUDIA: du / essen / gern / Fisch / ?
7. UWE: nein, / ich / essen / kein Fisch / und / auch / keine Wurst
8. UWE: ich / essen / aber / gern / Kuchen
9. CLAUDIA: heute / es / geben / leider / kein Kuchen

3. Beim Frühstück. Oliver is a German exchange student who just arrived last night in New York and is staying with the Schuberts. Harry and Anna Schubert, their two children, Hannah and Frank, and Oliver are sitting at the breakfast table. Give the German equivalent of their conversation.

1. MRS. SCHUBERT: Who needs the tea?
2. MR. SCHUBERT: Hannah, give Oliver the coffee.
3. HANNAH: Oliver doesn't drink coffee.
4. OLIVER: No, I always drink tea for breakfast.
5. MRS. SCHUBERT: Harry, what are you doing today?
6. MR. SCHUBERT: I'm working in the library. (in the = **in der**)
7. MRS. SCHUBERT: Oliver, whom do you know in New York?
8. OLIVER: I know a professor.
9. FRANK: Oliver, are there many cybercafés° in Germany?
10. OLIVER: Of course. Why do you ask, Frank?

das Internetcafé, -s

4. Nicht oder kein? Answer in the negative, using **nicht** or a form of **kein.**

→ Kauft Erika heute Kartoffeln? *Nein, sie kauft heute keine Kartoffeln.*

1. Kauft sie Kuchen?
2. Geht sie heute zum Bäcker?
3. Kauft sie das Fleisch im Supermarkt?
4. Kauft Gerd heute Käse?
5. Kauft er das Brot beim Bäcker?
6. Kauft er heute Milch?
7. Gibt es hier einen Supermarkt?

5. Frage-Ecke. Compare the picture of your room with that of your partner. **S1's** picture is below; **S2's** picture is in Appendix B.

S1: Mein Zimmer hat [eine Pflanze]. Hast du auch [eine Pflanze]?
S2: Ja, ich habe auch [eine Pflanze]./Nein, aber ich habe Blumen.

S1:

6. Gespräche. You invite a classmate back to your room or apartment for dinner.

1. She/He makes comments on your room/apartment.
2. Ask her/him what she/he likes to eat.
3. Either you don't have what she/he has mentioned or what you have is not fresh.
4. She/He asks if there is a grocery store nearby.
5. Make a list of what you will buy together for dinner.

7. Zum Schreiben

1. **a.** Assume that you are visiting Gisela in Tübingen. (See **Einkaufen am Wochenende,** pages 98–99.) Write a short letter to someone you are going to visit in Austria, in which you tell what you plan to do on the second weekend of your visit in Germany. It is O.K., incidentally, to do many of the same things that you did on the first weekend, especially if you enjoyed them.

   b. Or assume you are Gisela and you have guests from the U.S.A. or Canada. Write a letter to a friend in which you tell what you plan to do with them during their visit.

Hinweise (tips): Before you begin your letter turn back to *Kapitel 1* and review the format (opening, closing, etc.) for informal letters. Then make a list of activities you plan to write about, e.g., shopping, playing tennis.

2. Your friend Erik prefers to shop in **Supermärkte,** but your friend Lisa prefers **kleine Lebensmittelgeschäfte.** Write a paragraph in German in which you state your personal preference and your reasons for it.

Hinweise: Look over the reading (pp. 98–99) and **Land und Leute: Einkaufen** (page 101) before you begin writing. Think about which things appeal to you in the type of store you prefer. Write down your ideas and then organize them according to their order of importance. Begin your paragraph by stating which type of store you like: **Ich gehe gern [in den Supermarkt]. Da ...**

Grammatik: Zusammenfassung

Verbs with stem-vowel change e > i

essen		
ich esse	wir essen	
du **isst**	ihr esst	
er/es/sie **isst**	sie essen	
Sie essen		

geben		
ich gebe	wir geben	
du **gibst**	ihr gebt	
er/es/sie **gibt**	sie geben	
Sie geben		

nehmen		
ich nehme	wir nehmen	
du **nimmst**	ihr nehmt	
er/es/sie **nimmt**	sie nehmen	
Sie nehmen		

Several verbs with the stem vowel **e** (including **essen, geben, nehmen**) change **e > i** in the **du-** and **er/es/sie**-forms of the present tense.

Word order with expressions of time and place

	Time	Place
Monika geht	heute Abend	ins Kino.
Robert war	gestern	nicht hier.

In German, time expressions generally precede place expressions.

Imperative forms

	Infinitive	Imperative	Present
du	sagen	**Sag(e)** etwas, bitte.	Sagst du etwas?
ihr		**Sagt** etwas, bitte.	Sagt ihr etwas?
Sie		**Sagen Sie** etwas, bitte.	Sagen Sie etwas?
du	nehmen	**Nimm** das Brot, bitte.	Nimmst du das Brot?
ihr		**Nehmt** das Brot, bitte.	Nehmt ihr das Brot?
Sie		**Nehmen Sie** das Brot, bitte.	Nehmen Sie das Brot?

■ *Imperative of* **sein**

du	**Sei** nicht so nervös.
ihr	**Seid** ruhig.
Sie	**Seien Sie** so gut.

Accusative case of nouns

Nominative	Accusative
Subject	*Direct Object*
Der Kuchen ist frisch.	Er nimmt **den Kuchen**.
Die Uhr ist schön.	Sie kauft **die Uhr**.

A noun that is used as a direct object of a verb is in the accusative case.

Accusative case of masculine *N*-nouns

Nominative	der Herr	der Junge	der Mensch	der Nachbar	der Student
Accusative	den Herr**n**	den Junge**n**	den Mensch**en**	den Nachbar**n**	den Student**en**

A number of masculine nouns add **-n** or **-en** in the accusative singular.

Accusative case of the definite articles *der, das, die*

	der	das	die	Plural
Nominative	der ⎱ Käse	das ⎱ Brot	die ⎱ Butter	die ⎱ Eier
Accusative	den ⎰	das ⎰	die ⎰	die ⎰

Accusative case of demonstrative pronouns

Accusative nouns	Accusative pronouns
Ich finde **den Käse** gut.	**Den** finde ich auch gut.
Ich finde **das Brot** trocken.	**Das** finde ich auch trocken.
Ich finde **die Butter** frisch.	**Die** finde ich auch frisch.
Ich finde **die Eier** schlecht.	**Die** finde ich auch schlecht.

Accusative case of *wer* and *was*

Nominative	Accusative
Wer fragt?	**Wen** fragt er?
Was ist los?	**Was** fragst du?

Accusative of *ein*, *kein*, and possessive adjectives

	Masculine	Neuter	Feminine	Plural
	(der Kuli)	*(das Heft)*	*(die Uhr)*	*(die Kulis)*
Nominative	ein / kein / dein ⎱ Kuli	ein / kein / dein ⎱ Heft	eine / keine / deine ⎱ Uhr	keine / deine ⎱ Kulis
Accusative	einen / keinen / deinen ⎱ Kuli	ein / kein / dein ⎱ Heft	eine / keine / deine ⎱ Uhr	keine / deine ⎱ Kulis

Kein and the possessive adjectives (**mein, dein, sein, ihr, unser, euer, Ihr**) have the same endings as the indefinite article **ein**.

Accusative case of personal pronouns

Nominative	ich	du	er	es	sie	wir	ihr	sie	Sie
Accusative	mich	dich	ihn	es	sie	uns	euch	sie	Sie

[1]*inexpensive*   [2]*family vacation*   [3]*farm*

Prepositions with the accusative case

durch	through	Sie geht **durch** das Zimmer. [**durchs** Zimmer]
für	for	Sie kauft die Uhr **für** das Haus. [**fürs** Haus]
gegen	against	Sie hat nichts **gegen** den Mann.
ohne	without	Sie geht **ohne** Herrn Bauer.
um	around	Sie geht **um** das Haus. [**ums** Haus]

Impersonal expression es *gibt*

Es gibt keinen Kaffee mehr.   There is no more coffee.
Gibt es auch keine Brötchen?   Aren't there any rolls, either?

Es gibt is equivalent to English *there is* or *there are*. It is followed by the accusative case.

Was studierst du?

Studenten nach der Vorlesung. (Frankfurt)

LERNZIELE

Sprechintentionen

Borrowing and lending things
Talking about student life
Offering explanations/excuses
Describing one's family, nationality,
  and profession
Talking about personal interests
Inquiring about abilities
Discussing duties and requirements
Inquiring about future plans
Expressing regret

Lesestück

Studieren in Deutschland

Land und Leute

Hamburg
Higher education In Germany
University admission and financial
  aid in Germany
Foreign students in Germany
English vs. German terms
  (education)
The school system in Germany

Vokabeln

Professions and nationalities
Family members

Grammatik

Werden
Verbs with stem-vowel change
  e > ie
Wissen and *kennen*
Der-words
Modal auxiliaries
Separable-prefix verbs

Bausteine für Gespräche

Notizen für die Klausur

GISELA: Hallo, Michael. Kannst du mir bitte deine Notizen leihen?

MICHAEL: Ja, gern.

GISELA: Das ist nett. Für die Klausur muss ich noch viel arbeiten.

MICHAEL: Klar, hier hast du sie. Kannst du sie morgen bitte wieder mitbringen?

Ist das dein Hauptfach?

MICHAEL: Moin, Moin, Melanie. Seit wann gehst du denn in eine Literatur-Vorlesung? Studierst du nicht Geschichte?

MELANIE: Nein, nicht mehr. Ich mache jetzt Germanistik.

MICHAEL: Ah ja? Als Nebenfach?

MELANIE: Nein, als Hauptfach.

MICHAEL: Ach, wirklich? Du, möchtest du nachher Kaffee trinken gehen?

MELANIE: Ich kann leider nicht. Ich muss noch etwas lesen. Morgen habe ich ein Referat und bin nicht besonders gut vorbereitet.

Brauchbares

1. **Moin, Moin:** Michael, who is from Hamburg, greets Melanie in the popular greeting from North Germany: **Moin, Moin.** Young people in other parts of Germany are also using this greeting, which they find "cool."

2. There are various German equivalents of the English word *study:*

   a. **studieren** = *to study a subject,* e.g., **Ich studiere Geschichte** *(I'm majoring in history).* **Studieren** also means to be a student or attend college, e.g., **Ich studiere jetzt** *(I go to college now).*

   b. **machen** = *to do homework,* e.g., **Ich mache heute Abend Deutsch** *(I'm going to study German tonight).* **Machen** also means *to major in,* e.g., **Ich mache jetzt Deutsch** *(I'm majoring in German now).*

   c. **lernen** = *to study in the sense of doing homework,* e.g., **Ich lerne die Vokabeln** *(I'm studying the vocabulary words).*

Fragen

1. Warum möchte Gisela Michaels Notizen leihen?
2. Warum muss Gisela noch viel lernen?
3. Wann möchte Michael seine Notizen wiederhaben?
4. Warum geht Melanie jetzt in eine Literatur-Vorlesung?
5. Was ist Melanies Hauptfach?
6. Was möchte Michael nachher machen?
7. Warum kann Melanie nicht mitgehen?

Exams in university-level courses are given much less frequently in Germany than in the U.S. Most German courses do not have weekly or chapter exams, midterms, or finals. Because they are given infrequently, exams such as **Klausuren** tend to be major exams, comparable to a semester exam in the U.S.

Borrowing objects/lending objects

1. Sie brauchen etwas. Sie brauchen etwas. Vielleicht kann eine Kursteilnehmerin/ein Kursteilnehmer es Ihnen leihen. Fragen Sie sie/ihn. (You need something. Perhaps a fellow student can lend it to you. Ask her/him.)

S1:			S2:
Kannst du mir	**deine Notizen**	leihen?	Ja, gern.
	dein Referat		Klar.
	deine Seminararbeit[+]		Natürlich.
	deinen Kugelschreiber		Tut mir Leid[+]. Ich
	deine Disketten[+]		brauche ihn/es/sie
			selbst.

Land und Leute

Hamburg

 Go to the *Deutsch heute* website at
http://college.hmco.com.

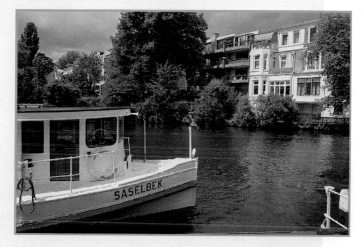

Since the Middle Ages, when Hamburg was a member of the Hanseatic League (**die Hanse**), the city has been a center of trade and industry. Located at the mouths of the Elbe and Alster rivers only one hundred kilometers from the North Sea, Hamburg calls itself "the Gateway to the World" (**das Tor zur Welt**). There are 3000 firms in the import/export business alone. Hamburg's harbor is one of the largest in the world and spreads out over 75 square kilometers within the city. With its 1.7 million inhabitants, Hamburg is Germany's second largest city after Berlin, and after the Ruhr valley area (**das Ruhrgebiet**), it is the second largest industrial center.

Wassertaxi auf der Alster (Hamburg)

Hamburg is also known as the green industrial center because over 12% of its area consists of green spaces and parks. One of the most famous green areas is **Planten un Blomen** (Low German for **Pflanzen und Blumen,** plants and flowers) in the middle of the city. Also in the center of the city, the Alster River forms two large lake-like bodies of water (**Außenalster** and **Binnenalster**) that provide both a popular place for water sports and a convenient taxi boat service. **Hagenbecks Tierpark,** built in 1907, was the first zoo in the world to keep animals in a natural setting rather than in cages. It has been the model for such zoos ever since.

Hamburg is not only the commercial but also the cultural center of all Northern Germany. It has eleven universities and technical schools, thirty-one theaters, six concert halls, and fifty public and private museums. Like many other large seaports, Hamburg is known for its nightlife, found especially in the entertainment quarter called **St. Pauli.** The Beatles' 1962 performances in the Star Club here marked the beginning of their international popularity.

Diskussion

1. Hamburg is a major port city. What advantages does this geographical feature have for a city? How has it influenced Hamburg's development? Can you compare Hamburg to another port city?
2. Hamburg applied to host the summer Olympic games in 2012. Would you like to attend the Olympics there? Why or why not?

Discussing college majors and minors

2. Hauptfach. Nebenfach. Interviewen Sie vier Studentinnen/Studenten in Ihrem Deutschkurs. Was sind ihre Hauptfächer und Nebenfächer? In den Supplementary Word Sets, Appendix C, finden Sie weitere Studienfächer. (Interview four students in your German class. What are their majors and minors? In the Supplementary Word Sets in Appendix C, you will find further college majors.)

S1:
Was ist dein | **Hauptfach?**
Nebenfach?

S2:
Ich studiere | **Germanistik.**
Mein Nebenfach ist | Psychologie⁺.

Schüttelkasten

Biologie⁺   Anglistik⁺   Philosophie⁺   Kunstgeschichte⁺   Physik⁺
Informatik⁺   Mathematik⁺   Chemie⁺

3. Was liest du? Was lesen die Studentinnen/Studenten in Ihrem Deutschkurs gern? Fragen Sie sie. (What do the students in your German class like to read? Ask them.)

S1:
Was liest du gern?

S2:
Artikel über | Sport/Musik/Schach.
Bücher über | Psychologie
Krimis⁺.
Liebesromane⁺.
Moderne⁺ Literatur.
Zeitung⁺

Offering explanations/ excuses

Land und Leute (p. 131): Departments set requirements for the number of graded certificates (**Seminarscheine**) a student must submit to be admitted to the final comprehensive exam. A student earns a Schein by writing a seminar paper. Some departments also require **Teilnahmescheine (Sitzscheine).** For this **Schein,** a student participates in a seminar, but does not write a paper.

4. Es tut mir Leid. Ihre Freundin/Ihr Freund möchte später mit Ihnen etwas zusammen machen. Sie können aber nicht. Sagen Sie warum. (Your friend would like to do something together later, but you can't. Say why.)

S2:
Willst du nachher | **Kaffee trinken gehen?**
einkaufen gehen?
fernsehen⁺?
spazieren gehen?
ein Video ausleihen⁺?
eine DVD ausleihen?

S1:
Ich kann leider nicht.
Ich muss **mein Referat vorbereiten.**

Schüttelkasten

Deutsch machen   meine Notizen durcharbeiten⁺

die Vokabeln lernen   wieder in die Bibliothek

Land und Leute

Hochschulen

www Go to the *Deutsch heute* website at
http://college.hmco.com.

Germany has some 350 institutions of higher learning (**Hochschulen**). Responsibility for higher education is shared by the states and the federal government. The best-known type of institution is the **Universität,** which has a long tradition in German-speaking countries. The oldest university in present-day Germany is the University of Heidelberg, founded in 1386. Universities offer a variety of academic degrees (**Abschlüsse**): the **Diplom** is the first degree for most areas in the sciences, engineering, and other similar fields. Students in humanities generally pursue a **Magister Artium.** All degrees require written and oral examinations as well as an academic dissertation. Students who plan to enter civil service or a profession regulated by the state such as medicine, teaching, or law conclude their studies with the state examination (**Staatsexamen**).

Professor und Architekturstudentin an der Technischen Hochschule in Frankfurt am Main.

Colleges that specialize in preparing students for careers in art or music are called **Kunsthochschulen** and **Musikhochschulen** respectively. A newer type of institution of higher learning, introduced in the 1960s, is the **Fachhochschule** that specializes in fields of study (**Studiengänge**) that are more oriented toward a specific career such as business or engineering. These institutions offer a more structured and limited curriculum than universities, and the course of study can usually be concluded in four and a half years. Most students at a university expect to spend more than five years to complete their studies. In 1998 the **Bachelor-Studiengang** was introduced in **Fachhochschulen.** This degree is modeled on the British Bachelor of Science degree. Students progress towards a degree by collecting credits similar to those used in the American system and can usually graduate within three years.

At some universities students bear the responsibility for their own progress. Courses taken by the student are listed in an official transcript book (**Studienbuch**), which individual students keep in their possession. There are few exams, papers, and daily assignments, and for many courses there are no exams. At the beginning of the semester students choose classes according to type and subject matter. A **Vorlesung** is a lecture with little discussion and no exams. An **Übung** is a course that often has daily assignments, discussion, and a test (**Klausur**) at the end. In a **Seminar**, students write papers and discuss the material. They have to write term papers (**Seminararbeiten**) as well.

After successful completion of a **Seminar** or **Übung,** students receive a certificate (**Schein**), which includes a grade. A minimum number of **Scheine** is necessary before the student may take the intermediate qualifying exam (**Zwischenprüfung**), which is usually taken after four to six semesters at the university. More **Scheine** are required before a student can write a master's thesis (**Magisterarbeit**) or take examinations for the degree.

Approximately 25% of German students attend a **Fachhochschule.**

Diskussion

Which type of German institution is closest in form to your college or university? Compare the course types and grading system at a German university to your experience of higher education.

Vokabeln 1

Substantive

die **Anglistik**   English studies (language and literature)

die **Arbeit, -en**   work; paper

der **Artikel, -**   article

die **Biologie**   biology

die **Chemie**   chemistry

die **Diskette, -n**   disk

die **DVD, -s**   DVD

das **Fernsehen**   television (the industry); der **Fernseher** television set

der **Film, -e**   film

die **Germanistik**   German studies (language and literature)

die **Geschichte, -n**   story; history

das **Hauptfach, ⁻er**   major (subject)

die **Informatik**   computer science

die **Klausur, -en**   test; **eine Klausur schreiben**   to take a test

der **Krimi, -s**   mystery (novel or film)

die **Kunstgeschichte**   art history

die **Liebe**   love; der **Liebesroman**   romance (novel)

die **Literatur**   literature

die **Mathematik**   mathematics; (used without article) **Mathe**   math

das **Nebenfach, ⁻er**   minor (subject)

die **Notiz, -en**   note

die **Philosophie, -n**   philosophy

die **Physik**   physics

die **Psychologie**   psychology

das **Referat, -e**   report

der **Roman, -e**   novel

das **Seminar, -e**   seminar

die **Seminararbeit, -en**   seminar paper

das **Video, -s**   video

die **Vorlesung, -en**   lecture

die **Zeitung, -en**   newspaper

Verben

Separable-prefix verbs are indicated with a raised dot: **durch·arbeiten.** (See *Grammatik und Übungen*, section 9, in this chapter.)

aus·leihen   to rent (e.g., video); to check out (e.g., book from library); to lend out

bringen   to bring

durch·arbeiten   to work through; to study

dürfen (darf)   to be permitted to, to be allowed to; may

fern·sehen (sieht fern)   to watch TV

können (kann)   to be able to; can

leihen   to lend; to borrow

lernen   to learn; to study

lesen (liest)   to read

mit·bringen   to bring along

müssen (muss)   to have to; must

sehen (sieht)   to see

sollen (soll)   to be supposed to

vor·bereiten   to prepare

wollen (will)   to want to, intend to

Andere Wörter

besonders   especially

klar   clear; of course, naturally

modern   modern

nachher   afterwards

noch etwas   something else

seit   since (temporal)

wieder   again

Besondere Ausdrücke

Deutsch machen   to do/study German (as homework); to study German (subject at the university)

(es) tut mir Leid   I'm sorry

ich bin (nicht) gut vorbereitet   I am (not) well prepared

ich kann leider nicht   unfortunately, I can't

kannst du mir [deine Notizen] leihen?   can you lend me [your notes]?

seit wann   since when, (for) how long

Land und Leute (p. 133): **Regelstudienzeit:** Only one in ten students finishes within the specified number of semesters. Most students study for 12–13 semesters.

Land und Leute

Finanzen und Studienplätze

Around 1.9 million students are enrolled in Germany's institutions of higher learning. In the 1960s only 8% of young people pursued academic studies; today one-third does. One of the reasons for this rapid growth is the availability of student aid. In 1971, a law called the **Bundesausbildungsförderungsgesetz (BAföG)** was passed to give everyone an equal chance to study at the university. Today approximately 340,000 students are subsidized through this program, which provides 50% of the aid as a grant and 50% as a no-interest loan. Generally, there is no tuition (**Studiengebühren**) at public universities, so the financial aid is for living expenses. However, a few states have introduced tuition under limited conditions. The German Supreme Court has ruled that students who are pursuing their first degree have a right to a tuition-free education. In Austria students pay tuition (**Studienbeitrag**) of 360 euros per semester, and in Switzerland sFr 600 to sFr 2000 a year. To finance their studies, most German students work part-time (**jobben**), either during the semester or during vacation (**Semesterferien**). Students may earn up to 325 euros each month almost tax-free through regular employment.

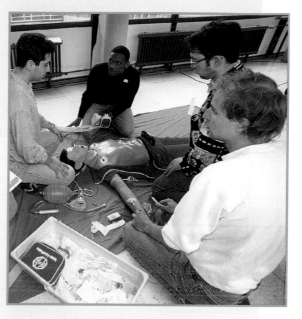

Diese Medizinstudenten haben einen Studienplatz bekommen. (Hannover)

This rapid expansion of higher education has led to problems of overcrowding in the universities. University officials are concerned that rooms are used beyond their capacity. Students complain about inadequate accessibility of teachers and research materials and that they cannot enroll in required courses. Occasionally students engage in strike actions to protest what they perceive as the underfunding and overcrowding of universities or the introduction of tuition.

In some subject areas, including medicine, law, and psychology, a system called **Numerus clausus (N.C.)** is used to limit the number of students. The subject areas involved may vary from year to year, depending on the enrollment capacity (**Studienplätze**). Places in **N.C.** programs are distributed by a central office mainly on the basis of high school grades (**Noten**) received during the last years of the **Gymnasium** and grades on the final comprehensive examination (**das Abitur**). Students who receive a place at a university they would rather not attend often attempt to trade places with a student at another university. There can be a waiting period of up to five years for admission in some disciplines. The **Regelstudienzeit,** in effect in some states, requires that the students finish their studies within a required number of semesters, on the average 8–12 semesters.

BAföG: In 2002 the basic award was around 466 euros per month. After the third semester students can use **BAföG** to study in any country of the EU.

For entrance requirements to attend a school of higher education see **Land und Leute,** p. 143.

Diskussion

1. What is your opinion of student strikes? For what reasons could you justify a strike?
2. Have a debate on the following subject: Resolved: Germany should charge tuition for higher education.

Studieren in Deutschland

Vorbereitung auf das Lesen

■ Vor dem Lesen

student life

In diesem Text lernen Sie etwas über die Universitäten und das Studentenleben° in Deutschland. Bevor Sie den Text lesen, sprechen Sie mit einer Kommilitonin/ einem Kommilitonen° über das Leben an Ihrer Universität und beantworten° Sie diese Fragen.

fellow student / answer

tuition
scholarships

1. Ist Ihre Uni oder Hochschule privat oder staatlich?
2. Wie teuer ist das Studium? Wie bezahlen Studenten die Studiengebühren° und andere Kosten? Durch Stipendien° oder durch Jobben? Oder bezahlen die Eltern?
3. Wie ist das akademische Jahr an Ihrer Hochschule organisiert? Was machen die Studenten in den Semesterferien?

enroll in
courses leading to the degree

4. Wie viele Kurse belegen° Sie jedes Semester? In welchen Fächern?
5. Wie viele Semester braucht man für einen Bachelor-Studiengang°?

■ Beim Lesen

compare

Vergleichen° Sie die Universitäten in Deutschland mit Ihrer Uni. Füllen Sie die Tabelle beim Lesen aus.

	meine Uni	in Deutschland
1. Studienplätze		
2. Studentenjobs		
3. Semesterferien		
4. Examen		

Möchten Sie in Deutschland studieren? Informationen für amerikanische Studenten

Wer kann studieren?

of those

in spite of that / space for
  students / (Latin) restricted
  admissions / that

vom = von dem: from the

language test

An deutschen Universitäten studieren heute etwa 1,9 Millionen Studenten. Davon° sind 140 000 Ausländer. Es gibt zu wenige Universitäten und die meisten Kurse sind deshalb überfüllt. Deutsche können nur mit dem Abitur studieren, trotzdem° gibt es mehr Studenten als Studienplätze°.
5 Daher haben viele Fächer den N.C., den Numerus clausus°. Junge Leute wissen also, dass° es schwer ist, einen Studienplatz zu finden. Nur mit sehr guten Noten vom° Gymnasium bekommen sie einen Studienplatz. Bevor Amerikaner in Deutschland studieren können, müssen sie in Amerika schon an einer Universität oder einem College Studenten sein. Sie
10 müssen für die deutsche Universität auch eine Sprachprüfung° machen.

Wie viel Geld braucht man?

Die Universitäten in Deutschland sind staatlich. Steuern° finanzieren das Studium. Deshalb gibt es keine Studiengebühren, aber die Studenten brauchen Geld für Essen und Wohnen. Leider gibt es nur wenige Studentenheime und Studenten müssen oft Zimmer in der Stadt suchen, und die sind oft teuer. Viele Studenten brauchen deshalb Geld vom Staat. Dieses Geld heißt BAföG°. Nur so kann jeder studieren. Die Hälfte° des Geldes müssen die Studenten dem Staat später zurückzahlen. Manche Studenten bekommen aber kein BAföG (z.B. wenn ihre Eltern zu viel verdienen) und brauchen deshalb Jobs. An deutschen Universitäten gibt es aber nicht viele Studentenjobs und die Studenten müssen andere Jobs finden. Diese Studenten jobben oft auch im° Semester, und sie studieren dann länger als BAföG-Empfänger°, im Durchschnitt° vierzehn Semester. BAföG-Empfänger studieren dagegen° im Durchschnitt nur elf Semester. Zehn Prozent der ausländischen° Studenten bekommen Stipendien.

(marginal glosses) taxes

BAföG: *see p. 133* / half

im = in dem: *here* during the recipients / im Durchschnitt: on the average / on the other hand / foreign

Wann studiert man?

Es gibt zwei Semester im Jahr, das Wintersemester (Mitte Oktober oder Anfang° November bis Mitte oder Ende Februar) und das Sommersemester (Mitte April oder Anfang Mai bis Mitte oder Ende Juli). Die Semesterferien sind lang, aber sie sind für die meisten Studenten keine freie Zeit. Viele Studenten müssen in den Ferien jobben oder ein Praktikum° machen. Oft lesen sie in der Bibliothek, schreiben dort ihre Seminararbeiten oder bereiten sich° auf das nächste Semester vor, denn in den Semesterferien ist die Bibliothek nicht so überfüllt.

(marginal glosses) beginning of

Internship

themselves

Was ist anders?

Studenten studieren ein oder zwei Fächer. Ihre Kurse sind alle in diesen Fächern. Nehmen wir° zum Beispiel Klaus Brendel aus Aachen. Er studiert Physik und Informatik und möchte Ingenieur werden. Er muss keine Kurse in Englisch, Geschichte und Biologie machen, denn das hat er in der Schule gemacht°. In Deutschland führen° Professoren keine Anwesenheitslisten°, und nur wenige Kurse haben jedes Semester Prüfungen. Dafür° gibt es nach vier Semestern eine Zwischenprüfung° und dann das große Examen am Ende.

(marginal glosses) nehmen wir: let's take

hat gemacht: studied / keep attendance lists
in place of that / qualifying exam

Brauchbares

1. l. 14, **Abitur:** In Austria and Switzerland the **Matura** is the equivalent of the **Abitur.**
2. Note that in dependent clauses—here those beginning with **dass** (l. 6), **bevor** (l. 8), and **wenn** (l. 18)—the finite verb is at the end of the clause, e.g., **dass es schwer ist.** (See *Kapitel 5*, section 3.)
3. l. 21, **jobben:** Two-thirds of all students have part-time jobs.
4. l. 22, **vierzehn Semester:** Note that German students measure their progress at the university in semesters instead of in years.
5. l. 34, **Nehmen wir:** *let's take.* English imperatives beginning with *let's* can be expressed in German with the **wir**-form of the present tense. The pronoun **wir** follows the verb as in **gehen wir:** *let's go.*

[l. 22] **14 Semester:** The average age at which Germans finish the university is 29, making them the oldest students compared with those of other countries, e.g., France 27, U.S. 24, Japan 23.

Nach dem Lesen

1. Fragen zum Lesestück

1. Wie viele Studenten gibt es in Deutschland?
2. Wer kann in Deutschland studieren?
3. Warum haben viele Fächer den Numerus clausus?
4. Was müssen Amerikaner machen, bevor sie in Deutschland studieren dürfen?
5. Wie viel kostet[+] das Studium in Deutschland?
6. Warum müssen Studenten oft Zimmer in der Stadt suchen?
7. Was ist BAföG?
8. Was machen viele deutsche Studenten in den Ferien?
9. Was studiert Klaus Brendel? Welche Kurse macht er nicht?
10. Wann gibt es Prüfungen an deutschen Universitäten?

answers
remark
use

2. Wie antwortet° eine Studentin/ein Student aus Deutschland? Schreiben Sie eine Antwort auf die Aussage° von der Amerikanerin/dem Amerikaner. Benutzen° Sie Informationen aus dem Text.

1. AMERIKANERIN/AMERIKANER: Morgen haben wir schon wieder eine Prüfung in Mathe!

    DEUTSCHE/DEUTSCHER: _____

2. AMERIKANERIN/AMERIKANER: Die Studiengebühren sind wirklich zu hoch[+] hier.

    DEUTSCHE/DEUTSCHER: _____

3. AMERIKANERIN/AMERIKANER: Ich wohne sehr gern im Studentenheim.

    DEUTSCHE/DEUTSCHER: _____

4. AMERIKANERIN/AMERIKANER: Ich jobbe 10 Stunden die Woche.

    DEUTSCHE/DEUTSCHER: _____

5. AMERIKANERIN/AMERIKANER: Hoffentlich bin ich in vier Jahren mit dem Studium fertig[+].

    DEUTSCHE/DEUTSCHER: _____

fits / expression

3. Was ist das? Welche Definition passt° zu dem Ausdruck°?

1. BAföG
2. Numerus clausus
3. jobben
4. Studentenheim
5. Abitur

a. die Prüfung und das Diplom am Ende vom Gymnasium
b. Geld für Studenten vom Staat
c. Studentenwohnungen° an der Uni
d. Fächer mit zu wenig Studienplätzen
e. ein anderes Wort für „arbeiten"

student residences

Let's report. / useful

4. Erzählen wir.° Machen Sie eine Liste von nützlichen° Wörtern und sprechen Sie dann über ein Thema.

Studenten und Geld ■ zu viele Studenten ■ zu viele Prüfungen

Ausländische Studenten

www Go to the *Deutsch heute* website at
http://college.hmco.com.

An den deutschen Universitäten studieren auch ausländische Studenten. (Universität Heidelberg)

German universities accept many foreign students. In 2001, 10% of university students in Germany were foreigners. Only the United States and England host more foreign students. Even in the **Numerus clausus** disciplines, spaces are available. Recently, Germany has introduced undergraduate and graduate programs in which the language of instruction is English. These programs are attractive to international students and to German students who see their future in an international environment; they are offered in subjects ranging from computer science and environmental studies to German studies. Like a German student, a foreigner pays no tuition (**Studiengebühren**), but all students pay 52 euros a month for health insurance and may also be liable for matriculation fees. A foreign student is not generally permitted a work permit. To be admitted for study in Germany, an American must usually have had at least two years of college and must pass a language exam.

To study at a Swiss university, an American needs a bachelor's degree and a working knowledge of the language of instruction, which may be German, French, or Italian. The tuition ranges from 1200 to 8000 Swiss francs per year. To study in Austria, international students who do not come from the European Union must pay 726 euros each semester for tuition (**Studienbeitrag**). They must also demonstrate proficiency in German and meet general admission standards.

Diskussion

Discuss the advantages and disadvantages of studying abroad. If you chose to attend a German university, would you choose a program which is taught primarily in German or primarily in English? Why?

5. Zur Diskussion

1. Was finden Sie an den deutschen Universitäten gut?
2. Was finden Sie an Ihrer Universität gut?
3. Möchten Sie in Deutschland studieren? Warum (nicht)?

Studenten-Witze[1]

Wie spät ist es?

Treffen sich zwei Studenten.[2]

„Wie spät ist es denn?"

„Mittwoch!"

„Sommer- oder Wintersemester?"

Bücher und Geld

Zwei Studenten treffen sich.

„Was ist denn mit dir los, warum bist du so gereizt[3]?"

„Ach, ich hab' meinen Alten um Geld für wichtige Bücher gebeten[4]."

„Na und?"

„Er hat mir die Bücher geschickt[5]."

Kurz-Kommunikation mit den Eltern

Ein Student schreibt eine E-Mail an seine Eltern:
„Wo bleibt das Geld?"
Die kurze Antwort: „Hier!"

[1]*jokes*   [2]**Treffen...Studenten:** *Two students meet.*

[3]*upset*   [4]*asked*   [5]*sent*

---

28 Semester? Was studierst Du denn?

Handy-Tarife.[1]

Das geht nun wirklich schneller:
D1, D2, E-Plus und Quam aus einer Hand, an einem Ort
mit objektiver Beratung.

debitel®
KOMMUNIKATION IST ALLES

[1]*fees*

Schule, Hochschule, Klasse, Student

Many words used in English to talk about university studies are not equivalent to the German words which appear to be cognates. In the German-speaking countries a greater distinction is made in words referring to education before college or university and post-secondary education.

- *school:* In German (**die**) **Schule** refers to an elementary or secondary school. When talking about post-secondary education German speakers use (**die**) **Universität** or (**die**) **Hochschule.** The equivalent of *What school do you go to?* is **An welcher Uni studierst du?**

- *high school:* A German equivalent of the U.S. or Canadian *high school* is (**die**) **Oberschule,** (**die**) **höhere Schule,** or (**das**) **Gymnasium.** A **Hochschule** is a post-secondary school such as a university.

- *student:* In German, **Studentin/Student** refers to someone at a post-secondary institution (i.e., at a **Universität** or **Hochschule**). The word (**die**) **Schülerin/(der) Schüler** is used for young people in elementary and secondary schools.

- *class:* The English word *class* refers to an instructional period or a group of students. The German word (**die**) **Klasse** refers only to a group of students (e.g., **meine Klasse** = *my class, my classmates*) or a specific grade (e.g., **die zweite Klasse** = *the second grade*). In a **Schule** the word for *class* meaning *instructional period* is **Stunde** (e.g., **die Deutschstunde** = *the German class*). At the university level in German-speaking countries there are several types of classes—**Vorlesung, Übung,** and **Seminar** (see *Land und Leute: Hochschulen,* p. 131). A very general word for a class is **Kurs.** To ask the question *How many students are in your German class?* a German might say: **Wie viele Kursteilnehmer gibt es in Ihrem Deutschkurs?**

Schüler und Schülerinnen in der ersten Klasse. (München)

www Go to the *Deutsch heute* website at http://college.hmco.com.

Diskussion

Many of the German words related to education look like the English words, but are used differently. Discuss what problems this causes for you learning the German language. You may also want to think about this question: Can you imagine what problems a student learning English would have with English words?

Erweiterung des Wortschatzes

1. Stating one's profession or nationality

Carsten ist Student.	Carsten is a student.
Barbara wird Ingenieurin.	Barbara is going to be an engineer.
Barbara ist Kanadierin.	Barbara is (a) Canadian.
Anton ist Deutscher.	Anton is (a) German.
Herr Becker ist **nicht (kein)** Ingenieur.	Mr. Becker is not an engineer.
Cordula ist **nicht (keine)** Österreicherin; sie ist Deutsche.	Cordula is not (an) Austrian; she's (a) German.

Either **nicht** or **kein** may be used to negate a sentence about someone's profession, nationality, or membership in a group. Remember that no indefinite article (**ein**) is used in the positive statement (see *Kapitel 2*). For names of additional professions, refer to the Supplementary Word Sets in Appendix C.

1. Neue Freunde. Auf einem Flug von Toronto nach Frankfurt lernen sich drei junge Leute kennen. Erzählen Sie von ihrem Flug. Geben Sie die Sätze auf Deutsch wieder. (On a flight from Toronto to Frankfurt three young people get acquainted. Tell about their flight. Give the German equivalents of the sentences.)

1. Robert is a Canadian.
2. He is a student.
3. Annette is not a Canadian.
4. She is also not an American; she's a German.
5. She is going to be an engineer.
6. Her brother Christoph lives in Frankfurt; he's a Frankfurter.
7. He is a pharmacist.

Describing one's nationality and profession

2. Persönliche Informationen. Schreiben Sie eine kurze Autobiografie. Geben Sie an: Name, Nationalität, Adresse und Telefonnummer, Hauptfach, Nebenfach. Was wollen Sie werden? (Write a short autobiography. Give: name, nationality, address and telephone number, college major, minor. What do you want to be?)

Was ist richtig?
TIPP: Mehr als eine Antwort ist richtig.
a. Ein Hamburger arbeitet bei McDonald's.
b. Ein Hamburger ist etwas zu essen.
c. Ein Hamburger ist eine Frau aus Hamburg.
d. Ein Hamburger ist ein Mann aus Hamburg.

1. Ich bin Berliner. 2. Ich bin ein Berliner. Welcher Satz bedeutet (*means*):
a. ein Mann aus Berlin?
b. etwas zu essen?

WILLI CLAUSEN
67

KÄTHE CLAUSEN
63

HANS PFEIFFER
39

KERSTEN CLAUSEN
35

VOLKER CLAUSEN
43

RENATE CLAUSEN
40

ANGELIKA PFEIFFER
13

JÜRGEN PFEIFFER
10

CHRISTOPH CLAUSEN
7

KATRIN GUMPERT
15

Kersten Clausen:
Beginning in 1991, married German women could choose to keep their maiden names. Married Austrian women were finally given the choice in 1995.

2. Die Familie

die **Mutter,** ⁻⁻	+	der **Vater,** ⁻⁻	=	die **Eltern** (*pl.*)
(die **Mutti,**		(der **Vati,**		
die **Mama**)		der **Papa**)		
die **Tochter,** ⁻⁻		der **Sohn,** ⁻e		
die **Schwester, -n**	+	der **Bruder,** ⁻⁻	=	die **Geschwister** (*pl.*)
die **Tante, -n**		der **Onkel, -**		
die **Kusine, -n**		der **Vetter, -n**		
die **Nichte, -n**		der **Neffe, -n, -n**		
die **Großmutter,** ⁻⁻	+	der **Großvater,** ⁻⁻	=	die **Großeltern** (*pl.*)
(die **Oma, -s**)		(der **Opa, -s**)		

Stief-: die **Stiefmutter;** der **Stiefvater**

Refer to the Supplementary Word Sets in Appendix C for names of additional family members.

3. Der Stammbaum. *(Family tree.)* Lesen Sie über Familie Clausen (Stammbaum auf Seite 141). Beantworten Sie dann die Fragen. (Read about the Clausen family tree on page 141. Then answer the questions.)

Willi und Käthe Clausen haben eine Tochter, Kersten, und einen Sohn, Volker. Kersten und ihr Mann, Hans Pfeiffer, haben zwei Kinder, Angelika und Jürgen. Die Kinder haben eine Großmutter, Oma Clausen, und einen Großvater, Opa Clausen. Volker Clausen ist geschieden°. Renate ist seine zweite° Frau. Sie hat eine Tochter, Katrin Gumpert, von ihrem ersten° Mann. Volker ist also Katrins Stiefvater. Renate und Volker haben einen Sohn, Christoph. Angelika Pfeiffer ist seine Kusine, und Jürgen ist sein Vetter. Die Eltern von Angelika und Jürgen sind natürlich Christophs Tante Kersten und sein Onkel Hans.

divorced / second

first

1. Wie heißt Jürgen Pfeiffers Vetter?
2. Wer ist Angelika Pfeiffers Onkel?
3. Wie heißen die Großeltern von Angelika und Jürgen?

4. Wie heißt Volker Clausens Frau?
5. Wie heißt Volkers Stieftochter?
6. Wie heißt Katrins Halbbruder°?

half brother

4. Frage-Ecke. Ergänzen Sie die fehlenden Informationen. Fragen Sie Ihre Partnerin/Ihren Partner. Die Informationen für *S1* finden Sie unten; die Informationen für *S2* finden Sie im Anhang (Appendix B). (Supply the missing information. Ask your partner. *S1*'s information is below; the information for *S2* is in Appendix B.)

S1: Wie heißt die Mutter von Angelika?
S2: Sie heißt Kersten Clausen.
S1: Wie alt ist Angelikas Mutter?
S2: Sie ist 35 Jahre alt.

S1:

	Vater	Mutter	Tante	Onkel	Großvater	Großmutter
Angelika	Hans Pfeiffer, 39		Renate Clausen, 40		Willi Clausen, 67	Käthe Clausen, 63
Christoph		Renate Clausen, 40		Hans Pfeiffer, 39		
ich						
Partnerin/Partner						

ÄCHZ...

LUKAS! KOMM MAL HER, MEIN SOHN!

WIR WOLLTEN DOCH BEIDE FITTER WERDEN... ...ICH VERSUCHE, MEINE ZEHEN[1] ZU BERÜHREN[2]... MACHST DU MIT?

...VON MIR AUS[3] ...

ABER WAS SOLL DAS BRINGEN?[4]

[1]*toes* [2]*touch* [3]**von mir aus:** *as far as I'm concerned*

[4]**Aber...bringen?:** *But what's the point?*

Land und Leute

Das Schulsystem in Deutschland

At the age of six all children go to a **Grundschule** (primary school, grades 1–4). After that they attend either a **Hauptschule, Realschule,** or **Gymnasium,** depending on their ability and the job or career they hope to have. The first two years (grades 5–6) are an orientation period during which the parents and child determine whether the child is in a school suitable to her/his interests and abilities.

Young people preparing to work in the trades or industry (e.g., as a baker or car mechanic) may attend a **Hauptschule** (grades 5–9 or 5–10). After obtaining their certificate (**Hauptschulabschluss**), they enter an apprenticeship program, which includes 3–4 days per week of work training at a business and 8–12 hours per week of study at a vocational school (**Berufsschule**) until at least the age of 18. Approximately one-third of the young people follow this path.

			Universitäten und technische[4] Hochschulen
13			
12	Berufsausbildung[2] in Betrieb[3] und Berufsschule		
11			Gymnasium
10			
9	Hauptschule	Realschule	
8			
7			
6	Orientierungsstufe[1]	Orientierungsstufe	Orientierungsstufe
5			
4	Grundschule		
3			
2			
1			
	Kindergarten		

[1]orientation stage   [2]vocational training   [3]firm, business   [4]technical

Another third of young people, those wanting a job in business, industry, public service, or the health field (e.g., as a bank clerk or nurse) attend a **Realschule** (grades 5–10). The certificate (**Mittlere Reife**) from a **Realschule** is a prerequisite for mid-level positions and permits the students to attend specialized schools (**Berufsfachschule** or **Fachoberschule**). Students who leave the **Gymnasium** after grade 10 also obtain a **Mittlere Reife.**

Young people planning to go to a university or a **Fachhochschule** (see page 131) attend all grades of a **Gymnasium** (grades 5–12/13, depending on the state). The certificate of general higher education entrance qualification (**Zeugnis der allgemeinen Hochschulreife**), which is the diploma from a **Gymnasium,** is granted on the basis of grades in courses and the passing of a comprehensive exam (**Abitur**).

In some areas, another type of school, the **Gesamtschule** (comprehensive school), offers secondary instruction for grades 5–10, and in some states the **Gesamtschule** extends to the thirteenth year.

Diskussion

www Go to the *Deutsch heute* website at http://college.hmco.com.

Imagine that you are in Germany and have been asked to make a presentation on the school system in your hometown. How would you compare your school system to the German system? Mention advantages and disadvantages.

Work experience may also qualify a person for study at the university.

Vokabeln 2

Substantive

das **Abitur** diploma from college-track high school [**Gymnasium**]

der **Ausländer, -/**die **Ausländerin, -nen** foreigner

das **Beispiel, -e** example; **zum Beispiel** (*abbrev.* **z.B.**) for example (*abbrev.* e.g.)

die **Eltern** (*pl.*) parents

das **Ende** end, conclusion; **am Ende** at (in) the end

das **Examen, -** comprehensive exam, finals; **Examen machen** to graduate from the university

das **Fach, ¨er** (academic) subject

die **Familie, -n** family

die **Ferien** (*pl.*) vacation; **in den Ferien** on vacation; die **Semesterferien** semester break

der **Film, -e** film

das **Gymnasium,** *pl.* **Gymnasien** college-track high school

die **Information, -en** information

der **Ingenieur, -e/**die **Ingenieurin, -nen** engineer

das **Internet** Internet; **im Internet surfen** to surf the Internet

der **Job, -s** job

die **Klasse, -n** class

der **Kurs, -e** course

die **Note, -n** grade; note

die **Party, -s** party

der **Platz, ¨e** place; seat; space

das **Prozent, -e** percent

die **Prüfung, -en** test, examination

die **Schule, -n** school

das **Semester, -** semester

der **Staat, -en** state, country

das **Stipendium,** *pl.* **Stipendien** scholarship

das **Studentenheim, -e** dormitory

das **Studium, Studien** study; studies

die **Zeit, -en** time

For additional family members, see p. 141.

Verben

erklären to explain

erzählen to tell, narrate, report

jobben (*colloq.*) to have a temporary job (e.g., a summer job)

kosten to cost

surfen to surf

verdienen to earn

werden (wird) to become

wissen (weiß) to know (a fact)

zahlen to pay

zurück·zahlen to pay back

Andere Wörter

amerikanisch American

an at; to

daher therefore, for that reason

denn (*conj.*) because, for

deshalb therefore, for that reason

dies- (-er, -es, -e) this, these

fertig finished; ready

frei free

hoch high

jed- (-er, -es, -e) each, every; **jeder** everyone

jung young

kanadisch Canadian

lang long; **länger** longer

manch- (-er, -es, -e) many a (*sg.*); some (*pl.*)

meist- most; **die meisten (Leute)** most of (the people)

privat private

schwer hard, difficult; heavy

staatlich public, government owned

wenig little; **ein wenig** a little; **wenige** few

wenn (*conj.*) if; when, whenever

zurück back, in return

zu viel too much

Was spielen die Männer? Wo spielen sie? Wer gewinnt wohl? Wann spielen sie? Wie ist das Wetter?

Am ersten Schultag bekommen die Kinder Schultüten mit Bonbons, Schokolade, Kulls usw. Wer geht mit dem Mädchen am ersten Tag mit? Wie alt ist das Mädchen? Was meinen Sie?

Grammatik und Übungen

1 Present tense° of *werden*

das Präsens

werden: to become	
ich werde	wir werden
du **wirst**	ihr werdet
er/es/sie **wird**	sie werden
Sie werden	
du-*imperative:* werde	

Werden is irregular in the **du-** and **er/es/sie**-forms in the present tense.

1. Wann wirst du ... ? *(When will you be . . . ?)* Hanna und Martin sprechen miteinander. Benutzen Sie die richtige Form von **werden.** (Hanna and Martin are talking to each other. Use the correct form of **werden.**)

HANNA: Sag mal, Martin, wann _____ du denn 21 Jahre alt?

MARTIN: Ich _____ im Mai 21.

HANNA: Und Kevin? Wann _____ er 21?

MARTIN: Er ist schon 21, er _____ im Mai 22.

HANNA: Was _____ Kevin nach dem Studium°?

nach ... Studium: after graduation

MARTIN: Kevin _____ Architekt, denke ich.

HANNA: Hmmm. Du auch. Ihr _____ also beide Architekten?

MARTIN: Ja, wir arbeiten dann beide in Deutschland und den USA.

② Verbs with stem-vowel change *e > ie*

sehen: to see	
ich sehe	wir sehen
du **siehst**	ihr seht
er/es/sie **sieht**	sie sehen
Sie sehen	
du-*imperative:* **sieh**	

lesen: to read	
ich lese	wir lesen
du **liest**	ihr lest
er/es/sie **liest**	sie lesen
Sie lesen	
du-*imperative:* **lies**	

Several verbs with the stem-vowel **e** change the **e** to **ie** in the **du-** and **er/es/sie-** forms of the present tense and in the **du**-imperative. Since the stem of **lesen** ends in a sibilant, the **du**-form ending contracts from **-st** to **-t** (see *Kapitel 1, Grammatik und Übungen,* section 7).

Talking about personal interests

2. Lesen und sehen – eine E-Mail-Umfrage. Gisela arbeitet in Sommer für amazon.de. Sie fragt, was für Videofilme die Leute gern sehen und welche Bücher sie lesen. Dann schreibt sie die Antworten. (Reading and watching—an e-mail questionnaire. Gisela is working for amazon.de during the summer. She asks what kind of videos people like to watch and what kind of books they read. Then she writes down the answers.)

➡ Erich Reimer / ernste Filme *Erich Reimer, was für Filme sehen Sie gern?*
 Erich Reimer sieht gern ernste Filme.

1. Ingrid / lustige Filme
2. Gabi und Jürgen / amerikanische Filme
3. Herr Meier / Science-Fiction-Filme
4. Du und Alex / Bücher über Musik
5. Detlev / Horrorgeschichten
6. Frau Ohnsorg und Professor Lange / Biografien

3. Filme und Bücher. Interviewen Sie drei Studentinnen/Studenten in Ihrem Deutschkurs. Was für Filme sehen sie gern? Was für Bücher lesen sie gern? Berichten Sie darüber. Benutzen Sie auch Wörter aus dem Anhang: Supplementary Word Sets, „Film" und „Literature". (Interview three students in your German class. What kind of films do they like to see? What kind of books do they like to read? Report on your findings. Also use words from Appendix C.)

 S1: Was für Filme siehst du gern?
 S2: [Tom]: Ich sehe gern [alte Filme, Krimis, Horrorfilme,
  Dokumentarfilme, Science-Fiction-Filme].
 S1: Was für Bücher liest du gern?
 S3: [Linda]: Ich lese gern [Biografien, Liebesromane, Horrorgeschichten,
  historische Romane, Krimis, Science-Fiction, Bücher über
  Politik/Musik, moderne Literatur].
 S1: [Tom] sieht gern [alte Filme]. [Linda] liest gern [Biografien].

③ Present tense of *wissen*

wissen: to know		
ich **weiß**	wir wissen
du **weißt**	ihr wisst
er/es/sie **weiß**	sie wissen
Sie wissen	

Wissen is irregular in the singular forms of the present tense. Note that the **du-**
form ending contracts from **-st** to **-t.**

4. Die Universität Heidelberg. David ist Amerikaner und möchte etwas über
die Universität Heidelberg wissen. Er spricht mit Barbara und Karin. Karin
studiert da. Ergänzen Sie ihren Dialog mit den passenden Formen von **wissen.**
(David is an American and would like to know something about Heidelberg
University. He is speaking with Barbara and Karin. Karin studies there. Complete
their dialogue with the appropriate forms of **wissen.**)

DAVID: Du Barbara. Was _____ du über die Universität Heidelberg?

BARBARA: Nicht viel. Aber ich glaube, Karin _____ viel darüber.

KARIN: Na, alle Leute _____, dass° Heidelberg die älteste° Universität   that / oldest
    Deutschlands ist.

BARBARA: So? Das _____ wir alle? _____ du denn, wie alt?

KARIN: Natürlich. Im Jahre 1986 war sie 600 Jahre alt.

DAVID: Das ist ja wirklich alt.

④ *Wissen* and *kennen*

Kennst du Martin?	Do you *know* Martin?
Weißt du, wo er wohnt?	Do you *know* where he lives?
Nein, aber ich **weiß** seine Telefonnummer.	No, but I *know* his telephone number.
Sie **kennt** Professor Schmidt gut.	She *knows* Professor Schmidt well.

There are two German equivalents for the English *to know:* **wissen**
and **kennen. Wissen** means *to know something as a fact.* **Kennen**
means *to be acquainted with a person, place, or thing.*

    Kennen was used as a verb in Middle English and is still
used in Scottish. The noun *ken* means perception or
understanding: "That is beyond my ken."

„Wer viel weiß, will noch mehr wissen."

BROCK HAUS
DIE ENZYKLOPÄDIE

IN 24 BÄNDEN

Brockhaus. Die Enzyklopädie.
Das Wissen der Welt – neuester Stand.

Wer will noch mehr wissen?
Was ist Brockhaus?

5. Was weißt du? Wen oder was kennst du? Fragen Sie Ihre Partnerin/Ihren Partner. (What do you know? Whom or what are you acquainted with? Ask your partner.)

> *S1:* Kennst du das neue Buch von [Stephen King]?
> *S2:* Nein, das kenne ich nicht. Kennst du den neuen Film von [Steven Spielberg]?

Kennst du ...

... den neuen Film von ...
... das neue Buch von ...
... die Freundin/den Freund von ...
... die Mutter/den Vater von ...
... Professor ...
... die Musikgruppe/die Band ...
... die Stadt ...

Weißt du ...

... den Vornamen von Frau/Herrn ...
... wie alt ... ist
... die E-Mail-Adresse von ...
... die Telefonnummer von ...
... wann ... Geburtstag hat
... die Adresse von ...
... wie die Universitätspräsidentin/der Universitätspräsident heißt

6. Die Stadt Heidelberg. Jetzt möchte David etwas über die Stadt Heidelberg wissen. Ergänzen Sie den Dialog mit den passenden Formen von **wissen** oder **kennen**. (Now David would like to know something about the town of Heidelberg. Complete the dialogue with the appropriate forms of **wissen** or **kennen**.)

DAVID: _____ ihr Heidelberg gut?

BARBARA: Ja, wir _____ die Stadt ganz gut.

DAVID: Dann _____ du, wo die Bibliothek ist.

KARIN: Natürlich _____ wir das. Du, David, ich _____ ein Buch über Heidelberg.

DAVID: _____ du, wo man das Buch kaufen kann?

KARIN: Ja, in jeder Buchhandlung.

DAVID: _____ du den Autor?

KARIN: Ja, den _____ wir alle. Das ist unser Professor.

⑤ Der-words

Diese Klausur ist schwer.	*This* test is hard.
Jede Klausur ist schwer.	*Every* test is hard.
Welche Klausur hast du?	*Which* test do you have?
Manche Klausuren sind nicht schwer.	*Some* tests are not hard.
Solche Klausuren sind nicht interessant.	*Those kinds of* tests aren't interesting.

In the singular, **so ein** is usually used instead of **solch-**: So eine Uhr ist sehr **teuer.** *That kind of/such a watch/clock is very expensive.*

	Masculine	Neuter	Feminine	Plural
	der	*das*	*die*	*die*
Nominative	dieser	dieses	diese	diese
Accusative	diesen	dieses	diese	diese

The words **dieser, jeder, welcher?, mancher,** and **solcher** are called **der**-words because they follow the same pattern in the nominative and accusative cases as the definite articles. **Jeder** is used in the singular only. **Welcher?** is an interrogative adjective, used at the beginning of a question. **Solcher** and **mancher** are used almost exclusively in the plural.

Der Stuhl (**da**) ist neu.　　*That* chair is new.

The equivalent of *that (those)* is expressed by the definite article (**der, das, die**). **Da** is often added for clarity.

7. Wie findest du diese Stadt? Beate ist Österreicherin und ihr Freund Mark ist Kanadier. Beate zeigt Mark einige Bilder. Geben Sie die richtige Form von den Wörtern in Klammern. (Beate is an Austrian and her friend Mark a Canadian. Beate is showing Mark some pictures. Give the correct form of the words in parentheses.)

BEATE: Kennst du _____ Stadt? (dieser)

MARK: Nein. Ich kenne viele Städte in Österreich, aber _____ nicht. (dieser)

BEATE: _____ Städte kennst du schon? (welcher)

MARK: Salzburg, zum Beispiel.

BEATE: Siehst du _____ Haus? (dieser) Da wohne ich.

MARK: Sind im Fenster immer _____ Blumen? (solcher)

BEATE: Ja, schön, nicht?

MARK: Hat _____ Haus _____ Garten? (jeder, so ein)

BEATE: Nein, das ist für viele Leute zu viel Arbeit. Aber mein Vater arbeitet gern im Garten.

⑥ Modal auxiliaries°

das Modalverb

Ich **muss** jetzt arbeiten.　　I *have to* work now.
Erika **kann** es erklären.　　Erika *can* explain it.
Ich **darf** nichts sagen.　　I am not *allowed* to say anything.

Both English and German have a group of verbs called *modal auxiliaries*. Modal auxiliary verbs (**muss, kann, darf**) indicate an attitude about an action; they do not express the action itself. In German, the verb that expresses the action is in the infinitive form (**arbeiten, erklären, sagen**) and is in last position.

Modals are irregular in the present-tense singular. They have no endings in the **ich**- and **er/es/sie**-forms, and five of the six modals show stem-vowel change, e.g., **können** > **kann**.

können: can, to be able to, to know how to do	
ich **kann** es erklären	wir **können** es erklären
du **kannst** es erklären	ihr **könnt** es erklären
er/es/sie **kann** es erklären	sie **können** es erklären
Sie **können** es erklären	

8. Was können diese Leute? Was können diese Leute tun? Erzählen Sie. (What can these people do? Tell [about it].)

→ Mark schwimmt gut. *Mark kann gut schwimmen.*

1. Karla spielt gut Tennis.
2. Wir machen Spaghetti.
3. Ich erkläre die Geschichte.
4. Du tanzt gut.
5. Herr Professor, Sie schreiben schön.
6. Karin und Peter tanzen wunderbar.
7. Ihr schwimmt gut.

Inquiring about abilities

9. Was kannst du? Interviewen Sie einige Studentinnen/Studenten in Ihrem Deutschkurs. Was können sie machen oder nicht machen? (Interview several students in your German class. What can they do or not do?)

S1: Kannst du Gitarre spielen?
S2: Ja, ich kann Gitarre spielen./Nein, ich kann nicht Gitarre spielen.

1. gut schwimmen
2. Golf spielen
3. gut tanzen
4. gut Geschichten erzählen
5. Schach spielen
6. im Sommer viel Geld verdienen

wollen: to want, wish; to intend to	
ich **will** arbeiten	wir **wollen** arbeiten
du **willst** arbeiten	ihr **wollt** arbeiten
er/es/sie **will** arbeiten	sie **wollen** arbeiten
Sie **wollen** arbeiten	

10. Was wollen diese Leute? Was wollen diese Leute tun oder nicht tun? (What do these people intend to do or not do?)

→ Erich geht einkaufen. *Erich will einkaufen gehen.*

1. Beatrice macht Musik.
2. Du gehst heute Abend tanzen, nicht?
3. Erich trinkt Kaffee.
4. Ich bezahle das Essen.
5. Die Kinder essen Kuchen.
6. Ihr macht Mathe.
7. Frau Kaiser studiert Geschichte.

11. Willst du? Sie und Ihre Partnerin/Ihr Partner machen für heute Abend oder morgen Pläne. Was wollen Sie machen? Was sagt Ihre Partnerin/Ihr Partner? (You and your partner are making plans for this evening. What do you want to do? What does your partner say?)

Making plans

S1:			*S2:*	
Willst du	**morgen**	**ins Kino** gehen?	Ja,	**gern.**
	heute Abend	joggen		vielleicht.
	am Samstag	tanzen	Nein, ich kann nicht.	

Schüttelkasten

fernsehen · Musik hören · spazieren gehen · Deutsch machen · zusammen für die Klausur arbeiten · Inlineskaten gehen · einkaufen gehen · im Internet surfen

sollen: to be supposed to	
ich **soll** morgen gehen	wir **sollen** morgen gehen
du **sollst** morgen gehen	ihr **sollt** morgen gehen
er/es/sie **soll** morgen gehen	sie **sollen** morgen gehen
Sie **sollen** morgen gehen	

12. Wir planen eine Party. Sie und Ihre Freunde planen eine Party. Was soll jede Person mitbringen, kaufen oder machen? (You and your friends are planning a party. What should everyone bring, buy, or do?)

→ Gabi und Moritz: Musik mitbringen *Gabi und Moritz sollen Musik mitbringen.*

1. wir: Käse kaufen
2. du: Salat machen
3. ich: Brot kaufen
4. Corinna: Wein mitbringen
5. ihr: Bier kaufen

müssen: must, to have to	
ich **muss** jetzt arbeiten	wir **müssen** jetzt arbeiten
du **musst** jetzt arbeiten	ihr **müsst** jetzt arbeiten
er/es/sie **muss** jetzt arbeiten	sie **müssen** jetzt arbeiten
Sie **müssen** jetzt arbeiten	

Discussing duties and requirements

13. Was müssen diese Leute tun? Sagen Sie, was diese Leute tun müssen. Ergänzen Sie die Dialoge mit der richtigen Form von **müssen.** (Say what these people have to do. Complete the dialogues with the correct form of **müssen.**)

1. BEATRIX: Was _____ du morgen machen?

   LIANE: Ich _____ eine Klausur schreiben.

   BEATRIX: Dann _____ du jetzt lernen, nicht?

2. NADJA: _____ ihr heute Abend wieder in die Bibliothek?

   STEFFI UND NILS: Ja, wir _____ noch zwei Kapitel durcharbeiten.

3. MARKUS: Was _____ Karin, Carsten und Beate am Wochenende machen?

   ROBERT: Karin _____ ein Buch über Psychologie lesen. Und Carsten und

   Beate _____ Referate vorbereiten.

Deutsch	Engl.	Mathe	Physik	Chemie	Kunst
Datum/Note	Datum/Note	Datum/Note	Datum/Note	Datum/Note	Datum/Note

14. Was musst du machen? Was muss Ihre Partnerin/Ihr Partner heute, morgen oder am Wochenende machen? Fragen Sie sie/ihn. (What does your partner have to do today, tomorrow, or on the weekend? Ask her/him.)

S1:		*S2:*	
Was musst du	**heute** machen?	**Heute** muss ich	**am Computer**
	morgen	Morgen	**arbeiten.**
	am Wochenende	Am Wochenende	

Schüttelkasten

arbeiten   einen Artikel schreiben

ein Referat vorbereiten   in die Bibliothek gehen

viele E-Mails schreiben   ein Buch für Geschichte lesen   Deutsch machen

dürfen: may, to be permitted to	
ich **darf** es sagen	wir **dürfen** es sagen
du **darfst** es sagen	ihr **dürft** es sagen
er/es/sie **darf** es sagen	sie **dürfen** es sagen
Sie **dürfen** es sagen	

15. Viele Regeln. *(Lots of rules.)* Dirk ist in einem neuen Studentenheim. Es gibt viele Regeln. Sehen Sie die Bilder an und beschreiben Sie die Regeln. Benutzen Sie ein logisches Modalverb. (Dirk is in a new dormitory. There are lots of rules. Look at the pictures and describe the rules. Use a logical modal verb.)

➜   nicht rauchen°   smoke
    Hier darf man nicht rauchen.

von 11:30 bis 13:00 Uhr

von ... bis ... essen

von 22 bis 8 Uhr

von ... bis ... nicht schwimmen

Trinkwasser

Wasser trinken

16-20 Uhr

von ... bis ... lernen

heute Abend

... Musik hören/tanzen gehen

Ruhe

immer ruhig sein

⑦ *Mögen* and the *möchte*-forms

mögen: to like	
ich **mag** keine Tomaten	wir **mögen** Erik nicht
du **magst** keine Eier	ihr **mögt** Melanie nicht
er/es/sie **mag** kein Bier	sie **mögen** Schmidts nicht
Sie **mögen** keinen Kaffee	

Mögen Sie Frau Lenz?   Nein, ich **mag** sie nicht.

The modal **mögen** is often used to express a fondness or dislike for someone or something. With this meaning it usually does not take a dependent infinitive.

16. Was für Musik magst du? Sagen Sie, was für Musik Sie mögen. Fragen Sie dann Ihre Partnerin/Ihren Partner. (Tell what kind of music you like. Then ask your partner.)

> *S1:* Ich mag Hardrock. Was für Musik magst du?
> *S2:* Ich mag Reggae.

Schüttelkasten

| Techno | Rap | Rock | klassische Musik | Blues | Jazz | Country |

ich **möchte** gehen	wir **möchten** gehen
du **möchtest** gehen	ihr **möchtet** gehen
er/es/sie **möchte** gehen	sie **möchten** gehen
Sie **möchten** gehen	

Möchte is a different form of the modal **mögen.** The meaning of **mögen** is *to like;* the meaning of **möchte** is *would like (to).*

17. Ja, das möchten wir. Was möchten Sie und Ihre Freundinnen/Freunde später machen? Erzählen Sie. (What would you and your friends like to do later? Tell about it.)

> → Dirk: heute Abend ins Kino gehen   *Dirk möchte heute Abend ins Kino gehen.*

1. wir: heute Nachmittag einkaufen gehen
2. du: mehr arbeiten
3. ihr: bestimmt hier bleiben
4. Gabi: im Café essen
5. Lotte und Erika: Musik hören
6. ich: ein interessantes Buch lesen
7. Rolf: am Wochenende wandern

Inquiring about future plans

18. Was möchtet ihr machen? Fragen Sie drei Studentinnen/Studenten, was sie tun möchten. Berichten Sie dann den Kursteilnehmerinnen/Kursteilnehmern. (Ask three students what they would like to do. Then report your findings to members of your class.)

> *S1:* Was möchtest du | **am Wochenende** | machen?
> heute Abend
> im Sommer
> *S2:* Ich möchte [einkaufen gehen].
> *S1:* [Tim] möchte [einkaufen gehen].

Schüttelkasten

| fernsehen | einen Krimi lesen | tanzen gehen | joggen gehen |

im Internet surfen   wandern   inlineskaten gehen   Fitnesstraining machen

19. Hören Sie zu. Gisela und David diskutieren. Hören Sie zu und geben Sie an, ob die folgenden Sätze richtig oder falsch sind. (Gisela and David are talking. Listen and indicate whether the following sentences are true or false.) Sie hören ein neues Wort (you will hear a new word): **schade** (that's too bad).

1. Gisela und David wollen morgen Abend ins Kino gehen.
2. David mag Julia Roberts.
3. Gisela kann um 6 Uhr gehen.
4. David muss bis halb neun Französisch lernen.
5. Um 8 Uhr 30 sehen Gisela und David einen französischen Film im Kino Blauc-Brücke.
6. Alex will auch ins Kino gehen.
7. Alex kann nicht kommen, er muss arbeiten.

8 Omission of the dependent infinitive with modals

Ich **kann** das nicht.	= Ich **kann** das nicht **machen**.
Ich **muss** in die Bibliothek.	= Ich **muss** in die Bibliothek **gehen**.
Das **darfst** du nicht.	= Das **darfst** du nicht **tun**.

Modals may occur without a dependent infinitive if a verb of motion (e.g., **gehen**) or the idea of to do (**machen, tun**) is clearly understood from the context.

Ich **kann** Deutsch.   I can speak German. (I know German.)

Können is used to say that someone knows how to speak a language.

20. In die Bibliothek? Nein. Christin und Mark studieren an der Universität Hamburg. Christin ist Deutsche, Mark ist Amerikaner. Sie trinken im Café Klatsch Kaffee. Geben Sie ihr Gespräch auf Englisch wieder. (Christin and Mark go to the University of Hamburg. Christin is German and Mark American. They're drinking coffee in the Klatsch café. Give the English equivalent of their conversation in German.)

1. CHRISTIN: Willst du jetzt nach Hause?
2. MARK: Nein, ich muss noch in die Bibliothek.
3. CHRISTIN: Was willst du da?
4. MARK: Ich muss Shakespeare lesen. Musst du auch in die Uni?
5. CHRISTIN: Nein, was soll ich denn da? Heute ist Sonntag!
6. MARK: Sag mal, kannst du gut Englisch?
7. CHRISTIN: Ja, ich kann aber auch Französisch.
8. MARK: Darf hier jeder in die Bibliothek?
9. CHRISTIN: Ja, wer° will, der° darf.   whoever / (that person)

21. Wie sagt man das?

1. Can you work this afternoon?
   No, I have to go home.
2. May I pay (for) the coffee?
   No, you may not. [Add **das.**]
3. Dirk wants to go to the movies tonight.
   What would he like to see?
4. Barbara intends to study German.
   Good. She already knows German well.
5. It's supposed to rain tomorrow.
   Really? That can't be.

22. Frage-Ecke. Ergänzen Sie die fehlenden Informationen. Fragen Sie Ihre Partnerin/Ihren Partner. Die Informationen für *S1* finden Sie unten; die Informationen für *S2* finden Sie im Anhang B (Appendix B). (Supply the missing information. Ask your partner. *S1*'s information is below; the information for *S2* is in Appendix B.)

> *S1:* Was muss Martina machen?
> *S2:* Sie muss jobben.

S1:

	müssen	dürfen	wollen	sollen	können
Martina		Kaffee trinken	tanzen gehen	einen Job suchen	
Kai und Sabine	Mathe machen			Blumen mitbringen	
Dominik		keine Eier essen	viel Geld verdienen		
Stefans Schwester	in die Bibliothek		fernsehen		gut Tennis spielen
ich					
Partnerin/ Partner					

23. Eine ideale Welt! Wie sollen/können/müssen/dürfen diese Personen und Dinge (nicht) sein? Benutzen Sie logische Modalverben und Adjektive! Sagen Sie mindestens zwei Dinge! (How should/can/must/may these people and things [not] be? Use logical modals and adjectives. Say at least two things.)

> ➡ mein Auto
> *Mein Auto soll modern sein. Mein Auto darf nicht teuer sein.*

1. mein Freund/meine Freundin
2. mein Professor/meine Professorin
3. ich
4. meine Arbeit
5. der Präsident
6. meine Freizeit
7. meine Universität
8. mein Auto

Schüttelkasten

gut   lustig   progressiv

billig

faul   intelligent   modern   teuer

fleißig   interessant   nett   tolerant

⑨ Separable-prefix verbs°

das trennbare Verb

to get up   I get up early
to throw away   Don't throw away all those papers!

English has a large number of two-word verbs, such as *to get up, to throw away.*
These two-word verbs consist of a verb, such as *get,* and a particle, such as *up.*

einkaufen   Monika **kauft** morgens **ein.**
mitbringen   **Bringen** Sie bitte Blumen **mit!**

German has a large number of "separable-prefix verbs" that function like certain
English two-word verbs. Examples are **durcharbeiten, einkaufen, fernsehen,
mitbringen, vorbereiten,** and **zurückzahlen.** In present-tense statements and
questions, and in imperative forms, the separable prefix (**durch-, ein-, fern-,
mit-, vor-, zurück-**) is in the last position.

Monika möchte Blumen **mit**bringen.

In the infinitive form, the prefix is attached to the base form of the verb.

Basic verb	Erik **sieht** gern lustige Filme.
	Erik likes to see amusing films.
Separable-prefix verb	Erik **sieht** gern **fern.**
	Erik likes to watch TV.

The meaning of a separable-prefix verb, such as **fernsehen,** is often different
from the sum of the meanings of its parts: **sehen** *(see),* **fern** *(far off).*

Ute will nicht **fern´**sehen.   Elfi sieht nicht **fern´.**

In spoken German, the stress falls on the prefix of separable-prefix verbs. In
vocabulary lists in this textbook, separable prefixes are indicated by a raised dot
between the prefix and the verb: **durch·arbeiten, fern·sehen, ein·kaufen,
mit·bringen, vor·bereiten, zurück·zahlen.**

24. Michaels Tagesplan. Michael erzählt Uwe von seinen Plänen für heute.
(Michael is telling Uwe about his plans for today.)

→   heute Nachmittag einkaufen   *Ich kaufe heute Nachmittag ein.*

1. Großmutter Blumen mitbringen
2. meine Notizen durcharbeiten
3. mein Referat vorbereiten
4. Melanie meinen CD-Player ausleihen
5. heute Abend fernsehen

25. Hören Sie zu. Gisela und Alex sprechen miteinander. Hören Sie, was Gisela
heute alles macht, und beantworten Sie dann die Fragen. (Gisela and Alex are
speaking with each other. Hear what Gisela is doing today and then answer the

questions.) Sie hören einen neuen Ausdruck (you will hear a new expression): **Was ist los?** (*What's going on?*)

1. Wer hat heute Geburtstag?
2. Was für Notizen arbeitet Gisela durch?
3. Was muss Gisela vorbereiten?
4. Wer bringt Blumen mit?
5. Wer geht spazieren und isst bei „Luigi"?
6. Wann sieht Gisela fern?

 Leserunde

Hans Manz is a journalist and author of children's poems, tales, and novels. Manz was born in Switzerland in 1931 and taught school for 30 years there. Since 1987 he has been a journalist and author. For Manz, language is primary, and the reader and listener enjoy discovering meaning between the lines. In the poem "Ferien machen: eine Kunst," Manz lists modal auxiliaries and interrogatives to talk about vacations. Such a listing of words is a technique characteristic of concrete poetry, as is the everyday topic (see **Leserunde,** *page 16).*

Ferien machen: eine Kunst[1]

Nichts müssen,
nichts sollen.
Nur dürfen
und wollen.
Jeder Tag
ein unvorbereitetes Fest[2]
Sich einigen[3],
wer
wann
wo
was wie
mit wem[4]
tut oder lässt[5].

Hans Manz

[1]*art, skill*   [2]**unvorbereitetes Fest:** *unanticipated holiday*   [3]**Sich einigen:** *to come to an agreement*
[4]*whom*   [5]*not do*

Wiederholung

1. Rollenspiel. Sie wollen morgen snowboarden gehen und Sie fragen Ihre Partnerin/Ihren Partner, ob sie/er mitkommen möchte. Sie/Er antwortet negativ mit Bedauern. (You plan to go snowboarding tomorrow and you ask your partner whether she/he wants to come along. She/he answers negatively, expressing regret.)

Redemittel: Bedauern ausdrücken (*Expressing regret*)

Nein, es geht leider nicht. ■ Leider kann ich morgen nicht.
■ Nein, es tut mir Leid. ■ Nein, leider nicht.

---

1. Kommst du morgen mit zum Snowboarden?
2. Kannst du Tanja dein Snowboard ausleihen?
3. Weißt du, wer ein Snowboard hat?
4. Weißt du, was ein Snowboard etwa kostet?
5. Weißt du, wo es billige Snowboards gibt?
6. Fährst du am Wochenende zum Skilaufen°?　　　　　　skiing
7. Jobbst du im Winter wieder als Skilehrer° in Österreich?　　ski instructor

2. Andrea muss zu Hause bleiben. Andrea möchte ins Kino gehen, aber sie muss leider zu Hause bleiben. Sagen Sie warum. (Andrea would like to go to the movies but unfortunately she has to stay home. Tell why.)

1. Andrea / (möchte) / gehen / heute Abend / ins Kino
2. sie / müssen / lernen / aber / noch viel
3. sie / können / lesen / ihre Notizen / nicht mehr
4. sie / müssen / schreiben / morgen / eine Klausur
5. sie / müssen / vorbereiten / auch noch / ein Referat
6. sie / wollen / studieren / später / in Kanada

3. Mach das. Sagen Sie Thomas, was er heute Morgen alles machen muss. Benutzen Sie den **du**-Imperativ. (Tell Thomas all the things he has to do this morning. Use the **du**-imperative form.)

→ essen / Ei / zum Frühstück　*Iss ein Ei zum Frühstück.*

1. gehen / einkaufen / dann
2. kaufen / alles / bei Meiers
3. kommen / gleich° / nach Hause　　　　　　　　　　immediately
4. vorbereiten / dein Referat
5. durcharbeiten / deine Notizen

4. Wer arbeitet für wen? Sie und Ihre Freundinnen und Freunde arbeiten für Familienmitglieder. Wer arbeitet für wen? Benutzen Sie die passenden Possessivpronomen. (You and your friends work for members of your families. Who works for whom? Use the appropriate possessive adjectives.)

→ Annette / Großmutter　*Annette arbeitet für ihre Großmutter.*

1. Felix / Tante
2. ich / Vater
3. du / Mutter / ?
4. Jürgen / Onkel
5. Karin und Sonja / Schwester
6. wir / Eltern
7. ihr / Großvater / ?

5. Wie sagt man das? Übersetzen Sie das Gespräch zwischen Julia und Christine. (Translate the conversation between Julia and Christine.)

CHRISTINE: Julia, may I ask something?
JULIA: Yes, what would you like to know?
CHRISTINE: What are you reading?
JULIA: I'm reading a book. It's called *Hello, Austria.*
CHRISTINE: Do you have to work this evening?
JULIA: No, I don't think so.
CHRISTINE: Do you want to go to the movies?
JULIA: Can you lend me money?
CHRISTINE: Certainly. But I would like to pay for you.

6. Bildgeschichte. Erzählen Sie, was Daniel heute alles macht. Schreiben Sie einen oder zwei Sätze zu jedem Bild. (Tell everything Daniel is doing today. Write one or two sentences for each picture.)

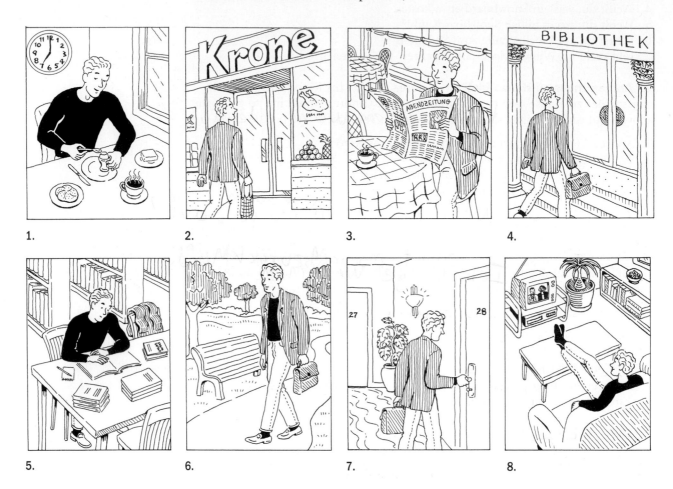

1. 2. 3. 4.

5. 6. 7. 8.

7. Rollenspiel

1. Ihre Freundin/Ihr Freund macht einen Kurs, der Sie interessiert. Fragen Sie sie/ihn, was man alles für den Kurs machen muss. (Your friend is taking a course that interests you. Ask her/him what you have to do for the course.)

2. Letzte Woche waren Sie nicht im Deutschkurs, denn Sie waren krank. Sie fragen drei andere Studentinnen/Studenten, ob sie Ihnen ihre Notizen leihen können. Alle sagen nein und erklären Ihnen, warum sie das nicht können. (Last week you weren't in German class because you were ill. You ask three other students whether they can lend you their notes. They all say no and explain why they can't.)

3. Sie und Ihre Mitbewohnerin/Ihr Mitbewohner unterhalten sich über den Abend – was können, sollen, wollen Sie machen. Am Ende gehen Sie Kaffee trinken und hören Musik. (You and your roommate are talking about the evening—what you can, should, or want to do. You end up going to have coffee and listening to music.)

Großeltern, Eltern und Enkelkinder (*grandchildren*).

8. Zum Schreiben

1. Choose one of the people in the photo above and make up a profile about
   that person. Give the person a name and describe her/him:

   a. age
   b. relationship to others in the photo
   c. nationality
   d. profession (see Appendix C: Supplementary Word Sets)
   e. what the person likes to do in her/his free time
   f. what the person likes to eat and drink

   You may find it helpful to review the *Vokabeln* sections in this and prior chapters and to write a few key words next to the points mentioned in a–f before
   you begin writing.

2. Describe in German a typical Friday at your college or university. Before you
   begin your description think about what you want to mention, e.g., your
   classes, where you eat, your shopping habits, and your plans for the evening.

Hinweise: After you have written your description(s), check over your work, paying particular attention to the following:

   • Check that each sentence has a subject and a verb and that the verb agrees
     with the subject.
   • Check the word order of each sentence.
   • Be sure you have used correct punctuation and capitalization.
   • Watch for the position of the prefix in separable-prefix verbs.
   • If you have used a modal auxiliary, be sure the dependent infinitive is at the
     end of the sentence.

Grammatik: Zusammenfassung

Present tense of *werden*

werden	
ich werde	wir werden
du **wirst**	ihr werdet
er/es/sie **wird**	sie werden
Sie werden	
du-*imperative:* werde	

Verbs with stem-vowel change *e > ie*

sehen	
ich sehe	wir sehen
du **siehst**	ihr seht
er/es/sie **sieht**	sie sehen
Sie sehen	
du-*imperative:* **sieh**	

lesen	
ich lese	wir lesen
du **liest**	ihr lest
er/es/sie **liest**	sie lesen
Sie lesen	
du-*imperative:* **lies**	

Present tense of *wissen*

wissen	
ich **weiß**	wir wissen
du **weißt**	ihr wisst
er/es/sie **weiß**	sie wissen
Sie wissen	

Der-words

	Masculine	Neuter	Feminine	Plural
	der	*das*	*die*	*die*
Nominative	dies**er** Mann	dies**es** Kind	dies**e** Frau	dies**e** Leute
Accusative	dies**en** Mann	dies**es** Kind	dies**e** Frau	dies**e** Leute

Der-words follow the same pattern in the nominative and accusative as the definite articles.

Meanings and uses of *der*-words

dies- (-er, -es, -e)	this; these *(pl.)*
jed- (-er, -es, -e)	each, every *(used in the singular only)*
manch- (-er, -es, -e)	many a, several, some *(used mainly in the plural)*
solch- (-er, -es, -e)	that kind of (those kinds of), such *(used mainly in the plural; in the singular* **so ein** *usually replaces* **solch-***)*
welch- (-er, -es, -e)	which *(interrogative adjective)*

Modal auxiliaries

Present tense

	dürfen	können	müssen	sollen	wollen	mögen	(möchte)
ich	darf	kann	muss	soll	will	mag	(möchte)
du	darfst	kannst	musst	sollst	willst	magst	(möchtest)
er/es/sie	darf	kann	muss	soll	will	mag	(möchte)
wir	dürfen	können	müssen	sollen	wollen	mögen	(möchten)
ihr	dürft	könnt	müsst	sollt	wollt	mögt	(möchtet)
sie	dürfen	können	müssen	sollen	wollen	mögen	(möchten)
Sie	dürfen	können	müssen	sollen	wollen	mögen	(möchten)

German modals are irregular in that they lack endings in the **ich-** and **er/es/sie-** forms, and most modals show stem-vowel changes.

> Stefanie muss jetzt **gehen.**   Stefanie has to leave now.

Modal auxiliaries in German are often used with dependent infinitives. The infinitive is in last position.

Meanings

Infinitive	Meaning	Examples	English equivalents
dürfen	permission	Ich **darf** arbeiten.	I'm allowed to work.
können	ability	Ich **kann** arbeiten.	I can (am able to) work.
mögen	liking	Ich **mag** es nicht.	I don't like it.
müssen	compulsion	Ich **muss** arbeiten.	I must (have to) work.
sollen	obligation	Ich **soll** arbeiten.	I'm supposed to work.
wollen	wishing, wanting, intention	Ich **will** arbeiten.	I want (intend) to work.

Ich **mag** Paul nicht.	I don't like Paul.
Mögen Sie Tee?	Do you like tea?
Möchten Sie Tee oder Kaffee?	Would you like tea or coffee?

Möchte is a different form of the modal **mögen.** The meaning of **mögen** is *to like;* the meaning of **möchte** is *would like (to).*

Separable-prefix verbs

mitbringen	**Bring** Blumen **mit!**	Bring flowers.
fernsehen	**Siehst** du jetzt **fern?**	Are you going to watch TV now?

Many German verbs begin with prefixes such as **mit** or **fern.** Some prefixes are "separable," that is, they are separated from the base form of the verb in the imperative (e.g., **bring ... mit**) and in the present tense (e.g., **siehst ... fern**). The prefix generally comes at the end of the sentence. Most prefixes are either prepositions (e.g., **mit**) or adverbs (e.g., **fern**).

The separable-prefix verbs you have had are **durcharbeiten, einkaufen, fernsehen, mitbringen, vorbereiten,** and **zurückzahlen.**

Warum **kauft** Stefan heute **ein?**	Warum will Stefan heute **einkaufen?**
Bringt er Blumen **mit?**	Kann er Blumen **mitbringen?**

The separable prefix is attached to the base form of the verb (e.g., **einkaufen, mitbringen**) when the verb is used as an infinitive.

Servus in Österreich

Alte und neue Architektur in Wien –
der Stephansdom und das Haas Haus.

LERNZIELE

Sprechintentionen

Discussing transportation
Discussing travel plans
Making plans for the weekend
Showing connections and
   relationships
Reporting on actions
Giving reasons
Discussing ideas for birthday
   presents
Making plans for a vacation
Sharing enthusiastic reactions

Lesestück

Österreich: Ein Porträt

Land und Leute

Youth hostels
Cafés
Importance of public transportation
Vienna, a cultural city
The House of Habsburg
Austrian neutrality

Vokabeln

Wo? and wohin?
Means of transportation

Grammatik

Verbs with stem-vowel change *a* > *ä*
Independent clauses and
   coordinating conjunctions
Dependent clauses and
   subordinating conjunctions
Dative case
Indirect object

Bausteine für Gespräche

Fährst du morgen mit dem Auto zur Uni?

UWE: Fährst du morgen mit dem Auto zur Uni?

CLAUDIA: Ja, warum? Willst du mitfahren?

UWE: Geht das? Ich hab' so viele Bücher für die Bibliothek. Kannst du mich vielleicht abholen?

CLAUDIA: Klar, kein Problem. Ich komme um halb neun bei dir vorbei. Ist das okay?

UWE: Ja, halb neun ist gut. Ich warte dann schon unten.

Fragen

1. Wer fährt mit dem Auto zur Uni?
2. Warum möchte Uwe mitfahren?
3. Wann holt Claudia Uwe ab?
4. Ist halb neun zu früh+?
5. Wo wartet Uwe?

In den Ferien

MICHAEL: Was machst du in den Ferien, Melanie?

MELANIE: Ich fahre nach Österreich.

MICHAEL: Fährst du allein?

MELANIE: Nein, ich fahre mit meiner Freundin Sibylle. Die kennt Österreich ziemlich gut.

MICHAEL: Fahrt ihr mit dem Auto?

MELANIE: Nein, mit der Bahn. Wir bleiben drei Tage in Wien und dann gehen wir wandern.

MICHAEL: Und wo übernachtet ihr?

MELANIE: In Wien schlafen wir bei Freunden. Und sonst zelten wir.

Brauchbares

The chapter title, **Servus in Österreich,** is equivalent to *Hello in Austria.* **Servus** is a common greeting in Austria among young people and good friends, that is, those with whom one would use **du.** Austrians find the use of this greeting with people one doesn't know very well, especially by non-Austrians, close to insulting.

Fragen

1. Wohin+ fährt Melanie in den Ferien?
2. Warum ist es gut, dass Melanies Freundin mitfährt?
3. Wie kommen Melanie und ihre Freundin nach Österreich?
4. Wo schlafen sie in Wien?
5. Wo schlafen sie, wenn sie nicht in Wien sind?

(*See photo, left:*) The world-famous Viennese architect Friedensreich Hundertwasser (1928–2000) was known for his unusually shaped buildings.

Germans love to travel to foreign countries. A very popular choice is Austria. They also frequently visit Switzerland, Italy, Spain, Portugal, and France.

For American travelers Vienna is a favorite destination outside the U.S.A.

Land und Leute

Generally anyone with a valid **Jugendherbergsausweis** can stay at a **Jugendherberge**.
If there is a lack of space, people under 25 are accepted first.

Jugendherbergen

In German-speaking countries young people can stay inexpensively at a youth hostel (**Jugendherberge**). Germany alone has over 780 **Jugendherbergen;** Austria and Switzerland have over 120 each. Originally established in the early twentieth century, **Jugendherbergen** were located no more than a day's hike apart. They are found not only near vacation spots and national parks, but also in cities and towns. The appearance of **Jugendherbergen** varies greatly. Some are found in modern buildings while others are in small country houses or even in old fortresses. All serve a simple, cafeteria-style breakfast and provide bedding, if needed. Many have curfews and some even require their guests to help with various chores.

Traveling to other European countries is very popular among German students, particularly since there are special railway fares for young people through the age of 26 (**BahnCard Junior**). (North Americans in that age group can also obtain reduced fares.)

Jugendherberge in Salzburg.

www Go to the *Deutsch heute* website at http://college.hmco.com.

Diskussion

Plan a trip through a German-speaking country in which you stay at **Jugendherbergen.**

Discussing transportation

Jugendherbergen: For information about obtaining an international youth hostel card and about youth hostels throughout the world, write to Youth Hosteling International: American Youth Hostels, Inc., 733 15th St. NW, Suite 840, Washington, DC 20005. Tel. (202) 783-6161, Fax (202) 783-6171.

1. Kann ich mitfahren? Ihr Auto ist kaputt. Vielleicht können Sie morgen mit einer Studentin/einem Studenten aus Ihrem Deutschkurs mitfahren. Fragen Sie sie/ihn.

S1:		*S2:*
Fährst du mit dem Auto zur	Uni?	Ja, willst du mitfahren?
	Arbeit?	Nein, **mein Auto ist kaputt**[+].
		ich nehme den Bus[+] / die U-Bahn[+].
		ich gehe immer zu Fuß[+].
		ich laufe[+].
		ich fahre mit dem Rad[+].

2. Um wie viel Uhr? Fragen Sie Ihre Partnerin/Ihren Partner, wann sie/er zur Uni, zur Arbeit und wieder nach Hause geht. Machen Sie Notizen.

S1: Wann gehst [fährst, kommst] du zur Uni [zur Arbeit, nach Hause]?
S2: Ich gehe [um acht] zur Uni.

3. Was machst du in den Ferien? Ihre Partnerin/Ihr Partner möchte
wissen, was Sie in den Sommerferien machen. Sagen Sie es ihr/ihm.

Discussing travel plans

S2:	*S1:*	
Hast du schon Pläne⁺ für die Ferien?	Ja, ich fahre/fliege⁺ nach Österreich.	
	ich möchte	**wandern.**
		zelten.
		viel schwimmen.
		Wasserski fahren⁺.
		schlafen⁺.
		snowboarden⁺.
		Ski laufen⁺.

Nein, ich habe keine.
Ich muss arbeiten.
Nein, die Ferien sind zu kurz⁺.

4. Rollenspiel. Erzählen Sie Ihrer Freundin/Ihrem Freund von Ihren
Plänen für morgen. Fragen Sie sie/ihn dann, was für Pläne sie/er hat.

Erweiterung des Wortschatzes

1. Wo? and *wohin?*

Wo ist Dieter?
Where is Dieter?

Wohin geht Erika?
Where is Erika going?

English *where* has two meanings: *in what place* and *to what place*. German has
two words for *where* that correspond to these two meanings: **wo** (*in what place,*
i.e., position) and **wohin** (*to what place,* i.e., direction).

1. Wie bitte? You don't understand what Nicole is saying. Ask her to repeat her
statements.

➡ Cornelia fährt zur Uni.   *Wohin fährt Cornelia?*
➡ Erik arbeitet im Supermarkt.   *Wo arbeitet Erik?*

1. Dieter fährt in die Schweiz.
2. Tanja arbeitet beim Bäcker.
3. Bärbel fährt nach Österreich.
4. Schmidts wandern in Österreich.
5. Fischers kaufen immer im Supermarkt ein.
6. Mark geht nach Hause.

Land und Leute

Das Kaffeehaus

www Go to the *Deutsch heute* website at http://college.hmco.com.

The **Kaffeehaus** was first introduced to the German-speaking areas in the seventeenth century. The Viennese **Kaffeehäuser** in the late nineteenth and early twentieth centuries were especially famous as gathering places for artists, writers, and even revolutionaries like Leon Trotsky. Today, **Cafés** are still popular meeting places throughout the German-speaking countries and often provide newspapers and magazines for their customers. People from all walks of life, business people, students and artists, enjoy taking a break for coffee and perhaps a piece of cake. In addition to **Kaffee** and a wide variety of **Kuchen** and **Torten,** many **Cafés** offer a small selection of meals (hot and cold), ice cream treats, and beverages.

A cup of coffee costs about 2 to 3 euros in Austria or Germany. A piece of cake to accompany the coffee will cost an additional 2 to 3 euros. In Switzerland a cup of coffee costs about 4 Swiss francs. There are no free refills in German-speaking countries. In most Viennese **Kaffeehäuser** coffee is served with a small glass of water on a small wooden or silver tray. A spoon is placed upside down across the top of the water glass. Coffee with **Schlagobers** *(whipped cream)* is a favorite in Vienna.

Cafés are usually not open evenings, but they are open six or seven days per week. The day on which a **Café** or restaurant is closed is called its **Ruhetag.** Most **Cafés** have a sign posted in a prominent place indicating their **Ruhetag.**

In vielen Wiener Kaffeehäusern kann man auch draußen sitzen.

The **Kaffeehaus** is the central spot for conversation, philosophizing, reading, and playing cards, billiards, and chess.

Diskussion

Historical research: Coffee was introduced to Europe by the Turks in the seventeenth century. Find out something about the relationship between the Ottoman Empire and Austria or how coffee came to Europe.

Leserunde

*Jürgen Becker was born in Cologne in 1932 and has lived there most of his life. Becker is known for his work in experimental literature and has published poetry, radio plays (**Hörspiele**), prose works, and in 1999 his first novel. The poem "Wo – vielleicht dort" is taken from his first collection of poetry, Felder (1964), which immediately drew a great deal of attention. The poem consists of common, everyday questions with common, everyday answers (see **Leserunde,** p. 16.) How much communication is there in these typical interchanges? What does this say about the way people interact?*

Wo – vielleicht dort

```
     wo
     vielleicht dort
     wohin
     mal sehen
 5   warum
     nur so
     was dann
     dann vielleicht da
     wie lange
10   mal sehen
     mit wem
     nicht sicher
     wie
     nicht sicher
15   wer
     mal sehen
     was noch
     sonst nichts
```

Jürgen Becker

2. Wie fährt man? Man fährt...

mit dem Fahrrad/Rad

mit dem Auto/mit dem Wagen

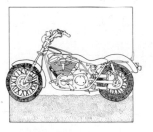

mit dem Motorrad

mit dem Bus

mit der Straßenbahn

mit der U-Bahn

mit der Bahn/mit dem Zug

mit dem Schiff

Das Flugzeug. (Man fliegt.)

2. Wie fahren Sie? Answer the following questions. For additional transportation terms, refer to the Supplementary Word Sets in Appendix C.

1. Haben Sie ein Fahrrad? Einen Wagen? Ein Motorrad?
2. Ist es/er neu oder alt?
3. Wie fahren Sie zur Uni? Mit dem Bus? Mit dem Auto? Mit dem Rad? Mit der
   U-Bahn?
4. Fliegen Sie gern? Viel?

Kulturstadt Wien

Go to the *Deutsch heute*
website at
http://college.hmco.com.

Die Wiener Oper ist in der ganzen Welt berühmt.

Austria has a very rich and diverse cultural tradition. The university of Vienna
(**Wien**), founded in 1365, is the oldest university in the present German-speaking
world. In the late eighteenth and early nineteenth cen-
turies, Vienna was the center of a musical culture associated with such names as Haydn, Mozart,
Beethoven, and Schubert. In the second half of the
nineteenth century the **Operette** reached its prime
with composers like Johann Strauss the Younger and
Franz Lehár. At the end of the nineteenth century
Vienna was a major intellectual and artistic center of
Europe. Two important names of that time are Sigmund Freud, who established psychoanalysis, and
Gustav Mahler, who continued the city's great musical
tradition. Today, Vienna continues to attract well-
known Austrian artists, performers, and writers,
as well as creative people from Eastern European
countries.

Diskussion

A 2002 survey by Mercer Human Resource Consulting
comparing the quality of life in 215 world cities ranked
Vienna third. Zurich ranked first, Vancouver ranked
second, Frankfurt fourth and Munich tenth. The ranking
is based on 39 criteria, including political, social,
economic, and environmental conditions, as well as
public safety, transportation, education, and health.

1. Choose a famous Austrian. In a few sentences describe the life and achievements of
   the person to your classmates without men-
   tioning the person's name. See if your classmates can guess the identity of the person.
2. Organize your own Austrian Music Festival.
   Bring a tape or CD of music by an Austrian
   composer or a composer who worked in
   Vienna.

Vokabeln 1

Substantive

das **Auto, -s** automobile, car
die **Bahn, -en** train; railroad
der **Bus, -se** bus
das **Fahrrad, ̈er** bicycle
das **Flugzeug, -e** airplane
der **Fuß, ̈e** foot
das **Motorrad, ̈er** motorcycle
der **Plan, ̈e** plan
das **Problem, -e** problem
das **Rad, ̈er** (*short for* **Fahrrad**) bike, bicycle

das **Schiff, -e** ship
der **Ski, -er** (**Ski** *is pronounced* **Schi**) ski
das **Snowboard, -s** snowboard
die **Straßenbahn, -en** streetcar
die **U-Bahn, -en** subway
der **Wagen, -** car
der **Wasserski, -er** water ski
der **Zug, ̈e** train

Verben

ab·holen to pick up
fahren (fährt) to drive, to travel; **mit (dem Auto) fahren** to go by (car)
fliegen to fly
laufen (läuft) to run; to go on foot; to walk
mit·fahren (fährt mit) to drive (go) along
Rad fahren (fährt Rad) to ride a bike; **ich fahre Rad** I ride a bike

schlafen (schläft) to sleep
Ski laufen (läuft Ski) to ski
snowboarden to snowboard
übernachten to spend the night/to stay (*in a hotel or with friends*)
vorbei·kommen to come by
warten (auf + *acc.*) to wait (for)
Wasserski fahren (fährt Wasserski) to water ski
zelten to camp in a tent

Andere Wörter

allein alone
dir (*dat.*) (to *or* for) you
früh early
kaputt broken; exhausted (*slang*)

kurz short, brief
unten downstairs; below
wem (*dat.* of **wer**) (to *or* for) whom
wohin where (to)

Besondere Ausdrücke

bei dir at your place
bei mir vorbeikommen to come by my place
Geht das? Is that OK?

mit (dem Auto) by (car)
zu Fuß on foot; **Ich gehe immer zu Fuß.** I always walk.

Land und Leute

Öffentliche Verkehrsmittel°

www Go to the *Deutsch heute* website at http://college.hmco.com.

public transportation

Public transportation is efficient and much utilized by the people in German-speaking countries. Buses, streetcars, subways, and trains are owned by either the federal or local government. While the popularity of the car continues to grow, governments subsidize public transportation because public transportation is better for the environment (**umweltfreundlich**) and ensures that everyone has access to transportation. Reduced rates are available for senior citizens (**Seniorenkarten**) and for students (**Schüler-/ Studentenkarten**) at all levels. In towns, villages, and suburbs there is convenient bus and sometimes streetcar (**Straßenbahn**) service. Major cities have a subway (**Untergrundbahn** or **U-Bahn**) and/or a modern commuter rail system (**Schnellbahn/Stadtbahn** or **S-Bahn**). The German, Austrian, and Swiss post offices provide extensive bus service between towns. If needed, even ferries are included in the public transportation network, such as the ferry on the Alster (**Alsterfähre**) in Hamburg.

Die Wiener Straßenbahn ist eine praktische Alternative zum Auto.

Trains are still a major part of the transportation system in German-speaking countries for both long and short distance travel. Larger cities have more than one train station (**Bahnhof**), but the main train station (**Hauptbahnhof**) is usually a prominent building located in the center of town. In addition to transportation facilities, larger train stations may also have a variety of restaurants and shops to serve the traveling public. To commute, people often use short-distance trains (**Nahverkehrszüge**). Fast, comfortable **Intercityexpress** (**ICE**) trains run hourly between major cities. This system is being supplemented with the **Interregiozüge,** which depart every two hours. The slightly slower "through" trains (**D-Züge**) also make long-distance runs, but stop more frequently than the **ICE** trains. A network of trains known as the **Eurocity** connects the major cities throughout Europe. Germany plans to have a magnetic elevated train (**Magnetbahn**), the **Metrorapid**, in operation for the world soccer championship (**Weltmeisterschaft**) in 2006. One stretch will run from Munich's **Hauptbahnhof** to the international airport (**Flughafen**), and the other will connect the cities Dortmund and Düsseldorf.

Diskussion

The **Intercityexpress (ICE)** is a high-speed train that averages 250 km/h (156 mph) and reaches a top speed of 280 km/h (175 mph). The trains feature telephones, equipped offices, and videos. Half as fast as a plane but twice as comfortable, the train is called an "aircraft on wheels."

Stores in train stations in Germany are allowed to be open weekends and late hours for travelers. Sometimes people who are not traveling use these shops as a way of circumventing the "shop closing law (**Ladenschlussgesetz**)."

Discuss your experience with public transportation. Consider these questions: Does your community have an extensive public transportation system? To what extent do you think that providing transportation is a responsibility of the government?

Österreich: Ein Porträt

Vorbereitung auf das Lesen

In diesem Text lernen Sie einiges° über Österreich.

some things

■ Vor dem Lesen

Sehen Sie sich die Landkarte° von Österreich am Anfang° des Buches an° und lesen Sie die folgenden° Informationen. Dann beantworten Sie die Fragen.

map / beginning / **Sehen Sie sich an:** look at / following

- **Größe°:** 83.855 qkm°
  etwa so groß wie Maine (86.027 qkm)
  etwas größer° als Neubraunschweig° (72.000 qkm)

size / qkm = **Quadratkilometer:** square kilometers (32,375 sq. miles)
larger / New Brunswick, Canada / low plain

- **Topografie:** Im Osten Tiefebene°, im Westen und in der Mitte hohe⁺ Berge⁺.
- **Bevölkerung°:** 8 Millionen Einwohner

population

- **Regierungsform°:** Bundesstaat° mit 9 Bundesländern°
  parlamentarische Demokratie

type of government / federation / federal states

- **Hauptstadt:** Wien (1, 5 Millionen Einwohner)
- **8 Nachbarn:** Italien (I)*, Fürstentum Liechtenstein (FL), die Schweiz (CH), Deutschland (D), die Tschechische Republik (ČZ), die Slowakei (SK), Ungarn (H), Slowenien (SLO)

Famous Austrian-Americans: directors: Fritz Lang, Billy Wilder, Erich von Stroheim, Otto Preminger, Max Reinhardt; actors: Peter Lorre, Arnold Schwarzenegger, Hedy Lamarr; John David Hertz, founder of Hertz car rental; John Kohler, founder of Kohler plumbing equipment business.

1. Welche anderen parlamentarischen Demokratien kennen Sie?
2. Österreich ist ein Land mit vielen Bergen. Das Gebirge heißt die Alpen⁺. Was kann man in den Bergen machen? Machen Sie gern Urlaub in den Bergen?
3. Welche berühmten⁺ Österreicher kennen Sie?
4. Haben Sie schon eine Vorstellung° von Österreich? Was wissen Sie schon über Österreich?

idea

5. Die Österreicher sagen, Österreich liegt im Herzen° von Europa. Warum sagen sie das?

heart

6. Herr Obermaier, der° in diesem Text über Österreich spricht, kommt aus Graz. Suchen Sie Graz auf der Landkarte⁺ von Österreich.

who

■ Beim Lesen

1. Herr Obermaier erwähnt° einige⁺ berühmte Österreicher. Machen Sie eine Liste von ihnen.

mentions

2. Was erfahren° Sie im Text über Österreichs Beziehungen° zu anderen Ländern?

find out / relationships

Andreas Obermaier aus Graz besucht seine amerikanische Kusine Sandra Heller. Sie ist Deutschprofessorin. Er kommt mit° in ihren Deutschkurs und spricht mit den Studenten über Österreich.

kommt mit: comes along

Guten Tag, meine sehr verehrten Damen und Herren°, vielen Dank, dass
5 ich heute als Gast in Ihrem Deutschkurs über mein Heimatland° sprechen darf.

meine...Herren: ladies and gentlemen / homeland

---

* The abbreviations in parentheses are the international symbols used on automobile stickers.

Nehmen wir: let's take

numerous

associate

medals
truth

which

in this connection / location
during
tried

refugees / **hat aufgenommen:**
accepted / seat of / important
(*genitive case*) / richest

Wussten Sie: did you know /
besides

finden statt: take place

es … gefallen: you liked it /
attention

Österreich liegt in Mitteleuropa und ist nur etwa so groß wie Maine, ein bisschen größer als die kanadische Provinz Neubraunschweig. Heute leben un- gefähr acht Millionen Menschen dort. Die meisten Menschen, 1,5 Millionen,
10 leben in Wien, der Hauptstadt. Seit 1995 gehört Österreich auch zur Europäi- schen Union.

Wahrscheinlich kennen Sie die meisten Österreich-Klischees schon. Sie sind nicht nur wahr, sondern meistens auch positiv. Nehmen wir° zum Beispiel das Klischee „Österreich – das Land der Musik". Musik war und ist sehr wichtig
15 für uns Österreicher. Viele weltberühmte Komponisten wie Haydn, Mozart und Schubert waren Österreicher und bis heute gibt es jedes Jahr zahlreiche° Musikfeste.

Ein anderes Klischee ist „Österreich – das Land der Kultur" – auch das ist wahr, denn es kommen doch relativ viele bekannte Schriftsteller, Künstler
20 und Wissenschaftler aus unserer kleinen Alpenrepublik. Franz Werfel, Gustav Klimt und Sigmund Freud sind auch in Ihrem Land bekannt.

Was assoziieren° Sie noch mit Österreich? Sport, vor allem Wintersport. Dass Österreichs Skiläuferinnen und Skiläufer in den Olympischen Winter- spielen immer wieder Medaillen° gewinnen ist kein Klischee, sondern die
25 Wahrheit°.

Ein letztes Klischee ist „das gemütliche Österreich". Überall gibt es Cafés, in denen° man gemütlich sitzen, Kaffee trinken und gute Torten essen kann. Dort trifft man seine Freunde oder liest die Zeitung und bleibt so lange, wie man will.
30 Wenn das Ihr Österreich-Bild ist, dann sind Sie nicht allein! Die meisten Leute denken an Österreichs Geschichte und Kultur. Doch, meine Damen und Herren, vergessen Sie dabei° nicht, dass Österreichs Lage° in Mitteleuropa poli- tisch und wirtschaftlich wichtig ist. Während° des Kalten Krieges hat Öster- reich versucht°, politisch, kulturell und wirtschaftlich neutral zu sein. Deshalb
35 hat dieses kleine Land seit dem Zweiten Weltkrieg nicht nur 2,1 Millionen Flüchtlinge° aufgenommen°, sondern ist auch Sitz° wichtiger° internationaler Organisationen wie der UNO* und OPEC**. Österreich ist heute eines der reichsten° Industrieländer der Welt und exportiert seine Produkte in die ganze Welt.
40 Wussten° Sie zum Beispiel, dass es neben° Hewlett-Packard und General Motors 350 amerikanische Firmen in Österreich gibt? Neben den klassischen Musikfesten finden jedes Jahr interessante Avantgarde-Feste statt°, und an den Universitäten arbeiten innovative Wissenschaftler mit den neuesten Technologien.
45 Und das, meine Damen und Herren, war mein Kurzporträt von Österreich. Ich hoffe, es hat Ihnen gefallen°. Vielen Dank für Ihre Aufmerksamkeit°. Ich bin jetzt gern bereit Ihre Fragen zu beantworten.

Brauchbares

[l.37]: Austria joined the U.N. in 1955, when the Allied occupation ended and it became a sovereign state. Vienna is headquarters for the U.N.'s International Development Org., as well as being the site for many other U.N. activities and conferences.

1. l.4. To start a speech German speakers generally begin with **Meine Damen und Herren** (*ladies and gentlemen*). **Meine sehr verehrten Damen und Herren,** which Andreas Obermeier uses, is very formal, something like *Most honored ladies and gentlemen.*

---

* *United Nations (Organization)*
** *Organization of Petroleum Exporting Countries*

[l.38]: A comparison of the 2002 estimated GDP per capita of selected countries: Germany $26,600, Austria $27,700, Japan $28,000, Canada $29,400, Switzerland $31,700, USA $36,300.

2. l.15–16. Three famous Austrian composers are mentioned: **Franz Josef Haydn** (1732–1809), friend of Mozart and inspiration for Beethoven, composed over 100 symphonies, 50 piano sonatas, and numerous operas, masses, and songs.

    Wolfgang Amadeus Mozart (1756–1791) is considered one of the greatest composers of all time. He was a child prodigy who began composing before he was five, at the age of six gave concerts throughout Europe, and by the age of 13 had written concertos, sonatas, symphonies, a German operetta, and an Italian opera. In his short lifetime he composed over 600 works—18 masses, 41 symphonies, 28 piano concertos, 8 well-known operas, and many chamber works.

    Franz Schubert (1797–1828) wrote his first composition at the age of 13 and his first symphony at 16. In one year at the age of 18 he wrote 140 songs. In his short lifetime Schubert wrote 998 works which include 9 symphonies, 7 masses, many piano pieces, and 606 songs.

3. l.20–21. The writer **Franz Werfel** (1890–1945) fled from Nazi-occupied Austria to France and then on to the United States. His work consists of poetry, dramas, and novels. He is best known in the United States for his novels *The Forty Days of Musa Dagh* (1934), which tells of the struggle of the Armenians against the Turks in World War I, and the *Song of Bernadette* (1942), which is about the saint from Lourdes.

    The painter **Gustav Klimt** (1862–1918) was the most famous painter of Art Nouveau in Vienna. He is best known for his portraits and landscapes. Some of his works are in the Museum of Modern Art, New York City.

    The psychiatrist **Sigmund Freud** (1856–1939) is known as the founder of psychoanalysis. When in 1938 the Nazis occupied Austria and made it part of Germany, Freud fled to England where he died the next year.

4. l.31. **doch:** You already know **doch** as a flavoring particle and as a positive response to a negative statement or question (see *Kapitel 3*). **Doch** is also a conjunction which means *nevertheless, still, however,* as in the line **Doch, meine Damen und Herren, vergessen Sie dabei nicht...**

5. l.34. **hat versucht** *(tried);* l.35–36, **hat aufgenommen** *(accepted);* and l.46, **hat gefallen** *(liked):* German has several past tenses. One of them is called the present perfect tense and is made up of a form of **haben** and a participle. This past tense will be practiced in *Kapitel 6.*

6. l.38–39, **exportiert seine Produkte:** Exports make up 52.2% of Austria's gross domestic product. In comparison, in the United States exports make up 11.2% of the GDP and in Canada it is 43.8% of the GDP.

7. l.46, **gefallen** means *to like:* You have already encountered other words meaning to like—**mögen** and **gern. Mögen** usually expresses stronger feelings than **gefallen:**
Deine Freunde **gefallen** mir nicht. (I don't like your friends = I don't care for them.)
Deine Freunde **mag** ich nicht. (I don't like your friends = I dislike them.)
Gern is used with verbs: Ich koche **gern.** (I like to cook.)

8. Andreas Obermaier could also have mentioned Austria's strong school system. Based on the "Global Competitiveness Report," published by the World Economic Forum, Austria's public school system was rated as one of the best in the world. Austria and Finland were ranked number one, followed by Belgium and Switzerland. Germany ranked 28th.

Land und Leute, p. 176: The Austro-Hungarian Empire and its satellite states in 1914 at the outbreak of WW I had 50 million people and included lands which comprise these modern countries: Austria, Hungary, Czech Republic, Slovakia, Slovenia, Croatia, Bosnia-Herzegovina, Romania, parts of Poland (Galicia), parts of the Ukraine.

Nach dem Lesen

1. Fragen zum Lesestück

1. Warum kommt Herr Obermaier in den Deutschkurs?
2. Ist Österreich größer oder kleiner als Ihr Bundesland/Ihre Provinz?
3. Was sind einige der weltbekannten Klischees über Österreich?
4. In welcher Sportart ist Österreich besonders erfolgreich°?
5. Möchten Sie in ein österreichisches Café gehen? Warum (nicht)?
6. Warum ist die geografische Lage Österreichs politisch und wirtschaftlich wichtig?
7. Welche internationalen Organisationen haben Büros° in Österreich?
8. Warum kann man sagen, dass Österreich ein Land der Kontraste ist?
9. Herr Obermaier erwähnt einige berühmte Österreicher. Welche kennen Sie?
10. Stellen Sie Herrn Obermaier eine Frage°.

2. Vokabeln.
Welches Wort oder welche Wendung° passt° zu welchem Thema°? Ordnen° Sie das Wort zu dem Thema, dann suchen Sie noch zwei Wörter oder Wendungen im Text zu den Themen.

Wörter/Wendungen: neutral ▪ Mozart ▪ Industrieland
Themen: Wirtschaft⁺ ▪ Außenpolitik° ▪ Musik

3. Erzählen wir.
Sprechen Sie über eines der folgenden Themen:

Warum ich Österreich besuchen will.
Wichtiges° über Österreich.
Ich möchte in Österreich arbeiten.

Margin glosses:
successful
offices
Stellen ... Frage: ask a question
phrase / fits / topic
match
foreign policy
important things

Land und Leute

Die Habsburger

www Go to the *Deutsch heute* website at http://college.hmco.com.

A significant period in Austria's history is the era under the rule of the House of Habsburg. In 1273 Rudolf von Habsburg was the first member of the Habsburg family to be elected emperor of the Holy Roman Empire (**Heiliges Römisches Reich**), which existed from 962 until 1806. In the first 400 years of Habsburg rule, the empire expanded greatly. The expansion was due to wars and to a successful **Heiratspolitik,** which deliberately aimed at advantageous marriages with the ruling European houses. Perhaps the most famous marriage was that of Marie Antoinette, daughter of Empress Maria Theresa of Austria, with Louis XVI of France. (Marie Antoinette and Louis XVI were guillotined in 1793 during the French Revolution.) The success of Napoleon's wars at the beginning of the nineteenth century led to the end of the empire in 1806. Members of the House of Habsburg continued to rule the Austro-Hungarian Empire until 1918, however, when Austria was declared a republic.

Diskussion

Find a map of early twentieth-century Europe and compare it to a current map. Which modern countries were part of the Austro-Hungarian Empire before World War I?

Vokabeln 2

Substantive

die **Alpen** *(pl.)*   Alps
der **Berg, -e**   mountain
der **Brief, -e**   letter
das **Café, -s**   café
die **Dame, -n**   lady
der **Dank**   thanks; **vielen
Dank**   many thanks
das **Fest, -e**   festival; party
die **Firma**, *pl.* **Firmen**   company
der **Gast, ⁼e**   guest
das **Klischee, -s**   cliché
der **Komponist, -en, -en**/die
Komponistin, -nen   composer
der **Krieg, -e**   war; der
Weltkrieg   world war
der **Künstler, -**/die **Künstlerin,
-nen**   artist

die **Landkarte, -n**   map
das **Porträt, -s**   portrait
das **Produkt, -e**   product
der **Regenschirm, -e**   umbrella
der **Schriftsteller, -**/die
Schriftstellerin, -nen   writer
der **Skiläufer, -**/die **Skiläuferin,
-nen**   skier
das **Taschenbuch, ⁼er**   paperback
book
die **Welt, -en**   world
die **Wirtschaft**   economy
der **Wissenschaftler, -**/die
Wissenschaftlerin, -nen   scientist

Verben

beantworten   to answer (a question,
a letter)
besuchen   to visit; to attend (e.g., a
lecture, school)
gefallen (gefällt) (+ *dat.*)   to please, be
pleasing to; **es gefällt mir**   I like it
gehören (+ *dat.*)   to belong to
gewinnen   to win

hoffen   to hope
leben   to live
schenken   to give (as a gift)
sitzen   to sit
sprechen (spricht)   to speak
treffen (trifft)   to meet
vergessen (vergisst)   to forget
versuchen   to try

Andere Wörter

bekannt   known, famous
bereit   ready, prepared; willing
berühmt   famous
bevor *(conj.)*   before
dass *(conj.)*   that
doch *(conj.)*   nevertheless, still,
however
einige   some, several
gemütlich   comfortable, informal
hoh- (**-er, -es, -e**)   high (the form of
hoch used before nouns, as in
hohe Berge   high mountains)
letzt- (**-er, -es, -e**)   last

meistens   mostly
obwohl *(conj.)*   although
österreichisch   Austrian *(adj.)*
reich   rich
sondern *(conj.)*   but (on the
contrary)
überall   everywhere
ungefähr   approximately
wahr   true; **nicht wahr?**   isn't that
true?
wahrscheinlich   probably
weil *(conj.)*   because
wirtschaftlich   economical

Besondere Ausdrücke

immer wieder   again and again
nicht nur ... sondern auch   not
only . . . but also

zu Hause   at home

Land und Leute

Neutralität

www   Go to the *Deutsch heute* website at http://college.hmco.com.

World War II ended in 1945, but because of the East-West conflict, Austria's sovereignty was not restored until 1955. The Soviet Union finally agreed to a peace treaty after Austria declared its policy of permanent neutrality (**immer während Neutralität**). Therefore, during the Cold War, Austria was a member neither of NATO nor of the Warsaw Pact. From the end of World War II until the end of the Cold War approximately 45 years later, Austria granted temporary or permanent asylum to about two million people from more than thirty countries. In fact, its decision to allow East German refugees to enter through its border with Hungary in 1989 was a contributing factor to the fall of the government of East Germany.

Until the end of World War I in 1918, Austria included lands that today are part of eastern European countries—the Czech Republic, Romania, Hungary, and the former Yugoslavia. Because of these ties, Austria served as an important link between eastern and western Europe during the Cold War, and it continues to play an important and special role in Europe today. Austria joined the European Union (**Europäische Union**) in 1995 but has not surrendered its neutrality. It is an active member of the United Nations and serves as the site of many international congresses and conferences. Vienna ranks among the leading convention cities in the world.

UNO-Gebäude in Wien.

Diskussion

Austria's national holiday is October 26, the day in 1955 when Austria regained its sovereignty.

Both Switzerland and Austria are neutral nations that are active in international organizations. Do you think that the policy of neutrality is a good one for a nation? How important do you think that international organizations such as the United Nations or the Red Cross are?

Grammatik und Übungen

1 Verbs with stem-vowel change *a* > *ä*

fahren: to drive	
ich fahre	wir fahren
du **fährst**	ihr fahrt
er/es/sie **fährt**	sie fahren
Sie fahren	
du-*imperative:* fahr(e)	

laufen: to run; to go on foot, walk	
ich laufe	wir laufen
du **läufst**	ihr lauft
er/es/sie **läuft**	sie laufen
Sie laufen	
du-*imperative:* lauf(e)	

Some verbs with stem-vowel **a** or **au** change **a** to **ä** in the **du-** and **er/es/sie**-forms of the present tense. The verbs you know with this change are **fahren, schlafen,** and **laufen.**

Wo die Zeit langsamer läuft.

Kleinkunstprogramm · Pianoabend · Biergarten · Cocktailgambling

BOUDOIR
Bar · Café · Restaurant

Stolzestr.1 50674 Köln Tel. 4201911 täglich 17°°Uhr bis 1°°Uhr

Was ist das „Boudoir"?
Wann kann man dort sein?
Was kann man im „Boudoir" alles machen?
Der Slogan bedeutet (*means*):
    a. Die Zeit läuft hier langsamer, weil es im „Boudoir" langweilig (*boring*) ist.
    b. Die Zeit läuft hier langsamer, weil man im „Boudoir" gut relaxen kann.

1. Zwei Gespräche

a. Ute fährt wieder nach Salzburg. Ergänzen° Sie die Sätze mit der passenden°   complete / appropriate
   Form von **fahren.**

KAI: Sag mal, Ute, _____ du übers Wochenende nach Salzburg?

UTE: Ja. Ich glaube schon.

KAI: _____ Katja mit?

UTE: Nein. Ich _____ allein. Katja und Tina _____ nach Wien. Aber so viel Zeit habe ich nicht.

KAI: Also dann, gute Reise.

b. Kais ganze Familie joggt gern. Ergänzen Sie die Sätze mit der passenden Form von **laufen**.

UTE: Du, Kai, _____ du jeden Morgen?

KAI: Nicht jeden Morgen, aber ich _____ viel. Mutti _____ aber jeden Morgen.

UTE: Deine Schwester Beatrix _____ auch viel, nicht?

KAI: Ja. Mein Vater und sie _____ vierzig Minuten nach der Arbeit. Morgens haben sie keine Zeit. Du und Erik, ihr _____ auch gern, nicht?

UTE: Ja, aber wir _____ nur am Wochenende.

lake

befindet sich: is located / ad

2. Restop Altea. Mondsee ist eine Stadt und auch ein See°. Restop Altea Motel befindet sich° in Mondsee. Was wissen Sie über das Motel? Lesen Sie die Anzeige° für das Motel und beantworten Sie die Fragen.

Mondsee is the name of a lake and a town on the lake in Austria, about 30 km east of Salzburg. In addition to the lake with camping facilities and water sports, the tourist attractions in Mondsee include one of the largest and most beautiful baroque churches in Austria, a castle, and its market square. The castle in Mondsee was originally a monastery, the oldest in Upper Austria. Salt has been mined in this area since prehistoric times. The **Salzkammergut** is a popular tourist area in Austria, famous for its many lakes and alpine landscape, which is often described as similar to the fjords in Norway.

RESTOP ♿

ALTEA
M O T E L

MONDSEE
Tel. 06232/2876–2879, Telex 633357 altea
Telefax 06232/2876/5

DER MONDSEE LIEGT IHNEN ZU FÜSSEN

Idealer Ausgangspunkt[1] für jung und alt in äußerst[2] ruhiger Lage[3]. Das ist unser Motel mit 46 Komfortzimmern, erreichbar[4] von beiden Fahrtrichtungen[5] der A-1-Autobahn. In unserem Panorama-Restaurant überraschen[6] wir Sie mit kulinarischen Spezialitäten. Hoteleigener Badestrand[7]!

Es lädt Sie ein[8]:

Der Mondsee: zum Segeln, Surfen, Wasserschilaufen und zu Schiffsrundfahrten[9].

Die Bergwelt Mondsee: zum Bergwandern und Bergsteigen[10]. zum Besuch von Kulturstätten[11] und Veranstaltungen[12].

Die Umgebung[13]: zum Tennisspielen, zum Golfen auf zwei Plätzen mit neun bzw. 18 Löchern[14], zu Ausflugsfahrten[15] ins Salzkammergut.

Unser Haus: mit dem Weekend-Hit, zahle 2 Nächte und bleibe 3!

Gute Erholung[16] und viel Vergnügen[17]!

[1]starting point [2]extremely [3]location [4]accessible [5]directions [6]surprise [7]swimming beach owned by the hotel [8]invite [9]boat excursions [10]mountain climbing [11]places of cultural interest [12]events [13]surroundings [14]holes [15]excursions [16]relaxation [17]fun

1. Welche Autobahn fährt nach Mondsee?
2. Wie viele Zimmer hat das Motel?
3. Was für Sport kann man treiben?
4. Was ist der Weekend-Hit?
5. Warum schläft man in diesem Motel gut?

Making plans for the weekend

3. Rollenspiel. Sie möchten ein Wochenende in Mondsee verbringen°. Versuchen Sie, Ihre Partnerin/Ihren Partner zu überreden° mitzukommen. Sagen Sie ihr/ihm, was man da alles machen kann. Hier sind einige Vorschläge°.

spend
persuade
suggestions

> **S1:** Fahren wir nach Mondsee? Komm doch mit! ▪ Wir kommen ganz leicht° nach Mondsee. ▪ Ich möchte gern auf dem See° segeln°. ▪ Kannst du surfen? ▪ Und ich möchte auch gerne gut essen. ▪ Wir können ins Salzkammergut fahren.
>
> **S2:** Hast du denn ein Auto? ▪ Ich kann nicht segeln. ▪ Kann man da auch gut wandern? ▪ Gibt es in Mondsee einen Golfplatz? ▪ Ist das nicht zu teuer? ▪ Ich möchte vor allem meine Ruhe° haben.

easily / lake / sail

peace and quiet

② Independent clauses° and coordinating conjunctions°

der Hauptsatz / die koordinierende Konjunktion

Wir wollen am Wochenende zelten. Es soll regnen.
Wir wollen am Wochenende zelten, **aber** es soll regnen.

An independent (or main) clause can stand alone as a complete sentence. Two (or more) independent clauses may be connected by a coordinating conjunction (e.g., **aber**). Because coordinating conjunctions are merely connectors and not part of either clause, they do not affect word order. Thus the subject comes before the verb. The coordinating conjunctions you know are **aber, denn, oder, sondern,** and **und.**

Erika kommt morgen, **aber** Christel kommt am Montag.

In written German, the coordinating conjunctions **aber, denn,** and **sondern** are generally preceded by a comma.

Erika kommt morgen **und** Christel kommt am Montag.

The conjunctions **und** and **oder** are generally not preceded by a comma, although writers may choose to use one for clarity.

4. Erika und Sabine. Sagen Sie, was Sabine und Erika diese Woche machen. Verbinden Sie jedes Satzpaar° mit einer koordinierenden Konjunktion.

pair of sentences

> → Die Studentin heißt Erika. Ihre Freundin heißt Sabine. (und)   *Die Studentin heißt Erika und ihre Freundin heißt Sabine.*

1. Erika wohnt bei einer Familie. Sabine wohnt bei ihren Eltern. (aber)
2. Erika arbeitet zu Hause. Sabine muss in die Bibliothek gehen. (aber)
3. Erika arbeitet schwer. Am Mittwoch hat sie eine Klausur. (denn)
4. Sabine hat ihre Klausur nicht am Mittwoch. Sie hat sie am Freitag. (sondern)
5. Was machen die Mädchen in den Ferien? Wissen sie es nicht? (oder)

▪ Sondern *and* aber

Paul fährt morgen nicht mit dem Auto, **sondern** geht zu Fuß.

Paul isn't going by car tomorrow, *but (rather)* is walking.

Sondern is a coordinating conjunction that expresses a contrast or contradiction. It connects two ideas that are mutually exclusive. It is used only after a negative clause and is equivalent to *but, on the contrary, instead, rather.* When the subject is the same in both clauses, it is not repeated. This is also true of a verb that is the same; it is not repeated.

Cordelia tanzt **nicht nur** viel, **sondern auch** gut.	Cordelia dances *not only* a lot, *but also* well.

The German construction **nicht nur ... sondern auch** is equivalent to *not only ... but also.*

Er fährt nicht mit dem Auto, **aber** sein Vater fährt mit dem Auto.	He isn't going by car, *but* his father is.

Aber as a coordinating conjunction is equivalent to *but* or *nevertheless.* It may be used after either positive or negative clauses.

5. Was macht Sabine? Erzählen Sie, was Sabine heute alles macht. Ergänzen Sie die Sätze mit **aber** oder **sondern.**

→ Sabine spielt heute nicht Fußball, _____ Tennis.
Sabine spielt heute nicht Fußball, sondern Tennis.

1. Sie spielt Tennis nicht gut, _____ sie spielt es sehr gern.
2. Sie geht nicht zur Vorlesung, _____ in die Bibliothek.
3. Im Café bestellt° sie Bier, _____ sie trinkt Julians Kaffee.
4. Sie möchte den Kaffee bezahlen, _____ sie hat kein Geld.
5. Sie fährt nicht mit dem Bus nach Hause, _____ geht zu Fuß.

orders

Showing connections and relationships

6. Hören Sie zu. Sabine und Julian sprechen über ihre Freunde. Hören Sie, was sie sagen. Geben Sie dann an, ob die Sätze richtig oder falsch sind. Sie hören ein neues Wort: **helfen** (*help*).

1. Monika ist Filmstudentin.
2. Sie studiert nicht nur, sondern arbeitet auch dreißig Stunden in der Woche.
3. Sie hat einen Job in einem Kino, aber sie sieht keine Filme.
4. Monika kauft oft Kinokarten.
5. Julian möchte nicht nur mit Monika, sondern auch mit Sabine ins Kino gehen.
6. Monika gibt nicht Julian, sondern David ihre Kinokarten.
7. David sagt, dass er besser Deutsch lernt, wenn er viele Filme sieht.

der Nebensatz / die subordinierende Konjunktion

③ Dependent clauses° and subordinating conjunctions°

Independent Clause	Conjunction	Dependent Clause
Rita sagt,	dass	sie nach Österreich **fährt.**
Sie übernachtet bei Freunden,	wenn	sie zu Hause **sind.**

A dependent (subordinate) clause is a clause that cannot stand alone; it must be combined with an independent clause to express a complete idea. Two signals distinguish a dependent clause from an independent clause: (1) it is introduced by a subordinating conjunction (**dass, wenn**) and (2) the finite verb (**fährt, sind**) is at the end. In writing, a dependent clause is separated from the independent clause by a comma. A few common subordinating conjunctions are: **bevor,** *before;* **dass,** *that;* **obwohl,** *although;* **weil,** *because;* **wenn,** *if; when.*

7. Österreicher fahren in die Ferien. Wie und wo verbringen° viele Öster-   spend
reicher die Ferien? Verbinden Sie die Sätze mit den Konjunktionen in Klammern.

→ In den Ferien fahren viele Österreicher nach Ungarn. Alles ist da
billiger. (weil)
*In den Ferien fahren viele Österreicher nach Ungarn, weil da alles
billiger ist.*

1. Die Österreicher finden es auch gut. Ungarn ist nicht so weit. (dass)
2. Sie können nicht vor Mitte Juli fahren. Die Sommerferien beginnen erst dann.
   (weil)
3. Nach Prag fahren sie auch oft. Die Ferien sind kurz. (wenn)
4. Viele Musikfans bleiben in Österreich. Im Sommer sind in Bregenz und
   Salzburg die Festspiele. (wenn)
5. In den Winterferien fahren viele Österreicher nach Italien. Das Skilaufen ist
   dort billiger. (weil)
6. Es ist gut für die Österreicher. Ihr Land liegt in Mitteleuropa. (dass)

„Schade, dass wir nur Freunde sind."

▶ Schülerticket und Geschwisterkarte
für Schüler – Berlin AB.

gültig ab 1. August 2001

VBB

S Bahn Berlin   Die Bahn DB

BVG

Für wen gibt es billige
Tickets?

■ *Dependent clauses and separable-prefix verbs*

Statement	Monika **kauft** gern im Supermarkt **ein.**
Dependent clause	Monika sagt, **dass** sie gern im Supermarkt **einkauft.**

In a dependent clause, the separable prefix is attached to the base form of the
verb, which is in final position.

Reporting on actions

8. Was sagt Gabi? Sagen Sie Mark, was Gabi über ihre Pläne sagt. Beginnen Sie jeden Satz mit: **Gabi sagt, dass ...**

    ➡ Sie kauft in der Stadt ein.   *Gabi sagt, dass sie in der Stadt einkauft.*

1. Renate kommt mit.
2. Renate kommt um neun bei ihr vorbei.
3. Sie kaufen auf dem Markt ein.
4. Sie bereitet dann zu Hause ein Referat vor.
5. Renate bringt ein paar° Bücher mit.
6. Sie bringt die Bücher am Freitag zurück.

a few

■ ***Dependent clauses and modal auxiliaries***

Statement	Rita **möchte** in die Schweiz fahren.
Dependent clause	Rita sagt, **dass** sie in die Schweiz fahren **möchte.**

In a dependent clause, the modal auxiliary is the finite verb and therefore is in final position, after the dependent infinitive.

9. Peter sagt das. Peter sagt, was er alles tun möchte und tun muss. Sagen Sie einem Freund, was Peter sagt.

    ➡ Ich soll meine Seminararbeit zu Ende schreiben.
       Peter sagt, dass er seine Seminararbeit zu Ende schreiben soll.

1. Ich muss meine E-Mails durchlesen.
2. Ich soll einen Brief an meine Großeltern schreiben.
3. Ich will mit dem Computer arbeiten.
4. Ich möchte ein bisschen im Internet surfen.
5. Ich möchte heute Abend ein bisschen fernsehen.

Giving reasons

10. Freizeit. Ihre Partnerin/Ihr Partner fragt, warum Sie nicht dies und das in Ihrer Freizeit und in den Ferien machen. Beginnen Sie Ihre Antwort mit **weil.** Unten finden Sie einige mögliche Antworten.

    S2: Warum gehst du nicht ins Kino?
    S1: Weil ich kein Geld habe.

S2:
1. Warum gehst du nicht inlineskaten?
2. Warum gehst du nicht mit Freunden ins Café?
3. Warum gehst du nicht tanzen?
4. Warum joggst du nicht?
5. Warum liest du nicht einen Krimi?
6. Warum machst du nicht Ferien in Österreich?
7. Warum spielst du nicht Golf?
8. Warum spielst du nicht mit uns Karten?
9. Warum bist du immer so müde?

S1:
    Ich will zu Hause bleiben.
    Ich muss eine Seminararbeit schreiben.
    Ich will allein sein.
    Ich muss arbeiten.
    Ich will in die Bibliothek gehen.

Ich habe kein Geld.
Ich habe keine Zeit.
Ich kann nicht tanzen.
Das interessiert mich nicht.
Ich kann nicht schlafen.

■ Dependent clauses beginning a sentence

	1	2	
	Paul	**fährt**	mit dem Bus.
1		2	
Weil sein Auto kaputt ist,		**fährt**	er mit dem Bus.

In a statement, the finite verb is in second position. If a sentence begins with a dependent clause, the entire clause is considered a single element, and the finite verb of the independent clause is in second position, followed by the subject.

11. Eine Radtour durch die Schweiz. Gerhard und Fabian planen eine Radtour° durch die Schweiz. Verbinden Sie jedes Satzpaar°. Beginnen Sie den neuen Satz mit der angegebenen° Konjunktion.

bicycle trip / pair of sentences
cued

➡ (wenn) Das Wetter ist gut. Gerhard und Fabian wollen in die Schweiz.
Wenn das Wetter gut ist, wollen Gerhard und Fabian in die Schweiz.

1. (weil) Sie haben wenig Geld. Sie fahren mit dem Rad.
2. (wenn) Sie fahren mit dem Rad. Sie sehen mehr vom Land.
3. (wenn) Es ist nicht zu kalt. Sie zelten.
4. (wenn) Das Wetter ist sehr schlecht. Sie schlafen bei Freunden.
5. (obwohl) Sie haben wenig Geld. Sie können vier Wochen bleiben.
6. (weil) Sie haben nur vier Wochen Ferien. Sie müssen im August wieder zu Hause sein.

4 Dative case°

der Dativ

Nominative	**Der** Mann heißt Falk.
Accusative	Kennst du **den** Mann?
Dative	Ich gebe **dem** Mann meine Zeitung.

In addition to nominative and accusative, German has a case called *dative*.

Masculine	**Neuter**	**Feminine**	**Plural**
dem Mann	dem Kind	der Frau	den Freunden
diesem Mann	diesem Kind	dieser Frau	diesen Freunden
einem Mann	einem Kind	einer Frau	keinen Freunden
ihrem Mann	unserem Kind	seiner Frau	meinen Freunden

The definite and indefinite articles, **der**-words, and **ein**-words change their form in the dative case. Nouns add an **-n** in the dative plural, unless the plural already ends in **-n** or **-s**: **meine Freunde > meinen Freunden;** but **die Frauen > den Frauen, die Autos > den Autos.**

5 Masculine N-nouns in the dative

Nominative	der Herr	der Student
Accusative	den Herr**n**	den Student**en**
Dative	dem Herr**n**	dem Student**en**

Masculine **N**-nouns, which add **-n** or **-en** in the accusative, also add **-n** or **-en** in the dative singular. The masculine **N**-nouns you know so far are: **der Herr, der Junge, der Komponist, der Mensch, der Nachbar, der Name, der Student,** and **der Tourist.**

6 Dative of *wer?*

Nominative	**Wer** sagt das?	*Who* says that?
Dative	**Wem** sagen Sie das?	*To whom* are you saying that?

The dative form of the interrogative **wer?** *(who?)* is **wem?** *([to] whom?).*

7 Dative verbs

Das Haus **gehört meinen** Eltern.   The house belongs to my parents.
Kerstin **glaubt ihrer** Schwester nicht.   Kerstin doesn't believe her sister.

Most German verbs take objects in the accusative. However, a few verbs take objects in the dative. The dative object is usually a person. Such verbs can be classified as "dative verbs." The dative verbs you've learned so far are **glauben, gefallen,** and **gehören.** A more complete list of dative verbs is found in section 17 of the Grammatical Tables in Appendix F.

Daniela **glaubt ihrem** Freund Erik.   Daniela believes her friend Erik.
Erik **glaubt es** nicht.   Erik doesn't believe it.

The verb **glauben** always takes personal objects (e.g., **ihrem Freund**) in the dative case. However, impersonal objects (e.g., **es**) after **glauben** are in the accusative case.

gone
things

12. Wem gehört das? Sie und Carsten kommen von einer Bustour nach Berlin zurück. Alle Passagiere sind schon fort°. Sie sind noch im Bus und sehen einige Dinge°. Carsten fragt, wem die Dinge gehören. Sie wissen es.

 → das Poster (dein Freund Uwe)
Wem gehört das Poster?   *Das Poster gehört deinem Freund Uwe.*

1. der Regenschirm
(dein Professor)

2. das Handy
(deine Professorin)

3. der Rucksack
(die Amerikanerin)

4. die Landkarte
(der Engländer)

5. das Taschenbuch
(deine Freundin Cornelia)

6. die Zeitung
(der Busfahrer)

Gefallen is equivalent to English *like.* When using the verb **gefallen,** what one likes is the subject and thus in the nominative case. The person who likes something is in the dative. Note that sentences with **gefallen** often begin with the dative.

Das Bild **gefällt mir.**	*I like* the picture.
Mir gefällt es nicht, dass Mark so wenig liest.	*I don't like* (the fact) that Mark reads so little.

13. Was bedeutet° das? Geben Sie die Sätze auf Englisch wieder°.

*means / **geben wieder:** render*

1. Wie gefällt deinem Freund Mark Hamburg?
2. Ihm gefällt es sehr.
3. Was gefällt deinem Freund nicht so gut?
4. Ihm gefällt es nicht, dass es so viel regnet.
5. Es gefällt Mark auch nicht, dass es so viele Autos gibt.

8 Dative personal pronouns

Singular						
Nominative	ich	du	er	es	sie	Sie
Accusative	mich	dich	ihn	es	sie	Sie
Dative	**mir**	**dir**	**ihm**	**ihm**	**ihr**	**Ihnen**

Plural				
Nominative	wir	ihr	sie	Sie
Accusative	uns	euch	sie	Sie
Dative	**uns**	**euch**	**ihnen**	**Ihnen**

Dative personal pronouns have different forms from the accusative pronouns, except for **uns** and **euch.**

roommate

räumen auf: are straightening up

14. Was denkt Aishe? Aishe ist Ihre Mitbewohnerin°. Sie räumen Ihre Wohnung auf°. Fragen Sie, wem die Dinge gehören und ob sie Aishe gefallen. Antworten Sie immer mit einem logischen Personalpronomen.

➡ Gehört der Regenschirm deinem Vater? (ja)
Ja, der Regenschirm gehört ihm.
➡ Gefällt dir das Poster? (nein) *Nein, das Poster gefällt mir nicht.*

1. Gehört der Rucksack deiner Schwester? (ja)
2. Gehört dir das Video? (nein)
3. Gefällt dir das Video? (ja)
4. Gehören die Disketten deinen Kusinen? (ja)
5. Gehört die Einkaufstasche deiner Mutter? (ja)
6. Gehören die CDs deinem Bruder? (ja)
7. Gefallen dir die CDs? (nein)

schreiben auf: write down

15. Was gefällt Ihnen? Was finden Sie gut? Schreiben Sie erst drei Dinge oder Aktivitäten auf°, die Ihnen gefallen. Dann interviewen Sie Ihre Partnerin/Ihren Partner und schreiben auf, was ihr/ihm gefällt.

S1: Skilaufen gefällt mir. Susanna, was gefällt dir?
S2: Snowboarden gefällt mir.
S1: schreibt: Snowboarden gefällt Susanna.

das indirekte Objekt

9 Indirect object°

	Indirect object	Direct object
Katrin schenkt	ihrem Freund	einen CD-Player.
Katrin is giving	her friend	a CD player.

In both English and German some verbs take two objects, which are traditionally called the direct object (e.g., **CD-Player**—*CD player*) and the indirect object (e.g., **Freund**—*friend*). The indirect object is usually a person and answers the question *to whom* or *for whom* the direct object is intended. Some verbs that can take both direct and indirect objects are **bringen, erklären, geben, kaufen, leihen, sagen, schenken,** and **schreiben.**

10 Signals for indirect object and direct object

	Indirect (dative) object	Direct (accusative) object
Katrin schenkt	ihren Eltern	einen CD-Player.
Katrin is giving	her parents	a CD player.

English signals the indirect object by putting it before the direct object or by using the preposition *to* or *for*, e.g., Katrin is giving a CD player *to* her parents. To determine in English whether a noun or pronoun is an indirect object, add *to* or *for* before it.

German uses case to signal the difference between a direct object and an indirect object. The direct object is in the accusative, and the indirect object is in the dative. Since the case signals are clear, **German never uses a preposition to signal the indirect object.**

16. Geburtstage. Einige Leute haben diesen Monat Geburtstag. Theresa und David diskutieren, was sie den Leuten schenken. Bestimmen° Sie das indirekte Objekt (Dativ) und das direkte Objekt (Akkusativ). Übersetzen° Sie die Sätze.

→ DAVID: Wem schenkst du die Blumen?
   indirect object: Wem
   direct object: die Blumen
   English equivalent: To whom are you giving the flowers?

1. THERESA: Diese Blumen bringe ich meiner Großmutter.
2. THERESA: Was kaufst du deiner Freundin?
3. DAVID: Meiner Freundin möchte ich ein T-Shirt schenken.
4. THERESA: Ich schreibe meinem Bruder einen Brief.
5. THERESA: Leider kann ich meinem Freund Christian nichts schenken. Ich habe kein Geld mehr.
6. THERESA: Das muss ich ihm erklären.

17. Was macht Dieter? Wem kauft, leiht, gibt, schenkt Dieter etwas? Ergänzen Sie die Sätze mit der Dativform der Wörter° in Klammern.

→ Dieter kauft _____ neue Weingläser. (seine Eltern)
   Dieter kauft seinen Eltern neue Weingläser.

1. Er leiht _____ sein neues Fahrrad. (ich)
2. _____ bringt er Blumen mit. (seine Großmutter)
3. Er leiht _____ seinen neuen Roman. (sein Freund Erik)
4. Will er _____ seinen Rucksack leihen? (du)
5. Er schenkt _____ seinen alten Computer. (sein Bruder)
6. Dieter gibt _____ eine interessante DVD. (wir)

11 Word order of direct and indirect objects

	Indirect object	**Direct-object noun**
Katrin leiht	*ihrem Freund*	ihr Fahrrad.
Katrin leiht	*ihm*	ihr Fahrrad.

The direct (accusative) object determines the order of objects. If the direct object is a noun, it usually follows the indirect (dative) object.

	Direct-object personal pronoun	**Indirect object**
Katrin leiht	**es**	*ihrem Freund.*
Katrin leiht	**es**	*ihm.*

If the direct (accusative) object is a personal pronoun, it always precedes the indirect (dative) object. Note that a pronoun, whether accusative or dative, always precedes a noun.

cued / pay attention / word order

18. Kleine Gespräche. Ergänzen Sie die kleinen Gespräche mit den angegebe-nen° Wörtern. Achten° Sie auf die richtige Wortstellung°.

→ PAUL: Schenkst du _____ _____ ? (den kleinen Tisch/Michaels Schwester) *Schenkst du Michaels Schwester den kleinen Tisch?*

→ HEIKE: Ja, ich schenke _____ _____ . (ihn/Michaels Schwester) *Ja, ich schenke ihn Michaels Schwester.*

1. PAUL: Schenkst du _____ _____ ? (deine Gitarre/Michael)

   HEIKE: Ja, ich schenke _____ _____ . (sie/ihm)

2. MUTTI: Schenkst du _____ _____ zum Geburtstag? (diesen DVD-Player/Christine)

   STEFFI: Ja, ich schenke _____ _____ . (ihn/Christine)

3. VATI: Schreibst du _____ oft _____ ? (E-Mails/deinen Freunden)

   DIRK: Ja, ich schreibe _____ _____ . (viele E-Mails/ihnen)

4. LIANE: Willst du _____ _____ leihen? (deinen Rucksack/mir)

   UTE: Ja. Ich leihe _____ _____ gern. (ihn/dir)

lottery / won

members of your family / presents

19. Frage-Ecke. Sie und einige Freundinnen und Freunde haben im Lotto° gewonnen°. Mit dem Geld kaufen Sie Ihren Freunden und Familien-mitgliedern° schöne Geschenke°. Wer bekommt was? Die Informationen für *S2* finden Sie im Anhang (Appendix B).

S1: Was schenkt Ralf seinen Eltern?
S2: Er schenkt ihnen zwei Wochen in Wien.

S1:

	Eltern	Schwester	Bruder	Melanie
Karsten	einen Porsche	einen Computer		
Stefanie	Winterferien in Spanien			einen Fernseher
Ralf		eine Gitarre	ein Fahrrad	
ich				
Partnerin/ Partner				

20. Wie sagt man das?

1. What are you giving your mother for her birthday?
   —I'm giving her flowers and a book.

2. Whom are you writing the card to?
   —[To] my cousin Martin.

3. Are you lending your friend money? He wants to buy his parents flowers.
   —No. I don't lend him money any more.

4. Is that motorcycle new? Does it belong to you?
   —No, to my sister.

21. Ausleihen und zurückgeben. Was leihen Sie Ihren Freunden (nicht) gern aus? Fragen Sie Ihre Partnerin/Ihren Partner und schreiben Sie!

Wem? Bruder ▪ Eltern ▪ Freund ▪ Freundin ▪ Schwester

Was? Auto ▪ Bücher ▪ Computerspiele ▪ Fahrrad ▪ Geld ▪ Handy ▪ Kulis ▪ Sweatshirt

Wann? sofort° ▪ (nicht) schnell ▪ (nicht) oft ▪ nie°   immediately / never

S1: Was leihst du deinen Freunden (nicht) gern aus?
S2: Ich leihe ihnen nicht gern [mein Auto] aus.
S1: Wem leihst du (nicht) gern deine Sachen° aus?   clothes
S2: Ich leihe [meiner Schwester] nicht gern meine Sachen aus.
S1: Gibst du geliehene° Dinge [schnell] zurück?   borrowed
S2: [Ja, sofort].

12 Dative prepositions

aus	out of	Nils geht morgens immer spät **aus** dem Haus.
	(to come) from [cities and countries]	Er kommt **aus** Berlin.
außer	besides, except for	**Außer** seinem Freund Paul kennt Nils nur wenige Leute in Wien.
bei	with (at the home of)	Nils wohnt **bei** seiner Tante.
	at (a place of business)	Er arbeitet **bei** Pizzeria Uno.
	near (in the proximity of)	Die Pizzeria ist **bei** der Universität.
mit	with	Nils fährt **mit** seinem Freund zur Uni.
	by means of (transportation)	Sie fahren **mit** dem Auto.
nach	to (with cities and countries used without an article)	Am Wochenende fahren sie **nach** Salzburg.
	after	Aber **nach** einem Tag kommen sie schon zurück.
seit	since (time)	Nils wohnt **seit** Januar in Wien.
von	from	Er hört jede Woche **von** seinen Eltern aus Berlin.
	of	Berlin ist eine Stadt **von** 3,4 Millionen Einwohnern.
	by	Heute Abend hört er eine Oper **von** Mozart.
zu	to (with people and some places)	Nils geht gern **zu** seinem Freund Paul.
		Sie fahren zusammen **zur** Pizzeria Uno.
	for (in certain expressions)	Heute Abend gibt es **zum** Abendessen Pizza.

The prepositions **aus, außer, bei, mit, nach, seit, von,** and **zu** are always followed by the dative. Some common translations are provided in the chart above.

Liebe Anna,
lieber Walter!

Herzlichen¹
Glückwunsch
zu eurer Silbernen
Hochzeit².
Auf weitere 25
glückliche Jahre
zusammen!

Eure Freunde vom
Tennisclub Leonberg

Liebe Mama,

bleib immer so lieb!
Du bist die beste
Mama auf der Welt!

Alles Liebe zum
Muttertag
von deinen Lukas,
Lea und Lilli

Wie lange sind Anna und Walter schon verheiratet (*married*)? Was machen Anna und Walter gern mit ihren Freunden in Leonberg?

Wie heißen die drei Kinder? Warum schreiben sie ihrer Mutter? Was schreiben sie?

¹**herzlichen Glückwunsch:** *warmest wishes* ²*wedding anniversary*

Wer gratuliert Nina? Was
macht Nina jetzt?

■ **bei**

In addition to the meanings listed above, **bei** has many uses that are hard to translate exactly. It is used, in a general way, to indicate a situation: **beim Lesen** (*while reading*), **bei der Arbeit** (*at work*), **bei diesem Wetter** (*in weather like this*).

■ **bei/mit**

Sarah wohnt **bei** ihren Eltern.	Sarah lives *with* her parents.
Sarah fährt morgen **mit** ihren Eltern.	Sarah's driving *with* her parents tomorrow.

One meaning of both **bei** and **mit** is *with*. However, they are not interchangeable. **Bei** indicates location. **Bei ihren Eltern** means at the home of her parents. **Mit** expresses the idea of doing something together (**mit ihren Eltern**).

Campus Reisebüro[1]

**Bei uns fliegen Jugendliche[2]
und Studenten besonders günstig[3].**

Campus Reisebüro
Wilhelmstr. 13
72074 Tübingen
Telefon: 07071-25028

Telefax: 07071-21439

Campus Reisebüro
Auf der Morgenstelle 26
72076 Tübingen
Telefon: 07071-66052
(Ring: -73908)

Telefax: 07071-66082

Wo ist das Campus Reisebüro?
Warum buchen (*book*) Studenten ihre
Reisen in diesem Reisebüro?

[1]*travel agency* [2]*young people* [3]*reasonably*

■ **nach/zu**

Schmidts fahren morgen **nach** Salzburg.	The Schmidts are going *to* Salzburg tomorrow.
Ich muss **zum** Bäcker.	I have to go *to* the bakery.

One meaning of both **zu** and **nach** is *to*. **Zu** is used to show movement toward people and many locations. **Nach** is used with cities and countries without an article.

■ **seit**

Tanja ist **seit** Montag in Hamburg.	Tanja has been in Hamburg *since* Monday.
Jürgen wohnt **seit** drei Wochen in Wien.	Jürgen has been living in Vienna *for* three weeks.

Seit plus the present tense is used to express an action or condition that started in the past but is still continuing in the present. Note that English uses the present perfect tense (e.g., *has been living*) with *since* or *for* to express the same idea.

Contractions

Brot kaufen wir nur **beim** Bäcker.	bei dem = **beim**
Jürgen kommt jetzt **vom** Markt.	von dem = **vom**
Monika geht **zum** Supermarkt.	zu dem = **zum**
Kerstin geht **zur** Uni.	zu der = **zur**

The prepositions **bei, von,** and **zu** often contract with the definite article **dem,** and **zu** also contracts with the definite article **der.** While contractions are generally optional, they are required in certain common phrases such as:

beim Arzt°   zum Frühstück/Mittagessen/Abendessen   doctor
beim Bäcker   zum Arzt gehen
vom Arzt kommen   zum Bäcker gehen
zum Beispiel   zur Uni/Schule gehen
zum Geburtstag

Contractions are not used when the noun is stressed or modified: **Gehen Sie immer noch zu dem Bäcker in der Bahnhofstraße?** (*Do you still go to the baker on Bahnhofstraße?*)

22. Christine in Wien. Daniela erzählt von ihrer Freundin Christine. Ergänzen Sie die Sätze mit den passenden Präpositionen und Artikeln und Possessivpronomen.

Christine kommt _____ d_____ Schweiz. _____ ein_____ Jahr wohnt

sie _____ ein_____ Familie in Wien. Sie will Musikerin° werden und geht   musician

jeden Tag _____ Konservatorium (das). Zwei Tage in der Woche muss sie

jobben. Sie arbeitet _____ ein_____ Bäcker. Nächsten Sommer macht sie

_____ ihr_____ Freundin Petra eine Radtour. Sie fahren _____ Salzburg

zu den Festspielen°. Ich höre nicht sehr oft _____ Christine, denn sie hat   famous festival of music and
                                                                                                                                                                theater
wenig Zeit. Aber _____ ihr_____ Bruder bekomme ich manchmal E-Mails.

Im September möchte ich _____ Wien fahren und Christine besuchen.

**Wien – Schloss
Schönbrunn, die
Sommerresidenz
der Habsburger
Kaiser.**

194

DEUTSCH
HEUTE

trip

*Making plans for a
vacation*

23. Hören Sie zu. Michael und Uwe planen eine Reise°. Hören Sie zu und beantworten Sie die Fragen. Sie hören fünf neue Wörter: **die Stadtrundfahrt** *(city tour);* **das Hofburg Museum** *(museum in the Hofburg castle);* **das Schloss Schönbrunn** *(Schönbrunn castle);* **der Prater** *(famous amusement park);* **die Jazzkneipe** *(jazz bar).*

1. Was hat Uwe für Michael?
2. Wie kommen Michael und Uwe nach Wien?
3. Wann fährt der Bus von der Uni ab?
4. Wie lange bleiben Michael und Uwe in Wien?
5. Was sehen sie in Wien?
6. Welche Stadt wollen sie außer Wien noch besuchen?
7. Was für Musik möchte Michael hören?
8. Um wie viel Uhr sind sie wieder in Tübingen?

¹*special prices* ²*reasonable* ³*lodgings* ⁴*rental cars* ⁵*travel consultation*

Wo kann man „mehr Welt" für sein Geld bekommen?
Was ist billiger? Eine Reise nach Nairobi oder eine Reise nach Sydney?
Wie ist die Adresse von Sta Travel?
Wo kann ich anrufen, wenn ich billig nach Nairobi reisen möchte?
Wohin kann ich ab 516 Euro fliegen?

24. Verkehrsmittel. Fragen Sie Ihre Partnerin/Ihren Partner, wie man am besten° von Ort° zu Ort fahren kann. Benutzen° Sie den Plan.

am besten: best / place / use

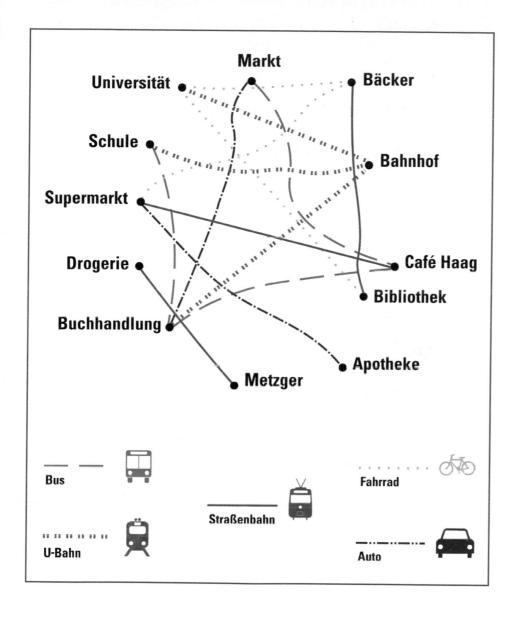

S1: Wie komme ich am besten von der Uni zur Bibliothek?
S2: Am besten fährst du mit dem Fahrrad.

1. Wie komme ich am besten von der Schule zum Bahnhof°?
2. Wie komme ich am besten vom Markt zum Café Haag?
3. Wie komme ich am besten vom Metzger zur Drogerie?
4. Wie komme ich am besten von der Buchhandlung zum Markt?
5. Wie komme ich am besten von der Uni zum Bäcker?

train station

Wiederholung

1. Rollenspiel. Sie wohnen in Wien und Ihre Partnerin/Ihr Partner besucht Sie. Ihre Partnerin/Ihr Partner möchte wissen, was sie/er dort alles machen kann. Geben Sie eine sehr positive Antwort.

Redemittel: Enthusiastische Reaktionen zeigen

Ja, sicher. ▪ Klar. ▪ Kein Problem. ▪ Ja, wirklich.
▪ Ja, natürlich.

---

1. Kann ich wirklich drei Tage hier bleiben?
2. Ist es denn okay, wenn ich so lange bei dir übernachte?
3. Kann ich hier abends etwas zu essen machen?
4. Kann man von hier mit dem Bus in die Stadt fahren?
5. Darf ich mir auch mal dein Fahrrad ausleihen?
6. Dann darf ich dir aber auch etwas schenken für deine Gastfreundschaft°.

hospitality

2. Eine Reise nach Österreich. Erzählen Sie von Davids Reise nach Österreich. Benutzen Sie die angegebenen° Wörter.

cued

1. David / sein / Amerikaner
2. er / fliegen / nach / Wien
3. er / sprechen / mit / einige / Studenten
4. sie / erzählen / von / diese Universität
5. nach / zwei Tage / David / fahren / mit / Zug / nach / Salzburg

complete
parentheses

3. Was macht Monika? Sandra erzählt von Monikas Tag. Ergänzen° Sie die Sätze mit den Wörtern in Klammern°.

1. Monika geht aus _____ . (das Haus)
2. Sie geht zu _____ . (der Bäcker)
3. _____ Andrea arbeitet bei _____ . (ihre Freundin / der Bäcker)
4. Monika arbeitet für _____ . (ihr Onkel)
5. Sie erklärt _____ auch viel über Computer. (er)
6. Sie fährt mit _____ zur Arbeit. (das Fahrrad)
7. Nach _____ geht sie in die Buchhandlung. (die Arbeit)
8. Sie kauft _____ über Österreich. (ein Buch)
9. _____ bringt sie Blumen mit. (ihre Mutter)
10. Jeden Freitag bringt sie _____ Blumen. (sie, *sing.*)
11. Morgen schenkt sie _____ das Buch zum Geburtstag. (ihr Vater)
12. Nächstes Jahr fährt sie mit _____ nach Österreich. (ihre Freunde)
13. Das sagt sie _____ heute am Telefon. (sie, *pl.*)

4. Jetzt weiß er es. In einem Café setzt sich° Dieter Meier an Karen Müllers Tisch. Nach zehn Minuten weiß Dieter einiges° über Karen. Sagen Sie, was Dieter alles weiß. Beginnen Sie jeden Satz mit **Er weiß, dass ...**

setzt sich: sits down
some things

KAREN: Ich bin Österreicherin.
DIETER: Kommst du aus Wien?
KAREN: Nein, aus Salzburg.
DIETER: Wohnst du in einem Studentenheim?
KAREN: Nein, bei einer Familie.
DIETER: Was studierst du denn?
KAREN: Wirtschaftswissenschaft° ist mein Hauptfach und Englisch mein Nebenfach. Ich möchte in Amerika arbeiten.
DIETER: Warst du schon in Amerika?
KAREN: Leider noch nicht.

economics

5. Wie sagt man das?

1. VERENA: Would you like to go to Austria this summer?
2. CARINA: Yes. Gladly. Do you want to go by car or by train?
3. VERENA: By bike. If the weather stays nice.

4. EIN FREUND: Can you lend me your German book?
5. SIE: Of course, I can give it to you.
6. EIN FREUND: And can you also explain the dative° to me?
7. SIE: Do we have enough time?

dative = **der Dativ**

6. Wo soll ich studieren? Ihre Partnerin/Ihr Partner möchte in Europa studieren. Sie/Er weiß aber nicht, ob sie/er in Deutschland oder Österreich studieren soll. Wählen° Sie ein Land und erzählen Sie von dem Land. Hier sind einige Fragen.

choose

Wie groß ist das Land?   Hat es viele Berge?
Wie viele Einwohner hat es? Hat es viel Industrie?
Wie viele Nachbarn hat es?   Wie heißt die Hauptstadt?

7. Zum Schreiben. Sie studieren in Wien und möchten Ihre Freundin/Ihren Freund überreden° auch in Wien zu studieren. In einem kurzen Brief schreiben Sie ihr/ihm von den Vorteilen°.

persuade
advantages

Wien, den 30. Dezember 2005

Liebe [Barbara],/Lieber [Paul],
ich bin ...

...
Viele Grüße
deine [Jennifer]/dein [David]

After you have finished your letter, check the following carefully:

• Subject and verb agreement
• Word order and punctuation in sentences with conjunctions
• Genders and cases of all nouns and pronouns
• Case used with each preposition

Österreich ist ein
Alpenland: Blick von
Salzburg auf die Alpen.

Grammatik: Zusammenfassung

Verbs with stem-vowel change *a* > *ä*

fahren	
ich fahre	wir fahren
du **fährst**	ihr fahrt
er/es/sie **fährt**	sie fahren
Sie fahren	
du-*imperative:* fahr(e)	

laufen	
ich laufe	wir laufen
du **läufst**	ihr lauft
er/es/sie **läuft**	sie laufen
Sie laufen	
du-*imperative:* lauf(e)	

Independent clauses and coordinating conjunctions

Erik **kommt** morgen, aber Christl **muss** morgen arbeiten.

In independent (main) clauses the finite verb (**kommt, muss**) is in second position. A coordinating conjunction (**aber**) does not affect word order. The five common coordinating conjunctions are **aber, denn, oder, sondern,** and **und.**

Dependent clauses and subordinating conjunctions

Ich weiß, dass Frank morgen **kommt.**
  dass Petra morgen **mitkommt.**
  dass Helmut nicht **kommen kann.**

In dependent (subordinate) clauses:

1. The finite verb (**kommt**) is in final position.
2. The separable prefix (**mit**) is attached to the base form of the verb (**kommt**) in final position.
3. The modal auxiliary (**kann**) is a finite verb and therefore is in final position, after the infinitive (**kommen**).

Some common subordinating conjunctions are **bevor, dass, obwohl, weil,** and **wenn.**

Wenn du mit dem Rad fährst, **siehst** du mehr vom Land.

When a dependent clause begins a sentence, it is followed directly by the finite verb (**siehst**) of the independent clause.

Dative case

Articles, der- and ein-words in the dative case

	Masculine	Neuter	Feminine	Plural
Nominative	der Mann	das Kind	die Frau	die Freunde
Accusative	den Mann	das Kind	die Frau	die Freunde
Dative	**dem** Mann	**dem** Kind	**der** Frau	**den** Freunden
	diesem Mann	**diesem** Kind	**dieser** Frau	**diesen** Freunden
	einem Mann	**einem** Kind	**einer** Frau	**keinen** Freunden
	ihrem Mann	**unserem** Kind	**seiner** Frau	**meinen** Freunden

Nouns in the dative plural

Nominative	die Männer	die Frauen	die Radios
Dative	den Männer**n**	den Frauen	den Radios

Nouns in the dative plural add **-n** unless the plural already ends in **-n** or **-s**.

Masculine N-nouns in the dative case

Nominative	der Herr	der Mensch
Accusative	den Herrn	den Menschen
Dative	**dem** Herrn	**dem** Menschen

For the masculine **N**-nouns used in this book, see the Grammatical Tables in Appendix F.

Dative of wer

Nominative	wer
Accusative	wen
Dative	**wem**

Dative personal pronouns

	Singular					
Nominative	ich	du	er	es	sie	Sie
Accusative	mich	dich	ihn	es	sie	Sie
Dative	**mir**	**dir**	**ihm**	**ihm**	**ihr**	**Ihnen**

	Plural			
Nominative	wir	ihr	sie	Sie
Accusative	uns	euch	sie	Sie
Dative	**uns**	**euch**	**ihnen**	**Ihnen**

Word order of direct and indirect objects

	Indirect object	Direct-object noun
Katrin schenkt	*ihrer Schwester*	**den Rucksack.**
Katrin schenkt	*ihr*	**den Rucksack.**

The direct (accusative) object determines the order of objects. If the direct object is a noun, it follows the indirect (dative) object.

	Direct-object pronoun	Indirect object
Katrin schenkt	**ihn**	*ihrer Schwester.*
Katrin schenkt	**ihn**	*ihr.*

If the direct (accusative) object is a personal pronoun, it precedes the indirect (dative) object.

Dative verbs

Das Fahrrad **gehört** meinem Bruder.
Ich **glaube** dir nicht.

Most German verbs take objects in the accusative. A few verbs take objects in the dative. The dative object is usually a person. For convenience such verbs can be classified as "dative verbs."

For dative verbs used in this book, see the Grammatical Tables in Appendix F.

Dative prepositions

aus	out of; from *(= is a native of)*
außer	besides, except for
bei	with *(at the home of)*; at *(a place of business)*; near *(in the proximity of)*; while *or* during *(indicates a situation)*
mit	with; by means of *(transportation)*
nach	to *(with cities, and countries used without an article)*; after
seit	since, for *(referring to time)*
von	from; of; by *(the person doing something)*
zu	to *(with people and some places)*; for *(in certain expressions)*

Contractions of dative prepositions

bei dem	=	**beim**
von dem	=	**vom**
zu dem	=	**zum**
zu der	=	**zur**

Was hast du vor?

Diese jungen Leute wollen ins Kino gehen.
(Potsdamer Platz, Berlin)

LERNZIELE

Sprechintentionen

Discussing leisure-time activities
Expressing likes and dislikes
Discussing clothes
Expressing opinions
Talking about the past
Apologizing

Lesestück

Freizeitpläne

Land und Leute

Work vs. leisure time in Germany
Television
Requirements for a driver's license
Theater in the German-speaking
  countries
Holidays in Germany
German film

Vokabeln

Television
Hobbies
Infinitives used as nouns
Clothing

Grammatik

Present perfect tense
Past participles
Use of auxiliaries **haben** and **sein**

201

Bausteine für Gespräche

 Was habt ihr vor?

UWE: Sagt mal, was macht ihr am
Wochenende?

MELANIE: Keine Ahnung.

MICHAEL: Ich habe am Freitag Probe mit
der Band. Am Samstag spielen wir in der
Musikfabrik.

UWE: Du, Melanie, da können wir doch
zusammen hingehen, oder?

MELANIE: Gute Idee. Das ist super. Vielleicht
geht auch Alex mit?

MICHAEL: Der kann nicht. Er muss fürs Examen arbeiten.

UWE: Also, Melanie, ich hole dich um acht ab. In Ordnung?

Fragen

1. Was hat Michael am Wochenende vor?
2. Wohin möchte Uwe gehen?
3. Warum kann Alex nicht mitgehen?
4. Wann holt Uwe Melanie ab?

 Ich habe im Internet gesurft.

GISELA: Sag mal, Alex, mit wem hast du denn gestern Abend so lange telefoniert?
Ich habe von acht bis elf immer wieder bei dir angerufen. Es war immer
besetzt.

ALEX: Ach, ich habe nur ein bisschen im Internet gesurft.

GISELA: Wie, drei Stunden lang gesurft?

ALEX: Ja, ich habe nach billigen Flügen in die USA gesucht. Außerdem habe ich
noch ein paar Informationen für meine Hausarbeit gebraucht. Und ich habe
dir eine E-Mail geschrieben. Hast du sie denn nicht bekommen?

GISELA: Weiß ich gar nicht. Ich sitze ja nicht wie du jeden Tag an meinem
Computer.

Fragen

1. Hat Alex gestern Abend lange telefoniert?
2. Was hat er von acht bis elf gemacht?
3. Warum hat Gisela die E-Mail von Alex noch nicht gelesen?

Brauchbares

1. To ask whether Melanie agrees with him, Uwe ends one sentence with
"oder?" and the other with **"In Ordnung?"** These two phrases are common in
German conversation. **Oder?** is equivalent to *Or don't you agree?* and **In Ordnung?** is equivalent to *Is that all right with you?*
2. **Es war immer besetzt.** = The line was always busy.

1. Was machst du in der Freizeit? Fragen Sie Ihre Partnerin/Ihren Partner, was sie/er in ihrer/seiner Freizeit macht. Erzählen Sie den Kursteilnehmern, was sie/er gesagt hat. Benutzen Sie auch Wörter aus dem Anhang (Supplementary Word Sets, „Free time" und „Sports and games", Appendix C).

S1:
Was sind deine Hobbys?

S2:
Rad fahren.

Schüttelkasten

Science-Fiction lesen

kochen[+]

Musik hören/machen

fotografieren[+]

im Internet surfen

inlineskaten gehen

Rad fahren[+]

joggen

Ski laufen/Wasserski fahren

S1:
Was hast du am
Wochenende vor?

S2:
Ich gehe | **schwimmen.**
Ski laufen/Wasserski fahren.
windsurfen[+].
tanzen.

Ich will | **viel lesen.**
faulenzen[+].
arbeiten.
Fußball/Tennis im
Fernsehen sehen.
im Internet chatten.

2. Was machst du alles mit dem Computer? In einer Gruppe von vier Personen, stellen Sie einander Fragen°. Finden Sie heraus°, was die anderen alles am Computer machen.

S1: Was machst du alles mit dem Computer?
S2: Ich [schreibe oft E-Mails, surfe gern im Internet, kaufe manchmal etwas übers Internet, suche Informationen für meine Hausarbeit, mache Computerspiele, chatte gerne].

stellen ... Fragen: ask each other
questions / finden heraus:
find out

3. Was hast du gestern Abend gemacht? Beantworten Sie die Frage erst selbst und fragen Sie dann Ihre Partnerin/Ihren Partner. Erzählen Sie den Kursteilnehmern, was sie/er gesagt hat.

S1: Gestern Abend habe ich etwas ferngesehen. Was hast du gestern Abend gemacht?
S2: Ich habe [mit einer Freundin/einem Freund telefoniert, im Internet gesurft, nach Informationen für meine Hausarbeit gesucht, E-Mails geschrieben, an meinem Computer gearbeitet, etwas ferngesehen, Musik gehört, ein bisschen gelesen, gar nichts gemacht].
S1: Kelsey hat [mit einem Freund telefoniert].

Land und Leute

Freizeit

www Go to the *Deutsch heute* website at
http://college.hmco.com.

Although the Germans have a reputation for being industrious, they are also known as the world champions in leisure time (**Freizeitweltmeister**). The average workweek in Germany is 37.2 hours. In the year 2000, Germans worked an average of 1480.1 hours a year. In contrast, American workers worked 1978.7 hours. Germany ranks near the top among the industrialized nations in paid vacation time (**Urlaub**). In addition to paid vacation time, many German companies pay their employees a vacation bonus (**Urlaubsgeld**) of several hundred euros. The United States and Canada bring up the rear among many nations in paid vacation time.

Germans spend much of their free time taking vacation trips abroad. In 2001, Germans spent approximately 52 billion euros on trips to other countries. The most popular European destinations for Germans are Spain, Italy, and Austria. Outside of Europe, the favorite destinations are the United States and Canada. About one-third of the vacation trips are taken in Germany.

Segeln ist ein beliebter Sport in Deutschland.
(Wannsee, Berlin)

Diskussion

Below is a chart with the average number of paid vacation days (not including paid holidays).

Country Average of Paid Vacation Days

Country	
Finland	35
Sweden	32
Germany	30
Austria	30
Ireland	28
Norway	21
Switzerland	21
USA	15
Canada	15

1. Studies have shown that workers are most productive when they receive a minimum of three weeks of vacation per year. Why do you think that some industrialized nations do not provide their workers with this amount of vacation? How many paid vacation days do employees receive in your area?
2. Most European nations have more paid vacation days than the United States. Do you think that so much vacation time is a good policy? Make a plan of how you would spend six weeks of vacation time. You do not have to take all six weeks at the same time.

The average vacation time in the United States, including holidays, is 23 days per year; in Canada it is 26 days.

Urlaubsgeld for public employees is approximately 300 euros.

Erweiterung des Wortschatzes

Fernsehprogramme

Freitag, 2. August			
ZDF		**RTL**	
5:30	Morgenmagazin	6:00	Punkt 6 – Magazin
9.00	Tagesschau[1]	7.00	Unter uns[16] – Soap
9.05	Volle Kanne[2]	7.30	Gute Zeiten, schlechte Zeiten
10.00	Tagesschau		Soap
10.03	Frauenarzt Dr. Merthin	8.05	RTL Shop
	Arztserie	9.00	Punkt 9 – Magazin
10.50	Reich und schön	9.30	Meine Hochzeit[17]
11.35	Genießen auf gut deutsch	10.00	Dr. Stefan Frank
	Esskultur[3]		Dt. Arztserie (1995)
12.00	Tagesschau	11.00	Mein Baby
12.15	drehscheibe[4] Deutschland		Dt. Doku-Soap
13.00	Tagesschau	11.30	Familien-Duell
13.05	Mittagsmagazin	12.00	Punkt 12 – Magazin
14.00	heute – in Deutschland	13.00	Oliver Geissen Show
	Nachrichten		Talk mit Gästen
14.15	Reiselust[5] Deutschlands	14.00	Bärbel Schäfer
	schönste Wälder[6]		Talk mit Gästen
15.00	heute / Sport	15.00	Die Wache[18]
15.10	Streit um drei[7]		Dt. Polizeiserie (1996)
	Politmagazin	16.00	Jugendgericht[19]
16.00	heute – in Europa		Mit Richterin[20] Dr. Herz
16.15	Risiko – Quiz	17.00	Die Nanny
17.00	heute / Wetter		US-Sitcom (1993)
17.10	hallo Deutschland	17.30	Unter uns
18.02	Tagesmillion		Dt. Seifenoper ('02)
18.05	Schlosshotel[8] Orth	18.00	Guten Abend RTL
	Dt.-österr. Serie ('00)		Ländermagazin
	Späte Rache[9]	18.30	Exclusiv – Stars
19.00	heute		Mit Frauke Ludowig
19.20	Wetter	18.45	RTL Aktuell[21]
19.25	Forsthaus Falkenau		Mit Sport und Wetter
	Dt.-österr. Serie ('00)	19.10	Explosiv
	Spuren[10] im Wasser		Magazin mit Markus Lanz
20.15	Wenn die Musik spielt	19.40	Gute Zeiten, schlechte Zeiten
	Open Air-Volksmusik		Dt. Seifenoper
22.30	heute-journal	19.25	Forsthaus Falkenau
22.45	Aspekte-Kulturmagazin		Dt.-österr. Serie ('00)
	Mit Wolfgang Herles	20.15	Nikola
23.15	Eine Liebe auf Mallorca		Dt. Sitcom (1998)
	Dt. Spielfilm ('98)	21.45	Ritas Welt
1.30	heute Nacht		Dt. Comedyserie (1999)
1.45	Hier war ich glücklich	22.15	Life! – Die Lust[22] zu leben
	Engl. Spielfilm (1965)		Lifestyle-Magazin
3.15	3sat-Börsennews[11]	23.15	Freitag Nacht News
3.50	Der Klitschko-Clan[12]		Comedyshow
	4teilig[13] – Aufbruch[14]	0.00	Nachtjournal
	und Abschied[15]	0.30	Caroline In The City
5.05	citydreams		US-Sitcom (1997)
		1.30	Die Nanny
		1.55	Nikola
		2.25	Ritas Welt
		2.50	Nachtjournal
		3.15	stern[23] TV
		4.40	RTL Shop

[1]daily news [2]full pot [3]to enjoy good German cooking [4]turntable [5]wanderlust [6]forests [7]fight at three (o'clock) [8]castle hotel [9]revenge [10]traces [11]stock market reports [12]the Klitschko clan (Russian boxers) [13]in four parts [14]starting out [15]farewell [16]among ourselves [17]wedding [18]police station [19]juvenile court [20]judge [21]current affairs [22]desire [23]stern is the name of a magazine

Sehen nach: look up

1. Fernsehen. Suchen Sie für jede Kategorie von Fernsehsendungen eine Sendung⁺ auf Seite 205 oder eine Sendung im amerikanischen Fernsehen. Geben Sie die Zeit an, wann die Sendung kommt.

Hinweis: Sehen Sie nach°: „TV programs" in Supplementary Word Sets, Appendix C.

Seifenoper
Fernsehserie
Musiksendung
Nachrichten
Spielfilm
Sportsendung

2. Fernsehprogramme. Sehen Sie die Fernsehprogramme von ZDF und RTL auf Seite 205 an⁺. Beantworten Sie die Fragen.

(TV) listings

1. In den Programmen° gibt es auch amerikanische Sendungen. Welche sind das?
2. Es gibt auch viele englische Wörter. Welche sind das?
3. Welches Programm hat mehr Talk-Shows?
4. Die Nachrichtensendungen im ZDF heißen „Tagesschau" und „heute". Wie oft kommen diese beiden Sendungen zum Beispiel am 2. August? Um welche Uhrzeit?
5. Wo und wann gibt es Sportsendungen?
6. Wo und wann kann man eine Kultursendung ansehen?

3. Deine Lieblingssendung. Interviewen Sie drei Studentinnen/Studenten in Ihrem Deutschkurs. Wie oft sehen sie fern? Welche Sendungen mögen sie? Welche mögen sie nicht? Warum? Was ist ihre Lieblingssendung?

S1:	*S2:*
Wie oft siehst du fern?	Einmal⁺ [zweimal, dreimal] die Woche.
Welche Sendungen magst du?	Ich sehe gern [...]. Es ist lustig.
Was ist deine Lieblingssendung?	Meine Lieblingssendung ist [...].

4. Was war im Fernsehen? Sagen Sie Ihrer Partnerin/Ihrem Partner, was Sie gestern im Fernsehen gesehen haben. Dann fragen Sie, was Ihre Partnerin/Ihr Partner gestern gesehen hat.

Hinweis: Sehen Sie nach: „TV programs" in Supplementary Word Sets, Appendix C.

S1: Ich habe gestern [einen Krimi] im Fernsehen gesehen.
S2: Wie war die Sendung?
S1: Die Sendung war [interessant, ganz gut, langweilig⁺, nicht besonders toll/gut]. Was hast du gestern im Fernsehen gesehen?

Fernsehen

Germany has both public (**öffentlich-rechtlich**) and private (**privat**) television, which is designated as **das duale System.** The public channels are run as nonprofit public corporations and supervised by broadcasting councils. Their programming is financed primarily by fees collected from owners of televisions and radios. These fees are 16.15 euros monthly. Cable TV costs the viewer an additional 14.50 euros. Each community has access to two national public channels and at least one regional channel. These are referred to respectively as **ARD (Arbeitsgemeinschaft der öffentlich-rechtlichen Rundfunkanstalten Deutschlands)** or **Erstes Programm, ZDF (Zweites Deutsches Fernsehen)** or **Zweites Programm,** and **Drittes Programm (Regionalprogramm).** The **ARD** includes both television and radio. Commercials on these channels are usually shown in two to three clusters per evening and are restricted to a maximum of twenty minutes per workday. There are no commercials after 8 P.M. or on Sundays or holidays. The private stations, which are available through subscription via cable, have become strong competitors to the public TV stations. The major cable stations are **RTL, SAT 1, SAT 2,** and **3 SAT.** Viewers find them attractive because they offer more light entertainment and feature films than the public stations, whose schedule consists of around 44% informational programs. More and more Germans are opting for TV via satellite instead of cable.

Statistically, the average German watches television a little over $2\frac{1}{7}$ hours a day. Popular programs on German TV include news shows (**Nachrichten**), game shows, sports (**Sportsendungen**), movies (**Spielfilme**), and series (**Serien**) such as situation comedies or detective shows (**Krimis**)—many of which are co-productions with Swiss and Austrian television or imported from the United States. Most movies and sitcoms are American-made with dubbed voices; many game shows are based on American models. American and other foreign films are usually with dubbed voices rather than subtitles. For many programs, stereo broadcasting makes it possible to hear the soundtrack either in German or in the original. People who live close to a border sometimes receive broadcasts from a neighboring country.

Nachrichten im deutschen Fernsehen.

Owners of both television sets and radios pay a fee of 16.15 euros per month, but for radio only, people pay 5.32 euros. Television alone still costs 16.15 euros.

Germans between 14 and 49 listen to the radio 3 hours per day and watch television 2½ hours per day.

www Go to the *Deutsch heute* website at http://college.hmco.com.

Diskussion

Gerd Bacher, a former Director-General of the public broadcasting system in Austria (**Österreichischer Rundfunk**), made the following statement: **"Öffentlich-rechtlicher Rundfunk braucht Geld, um Programm zu machen. Privatfernsehen braucht Programm, um Geld zu machen."** What do you think he meant by this statement? What is the role of public broadcasting in your community? In your life?

Vokabeln 1

Beginning in this chapter the past participles of strong verbs (see pp. 223–224) will be listed after the infinitive, e.g., **einladen, eingeladen.**

Substantive

die **Ahnung**   hunch; idea; **keine Ahnung!**   no idea!
die **Band, -s**   (musical) band
die **E-Mail, -s**   e-mail
das **Fernsehprogramm, -e**   TV channel
der **Flug, ⁻e**   flight

die **Freizeit**   free time
die **Hausarbeit**   homework
das **Hobby, -s**   hobby
die **Idee, -n**   idea
die **Probe, -n**   rehearsal
die **Sendung, -en**   TV or radio program

Verben

an·rufen, angerufen   to phone; **bei [dir] anrufen**   to call [you] at home
an·sehen, angesehen   to look at
chatten   to chat (Internet)
faulenzen   to lounge around, be idle
fotografieren   to photograph
hin·gehen, ist hingegangen   to go there
kochen   to cook

mit·gehen, ist mitgegangen   to go along
telefonieren   to speak on the telephone; (**mit jemandem**) **telefonieren**   to telephone someone
vor·haben   to intend, have in mind
windsurfen gehen   to go windsurfing; **surfen**   to surf

Andere Wörter

außerdem   besides, in addition, as well
besetzt   busy, occupied; **es war besetzt**   the line was busy
ein paar   a few, a couple

einmal   once, one time
langweilig   boring
gar nicht   not at all
super   super, great

Besondere Ausdrücke

gestern Abend   last night
in Ordnung?   is that all right (with you)?

oder?   or don't you agree?
übers Internet kaufen   to buy on the Internet

freizeitpläne

Vorbereitung auf das Lesen

■ *Vor dem Lesen*

am liebsten: most of all

expressions / use

1. Was machen Sie am liebsten° in Ihrer Freizeit? Sie können diese Wörter und Wendungen° in Ihren Antworten benutzen°:

   Am liebsten …   Meistens …

zur Entspannung: for relaxation

   In meiner Freizeit …   Zur Entspannung° …

Rad fahren ▪ joggen ▪ fernsehen ▪ am Computer arbeiten⁺ ▪ lesen
▪ wandern oder spazieren gehen ▪ mit Freunden zusammen sein ▪ ins
Kino, Theater⁺ oder Konzert⁺ gehen ▪ im Internet surfen/chatten
▪ faulenzen ▪ essen gehen ▪ telefonieren ▪ Sport treiben ▪ tanzen gehen
▪ Musik hören

2. Machen Sie eine Umfrage° unter den Studentinnen/Studenten.   survey

   ➡ *Was machst du am liebsten in deiner Freizeit?*

3. Sehen Sie die Anzeigen° an und beantworten Sie die Fragen.   ads
   a. Welche Art° von Musik macht Farin Urlaub?   kind
   b. Wo spielt er am 30. September?
   c. Mit welcher Band spielt Farin Urlaub?
   d. Wo kann man ein amerikanisches Musical sehen?
   e. Wo kann man die Theaterkarten⁺ von 10 bis 18 Uhr kaufen?
   f. Wann endet das Musical?
   g. Welche von den beiden Möglichkeiten° gefallen Ihnen?   possibilities

Farin Urlaub
Pop-Punk mit dem
Frontmann der „Ärzte"

30.9., 19h
Köln, Live Music Hall

Staatstheater am Gärtnerplatz
Telefon 2 01 67 67
Vorverkauf¹ im Theater
Mo.-Fr. 10-18 Uhr, Sa. 10-13 Uhr
Maximilianstr. 11-13
Mo.-Fr. 10-13, 15.30-17.30, Sa. 10-13 Uhr
Der Fiedler² auf dem Dach³ (Anatevka)
Musical Jerry Bock
Beginn: 19.30   Ende: 22.45 Uhr

¹*advance ticket sales* ²*fiddler* ³*roof*

Dieser junge Mann geht in seiner Freizeit gern inlineskaten.

cafe. SMILE .de
internet - cafe
am Zülpicherplatz
Jahnstr. 26–30
50676 Köln
Tel. (02 21) 9 65 91 45
www.cafe-smile.de
Montag– Sonntag 10.00–24.00 Uhr
surfen, drucken[1] downloaden, scannen, MP3
und vieles mehr..........
16

[1] *print*

Wie heißt das Internetcafé in Köln? Was kann man dort alles machen?

Beim Lesen

Was machen die Leute im Text in ihrer Freizeit? Machen Sie eine Liste.

Peter Bosch ist Reporter bei einer Studentenzeitung und macht Straßeninterviews für die Zeitung. Seine Frage: „Was hast du letztes Wochenende in deiner Freizeit gemacht?"

Silke, 23 Jahre:

„Freizeit? Ich habe schon ewig keine richtige Freizeit mehr gehabt. Ich studiere Informatik und bekomme BAföG, da möchte ich natürlich so schnell wie möglich mit dem Studium fertig werden. Ich jobbe in einem Internetcafé, meistens samstags und sonntags. Das ist aber fast wie Freizeit für mich, weil Computer und das Internet meine große Leidenschaft° sind. Und wenn im Café nicht so viel los ist, kann ich auch selbst° im Internet surfen. Ich chatte gern und viel. Ich finde, beim Chatten kann man Leute richtig gut kennen lernen, weil man offen und ehrlich miteinander spricht. Vor ein paar Wochen habe ich ‚XY' im Chatroom kennen gelernt. Letztes Wochenende haben wir uns verabredet° und wir sind zusammen essen gegangen. Es war toll – wie wenn sich zwei alte Freunde treffen."

passion
myself
made a date

Stefan, 19 Jahre:

„Ich habe seit zwei Monaten meinen Führerschein und fahre gern mit meinem Auto spazieren. Letzten Samstag bin ich sehr früh aufgestanden. Ich bin zu meinen Großeltern gefahren und habe sie besucht. Sie wohnen etwa hundertfünfzig Kilometer nördlich von München.

Ich höre gern Hip-Hop und Rock. Am Samstag sind meine Freunde und ich tanzen gegangen. Wir waren in der Sonderbar. Das ist ein ganz toller

Club. Mein Auto ist natürlich zu Hause geblieben, denn ich habe Bier getrunken. Ins Kino gehe ich nicht so gern. Das finde ich so passiv, denn man kann dort nicht mit Freunden sprechen. Eine Disco ist da schon viel besser oder eine Kneipe."

Evi, 31 Jahre:

25 „Viele Leute sagen, Deutsche arbeiten zu viel und sind sehr fleißig. Ich denke auch manchmal, ich arbeite zu viel. Ich bin Ärztin und muss oft viele Stunden im Krankenhaus sein. Letztes Wochenende habe ich aber frei gehabt. Ich habe am Samstag zuerst mit meinem Bruder Tennis gespielt, dann bin ich mit meinem Freund Rad gefahren. Ich treibe gern Sport. Und außerdem ist Sport 30 gesund. Am Abend hat meine Familie Geburtstag gefeiert, denn meine Großmutter ist 83 Jahre alt geworden! Am Sonntag sind mein Freund und ich ins Staatstheater am Gärtnerplatz gegangen. Wir haben das Musical ‚Der Fiedler auf dem Dach' gesehen. Mich hat das Stück interessiert, aber mein Freund hat es etwas langweilig gefunden. Ich gehe in meiner Freizeit gern aus. Manchmal 35 bin ich aber ganz einfach auch gern zu Hause, sehe fern, höre Radio, lese ein Buch oder tue nichts."

Brauchbares

1. 1. 7–8, **Computer und das Internet:** Many of the German terms for the computer and the Internet come from English or are guessable. A few such terms are **der Chatroom, chatten, downloaden, die E-Mail schicken** or **mailen, die Homepage, das Internet, im Internet surfen/chatten, klicken, kopieren, die Maus, das Modem, das Newsboard, das Netz, scannen, das Web, die Webseite.**

2. To an American it might seem that Stefan is getting his driver's license rather late. Reasons for this are found in **Land und Leute: Der Führerschein,** p. 213.

Nach dem Lesen

1. Fragen zum Lesestück

1. Lesen Sie Ihre Liste von den Freizeitbeschäftigungen° im Text. Und was machen Sie in Ihrer Freizeit? — leisure-time activities
2. Was studiert Silke?
3. Wo arbeitet Silke am Wochenende?
4. Was findet Silke am Chatten so gut?
5. Wie alt ist Stefan?
6. Wie lange hat Stefan schon seinen Führerschein?
7. Warum geht Stefan gern in eine Disco oder Kneipe?
8. Warum bleibt Stefans Auto zu Hause?
9. Was ist Evis Beruf°? — profession
10. Wann hat Evi frei gehabt?
11. Mit wem geht Evi ins Theater?
12. Welches Musical läuft im Staatstheater?
13. Was macht Evi gern zu Hause?
14. Mit wem (Silke, Stefan oder Evi) möchten Sie gern ein Wochenende verbringen°? Warum? — spend (time)

hätte sagen können: could
have said

2. Wer hätte das sagen können°? Silke, Stefan oder Evi?

1. Ich habe wenig Freizeit. _____
2. Ich spreche gern mit meinen Freunden. _____
3. Ich studiere in München. _____
4. Ich fahre gern spazieren. _____
5. Ins Kino gehen gefällt mir nicht. _____
6. Ich muss oft lernen. _____
7. Ich muss viele Stunden arbeiten. _____
8. Ich surfe gern im Internet. _____
9. Meine Großmutter ist 83 Jahre alt. _____
10. Ich höre gern Rockmusik. _____
11. Ich spiele gern Tennis. _____
12. Im Chatroom lerne ich oft nette Leute kennen. _____
13. Ich möchte bald mit dem Studium fertig sein. _____

discuss / **eins ... Themen**: one of
the following topics

3. Erzählen wir. Besprechen° Sie eins der folgenden Themen° in einer Gruppe von drei Studenten.

• Was ich in meiner Freizeit mache
• Warum ich keine Freizeit habe

Erweiterung des Wortschatzes

1. Infinitives used as nouns

Mein Hobby ist **Wandern.**
Frühmorgens ist **das Joggen** toll.

My hobby is *hiking.*
Jogging early in the morning is
    great.

German infinitives may be used as nouns. An infinitive used as a noun is always neuter. The English equivalent is often a gerund, that is, the *-ing* form of a verb used as a noun.

Arbeiten
soll Spaß
machen.
Lesen auch.

EXTRA-HELL
Mit 100 neuen
Super-Singles

AMICA im Mai: Ab 16.4. am Kiosk.

1. Was ist schön? Beantworten Sie die Fragen mit Slogans. Nehmen Sie die Wörter aus dem Schüttelkasten.

→ Was ist schön? *Laufen ist schön.*

1. Was ist toll?
2. Was soll Spaß machen?
3. Was ist gesund?

4. Was macht dumm?
5. Was macht fit?

Schüttelkasten

schlafen

laufen

faulenzen   arbeiten   schwimmen

einkaufen   fernsehen   chatten

Land und Leute

Der Führerschein

The minimum age for a driver's license (**Führerschein**) in the German-speaking countries is eighteen, although exceptions are sometimes made for people as young as sixteen who need a car to make a living. To obtain a license one must attend a private driving school (**Fahrschule**). In Germany a driving course for a passenger car consists of a minimum of fourteen 90-minute classes of theoretical instruction and a minimum of twelve hours of driving lessons (**Fahrstunden**). The driving lessons include practice in city driving, on the highway (**Autobahn**) and nighttime driving. At the end of the course, every student must pass both a theoretical test and a driving test. Approximately one-third of the students fail the test the first time. Each candidate must also complete a course in first aid before being issued a driver's license. The **Führerschein** is then issued temporarily for two years, after which time the driver can obtain it for life, if the driving record shows no entries for drunk driving or other at-fault violations. The total cost of the driving lessons plus the test fees can easily exceed 1000 euros.

The member nations of the EU have agreed to standards that apply to all member countries. Therefore, national driver's licenses are valid in all EU countries.

Fahrschule Hahn ist nur eine der vielen Hamburger Fahrschulen.

Diskussion

Go to the *Deutsch heute* website at http://college.hmco.com.

Some activists believe that a speed limit would reduce the auto emissions in the atmosphere and decrease the number of accidents.

Countries have different laws and regulations about driving. Comment on the following laws in German-speaking countries in comparison to regulations in your country or state.

1. Germany has no speed limit on most sections of the **Autobahnen.**
2. Austria, Switzerland, and Germany have laws prohibiting speaking on hand-held phones while driving. (See **Land und Leute, das Telefon,** page 10.)
3. In Germany, truck traffic is forbidden on Sundays and holidays, as well as on Saturdays at the height of the vacation season.
4. Switzerland and Austria charge a fee for using **Autobahnen.** In Germany there is a fee for large trucks, but none for small trucks or passenger cars.

articles of clothing

German fashion ads are filled
with American borrowings.
Current examples: das **T-Shirt**,
das **Sweatshirt**, der **Blazer**,
die **Jeans**, das **Make-up**, das
Outfit, die **Boots**.

2. Kleidungsstücke°

1. der **Anzug**, ¨e
2. der **Badeanzug**, ¨e
3. der **Handschuh**, -e
4. der **Hut**, ¨e
5. der **Pulli**, -s
6. der **(Regen)mantel**, ¨
7. der **(Regen)schirm**, -e
8. der **Rock**, ¨e
9. der **Schuh**, -e
10. der **Stiefel**, -

11. das **Hemd**, -en
12. das **Jackett**, -s
13. das **Kleid**, -er
14. das **Polohemd**, -en
15. das **T-Shirt**, -s

16. die **Badehose**, -n
17. die **Bluse**, -n
18. die **(Hand)tasche**, -n
19. die **Hose**, -n
20. die **Jacke**, -n
21. die **Jeans** (*sg. and pl.*)
22. die **Krawatte**, -n
23. die **Mütze**, -n
24. die **Shorts (die kurzen
    Hosen)**
25. die **Socke**, -n
26. die **(Sonnen)brille**, -n
27. die **Strumpfhose**, -n

For additional articles of clothing see Appendix C.

2. Was tragen⁺ die Leute? Beschreiben⁺ Sie, was eine der Personen auf dem Bild auf Seite 214 trägt oder auf einem Bild, das Sie mitgebracht haben. Ihre Partnerin/Ihr Partner soll Ihnen sagen, wen Sie beschrieben haben, und beschreibt Ihnen dann eine andere Person.

> *S1:* Diese Frau trägt einen Rock, eine ...
> *S2:* Das ist ...

3. Was tragen Sie? Beantworten Sie die Fragen erst selbst und fragen Sie dann Ihre Partnerin/Ihren Partner. Denken Sie daran, mit Ihrer Partnerin/Ihrem Partner **du** zu benutzen°.

Discussing clothes

use

1. Was tragen Sie im Winter? Im Sommer?
2. Was tragen Sie, wenn Sie in die Vorlesung gehen?
3. Was tragen Sie, wenn Sie tanzen gehen?
4. Was möchten Sie zum Geburtstag haben?
5. Welche Farben tragen Sie gern?

Expressing opinions and likes and dislikes

4. Wie gefällt es dir? Fragen Sie mehrere° Kursteilnehmer°, wie sie die Kleidungsstücke finden. Sie können dazu ein Bild aus diesem Buch nehmen oder Bilder von zu Hause mitbringen.

several / members of the class

> *S1:*
> Was hältst⁺ du von [dem Kleid]?
>
> *S2:*
> **[Das] muss furchtbar teuer sein.
> Was kostet [es]?**
> [Das] ist schön/toll/praktisch.
> [Das] sieht billig aus⁺.
> [Das] ist nichts Besonderes.

5. Wer ist das? Wählen Sie zusammen mit einer Partnerin/einem Partner eine Studentin/einen Studenten aus Ihrem Deutschkurs aus° und beschreiben Sie, was sie/er trägt. Die anderen Studenten sollen herausfinden, wen Sie beschreiben.

Wählen aus: choose

Vokabeln 2

Substantive

die **Antwort, -en**   answer
der **Arzt, ⸚e**/die **Ärztin, -nen**   doctor, physician
der **Chatroom, -s**   chat room
die **Disco, -s** (also **Disko**)   dance club
der **Führerschein, -e**   driver's license
das **Internetcafé, -s**   Internet café
das **Interview, -s**   interview
die **Karte, -n**   ticket; die **Theaterkarte, -n**   theater ticket
die **Kleidung**   clothing
die **Kneipe, -n**   bar, pub
das **Konzert, -e**   concert; **ins Konzert gehen**   to go to a concert

das **Krankenhaus, ⸚er**   hospital
das **Musical, -s**   musical
der **Reporter, -**/die **Reporterin, -nen**   reporter
die **Rockmusik**   rock (music)
die **Sache, -n**   thing; matter; **Sachen** *(pl.)* clothes
das **Stück, -e**   piece (of music); **Theaterstück**   play (theater)
die **Stunde, -n**   hour
das **Theater, -**   theater; **ins Theater gehen**   to go to the theater
For articles of clothing see page 214.

Verben

auf·stehen, ist aufgestanden   to get up; to stand up

aus·gehen, ist ausgegangen   to go out

aus·sehen (sieht aus), ausgesehen   to look like, seem

beschreiben, beschrieben   to describe

bleiben: ist geblieben

ein·laden (lädt ein), eingeladen   to invite

fahren: ist gefahren

feiern   to celebrate

gehen: ist gegangen

halten (hält), gehalten   to hold; **halten von**   to think of, have an opinion

interessieren   to interest

kennen lernen   to become acquainted with, to meet

schmecken   to taste; **der Käse schmeckt mir**   the cheese tastes good; **hat es geschmeckt?**   did it taste good? did you like it?

sehen: gesehen

spazieren fahren (fährt spazieren), ist spazieren gefahren   to go for a drive

tragen (trägt), getragen   to wear; to carry

tun (tut), getan   to do

werden: ist geworden   to become; **es wird kalt**   it's getting cold

Andere Wörter

ehrlich   honest

einander   one another, each other; **miteinander**   with each other

ewig   forever; eternally

frei: frei haben   to be off from work; **frei sein**   to be unoccupied

gesund   healthy

möglich   possible

offen   frank

passiv   passive

richtig   correct, right; proper

vor   ago; **vor zwei Wochen**   two weeks ago

zuerst   first, first of all, at first

Besondere Ausdrücke

am Computer arbeiten   to work at the computer

beim Chatten   while chatting

es ist nicht viel los   there's not much going on

 ### Leserunde

*Wolf Biermann is a poet, singer, and songwriter (**Liedermacher**) and one of the best known literary figures in Germany. He was born in 1936 in Hamburg. Because of his socialist beliefs, he emigrated to the German Democratic Republic in 1953. Due to his criticism of the communist regime there, however, he was forbidden to publish and perform. In 1982 the East German government allowed him to go to West Germany to perform, but did not allow him to return. Today he lives in Hamburg and remains a very controversial political and literary figure. In his song **Kleinstadt-sonntag**, Biermann uses everyday language in an everyday situation and brings us a subtle and ironic look at leisure time on Sunday.*

Kleinstadtsonntag

Gehn wir mal hin?
Ja, wir gehn mal hin.
Ist hier was los?
Nein, es ist nichts los.
5 Herr Ober[1], ein Bier!
Leer[2] ist es hier.
Der Sommer ist kalt.
Man wird auch alt.
Bei Rose gabs Kalb[3].
10 Jetzt isses[4] schon halb.
Jetzt gehn wir mal hin.
Ja, wir gehn mal hin.
Ist er schon drin[5]?
Er ist schon drin.
15 Gehn wir mal rein[6]?
Na gehn wir mal rein.
Siehst du heut fern?
Ja, ich sehe heut fern.
Spielen sie was?
20 Ja, sie spielen was.
Hast du noch Geld?
Ja, ich habe noch Geld.
Trinken wir ein'?
Ja, einen klein'.
25 Gehn wir mal hin?
Ja, gehn wir mal hin.
Siehst du heut fern?

Ja, ich sehe heut fern.

Wolf Biermann

[1]**Herr Ober:** *waiter* [2]*empty* [3]*veal for dinner* [4]**isses = ist es** [5]*inside* [6]*in*

Grammatik und Übungen

1 The present perfect tense°

das Perfekt

Ich **habe** mit Karin **gesprochen.**	I *have spoken* with Karin.
	I *spoke* with Karin.
Sie **ist** nach Hause **gegangen.**	She *has gone* home.
	She *went* home.

German has several past tenses. One of them is the present perfect tense, which is commonly used in conversation to refer to past actions or states.

The present perfect tense is made up of the present tense of the auxiliary **haben** or **sein** and the past participle of the verb. In independent clauses, the past participle is the last element. (For dependent clauses see section 10.)

Land und Leute

Das Theater

www Go to the *Deutsch heute* website at
http://college.hmco.com.

Theater in the German-speaking countries has a long tradition. The present system of theaters with resident staffs goes back to the eighteenth century. Many theaters were founded then by local rulers to provide entertainment for the court. Today there are more than 500 theaters in the German-speaking countries. In Germany, most of the theaters are repertory theaters under the jurisdiction of city governments (**Stadttheater**), some are under the jurisdiction of an individual state (**Staatstheater**), and some are private theaters (**Privattheater**).

In addition to the repertory theaters there are also many experimental theaters (**Freie Theatergruppen**). Some of the private theaters are small stages run in conjunction with a pub (**Kneipe** or **Wirtschaft**), which helps to finance the theater. Many theaters receive government subsidies for their productions. The repertory (**Spielplan**) of German-speaking theaters usually includes a variety of German and foreign plays. The top three playwrights performed in German-speaking theaters are Shakespeare, Goethe, and Brecht. The American author Neil Simon ranks tenth.

Was Sie in München im Theater sehen können.

Diskussion

Imagine that you are a member of a group trying to open a new theater in your community. What kind of financing could you get? Where would you locate the theater? What authors would you produce?

das Partizip Perfekt / das
regelmäßige schwache Verb

② Past participles° of regular weak verbs°

Infinitive	Past participle	Present perfect tense
spielen	ge + spiel + t	Tania **hat** gestern nicht **gespielt.**
arbeiten	ge + arbeit + et	Sie **hat gearbeitet.**

German verbs may be classified as weak or strong according to the way in which they form their past tenses. A German weak verb is a verb whose infinitive stem (**spiel-, arbeit-**) remains unchanged in the past tense forms.

In German, the past participle of a weak verb is formed by adding **-t** to the unchanged infinitive stem. The **-t** expands to **-et** in verbs whose stem ends in **-d** or **-t** (**arbeiten > gearbeitet**), and in some verbs whose stem ends in **-m** or **-n** (**regnen > geregnet**). Most weak verbs also add the prefix **ge-** in the past participle. In English, the past participle of corresponding verbs (called "regular" verbs) is formed by adding **-ed** to the stem, e.g., *play > played, work > worked.*

3 **Auxiliary *haben* with past participles**

ich **habe** etwas **gefragt**	wir **haben** etwas **gefragt**
du **hast** etwas **gefragt**	ihr **habt** etwas **gefragt**
er/es/sie **hat** etwas **gefragt**	sie **haben** etwas **gefragt**
Sie **haben** etwas **gefragt**	

The chart above shows how the present perfect tense of a weak verb is formed, using the auxiliary **haben.**

1. Wir haben es schon gehört. Ihre Freundin/Ihr Freund möchte anderen ein paar Neuigkeiten° erzählen. Sagen Sie Ihrer Freundin/Ihrem Freund, dass diese Leute die Neuigkeiten schon gehört haben.   pieces of news

➡ Frau Fischer   *Frau Fischer hat es schon gehört.*

1. Klaus
2. ich
3. Professor Weber
4. unsere Freunde
5. wir
6. Karin

2. Am Wochenende. Sabine erzählt vom Wochenende. Ergänzen Sie die Sätze. Benutzen Sie das Perfekt.

➡ Am Wochenende war sehr viel los. Am Freitagabend _____ Julian und ich Tennis _____ . (spielen)
   Am Freitagabend haben Julian und ich Tennis gespielt.

1. Du _____ mich _____ , was am Wochenende los war. (fragen)

2. Also, Bettina _____ am Samstag wieder _____ . (jobben)

3. Ich _____ heute Morgen für meine Matheklausur _____ , aber am Nachmittag nur _____ . (lernen/faulenzen) gefaulenzt

4. Am Sonntag _____ wir den Geburtstag meiner Mutter _____ . (feiern)

5. Meine Schwester _____ ihr wirklich schöne Blumen _____ . (schenken)

6. Vati _____ das ganze Essen _____ . (kochen)

7. _____ es wirklich gut _____ ? (schmecken)

8. Leider _____ es _____ . (regnen)

9. Aber es war eigentlich okay. Wir _____ Karten _____ . (spielen)

Past participles of irregular weak verbs°

Infinitive	Past participle	Present perfect tense
bringen	ge + brach + t	Wer **hat** die Blumen **gebracht?**
denken	ge + dach + t	Jens **hat** an den Wein **gedacht.**
kennen	ge + kann + t	Sie **hat** Thomas gut **gekannt.**
wissen	ge + wuss + t	Wir **haben** es **gewusst.**

A few weak verbs, including **bringen, denken, kennen,** and **wissen,** are irregular. They are called irregular weak verbs because the past participle has the prefix **ge-** and the ending **-t,** but the verb also undergoes a stem change. The past participles of irregular weak verbs are noted in the vocabularies as follows: **denken, gedacht.**

3. Alles vorbereitet. Sabine und Julian bereiten eine Party vor. Lesen Sie die Sätze und sagen Sie, was sie schon gemacht haben. Benutzen Sie das Perfekt.

➜ Julian denkt an alle Freunde.
Julian hat an alle Freunde gedacht.

1. Sabine denkt an den Wein.
2. Julian kennt ein gutes Weingeschäft.
3. Julian weiß Erikas Telefonnummer nicht.
4. Marion bringt Pizza mit.
5. Leila und Klaus bringen Mineralwasser mit.
6. Sabine kennt ein paar gute Musik-CDs.

denken aus: think up / weak

4. Was wollen Sie sagen? Denken Sie sich mit einer Partnerin/einem Partner eine Geschichte aus°. Benutzen Sie zehn schwache° Verben. Erzählen Sie im Perfekt.

arbeiten ■ brauchen ■ bringen ■ chatten ■ denken ■ faulenzen ■ feiern ■ fragen ■ glauben ■ hören ■ jobben ■ kaufen ■ kennen ■ kennen lernen ■ kochen ■ kosten ■ leben ■ lernen ■ machen ■ regnen ■ sagen ■ schenken ■ schneien ■ spielen ■ suchen ■ surfen ■ tanzen ■ wandern ■ warten ■ wissen ■ wohnen ■ zahlen ■ zelten

5 **Use of the present perfect tense**

In English, the present perfect tense and the simple past tense have different meanings.

What are you doing today?
Gerd has invited me to dinner (and I'm going this evening).

The present perfect tense (e.g., *has invited*) in English refers to a period of time that continues into the present and is thus still uncompleted.

What did you do today?
Gerd invited me to dinner (and I went).

The simple past tense (e.g., *invited*) in English, on the other hand, refers to a period of time that is completed at the moment of speaking.

Gerd hat mich zum Essen eingeladen. $\begin{cases} \text{Gerd has invited me to dinner.} \\ \text{Gerd invited me to dinner.} \end{cases}$

In German, the present perfect tense (e.g., **hat eingeladen**) refers to all actions or states in the past, whereas in English the simple past tense is used for completed actions and the present perfect tense for uncompleted actions. Context usually makes the meaning clear.

In German, the present perfect tense is most frequently used in conversation to refer to past actions or states, and is therefore often referred to as the "conversational past." German also has a simple past tense (see *Kapitel 10*) that is used to narrate connected events in the past, and which is, therefore, frequently called the "narrative past."

5. Ich hab' das nicht gewusst. Beantworten Sie die folgenden Fragen erst selbst und fragen Sie dann eine Partnerin/einen Partner. Denken Sie daran **du** zu benutzen.

Talking about the past

1. Wo hast du als° Kind gewohnt?   *as*
2. Wie viele Bücher hast du für deine Kurse gekauft?
3. Wie viel haben die Bücher gekostet?
4. Hast du dieses Semester schon viel Deutsch gelernt?
5. Bis wann hast du gestern Abend gearbeitet?
6. Wie hat das Essen gestern Abend geschmeckt?
7. Was hast du letzte Woche in deiner Freizeit gemacht?

6. Wie sagt man das? Geben Sie die folgenden Kurzdialoge auf Deutsch wieder und benutzen Sie das Perfekt.

➡   What did Erik say?   *Was hat Erik gesagt?*
    —I didn't hear it.   *—Ich habe es nicht gehört.*

1. Christel bought a jacket.
   — What did it cost?
2. Why didn't the men work yesterday?
   — It rained.
3. Why didn't Barbara buy the purse?
   — She didn't have any money.
4. Markus cooked the dinner last night.
   — Really? I didn't know that.
5. Who brought the wine?
   — I don't know. I didn't ask.

7. Hören Sie zu. Gisela und Alex sind an der Uni. Gisela hat eine Einkaufstasche und Alex will wissen, was Gisela gekauft hat. Hören Sie zu und geben Sie an, ob die Sätze unten richtig oder falsch sind. Sie hören vier neue Wörter: **pleite** *(broke [out of money])*; **du Armer** *(you poor thing)*; **neugierig** *(curious)*; **zum Spaß** *(for fun)*.

1. Alex hat viel Geld und will einkaufen gehen.
2. Gisela hat Schuhe gekauft.
3. Professor Huber hat zwei Bücher für das Seminar gekauft.
4. Gisela hat Alex einen Kalender gekauft.

Land und Leute

Feiertage

www Go to the *Deutsch heute* website at http://college.hmco.com.

Germans enjoy a minimum of nine legal, paid holidays per year. These holidays are days off in addition to vacation time. In some states, such as Bavaria, the people have twelve holidays. With the exception of some transportation facilities, some restaurants and recreational facilities, businesses in Germany must be closed on legal holidays.

Germany celebrates both secular and religious holidays. Among the secular holidays are New Year's Eve (**Silvester**), New Year's Day (**Neujahr**), and **Tag der Arbeit** on May 1, which is celebrated in honor of workers. The newest holiday is the national holiday, **Tag der deutschen Einheit** (Day of German Unity), celebrated on October 3 to commemorate the unification of East and West Germany in 1990.

The following Christian holidays are observed throughout the country: Good Friday (**Karfreitag**); Easter (**Ostern**—both **Ostersonntag** and **Ostermontag**); Ascension Day (**Christi Himmelfahrt**), the sixth Thursday after Easter; Pentecost (**Pfingsten**), the seventh Sunday and Monday after Easter; Christmas Eve (**Heiligabend**), and December 25 and 26 (**erster Weihnachtstag** and **zweiter Weihnachtstag**). Four other Christian holidays are observed in some states, but not all.

Prost Neujahr! – Feuerwerk in Mittenwald (Bayern).

Diskussion

1. Many countries around the world have a holiday to honor workers on May 1. Do some historical research and find out why this is a popular date for this holiday. Hint: An important event in the history of the union movement in the United States took place in May.
2. Do you think that it is a good idea for businesses to be closed on holidays? Why or why not?

6 Past participles of strong verbs°

das starke Verb

Infinitive	Past participle	Present perfect tense
sehen	ge + seh + en	Ich **habe** es **gesehen.**
finden	ge + fund + en	Ich **habe** es **gefunden.**
nehmen	ge + nomm + en	Ich **habe** es nicht **genommen.**

The past participle of a strong verb ends in **-en.** (Note the exception **getan.**) Most strong verbs also add the **ge-** prefix in the past participle. Many strong verbs have a stem vowel in the past participle (**gefunden**) that is different from that in the infinitive, and some verbs also have a change in the consonants (**genommen**). Past participles of strong verbs are noted in the vocabularies as follows: **schreiben, geschrieben.**

For a list of strong verbs, see #24 of the Grammatical Tables in Appendix F.

Infinitive	Past participle
halten	gehalten
schlafen	geschlafen
tragen	getragen
tun	getan

8. Pizza machen. Aylin und Songül sprechen über Mustafa. Ergänzen Sie die Sätze im Perfekt.

→ AYLIN: Warum _____ Mustafa heute so lange _____ ? (schlafen)
Warum hat Mustafa heute so lange geschlafen?

1. SONGÜL: Er _____ heute nicht viel _____ . (tun)

2. Er _____ nur eine Pizza _____ . (machen)

3. AYLIN: Was _____ die Freunde von seinem Plan _____ ? (halten)

4. SONGÜL: Sie _____ auch eine Pizza _____ . (machen)

5. Dann _____ sie die Pizzas zu den Nachbarn _____ . (tragen)

6. AYLIN: Was _____ die Nachbarn dann _____ ? (tun)

7. SONGÜL: Sie _____ die Pizzas natürlich _____ . (essen)

    Sie _____ gut _____ . (schmecken)

Infinitive	Past participle
geben	gegeben
lesen	gelesen
sehen	gesehen
essen	gegessen
liegen	gelegen
sitzen	gesessen

9. Ein Abend bei mir. Sie haben Klaus gestern Abend eingeladen. Erzählen Sie, was Sie gemacht haben. Benutzen Sie das Perfekt.

➔ Ein Buch über die Schweiz liegt da.   *Ein Buch über die Schweiz hat da gelegen.*

1. Was machst du mit dem Buch?
2. Ich gebe es Klaus.
3. Zuerst liest er das Buch.
4. Dann essen wir ein Wurstbrot°.   cold meat sandwich
5. Ich esse auch einen Apfel.
6. Später sehen wir einen Film im Fernsehen.

Infinitive	Past participle
nehmen	genommen
sprechen	gesprochen
treffen	getroffen
finden	gefunden
trinken	getrunken
leihen	geliehen
schreiben	geschrieben

 10. Was haben sie getan? Geben Sie die folgenden Kurzdialoge im Perfekt wieder.

➔ Nehmen Paul und Manuel den Zug?   *Haben Paul und Manuel den Zug genommen?*

  — Nein, ich leihe ihnen mein Auto.   *— Nein, ich habe ihnen mein Auto geliehen.*

1. Trinken Sie Kaffee?
   — Nein, ich nehme Tee.
2. Schreibst du die Karte?
   — Nein, ich finde sie nicht.
3. Sprechen Gerd und Susi mit euch Englisch?
   — Ja, wir finden das toll.

11. Mein Tag war langweilig/interessant. Sprechen Sie mit einer Partnerin/einem Partner oder in einer Gruppe darüber, was Sie in den letzten 24 Stunden gemacht haben. Benutzen Sie die Fragen. Dann entscheiden° Sie, welche Person den interessantesten und welche Person den langweiligsten Tag hatte. Wenn Sie Ihren Tag interessanter machen wollen, übertreiben° Sie ruhig ein bisschen! Erzählen Sie dann den anderen Studenten im Deutschkurs, was Sie gemacht haben.

decide

exaggerate

S1:
Hast du gut geschlafen?

S2:
Ja.
Nein, ich habe die ganze Nacht getanzt.

1. Bis wann hast du geschlafen?
2. Was hast du zum Frühstück gegessen?

3. Was hast du zum Frühstück getrunken?
4. Was für Kleidung hast du getragen?
5. Was hast du gelesen?
6. Wen hast du heute in der Uni gesehen?
7. Mit wem hast du heute gesprochen?

 7 **Separable-prefix verbs° in the present perfect tense**   das trennbare Verb

Infinitive	Past participle	Present perfect tense
anrufen	an + ge + rufen	Kirstin **hat** gestern **angerufen**.
einkaufen	ein + ge + kauft	Ingrid **hat** heute **eingekauft**.

The prefix **ge-** of the past participle comes between the separable prefix and the stem of the participle. Some separable-prefix verbs are weak; others are strong. In spoken German the separable prefix receives stress: **an′gerufen.** A list of some separable-prefix verbs you have encountered follows.

Infinitive	Past participle
anrufen	angerufen
aussehen	ausgesehen
durcharbeiten	durchgearbeitet
einkaufen	eingekauft
einladen	eingeladen
fernsehen	ferngesehen
mitbringen	mitgebracht
vorhaben	vorgehabt
zurückzahlen	zurückgezahlt

12. Studentenleben. Geben Sie die folgenden Kurzdialoge im Perfekt wieder.

→   Lädt Klaus für Samstag einige   *Hat Klaus für Samstag einige Freunde*
     Freunde ein?   *eingeladen?*
     — Natürlich. Er lädt alle seine   *— Natürlich. Er hat alle seine*
     Freunde ein.   *Freunde eingeladen.*

1. Kauft er auch Wein ein?
   — Na klar. Er kauft auch Käse, Wurst und Brot ein.
2. Bringen seine Freunde etwas mit?
   — Natürlich. Sie bringen viel mit.
3. Lädt Klaus auch Evi ein?
   — Ja, aber sie hat etwas vor.
4. Sieht sie fern?
   — Nein, sie arbeitet ihre Vorlesungsnotizen durch.

13. Wer hat was gemacht? Sagen Sie, was die Leute auf den Bildern gestern in ihrer Freizeit gemacht haben. Denken Sie sich Namen für die Personen aus°.

Vokabeln: am Computer arbeiten ■ einen Brief schreiben ■ fernsehen ■ im Supermarkt einkaufen ■ Spaghetti kochen ■ viel schlafen ■ Zeitung lesen

➤ *(Tina) hat die Zeitung gelesen.*

1.

2.

3.

4.

5.

6.

⑧ Past participles without the *ge-* prefix

■ *Verbs ending in* -ieren

Infinitive	Past participle	Present perfect tense
studieren	studiert	Dirk **hat** in München **studiert**.
interessieren	interessiert	Der Film **hat** mich nicht **interessiert**.

Verbs ending in **-ieren** do not have the prefix **ge-** in the past participle. They are always weak verbs whose participle ends in **-t.** These verbs are generally based on words borrowed from French and Latin; they are often similar to English verbs.

14. Worüber hat man diskutiert? Ergänzen Sie die Kurzdialoge im Perfekt.

➤ DIRK: Wo _____ du _____ , Katja? (studieren)
Wo hast du studiert, Katja?

KATJA: Ich _____ in München _____ . (studieren)
Ich habe in München studiert.

1. JÖRN: Mit wem _____ Gerd so lange _____ ? (telefonieren)

   KEVIN: Mit Laura. Er _____ ihr zum Geburtstag _____ . (gratulieren)

2. UTE: Dirk _____ mit seinem Freund über ein Problem _____ . (diskutieren)

   BETTINA: Schön. Aber warum _____ sie so lange _____ ? (diskutieren)

3. UTE: Die Professoren _____ wieder für mehr Mathematik _____ .
   (plädieren°)   plead

   CARSTEN: Die Studenten _____ wieder gegen diesen Plan _____ , nicht
   wahr? (protestieren)

■ *Verbs with inseparable prefixes°*   das untrennbare Verb

Infinitive	Past participle	Present perfect tense
beantworten	beantwortet	Du **hast** meine Frage nicht **beantwortet**.
bekommen	bekommen	Ich **habe** nichts **bekommen**.
besuchen	besucht	Paul **hat** seine Tante **besucht**.
bezahlen	bezahlt	Wer **hat** das **bezahlt**?
erklären	erklärt	Ich **habe** es schon **erklärt**.
erzählen	erzählt	Erik **hat** es **erzählt**.
gefallen	gefallen	**Hat** es dir **gefallen**?
gehören	gehört	Wem **hat** diese alte Uhr **gehört**?
gewinnen	gewonnen	Wer **hat** das Fußballspiel **gewonnen**?
vergessen	vergessen	Ich **habe** seinen Namen **vergessen**.
versuchen	versucht	**Hast** du wirklich alles **versucht**?

Some prefixes are never separated from the verb stem. These prefixes are **be-,**
emp-, ent-, er-, ge-, ver-, and **zer-.** Inseparable-prefix verbs do not add the prefix
ge- in the past participle. Some inseparable-prefix verbs are weak; others are
strong.

An inseparable prefix is not stressed in spoken German: **bekom′men.**

15. Petras Reise° in die Schweiz. Petra hat eine Reise in die Schweiz gemacht.   trip
Erzählen Sie von ihrer Reise und geben Sie jeden Satz im Perfekt wieder.

→ Petra erzählt von ihren Ferien. *Petra hat von ihren Ferien erzählt.*

1. Sie bezahlt die Reise selbst.
2. Die Schweiz gefällt Petra sehr.
3. Sie besucht da Freunde.
4. Sie bekommt da auch guten Käse.
5. Ein Schweizer erklärt ihr vieles.
6. Er erzählt viel Lustiges°.   amusing things

⑨ Auxiliary *sein* with past participles

ich **bin gekommen**	wir **sind gekommen**
du **bist gekommen**	ihr **seid gekommen**
er/es/sie **ist gekommen**	sie **sind gekommen**
Sie **sind gekommen**	

Some verbs use **sein** instead of **haben** as an auxiliary in the present perfect.

Warum **ist** Silke so früh **aufgestanden?**   Why did Silke get up so early?
Sie **ist** nach Freiburg **gefahren.**   She drove to Freiburg.

Verbs that require **sein** must meet two conditions. They must:

1. be intransitive verbs (verbs without a direct object) and
2. indicate a change in condition (e.g., **aufstehen**) or motion to or from a place (e.g., **fahren**).

Infinitive		Past participle
aufstehen		aufgestanden
fahren		gefahren
fliegen	ist	geflogen
gehen		gegangen
kommen		gekommen

Infinitive		Past participle
laufen		gelaufen
schwimmen		geschwommen
wandern	ist	gewandert
werden		geworden

Wer **ist** wieder so lange bei Helmut **geblieben?**	Who stayed so late at Helmut's again?
Ich **bin** es nicht **gewesen.**	It wasn't I.

The verbs **bleiben** and **sein** require **sein** as an auxiliary in the present perfect tense, even though they do not indicate a change in condition or motion to or from a place.

Wie **war** der Kaffee?	How was the coffee?
Der Kuchen **war** gut.	The cake was good.

The simple past tense of **sein (war)** is used more commonly than the present perfect tense of **sein (ist gewesen),** even in conversation.

Deutsche Bahn **DB**

Lieber[1] clever gefahren
als dumm gelaufen.

Das StadtTicket.

[1]*rather, better*

Richtig oder falsch?

Die Füße sind kaputt, weil der Mann mit der Bahn gefahren ist.
Ein intelligenter Mann fährt mit der Bahn und läuft nicht.
Mit dem StadtTicket kann man mit der Bahn fahren und muss nicht laufen.

16. So war es. Ergänzen Sie die Kurzdialoge im Perfekt.

→ JÖRG: Sag mal, Bettina, _____ du mit dem Auto _____ ?
(fahren) *Sag mal, Bettina, bist du mit dem Auto gefahren?*

→ BETTINA: Nein, ich _____ _____ .
(fliegen) *Nein, ich bin geflogen.*

1. LIANE: _____ du nach Österreich _____ , Tim? (fahren)

   TIM: Nein, ich _____ auch in den Ferien zu Hause _____ . (bleiben)

2. HERR LEHMANN: _____ Müllers auch schwimmen _____ ? (gehen)

   FRAU LEHMANN: Ja, aber sie _____ erst° später _____ . (kommen)   only

3. MUTTI: Warum _____ ihr nicht schwimmen _____ ? (gehen)

   KINDER: Es _____ zu kalt _____ . (werden)

4. INA: _____ du auch in den Ferien jeden Tag so früh _____ ? (aufstehen)

   STEFFI: Ja, ich _____ mit meinem Hund im Park _____ . (laufen)

17. Hören Sie zu. Stefan hat ein kurzes Interview mit einem Freizeitmagazin. Die Reporterin ist eine alte Schulfreundin von Stefan und will herausfinden, was ein typischer Student in seiner Freizeit macht. Geben Sie an, was Stefan gesagt hat. Sie hören einen neuen Ausdruck: **Du hast Recht** *(You're right)*.

1. Stefan hat Ulrike schon lange nicht mehr gesehen.
2. Stefan ist in die Vorlesung gegangen.
3. Stefan hat eine Prüfung geschrieben.
4. Stefan will nächstes Jahr in Finnland Kajak fahren.
5. Stefan hat viele E-Mails geschrieben.
6. Stefan hat Freunde in der Disco gesehen.
7. Stefan isst jeden Tag Pizza.
8. Stefan hat viel Kaffee getrunken.

18. Frage-Ecke. Sprechen Sie mit Ihrer Partnerin/Ihrem Partner darüber°,   about was Evi, Dirk, Stefan, Silke, Sie und Ihre Partnerin/Ihr Partner am Wochenende gemacht haben. Die Informationen für *S2* finden Sie im Anhang (Appendix B).

S1: Was hat Evi gemacht?
S2: Evi ist spazieren gegangen und hat einen Roman gelesen.

S1:

	Evi	Dirk	Stefan	Silke	ich	Partnerin/Partner
im Restaurant essen				X		
spazieren gehen						
fernsehen						
Rad fahren		X				
faulenzen		X				
in die Kneipe gehen						
einen Roman lesen				X		
mit Freunden telefonieren						

Talking about past activities

denken ... aus: think up your own questions

 19. Was haben Sie gemacht? Sprechen Sie mit Ihrer Partnerin/Ihrem Partner darüber, was Sie beide gemacht haben. Benutzen Sie die Fragen oder denken Sie sich Ihre eigenen Fragen aus°.

- Wann bist du gestern aufgestanden? Am Sonntag?
- Wohin bist du nach dem Frühstück gegangen? Oder bist du [zu Hause/im Studentenheim] geblieben?
- Wo hast du gestern Abend gegessen?
- Was hast du gestern Abend getrunken?
- Wann bist du heute zur Uni gefahren?
- Wie viele Vorlesungen hast du gehabt?
- Wann bist du gestern wieder nach Hause gegangen?
- Was hast du im Fernsehen gesehen?
- Was hast du letzte Woche gekauft?
- Wann bist du am Samstag ins Bett gegangen?

10 Dependent clauses in the present perfect tense

> Silke erzählt, dass sie gestern einen guten Film gesehen **hat.**
> Sie sagt, dass sie mit Freunden ins Kino gegangen **ist.**

In a dependent clause, the present-tense form of the auxiliary verb **haben** or **sein** follows the past participle and is the last element in the clause.

20. Neugierig *(curious).* Ihre Freundin/Ihr Freund möchte viel über Nicole wissen. Beantworten Sie ihre/seine Fragen mit den Sätzen in Klammern. Beginnen Sie jeden Satz mit **weil.**

trip

➡ Warum hat Nicole im Sommer keine Reise° gemacht? (Sie hat bei einer Computerfirma gearbeitet.)
Weil sie bei einer Computerfirma gearbeitet hat.

1. Warum hat Nicole in den Ferien gearbeitet? (Sie hat das Geld fürs Studium gebraucht.)
2. Warum hat sie so viel Geld gebraucht? (Alles ist so teuer geworden.)
3. Warum ist sie in die Buchhandlung gegangen? (Sie hat ein Buch gesucht.)
4. Warum hat sie dieses Buch gekauft? (Es hat ihr gefallen.)

language
5. Warum hat sie Deutsch gelernt? (Sie hat die Sprache° interessant gefunden.)
6. Warum ist sie noch nicht nach Deutschland gefahren? (Sie hat nicht genug Geld gehabt.)

Ruf doch mal an!

Die Telefon-Information für Österreich-Reisende

So einfach ist es, zu Hause anzurufen:
Von allen öffentlichen[1] Telefonen. Ausgenommen[2] sind Ortsmünztelefone[3].

[1]*public* [2]*excluded* [3]*local coin telephones*

Der deutsche Film

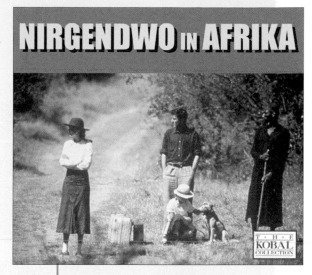

Caroline Link bekommt für *Nirgendwo in Afrika* den Oscar 2003 für den besten ausländischen Film.

Going to the movies is a favorite pastime of people in the German-speaking countries. Movies were invented over 100 years ago. Some of the earliest film premieres were in Germany. In Berlin in 1885 Max and Emil Skladanowsky produced a seven-minute film which is still in existence. The German movie industry flourished during the era of silent films and early "talkies" (1919–1932). Directors like Fritz Lang, F. W. Murnau, and F. W. Pabst were considered among the finest in the world, and the German use of the "moving camera" influenced many directors.

During the Nazi era (1933–1945), many great German and Austrian filmmakers emigrated to the United States and other countries. Some of them never returned; this loss led to a period of mediocrity in German filmmaking that lasted until the mid-sixties. At that point a generation of young filmmakers began to introduce the New German Cinema (**Neuer deutscher Film**). Those directors, many of them now famous, include Werner Herzog, Wim Wenders, Wolfgang Petersen, and the late Rainer Werner Fassbinder. Since then, despite the fact that the majority of films shown in German movie theaters today are American, with dubbed voices, other German directors such as Margarethe von Trotta, Volker Schlöndorff, Doris Dörrie, Percy Adlon, Tom Twyker, and Caroline Link have gained international recognition.

Three of these leading German filmmakers are women. Margarethe von Trotta (b. 1942) now resides in Italy, but her films are "German" with German themes. Her film *Das Versprechen* (The Promise) opened the 45th **Internationale Filmfestspiele** in Berlin in 1995. Doris Dörrie (b. 1955) made a name for herself with her early movie *Männer* and continues to fulfill her promise with other films such as *Bin ich schön* (1998) and *Nackt* (Naked) (2002). Caroline Link (b. 1964) directed *Nirgendwo in Afrika* (Nowhere in Africa), which won the American Academy Award for best foreign language film in 2003. It was the highest grossing German film in 2002 and received German Film Awards for Best Film and Best Director.

www Go to the *Deutsch heute* website at http://college.hmco.com.

Diskussion

Many people from German-speaking countries or of German heritage have been successful in the American movie industry. See if you can find information about one of the following people: Marlene Dietrich, Billy Wilder, Nastassja Kinski, Leonardo DiCaprio, Wolfgang Petersen, Fritz Lang.

21. Bildgeschichte. Erzählen Sie, was Steffi am Montag gemacht hat. Schreiben Sie zu jedem Bild einen oder zwei Sätze im Perfekt.

1.

2.

3.

4.

5.

6.

7.

Wiederholung

1. Rollenspiel. Sie sind Bedienung° in einem Café und heute ist Ihr erster Tag. Ihre Partnerin/Ihr Partner ist der Gast und ist nicht sehr zufrieden° mit dem Service. Sie antworten mit Entschuldigungen° auf ihre/seine Aussagen.

waitress/waiter
satisfied
apologies

Redemittel: sich entschuldigen *(apologizing)*		
Bitte entschuldigen Sie mich.	Entschuldigen Sie.	Entschuldigung°.
Es tut mir Leid, aber ...	Leider nicht.	Verzeihung°.
Das habe ich nicht so gemeint°.	Das wollte ich nicht.	

Excuse me.
Pardon me.
meant

1. Bedienung, ich warte schon zwanzig Minuten. Kann ich jetzt endlich°   finally
bestellen°, bitte?   order
2. Gibt es denn heute keinen Apfelkuchen?
3. Ich möchte bitte Karameleis. Haben Sie das?
4. Autsch, jetzt haben Sie mir Kaffee auf die Hose geschüttet°.   poured
5. Seien Sie nicht so hektisch!
6. Ich finde den Service hier wirklich nicht besonders gut.
7. Kann ich jetzt bitte endlich bezahlen? Ich warte schon seit einer halben
Stunde.

2. Das gefällt ihnen nicht. Sie suchen Geschenke für Ihre Freundinnen/
Freunde. Sandra möchte Ihnen helfen° Bücher, CDs und Videos für sie   help
auszusuchen. Beantworten Sie ihre Fragen mit *nein*.

➡ Liest Kevin gern klassische Literatur?
Nein, klassische Literatur gefällt ihm nicht.
➡ Liest Claudia gern Krimis?
Nein, Krimis gefallen ihr nicht.

1. Hört Anna gern klassische Musik?
2. Hört Benjamin gern Rockmusik?
3. Sieht Marion gern Actionfilme?
4. Sehen Hans und Lisa gern Dokumentarfilme?
5. Liest Alex gern Romane?
6. Und du: Hörst du gern Jazz?
       Liest du gern Liebesromane?
       Siehst du gern alte Filme?

3. Frank hat Freunde zum Essen eingeladen. Erzählen Sie über Frank und
ergänzen Sie die fehlenden° Präpositionen.   missing

1. Frank lebt _____ zwei Monaten in Bremen.

2. Er arbeitet _____ einer amerikanischen Firma.

3. _____ Samstag hat er einige Freunde _____ Essen eingeladen.

4. Am Wochenende kommen seine Freunde oft _____ ihm.

5. Sie sind _____ zwölf gekommen.

6. Frank hat _____ seine Freunde einen Fisch gegrillt.

7. _____ dem Wein trinken sie eine ganze Flasche°.   bottle

8. Der Wein kommt _____ Italien.

9. _____ dem Essen gehen sie _____ einem Fußballspiel.

4. Pizza oder Spaghetti? Beschreiben Sie, wie Renate ein Essen für ihre
Freunde vorbereitet hat. Benutzen Sie das Perfekt und die folgenden Wörter.

1. Renate / einladen / am Samstag / Freunde / zum Essen
2. sie / machen / eine Pizza
3. sie / haben / keinen Käse // und / ihre Freundin Monika / laufen / zu /
Supermarkt
4. die Pizza / aussehen / ein bisschen schwarz
5. dann / sie / kochen / Spaghetti

5. Wie sagt man das?

1. — Why did you come by bus?
   — My car is broken down.
   — I'm sorry.
2. — Did you like Denmark?
   — Yes. We hiked a lot.
   — Did you camp (in a tent)?
   — No. It rained too much. We slept at friends' (houses).
3. — Would you like a piece (of) cake?
   — Gladly. I'm hungry.
   — How does it taste?
   — Very good.

6. Fragen über die Uni. Was hat David über das Studium in Deutschland herausgefunden? Verbinden Sie die Sätze mit den Konjunktionen in Klammern.

1. David hat viele Fragen. (weil) Er möchte in Deutschland studieren.
2. Er studiert vielleicht vier Semester dort. (wenn) Die Uni ist nicht zu teuer.
3. Nicole sagt ... (dass) Es kostet nichts.
4. Dann studiert er. (wenn) Er kann einen Studentenjob finden.
5. Nicole sagt ... (dass) Es gibt leider wenige Studentenjobs.

7. Rollenspiel. Ihre Partnerin/Ihr Partner ist gestern Abend mit einer Freundin/einem Freund ausgegangen. Fragen Sie sie/ihn, was sie gemacht haben.

8. Zum Schreiben

various/choose

1. Jörg und Anja sprechen über verschiedene° Themen. Wählen° Sie eins von den Themen und schreiben Sie ein Gespräch zwischen Jörg und Anja.

   das Wetter ▪ einkaufen ▪ die Vorlesung ▪ Ferien
   ▪ eine Seminararbeit vorbereiten ▪ das Essen ▪ das Wochenende

diary

2. Schreiben Sie eine Woche lang ein Tagebuch° auf Deutsch. Schreiben Sie auf, was Sie jeden Tag gemacht haben. Sie können die folgenden Verben benutzen:

   arbeiten ▪ aufstehen ▪ besuchen ▪ fernsehen ▪ gehen ▪ kaufen
   ▪ lernen ▪ spielen ▪ sprechen (mit)

Hier gibt es Sachen für den neuen Mann. (Stuttgart)

3. Stellen Sie sich vor°, dass Sie ein Jahr lang an einer Universität in Deutschland studieren. Schreiben Sie einen Brief an eine Freundin oder einen Freund in Deutschland und beschreiben Sie die letzten paar Wochen. Mögliche Themen sind: das Wetter, die Kurse, Leute, die° Sie jetzt kennen, Freizeitaktivitäten wie Sport, Fernsehen, Musik, Konzerte, Kneipen, Filme.

stellen vor: imagine

whom

Hinweise: After you have completed the writing assignment, check over your work, paying particular attention to the following:

- agreement between subject and verb
- gender and case of all nouns and pronouns (see all chapters, especially *Einführung, Kapitel 3, 5*)
- choice of prepositions and correct case used with the prepositions (see *Kapitel 3* and *5*)
- choice of auxiliary verb in the present perfect tense (see this chapter)
- word order in sentences with dependent and independent clauses (see *Kapitel 5*)
- word order in sentences with the present perfect tense (see this chapter)

Grammatik: Zusammenfassung

The present perfect tense

Hast du gestern Abend **ferngesehen?**   Did you watch TV last night?
Nein, ich **bin** ins Kino **gegangen.**   No, I went to the movies.

The German present perfect tense, like the English present perfect, is a compound tense. It is made up of the present tense of the auxiliary **haben** or **sein** and the past participle. In independent clauses, the past participle is in final position. (For dependent clauses, see below.)

Past participles of regular weak verbs

Infinitive	Past participle	Present perfect tense
sagen	ge + sag + t	Er **hat** es **gesagt.**
arbeiten	ge + arbeit + et	Sie **hat** schwer **gearbeitet.**
baden°	ge + bad + et	Er **hat** gestern nicht **gebadet.**
regnen	ge + regn + et	Es **hat** gestern **geregnet.**

to bathe

The past participle of a weak verb is formed by adding **-t** to the unchanged infinitive stem. The **-t** expands to **-et** in verbs like **arbeiten, baden,** and **regnen.** In the past participle, most weak verbs also have the prefix **ge-.**

Past participles of irregular weak verbs

Infinitive	Past participle	Present perfect tense
bringen	ge + brach + t	Wer **hat** das **gebracht?**
denken	ge + dach + t	Sie **hat** nicht an die Zeit **gedacht.**
kennen	ge + kann + t	Sie **hat** deinen Freund gut **gekannt.**
wissen	ge + wuss + t	Sie **hat** es **gewusst.**

A few weak verbs are irregular. The past participle has the prefix **ge-** and the ending **-t;** there is also a change in the stem vowel and in the consonants of several verbs.

Past participles of strong verbs

Infinitive	Past participle	Present perfect tense
nehmen	ge + nomm + en	Ich **habe** das Brot **genommen.**
essen	ge + gess + en	Ich **habe** heute wenig **gegessen.**
tun	ge + ta + n	Ich **habe** das nicht **getan.**

The past participle of a strong verb ends in **-en.** (Note the exception **getan.**) Most strong verbs also add the **ge-** prefix in the past participle. Many strong verbs have a stem vowel of the past participle that is different from that of the infinitive, and some verbs also have a change in the consonants.

For a list of strong verbs, see #24 of the Grammatical Tables in Appendix F.

Past participles of separable-prefix verbs

Infinitive	Past participle	Present perfect tense
aufhören	auf + **ge** + hört	Lisa **hat** mit der Arbeit **aufgehört.**
anrufen	an + **ge** + rufen	Gerd **hat** sie **angerufen.**

The prefix **ge-** of the past participle comes between the separable prefix and the stem of the participle. Some separable-prefix verbs are weak (e.g., **aufhören**); others are strong (e.g., **anrufen**).

Past participles without the *ge-* prefix
■ *Verbs ending in* -ieren

Present tense	Present perfect tense
Jutta **studiert** in Heidelberg.	Jutta **hat** in Heidelberg **studiert.**
Jens **repariert** sein Auto.	Jens **hat** sein Auto **repariert.**

Verbs ending in **-ieren** do not have the prefix **ge-** in the past participle. They are always weak verbs whose participle ends in **-t.** These verbs are generally based on words borrowed from French and Latin; they are often similar to English verbs.

Musiker proben.

■ *Verbs with inseparable prefixes*

Present tense	Present perfect tense
Birgit **erzählt** von ihrer Arbeit.	Sie **hat** von ihrer Arbeit **erzählt.**
Sie **bekommt** einen neuen Computer.	Sie **hat** einen neuen Computer **bekommen.**

Some prefixes are never separated from the verb stem. These prefixes are **be-, emp-, ent-, er-, ge-, ver-,** and **zer-.** Inseparable-prefix verbs do not add the prefix **ge-** in the past participle. Some inseparable-prefix verbs are weak (e.g., **erzählen**); others are strong (e.g., **bekommen**).

Use of the auxiliary *haben*

| Christine **hat** heute schwer **gearbeitet.** | Christine worked hard today. |
| Sie **hat** ein Referat **geschrieben.** | She wrote a report. |

Haben is used to form the present perfect tense of most verbs.

Use of the auxiliary *sein*

| Schmidts **sind** spät nach Hause **gekommen.** | The Schmidts came home late. |
| Sie **sind** dann spät **aufgestanden.** | Then they got up late. |

The auxiliary **sein** is used to form the present perfect tense of intransitive verbs (i.e., verbs that do not have a direct object) when these verbs denote a change in condition (e.g., **aufstehen**) or motion to or from a place (e.g., **kommen**).

| Warum **bist** du so lange **geblieben?** | Why did you stay so long? |
| Es **ist** so schön **gewesen.** | It was so nice. |

The intransitive verbs **bleiben** and **sein** require the auxiliary **sein,** even though they do not indicate a change in condition or motion to or from a place.

Verbs using the auxiliary *sein*

You have already encountered some verbs that take the auxiliary **sein** in the present perfect tense. They are shown in the table below.

Infinitive	Auxiliary	Past participle
aufstehen	ist	aufgestanden
bleiben	ist	geblieben
fahren	ist	gefahren
fliegen	ist	geflogen
gehen	ist	gegangen
kommen	ist	gekommen
laufen	ist	gelaufen
schwimmen	ist	geschwommen
sein	ist	gewesen
wandern	ist	gewandert
werden	ist	geworden

Use of the present perfect tense in dependent clauses

Klaus sagt, dass David ihm eine Karte geschrieben **hat.**
Er sagt, dass David nach Österreich gefahren **ist.**

In a dependent clause, the auxiliary **haben** or **sein** follows the past participle and is the last element in the clause, because it is the finite verb.

Andere Länder— andere Sitten

In Deutschland ist Radfahren eine beliebte Freizeitbeschäftigung. (Berlin)

LERNZIELE

Sprechintentionen

Making plans and preparations
Discussing and scheduling
   household chores
Seeking information about someone
Expressing agreement and
   disagreement
Discussing cultural differences

Lesestück

Ein Austauschstudent in
   Deutschland

Land und Leute

Munich
Pedestrian zones
Freunde vs. *Bekannte*
Homes and apartments in German-
   speaking countries
Closed doors
Eating at home and as a guest
Germans in the U.S.A.

Vokabeln

Household chores
Furniture
Kitchen appliances

Grammatik

Hin and *her*
Verbs *legen/liegen, stellen/stehen,*
   setzen/sitzen, hängen, stecken
Two-way prepositions
Special meanings of prepositions
Time expressions in dative and
   accusative
Da-compounds
Wo-compounds
Indirect questions

239

Bausteine für Gespräche

München im Sommer

Peter besucht seine Freundin Christine in München.

PETER: Was machst du nach der Vorlesung? Musst du in die Bibliothek?

CHRISTINE: Nein, ich habe Zeit. Sollen wir nicht mal in einen typisch bayerischen Biergarten gehen? Bei dem Wetter können wir doch schön draußen sitzen.

PETER: Au ja, gern. Im Englischen Garten?

CHRISTINE: Hmmm. Dort gibt es natürlich einige Biergärten, aber dort sind immer so viele Touristen. Außerdem ist es dort ziemlich teuer. Ich bin im Moment etwas pleite.

PETER: Macht nichts. Ich lade dich ein. Wenn ich schon in München bin, möchte ich doch in den Englischen Garten gehen!

Fragen

1. Muss Christine nach der Vorlesung arbeiten?
2. Welche Idee hat Christine?
3. Was hält Peter davon?
4. Warum möchte Christine zuerst nicht in den Englischen Garten?
5. Was sagt Peter dazu⁺?

Vorbereitungen für ein Fest

MONIKA: Sag, willst du nicht endlich mal das Wohnzimmer aufräumen? Da liegen überall deine Bücher herum.

STEFAN: Muss das sein?

MONIKA: Klar, wir müssen das Essen vorbereiten und den Tisch decken. In einer Stunde kommen die Leute.

STEFAN: Was? Schon in einer Stunde? Du meine Güte! Und wir müssen noch Staub saugen, Staub wischen, abwaschen, abtrocknen, die Küche sieht aus wie ...

MONIKA: Jetzt red nicht lange, sondern mach schnell. Ich helf' dir ja.

Fragen

1. Warum soll Stefan das Wohnzimmer aufräumen?
2. Wann kommen die Gäste?
3. Was müssen Monika und Stefan noch machen?

Land und Leute

München

www Go to the *Deutsch heute* website at
http://college.hmco.com.

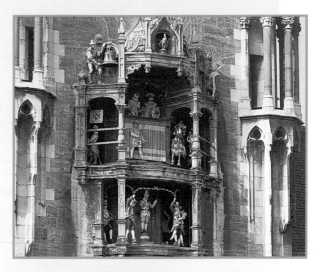
Das Münchner Glockenspiel

Munich (**München**), the capital of Bavaria (**Bay-ern**), is called **die Weltstadt mit Herz** (the world city with a heart). No doubt many of the six million people who visit the **Oktoberfest** each year in September can attest to the appropriateness of this nickname. Not only foreign tourists visit Munich. It is also the most popular domestic vacation destination for Germans. The **Marienplatz** is the location of several world-famous sights, including the **Hofbräuhaus** as well as the **Glockenspiel** on the **Neues Rathaus** (New City Hall).

Munich is more than a tourist attraction; it is also a dynamic center of business, commerce, science, and culture with 1.4 million residents, of whom 23% are foreigners. Founded in 1158, Munich got its name from the phrase **"bei den Mönchen"** (home of the monks). It quickly became the residence of the Wittelsbach family, who ruled Bavaria until 1918. Munich has been a center of education and science since the sixteenth century, and today it has three universities and five **Hochschulen,** among them the Munich **Hochschule für Film und Fernsehen.** Munich has become a center for media industries (movies, television, advertising, and music). Since 1983, the Munich Film Festival has attracted some 60,000 visitors each year to its screenings of international films and student productions. Munich is also a center for the financial industry, high-tech industries, and biotechnology.

The city offers a wide variety of museums and parks, including the well-known **Englischer Garten.** Among the most famous museums are the **Alte Pinakothek,** which possesses one of the most important collections of European paintings from the fourteenth through the eighteenth centuries, and the **Neue Pinakothek,** devoted to nineteenth century art. The **Deutsches Museum** has exhibitions on science and history, and for car fans, there is the BMW museum. If these museums are too conventional, the Center for Unusual Museums is also located in Munich. The Olympia Park, site of the 1972 Olympic Games, is another popular attraction.

Munich has excellent public transportation. One can also tour the city by bicycle or on skates. There is even a city map specifically for in-line skaters.

In a study of 83 German cities sponsored in 2001 by the magazine *Hörzu,* Munich was named the most attractive. Criteria considered were safety, work, education, living conditions, health, environment, leisure time activities, and culture.

Diskussion

1. Every region has its own specialties. See what you can find out about the following Bavarian specialties: **Brezel, Kalbshaxe, Semmelknödel, Weißwurst.**
2. A walking tour of downtown Munich beginning at the **Marienplatz** takes about two hours. Because most of this area is a pedestrian mall, you cannot drive past the sights. Would you rather walk, ride a bike, or go in-line skating for sightseeing? Why?

Brauchbares

1. The **Englischer Garten,** with its 373 hectares (921,683 acres), one of the largest urban parks in the world, was created in 1789 on a former hunting ground. On nice days it is very busy with people sunbathing, boating on the lake, horseback riding, bicycling, strolling, or visiting one of the beer gardens. Munich's surfers meet to go river surfing on the Isar, which flows nearby. Or, you can board one of the traditional wooden rafts and allow yourself to be carried toward the city center as the Isar boatmen used to do. The close proximity of the Garden to the Ludwig-Maximilians-Universität makes it popular with students.

2. **Englischer Garten/im Englischen Garten.** In German, adjectives that precede nouns take various endings depending on the gender and case of the noun. Thus, **Englischer Garten** is nominative and **im Englischen Garten** is dative. The treatment of adjectives is discussed in *Kapitel 8.*

3. Christine suggests going to a beer garden. Outdoor cafés and restaurants are very common in German-speaking countries. Even restaurants at rest stops on the **Autobahn** have patios so patrons can eat outside. The moderate climate of the summers lends itself to pleasant outdoor dining.

4. Monika's last sentence is **"Ich helf' dir ja."** In colloquial German the ending **e** is often dropped from the verb in the **ich**-form. **Ja** is a flavoring particle here.

fellow student

1. Was machst du? Eine Kursteilnehmerin/ein Kursteilnehmer° möchte etwas machen und fragt, was Ihre Pläne zu bestimmten Zeiten sind.

Making plans

S1:		S2:	
Was machst du	**nach der Vorlesung?**	Ich gehe	**in einen Biergarten.**
	nach dem Seminar?		in die Bibliothek.
	heute Nachmittag?		ins Café.
	am Wochenende?		ein Video ausleihen.
			nach Hause.

Ich treffe [Michael]	**im Café.**
	in einem Biergarten.
	in der Bibliothek.

Täglich ab
10 Uhr
Frühstück, Café,
Restaurant
und im Sommer
Biergarten
zwischen Uni,
Unisee und
Stadtwald.

HAUS AM WALDE
CAFÉ · BIERGARTEN · RESTAURANT
KUHGRABENWEG 2 · TEL. 0421/21 27 65

Was kann man im „Haus am Walde" machen?
Wo ist das „Haus am Walde"?
Ab wann kann man im „Haus am Walde" frühstücken?

2. Ein Fest. Ein Freund/Eine Freundin hat Sie zu einem Fest eingeladen.   *Preparing for a party*
Fragen Sie, was geplant ist und was Sie mitbringen sollen.

S1:
Was macht ihr auf
   dem Fest?

S2:
Wir | **tanzen.**
     | hören Musik.
     | essen viel.
     | reden viel.
     | schauen[+] ein Video an.

Was soll ich zu dem
   Fest mitbringen?

Bring doch | **die Bilder von**
           | **deiner Ferienreise[+]** | mit.
etwas zu | **essen**
         | trinken
ein paar | **Flaschen[+] Cola**
         | CDs
         | Videos
         | DVDs

Erweiterung des Wortschatzes

Hausarbeit

die Spülmaschine
einräumen

den Tisch decken

Geschirr spülen

abtrocknen

das Bad putzen

die Spülmaschine
ausräumen

die Küche sauber
machen

Staub wischen

Staub saugen

die Wäsche waschen

Diese Studenten aus Hannover feiern ein Fest.

several

Talking about household chores

1. Hausarbeit. Fragen Sie mehrere° Kursteilnehmer und finden Sie heraus, welche Hausarbeiten sie zu Hause machen und welche sie nicht machen. Benutzen Sie die Bilder. Weitere Wörter finden Sie im Anhang (Supplementary Word Sets, „Chores," Appendix C).

> *S1:* Welche Arbeiten machst du zu Hause?
> *S2:* Ich räume die Spülmaschine ein.
> *S1:* Welche Arbeiten machst du nicht?
> *S2:* Ich sauge nicht Staub.

stellen auf: draw up

Scheduling chores

2. Frage-Ecke. Sie und Ihre Partnerin/Ihr Partner stellen den Plan für die Hausarbeit am Wochenende auf°. Sagen Sie, was Julia, Lukas, Alex, Lena, Sie und Ihre Partnerin/Ihr Partner am Freitag und Samstag machen. Die Informationen für *S2* finden Sie im Anhang (Appendix B).

> *S1:* Was macht Julia am Freitag?
> *S2:* Sie kocht das Abendessen.

S1:

	Freitag	Samstag
Julia		das Wohnzimmer aufräumen
Lukas	das Abendessen kochen	
Alex		die Küche sauber machen
Lena	abwaschen	
ich		
Partnerin/ Partner		

Vokabeln 1

Substantive

das **Bad, ¨-er**   bath; bathroom
der **Biergarten, ¨-**   beer garden
die **Cola, -s**   cola drink
die **Ferienreise, -n**   vacation trip
das **Fest, -e**   party; celebration; feast;
 auf dem Fest   at the party; **ein Fest
 geben**   to give a party
die **Flasche, -n**   bottle; **eine Flasche
 Mineralwasser**   a bottle of mineral
 water
das **Geschirr**   dishes
die **Hausarbeit**   housework; chore
die **Küche, -n**   kitchen

der **Moment, -e**   moment; **im
 Moment**   at the moment
die **Reise, -n**   trip, journey
die **Spülmaschine, -n**
 dishwasher
der **Staub**   dust
der **Tourist, -en, -en**/die **Touristin,
 -nen**   tourist
die **Vorbereitung, -en**
 preparation
die **Wäsche**   laundry
das **Wohnzimmer, -**   living room

Verben

ab·trocknen   to dry dishes; to wipe
 dry
**ab·waschen (wäscht ab),
 abgewaschen**   to do dishes
an·schauen   to look at, watch (e.g.,
 ein Video)
auf·räumen   to straighten up
 (a room)
aus·räumen   to unload (dishwasher);
 to clear away
decken   to cover; **den Tisch
 decken**   to set the table
ein·laden (lädt ein), eingeladen   to
 invite; to treat (pay for someone);
 Ich lade dich ein   It's my treat
ein·räumen   to load (dishwasher);
 ich räume die Spülmaschine ein
 I load the dishwasher; **ich räume
 das Geschirr in die Spülmaschine**

 ein   I put the dishes in the
 dishwasher
helfen (hilft), geholfen (+ *dat.*)   to
 help; **hilf mir**   help me
herum·liegen, herumgelegen   to be
 lying around
putzen   to clean
sitzen: gesessen
spülen   to rinse; to wash; **Geschirr
 spülen**   to wash dishes
Staub saugen   to vacuum; **ich sauge
 Staub**   I vacuum; **ich habe Staub
 gesaugt**   I vacuumed
Staub wischen   to dust; **ich wische
 Staub**   I'm dusting; **ich habe Staub
 gewischt**   I dusted
waschen (wäscht), gewaschen   to
 wash

Andere Wörter

bay(e)risch   Bavarian
dazu   to it
draußen   outside
endlich   finally
herum   around

nun   now, at present
pleite   broke, out of money
sauber   clean; **sauber machen**   to
 clean
typisch   typical

Besondere Ausdrücke

Du meine Güte!   Good Heavens!
Mach schnell!   Hurry up!

Macht nichts!   Doesn't matter!

Ein Austauschstudent in Deutschland

Vorbereitung auf das Lesen

▉ *Vor dem Lesen*

1. Viele Leute sprechen gern über ihre Zeit im Ausland. Mögliche Themen sind das Essen oder die Reise selbst°, z.B. der Flug. Welche anderen Themen können Sie nennen°?

2. Denken Sie an° ein Land – Kanada, Deutschland, die USA. Was assoziieren Sie mit diesem Land? Was ist typisch oder stereotyp für das Land?

▉ *Beim Lesen*

1. Machen Sie eine Liste von den Themen, über die° Christine und Peter sprechen.

2. Welche Bemerkungen° von Peter und Christine finden Sie stereotyp?

Der Austauschstudent Peter Clasen studiert seit drei Monaten an der FU° in Berlin. Dieses Wochenende ist er nach München gekommen, wo er seine Freundin Christine trifft. Er hat sie letztes Jahr an seiner Uni in Amerika kennen gelernt. Christine war dort für ein Jahr als Austauschstuden-
5 tin und sie studiert jetzt in München. Peter und Christine sitzen in einem Straßencafé in der Fußgängerzone und Christine möchte wissen, wie es Peter in Deutschland gefällt. Sie fragt ihn: „Sag mal, Peter, wie findest du das Leben in Deutschland? Was ist für dich anders hier als in Amerika?"

PETER: Vieles ist ja genauso wie in Amerika. Aber vieles ist doch auch anders.
10 Da war zum Beispiel meine erste° Fahrt° auf der Autobahn. Furchtbar, sag' ich dir. Die fahren wie die Wilden, hab' ich gedacht. Seitdem° fahr' ich richtig gern mit dem Zug. Außerdem hat fast jede größere° Stadt einen Bahnhof und es gibt genug Züge. Sie sind sauber. Sie fahren meistens pünktlich ab und kommen pünktlich an. Überhaupt funktioniert alles.
15 CHRISTINE: Ja, das habe ich in Amerika vermisst° – die öffentlichen Verkehrsmittel. Es gibt zwar Busse, aber die fahren nicht so oft. Alles ist auch so weit auseinander°. Deswegen° braucht man wirklich ein Auto. – Aber Peter, es tut mir Leid, ich habe dich unterbrochen°. Was ist sonst noch anders in Deutschland?
20 PETER: Also mit den Bussen hast du ja Recht. Was noch? Vielleicht die Parks in jeder Stadt und auch die Fußgängerzonen mit den vielen Straßencafés, so wie hier. Die machen eine Stadt gleich gemütlich. Schön sind auch die vielen Blumen in den Fenstern, auf den Märkten und in den Restaurants. Und dann das Essen. Erstens° ist das Essen selbst anders – anderes Brot und
25 Bier, mehr Wurst und so. Dann wie man isst – wie man Messer und Gabel benutzt, meine ich. Und schließlich° hab' ich auch gefunden, dass das Essen mehr ein Ereignis° ist. Man sitzt länger° am Tisch und spricht miteinander.
CHRISTINE: Ja, da hast du auch wieder Recht. Aber ich weiß nicht, ob das in allen Familien so ist. In vielen Familien arbeiten beide Eltern. Da bleibt
30 auch nicht mehr so viel Zeit fürs Reden.

Glossary (left margin):

itself
name

Denken Sie an: think of

which

observations

FU = Freie Universität

first / ride
since then
larger

missed

apart / therefore
interrupted

first of all

finally
event / for a longer time

Of all Europeans, Germans spend the most for cut flowers – 81 euros a year. Favorite flowers are, in order, **Rosen, Tulpen** *(tulips),* **Nelken** *(carnations).*

PETER: Ach ja, und noch etwas. Alles ist so sauber in Deutschland, aber
manchmal gehen die Deutschen ein bisschen zu weit. Ich habe einmal im
Dezember eine Frau in Gummistiefeln° gesehen. Sie hat eine öffentliche   rubber boots
Telefonzelle° geputzt. Das kann doch wohl nur in Deutschland passieren!   telephone booth
35   Aber nun mal zu dir. Was hast du denn in Amerika so beobachtet?
CHRISTINE: Einige Sachen haben mir ausgesprochen° gut gefallen. Zum   really
Beispiel kann man in Amerika auch abends und am ganzen Wochenende
einkaufen gehen. Das finde ich toll. Und ich finde die Amerikaner
unglaublich freundlich. In den Geschäften und Restaurants waren alle
40   einerseits° sehr hilfsbereit°...   on the one hand / helpful
PETER: Und, andererseits°, was hat dir weniger° gefallen?   on the other hand / less
CHRISTINE: Na ja, also sei mir bitte nicht böse, aber diese Freundlichkeit°   friendliness
erscheint° mir manchmal doch auch sehr oberflächlich. Einmal war ich zum   appears
Beispiel beim Arzt, und die Krankenschwester hat „Christine" zu mir gesagt
45   und nicht „Miss" oder „Ms. Hagen". Sie hat mich doch gar nicht gekannt!
Wir benutzen den Vornamen nur unter Freunden.
PETER: Das sehen wir eben anders. Ein nettes Lächeln und ein freundliches
Wort im Alltag° machen das Leben eben einfacher.   everyday life

Brauchbares

1. l. 11, **"Die fahren wie die Wilden . . ."**: On much of the **Autobahn** there is no
speed limit (**die Geschwindigkeitsbegrenzung** or **das Tempolimit**). Although
environmentalists keep advocating a speed limit of 100 km per hour everywhere, polls show that 80% of the German population opposes limits of any
kind.

Im Münchner
Hauptbahnhof.

2. l. 13, **"Bahnhof/sauber"**: In a test of 23 European train stations conducted in 2002 by the ADAC (Allgemeiner Deutscher Automobil-Club), seven German stations occupied the top positions for service, comfort, and safety. There are 6,000 train stations in Germany, used by 4.1 billion travelers per year.

3. l. 25, **"Dann wie man isst ... "**: If only a fork or spoon is needed, the other hand rests on the table next to the plate. If both a knife and fork are used, the knife is held in the right hand all during the meal. Open-faced sandwiches are common and eaten with a knife and fork.

4. l. 43–44, **"Einmal war ich zum Beispiel beim Arzt ..."**: Another example of American "friendliness" that would be rare in German culture is the supermarket cashier who greets the customer with a "Hi, how are you?", perhaps makes an additional comment, and then says, "Have a good day."

5. l. 46, **"Wir benutzen den Vornamen nur unter Freunden"**: Adult Germans use **du** and first names only with close friends. Although students use first names and **du** with each other immediately, it is still prudent in most situations for a foreign visitor to let a German-speaking person propose the use of the familiar **du.**

6. In l. 47 Peter says, **"Das sehen wir eben anders"**: **Eben** is a flavoring particle that can be used by a speaker in a discussion in a final or closing statement to imply that she/he has no desire or need to discuss the point further. In other contexts it is used to support or strengthen a previous statement or idea or even to express strong agreement with what someone has said.

Nach dem Lesen

1. Fragen zum Lesestück

1. Über welche Themen haben Christine und Peter gesprochen?
2. Wie fahren die Deutschen auf der Autobahn?
3. Mit welchem Verkehrsmittel fährt Peter gern?
4. Wie sind die Züge in Deutschland?
5. Warum ist Christine in Amerika nicht gern mit dem Bus gefahren?
6. Peter findet, dass die Deutschen vielleicht zu sauber sind. Warum glaubt er das?
7. Wie ist das Einkaufen anders in Amerika?
8. Was hat Christine bei dem amerikanischen Arzt nicht gefallen?
9. Findet Peter, dass die Amerikaner zu freundlich sind?

2. Vokabeln sammeln. *(Gathering vocabulary.)* Suchen Sie Wörter und Wendungen° im Text zu den folgenden Themen:

expressions

- das Essen
- Verkehrsmittel

3. Positives und Negatives. Peter und Christine machen Notizen über ihre Erlebnisse° im Ausland⁺. Was steht° auf den Listen?

experiences / steht: stands, here: is

	Positives	Negatives
Peter über Deutschland		
Christine über Amerika		

4. Zur Diskussion. Sind Amerikaner freundlich oder zu freundlich? Geben Sie Beispiele, warum Ausländer sagen, dass Amerikaner freundlich sind. Geben Sie Beispiele, wann Amerikaner vielleicht oberflächlich sind.

5. Erzählen wir. Sprechen Sie über eines der folgenden° Themen. Was ist in Deutschland anders als hier? Was ist genauso wie bei Ihnen?

following

Autofahren	Fernsehen
Blumen	Freundlichkeit
Essen	Vornamen
Einkaufen	Züge

Fußgängerzonen

In der Fußgängerzone in München

Most people in German-speaking countries live in urban areas. Three-fourths of the German population live in cities, and two-thirds live in cities with a population of more than 100,000.

The physical layout of cities in the German-speaking countries is generally different from that of cities in the United States. The concept of building large suburbs and shopping malls around a city is uncommon in most of Europe. A city (**Großstadt**) or town (**Stadt**) in German-speaking countries has a center containing office buildings as well as apartment buildings, stores, and places for cultural events. Many downtown areas have been converted to traffic-free pedestrian zones (**Fußgängerzonen**). A typical pedestrian zone has large department stores as well as small specialty stores and street vendors, restaurants, and outdoor cafés. The streets are often lined with flowers, bushes, and trees and sometimes lead into small squares, where people can rest on benches. The downtown shopping areas are used not only by people who live in the city, but also by people who live in the outskirts or in nearby villages.

Diskussion

Describe the shopping area and downtown where you live. Using the information in the cultural note, compare your shopping and downtown areas to those in German-speaking countries. Do you see any major advantages or disadvantages to having a city center as is common in German-speaking countries?

www Go to the *Deutsch heute* website at http://college.hmco.com.

kitchen appliances

Erweiterung des Wortschatzes

Möbel und Küchengeräte°

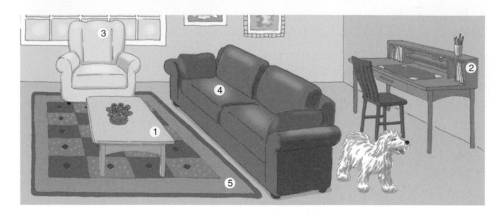

das Wohnzimmer

1. der **Couchtisch, -e**
2. der **Schreibtisch, -e**
3. der **Sessel, -**
4. das **Sofa, -s**
5. der **Teppich, -e**

das Schlafzimmer

6. das **Bett, -en**
7. die **Kommode, -n**
8. der **Nachttisch, -e**
9. der **Schrank, ⸚e**
10. der **Spiegel, -**
11. die **Bettdecke, -n**
12. das **Kissen, -**

die Küche

13. der **Herd, -e**
14. der **Kühlschrank, ⸚e**
15. die **Spülmaschine, -n**

ziehen um: are moving

1. Was steht wo? Sie ziehen um°. Machen Sie eine Liste und schreiben Sie auf, was in jedes Zimmer kommt.

die Küche	das Wohnzimmer	das Esszimmer⁺	das Schlafzimmer

2. Frage-Ecke. Ihre Partnerin/Ihr Partner und verschiedene andere Leute haben einige neue Möbel und andere neue Sachen in ihren Wohnungen⁺. Finden Sie heraus, was sie haben und in welchen Zimmern die Sachen sind. Die Informationen für *S2* finden Sie im Anhang (Appendix B).

> *S1:* Was ist im Wohnzimmer und im Schlafzimmer von Herrn Becker neu?
> *S2:* Im Wohnzimmer ist die Pflanze und im Schlafzimmer ist der Schrank neu.

S1:

	in der Küche	im Wohnzimmer	im Esszimmer	im Schlafzimmer
Herr Becker	Herd		Tisch	
Frau Hauff		Sofa	4 Stühle	
Andrea	Geschirr			Schreibtisch
Jens		Bücherregal		Kommode
ich				
Partnerin/ Partner				

3. Meine Wohnung. Beschreiben Sie Ihrer Partnerin/Ihrem Partner ein Zimmer in Ihrem Haus oder in Ihrer Wohnung. Sprechen Sie auch über Details wie Farbe und Größe von den Sachen in Ihrem Zimmer und ob sie alt oder neu sind.

> → *Im Schlafzimmer habe ich ein Bett, einen Schreibtisch, ein Bücherregal und eine Lampe. Der Schreibtisch ist modern und groß. Das Bücherregal ist...*

Was ist alles in diesem Wohnzimmer?

Vokabeln 2

Substantive

die **Angst, ⸚e** fear
das **Ausland** *(no pl.)* foreign
countries; **im Ausland** abroad
der **Austauschstudent, -en, -en**/die
Austauschstudentin, -nen
exchange student
die **Autobahn, -en** freeway,
expressway
der **Bahnhof, ⸚e** train station
der **Boden, ⸚** floor
die **Ecke, -n** corner
das **Esszimmer, -** dining room
die **Fußgängerzone, -n** pedestrian
zone
die **Gabel, -n** fork
der **Hund, -e** dog
die **Katze, -n** cat
die **Krankenschwester, -n** nurse

das **Leben, -** life
der **Löffel, -** spoon
das **Messer, -** knife
die **Möbel** *(pl.)* furniture;
das **Möbelstück** piece of
furniture
der **Name, -n, -n** name
der **Park, -s** park
das **Restaurant, -s** restaurant
das **Schlafzimmer, -** bedroom
die **Vase, -n** vase
das **Verkehrsmittel, -** means of
transportation
der **Vorname, -n, -n** first name
die **Wohnung, -en** dwelling,
apartment
*For items of furniture and kitchen
appliances see p. 250.*

Verben

**ab·fahren (fährt ab), ist
abgefahren** to depart (by vehicle)
an·kommen, ist angekommen (**in** +
dat.) to arrive (in)
benutzen to use
beobachten to observe
hängen to hang (something), put
hängen, gehangen to be hanging
lächeln to smile
legen to lay, put (horizontal)
meinen to mean; to think, have an

opinion; **was meinst du?** what do
you think?
passieren, ist passiert (+ *dat.*) to
happen; **was ist dir passiert?** what
happened to you?
setzen to set, put
stecken to stick, put into, insert
stehen, gestanden to stand; to be
located
stellen to place, put (upright)

Andere Wörter

böse (**auf** + *acc.*) angry (at)
eben *(flavoring particle)* just; simply;
even
genau exact(ly); **Genau!** That's
right!
genauso exactly the same
gleich immediately, at once; same;
similar
nächst (-er, -es, -e) next
ob *(conj.)* whether, if
oberflächlich superficial

öffentlich public
pünktlich punctual
selbst oneself, myself, itself, etc.
überhaupt generally (speaking);
actually, altogether; **überhaupt
nicht** not at all
unglaublich unbelievable
unter (+ *acc. or dat.*) under; among
zwar it's true; to be sure; indeed
zwischen (+ *acc. or dat.*) between

Eben is a flavoring particle used
to support a previous statement,
express agreement. Made as a
final statement, it implies the
speaker has no desire to discuss
a point further.

Besondere Ausdrücke

Recht haben to be right; **Du hast
Recht.** You're right.

sei [mir] nicht böse don't be mad
[at me]
was noch? what else?

Freunde *vs.* Bekannte

Germans do not use the word **Freund/Freundin** as freely as Americans use *friend*. A **Freund/Freundin** is a person with whom one is on intimate terms, a person who is often called "a very good friend" by Americans. Germans tend to have fewer **Freunde** and a larger circle of acquaintances (**Bekannte**). Even acquaintances of years' standing, e.g., neighbors and co-workers, do not necessarily become **Freunde.**

Most teenagers and young adults in German-speaking countries spend their free time with a group of friends, rather than with one friend or a date. This is true for single men and women as well as for many couples in that age group. While an American college student might say "I'm going on a date," a German student is more likely to say **Ich treffe mich mit meinen Freunden** (*I'm meeting with my friends*).

Studenten an der Berliner Humboldt-Universität machen eine Pause.

 Go to the *Deutsch heute* website at
http://college.hmco.com.

Diskussion

What is a good friend? Make a list of five qualities that you expect to find in a "good friend." Find the German equivalents of the words and compare your list with the lists of other students. Can you make any distinctions between the qualities you expect from "good friends" (**Freunde**) and "friends" (**Bekannte**)? Would your list of characteristics be any different?

Grammatik und Übungen

1 *Hin* and *her*

Meine Tante wohnt nicht hier, sondern in Hamburg.	My aunt doesn't live here, but rather in Hamburg.
Wir fahren einmal im Jahr **hin.**	Once a year we go *there.*
Und zweimal im Jahr kommt sie **her.**	And twice a year she comes *here.*

Hin and **her** are used to show direction. **Hin** shows motion away from the speaker, and **her** shows motion toward the speaker. **Hin** and **her** occupy last position in the sentence.

Er war letztes Jahr in Europa. Er möchte wieder **dorthin.**	He was in Europe last year. He wants to go there again.
Kommen Sie mal **herauf.**	Come on up here.

Hin and **her** may be combined with several parts of speech, including adverbs, prepositions, and verbs.

Woher kommen Sie?	**Wo** kommen Sie **her?**	Where are you from?
Wohin fahren Sie?	**Wo** fahren Sie **hin?**	Where are you going?

In spoken German, **hin** and **her** are often separated from **wo. Hin** and **her** occupy last position in the sentence.

1. Ilse und Axel. Stellen Sie Fragen über Ilse und Axel. Benutzen Sie **wo, wohin** oder **woher.**

> ➜ Ilse und Axel wohnen bei München.
> *Wo wohnen sie?*
> ➜ Sie fahren jeden Morgen nach München.
> *Wohin fahren sie? / Wo fahren sie hin?*

1. Sie arbeiten in einer Buchhandlung.
2. Sie gehen am Samstag in den Supermarkt.
3. Die Blumen kommen vom Markt.
4. Sie fahren am Sonntag in die Berge.
5. Sie wandern gern in den Bergen.
6. Nach der Wanderung° gehen sie in ein Restaurant.
7. Sie essen gern im Restaurant.
8. Nach dem Essen fahren sie wieder nach Hause.
9. In den Ferien fahren sie in die Schweiz.
10. Axel kommt aus der Schweiz.

hike

Was soll man wissen?
Was machen die beiden Personen?

Häuser und Wohnungen

Most people in German-speaking countries live in apartments, either rented (**Miet-wohnung**) or owned (**Eigentumswohnung**). Inhabitants of **Mietwohnungen** share the cleaning of the stairway, attic, and basement, unless the owner has hired a superintendent (**Hausmeisterin/Hausmeister**).

Only 43% of the people in western Germany and 28% in eastern Germany own a single family home (**Einfamilienhaus**) — compared to more than 66% of the people in the U.S. Even though the federal government, cities, and counties have tried to make it easier and more affordable to become a homeowner, land remains limited and expensive; construction materials and wages remain costly; planning, licensing, and building codes are complex; and mortgages still require very large down payments.

A typical house has stucco-coated walls and a tile or slate roof. Normally there is a full basement (**der Keller**) that is used primarily for storage or as a work area. The first floor (**erster Stock** or **erste Etage**) is what is usually considered the second story in American homes. The ground floor is called **das Erdgeschoss** or **Parterre**. Privacy is assured not only by closed doors but also by window curtains (**Gardinen**) and drapes (**Vorhänge**). Many homes and apartments are equipped with outdoor shutters (**Rollläden**) that unfold vertically over the windows.

In addition to the modern houses, each region of Germany has its own traditional architecture. **Fachwerkhäuser** (half-timbered houses) lend charming character to many town centers.

Einfamilienhaus in Bielefeld.

www Go to the *Deutsch heute* website at http://college.hmco.com.

Diskussion

Research project: What differences do you find between German homes and North American homes?

Der Trend geht wieder zum Eigenheim[1] mit *Gartenzwergen.*

Wohin geht der Trend?
Was soll das Eigenheim haben?

[1]*owner-occupied home*

2 The verbs *legen/liegen, stellen/stehen, setzen/sitzen, hängen, stecken*

Wohin?   **Wo?**

Lisa **legt** das Buch auf den Schreibtisch.

Das Buch **liegt** auf dem Schreibtisch.

Herr Schumann **stellt** die Lampe in die Ecke.

Die Lampe **steht** in der Ecke.

Anna **setzt** die Katze auf den Boden.

Die Katze **sitzt** auf dem Boden.

Jessica **steckt** die Zeitung in die Tasche.

Die Zeitung **steckt** in der Tasche.

Wohin?

Felix **hängt** das Poster an die Wand.

Wo?

Das Poster **hängt** an der Wand.

In English, the all-purpose verb for movement to a position is *to put,* and the all-purpose verb for the resulting position is *to be.* German uses several verbs to express the meanings *put* and *be.*

Position			
to put ~ accusativ		*to be* dativ	~~(sein 30)~~
legen, gelegt	*to lay*	liegen, gelegen	*to be lying*
stellen, gestellt	*to place upright*	stehen, gestanden	*to be standing*
setzen, gesetzt	*to set*	sitzen, gesessen	*to be sitting*
stecken, gesteckt	*to stick (into)*	stecken, gesteckt	*to be inserted (in)*
hängen, gehängt	*to hang*	hängen, gehangen	*to be hanging*

The German verbs expressing *to put* all take direct objects and are weak.

Ich **habe** das Buch auf den Tisch **gelegt.**

The German verbs expressing stationary position *(to be)* do not take direct objects and, except for **stecken,** are strong.

Das Buch **hat** auf dem Tisch **gelegen.**

Two-way prepositions following verbs expressing *to put* take the accusative case, e.g., auf **den** Tisch. Two-way prepositions following verbs expressing *to be* take the dative case, e.g., auf **dem** Tisch. See Section 3, Two-way prepositions, page 258.

2. Wir räumen auf. Sie räumen zusammen mit Anja Ihr Zimmer auf. Beschreiben Sie, was Sie tun. Benutzen Sie passende Verben aus der Tabelle.

➡ Anja _____ das Buch auf den Tisch.
    Anja legt das Buch auf den Tisch.

1. Ich _____ das Poster an die Wand.
2. Anja _____ den Sessel in die Ecke.
3. Die Lampe muss über dem Tisch _____ .

4. Die Hefte _____ auf der Kommode.

5. Ich _____ das Geld in die Tasche.

6. Der Fernseher _____ unter dem Fenster.

7. Ich _____ die Schuhe in den Schrank.

8. Der Mantel _____ schon in dem Schrank.

9. Der Regenschirm _____ auch in dem Schrank.

10. Die Katze _____ auf dem Schreibtisch.

11. Anja _____ die Katze auf den Boden.

12. Die Bücher müssen in dem Bücherregal _____ .

13. Ich _____ die Vase auf das Bücherregal.

die Präposition mit Dativ oder
Akkusativ

3 Two-way prepositions°

Preposition	Meaning	Wo? (Preposition + dative)	Wohin? (Preposition + accusative)
an	on (vertical surfaces) at (the side of) to	Kurts Bild hängt **an der** Wand. Ute steht **am** (**an dem**) Fenster.	Sabine hängt ihr Bild **an die** Wand. Benno geht **ans** (**an das**) Fenster.
auf	on top of (horizontal surfaces) to	Kurts Buch liegt **auf dem** Tisch.	Sabine legt ihr Buch **auf den** Tisch. Ich gehe **auf den** Markt.
hinter	behind/in back of	Inge arbeitet **hinter dem** Haus.	Nils geht **hinter das** Haus.
in	in, inside (of) into to	Paula arbeitet **im** (**in dem**) Wohnzimmer.	Jürgen geht **ins** (**in das**) Wohnzimmer. Wir gehen **ins** (**in das**) Kino.
neben	beside, next to	Ritas Stuhl steht **neben dem** Fenster.	Jan stellt seinen Stuhl **neben das** Fenster.
über	over, above across (direction)	Eine Lampe hängt **über dem** Tisch.	Hugo hängt eine andere Lampe **über den** Tisch. Ich gehe **über die** Straße.
unter	under	Ein Schuh steht **unter dem** Bett.	Kurt stellt den anderen Schuh **unter das** Bett.
vor	in front of	Ilses Auto steht **vor dem** Haus.	Armin fährt sein Auto **vor das** Haus.
zwischen	between	Die Seminararbeit liegt **zwischen den** Büchern.	Judith legt die Seminararbeit **zwischen die** Bücher.

Dative: **wo?**

Ilse arbeitet **in der Küche.**
Ilse is working *in the kitchen.*

Accusative: **wohin?**

Axel kommt **in die Küche.**
Axel comes *into the kitchen.*

German has nine prepositions that take either the dative or the accusative. The dative is used when position *(place where)* is indicated, answering the question **wo?** (e.g., **in der Küche**). The accusative is used when a change of location *(place to which)* is indicated, answering the question **wohin?** (e.g., **in die Küche**).

In their basic meanings, the two-way prepositions are "spatial," referring to positions in space (dative) or movements through space (accusative). To distinguish place *where* from place *to which*, German uses different cases; English sometimes uses different prepositions (e.g., *in* vs. *into*).

4 Prepositional contractions

Er geht **ans** Fenster.	an das = **ans**
Er steht **am** Fenster.	an dem = **am**
Sie geht **ins** Zimmer.	in das = **ins**
Sie ist **im** Zimmer.	in dem = **im**

The prepositions **an** and **in** often contract with **das** and **dem.** Other possible contractions are **aufs, hinters, hinterm, übers, überm, unters, unterm, vors,** and **vorm.**

3. Was ist wo? Sehen Sie sich das Bild an und ergänzen Sie die Sätze mit passenden Präpositionen, Artikeln und Substantiven.

➡ Der Hund liegt _____ .
Der Hund liegt unter dem Tisch.

1. Der Stuhl steht _____ .
2. Die Vase steht _____ .
3. Die Bücher stehen _____ .
4. Der Tisch steht _____ .
5. Das Bild hängt _____ .
6. Die Katze sitzt _____ .
7. Der Sessel steht _____ .
8. Die Lampe hängt _____ .

4. Das habe ich gemacht. Erzählen Sie, was Sie mit einigen Sachen in Ihrem Zimmer gemacht haben.

→ Ich habe das Bild _____ Wand gehängt.
Ich habe das Bild an die Wand gehängt.

1. Ich habe den Stuhl _____ Tisch gestellt.
2. Ich habe die Vase _____ Bücherregal gestellt.
3. Ich habe die Bücher _____ Bücherregal gestellt.
4. Ich habe den Tisch _____ Bücherregal gestellt.
5. Ich habe die Lampe _____ Tisch gehängt.
6. Ich habe den Sessel _____ Bücherregal und _____ Tür gestellt.
7. Der Hund ist _____ Tisch gegangen.
8. Die Katze ist _____ Sessel gegangen.

⑤ An and *auf* = on

Der Spiegel hängt **an der Wand.**   The mirror is hanging on the wall.
Mein Buch liegt **auf dem**   My book is lying on the desk.
   Schreibtisch.

An and **auf** can both be equivalent to *on*. **An** = *on (the side of)* is used in reference to vertical surfaces. **Auf** = *on (top of)* is used in reference to horizontal surfaces.

⑥ An, *auf*, and *in* = to

Veronika geht **an** die Tür.   Veronika goes to the door.
Bernd geht **auf** den Markt.   Bernd goes to the market.
Lore geht **in** die Stadt.   Lore goes to town.

The prepositions **an, auf,** and **in** can be equivalent to the English preposition *to*.

5. Julia hat endlich ein Zimmer. Julia richtet ihr neues Zimmer ein°. Ergänzen Sie die Sätze mit den fehlenden° Präpositionen **an** oder **auf**.

→ Julia stellt den Schreibtisch _____ Fenster.
Julia stellt den Schreibtisch ans Fenster.

1. Den Stuhl stellt Julia _____ Schreibtisch.
2. Sie hängt das Bild _____ Wand.
3. Sie legt die Bücher _____ Schreibtisch.
4. Der Schirm hängt _____ Tür. Das gefällt ihr nicht und sie legt ihn _____ Schrank.
5. _____ Stuhl liegt ihr Mantel. Den hängt sie _____ Tür.
6. Die Blumen stellt sie _____ Bücherregal.
7. Und jetzt geht sie _____ Markt und kauft ein.

richtet ein: is arranging
missing

Land und Leute

Geschlossene Türen

www Go to the *Deutsch heute* website at http://college.hmco.com.

An American visiting a business or a home in a German-speaking country will be struck by the fact that inside doors are mostly closed. Doors to offices in American businesses, public buildings, and universities tend to be open. An open door in a German, Austrian, or Swiss firm, however, might bother the employee. Open doors imply lack of privacy. If the door has a glass pane it is usually of milk glass so that one can't see through it.

Doors also tend to be shut in private homes. When one enters a typical German home there is an entrance hall (**die Diele/der Flur**). From this hall, doors lead into the living room, kitchen, bathroom, and bedrooms. These doors remain closed so that a visitor cannot look into the rooms.

The people in German-speaking countries take their privacy seriously. They feel their privacy is violated if they can be seen or if outside noise disturbs them in their homes. Therefore, while Americans tend to solve noise problems by sound-proofing, most people in German-speaking countries observe regulations that require a quiet time around midday (**Ruhezeit**) and after 10 P.M. During these hours, people try not to engage in activities that might disturb the neighbors. In a country like Germany that is half the size of Texas but with a population of 82.6 million and where most people live in apartment houses, the need to preserve privacy is understandable.

Zimmertüren bleiben meistens geschlossen.

Diskussion

Germany is one of the most densely populated countries in Europe. It has approximately 230 inhabitants per square kilometer or 601 per square mile. The close proximity of living conditions has an effect on ideas of privacy and influences housing patterns. Find out the density of population in your country and state and discuss ideas of privacy in your culture. You may want to consider the following issues: the differences between living in an apartment, single-family home, or dormitory room; times and levels of noise that you consider acceptable; how you define your private space, the role of doors, your relationship with neighbors.

6. Am Wochenende. Susan ist ein Jahr lang als Austauschstudentin in Deutschland. Sie wohnt mit Erika zusammen. Erzählen Sie, was Susan am Wochenende macht. Benutzen Sie die Wörter.

➡ Susan / gehen / auf / Markt
Susan geht auf den Markt.

1. auf / Markt / sie / kaufen / Blumen / für / ihr Zimmer
2. dann / sie / gehen / in / Buchhandlung
3. Erika / arbeiten / in / Buchhandlung

4. Susan / müssen / in / Drogerie
5. in / Drogerie / sie / wollen / kaufen / Kamm
6. sie / gehen / dann / in / Café
7. in / Café / sie / treffen / Erika
8. sie / sitzen / an / Tisch / in / Ecke

Special meanings of prepositions

In addition to their basic meanings, prepositions have special meanings when combined with specific verbs (e.g., **denken an,** *to think of*) or with certain nouns (e.g., **Angst vor,** *fear of*). Each combination should be learned as a unit, because it cannot be predicted which preposition is associated with a particular verb or noun. The prepositions **durch, für, gegen, ohne, um** and **aus, außer, bei, mit, nach, seit, von, zu** take the accusative and dative respectively. The case of the noun following two-way prepositions must be learned. When **über** means *about/concerning,* it is always followed by the accusative case. A few combinations are given below.

denken an (+ *acc.*) Ich **denke** oft **an** meine Freunde.	*to think of/about* I often *think of* my friends.
schreiben an (+ *acc.*) Martina **schreibt an** ihren Vater.	*to write to* Martina *is writing to* her father.
studieren an/auf (+ *dat.*) Mark **studiert an/auf** der Universität München.	*to study at* Mark *is studying at* the University of Munich.
warten auf (+ *acc.*) Wir **warten auf** den Bus.	*to wait for* We *are waiting for* the bus.
helfen bei **Hilf** mir bitte **bei** meiner Arbeit.	*to help with* Please *help* me *with* my work.
fahren mit Wir **fahren mit** dem Auto nach Ulm.	*to go by (means of)* We *are going* to Ulm *by* car.
reden/sprechen über (+ *acc.*) Meine Eltern **sprechen** oft **über** das Wetter.	*to talk/speak about* My parents often *talk about* the weather.
schreiben über (+ *acc.*) Anna **schreibt über** ihre Arbeit.	*to write about* Anna *is writing about* her work.
halten von Sarah **hält** nicht viel **von** dem Plan.	*to think of, have an opinion of* Sarah doesn't *think* much *of* the plan.
reden/sprechen von Kevin **redet** wieder **von** seinem Porsche.	*to talk/speak about/of* Kevin *is talking about* his Porsche again.
Angst haben vor (+ *dat.*) Tobias **hat Angst vorm** Fliegen.	*to be afraid of* Tobias *is afraid of* flying.

7. Mein Bruder. Ihr Freund Lukas erzählt Ihnen von seinem Bruder. Ergänzen Sie die Sätze.

1. Mein Bruder geht _____ die Universität.

2. Oft schreibt er Briefe _____ mich und meine Eltern.

3. Ich denke oft _____ ihn, weil er mir immer _____ meinen Hausaufgaben°   homework
   geholfen hat.

4. Wie oft haben wir stundenlang _____ Politik, Sport und Frauen gesprochen!

5. In seinem letzten Brief hat er mir _____ seiner Freundin Cornelia erzählt.

6. Soll ich ihm auch _____ meiner Freundin erzählen?

8. Ein Jahr in Deutschland. Geben Sie die Sätze über Peters Jahr in Deutschland auf Deutsch wieder.

1. Peter lives behind a supermarket.
2. There are parks in every city.
3. In the restaurants there are flowers on every table.
4. Peter goes to the university by bus.
5. He doesn't like to drive on the freeway.
6. One can buy aspirin only in the pharmacy.
7. After a meal his friends sit at the table a long time.
   (*Word order:* long time / table)
8. They talk about sports, books, and their seminar reports.

9. So bin ich. Ihre Partnerin/Ihr Partner möchte Sie besser kennen lernen und fragt Sie nach Ihren Interessen und wie Sie auf Dinge° reagieren. Ergänzen Sie° die Sätze und bereiten Sie sich auf die Konversation vor°. Ihre Partnerin/Ihr Partner erzählt dann einer dritten Person, was Sie gesagt haben.

     S2: Woran denkst du oft?
     S1: Ich denke oft an die Sommerferien.
     S2: [Rita/Thomas] denkt oft an die Sommerferien.

things

complete / **bereiten ... vor:**
prepare yourself for the
conversation

*Getting to know someone
better*

1. Ich denke oft an _____
2. Ich spreche gern über _____
3. Ich weiß viel/wenig über _____
4. Ich halte nicht viel von _____
5. Ich rede oft mit _____ .
6. Ich schreibe oft an _____ .
7. Ich habe oft Probleme mit _____ .
8. Ich muss oft über _____ lächeln.

10. Hören Sie zu. Uwe war letztes Jahr in Michigan und Melanie spricht mit ihm. Hören Sie gut zu und geben Sie an, ob die Sätze richtig oder falsch sind. Sie hören zwei neue Wörter: **nie** *(never);* **komisch** *(strange).*

1. Melanie will nächstes Jahr in Michigan studieren.
2. Uwe hat sein Jahr in den USA gut gefallen.
3. Uwe findet es gut, dass man in den USA ein Auto braucht.
4. Uwe findet die Amerikaner zu freundlich.
5. Uwe hat mit seinen Professoren den Vornamen benutzt.
6. Uwe sagt, dass Melanie nicht nach Boston gehen soll.

Warum sollen Sie auf die
Straße gehen?
Wo finden Sie coole
Partytermine (*party
times*)?

8 Time expressions° in the dative

Am Montag bleibt Karla immer zu Hause.	On Monday Karla always stays home.
Philipp kommt **in** einer Woche.	Philipp's coming in a week.
Ich lese gern **am** Abend.	I like to read in the evening.
Marcel arbeitet **vor** dem Essen.	Marcel works before dinner.
Laura war **vor** einer Woche hier.	Laura was here a week ago.

With time expressions, **an, in,** and **vor** take the dative case. The use of **am** + a day may mean *on that one day* or *on all such days.*

time expressions

11. Wann machst du das? Ein Freund von Ihnen denkt, dass er weiß, wann Sie was machen. Korrigieren Sie ihn und benutzen Sie dazu die Zeitausdrücke° im Dativ.

→ Du arbeitest nur am Morgen, nicht? (Abend)   *Nein, nur am Abend.*

1. Frank kommt in fünf Minuten, nicht? (zwanzig Minuten)
2. Sollen wir vor dem Seminar Kaffee trinken gehen? (Vorlesung)
3. Du gehst am Donnerstag schwimmen, nicht? (Wochenende)
4. Du fährst am Samstagnachmittag nach Hause, nicht? (Sonntagabend)
5. Rita kommt in zwei Wochen, nicht? (eine Woche)
6. Du musst die Arbeit vor dem Wintersemester fertig haben, nicht? (Sommersemester)
7. Im Sommer fährst du in die Berge, nicht? (Herbst)
8. Du gehst nur einmal im Monat in die Bibliothek, nicht? (Woche)

9 Time expressions in the accusative

Definite point	Martin kommt **nächsten Sonntag.**	Martin is coming next Sunday.
Duration	Er bleibt **einen Tag.**	He's staying (for) one day.

Nouns expressing a definite point of time or a duration of time are in the accusative, and do not use a preposition.

12. Wann und wie lange? Eine Pianistin kommt und Michael möchte gern wissen, wie lange sie bleibt. Ergänzen Sie die Sätze.

→ Wann war die Pianistin in Hamburg? —Sie war *letzten Mittwoch* in Hamburg. (*last Wednesday*)

1. Wann kommt sie zu uns? —Sie kommt _____ zu uns. (*this weekend*)

2. Wie lange bleibt sie? —Sie bleibt _____ . (*a day*)

practice

3. Wie oft übt° sie? —Sie übt _____ . (*every morning*)

4. Wann fährt sie wieder weg? —Sie fährt _____ wieder weg. (*next Monday*)

5. Wann kommt sie wieder? —Sie kommt _____ wieder. (*next year*)

6. Wie lange bleibt sie dann? —Dann bleibt sie _____ . (*a month*)

Essen zu Hause und als Gast

Although a growing number of Germans eat their main hot meal in the evening (**Abendessen**), many Germans still eat their main meal at noon (**Mittagessen**). It may consist of up to three courses: appetizer (**Vorspeise**), entrée (**Hauptgericht** or **Hauptspeise**), and dessert (**Nachtisch** or **Dessert**), which is usually fruit, pudding, or ice cream. Cakes and pastries are served at afternoon coffee time (**Kaffee**).

Before a meal, it is customary to say **Guten Appetit** or **Mahlzeit,** and others may wish you the same by responding **Danke, gleichfalls.** Even in a restaurant, when sharing a table with a stranger who has asked if it is all right to sit at the table by saying **Ist hier noch frei?,** one wishes the stranger **Guten Appetit** when the meal arrives.

Most restaurants post their menus outside. After the meal, one pays the server. A service charge (**Bedienung**) is included in the bill. However, it is customary to add a tip (**Trinkgeld**) by rounding off the bill for small amounts (e.g., 4 euros instead of 3.70) and giving a 5 to 10 percent tip for larger amounts.

When people are invited to a friend's house for dinner or for **Kaffee,** it is customary to bring a small gift. Most often the guest will bring a small bouquet, a box of chocolates, or a bottle of wine.

Abendessen bei einer Familie in Ostdorf bei Balingen.

Diskussion

Imagine that your German e-mail pen pal is coming to visit. Explain to her/him what kind of eating habits to expect in your area and how they might be different from those in Germany.

JE FACHINGER[1] -
DESTO[2] GESÜNDER

ORIGINAL STAATL. FACHINGEN JETZT
Mit Schraubverschluß und neuem Etikett
In neuer Flasche und 12er Kasten

[1]*Fachinger:* ein Mineralwasser; [2]*je ... desto: the more . . . the more*

13. Hören Sie zu. Sabine arbeitet für die Uni-Zeitung und sie interviewt Ari Izmir, den Gitarristen von der Band „Supermann". Hören Sie zu und beantworten Sie die Fragen zu dem Interview. Sie hören drei neue Wörter: **üben** *(to practice);* **viel Glück** *(good luck);* **sicher** *(definitely).*

1. Warum spricht Sabine mit Ari?
2. Warum sagen Sabine und Ari „du" und nicht „Sie"?
3. Wie lange sind Ari und seine Band „Supermann" schon zusammen?
4. Seit wann kennt Ari seine Bandmitglieder?
5. Wie lange spielen Ari und seine Band im „Café Eulenspiegel"?
6. Wie oft übt Ari Gitarre?
7. Wann studiert Ari?

 14. Pläne. Sprechen Sie mit Ihrer Partnerin/Ihrem Partner darüber, was Sie am Wochenende oder in den Ferien machen wollen.

> *S2:* Was machst du [am Wochenende]?
> *S1:* Ich will [nichts tun].

Times: am Wochenende ■ am Mittwoch ■ nach dem Abendessen ■ im Sommer ■ in den Ferien

Activities: ins Kino gehen ■ mit Freunden kochen ■ lesen ■ ein Video anschauen ■ Freunde treffen ■ tanzen gehen ■ eine Wanderung machen ■ im Internet surfen/chatten ■ Fitnesstraining machen

das da-Kompositum

⑩ Da-compounds°

Erzählt Bianca **von ihrem Freund?**   Ja, sie erzählt viel **von ihm.**
Erzählt Bianca **von ihrer Arbeit?**   Ja, sie erzählt viel **davon.**

In German, pronouns used after prepositions normally refer only to persons (**Freund**). To refer to things and ideas (**Arbeit**), a **da**-compound consisting of **da** + a preposition is generally used: **dadurch, dafür, damit,** etc. **Da**- expands to **dar**- when the preposition begins with a vowel: **darauf, darin, darüber.**

 15. Was hält Christine von Amerika? Christine und Peter sind in den USA. Christines Freund Alex fragt, was sie in den USA macht und wie es ihr gefällt. Beantworten Sie Alex' Fragen mit „ja" und benutzen Sie ein **da**-Kompositum oder eine Präposition mit einem Pronomen.

> ➔ Gefällt es Christine bei ihren amerikanischen Freunden?
>   *Ja, es gefällt Christine bei ihnen.*

> ➔ Hat sie Hunger auf deutsches Brot?
>   *Ja, sie hat Hunger darauf.*

differences

1. Redet sie gern mit Peter?
2. Reden sie oft über kulturelle Unterschiede°?
3. Hilft sie Peter oft mit seinem Deutsch?
4. Geht sie gern mit ihren Freunden essen?
5. Denkt Christine oft an zu Hause?
6. Erzählt sie gern von ihrem Leben in Deutschland?
7. Fährt sie oft mit dem Fahrrad?
8. Erzählt sie oft von ihren Freunden?

11 Wo-compounds°

das wo-Kompositum

| **Von wem** spricht Bianca? | Sie spricht **von ihrem Freund.** |
| **Wovon (Von was)** spricht Bianca? | Sie spricht **von ihrer Arbeit.** |

The interrogative pronouns **wen** and **wem** are used with a preposition to refer only to persons. The interrogative pronoun **was** refers to things and ideas. As an object of a preposition, **was** may be replaced by a **wo**-compound consisting of **wo** + a preposition: **wofür, wodurch, womit,** etc. Wo- expands to **wor-** when the preposition begins with a vowel: **worauf, worin, worüber.** A preposition + **was** (**von was, für was**) is colloquial.

| Matthias wohnt seit September in München. | **Seit wann** wohnt er in München? |

Wo-compounds are not used to inquire about time. To inquire about time, **wann, seit wann,** or **wie lange** is used.

16. Wie bitte? Rolf nuschelt°, weil er müde ist. Sie hören nicht genau, über wen oder worüber er spricht. Fragen Sie ihn, was er gesagt hat. Benutzen Sie ein **wo**-Kompositum oder eine Präposition mit Pronomen und ersetzen° Sie die fett gedruckten° Ausdrücke.

mumbles

replace

fett gedruckt: boldfaced

| → | Klaus hat die Arbeit **mit dem Kugelschreiber** geschrieben. | *Womit hat er sie geschrieben?* |
| → | Er hat die Arbeit **mit Annette** geschrieben. | *Mit wem hat er sie geschrieben?* |

1. Susanne hat **von ihrer Vorlesung** erzählt. _____ hat sie erzählt?

2. Sie hat auch **von Professor Weiß** erzählt. _____ hat sie erzählt?

3. Udo arbeitet **für Frau Schneider.** _____ arbeitet er?

4. Sabine ist **mit Gerd** essen gegangen. _____ ist sie essen gegangen?

5. Beim Essen hat sie **von ihrer Arbeit** erzählt. _____ hat sie beim Essen erzählt?

6. Nachher hat sie **mit Udo** Tennis gespielt. _____ hat sie nachher Tennis gespielt?

7. Sie hat nur **über das Tennisspiel** geredet. _____ hat sie geredet?

8. Sie denkt nur **an Tennis.** _____ denkt sie nur?

9. Sie wohnt jetzt wieder **bei ihren Eltern.** _____ wohnt sie jetzt wieder?

10. Sie denkt nicht mehr **an eine eigene° Wohnung.** _____ denkt sie nicht mehr?

her own

Land und Leute

Die Deutschen in Amerika

 Go to the *Deutsch heute* website at http://college.hmco.com.

German immigration in the New World began on an organized basis in 1683 when 33 Germans from Krefeld arrived in Philadelphia on the ship Concord. They were looking for religious and political freedom and came to Pennsylvania through the auspices of William Penn and a German named Franz Daniel Pastorius. The settlers called the community they built Germantown, which in 1854 became a part of Philadelphia. Seven million German emigrants have come to the U.S.A. Between 1820 and 1920 alone, more than six million German immigrants arrived, many of them farmers and artisans.

Today approximately 46.5 million Americans out of a total population of 281 million claim German ancestry. This total makes German the largest single ancestry group in the United States. The states with the largest populations of German ancestry are Wisconsin, Indiana, Ohio, Texas, Kansas, Missouri, and Pennsylvania. In Canada, Germans comprise the third largest European ethnic group.

Das Pastorius-Haus in Germantown.

Diskussion

Do some historical research. The following famous Americans all have roots in a German-speaking country. How many of the names do you know? Look up information about a name that you do not know or add another name to the list.

Hannah Arendt, John Jacob Astor, Maximilian Berlitz, Wernher von Braun, Walter Chrysler, Albert Einstein, Karen Louise Erdrich, Milton S. Hershey, Paul Hindemith, Henry Kissinger, Franz Daniel Pastorius, Margarethe Meyer Schurz, Levi Strauss, John Sutter

Deutsche in Amerika: Do a survey of your class and find out the following information: How many students are of German heritage? How many of the students speak German at home? How many of the students speak a language other than English or German at home? How many famous Americans of German-speaking heritage can the class name?

 Indirect questions

Direct question	Indirect question
Wann kommt Paul nach Hause? When is Paul coming home?	Weißt du, **wann Paul nach Hause kommt?** Do you know *when Paul is coming home?*
Kommt er vor sechs? Is he coming before six?	Ich möchte wissen, **ob er vor sechs kommt.** I'd like to know *whether (if) he's coming before six.*

An indirect question (e.g., **wann Paul nach Hause kommt; ob er vor sechs kommt**) is a dependent clause. It begins with a question word (**wann**) or, if there is no question word, with the subordinating conjunction **ob.** The finite verb (**kommt**) is therefore in final position.

   An indirect question is introduced by an introductory clause such as:

Weißt du, ... ?   **Kannst du mir sagen, ... ?**
Ich möchte wissen, ...   **Ich weiß nicht, ...**

■ Indirect informational questions

Direct informational question	Wann fährt Birgit zur Uni?
Indirect informational question	Ich weiß nicht, wann Birgit zur Uni fährt.

¹*suits*

Indirect informational questions are introduced by the same question words that are used in direct informational questions (**wer, was, wann, wie lange, warum,** etc.). The question word functions as a subordinating conjunction.

17. Lia hat einen neuen Freund. Barbara and Gerd sprechen über Lias neuen Freund. Führen Sie das Gespräch nach dem folgenden Muster° weiter°.

model / **führen weiter:** continue

   → BARBARA: Wie heißt er?   GERD: *Ich weiß nicht, wie er heißt.*

1. Was macht er?
2. Wie lange kennt sie ihn schon?
3. Wo wohnt er?
4. Wie alt ist er?
5. Wo arbeitet er?
6. Warum findet sie ihn so toll?
7. Wann sieht sie ihn wieder?

■ Indirect yes/no questions

Yes/No question	Fährt Birgit heute zur Uni?
	Is Birgit driving to the university today?
Indirect question	Weißt du, **ob** Birgit heute zur Uni fährt?
	Do you know *if/whether* Birgit is driving to the university today?

Indirect yes/no questions are introduced by the subordinating conjunction **ob.** **Ob** has the meaning of *if* or *whether* and is used with main clauses such as **Sie fragt, ob ...** and **Ich weiß nicht, ob ...**

■ ob *vs.* wenn

Paul fragt Birgit, **ob** sie zur Uni fährt.   Paul is asking Birgit *if/whether* she's driving to the university.

Er möchte mitfahren, **wenn** sie zur Uni fährt.   He would like to go along, *if* she's driving to the university.

Both **wenn** and **ob** are equivalent to English *if.* However, they are not interchangeable. **Wenn** begins a clause that states the condition under which some event may or may not take place. **Ob** begins an indirect yes/no question.

blanks / **setzen ein:** insert

only

18. Ob Birgit zur Uni fährt? Gerd möchte mit Birgit zur Uni fahren und fragt Paul, ob er ihre Pläne kennt. Setzen Sie **ob** oder **wenn** in die Lücken° ein°.

1. GERD: Weißt du, _ob_ Birgit morgen zur Uni fährt?

2. PAUL: Ich glaube, sie fährt, _wenn_ ihr Auto wieder läuft.

3. GERD: Ich muss sie dann fragen, _____ das Auto wieder in Ordnung ist.

4. PAUL: Ich weiß aber nicht, _____ sie um acht Uhr oder erst° um neun fährt.
   Weißt du, _ob_ sie manchmal mit dem Rad zur Uni fährt?

5. GERD: Nein, und ich frage mich, warum sie immer mit dem Auto fährt,
   besonders _____ sie immer lange suchen muss, bis sie endlich parken kann.

6. PAUL: Ich habe sie mal gefragt, _ob_ wir vielleicht zusammen mit dem Rad
   fahren sollen, aber ich denke, das macht sie erst, _wenn_ ihr Auto total kaputt
   ist.

 Leserunde

*The Austrian writer Ernst Jandl (1925–2000) was a very popular and influential figure in German literature. His works are numerous and cover a broad range—concrete poetry, experimentally acoustical and visual poems, radio plays (**Hörspiele**), and dramas, many of which straddle the fence between the humorous and the serious. His characteristic wordplay is seen in the poem "fünfter sein," one of his best-known poems and one that became the basic text of a picture book for children and of a children's play. Using simple repetition of the adverbs **raus** and **rein,** Jandl creates a scene and a mood.*

fünfter sein

tür auf[1]
einer raus[2]
einer rein[3]
vierter sein

5 tür auf
einer raus
einer rein
dritter sein

tür auf
10 einer raus
einer rein
zweiter sein

tür auf
einer raus
15 einer rein
nächster sein

tür auf
einer raus
selber rein
20 tagherrdoktor

Ernst Jandl

[1]open   [2]*raus = heraus*   [3]*rein = herein*

Wiederholung

1. Rollenspiel. Ihre Partnerin/Ihr Partner kommt aus Österreich und Sie sprechen mit ihr/ihm über Alltag° und Kultur in den USA. Sie/Er macht die folgenden acht Aussagen° und Sie stimmen mit ihr/ihm in manchen Aussagen überein°, in manchen nicht.

everyday life
statements
stimmen überein: agree

Redemittel: übereinstimmen oder nicht übereinstimmen *(Expressing agreement or disagreement)*

Richtig. ■ Genau. ■ Natürlich. ■ Eben. ■ Du hast Recht. ■ Wirklich? ■ Meinst du? ■ Ja, vielleicht. ■ Vielleicht hast du Recht. ■ Das finde ich gar nicht. ■ Was hast du gegen [Freundlichkeit]? ■ Ich sehe das ganz anders. ■ Das siehst du nicht richtig.

---

1. Amerikaner sind zu freundlich. Das kann nicht echt° sein.
2. Das amerikanische Fernsehen ist toll.
3. In amerikanischen Städten braucht man immer ein Auto.
4. Die Amerikaner gehen wenig zu Fuß.
5. In Amerika gibt es nicht so viele Straßencafés.

genuine

Pommes frites: French fries

6. Die Amerikaner essen zu viele Hamburger und Pommes frites°.
7. Die Amerikaner treiben mehr Sport als die Europäer.
8. Die Amerikaner sind generell tolerant.

2. Das hat Mark in Deutschland beobachtet. Erzählen Sie von Marks Erfahrungen° in Deutschland. Benutzen Sie die folgenden Wörter.

experiences

1. Mark / fahren / nicht gern / auf / Autobahn
2. Leute / fahren / wie die Wilden
3. viele Kinder / sehen / im Fernsehen / *Sesamstraße*°
4. die vielen Blumen und Parks / gefallen / er
5. viele Leute / trinken / an / Sonntag / um vier / Kaffee
6. man / benutzen / Messer und Gabel / anders
7. man / sitzen / nach / Essen / lange / an / Tisch

Sesame Street

3. Ferien. Ergänzen Sie die folgenden Sätze über Urlaub° in Deutschland, Österreich und der Schweiz mit den passenden Präpositionen.

vacation

1. Im Sommer kommen viele Ausländer _____ Deutschland. (an, nach, zu)
2. Manche kommen _____ ihre Kinder. (mit, ohne, von)
3. Sie fahren natürlich _____ der Autobahn. (an, über, auf)
4. Junge Leute wandern gern _____ Freunden. (bei, ohne, mit)
5. Einige fahren _____ dem Fahrrad. (bei, an, mit)
6. Viele Kanadier fahren gern _____ Salzburg. (zu, auf, nach)
7. Sie fahren auch gern _____ die Schweiz. (an, in, nach)
8. _____ den Märkten kann man schöne Sachen kaufen. (auf, an, in)
9. Zu Hause erzählen die Kanadier dann _____ ihrer Reise. (über, von, um)

4. Etwas über Musik. Beantworten Sie die folgenden Fragen. Benutzen Sie entweder ein Pronomen oder° ein **da**-Kompositum für Ihre Antwort.

entweder ... oder: either . . . or

→ Hast du gestern mit deiner Freundin gegessen? (Ja)
  Ja, ich habe gestern mit ihr gegessen.

→ Habt ihr viel über Musik geredet? (Ja)
  Ja, wir haben viel darüber geredet.

works

1. Kennst du viele Werke° von Schönberg? (Ja)
2. Hältst du viel von seiner Musik? (Nein)
3. Möchtest du Frau Professor Koepke kennen lernen? (Ja)
4. Sie weiß viel über Schönberg, nicht? (Ja)
5. Liest sie° dieses Semester über seine Musik? (Ja)
6. Meinst du, ich kann die Vorlesung verstehen°? (Nein)

Liest sie: Is she lecturing

understand

5. Wie sagt man das? Erik Schulz studiert an der Universität Zürich. Erzählen Sie auf Deutsch ein bisschen, was er dort macht.

1. Erik Schulz goes to the University of Zurich.
2. In the summer he works for his neighbor.
3. On the weekend he goes with his girlfriend Karin to the mountains.
4. They like to hike.
5. Afterwards they are hungry and thirsty.
6. Then they go to a café, where they have coffee and cake. (Use **trinken** and **essen.**)

6. Wer weiß das? Stellen Sie den anderen Studentinnen und Studenten die folgenden Fragen. Schreiben Sie auf°, wer die Antworten weiß und wer sie nicht weiß.

schreiben auf: write down

➡ *Mark weiß, wie die Hauptstadt der° Schweiz heißt.*
➡ *Tom weiß nicht, wo Mozart gelebt hat.*

of the

Discussing cultural differences

Fragen:

1. Wie heißt die Hauptstadt der Schweiz?
2. Wo hat Mozart gelebt?
3. In welchem Land liegt Konstanz?
4. In welchen Ländern machen die Deutschen gern Ferien?
5. Was trinken die Deutschen gern?
6. Wie viele Sprachen° spricht man in der Schweiz?
7. Wie viele Nachbarländer hat Österreich?

languages

7. Zum Schreiben

1. Wählen Sie eines der folgenden Themen und schreiben Sie dazu auf Deutsch mehrere Sätze über Deutschland und Ihr Land.

   Blumen ▪ Wetter ▪ Autofahren ▪ Fernsehen ▪ Essen ▪ Universität ▪ Einkaufen

2. Stellen Sie sich vor°, Sie sind Christine Hagen. Schreiben Sie Ihrer Freundin Kerstin einen Brief über den amerikanischen Austauschstudenten Peter Clasen. Schreiben Sie darüber:

   Stellen ... vor: imagine

   a. wo Sie Peter getroffen haben
   b. wie Peter aussieht
   c. woher er kommt
   d. worüber Sie und Peter geredet haben
   e. was Sie und Peter am Wochenende machen

Hinweise: Before beginning the writing assignments, make notes of the points you want to mention. Try to use two-way prepositions and some of the verbs that require special prepositions. Pay close attention to the case used with two-way prepositions.

For a list of other things to pay attention to when writing or reviewing your writing, see *Hinweise,* page 235.

Grammatik: Zusammenfassung

Hin and *her*

Komm bitte **her.**   Please come here.
Fall nicht **hin!**   Don't fall down.

Hin and **her** are used to show direction. **Hin** indicates motion in a direction away from the speaker, and **her** shows motion toward the speaker. **Hin** and **her** function as separable prefixes and therefore occupy final position in a sentence.

| Komm mal **herunter!** | Come on down here! |
| Wann gehen wir wieder **dorthin?** | When are we going there again? |

In addition to verbs, **hin** and **her** may be combined with other parts of speech such as adverbs (e.g., **dorthin**) and prepositions (e.g., **herunter**).

The verbs *legen/liegen, setzen/sitzen, stellen/stehen, hängen, stecken*

| Nils **stellt** die Lampe **in die Ecke.** | Nils *puts* the lamp in the corner. |
| Die Lampe **steht** jetzt **in der Ecke.** | The lamp *is* now in the corner. |

In English, the all-purpose verb for moving something to a position is *to put;* the all-purpose verb for the resulting position is *to be.*

German uses several verbs to express the meaning of *to put* and *to be.*

Movement to a position, *to put*		Stationary position, *to be*	
legen, gelegt	*to lay*	liegen, gelegen	*to be lying*
setzen, gesetzt	*to set*	sitzen, gesessen	*to be sitting*
stellen, gestellt	*to place (upright)*	stehen, gestanden	*to be standing*
stecken, gesteckt	*to stick (into)*	stecken, gesteckt	*to be inserted (in)*
hängen, gehängt	*to hang*	hängen, gehangen	*to be hanging*

The German verbs describing movement to a position (**wohin?**) take the accusative case after two-way prepositions:

Nils stellt die Lampe **in die Ecke.**

The German verbs describing a stationary position (**wo?**) take the dative case after two-way prepositions:

Die Lampe steht **in der Ecke.**

Two-way prepositions and their English equivalents

an	at; on; to
auf	on, on top of; to
hinter	behind, in back of
in	in, inside (of); into; to
neben	beside, next to
über	over, above; across; about
unter	under; among
vor	in front of; before; ago
zwischen	between

Nine prepositions take either the dative or the accusative. The dative is used for the meaning *place where*, in answer to the question **wo?** The accusative is used for the meaning *place to which*, in answer to the question **wohin?** The English equivalents of these prepositions may vary, depending on the object with which they are used. For example, English equivalents of **an der Ecke** and **an der Wand** are *at the corner* and *on the wall.*

Prepositional contractions

am	= an dem	**im**	= in dem
ans	= an das	**ins**	= in das

The prepositions **an** and **in** may contract with **das** and **dem.** Other possible contractions are **aufs, hinters, hinterm, übers, überm, unters, unterm, vors,** and **vorm.**

Special meanings of prepositions

Prepositions have special meanings when combined with specific verbs (e.g., **denken an**) or with certain nouns (e.g., **Angst vor**).

denken an (+ *acc.*)	to think of/about
schreiben an (+ *acc.*)	to write to
studieren an/auf (+ *dat.*)	to study at
warten auf (+ *acc.*)	to wait for
helfen bei	to help with
fahren mit	to go by (means of)
reden/sprechen über (+ *acc.*)	to talk/speak about
schreiben über (+ *acc.*)	to write about
halten von	to think of, have an opinion of
reden/sprechen von	to talk/speak about/of
Angst haben vor (+ *dat.*)	to be afraid of

Time expressions in the dative

am Montag	on Monday, Mondays
am Abend	in the evening, evenings
in der Woche	during the week
in einem Jahr	in a year
vor dem Essen	before the meal
vor einem Jahr	a year ago

In expressions of time, the prepositions **an, in,** and **vor** are followed by the dative case.

Time expressions in the accusative

Definite point	Katrin kommt **nächsten Freitag.**	Katrin is coming *next Friday.*
Duration	Sie bleibt **einen Tag.**	She's staying *(for) one day.*

Nouns expressing a definite point in time or a duration of time are in the accusative. No preposition is used in these expressions. Note that words such as **nächst** and **letzt** have endings like the endings for **dies: diesen / nächsten / letzten Monat; dieses / nächstes / letztes Jahr**.

Da-compounds

Spricht Sabrina gern **von ihrem Freund?**	Ja, sie spricht gern **von ihm.**
Spricht Sabrina oft **von der Arbeit?**	Ja, sie spricht oft **davon.**

In German, pronouns after prepositions normally refer only to persons. German uses a **da**-compound, consisting of **da** + preposition, to refer to things or ideas.

Wo-compounds

Von wem spricht Sabrina?	Sie spricht **von ihrem Freund.**
Wovon (Von was) spricht Sabrina?	Sie spricht **von der Arbeit.**

The interrogative pronoun **wen** or **wem** is used with a preposition to refer to persons. The interrogative pronoun **was** refers to things and ideas. As an object of a preposition, **was** may be replaced by a **wo**-compound consisting of **wo** + a preposition. A preposition + **was** is colloquial: **von was.**

Patrick wohnt seit September in München.	**Seit wann** wohnt er in München?

Wo-compounds are not used to inquire about time. To inquire about time, **wann, seit wann,** or **wie lange** is used.

Indirect questions

Weißt du, **warum** Petra heute nicht kommt?	Do you know *why* Petra isn't coming today?
Ich weiß auch nicht, **ob** sie morgen kommt.	I also don't know *if/whether* she's coming tomorrow.

An indirect question is a dependent clause. The finite verb is therefore in last position. An indirect question is introduced by an introductory clause such as: **Weißt du, ... ?; Ich möchte wissen, ... ; Kannst du mir sagen, ... ?; Ich weiß nicht, ...**

An indirect informational question begins with the same question words that are used in direct informational questions (**warum, wann, wer, was, wie lange,** etc.).

An indirect yes/no question begins with **ob. Ob** can always be translated as *whether.*

Modernes Leben

Ein junger Vater bei der Hausarbeit mit seinen Kindern.

LERNZIELE

Sprechintentionen

Giving factual information
Expressing importance
Discussing friends and family
Describing things
Stating wants/desires
Asking for personal information
Inquiring about an opinion

Lesestück

Modernes Leben: Zwei Familien

Land und Leute

Milestones in the progress toward
  equal rights for women
German federal policy toward
  families

Vokabeln

Word families
Noun suffixes *-heit* and *-keit*

Grammatik

Genitive case
Adjectives
Ordinal numbers
Dates

Bausteine für Gespräche

Stellenanzeigen

ALEX: Na, was gibt's Neues in der Zeitung?
UWE: Ich weiß nicht. Ich hab' bis jetzt nur
die Anzeigen durchgesehen.
ALEX: Welche? Die Heiratsanzeigen?
UWE: Quatsch. Die Stellenanzeigen! Ich suche
Arbeit. Ich hätte gern einen interessanten
Job, wo man gut verdient.
ALEX: Ja, das wäre toll. Du suchst ja schon
eine ganze Weile. Viel Glück!

Fragen

1. Warum weiß Uwe nicht, was in der Zeitung steht?
2. Was denkt Alex, welche Anzeigen Uwe liest?
3. Wie reagiert Uwe darauf?
4. Was für einen Job sucht Uwe?

Brauchbares

1. Besides looking at **Stellenanzeigen** (want ads) in the newspaper, Uwe can
   search the Internet, where thousands of jobs are listed. However, he will not
   be searching for **Heiratsanzeigen** (ads for a marriage partner).

2. **Ich hätte gern ...** (I would like . . .) and **das wäre toll** (that would be great):
   Hätte and **wäre** are both subjunctive forms that express possibility. The subjunctive is practiced in *Kapitel 11*.

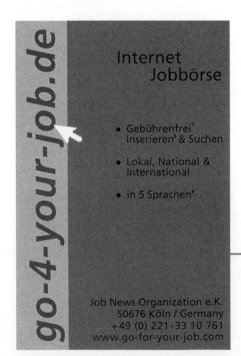

go-4-your-job.de

Internet
Jobbörse

- Gebührenfrei[1]
  Inserieren[2] & Suchen

- Lokal, National &
  International

- in 5 Sprachen[3]

Job News Organization e.K.
50676 Köln / Germany
+49 (0) 221-33 10 761
www.go-for-your-job.com

Wo kann man bei „go-4-your-job.de"
Arbeit finden?
In wie vielen Sprachen kann man auf
dieser Webseite Arbeit finden?
Wie ist die Postadresse dieser
Internet-Jobbörse?

[1]no charge   [2]place an ad   [3]languages

1. Die Zeitung. Fragen Sie drei Kursteilnehmerinnen/Kursteilnehmer, welche Zeitung sie lesen und warum sie die Zeitung lesen. Notieren Sie sich die Antworten und berichten Sie den anderen Studentinnen/Studenten, was Sie herausgefunden haben.

Giving factual information

S1:
Welche Zeitung liest du?
Warum liest du Zeitung – was
    interessiert dich?

S2:
Ich lese [*Die Zeit*].
Politik.

Schüttelkasten

Wirtschaft   Musik   Comics⁺

Sport   Theater   Literatur

2. Was ist wichtig? Fragen Sie vier Kursteilnehmerinnen/Kursteilnehmer, was sie in ihrem Beruf⁺ wichtig finden. Hier sind einige Möglichkeiten.

Expressing importance

sicherer⁺ Arbeitsplatz⁺   gut verdienen
den Menschen helfen   Teilzeitarbeit⁺
interessante oder leichte¹ Arbeit viel Freizeit
nicht [den ganzen Tag] im Büro⁺ sitzen nette Kollegen⁺

3. Heiraten/Bekanntschaften°. Im Dialog auf S. 278 hat Alex gefragt, ob Uwe die Heiratsanzeigen liest. Sehen Sie sich die Heiratsanzeigen an und beantworten Sie die folgenden Fragen.

acquaintances

Heiraten/Bekanntschaften

2 junggebliebene Freundinnen, verwitwet¹ 60 u. 65 J., suchen 2 nette Herrn. mögl. mit Auto, die mit ihnen Tanzen. Schwimmen und gemeinsame² nette Stunden verbringen³ Zuschr.⁴ mögl. mit Bild unt. Nr. 2/835083/G-Z.

ER, 28 J., 189 cm. schlank⁵ sucht nette SIE, meine Hobbys sind Bodybuilding. Motorrad fahren. Kino u. Essen gehen. Bitte schreibe mir an WT 1/167

Elfi ist von Beruf Küchenhilfe⁶ und ist **21 J.** alt. Sie hat blonde Haare, geht gerne schwimmen und spazieren. Wenn Du sie kennenlernen möchtest, dann schreibe unter AA 2154.

¹*widowed* ²*shared; joint* ³*spend* ⁴**Zuschriften:** *replies* ⁵*slender* ⁶*kitchen help*

1. Wie alt sind die Leute, die die Anzeigen aufgegeben° haben?
2. Wie alt sollen die Partnerinnen/Partner sein?
3. Wer möchte mit der Antwort zusammen ein Bild haben?
4. In welchen Anzeigen ist das Aussehen° wichtig?
5. Was für Menschen finden Sie sympathisch?

placed

appearance

Vokabeln 1

Substantive

die **Anzeige, -n** announcement; ad
der **Arbeitsplatz, ⸚e** job, position;
  workplace
der **Beruf, -e** profession, occupation,
  job
das **Büro, -s** office
die **Comics** *(pl.)* comics
das **Glück** luck; happiness; **viel
  Glück!** good luck
die **Heirat** marriage

der **Kollege, -n, -n/die Kollegin, -nen**
  colleague
die **Politik** politics; political science
der **Quatsch** nonsense;
  Quatsch! nonsense!
die **Stelle, -n** job; position; place;
  spot
die **Teilzeitarbeit** part-time work
die **Weile** while; **eine ganze Weile** a
  long time

Verben

**durch·sehen (sieht durch), sah durch,
  durchgesehen** to look through; to
  glance over; to examine

haben: hätte would have
heiraten to marry, get married
sein: wäre would be

Andere Wörter

leicht light; easy

sicher safe; secure; certain(ly)

Besondere Ausdrücke

das wäre toll that would be great

Was gibt's Neues? What's new?

Modernes Leben: Zwei Familien

Vorbereitung auf das Lesen

■ Vor dem Lesen

passt auf: looks after

1. Beschreiben Sie die traditionelle Familie. Gibt es eine Mutter und einen Vater?
   Wer arbeitet? Was machen die Kinder? Wer passt auf die Kinder auf°?

nowadays / kinds

2. Heutzutage° gibt es viele neue Arten° von Familien. Beschreiben Sie eine nicht
   traditionelle Familie.

stressful
child rearing

3. Viele Eltern, besonders Mütter, sagen, dass sie gestresst sind. Warum ist
   das so? Machen Sie eine Liste von drei anstrengenden° Dingen⁺ bei der
   Kindererziehung°.

■ Beim Lesen

rearing a child alone
while

Dieses Lesestück beschreibt die berufstätige Mutter Gabi Röttgen und den allein
erziehenden° Vater Rainer Valentin. Machen Sie Notizen zu den folgenden
Themen, während° Sie den Text lesen.

childcare

• die Kinder
• die Kinderbetreuung°
• ihre Karrieren

• das Geld
• der Stress

Familie und Ehe haben in den letzten Jahren stark an Bedeutung° verloren. [significance]
Heutzutage° gibt es neben der traditionellen Familie – Ehepaar mit einem [nowadays]
oder mehreren Kindern – zunehmend° andere Formen des Zusammenlebens. [increasingly]
Familien mit nur einem Elternteil°, Paare – verheiratet oder unverheiratet – [einem Elternteil: one parent]
5 ohne Kinder und so genannte° Patchwork-Familien, in denen° Partner mit [so-called / which]
Kindern aus anderen Verbindungen° zusammenleben. Vor allem in Großstäd- [unions]
ten gibt es immer mehr Menschen, die° alleine leben. Auch die Zahl der Ge- [who]
burten hat stark abgenommen°, weil es viele Menschen zu schwierig finden, [decreased]
Beruf und Kinder zu vereinbaren°. Lesen Sie hier zwei Beispiele von Familien [combine]
10 mit Kindern, wie sie leben und wie sie ihren Alltag° organisiert haben. [daily life]

Die berufstätige Mutter

Fünf Jahre hat Gabi Röttgen aus Lindlar Babypause gemacht, um ganz für ihre
Söhne, jetzt fünf und sieben, da zu sein°. In dieser Zeit hat ihr Mann den [um da zu sein: in order to be there]
Lebensunterhalt° der Familie verdient. Nun sind die Kinder in Schule und [livelihood]
Kindergarten und Gabi Röttgen arbeitet wieder halbtags in ihrem Beruf als
15 Sozialarbeiterin°. Doch obwohl sie nur 20 Stunden pro Woche arbeitet, klagt [social worker]
sie über die organisatorischen Probleme. „Ich arbeite morgens von acht bis
zwölf. Die Schule ist meistens um 12 Uhr 30 zu Ende, genauso der Kindergarten. Eine Betreuung° über Mittag gibt es zwar, doch wir haben leider keinen [childcare]
Platz bekommen. Jeden Tag hoffe ich, dass ich rechtzeitig° ankomme und von [on time]
20 der Erzieherin° nicht schon wieder hören muss, wie unpünktlich ich bin. [teacher]
Schlimm ist auch, wenn ich bei der Arbeit weggehen muss, obwohl ich mir
noch mehr Zeit nehmen möchte. Als Sozialarbeiterin habe ich ja oft mit Men-
schen mit Problemen zu tun. Da° dann zu sagen ‚Tut mir Leid, es ist zwölf [under the circumstances]
Uhr, kommen Sie morgen wieder‘ ist schon schwierig. Ich habe oft das Gefühl,
25 dass ich in beidem – Beruf und Muttersein° – immer gestresst bin und nie ge- [being a mother]
nug Zeit habe. Das macht keinen Spaß und das Familienleben leidet auch.
Manchmal frage ich mich, ob ich nicht noch ein oder zwei Jahre Elternzeit° [child-rearing leave]
nehmen soll. Da ich Beamtin° bin, geht das, weil ich danach° wieder ein Recht [civil service employee / afterwards]
auf eine Stelle als Sozialarbeiterin habe. Da bin ich schon privilegiert. Für
30 Frauen in anderen Berufen ist das schwieriger.“

Der alleinerziehende° Vater [rearing a child alone]

Seit fünf Jahren ist Rainer Valentin schon alleinerziehender Vater und er ist,
wie er sagt, „stolz auf seine intakte Familie“. Als er und seine Frau sich 1999
trennten°, war es klar, dass er das Sorgerecht° für die beiden Töchter Sarah [separated / custody]
und Anne, damals° drei und eins, bekommen sollte°. Er hatte sie die Jahre [at that time / should]
35 zuvor° versorgt°, weil er als selbstständiger° Architekt flexible Arbeitszeiten [before / hatte ... versorgt: had looked after them / independent / wanted / in any case / more home-oriented]
hatte. Seine Frau aber wollte° ihre gut bezahlte Stelle als Produktmanagerin
nicht aufgeben. „Ich war sowieso° immer häuslicher° und die Karriere war mir
nie so wichtig. So war der Schritt vom Hausmann zum alleinerziehenden Vater
gar nicht so groß. Mein Büro ist ja im Haus und so bin ich zwischen Schreib-
40 tisch und Wickeltisch° hin- und hergelaufen. Na ja, ganz so einfach war es na- [changing table]
türlich nicht – die Kinder waren ja noch sehr klein. Und wenn ich an die
schlaflosen Nächte denke oder wenn sie krank waren ... Am Anfang war es
für mich auch ein Problem, dass die ‚anderen Mütter‘ zum Beispiel in Spiel-
gruppen° oft ein bisschen skeptisch waren. Und wenn die Kinder schwierig [play groups]
45 waren – was ja alle Kinder mal sind – hatte ich das Gefühl, dass sie dachten°: [thought]
‚Na ja, ist ja kein Wunder, wenn nur der Vater erzieht!‘ Gut war, dass meine
Ex-Frau und ich immer einen guten Kontakt hatten, schon wegen der Kinder

could

supported

natürlich. Wenn ich mal ganz kaputt war, hat sie die Kinder genommen und
ich konnte° auch mal ausgehen oder Freunde treffen. Außerdem hat sie uns
50 natürlich finanziell unterstützt°. Heute sind wir wieder gute Freunde und im
Sommer wollen wir sogar alle zusammen Urlaub machen."

Brauchbares

1. This reading contains several verbs in the simple past, also called the narrative
past. The simple past tense is used mostly in writing. The meaning is the same
as the simple past in English and is discussed in *Kapitel 10*. You are already familiar with **war,** the simple past of the verb **sein.** Other verbs used here are as
follows: ll. 32–33 **sich trennten:** separated; l. 34 **sollte:** should; l. 36 **wollte:**
wanted; l. 45 **dachten:** thought; l. 49 **konnte:** could.

2. l. 7, **alleine leben:** A third of all German households contain a single person.
Germans refer to such people as **Singles.**

3. ll. 7–8, **Zahl der Geburten:** The number of births has been declining for years
in Germany. In 2002, there were more deaths than births, marking a negative
population growth that had persisted for ten years.

4. **berufstätige Mutter** (heading): 60% of mothers with underage children are
gainfully employed and many of these work part-time. Those women who
withdraw from the work force or work part-time during child-rearing years
very often find themselves at a disadvantage when they resume their careers.

5. l. 13, **Schule:** The family situation of working parents is complicated by a
shortage of childcare facilities and the fact that most German schools run only
to noon or slightly later. The government is responding to the request for
Ganztagsschulen. In the next few years 10,000 of the 40,000 schools are to be
restructured so that students can eat lunch at school and have afternoon
classes.

6. l. 27, **Elternzeit:** For information on **Elternzeit** see **Familienpolitik,** p. 291.

7. **Der alleinerziehende Vater** (heading): Single mothers are more prevalent than
single fathers. Fathers constitute only 14% of single parents.

8. l. 38, **Hausmann:** Like single fathers, house husbands are also relatively rare.
Doing housework also seems to be rare for men. In marriages, with or without children, only 15% of the husbands share housework with their wives,
even when the wives have an outside job. That means, of course, that unlike
her husband, the wife has two jobs.

9. l. 51, **Urlaub:** A 2002 survey reports that 73% of men at the manager level
take vacations with their families.

Nach dem Lesen

1. Fragen zum Lesestück

1. Wie lange ist Gabi Röttgen mit ihren Söhnen zu Hause geblieben, bevor sie
wieder gearbeitet hat?
2. Wie viele Stunden arbeitet Frau Röttgen am Tag?
3. Warum findet Frau Röttgen es manchmal schwierig, ihre Arbeit um 12 Uhr
zu verlassen°?

leave

4. Wann ist die Erzieherin mit Frau Röttgen ärgerlich°?

annoyed

5. Was für ein Gefühl hat Frau Röttgen oft?

6. Welche Lösung° sieht Frau Röttgen?   solution
7. Wie lange ist Rainer Valentin schon alleinerziehender Vater?
8. Warum hat er das Sorgerecht für die Töchter bekommen?
9. Was für Probleme hat er manchmal mit „den anderen Müttern"?
10. Wie hilft ihm seine Ex-Frau?

2. Vokabeln

A. Erklären Sie die Bedeutung° dieser Wörter. Benutzen Sie einen Satz mit **dass**   meaning
oder **wenn**.

➜ Babypause. *Eine Babypause ist, wenn die Mutter oder der Vater mit dem*
Baby zu Hause bleibt und nicht arbeitet.

berufstätig ■ flexible Arbeitszeit ■ gestresst ■ halbtags ■ Spaß ■ Urlaub

B. Rainer Valentin ist „stolz auf seine intakte Familie". Sagen Sie, wann Ihre
Eltern stolz oder nicht stolz auf Sie sind.

Meine Mutter/Mein Vater ist (nicht) stolz auf mich, wenn …

gute Noten bekommen
gut arbeiten
mein Zimmer aufräumen
spät nach Hause kommen
zu viel Geld ausgeben°   spend
meinen Freunden helfen

3. Erzählen wir. Sprechen Sie über eins der folgenden Themen.

Was für Probleme haben berufstätige Eltern?
Zwei Jahre Elternzeit: Eine gute oder schlechte Idee?
Wann sind Sie gestresst?

Erweiterung des Wortschatzes

1. Word families

arbeiten   *to work*
die **Arbeit**   *work*
der **Arbeiter**/die **Arbeiterin**   *worker*

Like English, German has many words that belong to families and are derived
from a common root.

1. Noch ein Wort. Ergänzen Sie die fünf Sätze mit einem sinnverwandten° Wort   related
und geben Sie dann die Bedeutung° aller fett gedruckten° Wörter wieder.   meaning / **fett gedruckt:** boldfaced

1. München hat 1,3 Millionen **Einwohner.** Viele Münchner _____ in kleinen
   Wohnungen.

2. Der **Koch** und die **Köchin** in diesem Restaurant benutzen nie ein **Kochbuch,**
   aber sie _____ sehr gut.

3. Auf unserer **Wanderung** haben wir viele **Wanderer** getroffen. Der **Wanderweg**
   war schön. Wir _____ wirklich gern.

4. —Ich muss jetzt zum **Flughafen.**

   —Wann geht dein **Flugzeug?**

   —Ich _____ um 10 Uhr 30.

5. In dieser **Bäckerei backen** sie gutes Brot. Ich finde, der _____ macht auch guten Kuchen.

2. Noun suffixes -*heit* and -*keit*

die **Freiheit**	*freedom*	die **Wirklichkeit**	*reality*
frei	*free*	**wirklich**	*really*

Nouns ending in -**heit** and -**keit** are feminine nouns. Many nouns of this type are related to adjectives. The suffix -**keit** is used with adjectives ending in -**ig** or -**lich**.

comments

related

lasts

2. Dieses Wetter! Ergänzen Sie Sandras Aussagen° über das Wetter. Benutzen Sie ein Substantiv, das auf -**heit** endet und das mit dem fett gedruckten Adjektiv verwandt° ist.

1. Der Garten ist sehr **trocken.** Wie lange dauert° diese _____ noch?

2. Dieses Wetter ist nicht **gesund.** Es ist nicht gut für die _____ .

3. Ich werde ganz **krank.** Hoffentlich ist es keine ernste _____ .

4. Aber die Natur ist immer **schön.** Mir gefällt ihre _____ .

5. In der Natur lebt man **frei.** Da ist die _____ groß.

3. Was für ein Mensch ist Dirk? Erzählen Sie, was für ein Mensch Dirk ist. Benutzen Sie ein Substantiv, das auf -**keit** endet und das mit dem fett gedruckten Adjektiv verwandt ist.

1. Für Dirk muss alles **natürlich** sein. Auch bei Mädchen findet er _____ besonders schön.

2. Dirk ist besonders **freundlich.** Die Mädchen mögen seine _____ .

3. Er findet es **wichtig,** dass man sehr nett ist. Es ist für ihn von großer _____ .

4. Es ist **schwierig** für ihn, dass die Leute manchmal unfreundlich sind. Diese _____ hat er besonders bei seinem neuen Job.

Vokabeln 2

Substantive

der **Anfang,** ̈e beginning; **am Anfang** in the beginning
der **Architekt, -en, -en**/die **Architektin, -nen** architect
das **Ding, -e** thing
die **Ehe, -n** marriage
das **Ehepaar, -e** married couple
die **Erziehung** rearing; education
die **Freiheit, -en** freedom

die **Geburt, -en** birth
das **Gefühl, -e** feeling
die **Großstadt,** ̈e city
der **Kindergarten,** ̈ nursery school
der **Mittag, -e** noon
das **Paar, -e** pair; couple
das **Recht, -e** right; law; **das Recht auf** (+ *acc.*) right to
der **Schritt, -e** step

der **Spaß** fun; enjoyment; **das macht Spaß** that's fun
der **Urlaub** vacation; **Urlaub machen** to go on vacation; **in** or **im** or **auf Urlaub sein** to be on vacation; **in Urlaub fahren** to go on vacation
die **Wirklichkeit** reality
das **Wunder,** - wonder; miracle; **kein Wunder** no wonder

Verben

auf·geben (gibt auf), aufgegeben to give up
erziehen, erzogen to bring up, rear; to educate

klagen to complain
leiden, gelitten to suffer; to tolerate; to endure
verlieren, verloren to lose

Andere Wörter

als (*sub. conj.*) when
berufstätig working, gainfully employed
da (*sub. conj.*) because, since (*causal*)
gestresst stressed
mehrere several; various
nie never
pro per

schlimm bad; serious, severe
schwierig difficult
sogar even
stark strong; greatly, very much
stolz proud; **stolz auf** (+ *acc.*) proud of
verheiratet married

Besondere Ausdrücke

immer mehr more and more

Leserunde

Maria Kaldewey (b.1963) began writing poetry at an early age and has seen her work published in a number of anthologies. Born in Westphalia, Kaldewey now lives in Neuried, near Munich, where she works as a bilingual secretary. In a statement for **Deutsch heute,** *Maria Kaldewey says: "Ich schreibe, weil Gedanken flüchtig sind, Worte aber bleiben. (I write because thoughts are fleeting, words however endure.)" In her five-line aphorism "Für immer," the poet has used simple, everyday words to state a deep thought about relationships between human beings. Does the simplicity of her language make the comment commonplace or more universally true?*

Für immer

Einen Menschen,
den man wahrhaft[1] liebt,
kann man nicht verlieren.
Es sei denn[2],
man vergisst ihn.

Maria Kaldewey

[1]*truly* [2]**Es sei denn:** *unless*

Grammatik und Übungen

der Genitiv

1 Genitive case°

■ Showing possession and close relationships

Ich habe mit dem Sohn **des Bäckers** gesprochen.	I talked to *the baker's* son.
Das ist die Frage **eines Kindes.**	That is *a child's* question.
Die Farbe **der Wände** gefällt mir.	I like the color *of the walls.*

English shows possession or other close relationships by adding 's to a noun or by using a phrase with *of.* English generally uses the 's form only for persons. For things and ideas, English uses the *of*-construction.

German uses the genitive case to show possession or other close relationships. The genitive is used for things and ideas as well as for persons. The genitive generally follows the noun it modifies (**die Frage eines Kindes**).

die Freundin **von meinem Bruder** (meines Bruders)
zwei **von ihren Freunden** (ihrer Freunde)
ein Freund **von Thomas** (Thomas' Freund)

In spoken German the genitive of possession is frequently replaced by **von +** *dative.*

ein Freund **von mir**
ein Freund **von Nicole**

Von + *dative* is also used in phrases similar to the English *of mine, of Nicole,* etc.

■ Masculine and neuter nouns

Hast du den Namen **des Kindes** verstanden?	Did you understand *the child's* name?
Das ist die Meinung **meines Professors.**	That is *my professor's* opinion.

Masculine and neuter nouns of one syllable generally add **-es** in the genitive; nouns of two or more syllables add **-s.** The corresponding articles, **der**-words, and **ein**-words end in **-es** in the genitive.

Wann ist die „Lange Nacht der Museen" in Stuttgart? Um welche Uhrzeit? Was sind die normalen Öffnungszeiten eines Museums?

Was für Veranstaltungen (*events*) gibt es bei der „Langen Nacht"? Aus welchen Bereichen (*areas*)?

Mit welchem Verkehrsmittel kann man zu den Veranstaltungen fahren?

Land und Leute

Gleichberechtigung°:   equal rights
Wichtige Daten

A few milestones in the progress of women toward
equality:

1901   German universities begin to admit women.

1918   German women receive the right to vote and to
be elected to parliament.

1949   The Basic Law of the Federal Republic
(**Grundgesetz**) guarantees the right of a person
to decide on her or his role in society.

1955   The Federal Labor Court (**Bundesarbeits-
gericht**) states that there should be no discrimination on the basis of gender in compensation
for work performed.

1977   Women and men are judged by law to be equal
in a marriage. Either can take the surname of
the other, or a combination of both names. A
divorce may now be granted on the principle of
irreconcilability rather than guilt, and all pension rights that the spouses accrued during
marriage are equally divided.

1979   Women are entitled to a six-month leave to
care for a newborn child. By 1990 the leave-
time had increased to 12 months and was available to women or men.

Vielleicht haben diese Frauen Erziehungsurlaub
genommen.

1980   The law prohibits gender discrimination in hiring
practices, wages, working conditions, opportunities for advancement, and ter-
mination policies.

1986   Years spent raising children are included in the calculation of retirement pen-
sions.

1991   Married partners may keep separate names. Children may have the name of
either parent.

1994   Married couples have the right to decide on a common married name. A law
forbidding sexual harassment at the workplace is passed. Parents may take
turns staying at home for three years
to care for their child.

2001   One or both parents may stay home and the
option to convert a former full-time position
into a part-time position should be generally
supported by the employer.

Diskussion

Historical research. Compare the milestones
in the progress of German women with important milestones in your country's policies
concerning women.

www   Go to the *Deutsch heute* website at
http://college.hmco.com.

Since unification, the laws of equality passed in 1977,
1978, and 1980 now apply to all of Germany.

Masculine N-nouns

Die Frau **des Herrn** da kommt aus
  Österreich.
Haben Sie die Frage **des Jungen**
  verstanden?

The wife *of the man* there is from
  Austria.
Did you understand *the boy's*
  question?

Masculine nouns that add **-n** or **-en** in the accusative and dative singular also add
-n or **-en** in the genitive. A few masculine nouns add **-ns: des Namens**.
  For a list of masculine **N-nouns**, see Appendix F, Grammatical Tables, #9.

1. Einige Fragen. Sie und Ihre Partnerin/Ihr Partner sprechen über ver-
schiedene° Dinge. Sehen Sie die zwei Listen an und verbinden Sie die Wörter.
Benutzen Sie den Genitiv der Wörter von der Liste auf der rechten Seite.

various

→ Wer war der Mann des Jahres?
→ Ist das Frau Meiers Buch?

das Buch	das Auto
die Designerin	der Film
das Deutschbuch	das Haus
die Farbe	Herr/Frau Meier
die Frau	das Jahr
der Mann	der Junge
der Name	der Professor
der Rucksack	der Pulli
der Titel	Sebastian

Feminine and plural nouns

Die Farbe **der Bluse** gefällt mir.
Schmidts sind Freunde **meiner
  Eltern.**

I like the color *of the blouse.*
The Schmidts are friends *of my parents.*

Feminine and plural nouns do not add a genitive ending. The corresponding articles, **der**-words, and **ein**-words end in **-er** in the genitive.

*is moving / **Ihre Nähe:** near where
you live*

2. Hast du die Adresse? Ihre Freundin/Ihr Freund zieht° in Ihre Nähe° und
braucht einige Adressen. Helfen Sie ihr/ihm.

→ Kennst du eine Apotheke?   *Hier ist die Adresse einer Apotheke.*

1. Kennst du eine Bäckerei?
2. Und eine Metzgerei?
3. Wo ist eine Drogerie?
4. Gibt es hier eine Buchhandlung?
5. Wo ist die Bibliothek?

The interrogative pronoun wessen?

Wessen CD-Spieler ist das?
Wessen CDs sind das?

Whose CD player is that?
Whose CD's are those?

The question word to ask for nouns or pronouns in the genitive is **wessen**. It is
the genitive form of **wer** and is equivalent to English *whose*.

■ *Possessive adjectives*

Theresa ist die Freundin **meines Bruders.**	Theresa is *my brother's* girlfriend.
Hast du die Telefonnummer **seiner Freundin?**	Do you have *his girlfriend's* telephone number?

Possessive adjectives take the case of the noun they modify. Even though a possessive adjective already shows possession (**mein** = my, **sein** = his), it must itself be in the genitive case when the noun it goes with is in the genitive (**meines Bruders** − of my brother); **die Freundin meines Bruders** shows *two* possessive relationships.

Die Quelle¹ der Schönheit

Mineralwasser
oder
Stille Quelle

STEINSIEKER

Viel Calcium
595mg/kg
Wenig Natrium²
19,4 mg/kg

12x0,7/0,75Ltr.

4.39
€uro

zuzgl.³ 3,30€ Pfand⁴
Preis/Ltr: 0,52€

Was ist die Quelle der Schönheit?
Wovon hat die Quelle der Schönheit viel?
Wie viel kostet die Quelle der Schönheit?

¹*source, spring* ²*sodium* ³**zuzüglich:** *in addition* ⁴*deposit*

3. Wessen Telefonnummer ist das? Beantworten Sie die folgenden Fragen und benutzen Sie den Genitiv. Lesen Sie das Beispiel.

→ meine Eltern *Wessen Telefonnummer ist das?*
Das ist die Telefonnummer meiner Eltern.

1. meine Tante
2. sein Bruder
3. ihr Freund Mark
4. seine Schwester
5. ihre Großeltern
6. unser Nachbar

4. Eine Fußballmannschaft° plant ihr Jahresfest°. Alle sprechen gleichzeitig°. Wiederholen° Sie die Sätze mit der Genitivform der Wörter in Klammern.

soccer team / annual party / at the same time / repeat

→ KEVIN: Der Termin° des Festes ist nächsten Samstag. (die Party)
Der Termin der Party ist nächsten Samstag.

date

1. MARTIN: Wie ist die Adresse des Biergartens? (das Café)
2. DOMINIK: Kennst du die Ideen seiner Freundin? (unser Nachbar)
3. STEFAN: Wie heißt die Freundin deines Bruders? (deine Schwester)
4. ALEX: Kennst du den Namen dieser Firma? (dieses Geschäft)
5. MARIO: Das ist die Telefonnummer meines Vetters. (meine Kusine)
6. PATRICK: Ich hole dich mit dem Auto meines Vaters ab. (meine Mutter)

choose

stellen ... Fragen: ask each other questions

Discussing friends and family

acquaintances

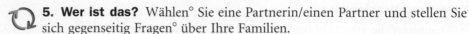

5. Wer ist das? Wählen° Sie eine Partnerin/einen Partner und stellen Sie sich gegenseitig Fragen° über Ihre Familien.

1. Wo wohnt der Freund deiner Schwester?
2. Wo wohnt die Freundin deines Bruders?
3. Wie ist die Telefonnummer deines Freundes? Deiner Freundin?
4. Hast du die Adresse deiner Tante? deines Onkels? Deiner Großeltern?
5. Was für ein Auto hat der Freund deiner Schwester? Die Freundin deines Bruders?
6. Wie heißen die Bekannten° deiner Eltern?

6. Hören Sie zu. Henning bekommt heute Besuch von seinen Eltern. Stefanie kommt vorbei. Hören Sie zu und beantworten Sie die Fragen dazu. Sie hören einige neue Ausdrücke: **Ich muss los** *(I have to leave);* **morgen früh** *(tomorrow morning).*

1. Warum hat Henning Stress?
2. Wie ist das Wetter?
3. Was muss Henning alles kaufen?
4. Warum ist Hennings Mutter kritisch, wenn sie Brot isst?
5. Wo finden Henning und Stefanie die Adresse der Bäckerei?
6. Bis wann bleiben Hennings Eltern bei ihm?
7. Wann will Stefanie Henning anrufen?

2 Genitive of time

Indefinite past	**Eines Tages** hat mir Melanie alles erklärt.	*One day* Melanie explained everything to me.
Indefinite future	**Eines Tages** mache ich das vielleicht.	*Someday* maybe I'll do that.

Nouns expressing an indefinite point in time are in the genitive.

3 Prepositions with the genitive

(an)statt	*instead of*	Kommt Anna **(an)statt** ihrer Schwester?
trotz	*in spite of*	**Trotz** des Wetters fahren wir in die Berge.
während	*during*	**Während** des Sommers bleiben wir nicht in Hamburg.
wegen	*on account of*	**Wegen** des Wetters gehen wir nicht schwimmen.

The prepositions **anstatt** or **statt, trotz, während,** and **wegen** require the genitive case.

    wegen **dem Wetter** (des Wetters)   trotz **dem Regen** (des Regens)

In colloquial usage many people use the prepositions **statt, trotz, wegen,** and sometimes **während** with the dative.

    trotz **ihm**   wegen **dir**

In colloquial usage dative pronouns are frequently used with the prepositions: **statt ihr, trotz ihm, wegen mir.**

7. Eine Wanderung. Die Firma, bei der° Ihr Vater arbeitet, macht manchmal   which
eine Wanderung. Ihre Freundin/Ihr Freund fragt Sie, wie die letzte Wanderung
war. Beantworten Sie die Fragen mit den Wörtern in Klammern.

→   Bist du auch mitgegangen? (ja, trotz / das Wetter)
      Ja, trotz des Wetters.

1. Warum ist dein Bruder zu Hause geblieben? (wegen / seine Arbeit)
2. Ist deine Schwester mitgegangen? (ja, statt / mein Bruder)
3. Sind viele Leute gekommen? (nein, wegen / das Wetter)
4. Wann macht ihr Pläne für die nächste Wanderung? (während / diese Woche)
5. Warum gehen die Leute eigentlich wandern? (wegen / das Café)

Familienpolitik

www   Go to the *Deutsch heute* website
at http://college.hmco.com.

**Diese Frau hat Recht auf sechs Wochen
Schwangerschaftsurlaub.**

In Germany federal policy concerning families (**Familienpolitik**) covers a number of areas in the lives of
women, men, and children. One aim is to help both
women and men reconcile their professional and personal lives. In recent years, opportunities for flexible
work hours (**Gleitzeit**), part-time work (**Teilzeitarbeit**) with full benefits, or sharing jobs have improved.
Many single mothers and fathers receive financial aid
(**Unterhaltsvorschüsse**) and every woman has the
right to a maternity leave of six weeks preceding and
eight weeks after the birth of the child while receiving
her full salary (**Mutterschutzurlaub**), the cost of
which is shared by the government and her employer.
One or both parents may stay home and care for the
child for the first three years (**Elternzeit**). With the
consent of the employer, twelve months of the three
years of **Elternzeit** may be taken at another time up until the child reaches her/his
eighth birthday. At the age of three, the child has a legal right to a place in a nursery
school, although in reality many children are three and a half or four before a place
becomes available.

    The government also provides a number of financial benefits. If the parent on
leave during **Elternzeit** has an income below a certain level (38,347 euros in 2002),
she/he receives a monthly stipend (**Erziehungsgeld**) of 307 euros for two years. This
is in addition to the child benefit (**Kindergeld**) of
154 euros per month. **Kindergeld** is paid until the
child is 18 or, if she/he continues her/his education
or training, up to age 25. As much as three years of
the time spent caring for a child can be applied
towards the caregiver's pension claim.

Diskussion

Many of the benefits that are available to
mothers and families in Germany are expensive for both the government and businesses.
To what extent do you think that the benefits
for families are worth the high cost?

das Adjektiv

④ Adjectives°

■ Predicate adjectives

> Die CD ist **toll.**
> Der Wein wird sicher **gut.**
> Das Wetter bleibt jetzt **schön.**

Predicate adjectives are adjectives that follow the verbs **sein, werden,** or **bleiben** and modify the subject. Predicate adjectives do not take endings.

■ Attributive adjectives

> Das ist eine **tolle** CD.
> Das ist ein **guter** Wein.
> Wir haben jetzt **schönes** Wetter.

Attributive adjectives are adjectives that precede the nouns they modify. Attributive adjectives have endings.

Was für Essen gibt es hier?
Was kostet 9 Euro?
Wie viel kostet eine türkische Pizza?

⑤ Preceded adjectives

■ Adjectives preceded by a definite article or der-word

	Masculine	Neuter	Feminine	Plural
Nom.	der alte Mann	das kleine Kind	die junge Frau	die guten Freunde
Acc.	den alten Mann	das kleine Kind	die junge Frau	die guten Freunde
Dat.	dem alten Mann	dem kleinen Kind	der jungen Frau	den guten Freunden
Gen.	des alten Mannes	des kleinen Kindes	der jungen Frau	der guten Freunde

	M.	N.	F.	Pl.
Nom.	e	e	e	en
Acc.	en	e	e	en
Dat.	en	en	en	en
Gen.	en	en	en	en

Definite articles and **der**-words indicate gender and/or case. Therefore, attributive adjectives do not have to. Their endings are simply **-e** or **-en.**

Diese Handschuhe sind **teuer**.   Willst du diese **teuren** Handschuhe
wirklich kaufen?

Adjectives ending in **-er** may omit the **-e** when the adjective takes an ending.

8. Neue Sachen. Viktoria und Anna schauen sich im Warenhaus° um°. Sie sehen viele schöne Sachen, aber sie kaufen nichts. Ergänzen Sie die Sätze mit den
passenden Endungen im Nominativ oder Akkusativ.

department store / **schauen sich um:** look around, browse

1. VIKTORIA: Sag' mal, Anna, wie findest du dies_en_ rot_en_ Pulli?

2. ANNA: Ganz gut, aber d_er_ blau_e_ Pulli hier gefällt mir besser.

3. VIKTORIA: Vielleicht kaufe ich dies_en_ kurz_en_ Rock.

4. ANNA: Der Rock gefällt mir auch. Willst du lieber° d_en_ braun_en_

   rather

   oder d_en_ schwarz_en_?

5. VIKTORIA: Ich weiß nicht. Vielleicht kaufe ich anstatt des Rocks dies_e_

   toll_e_ Hose.

6. ANNA: Gute Idee. Du, schau° mal! D_as_ weiß_e_ Hemd da ist klasse°.

   look

   Es passt° gut zu der Hose.

   great / goes with

7. VIKTORIA: Meinst du? Ja, doch. Gut, ich kaufe auch d_as_ weiß_e_

   Hemd. Aber Moment mal, ich kann ja gar nichts kaufen. Ich habe ja gar kein
   Geld.

9. Woher hast du das? Fragen Sie vier Kursteilnehmerinnen/Kursteil-
nehmer, woher sie bestimmte Dinge haben (z.B. ein Kleidungsstück, eine
Tasche). Beschreiben Sie die Dinge genau (Farbe, Größe° usw.).

Describing things

size

S1:
Woher hast du/haben Sie [die
schöne braune Tasche]?

S2:
[Die] habe ich [von meiner Mutter].
[Die] habe ich [in einem kleinen
Geschäft gekauft].

10. Wie sind diese Orte°? Verena und Mario sprechen über ihre tägliche Routine. Geben Sie die Sätze mit einem passenden Adjektiv wieder.

places

→ Mario isst gern in dem Café an der Uni.
   Mario isst gern in dem billigen Café an der Uni.

Schüttelkasten

schön   laut

alt   modern   neu

   gut   groß

klein   ruhig   billig

                 gemütlich

1. Verena isst lieber in dem Biergarten in der Fußgängerzone.
2. Abends sitzen die beiden gern in der Kneipe an der Uni.
3. Nachmittags arbeitet Verena in der Buchhandlung am Markt.
4. Mario arbeitet in dem Musikgeschäft in der Altstadt°.

   old part of town

5. Abends laufen sie zusammen in dem Park im Stadtzentrum.

11. Viele Fragen. Peter hat viele Fragen. Ergänzen Sie die Sätze mit den passenden Endungen für **der**-Worte und für Adjektive im Plural.

1. Warum trägst du immer noch dies_e_ alt_en_ Schuhe?
2. D_iese_ neu_en_ Schuhe finde ich viel schöner.
3. Wann hast du dies_e_ toll_en_ Hemden bekommen?
4. Wer hat dies_e_ warm_en_ Handschuhe gekauft?
5. Was hältst du von dies_en_ neu_en_ CDs?
6. Was hältst du von dies_en_ viel_en_ Fragen?

noch einmal: once again
pay attention

12. Hier ist alles klein. Erzählen Sie die Geschichte noch einmal° mit dem Adjektiv **klein** vor jedem Substantiv. Achten° Sie auf die richtigen Endungen.

➜ Das Haus steht in der Sonnenstraße.
Das kleine Haus steht in der kleinen Sonnenstraße.

bench

Der Junge wohnt in dem Haus. Hinter dem Haus ist der Garten. In dem Garten steht die Bank°. Auf der Bank sitzt der Junge. Unter der Bank liegt der Ball von dem Jungen. Er will mit dem Ball spielen. Er nimmt den Ball in die Hand und kickt ihn durch das Fenster. Peng! Da ist das Fenster kaputt.

■ *Adjectives preceded by an indefinite article or **ein-word***

	Masculine	Neuter	Feminine	Plural
Nom.	ein alt**er** Mann	ein klein**es** Kind	eine jung**e** Frau	meine gut**en** Freunde
Acc.	einen alt**en** Mann	ein klein**es** Kind	eine jung**e** Frau	meine gut**en** Freunde
Dat.	einem alt**en** Mann	einem klein**en** Kind	einer jung**en** Frau	meinen gut**en** Freunden
Gen.	eines alt**en** Mannes	eines klein**en** Kindes	einer jung**en** Frau	meiner gut**en** Freunde

	M.	N.	F.	Pl.
Nom.	er	es	e	en
Acc.	en	es	e	en
Dat.	en	en	en	en
Gen.	en	en	en	en

Adjectives preceded by an indefinite article or an **ein**-word have the same endings as those preceded by **der**-words (**-e** or **-en**), except when the **ein**-word itself has no ending. These are **-er** for masculine nominative and **-es** for neuter nominative and accusative. Since in these instances **ein** does not indicate the gender of the noun, the adjective has to take on that function. Note the following table.

Nom.	ein alt**er** Mann	ein klein**es** Kind
Acc.	—	ein klein**es** Kind

WENN'S UM BÜCHER GEHT

**Berliner
Universitätsbuchhandlung**
SPANDAUER STRASSE 2 · 10178 BERLIN
FON (0 30) 2 40 94 31 · FAX (0 30) 2 42 31 13
Internet: http://www.unibuch-berlin.de   E-mail: info@unibuch-berlin.de

EINE DER DREI GROSSEN IN BERLIN
für Hoch-, Fachschulen und Universitäten

Wie viele große Universitätsbuchhandlungen
  gibt es in Berlin?
Wie oder wo können Sie mehr Informationen
  über die Buchhandlung finden?

13. Du hast Recht. Regina sagt einige Dinge über den Kurs. Stimmen Sie zu°
und benutzen Sie Adjektive im Nominativ für Ihre Antworten.

Stimmen zu: agree

→   Professor Schmidts Musikvorlesung war trocken, nicht?
    Ja, das war wirklich eine trockene Vorlesung.

1. Das Buch ist auch trocken, nicht?
2. Aber das Bier nachher war gut, nicht?
3. Die Klausur in Deutsch war lang und schwer, nicht?
4. Professor Langes Seminar ist interessant, nicht?
5. Eriks Referat war ziemlich kurz, nicht?
6. Das Referat war auch ziemlich schlecht, nicht?
7. Professor Memmels Kurs ist leicht, nicht?

14. Frage-Ecke. Sie und Ihre Partnerin/Ihr Partner sprechen über
Geburtstagsgeschenke. Finden Sie erst heraus, was Ihre Freunde ihrer Familie und ihren Freunden schenken. Fragen Sie dann Ihre Partnerin/Ihren Partner,
was sie/er ihrer/seiner Familie und ihren/seinen Freunden schenken möchte. Die
Informationen für *S2* finden Sie im Anhang (Appendix B).

S1: Was möchte Susi ihren Eltern schenken?
S2: Sie möchte ihren Eltern einen neuen Computer schenken.

S1:

	Eltern	Schwester	Bruder	Freundin/ Freund
Gerhard	ein teurer DVD-Player	eine blaue Bluse		
Susi			ein neues Fahrrad	eine tolle CD
Anna		eine kleine Katze	ein australischer Hut	
ich				
Partnerin/ Partner				

suggest

15. Ich habe gewonnen. Sie haben im Lotto gewonnen. Sagen Sie Ihrer Partnerin/Ihrem Partner, was Sie sich kaufen. Ihre Partnerin/Ihr Partner kann Ihnen vorschlagen°, was Sie ihr/ihm kaufen sollen. Benutzen Sie die Bilder und passende Adjektive.

> *S1:* Ich kaufe mir einen neuen teuren CD-Player. Was kann ich dir kaufen?
> *S2:* Du kannst mir ein neues Radio kaufen.

changed

16. Alles ist neu. In Andreas Leben hat sich viel verändert°. Fragen Sie sie nach Details.

> → Ich hab' ein neues Auto.
>   *Erzähl mal von deinem neuen Auto.*

1. Ich hab' eine neue Freundin.
2. Ich hab' einen neuen DVD-Player.
3. Ich hab' ein neues Fahrrad.
4. Ich hab' eine neue Wohnung.
5. Ich hab' neue Freunde.
6. Ich hab' einen neuen Deutschprofessor.
7. Ich hab' neue Vorlesungen.

dreams

17. Träume. In einer Gruppe von vier Personen sprechen Sie über Ihre Träume. Eine Person beginnt und erzählt, wovon sie/er träumt° oder was sie/er haben möchte, und fragt dann die nächste Person.

Stating wants/desires

> *S1:* Ich träume von [einem schönen Wochenende]. Wovon träumst du?
> *S2:* Ich träume von [einem tollen Motorrad].

Träume: Reise ■ Auto ■ Frau ■ Haus ■ Mann ■ Motorrad
■ Wochenende

Adjektive: schnell ■ klein ■ reich ■ schön ■ interessant ■ weiß
■ groß ■ toll ■ lang

6 Unpreceded adjectives

	Masculine	Neuter	Feminine	Plural
Nom.	guter Wein	gutes Brot	gute Wurst	gute Brötchen
Acc.	guten Wein	gutes Brot	gute Wurst	gute Brötchen
Dat.	gutem Wein	gutem Brot	guter Wurst	guten Brötchen
Gen.	guten Weines	guten Brotes	guter Wurst	guter Brötchen

	M.	N.	F.	Pl.
Nom.	er	es	e	e
Acc.	en	es	e	e
Dat.	em	em	er	en
Gen.	en	en	er	er

Adjectives not preceded by a definite article, a **der**-word, an indefinite article, or an **ein**-word must indicate the gender and/or case of the noun. They have the same endings as **der**-words, with the exception of the masculine and neuter genitive.

18. Peter isst gern. Geben Sie die Sätze mit der richtigen Form der Adjektive in Klammern wieder.

➡ Brötchen schmecken gut. (frisch)   *Frische Brötchen schmecken gut.*

1. Bier schmeckt auch gut. (deutsch)
2. Ich trinke gern Wein. (trocken)
3. Blumen auf dem Tisch gefallen mir. (frisch)
4. In vielen Städten kann man Fisch kaufen. (frisch)
5. Ich koche gern mit Wein. (deutsch)
6. Ich habe Hunger. (groß)
7. Zum Mittagessen esse ich gern Steak (*n.*). (amerikanisch)
8. Zum Abendessen esse ich gern Wurst. (deutsch)

19. Ein Geburtstagsfest. Sie und Ihre Partnerin/Ihr Partner planen ein Geburtstagsfest für eine Freundin. Diskutieren Sie darüber, was es zu essen geben soll, und schließen Sie dann einen Kompromiss°.

schließen ... Kompromiss: come to a compromise

S1: Ich möchte ungarischen Käse servieren.
S2: Ich möchte lieber holländischen Käse servieren.

Schüttelkasten

der Wein   der Fisch   das Brot

der Tee   das Bier   die Salami   der Kaffee

der Käse   der Kuchen   das Steak   die Orangen

Adjektive: italienisch ▪ türkisch ▪ englisch ▪ ungarisch° ▪ brasilianisch ▪ französisch ▪ amerikanisch ▪ deutsch ▪ holländisch ▪ spanisch

Hungarian

Ihr kulinarischer Treffpunkt[1]

Kreative italienische Küche genießen[2] Sie bei uns in südländischem Ambiente und im Sommer auch auf unserer grossen Terrasse.

Ristorante Pizzeria Molino

Theaterstrasse 7, 6003 Luzern, Telefon 041/210 77 71
7 Tage offen von 09.30 bis 24.00 Uhr
durchgehend[3] warme Küche

Was für Essen kann man im „Molino"
bekommen?
Wie lang kann man dort warm essen?
Wo kann man sitzen, wenn es warm ist?
In welchem Land ist das „Molino"?

[1]meeting place   [2]enjoy   [3]continuous

just

20. Hören Sie zu. Katrin und Leon sprechen über Katrins Bruder. Seine Frau hat gerade° ein Baby bekommen. Sie geht wieder arbeiten und er bleibt mit dem Baby zu Hause. Geben Sie an, ob die Informationen zu dem Dialog richtig oder falsch sind. Sie hören einige neue Wörter: **Wie fühlst du dich?** (*How do you feel?*); **süßeste** (*sweetest*); **stressig** (*stressful*).

1. Katrin ist als Tante nervös.
2. Ihr Bruder ist nicht gern Hausmann, er hat zu viel Stress.
3. Der Bruder muss das Haus sauber machen und kochen.
4. Katrin geht jetzt in den Park, weil schönes Wetter ist.
5. Leon geht mit.

Stating wants/desires

wishes

21. Welche Wünsche haben Sie? Sehen Sie sich zusammen mit Ihrer Partnerin/Ihrem Partner die folgende Tabelle an. Beantworten Sie die folgenden Fragen dazu. Sprechen Sie dann mit Ihrer Partnerin/Ihrem Partner über Ihre eigenen Wünsche°.

Umfrage: Welche Wünsche sind Ihnen besonders wichtig?
glückliches Familienleben 89%
Sicherheit und Ordnung im öffentlichen Leben 84%
persönliche Sicherheit 82%
Liebe und Partnerschaft 78%
das Leben genießen° 74%
Geld und Wohlstand° 60%
beruflicher Erfolg° 57%
Urlaub und reisen 57%
viele Freizeitaktivitäten 51%
Regierungswechsel° in Berlin 46%
neue Wohnung/neues Haus 16%

enjoy
affluence
success

change of government

am wichtigsten: most important

1. Welche Wünsche sind den Deutschen am wichtigsten°?
2. An welcher Stelle stehen
   a. Liebe und Partnerschaft?
   b. Erfolg im Beruf?
   c. Freizeit?

Stellen auf: draw up

3. Was ist Ihnen wichtig? Stellen Sie Ihre eigene Liste von Wünschen auf°.
4. Vergleichen Sie Ihre Liste mit der Liste Ihrer Partnerin/Ihres Partners. Was ist Ihnen wichtiger als Ihrer Partnerin/Ihrem Partner und was ist Ihnen nicht so wichtig? Erklären Sie warum.

Ordinal numbers

1. erst-	6. sechst-	21. einundzwanzig**st**-
2. zweit-	7. sieb**t**-	32. zweiunddreißig**st**-
3. dritt-	8. ach**t**-	100. hundert**st**-
		1000. tausend**st**-

An ordinal number is a number indicating the position of something in a sequence (e.g., the first, the second). In German, the ordinal numbers are formed by adding **-t** to numbers 1–19 and **-st** to numbers beyond 19. Exceptions are **erst-, dritt-, siebt-,** and **acht-.**

Die neue Wohnung ist im **dritten** Stock°.   floor
Am **siebten** Mai habe ich Geburtstag.

The ordinals take adjective endings.

8 **Dates°**   das Datum

Der Wievielte ist heute?	What is the date today?
Heute ist **der 1. (erste)** März.	Today is March first.
Den Wievielten haben wir heute?	What is the date today?
Heute haben wir **den 1. (ersten)** März.	Today is March first.

In German, there are two ways to express dates. Dates are expressed with ordinal numbers preceded by the masculine form of the definite article (referring to the noun **Tag**). A period after a number indicates that it is an ordinal. The day always precedes the month.

Hamburg, **den 2. März 2005.**

Dates in letter headings or news releases are always in the accusative.

22. Zwei Tage später. Frank vergisst immer, wann seine Freunde Geburtstag haben. Ihr Geburtstag ist immer zwei Tage später als er denkt. Beantworten Sie seine Fragen.

Asking for personal information

➡ Hat Inge am neunten Mai Geburtstag?
   Nein, am elften.

1. Hat Gisela am dreizehnten Juli Geburtstag?   *fünfzenten*
2. Hat Willi am ersten Januar Geburtstag?
3. Hat Uwe am zweiten März Geburtstag?
4. Hat Elke am sechsten November Geburtstag?
5. Hat Claudia am achtundzwanzigsten April Geburtstag?
6. Hat Gerd am fünfundzwanzigsten Dezember Geburtstag?

 23. Zwei Fragen. Fragen Sie vier Kursteilnehmerinnen/Kursteilnehmer, wann sie Geburtstag haben und in welchem Semester sie studieren.

S1: Wann hast du Geburtstag?
S2: Am [siebten Juni].
S1: In welchem Semester/Jahr bist du?
S2: [Im zweiten.]

Wiederholung

1. Meinungen erfragen. Fragen Sie zwei Kursteilnehmerinnen/Kursteilnehmer, was sie zu den folgenden Aussagen zum Thema Familie meinen. Benutzen Sie die Fragen aus der Liste.

Redemittel: Meinungen erfragen *(Inquiring about opinions)*

Wie findest du das? ■ Findest du es gut (nicht gut), dass ... ■ Was meinst du? ■ Was glaubst du? ■ Wie siehst du das? ■ Was hältst du davon? ■ Bist du dafür oder dagegen?

---

participate

decide / takes care of

different

are considered as

1. Ich bin dafür, dass die Mutter oder der Vater die ersten Monate beim Baby bleibt.
2. Ich finde es gut, dass immer mehr Väter an der Erziehung ihrer Kinder teilhaben°.
3. Ich glaube, dass jede Familie selbst entscheiden° soll, wer die Kinder versorgt°.
4. Ich halte nichts davon, dass oft nur die Mütter die Kinder erziehen.
5. Ich glaube, dass die moderne Familie sehr unterschiedlich° aussehen kann.
6. Ich bin dagegen, dass berufstätige Mütter als egoistisch gelten°.
7. Ich bin genauso dagegen, dass viele den Beruf Hausfrau und Mutter unwichtig finden.

Wie viele Personen können für 79 Euro mit dem „Weekender Plus" - Wochenendangebot im Hotel übernachten?
Wer muss nicht für das Essen zahlen und für wen ist nur das Frühstück inklusive?
Ist das „Weekender Plus" - Angebot nur für das Wochenende?

bright

2. Vorbereitungen. Bilden Sie Sätze und beschreiben Sie, wie Sie das Haus aufräumen, bevor Ihre Gäste kommen.

1. du / wollen / einräumen / Spülmaschine / jetzt / ?
2. ich / müssen / sauber machen / Küche / nachher
3. du / möchten / aufräumen / Wohnzimmer / ?
4. wer / sollen / sauber machen / Badezimmer / ?
5. nachher / ich / wollen / noch / Staub saugen
6. du / können / Staub wischen

3. Ein Amerikaner in Deutschland. Ergänzen Sie die Sätze mit den passenden Adjektivendungen.

Ein amerikanisch_en_ Student studiert an einer deutsch_en_ Universität. Er wohnt in einem schön_en_ , hell_en_° Zimmer bei einer nett_en_ Familie. In seinem Zimmer gibt es alles – ein bequem_es_° ___comfortable___
Bett, eine groß_e_ Kommode, einen modern_en_ Schreibtisch, Platz für viel_e_ Bücher auf einem groß_en_ Bücherregal – aber keinen Fernseher. Im ganz_en_ Haus ist kein Fernseher. Im Wohnzimmer steht neben dem grün_____ Sofa eine toll_____ Stereoanlage°, in seinem ___stereo system___
Zimmer hat er ein klein_____ Radio, aber das ganz_____ Haus hat nicht einen einzig°_____ Fernseher. Das gibt es!° ___single / **Das gibt es!:** There is such a thing!___

4. Eine Schweizerin in Deutschland. Erzählen Sie, wo Susanne studiert und was sie in den Sommerferien macht. Benutzen Sie die Wörter in Klammern.

1. Susanne studiert an _____ . (die Universität Tübingen)
2. Sie wohnt in _____ . (ein großes Studentenheim)
3. Sie denkt oft an _____ . (ihre Freunde zu Hause)
4. Sie kommt aus _____ . (die Schweiz)
5. In _____ fährt sie nach Hause. (die Sommerferien)
6. Sie arbeitet bei _____ . (ihre Tante)
7. Sie fährt mit _____ zur Arbeit. (der Bus)
8. Am Sonntag macht sie mit _____ eine kleine Wanderung. (ihr guter Freund)
9. Nach _____ gehen sie in ein Café. (die Wanderung)
10. Leider hat sie _____ . (kein Geld)
11. Ihr Freund muss _____ etwas Geld leihen. (sie)
12. Nachher gehen sie auf _____ . (ein Fest)

5. Wie sagt man das?

1. —My friend Karin is studying at the University of Tübingen.
   —Does she live with a family?
   —Yes. The family is nice, and she likes her large room.
2. —What's the date today?
   —It's February 28.
   —Oh oh. Karin's birthday was yesterday.
3. —Awful weather today, isn't it?
   —Yes, but I'm going hiking, in spite of the weather.

6. Letzte Woche. Erzählen Sie, was diese Leute letzte Woche gemacht haben.

→ Stefanie macht Hausarbeit.
Stefanie hat Hausarbeit gemacht.

1. Sie räumt ihr Schlafzimmer auf.
2. Gerd wäscht jeden Tag ab.
3. Stefanie trocknet manchmal ab.
4. Ich kaufe ein.
5. Ich fahre mit dem Fahrrad auf den Markt.
6. Gerd kocht am Wochenende.
7. Stefanie putzt das Badezimmer.

7. Was meinst du? Beantworten Sie die folgenden Fragen und finden Sie dann heraus, wie Ihre Partnerin/Ihr Partner sie beantwortet hat. Sie können Ihrer Partnerin/Ihrem Partner auch noch mehr Fragen stellen.

macht ... Haushalt: keeps house

1. Wer macht den Haushalt° bei dir zu Hause?
2. Welchen Beruf hat deine Mutter? Was macht sie da? (Hausfrau ist auch ein Beruf.)

having equal rights

3. Wie gleichberechtigt° sind Männer und Frauen hier in diesem Land? In der Wirtschaft? Zu Hause?
4. Wer war die erste berufstätige Frau in Ihrer Familie? (Großmutter? Mutter? Tante?)
5. Wann sitzt die erste Frau auf dem Präsidentenstuhl in den USA?

8. Zum Schreiben

denken Sie sich aus: invent

1. Schreiben Sie eine kurze Biografie von Gabi Röttgen oder Rainer Valentin. Denken Sie sich etwas über ihr Leben aus°, was Sie nicht im Text gelesen haben. Hier sind einige Möglichkeiten.

   • wo Gabi Röttgen ihren Mann oder Rainer Valentin seine Frau kennen gelernt hat

   • was Gabi an ihrem Mann oder Rainer an seiner Frau besonders gefallen hat

to what extent / satisfied

   • inwiefern° Gabi mit ihrem oder Rainer mit seinem Leben zufrieden° ist und inwiefern nicht

   • was Gabi in ihrer oder Rainer in seiner Freizeit gern macht

single

2. Im Lesestück steht etwas über alleinstehende° Mütter. Glauben Sie, dass es schwer ist, eine alleinstehende Mutter oder ein alleinstehender Vater zu sein? Erklären Sie auf Deutsch, warum das schwer ist oder warum nicht. Hier sind

cues

einige Stichwörter°:

   • Zeit

   • Geld

discipline

   • Disziplin°

by what means

3. Beschreiben Sie eine Person, die Ihr Leben beeinflusst hat, und wodurch° sie es beeinflusst hat.

Hinweise: Before beginning your German paragraph, make notes for each point you wish to include. Try to make your account more graphic and descriptive by using attributive adjectives. After you have finished writing, check the case endings of each adjective. Also pay particular attention to the case used with each preposition. For other things to watch for in your writing, refer to page 235.

Forms of the genitive

▣ Forms of articles, der-words, and ein-words

	Masculine	Neuter	Feminine	Plural
Definite article	des Mannes	des Kindes	der Frau	der Freunde
Der-words	dieses Mannes	dieses Kindes	dieser Frau	dieser Freunde
Indefinite article	eines Mannes	eines Kindes	einer Frau	—
Ein-words	ihres Mannes	unseres Kindes	seiner Frau	meiner Freunde

▣ Forms of nouns

Masculine/Neuter	Feminine/Plural
der Name **des Mannes**	der Name **der Frau**
ein Freund **des Mädchens**	ein Freund **der Kinder**

Masculine and neuter nouns of one syllable generally add **-es** in the genitive;
masculine and neuter nouns of two or more syllables add **-s**. Feminine and plural
nouns do not add a genitive ending.

▣ Forms of masculine N-*nouns*

Nom.	der Herr	der Student
Acc.	den Herrn	den Studenten
Dat.	dem Herrn	dem Studenten
Gen.	des Herrn	des Studenten

▣ The interrogative pronoun wessen?

Nom.	wer?
Acc.	wen?
Dat.	wem?
Gen.	wessen?

Uses of the genitive

▣ Possession and other relationships

das Buch **meines Freundes**	my friend's book
die Mutter **meines Freundes**	my friend's mother
die Farbe **der Blumen**	the color of the flowers

■ Prepositions

(an)statt	*instead of*	Kommt Erika **(an)statt** ihrer Freundin?
trotz	*in spite of*	**Trotz** des Wetters wandern wir.
während	*during*	**Während** der Ferien wandern wir.
wegen	*on account of*	**Wegen** des Wetters bleiben sie zu Hause.

■ Genitive of time

Indefinite past	**Eines Tages** hat mir Julia alles erklärt.	*One day* Julia explained everything to me.
Indefinite future	**Eines Tages** mache ich das vielleicht.	*Someday* maybe I'll do that.

Adjectives

■ Adjectives preceded by a definite article or der-word

	Masculine	Neuter	Feminine	Plural
Nom.	der alte Mann	das kleine Kind	die junge Frau	die guten Freunde
Acc.	den alten Mann	das kleine Kind	die junge Frau	die guten Freunde
Dat.	dem alten Mann	dem kleinen Kind	der jungen Frau	den guten Freunden
Gen.	des alten Mannes	des kleinen Kindes	der jungen Frau	der guten Freunde

	M.	N.	F.	Pl.
Nom.	e	e	e	en
Acc.	en	e	e	en
Dat.	en	en	en	en
Gen.	en	en	en	en

■ Adjectives preceded by an indefinite article or ein-word

	Masculine	Neuter	Feminine	Plural
Nom.	ein alter Mann	ein kleines Kind	eine junge Frau	meine guten Freunde
Acc.	einen alten Mann	ein kleines Kind	eine junge Frau	meine guten Freunde
Dat.	einem alten Mann	einem kleinen Kind	einer jungen Frau	meinen guten Freunden
Gen.	eines alten Mannes	eines kleinen Kindes	einer jungen Frau	meiner guten Freunde

	M.	N.	F.	Pl.
Nom.	er	es	e	en
Acc.	en	es	e	en
Dat.	en	en	en	en
Gen.	en	en	en	en

■ *Unpreceded adjectives*

	Masculine	Neuter	Feminine	Plural
Nom.	guter Wein	gutes Brot	gute Wurst	gute Brötchen
Acc.	guten Wein	gutes Brot	gute Wurst	gute Brötchen
Dat.	gutem Wein	gutem Brot	guter Wurst	guten Brötchen
Gen.	guten Weines	guten Brotes	guter Wurst	guter Brötchen

	M.	N.	F.	Pl.
Nom.	er	es	e	e
Acc.	en	es	e	e
Dat.	em	em	er	en
Gen.	en	en	er	er

Ordinal numbers

1. erst-	6. sechst-	21. einundzwanzigst-
2. zweit-	7. siebt-	32. zweiunddreißigst-
3. dritt-	8. acht-	100. hundertst-
		1000. tausendst-

The ordinals (numbers indicating position in a sequence) are formed by adding
-t to the numbers 1–19 and -st to numbers beyond 19. Exceptions are **erst-**,
dritt-, **siebt-**, and **acht-**.

Dies ist mein **drittes** Semester.   This is my third semester.

The ordinals take adjective endings.

KAPITEL 9

Grüezi in der Schweiz

Die Baseler Straßenbahn wünscht schöne Ferien.

LERNZIELE

Sprechintentionen

Inquiring about someone's health
Talking about injuries
Discussing wishes
Describing one's daily routine
Talking about household chores
Making comparisons
Stating preferences
Discussing personal information
Expressing sympathy

Lesestück

Ein Brief aus der Schweiz

Land und Leute

Switzerland
    Languages
    Swiss dialect
    History
    Government
    Zurich and Basel

Vokabeln

Parts of the body
Personal care and hygiene
Adjectives used as nouns
Viel and *wenig*

Grammatik

Reflexive constructions
Definite article with parts of the body
Infinitives with *zu*
The construction *um ... zu* + infinitive
Comparison of adjectives and adverbs

Bausteine für Gespräche

Hast du dich erkältet?

CLAUDIA: Hallo, Uwe! Was ist los? Du hustest ja füchterlich.

UWE: Ja, ich habe mich erkältet. Der Hals tut mir furchtbar weh.

CLAUDIA: Hast du auch Fieber?

UWE: Ja, ein bisschen – 38.

CLAUDIA: Du Armer! Du siehst auch ganz blass aus!

UWE: Ich fühle mich auch wirklich krank. Vielleicht gehe ich lieber zum Arzt.

CLAUDIA: Na, das würde ich aber auch sagen! Vergiss nicht, dass wir ab Samstag eine Woche lang mit Gisela and Alex in Zermatt Ski laufen wollen!

Fragen

1. Beschreiben Sie Uwes Krankheit[+].
2. Warum ist es besser, dass er zum Arzt geht?
3. Mit wem wollen Uwe und Claudia Ski laufen gehen?

(Drei Tage später ...)

Wie fühlst du dich heute?

CLAUDIA: Wie fühlst du dich heute? Bist du gestern zum Arzt gegangen?

UWE: Ja, ich war in der Uni-Klinik. Die Ärztin hat mir was verschrieben und es geht mir jetzt schon wesentlich besser. Das Fieber ist weg.

CLAUDIA: Willst du immer noch am Samstag mit in die Schweiz fahren?

UWE: Aber klar doch! Den Urlaub haben wir doch schon seit Monaten geplant.

CLAUDIA: Das Wetter soll nächste Woche toll sein. Vergiss nicht deine Sonnenbrille mitzubringen.

Fragen

1. Warum geht es Uwe nach drei Tagen besser?
2. Wie soll das Wetter nächste Woche in den Alpen sein?

Brauchbares

1. In Uwe's two sentences, **"Ich habe mich erkältet"** and **"Ich fühle mich auch wirklich krank"** note that in German there is the pronoun **mich**. These pronouns are reflexive pronouns and the verbs that use them are called reflexive verbs. The English equivalents of these two verbs have no reflexive pronouns. For more discussion of reflexive verbs see pages 323–324.

Wann soll man Emser Pastillen nehmen?

[1]scratchy throat [2]voice

2. Uwe's temperature of 38°C = 100.4°F. Normal body temperature is 37°C.

3. Claudia's exclamation, **"Na, das würde ich aber auch sagen!"** is the equivalent of English *I would also say so.* **Würde** is the equivalent of the English *would*-construction. Like *would,* **würde** is used to express polite requests, hypothetical situations, or wishes. **Würde** is derived from the verb **werden,** and it is the subjunctive form.

4. Zermatt is considered by many to be Switzerland's best all-round ski resort. At 1620 meters (5,250 ft.) Zermatt is dominated by the Matterhorn (4478 m or 14,691 ft.), one of the world's most photographed and recognized mountains. All three of Zermatt's ski areas are above 3100 m (10,200 ft.) and are open from late November to early May, giving it the longest winter season in the Alps. Zermatt can only be reached by rail; no cars are allowed.

5. Uwe speaks about **Urlaub. Urlaub** is used to express the idea of being or going on vacation (British English: *on holiday*). **Ferien** is used when speaking about a break from study or work: **Sommerferien** (*university break*).

Das idyllische Bergdorf Zermatt am Fuße des Matterhorns (4478 m) ist auch im Sommer attraktiv.

Inquiring about someone's health

 1. Was hast du? Ihre Partnerin/Ihr Partner sieht blass aus. Fragen Sie, was mit ihr/ihm los ist.

S1:
Du siehst blass aus. Was hast du?[+]

S2:
Mir geht es nicht gut.[+]
Ich fühle mich nicht wohl.[+]
Mir ist schlecht.[+]
Ich habe │ **Kopfschmerzen.**
　　　　　　 Zahnschmerzen[+].
　　　　　　 Magenschmerzen[+].
　　　　　　 Rückenschmerzen[+].
Ich bin erkältet.

2. Geht es dir besser? Fragen Sie eine Freundin/einen Freund nach° ihrer/seiner Erkältung.

fragen nach: inquire about

I want this to work

S1:
Was macht deine Erkältung?⁺

S2:
Es geht mir | **besser.**
           | schon besser.
           | schlechter.⁺
Ich fühle mich | **krank.**
               | schwach.⁺
               | schwächer als gestern.

3. Wie fühlst du dich? Fragen Sie eine Kursteilnehmerin/einen Kursteilnehmer, wie sie/er sich fühlt.

1. Was machst du, wenn du Fieber hast?
2. Was machst du, wenn du dich erkältet hast?
3. Wie oft gehst du zum Zahnarzt?

Erweiterung des Wortschatzes

1. Der Körper⁺

1. der **Hals,** ⸚e
2. der **Arm,** -e
3. die **Hand,** ⸚e
4. der **Finger,** -
5. der **Bauch,**
   pl. Bäuche
6. das **Bein,** -e
7. das **Knie,** -
8. der **Fuß,** ⸚e
9. der **Rücken,** -

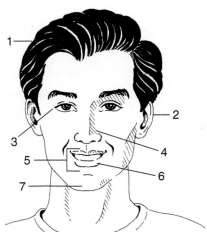

2. Der Kopf⁺

1. das **Haar,** -e
2. das **Ohr,** -en
3. das **Auge,** -n
4. die **Nase,** -n   das **Gesicht,** -er
5. der **Mund,** ⸚er
6. die **Lippe,** -n
7. das **Kinn,** -e

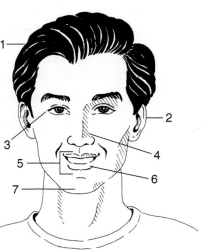

soccer team

team member

1. Jeder ist verletzt. Alexanders Fußballmannschaft° hat nicht nur das Fußballspiel verloren, sondern sich auch verletzt⁺. Fragen Sie Ihre Partnerin/Ihren Partner, wo jedes Mannschaftsmitglied° verletzt ist.

> *S1:* Wo ist Nummer 1 verletzt?
> *S2:* Der Arm tut ihm weh⁺.

2. Wer ist es? Sehen Sie sich alle Studenten in Ihrem Deutschkurs an und wählen Sie eine/einen aus°. Ihre Partnerin/Ihr Partner wird Ihnen Fragen stellen und raten°, wen Sie sich ausgesucht haben.

wählen aus: choose

guess

> *S2:* Ist sie/er groß oder klein?
> Hat sie/er blonde⁺/schwarze/braune /rote / dunkle⁺/
> hellbraune⁺ Haare?
> Sind die Haare kurz/lang?
> Trägt sie/er eine Brille?

Vokabeln 1

Adjectives and adverbs that add umlauts in the comparative and superlative are indicated as follows: **arm (ä).**

Substantive

die **Erkältung, -en**   cold *(illness)*
das **Fieber**   fever
das **Gesicht, -er**   face
der **Hals, ⸚e**   throat, neck
die **Klinik, -en**   clinic
der **Kopf, ⸚e**   head
der **Körper, -**   body
die **Krankheit, -en**   illness

der **Magen, -**   stomach; die
   Magenschmerzen *(pl.)* stomachache
der **Rücken, -**   back; die
   Rückenschmerzen   back pain
der **Schmerz, -en**   pain
der **Zahn, ⸚e**   tooth; die
   Zahnschmerzen *(pl.)*   toothache
*For additional parts of the body, see
   page 309.*

Verben

sich erkälten   to catch a cold; **erkältet: ich bin erkältet**   I have a cold
sich fühlen   to feel (*ill, well, etc.*)
husten   to cough
planen   to plan
verletzen   to injure, hurt; **ich habe mir den Arm verletzt**   I've injured/ hurt my arm; **ich habe mich verletzt**   I hurt myself

verschreiben, verschrieben   to prescribe
weh·tun (+ *dat.*)   to hurt; **Die Füße tun mir weh.**   My feet hurt.
würde (*subjunctive of* **werden**)   would; **ich würde das auch sagen**   I would also say that

Andere Wörter

ab   from a certain point on; away (from); **ab heute**   from today
arm (ä)   poor
blass   pale; **ganz blass**   pretty pale
blond   blond
dunkel   dark
fürchterlich   horrible, horribly
hell   light; bright; **hellbraun**   light brown

lieber   preferably, rather
schlecht: schlechter   worse
schwach (ä)   weak
wesentlich   essential, substantial, in the main
wohl   well

Besondere Ausdrücke

du Armer   you poor fellow
immer noch   still
Mir geht es (nicht) gut.   I am (not) well.
Mir ist schlecht.   I feel nauseated.

Was hast du?   What is wrong with you? What's the matter?
Was macht deine Erkältung?   How's your cold?

Ein Brief aus der Schweiz

Vorbereitung auf das Lesen

◾ Vor dem Lesen

1. Viele Leute haben Brieffreunde⁺. Was schreibt man einer Brieffreundin oder einem Brieffreund im ersten Brief?

2. Was möchten Sie Ihren Brieffreunden über Ihre Stadt oder Ihr Land erzählen? Nennen° Sie zwei Dinge.   name

3. Welche Stichwörter° assoziieren Sie mit der Schweiz?   key words

4. Sehen Sie sich die Landkarte von der Schweiz am Anfang des Buches an und lesen Sie die folgenden Informationen.

   • **Größe°:** 41.290 qkm°; etwa halb so groß wie Österreich (83.855 qkm) oder Maine (86.027 qkm); etwas kleiner als Neuschottland° (52.841 qkm)   size / **qkm = Quadratkilometer:** square kilometers / Nova Scotia

   • **Bevölkerung°:** ca.° 7,3 Millionen Einwohner   population / **ca.** (abbrev. for **circa**): approximately

   • **Topografie:** $\frac{2}{3}$ des Landes sind hohe Berge

type of government / federal state /
cantons

principality

state, province / larger / smaller

fewer

- **Regierungsform°:** Bundesstaat° mit 26 Kantonen°, parlamentarische Demokratie
- **Hauptstadt:** Bern
- **5 Nachbarn:** Frankreich (F)*, Deutschland (D), Österreich (A), Fürstentum° Liechtenstein (FL), Italien (I)

a. Ist Ihr Land oder Bundesland° größer° oder kleiner° als die Schweiz?
b. Ist die Schweiz größer als Österreich oder nur halb so groß?
c. Hat die Schweiz mehr Einwohner als Österreich oder weniger°?
d. Wie heißen die Nachbarn der Schweiz?

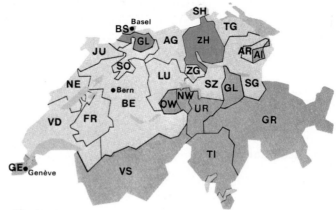

Kantone

ZH	Zürich	FR	Freiburg	AG	Aargau
BE	Bern	SO	Solothurn	TG	Thurgau
LU	Luzern	BS	Basel-Stadt	TI	Tessin
UR	Uri	BL	Basel-Land	VD	Waadt
SZ	Schwyz	SH	Schaffhausen	VS	Wallis
OW	Obwalden	AR	Appenzell A.-Rh.	NE	Neuenburg
NW	Nidwalden	AI	Appenzell I.-Rh.	GE	Genf
GL	Glarus	SG	St. Gallen	JU	Jura
ZG	Zug	GR	Graubünden		

▨ Beim Lesen

Beantworten Sie diese Fragen:

1. Schreibt Claudia „du" oder „Sie" in ihrem Brief an Thomas?
2. Welche Fragen stellt⁺ Claudia an Thomas?
3. Machen Sie Stichwörter zu Claudias wichtigen Themen.

---

partnerships / pen pals
(correspondence friendships)

Viele Schweizer sind nach Amerika ausgewandert. Deswegen gibt es in Amerika auch einige Orte mit Schweizer Namen. Einige amerikanische und Schweizer Städte haben Partnerschaften° und organisieren Brieffreundschaften° mit dem Ziel junge Amerikaner und Schweizer zusammenzubringen. Thomas
5 Wild aus New Glarus in Wisconsin und Claudia Handschin aus Glarus in der Schweiz möchten eine Brieffreundschaft beginnen. In ihrem ersten Brief an Thomas beschreibt Claudia ihr Land:

Lieber Thomas,

mein Name ist Claudia Handschin und ich bin 22 Jahre alt. Ich studiere
10 Chemie in Basel, aber ich komme aus Glarus. Ich interessiere mich für

---

* The abbreviations in parentheses are the international symbols used on automobile stickers.

Amerika. Da unsere zwei Städte eine Partnerschaft haben, habe ich deine
Adresse und ein paar Informationen über dich bekommen. Deine Urgroßeltern°   *great-grandparents*
sind voriges° Jahrhundert von Glarus nach Amerika ausgewandert, nicht wahr?   *last*
Du studierst Deutsch, nicht wahr? Sprichst du auch Deutsch zu Hause
15 oder sprechen nur die älteren Leute in New Glarus noch Deutsch? Hast du
Verwandte hier in Glarus?

     65% aller° Schweizer sprechen Deutsch. Deutsch ist jedoch nur eine von   *of all*
den offiziellen Sprachen unseres Landes. Italienisch, Französisch und Rätoro-
manisch° sind die anderen. Deswegen hat unser Land auch offiziell keinen   *Rhaeto-Romanic*
20 deutschen, französischen oder italienischen Namen, sondern einen lateini-
schen: „Confoederatio Helvetica". Das heißt auf deutsch „Schweizerische
Eidgenossenschaft°". Unsere kleine Schweiz hat nämlich° 26 autonome Kan-   *Confederation / you see*
tone und Bern ist die Hauptstadt.

     Glarus liegt in der deutschen Schweiz. Wir sprechen zu Hause Dialekt, du
25 auch? Im Kindergarten sagen wir noch „grüezi" und „woane gaasch", aber in
der Schule lernen wir Hochdeutsch° und müssen dann „grüß Gott" und   *High German*
„wohin gehst du?" sagen. Hochdeutsch sprechen wir auch noch mit Ausländern, mehr unter formellen Umständen° und oft im Radio und Fernsehen.   *circumstances*
Wenn wir schreiben, benutzen wir selten Dialekt.

30   Was kann ich dir weiter von der Schweiz erzählen? Du weißt wohl, dass die
Schweiz eine starke Wirtschaft hat. Aber du weißt vielleicht nicht, dass unser
kleines Land fast keine Rohstoffe hat. Wir müssen Rohstoffe und Lebensmittel
importieren. Um die bezahlen zu können, müssen wir auf den Weltmärkten
konkurrieren° können. Das können wir nur durch Qualität. Wir Schweizer   *compete*
35 machen alles sehr präzis: Maschinen, Instrumente, chemische Produkte und
Apparate. Diese Qualitätsprodukte sind zusammen mit dem Tourismus die
Basis für die starke Wirtschaft der Schweiz. Und eine starke Wirtschaft ist
wiederum° die Basis für unseren hohen Lebensstandard. Die Schweiz ist kein   *in turn*
Mitglied der EU (Europäischen Union). Doch viele Leute – vor allem junge
40 Leute – finden, dass unser Land Mitglied werden soll, weil sonst die Wirtschaft
auch schwächer werden könnte°. Schließlich werden Welt und Wirtschaft im-   *could*
mer° internationaler. Konservativere und ältere Leute jedoch argumentieren   *more and more*
dagegen. Für sie ist es ein Schritt gegen die Autonomie der Schweiz, wenn die
Schweiz zur EU gehört.

45   Viele Menschen waren aber auch dagegen, dass die Schweiz Mitglied der
Vereinten Nationen (UN) wird. Doch seit 2002 gehört die Schweiz zur UN
und hat damit° einen Teil ihrer 500-jährigen° Neutralität aufgegeben. Darüber   *thereby / 500-year-old*
hat es eine große Kontroverse gegeben. Die Gegner – oft ältere Leute – haben
die positiven Seiten der Neutralität in den beiden Weltkriegen betont°. Ich und   *emphasized*
50 viele andere jedoch haben befürchtet°, dass die Schweiz zwar neutral, aber   *feared*
auch isoliert von der Welt wäre°. Nun ist die Schweiz in der UN und die hatte°   *would be / had*
ihren europäischen Sitz° ja schon immer in der Stadt Genf, im französischen
Teil der Schweiz.

     So, lieber Thomas, für heute ist das alles aus der Schweiz. Bitte schreibe
55 mir bald etwas über Amerika. Ich freue mich schon auf deinen Brief!

Liebe Grüße

deine Claudia

[l.47]: After being defeated by
the French army in Italy in 1515,
Switzerland avoided political
entanglements with other powers.
Since then it has successfully
preserved its neutral status.

Brauchbares

1. Nouns ending in **-schaft** designate a group or condition. English equivalents often end in *-ship:* **Partnerschaft** (l. 3), *partnership;* **Brieffreundschaft** (l. 3), *pen pals (correspondence friendship).* Note also **Eidgenossenschaft** (l. 22), *confederation.* Nouns ending in **-schaft** are feminine and their plural ending is **-en.**

2. l. 38, **unser hoher Lebensstandard:** Switzerland's gross domestic product (GDP) per capita is 20% higher than that of other Western European countries (est. 2000): Switzerland $28,600, Austria $25,000, Germany $23,400. (Other industrial countries: USA $36,200; Japan $24,900; Canada $24,800). The actual average income in Switzerland is the highest in the world (2000): 1. Switzerland $38,000, 3. Japan $32,200, 5. USA $30,000, 7. Austria $25,900, 8. Germany $25,300.

3. Part of Switzerland's economic power owes something to its excellent public school system, which is considered one of the best in the world. Based on the 2002 *Global Competitiveness Report* (World Economic Forum), Switzerland's public schools ranked third in the world. Austria and Finland were first and Belgium second.

4. The verbs **könnte** (l. 41) and **wäre** (l. 51) are subjunctive forms of **können** and **sein.** The subjunctive is discussed in *Kapitel 11.*

5. The verb **hatte** (l. 51) is the simple past tense form of **haben.** The simple past is covered in *Kapitel 10.*

Nach dem Lesen

1. Fragen zum Lesestück

1. Warum schreibt Claudia Handschin an Thomas?
2. Warum interessiert sich Thomas wohl für die Schweiz?
3. Welcher Prozentsatz° von Schweizern spricht Deutsch?
4. Warum ist der offizielle Name der Schweiz ein lateinischer Name?
5. Wann lernen die Kinder Hochdeutsch?
6. Warum schreibt Claudia den Brief auf Hochdeutsch?
7. Was importieren und was exportieren die Schweizer?
8. Was ist die Basis für die starke Wirtschaft der Schweiz?
9. Seit wann ist die Schweiz Mitglied der UN?

percentage

2. Claudia Handschin. Ergänzen° Sie die fehlenden° Informationen über Claudia und schreiben Sie dann einen kurzen Absatz° über sie.

complete / missing
paragraph

Alter° _____   Wohnort° _____   Universität _____   Hauptfach _____

age / place where you live

3. Die Schweiz und ihre Rolle in der Welt. Suchen Sie im Text die Stellen über die Wirtschaft und die internationale Politik der Schweiz. Dann sagen Sie, wer laut° Claudia die folgenden Bemerkungen° machen könnte° – ein junger Schweizer oder ein älterer, konservativer Schweizer.

according to / comments / could

1. Wir dürfen nicht Mitglied der EU werden. Da geben wir unsere Autonomie auf.
2. Unsere Wirtschaft wird schwächer, wenn wir nicht Mitglied der EU werden.
3. Wir dürfen uns auch wirtschaftlich nicht isolieren.
4. Aus der Geschichte wissen wir, dass Neutralität für uns das Beste ist.
5. 500 Jahre Neutralität sind genug. Wir müssen aktiv an der Weltpolitik teilhaben°.

participate (in)

4. Hören Sie zu. Thomas ruft Claudia an. Er will nächsten Sommer in die
Schweiz reisen und Claudia besuchen. Hören Sie das Gespräch an und beantworten Sie die Fragen.

1. Wo ist Thomas, als er Claudia anruft?
2. Was möchte Thomas von Claudia wissen?
3. Wo ist Claudia in den ersten zwei Wochen im Juli?
4. Warum kann Thomas nicht lang in der Schweiz bleiben?
5. Bleiben Claudia und Thomas nur in Basel?
6. Wann kommt Thomas in die Schweiz?
7. Was möchte Claudia vielleicht nächstes Jahr machen?

Land und Leute

Die viersprachige Schweiz

Invasions by different ethnic tribes over a period of many hundred years shaped
Switzerland's linguistic character. Today there are four national languages, each one
spoken in a specific region or regional pocket. About 65% of the population speaks
German, 19% speaks French, and 8% speaks Italian.
The fourth national language, Rhaeto-Romanic
(**Rätoromanisch**) is only spoken by 0.8% of the population. In a conscious effort to preserve the language,
the Swiss voted in a constitutional referendum in 1996
to elevate Rhaeto-Romanic to the status of an official
language (**Amtssprache**) of the Swiss Confederation.
However, German, French, and Italian are the primary
Amtssprachen used to conduct business and political
affairs. Every Swiss can learn these languages at school
and usually gains at least a passive understanding of
them. Each of the four national languages has many
dialects; Rhaeto-Romanic alone has five dialects, Swiss
German has many more. Although High German
(**Hochdeutsch**) is taught in the schools, many Swiss
resist speaking it. **Hochdeutsch** is referred to as writ-
ten German (**Schriftdeutsch**). The primary spoken language of the German-speaking
Swiss is the dialect called **Schwyzerdütsch.**

Deutsch, Französisch, Itallenisch und Rätoromanisch
sind die vier Sprachen der Schweiz.

Considering its small size—the longest North-South distance is 137 miles (220
km) and the longest East-West distance is
216 miles (348 km)—and considering its
multitude of languages and dialects, Switzerland is linguistically and culturally a highly
diversified country. Only in a political sense
do the Swiss see themselves as a unity.

Diskussion

About 9% of the population speaks languages
other than the four national languages.

Switzerland has established a long history of linguistic and cultural diversity while maintaining political
unity. Quickly write down three things (concepts or
institutions) that you think are important for the
political unity of a country. Compare your list with
that of your classmates. How important does the
class think that a common language is for political
unity?

Schwyzerdütsch

www Go to the *Deutsch heute* website at http://college.hmco.com.

Differences between Swiss German (**Schwyzerdütsch**) and High German (**Hochdeutsch**) include vocabulary, grammar endings, pronunciation, and sentence rhythm. Below are two examples of Swiss German—one in a song, the other in a newspaper advertisement.

I schänke dr mis härz is a song by **Züriwest,** the most successful Swiss rock band of the last twenty years. The song is performed on their 1994 album *ZüriWest. Radio zum Glück* (Radio to Happiness), an album released in 2001, was also the title of a very successful tour. *I schänke dr mis härz* is in the dialect spoken in Bern. The band calls itself **Züriwest** because they are from Bern, which is west of Zurich (**Zürich**).

Refrain

i schänke dr mis härz – meh han i nid
du chasch es ha we de wosch
es isch es guets u es git
no mängi wo's würd näh
aber dr würd i's gä

The High German translation is:

Ich schenke dir mein Herz[1] – mehr habe ich nicht
Du kannst es haben wenn du willst
Es ist gut und es gibt
Noch eine Menge[2], die es nehmen würden[3]
Aber dir würde ich es geben.

[1]heart [2]many people [3]would

The advertisement looking for singers for the **Heimet-Chörli Basel** (a chorus) is from the *Baslerstab,* a newspaper in Basel. While the newspaper is written in High German, some advertisements, such as this one, are written in the dialect spoken in Basel.

*Heimet-Chörli Basel
Singsch au vo
Härze gärn?
Jodlerchörli suecht
Sängerinne,
probe dien mir
am Donnschtig Zobe
am achti im
Allmändhuus.
Uskunft 061 641 15 48*

The High German translation of this advertisement is:

homeland	Heimat°-Chor Basel
	Singst du auch von
heart	Herzen° gern?
	Jodlerchor sucht
	Sängerinnen,
proben ... wir: we rehearse	Proben tun wir°
	am Donnerstagabend
	um acht im
German house	Alemannenhaus°
information	Auskunft° 061 641 15 48

Diskussion

Compare the two versions of the song and the two versions of the advertisement. What differences do you see in vocabulary, grammar endings, and probable pronunciation?

Erweiterung des Wortschatzes

1. Adjectives used as nouns

Herr Schmidt ist **ein Bekannter** von mir.	Mr. Schmidt is *an acquaintance* of mine.
Frau Schneider ist **eine Bekannte** von mir.	Ms. Schneider is *an acquaintance* of mine.
Thomas hat **keine Verwandten** mehr in der Schweiz.	Thomas has *no relatives* in Switzerland any more.

Many adjectives can be used as nouns. They retain the adjective endings as though a noun were still there: **ein Deutscher (Mann), eine Deutsche (Frau)**. In writing, adjectives used as nouns are capitalized.

1. Ein guter Bekannter. Aische und Mustafa sind beim Einkaufen im Supermarkt und Mustafa sieht dort einen Bekannten. Aische möchte wissen, wer das ist. Setzen Sie die fehlenden Adjektivendungen ein.

AISCHE: Kennst du den groß_en_ Blond_en_ dort? Er hat dir gewinkt°.   waved

MUSTAFA: Ja, er ist ein gut_en_ Bekannt_en_ von mir. Er ist Arzt im

Marienhospital, und zwar Orthopäde. Die Krank_en_ dort sind bei ihm in besten Händen.

AISCHE: Ist er Deutsch_er_ ?

MUSTAFA: Nein, Kanadier.

AISCHE: Und die Klein_e_ neben ihm ist sicher seine Tochter, nicht?

MUSTAFA: Ja, und dort beim Obst steht seine Frau. Sie ist Deutsch_e_. Sie hat in Kanada studiert und da haben sie sich kennen gelernt.

AISCHE: In Kanada?

MUSTAFA: Ja, viele Deutsch_e_ studieren in den USA oder in Kanada. ... Ach, hallo James, wie geht es dir ...

Uni-Shop

Lust auf etwas Neues?

Neue Aula, Mo.– Fr. 11.30-13.30 Uhr
Osiander Mensa Morgenstelle

Das Gute daran ist, dass es billig ist.	*The good [thing]* about it is that it is cheap.
Hast du **etwas Neues** gehört?	Have you heard *anything new?*
Ja, aber **nichts Gutes.**	Yes, but *nothing good.*

Adjectives expressing abstractions (**das Gute,** the good; **das Schöne,** the beautiful) are neuter nouns. They frequently follow words such as **etwas, nichts, viel,** and **wenig,** and take the ending **-es** (etwas Schönes). Note that **anderes** is not capitalized in the expression **etwas anderes.**

2. Wie war das Wochenende? Melanie und Claudia sitzen nach der Vorlesung im Café und sprechen über das letzte Wochenende. Setzen Sie die fehlenden Adjektivendungen ein.

CLAUDIA: Hast du am Wochenende etwas Schön_____ gemacht?

MELANIE: Nein, ich habe nichts Besonder_____ gemacht. Das Interessant_____ war vielleicht noch der alte Spielfilm Sonntagabend im Fernsehen.

CLAUDIA: Bei mir war das Wochenende eigentlich ganz nett. Ich habe einen neuen französisch_____ Film mit Gerard Depardieu gesehen. Und das Best_____ war, Uwe hat mich eingeladen.

MELANIE: War der Film auf Französisch?

CLAUDIA: Ja. Das war ja das Gut_____ daran! Und ich habe sogar fast alles verstanden°.

understood

MELANIE: Ach, wie schön für dich. Aber so etwas Langweilig_____ wie dieses Wochenende habe ich lange nicht gehabt. Können wir jetzt von etwas ander *em*_____ reden?

2. The adjectives *viel* and *wenig*

Wir haben **wenig** Geld, aber **viel** Zeit.	We have *little* money but *lots of* time.

When used as adjectives, **viel** and **wenig** usually have no endings in the singular.

Dieter hat **viele** Freunde.	Dieter has *lots of* friends.
Das kann man von **vielen** Menschen sagen.	You can say that about *many* people.

In the plural, **viel** and **wenig** take regular adjective endings.

appropriate

3. Viel oder wenig? Suchen Sie sich passende° Wörter aus und fragen Sie Ihre Partnerin/Ihren Partner danach. Benutzen Sie folgende Fragewörter: wie viel?/wie viele? warum? welche?

Freunde ▪ Freundinnen ▪ Kurse dieses Semester ▪ CDs ▪ Kassetten ▪ Freizeit ▪ Geld ▪ Kreditkarten⁺ ▪ Videos ▪ Uhren

Vokabeln 2

Substantive

der **Apparat, -e** apparatus, appliance

der/die **Bekannte** (*noun declined like adj.*) acquaintance

der **Brieffreund, -e**/die **Brieffreundin, -nen** pen pal

der **Dialekt, -e** dialect

die **Digitalkamera, -s** digital camera

der **Gruß, -̈e** greeting; **Viele/Liebe Grüße** (*closing of a letter*) best regards

das **Instrument, -e** instrument

das **Jahrhundert, -e** century

die **Kamera, -s** camera

die **Kreditkarte, -n** credit card

der **Lebensstandard** standard of living

die **Maschine, -n** machine

das **Mitglied, -er** member

der **Ort, -e** place (geographical)

die **Qualität, -en** quality

der **Rohstoff, -e** raw material
die **Seite, -n** side; page
die **Sprache, -n** language
der **Teil, -e** part

der/die **Verwandte** (*noun declined like adj.*) relative
das **Ziel, -e** goal

Verben

aus·wandern, ist ausgewandert to emigrate
beginnen, begonnen to begin
sich **freuen (auf** + *acc.*) to look forward to; **sich freuen (über** + *acc.*) to be pleased (about/with)
(sich) interessieren (für) to be interested (in)

verstehen, verstanden to understand
wünschen (du wünschst) to wish; **was wünschst du dir zum Geburtstag?** what do you want for your birthday?

Andere Wörter

alt: älter older
deswegen therefore, for that reason
dick fat; thick
dumm (ü) dumb, stupid
dünn thin
erst (*adj.*) first; **erst** (*adv.*) not until, only, just
gerade just; straight

jedoch however, nonetheless
langsam slow(ly)
neutral neutral
schlank slender
schließlich finally, after all
Schweizer (*adj.*) Swiss
selten seldom
stark: stärker stronger

Besondere Ausdrücke

auf [Deutsch] in [German]
[sie] schreibt an [ihn] + *acc.* [she] writes to [him]; **sie schreibt einen Brief an ihn** she writes a letter to him (Also: **sie schreibt ihm einen Brief.**)

[sie] stellt Fragen an [ihn] [she] asks questions of [him] (Also: **sie stellt ihm Fragen.**)
um ... zu (+ *infinitive*) (in order) to; **um neutral zu bleiben** in order to remain neutral
vor allem above all

Grammatik und Übungen

1 Reflexive constructions

| Accusative | Ich habe **mich** gewaschen. | I washed (*myself*). |
| Dative | Kaufst du **dir** einen neuen Farbfernseher? | Are you buying (*yourself*) a new color TV? |

A reflexive pronoun indicates the same person or thing as the subject. A reflexive pronoun may be in either the accusative or the dative case, depending on its function in the sentence.

Land und Leute

Schweizer Geschichte

Switzerland's roots reach back more than 2,000 years, when a Celtic people called the Helvetians lived in the area that is now Switzerland. Over the course of several hundred years, the Alemanni, the Burgundians, and the Franks settled there as well. The Holy Roman Empire came into existence in A.D. 962. Most of this area became part of it in A.D. 1033. In the 13th century, the Habsburg family, the ruling house of Austria (1282–1918) and rulers of the Empire, gained control over these regions. The cantons (**Kantone**) Schwyz, Uri, and Unterwalden started the Swiss Confederation (1291) and fought for their independence. August 1 is now a national holiday celebrating the alliance of the three cantons. Between 1315 and 1388 Switzerland defeated Austria in three different wars and finally gained independence from the Holy Roman Empire in 1499. The period of greatest expansion came to an end in the sixteenth century. From that point on the Swiss Confederation began to embrace a policy of neutrality which was internationally recognized by the Congress of Vienna in 1815. Switzerland never participated in World War I or World War II. During the Nazi era in Germany, Switzerland accepted approximately 30,000 refugees, but it also turned a similar number away. In 1996 it became known that Swiss banks had done business with the Nazi party and that the banks had either lost track of the accounts of many German Jews or had plundered the accounts. Consequently, the Swiss banks set up a fund to aid Holocaust survivors. As the result of litigation in the United States, Swiss banks were ordered in 1998 to pay some $1.25 billion to Holocaust survivors or heirs of victims who had deposited money in Swiss banks.

Ein Beispiel für Schweizer Architektur aus dem Kanton Schwyz.

Today Switzerland is composed of 26 cantons, three of which are divided into half-cantons. Although the possibility of joining the European Union is being explored, it remains independent and neutral. It has an army to defend these principles if necessary. Military service is compulsory for all men. After completing their service, soldiers take home their rifles and uniforms, for they are still obligated to spend several weeks at regular intervals retraining. They remain members of the armed forces and on inactive status.

Diskussion

Wilhelm Tell is the national hero of Switzerland and the inspiration for works of music and literature. See what you can find out about this figure and why he represents an important event in Swiss history.

www Go to the *Deutsch heute* website at http://college.hmco.com.

② **Forms of reflexive pronouns°**

das Reflexivpronomen

	ich	du	er/es/sie	wir	ihr	sie	Sie
Accusative	mich	dich	**sich**	uns	euch	**sich**	**sich**
Dative	mir	dir	**sich**	uns	euch	**sich**	**sich**

Reflexive pronouns differ from personal pronouns only in the **er/es/sie-, sie-** *(pl.),* and **Sie**-forms, which are all **sich.**

■ *Use of accusative reflexive pronouns*

Direct object	Ich habe **mich** schnell gewaschen.	I washed *(myself)* in a hurry.
Object of preposition	Max erzählt etwas über **sich.**	Max is telling something about *himself.*

A reflexive pronoun is in the accusative case when it functions as a direct object or as the object of a preposition that requires the accusative.

1 Sie fühlen sich heute besser. Sie und Ihre Freunde hatten° denselben Virus, doch heute fühlen sich alle wieder besser. Bilden° Sie Sätze und benutzen Sie das passende Reflexivpronomen im Akkusativ.

had
form

→ *Veronika fühlt sich heute besser.*

1. Gabi und Rolf
2. du
3. ich
4. wir
5. Philipp
6. ihr

■ *Use of dative reflexive pronouns*

Indirect object	Kaufst du **dir** einen neuen Computer?	Are you going to buy *yourself* a new computer?
Object of preposition	Sprichst du von **dir?**	Are you talking about *yourself?*

A reflexive pronoun is in the dative case when it functions as an indirect object or as the object of a preposition that requires the dative case.

Früher war Nippes eine typische Arbeitergegend (*working class neighborhood*) in Köln. Heute aber ist es eine ziemlich teure Gegend (*area*) - multikulturell und im Trend - mit vielen Restaurants und Cafés. Was, denken Sie, wollen die Besitzer (*owners*) von Gernots sagen? Wählen Sie eine der Aussagen und finden Sie Argumente dafür.
a. „Wir sind modern."
b. „Wir sind alt und haben viel Tradition."
c. „Weil wir in Nippes sind, sind wir im Trend."

*Die Zeiten
ändern sich*[1]*.
Nippes auch.*

Gernots

Mauenheimer Straße 32 · 50733 Köln (Nippes)
Telefon 0221 / 76 63 05
Geöffnet: täglich 10–1h · 10–15 h Frühstück
12–15 h Mittagessen · 18–23 h Abends à la Carte

[1]*change*

2. Was wünschen sie sich aus der Schweiz? Frau Schmidt fährt zu einer Konferenz in die Schweiz und bringt ihrer Familie und ihren Freunden Souvenirs mit. Bevor sie in die Schweiz gereist ist, hat sie alle gefragt, was sie sich wünschen. Frau Schmidts Nachbarin spricht mit ihrer Tochter über ihre Wünsche. Ergänzen Sie den Text mit den richtigen Formen von **wünschen** und den Reflexivpronomen im Dativ.

wool jacket

wristwatch

Frau Schmidts Tochter Margot *wünscht sich* eine Wolljacke°. Ihr Mann _____ _____ eine Schweizer Armbanduhr°. Oliver, ihr Sohn, _____ _____ ein Buch über die Schweiz. Ihre Eltern _____ _____ Schweizer Schokolade. Ich _____ _____ einen schönen Fotokalender. Was hast du _____ _____ ? Letztes Jahr hast du _____ von Frau Schmidt eine CD von einer Schweizer Techno-Gruppe _____ , nicht wahr? Du und Sven – _____ ihr _____ wieder CDs? Hoffentlich bekommen wir alles, was wir _____ _____ .

Discussing wishes

individual

leather jacket
chic

3. Was wünschen sie sich? Stefan und seine Freunde sprechen darüber, was sie sich zum Geburtstag wünschen. Sehen Sie sich die Bilder an und fragen Sie Ihre Partnerin/Ihren Partner, was die einzelnen° Personen sich wünschen. Dann fragen Sie Ihre Partnerin/Ihren Partner, was sie/er sich wünscht.

ein neues Fahrrad ■ eine gute Digitalkamera ■ eine teure Lederjacke°
■ neue Schuhe ■ ein Handy ■ eine schicke° Sonnenbrille

S1: Was wünscht sich Stefan?
S2: Stefan wünscht sich eine teure Lederjacke.

S1: die Eltern? Claudia? mein Bruder Dirk? Partnerin/Partner?
S2: Stefan? Michaela? Sabine? Partnerin/Partner?

€219,00   €69,99   €45,00   €58,90   €39,90   €162,00

Stefan   **Michaela**   **Sabine**   **die Eltern**   **Claudia**   **mein Bruder Dirk**

Wanderer mit Blick auf das Matterhorn (4,478 Meter).

③ Verbs of personal care and hygiene

Wann badest du?
Ich bade abends.

Wann duschst du?
Ich dusche morgens.

Wann putzt du dir die Zähne?
Ich putze mir morgens die Zähne.

Wann rasierst du dich?
Ich rasiere mich morgens.

Wann schminkst du dich?
Ich schminke mich morgens.

Wann ziehst du dich an?
Ich ziehe mich morgens an.

Wann kämmst du dich?
Ich kämme mich morgens.

Wann ziehst du dich aus?
Ich ziehe mich abends aus.

Wann wäschst du dir Gesicht und
Hände?
Ich wasche mir abends Gesicht
und Hände.

■ **Verben**

sich an·ziehen, angezogen   to get dressed; **ich ziehe mich an**   I get dressed
sich aus·ziehen, ausgezogen   to get undressed; **ich ziehe mich aus**   I get
  undressed
baden   to take a bath; **ich bade**   I take a bath
(sich) duschen   to shower; **ich dusche (mich)**   I take a shower (**duschen**
  can be used with or without the reflexive pronoun; the meaning is the same.)
sich kämmen   to comb; **ich kämme mich**   I comb my hair; **ich kämme mir
  die Haare**   I comb my hair
putzen   to clean; **ich putze mir die Zähne**   I brush/clean my teeth
sich rasieren   to shave; **ich rasiere mich**   I shave
sich schminken   to put on make-up; **ich schminke mich**   I put on make-
  up; **ich schminke mir die Lippen/Augen**   I put on lipstick/eye make-up
sich waschen (wäscht), gewaschen   to wash; **ich wasche mich**   I wash myself; **ich wasche mir die Hände**   I wash my hands

*Describing one's daily
routine*

4. Wann machst du das? Fragen Sie Ihre Partnerin/Ihren Partner nach
ihrer/seiner täglichen Routine.

S1:		*S2:*
Wann	**stehst du auf?**	**Um (sieben).**
	duschst du?	Morgens.
	ziehst du dich an?	Abends.
	putzt du dir die Zähne?	Vor/Nach dem Frühstück.
	kämmst du dir die Haare?	Vorm Schlafengehen.
	wäschst du dir die Hände?	Vor/Nach dem Essen.
	ziehst du dich aus?	Nach einer schmutzigen° Arbeit.
	badest du?	[Drei]mal° am Tag.
	gehst du schlafen?	

dirty
times

fit ... halte ich mich,
... fühle ich mich!

Fitness · Gymnastik
Squash · Badminton
Sauna · Kosmetik
Kinderbetreuung[1]
Gastronomie
Shop · Sonne

Wir seh'n uns im...

*sportpark
am kreuzeck*®

34-05-00

Am Kreuzeck 2a
St. Augustin-Npl.
0 22 41/34 24 86

Womit kann man sich im
Sportpark fit halten?
Was kann man noch alles im
Sportpark machen?

[1]*childcare*

4   **Reflexive verbs in German vs. English**

Setz dich.	Sit down.
Fühlst du **dich** nicht wohl?	Don't you feel well?
Hast du **dich** gestern **erkältet?**	Did you catch a cold yesterday?
Hast du **dich** zu leicht **angezogen?**	Did you dress too lightly?
Mark hat **sich** heute nicht **rasiert.**	Mark didn't shave today.
Ich **freue mich** auf deinen Brief.	I'm looking forward to your letter.
Anna **interessiert sich** für Musik.	Anna is interested in music.

In German, some verbs regularly have a reflexive pronoun as part of the verb pattern. The English equivalents of these verbs do not have reflexive pronouns. In general, the reflexive construction is used more frequently in German than in English. In the vocabularies of this book, reflexive verbs are listed with the pronoun **sich: sich fühlen.**

5. Wie sagt man das?

1. Do you feel better today, Mr. Meier?
   —No, I don't feel well.
2. How did Astrid catch cold?
   —I don't know. Did she catch cold again?
3. Lotte, why haven't you dressed yet?
   —It's still early. I'll get dressed later.
4. Please sit down, Erna.
   —Thanks, I'll sit on this chair.
5. Are you interested in old films?
   —Yes, I'm looking forward to Casablanca on TV. (*on* = **im**)

⑤ Definite article with parts of the body

Ich habe **mir die** Hände gewaschen.	I washed *my* hands.
Hast du **dir die** Zähne geputzt?	Did you brush *your* teeth?

In referring to parts of the body, German uses a definite article (e.g., **die**) and a reflexive pronoun (e.g., **mir**) where English uses a possessive adjective (e.g., *my*).

Ich muss **mir die** Schuhe anziehen.	I have to put on *my* shoes.

In German the definite article is also often used with clothing.

6. Schon fertig. Sagen Sie, was Sie gemacht haben.

➡ Gesicht waschen
Ich habe mir das Gesicht gewaschen.

1. Hände waschen
2. Haare waschen
3. Haare kämmen
4. Zähne putzen
5. saubere Jeans anziehen
6. ein sauberes Hemd anziehen

7. Was sagen Sie? Beantworten Sie die Fragen erst selbst und vergleichen° Sie dann Ihre Antworten mit den Antworten anderer Kursteilnehmer/innen.

compare

1. Wann duschst oder badest du?
2. Wäschst du dir abends oder morgens die Haare?
3. Mit was für einem Shampoo wäschst du dir die Haare?
4. Wann putzt du dir die Zähne?
5. Mit welcher Zahnpasta° putzt du dir die Zähne?
6. Ziehst du dir die Schuhe aus, wenn du fernsiehst?
7. Ziehst du dir alte Sachen an, wenn du abends nach Hause kommst?

toothpaste

Land und Leute

Die politischen Institutionen der Schweiz

www Go to the *Deutsch heute* website at http://college.hmco.com.

Although political life in Switzerland is essentially based in the cantons (comparable to states in the U.S. and provinces in Canada), federal affairs are represented by several constitutional bodies.

Swiss citizens who are 18 years and older have the right to vote for the National Council (**Nationalrat**). Each citizen can vote for a party and a candidate. Elections for the Council of States (**Ständerat**) vary according to cantonal law. The National Council and the Council of States form the Federal Assembly (**Bundesversammlung**), which elects a cabinet of Federal Ministers (**Bundesrat**) and the Federal President (**Bundespräsident/Bundespräsidentin**). Although the President is the head of state, his/her duties are largely ceremonial and he/she does not hold special power within the government.

The Federal Assembly decides on new or amended laws. However, if within three months of such a decision, 50,000 signatures are collected from voters, the law must be put to the Swiss people for a vote. The law then only takes effect if the majority vote in favor. Some selected recent referenda: (1) In 1992 voters approved Switzerland's joining the International Monetary Fund and the World Bank. (2) In 1993 voters approved a rise in the price of gasoline and the introduction of a value-added tax to replace the sales tax. They rejected an initiative to ban ads for alcohol and tobacco products. (3) In 1994 the people approved a referendum for an outright ban in 10 years on all heavy trucks traveling through Switzerland to other European countries. Such vehicles will have to be hauled by rail. No new major highways may be built. (4) In 1996 the voters rejected a referendum that would have drastically limited immigration to Switzerland and ultimately denied asylum to refugees and illegal immigrants. (5) In 2001, the referendum to join the European Union was defeated for the third time. However, in 2002 the Swiss passed a referendum to join the UN.

Despite its long democratic tradition, it was not until 1971 that a referendum gave women the right to vote in federal elections and to hold federal office. In 1981 a referendum was passed that bars discrimination against women under canton as well as federal law.

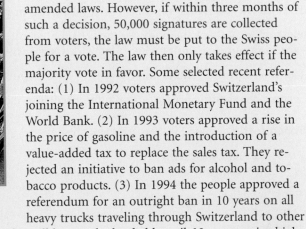

Der Nationalrat tagt in Bern.

Diskussion

Look at the issues recently decided by referendum in Switzerland. Do you believe that it is a good idea for voters to decide on such issues directly and on a regular basis? Which issue would you suggest for a national referendum in your country?

Leserunde

Burckhard Garbe (b. 1941) is a professor at the University of Göttingen, author of numerous books, and recipient of many literary prizes. He writes concrete poetry, visual texts, experimental texts, aphorisms, and ironic-satiric prose works. Garbe says that he loves word play: It amuses but also causes one to reflect on the trite expressions in everyday speech. Garbe's poem "für sorge" is a perfect example of his intentions, as he uses the mechanical declension of reflexive pronouns to end with a serious comment on human nature.

für sorge[1]

ich für mich
du für dich
er für sich
wir für uns
ihr für euch

jeder für sich

Burckhard Garbe

[1]**die Fürsorge:** *care*

6 Infinitives with *zu*

Infinitives with *zu*	Ich brauche heute nicht **zu** arbeiten.	I don't have to [need to] work today.
Modals and infinitive	Musst du morgen arbeiten?	Do you have to work tomorrow?

In English, dependent infinitives used with most verbs are preceded by *to*. In German, dependent infinitives used with most verbs are preceded by **zu**. Dependent infinitives used with modals are not preceded by **zu**.

Du brauchst nicht mit**zu**kommen.	You don't need to come along.
Wir haben vor übers Wochenende da**zu**bleiben.	We're planning to stay here over the weekend.

When a separable-prefix verb is in the infinitive form, the **zu** comes between the prefix and the base form of the verb.

Infinitive phrases need not be set off by commas although writers may choose to use a comma for clarity.

Some verbs you know that can be followed by **zu** + an infinitive are **beginnen, brauchen, lernen, scheinen, vergessen,** and **vorhaben.**

8. Das haben wir vor. Dieter hat gerade sein Examen an der Universität bestanden°. Sie und Ihre Freunde feiern sein Examen mit einer Party. Erzählen Sie noch einmal°, was Sie gemacht haben, und verbinden Sie dabei jeweils die beiden Sätze.

passed
once more

➜ Wir laden 20 Gäste ein. Das haben wir vor.
   Wir haben vor 20 Gäste einzuladen.

1. Ich bereite das Essen vor. Das muss ich noch.
2. Ich koche Spaghetti. Das habe ich vor.
3. Dieter geht einkaufen. Das will Dieter.
4. Er kauft eine besonders gute Torte. Das hat er vor.

5. Ich räume (nicht) auf. Das brauche ich nicht. (In your answer, omit the **nicht** in parentheses.)
6. Dieter macht alles. Das muss Dieter.
7. Er putzt das Bad (nicht). Das braucht er nicht. (In your answer, omit the **nicht** in parentheses.)

Talking about household chores

9. Hausarbeit. Sie und Ihre Freundin/Ihr Freund sprechen über die Hausarbeit, die Sie machen.

einkaufen ◼ kochen ◼ das Bett machen ◼ [bei der Hausarbeit] helfen ◼ Geschirr spülen ◼ abtrocknen ◼ aufräumen ◼ [die Küche] sauber machen ◼ Fenster putzen ◼ [die Wäsche/das Auto] waschen ◼ [im Garten] arbeiten ◼ die Spülmaschine ein- und ausräumen ◼ Staub saugen

S1:
Ich muss [jeden Tag] [abwaschen], und du?

S2:
Ja, ich muss auch [Geschirr spülen].
Ich brauche nicht [Geschirr zu spülen].

Wer lange lebt, hat mehr Zeit, krank zu werden

◼ *Expressions requiring infinitives with* **zu**

Es ist schön frühmorgens zu joggen.   It's nice to jog early in the morning.
Aber es ist schwer früh aufzustehen.   But it's hard to get up early.

Infinitives with **zu** are used after a number of expressions, such as **es ist schön, es ist schwer, es macht Spaß, es ist leicht,** and **es ist Zeit.** A writer may choose to set off the infinitive phrase for the sake of clarity: **Ich habe vor, vier Tage zu bleiben.**

10. Nicole studiert in Zürich. Erzählen Sie, wie es Nicole in Zürich geht. Benutzen Sie die Ausdrücke unten.

→ Sie steht früh auf.
Es ist schwer früh aufzustehen.

1. Sie fährt mit dem Zug.
2. Sie versteht die Vorlesungen.
3. Sie sitzt mit Freunden im Biergarten.
4. Sie findet einen Studentenjob.
5. Sie geht mit Freunden inlineskaten.

Schüttelkasten

Es ist gut

Es ist schwer   Es macht Spaß   Es ist nicht leicht   Es ist schön

11. Es macht Spaß ... Sie und Ihre Partnerin/Ihr Partner wollen sich besser kennen lernen: Erzählen Sie einander, was Sie gut, schlecht, schwer und leicht finden und was Ihnen Spaß macht.

> *S1:* Es ist schön [am Sonntag nichts zu tun].
> *S2:* Es ist schwer [zu schlafen].

Es macht Spaß ...	Es ist leicht ...
Es ist schön ...	Es ist gut ...
Es ist schwer ...	Ich habe keine Zeit ...

7 The construction *um ... zu* + infinitive

Die Schweiz muss wirtschaftlich stark sein, **um** neutral **zu** bleiben.	Switzerland has to remain economically strong *in order to* remain neutral.

The German construction **um ... zu** + infinitive is equivalent to the English construction *(in order) to* + infinitive. A comma is optional with an **um ... zu** construction. However, it is common practice in newspapers and magazines to use one to set the construction off, even though the sentence may be clear without it.

 12. Was meinen Sie? Ergänzen Sie die Sätze und vergleichen Sie dann Ihre Sätze mit den Sätzen von Ihrer Partnerin/Ihrem Partner.

➡ *Um gesund zu bleiben, [muss man viel Sport treiben].*

Um schöne Ferien zu haben, ...	Um glücklich zu sein, ...
Um gute Noten zu bekommen, ...	Um reich zu werden, ...
Um ein gutes Examen zu machen, ...	[Um ... zu ..., ...]
Um viele Freunde zu haben, ...	

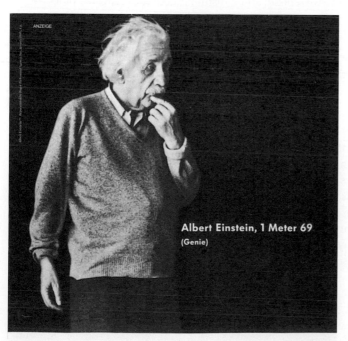

Albert Einstein, 1 Meter 69
(Genie)

Man muß nicht groß sein, um groß zu sein.

Land und Leute

Zürich und Basel

Zurich (**Zürich**), with 339,000 inhabitants, is Switzerland's largest city and one of the leading financial centers of the world. It is a city with global influence and tremendous wealth. The Zurich stock exchange is the fourth largest in the world, after New York, London, and Tokyo. Zurich is a beautiful city in an attractive setting. **Zürichsee** (Lake Zurich) is at one end; pleasant parks and gardens line the banks of the Limmat river, which bisects the city; and snow-clad peaks of the Alps are visible in the distance. Like many European cities, Zurich has a very old part, **die Altstadt,** and a new part built mostly in the nineteenth century. **Die Altstadt** is characterized by narrow streets and many well-preserved old buildings, including the houses of thirteen medieval guilds which were so crucial for Zurich's rise to financial importance. Among the churches in the area, the **Fraumünster** goes back to 853, but the new part was constructed mainly in the nineteenth century and today contains stained-glass windows by Marc Chagall. Unlike most other important cities, Zurich has only three high-rise buildings of modest size. Here is also found the **Bahnhofstraße,** an elegant world-famous shopping street with expensive fashion, jewelry, and watch shops. The University of Zurich, with 21,000 students, is the largest in Switzerland and occupies a beautiful setting on small hills not far from the center of the city.

In spite of its relatively small size, Zurich has an internationally recognized orchestra, **Zürich Tonhalle Orchester,** a widely recognized opera company, and an impressive theater housed in the **Schauspielhaus.** The Irish author James Joyce lived and wrote in Zurich and is buried there.

Citizens of **Basel** claim their city has the advantages of a small city (171,000 inhabitants) and all the advantages of a large city. Its position on the Rhine has furthered both commerce and intellectual activity. It has forty museums, a dozen theaters, the most modern music hall in Switzerland, and a distinguished university, the oldest in Switzerland (founded in 1456). Its very location lends itself to internationalism, for it is situated in the triangle (**Dreieck**) where Switzerland, Germany, and France meet. Every day almost 30,000 German and French commuters cross the border to work in Basel. It is a center of international banking, surpassed as a banking center only by Zurich and Geneva, and is the home of several immense pharmaceutical companies.

Basel is an old city with a history that goes back 2000 years to Celtic and Roman times. The Romans called the town **Basilia** (royal stronghold). The famous Dutch humanist Erasmus (ca. 1469–1536) lived there and is buried in the cathedral. By the middle ages, Basel was a center of commerce and learning, and it flourished into the Renaissance period. One can experience earlier times in Basel—city gates, narrow streets with medieval houses, the gothic cathedral (**Münster**), and the 500-year-old city hall (**Rathaus**), which is a Basel landmark.

One of the most famous Mardi Gras celebrations in Europe is the **Basler Fasnacht.** Unlike the celebrations in Germany, which are observed on the Monday (**Rosenmontag**) and Tuesday (**Fastnachtdienstag**) before Ash Wednesday (**Aschermittwoch**), **Fasnacht** in Basel begins the morning of Ash Wednesday and lasts three days.

Die Basler Fasnacht ist bekannt für ihre kunstvollen *(artistic)* **Masken.**

A 2002 survey by Mercer Human Resource Consulting, comparing the quality of life in 215 world cities, ranked Zurich first. For rankings of some other cities see note on page 170.

www Go to the *Deutsch heute* website at http://college.hmco.com.

Diskussion

1. **Karneval, Fasching, Fastnacht,** and **Fasnacht** are all names for the Mardi Gras holiday in German-speaking countries. Several centers for this celebration are in **Köln, München,** and **Düsseldorf.** Investigate the history and traditions of this holiday.
2. **Zürich** has preserved its natural beauty and its historic heritage by strictly limiting the building of skyscrapers. Are there any limitations on the height of buildings in your community? To what extent do you think municipalities should determine what kind of structures can be built?

 **8** **Comparison of adjectives and adverbs**

Comparison of equality

Die Schweiz ist halb **so** groß **wie** Österreich.	Switzerland is half *as* large *as* Austria.
Erik schwimmt nicht **so** gut **wie** Klaus.	Erik doesn't swim *as* well *as* Klaus does.
Diese Reise ist genau**so** schön **wie** die letzte.	This trip is just *as* nice *as* the last one.

The construction **so ... wie** is used to express the equality of a person, thing, or activity to another. It is equivalent to English *as ... as.*

13. Vier Bekannte

A. Ihre Partnerin/Ihr Partner möchte etwas über vier Bekannte von Ihnen wissen. Beschreiben Sie die Bekannten.

Mustafa   **Udo**   **Olaf**   **Luigi**

groß/klein ■ schlank/dick ■ attraktiv/unattraktiv ■ wenig/viel
Haare: blond ■ dunkel ■ lang/kurz ■ hellbraun
Nase: groß/klein ■ dünn ■ lang
Mund: groß/klein
Brille? eine dunkle Brille?

➜ Wie ist Mustafa?
   Er ist groß und hat dunkle Haare.

compare

B. Ihre Partnerin/Ihr Partner sagt etwas über einen der vier Bekannten. Vergleichen° Sie diesen mit einem anderen.

➜ Mustafa ist groß.
   Ja, Mustafa ist so groß wie Olaf.

1. Mustafa ist sportlich.
2. Luigi ist unfreundlich.
3. Olaf ist schlank.

4. Udo spricht gut Englisch.
5. Luigi kann gut kochen.
6. Udo spielt oft Gitarre.

der Komparativ

■ *Comparative forms*°

Base form	klein	Österreich ist **klein**.	Austria is *small*.
Comparative	kleiner	Die Schweiz ist noch **kleiner**.	Switzerland is even *smaller*.

The comparative of an adjective or adverb is formed by adding **-er** to the base form.

Ina arbeitet **schwerer als** Kai.   Ina works *harder than* Kai.
Ina ist **fleißiger als** Kai.   Ina is *more industrious than* Kai.

The comparative form plus **als** is used to compare people, things, or activities. **Als** is equivalent to English *than*.

Base form	dunkel	teuer
Comparative	dunkler	teurer

Adjectives ending in **-el** drop the final **-e** of the base form before adding **-er.** Adjectives ending in **-er** may follow the same pattern.

Base form	groß	Hamburg ist **groß.**
Comparative	größer	Hamburg ist **größer** als Bremen.

Many common one-syllable words with stem vowel **a, o,** or **u** add an umlaut in the comparative form, including **alt, dumm, jung, kalt, kurz, lang, oft, rot, stark,** and **warm.** Adjectives and adverbs of this type are indicated in the vocabularies of this book as follows: **kalt (ä).**

Base form	gern	gut	hoch	viel
Comparative	lieber	besser	höher	mehr

A few adjectives and adverbs have irregular comparative forms.

Jörg sieht **gern** fern.　　Jörg likes to watch TV.
Karin liest **lieber.**　　Karin prefers [likes more] to read.

The English equivalent of **lieber** is *to prefer,* or *preferably,* or *rather* with a verb.

14. Vergleichen Sie. Sehen Sie sich die Bilder auf Seite 322 an und beantworten Sie die Fragen.

Making comparisons

→　Was kostet mehr – Dirks Fahrrad oder Michaelas Handy?
　　Dirks Fahrrad kostet mehr als Michaelas Handy.

1. Was kostet mehr – Sabines Sonnenbrille oder Stefans Jacke?
2. Wessen Haare sind länger – Claudias oder Sabines?
3. Wer ist jünger – Stefan oder Dirk?
4. Wer ist älter – Michaela oder Dirk?
5. Was ist größer – das Fahrrad oder das Handy?
6. Was ist billiger – die Sonnenbrille oder die Digitalkamera?

15. Was ist besser? Sehen Sie sich die Bilder auf Seite 322 an. Vergleichen Sie mit Ihrer Partnerin/Ihrem Partner die Dinge, die Sie sich wünschen.

S1: Die Jacke sieht gut aus.
S2: Aber diese Jacke sieht besser aus.

1. Das Handy ist billig.
2. Die Sonnenbrille ist modern.
3. Die Digitalkamera ist praktisch.
4. Das Fahrrad ist gut.
5. Die Schuhe sind elegant.

16. Was machst du lieber? Ihre Partnerin/Ihr Partner fragt Sie, welche Aktivitäten Sie lieber als andere machen.

S2: Was machst du lieber? **Joggen oder Rad fahren?**
Zeitungen oder Bücher lesen?
Klassische Musik oder Rock hören?
Das Badezimmer sauber machen oder
 das Wohnzimmer aufräumen?
Staub wischen oder Staub saugen?
Gartenarbeit oder Hausarbeit?
Ins Kino oder zu einer Party gehen?
Italienisch oder chinesisch essen gehen?

S1: Ich fahre lieber Rad.

■ *Preceded comparative adjectives*

Das ist kein besser**er** Plan. That's not a better plan.
Hast du eine besser**e** Idee? Do you have a better idea?

Comparative adjectives that precede nouns take adjective endings.

dissatisfied

17. Unzufrieden°. Stefanie ist mit allem unzufrieden und will alles besser haben. Ergänzen Sie die Sätze mit einer passenden Komparativform.

➔ Stefanie hat eine schöne Wohnung, aber sie möchte eine _____ haben.
Stefanie hat eine schöne Wohnung, aber sie möchte eine schönere haben.

1. Sie hat ein großes Auto, aber sie möchte ein *größeres* haben.

2. Sie kauft immer teure Kleider, aber sie wünscht sich noch *teurere* .

3. Sie isst oft in guten Restaurants, aber sie möchte in *besseren* essen.

4. Sie hat einen schnellen Computer, aber sie kauft sich bald einen *schnelleren.*

5. Sie macht schöne Ferien, aber sie wünscht sich _____ .

6. Stefanie hat einen guten Job, aber sie braucht bestimmt einen _____ .

18. Hören Sie zu. Monika und Yvonne gehen einkaufen, weil Monikas Bruder Stefan Geburtstag hat. Hören Sie das Gespräch an. Geben Sie dann an, ob die Sätze richtig oder falsch sind. Sie hören zwei neue Wörter: **die Herrenabteilung** (*men's department*), **die Musikabteilung** (*music section*).

1. Monika weiß genau, was ihr Bruder Stefan zum Geburtstag haben möchte.
2. Monika möchte ihrem Bruder etwas kaufen, weil er ihr immer etwas zum Geburtstag schenkt.
3. Yvonne und Monika sehen sich zuerst Lederjacken an.
4. Sie finden eine gute, billige Lederjacke und kaufen sie.
5. Monika findet 120 Euro nicht zu teuer.
6. Yvonne und Monika suchen lieber eine CD für Stefan.

der Superlativ

■ *Superlative forms°*

Base form	alt	Trier ist sehr **alt**.	Trier is very *old*.
Superlative	**ältest-**	Es ist die **älteste** Stadt in Deutschland.	It is the *oldest* city in Germany.

The superlative of an adjective is formed by adding **-st** to the base form. The **-st** is expanded to **-est** if the adjective stem ends in **-d, -t,** or a sibilant. The superlative of **groß** is an exception: **größt-**. The words that add umlaut in the comparative also add umlaut in the superlative. Superlative adjectives that precede nouns take adjective endings.

Sternen-Stunden erleben[1]...

**GASTHOF[2]
ZUM GOLDENEN
STERNEN**

-liegt direkt am Rhein
-mit historischen Räumen[3] bis 80 Pers.
-Rheinterasse und Hofgarten[4]
-kreative, saisonale Küche

Johannes Tschopp, St. Alban-Rheinweg 70, CH - 4052 Basel
Tel.061 272 16 66 // Fax 061 272 16 67 // info@sternen-basel.ch

...im ältesten Gasthof von Basel

[1]experience [2]inn [3]rooms [4]garden in courtyard

Wie heißt der älteste
Gasthof von Basel?
Wo liegt der Gasthof?
Finden Sie den Gasthof
groß oder klein?

19. Was weißt du über Deutschland? Ihre Freundin/Ihr Freund spricht mit Ihnen über Deutschland. Erklären Sie ihr/ihm, dass die Orte die ältesten, größten usw. sind.

→ Trier ist eine alte Stadt, nicht?
   Ja, Trier ist die älteste Stadt Deutschlands.

1. Die Universität Heidelberg ist eine alte Universität, nicht?
2. Bayern ist ein großes Land, nicht?
3. Bremen ist ein kleines Land, nicht?
4. Berlin ist sicher eine sehr große Stadt.
5. Der Rhein ist bestimmt ein langer Fluss°.   river

| Im Winter arbeitet Frau Greif **am schwersten.** | In the winter Mrs. Greif works *(the) hardest.* |
| Im Winter sind die Tage **am kürzesten.** | In the winter the days are *(the) shortest.* |

The superlative of adverbs (e.g., **am schwersten**) and predicate adjectives (e.g., **am kürzesten**) is formed by inserting the word **am** in front of the adverb or adjective and adding the ending **-(e)sten** to it. The construction **am** + superlative is used when it answers the question **wie?** (*how?*) as in: **Wie arbeitet Frau Greif im Winter? Sie arbeitet am schwersten.**

20. Alles ist am größten. Claudia spricht im Superlativ. Wenn jemand etwas sagt, wiederholt° sie es und sagt, dass es am größten, am kältesten, am langsamsten usw. ist. Stellen Sie sich vor°, Sie sind Claudia.

repeats

Stellen ... vor: imagine

→ Im Sommer sind die Tage lang.
   Im Sommer sind die Tage am längsten.

1. Im Herbst sind die Farben interessant. - Am interessanter interessantesten.
2. Im Frühling sind die Blumen schön.

3. Im Winter sind die Tage kalt.
4. Regina fährt langsam.
5. Hans-Jürgen arbeitet schwer.
6. Ingrid und Thomas tanzen schön.

Lukas ist der jüngste Sohn und Fabian ist **der älteste (Sohn).**	Lukas is the youngest son and Fabian is *the oldest (son).*

The superlative of attributive adjectives (with a following noun expressed or understood) is formed by inserting **der/das/die** in front of the adjective and adding the appropriate ending to the superlative form of the adjective.

1. Im Juni sind die Rosen **am schönsten.**
2. Diese Rose ist **die schönste.**
   Diese Rosen sind **die schönsten.**

The above chart shows the two patterns of superlative predicate adjectives. The adjectives preceded by **der/das/die** have **-e** in the singular and **-en** in the plural.

Blick ist eine bekannte Schweizer Bild-Zeitung. Was kann man über die News sagen? Über die Leser? Über die Konsumenten?

[1]*consumers*

 21. Die schönsten, neuesten Sachen. Wie Claudia findet auch Peter alles am besten. Stellen Sie sich vor, Sie sind Peter.

→ Diese Schuhe sind sehr billig.   *Diese Schuhe sind die billigsten.*

1. Diese Blumen sind sehr schön.
2. Dieses Auto ist sehr teuer.
3. Diese Jacke ist sehr warm.
4. Dieses T-Shirt ist toll.

5. Dieser CD-Player ist billig.
6. Diese Digitalkamera ist ziemlich teuer.

Base form	gern	gut	hoch	viel
Comparative	lieber	besser	höher	mehr
Superlative	liebst-	best-	höchst-	meist-

The adjectives and adverbs that are irregular in the comparative are also irregular in the superlative. Irregular forms are indicated in the vocabularies of this book as follows: **gern (lieber, liebst-).**

22. Was sind das alles für Leute in diesem Sportclub? Beantworten Sie die Fragen über den Sportclub im Superlativ.

→ Frank spielt lieber Tennis als Basketball. Und Fußball?
Fußball spielt er am liebsten.

1. Peter spielt aber besser als Frank. Und Georg?
2. Inge treibt mehr Sport als ihr Bruder. Und ihre Schwester?
3. Gudrun schlägt° den Ball höher als Lisa. Und Karoline?   hits
4. Julians Tennisschuhe kosten mehr als Ullis Schuhe. Und Marks Schuhe?
5. David joggt lieber morgens als mittags. Und abends?
6. Nach dem Sport hören sie lieber Reggae als klassische Musik. Und Rockmusik?

23. Was meinst du? Beantworten Sie die Fragen erst selbst und vergleichen Sie dann Ihre Antworten mit den Antworten Ihrer Partnerin/Ihres Partners.   *Discussing personal information*

1. Was trinkst du am liebsten?
2. Was isst du am liebsten?
3. An welchem Tag gehst du am spätesten ins Bett?
4. Welche Sprache sprichst du am besten?
5. Was studierst du am liebsten?
6. Wer arbeitet in deiner Familie am schwersten?
7. Welchen Sport treibst du am liebsten?
8. Welcher Politiker spricht am besten?
9. Welche Stadt ist die schönste?
10. Wer ist der beste Profi-Basketballspieler? Der beste Tennisspieler? Der beste Golfspieler?

24. Was wissen Sie schon über diese Länder? Vergleichen Sie die folgenden Länder und diskutieren Sie mit Ihrer Partnerin/Ihrem Partner. Jeder gibt Informationen über das Land. Achtung!° Geben Sie auch Informationen, die nicht in der Tabelle sind.   *Attention!*

Land	Größe (qkm)	Einwohner
Deutschland	357.021	83.000.000
Italien	301.230	57.700.000
Österreich	83.858	8.150.000
Portugal	92.391	10.100.000
die Schweiz	41.290	7.300.000
Spanien	504.782	40.100.000

→ Österreich und die Schweiz

S1: Die Schweiz ist kleiner als Österreich.
S2: Sie hat auch weniger Einwohner.
S1: In der Schweiz und Österreich spricht man Deutsch.
S2: Ja, mehr Leute sprechen in der Schweiz Deutsch als Französisch.

1. Spanien und Deutschland
2. Portugal und Italien
3. die Schweiz und Spanien
4. Deutschland und Österreich
5. Portugal und Spanien

Wiederholung

files

drücken ... aus: express your
sympathy / in each instance

1. Rollenspiel. Ihre Partnerin/Ihr Partner erzählt Ihnen, dass ihr/sein Computer kaputt gegangen ist und alle Dateien° weg sind. Sie drücken ihr/ihm Ihr Mitgefühl aus° und wählen dafür jeweils° eine passende Formulierung unten.

too bad / stupid / annoying

Redemittel: Mitgefühl ausdrücken *(Expressing sympathy)*

Schade°. ▪ Du Armer/Du Arme! ▪ Das ist ja dumm/blöd°/ärgerlich°/ schade. ▪ Was hast du denn? ▪ Das verstehe ich. ▪ Geht es dir nicht gut? ▪ Das tut mir aber Leid für dich. ▪ Dass dir das passieren muss!

---

hard drive
back-up copies
in vain

ärgere mich: am annoyed

1. Am Wochenende ist mir mein Computer kaputt gegangen.
2. Der Monitor war auf einmal schwarz.
3. Leider kann niemand den Computer reparieren.
4. Alle Dateien sind weg.
5. Das ganze Material für meine Magisterarbeit war auf der Festplatte°.
6. Und ich habe keine Sicherheitskopien°.
7. Die ganze Arbeit war umsonst°.
8. Und jetzt muss ich mir einen neuen Computer kaufen.
9. Ach, ich ärgere mich° so!

begins

2. So beginnt mein Tag. Beschreiben Sie, wie Ihr Tag anfängt°. Benutzen Sie die folgenden Wörter und Wortverbindungen.

> aufstehen ▪ baden oder duschen ▪ sich anziehen ▪ tragen ▪ etwas trinken und essen ▪ sich die Zähne putzen ▪ sich die Haare kämmen

appropriate

3. In der Schweiz ist es anders. Verbinden Sie die Sätze mit einer passenden° Konjunktion aus der Liste.

> aber ▪ da ▪ dass ▪ denn ▪ ob ▪ oder ▪ und ▪ weil ▪ wenn

→ Diane Miller studiert in der Schweiz. Sie möchte mehr Deutsch lernen.
Diane Miller studiert in der Schweiz, denn sie möchte mehr Deutsch lernen.

surprised

1. Sie geht mit ihrer Freundin Nicole. Ihre Freundin geht einkaufen.
2. Diane ist erstaunt°. Nicole geht jede Woche dreimal einkaufen.
3. Sie nimmt eine Einkaufstasche mit. Sie geht zum Supermarkt.
4. Nicole kauft fast alles im Supermarkt. Die Sachen sind da oft billiger.
5. Sie kauft Tabletten in der Apotheke. Sie kauft einen Kamm in der Drogerie.
6. Beim Bäcker kauft sie frischen Kuchen. Sie kauft kein Brot.
7. Diane ist erstaunt. Nicole geht in so viele Geschäfte.

4. Bei Beckers in Zürich. Robert, ein amerikanischer Student, wohnt bei Familie Becker in Zürich. Im folgenden Dialog laden Anja Becker und ihre Freundin Bianca Robert ein, mit ihnen eine Reise nach Österreich zu machen. Ergänzen Sie den Text mit den passenden Possessivpronomen.

1. ANJA: Komm, Robert, wir machen gerade _____ Ferienpläne. Wir fahren nach Österreich zu _____ Freunden. Du kommst doch mit, oder?

2. ROBERT: Ja, gern. Wie lange bleibt ihr denn bei _____ Freunden?

3. BIANCA: Eine Woche. Du kannst _____ Arbeit mitnehmen.

4. ROBERT: Ja, das muss ich. Ich muss _____ Referat vorbereiten.

5. ANJA: Das Schöne ist, dass Vater gesagt hat, wir können _____ Auto nehmen.

6. ROBERT: Das finde ich sehr nett von _____ Vater, Anja.

7. BIANCA: Ja, das ist toll! Ich wollte schon _____ Schwester fragen, ob sie uns _____ Wagen gibt.

8. ANJA: Na, den brauchen wir jetzt nicht. Ich glaube, _____ Reise wird super!

5. Mein Bruder. Sebastian spricht über seinen Bruder. Er benutzt in seinen Sätzen Wörter, die miteinander verwandt sind. Manche Wörter sind für Sie neu, aber vielleicht können Sie ihre Bedeutung° erraten°, weil Sie das verwandte Wort kennen. Geben Sie die Sätze auf Englisch wieder.

meaning / guess

1. Ich habe meinem Bruder geholfen. Er hat meine Hilfe gebraucht.
2. Er ist Student. Er studiert in Leipzig. Mit dem Studium ist er erst in vier Jahren fertig.
3. Weil er Geld braucht, will er sein Motorboot verkaufen. Dann will er sich ein Motorrad kaufen.
4. Motorrad fährt er sehr gern. Aber der Fahrschulkurs war teuer. Die Fahrschule hat er letztes Jahr besucht.
5. Im Sommer will er dann durch Deutschland reisen. Die Reise wird bestimmt ganz toll.
6. Wenn das Wetter gut ist, will er zelten. Sein Zelt ist klein und praktisch.

6. Erik fühlt sich nicht wohl. Annette denkt, dass Erik krank aussieht. Geben Sie die Sätze auf Deutsch wieder.

ANNETTE: Why did you get up so late?
ERIK: I don't feel well.
ANNETTE: Do you have a fever?
ERIK: No. I caught a cold. My throat hurts.
ANNETTE: You look pale. Maybe it's better if you go to the doctor.
ERIK: You're right. I do feel weak.

7. Rollenspiel. Sie sind Ärztin/Arzt. Ihre Partnerin/Ihr Partner ist Ihre Patientin/Ihr Patient. Sie/Er sagt Ihnen, dass sie/er sich nicht wohl fühlt, und beschreibt viele verschiedene Symptome. Sie glauben, dass die Patientin/der Patient gestresst ist, und sagen ihr/ihm, sie/er soll die tägliche Routine ändern.

8. Zum Schreiben. Sie haben hier zwei mögliche Themen. Wählen Sie sich eins aus° und schreiben Sie.

wählen aus: select

1. Stellen Sie sich vor°, Sie sind Thomas, an den Claudia den Brief über die Schweiz auf Seite 312–313 geschrieben hat. Antworten Sie auf Claudias Brief. Vergessen Sie nicht die folgenden Informationen:

stellen vor: pretend

- Danken Sie Claudia für den Brief.
- Schreiben Sie etwas über sich selbst, ähnlich° wie Claudia es im ersten Abschnitt° ihres Briefes getan hat.

similarly
paragraph

request

denken aus: make up

- Beantworten Sie Claudias Fragen.
- Schreiben Sie ein bisschen über Ihre Stadt, Ihren Staat oder Ihre Provinz, z.B., wo liegt sie/er, welche Städte, was ist besonders?
- Erklären Sie ihr, warum Sie gern oder ungern dort leben.
- Bitten° Sie sie zurückzuschreiben.
- Erklären Sie ihr, dass Sie sich auf Ihre Antwort freuen.

2. In ihrem Brief hat Claudia ein bisschen über sich selbst geschrieben. Wie ist Claudia? Denken Sie sich noch ein bisschen mehr über sie aus°, zum Beispiel über ihre Familie und was sie gern tut.

Hinweise: As you write your letter, remember to use **du**-forms and to give your letter the proper German heading, salutation, and closing.

After you have written your letter, or description, review it, paying particular attention to the following:

- subject-verb agreement
- word order
- case used with prepositions
- adjective endings
- reflexive pronouns

Grammatik: Zusammenfassung

Reflexive constructions
Forms of reflexive pronouns

	ich	du	er/es/sie	wir	ihr	sie	Sie
Accusative reflexive	mich	dich	sich	uns	euch	sich	sich
Dative reflexive	mir	dir	sich	uns	euch	sich	sich

Use of reflexive constructions
Accusative reflexive pronouns

Direct object	Ich habe **mich** gewaschen.	I washed (*myself*).
Object of preposition	Hast du das für **dich** gemacht?	Did you do that for *yourself?*

Dative reflexive pronouns

Indirect object	Hast du **dir** ein neues Auto gekauft?	Did you buy *yourself* a new car?
Dative verb	Ich kann **mir** nicht helfen.	I can't help *myself.*
Object of preposition	Spricht Edith von **sich** selbst?	Is Edith talking about *herself?*

■ *Reflexive vs. personal pronouns*

Reflexive	Max hat das für **sich** gemacht.	Ich kann **mir** nicht helfen.
	Max did it for *himself.*	I can't help *myself.*
Personal	Max hat das für **ihn** gemacht.	Max kann **mir** nicht helfen.
	Max did it for *him.*	Max can't help *me.*

Definite articles with parts of the body

Ich habe **mir die** Hände gewaschen.	I washed *my* hands.
Sophia hat **sich die** Haare gekämmt.	Sophia combed *her* hair.

In referring to parts of the body, German often uses a definite article and a dative pronoun. English uses a possessive adjective.

Infinitives with *zu*

Theo versucht alles **zu** verstehen.	Theo tries to understand everything.
Er kann alles verstehen.	He can understand everything.

Dependent infinitives used with most verbs are preceded by **zu.** Dependent infinitives used with modals are not preceded by **zu.**

Hannah hat keine Zeit die Arbeit **zu** machen.	Hannah has no time to do the work.
Es war schwer die Vorlesung **zu** verstehen.	It was difficult to understand the lecture.

Infinitives with **zu** are also used after a large number of expressions like **sie hat keine Zeit** and **es ist schwer.** While a comma is not required to set off an infinitive phrase, a writer may choose to use a comma for the sake of clarity.

Es ist schwer so früh auf**zu**stehen.
Es ist Zeit jetzt auf**zu**hören.

When a separable prefix is in the infinitive form, the **zu** comes between the prefix and the base form of the verb.

The construction *um ... zu* + infinitive

Amerikaner kommen oft nach Deutschland, **um** dort **zu** studieren.	Americans often come to Germany *in order to* study there.

The German construction **um ... zu** + infinitive is equivalent to the English construction *(in order) to* + infinitive. While a comma is not required to set off an **um ... zu** construction, newspapers and magazines tend to use a comma.

Comparison of adjectives and adverbs

■ *Forms of the comparative and superlative*

Base form	klein	small	schön	beautiful
Comparative	kleiner	smaller	schöner	more beautiful
Superlative	kleinst-	smallest	schönst-	most beautiful

German forms the comparative by adding the suffix **-er** to the base form. It forms the superlative by adding the suffix **-st** to the base form. The ending **-est** is added to words ending in **-d** (**gesündest-**), **-t** (**leichtest-**), or a sibilant (**kürzest-**). An exception is **größt-**.

Base form	alt	groß	jung
Comparative	älter	größer	jünger
Superlative	ältest-	größt-	jüngst-

Many one-syllable adjectives and adverbs with stem vowel **a, o,** or **u** add an umlaut in the comparative and the superlative.

Base form	gern	gut	hoch	viel
Comparative	lieber	besser	höher	mehr
Superlative	liebst-	best-	höchst-	meist-

A few adjectives and adverbs are irregular in the comparative and superlative forms.

■ *Special constructions and uses*

Bernd ist nicht **so groß wie** Jens.   Bernd is not *as tall as* Jens.
Es ist heute **so kalt wie** gestern.   Today it is just *as cold as* yesterday.

In German the construction **so ... wie** is used to make comparisons of equality. It is equivalent to English *as . . . as.*

Erika ist **größer als** ihre Mutter.   Erika is *taller than* her mother.
Es ist **kälter als** gestern.   It is *colder than* yesterday.

The comparative form of an adjective or adverb is used to make comparisons of inequality. **Als** is equivalent to English *than.*

Verena singt **am schönsten.**   Verena sings *the best.*
Im Frühling ist das Wetter hier   The weather here is *nicest* in the
 am schönsten.   spring.
Die kleinsten Blumen sind **die**   The smallest flowers are *the pret-*
 schönsten.   *tiest* (flowers).

The pattern **am** + superlative with the ending **-en** is used for adverbs (as in the first example above), and for predicate adjectives (as in the second example). The superlative of attributive adjectives, with a following noun that is expressed or understood, is preceded by the article **der/das/die** (as in the third example). The superlative form of the adjective therefore has an ending.

Deutschland: 1945 bis heute

KAPITEL 10

Die Kirchenruine und der neue Teil der Gedächtniskirche in Berlin.

LERNZIELE

Sprechintentionen

Talking about cultural events
Making and responding to an invitation
Asking about cultural interests
Asking someone about her/his past
Expressing perplexity

Lesestück

Deutschland: 1945 bis heute

Land und Leute

Bertolt Brecht
Two German states
After unification
Leipzig and Dresden
Germany: The government

Vokabeln

The suffix *-ung*
City names used as adjectives
Immer + comparative
Dates

Grammatik

Simple past tense
Past perfect tense
Conjunctions *als*, *wenn*, and *wann*

Bausteine für Gespräche

Wie war's?

Gisela und Alex sind für ein paar Tage in Berlin bei Giselas Freunden Monika und Stefan. Morgens beim Frühstück sprechen sie über ihre Aktivitäten.

STEFAN: Na, wie findet ihr das Berliner Nachtleben? Wo wart ihr denn gestern Abend?

GISELA: Monika ging ja zu dem Volleyball-spiel, aber Alex und ich waren im Berliner Ensemble.

STEFAN: Ah, und was gab es?

GISELA: Sie spielten das Brecht-Stück *Das Leben des Galilei*. Es war sehr interessant.

STEFAN: Ach ja, darüber stand in der Zeitung eine gute Kritik. Hattet ihr denn gute Plätze?

ALEX: Ja, wir hatten sogar prima Plätze, obwohl wir Studentenkarten hatten. Die kosteten nur 8 Euro.

STEFAN: Ich hätte ja mal große Lust wieder ins Theater zu gehen. Könnt ihr das Stück denn empfehlen?

GISELA: Ja, unbedingt. Ich wollte es zuerst gar nicht sehen, aber dann fand ich es absolut toll.

STEFAN: Und was habt ihr danach gemacht? Ihr kamt doch erst so spät nach Hause.

ALEX: Wir waren noch in der Wunder-Bar, tranken etwas und unterhielten uns lange über das Stück.

STEFAN: Ach, ihr Glücklichen! Ich wäre auch gern dabei gewesen! Ich war zwar auch bis zwei Uhr wach, aber ich musste für meine Prüfung lernen!

Leben des Galilei was first performed in 1943. In 1947 Brecht adapted it for the American stage. One of Brecht's major plays, it treats the problem of the scientist's freedom of inquiry and control by the state — or, put differently, it investigates the problem of the scientist who pursues knowledge without regard for its social implications.

In the play, Galileo officially recants before the Inquisition. As a prisoner, however, he secretly writes down his discoveries, and a student smuggles out Galileo's notes.

Fragen

1. Wo waren Gisela und Alex gestern Abend?
2. Warum war Monika nicht dabei?
3. Was haben Gisela und Alex gesehen?
4. Was für Karten hatten sie?
5. Wie war das Stück?
6. Warum war Stefan bis 2 Uhr wach?

Brauchbares

1. Note that to say something is written or printed somewhere, e.g., in a newspaper or sentence, German uses the verb **stehen**. Thus Stefan says, **"darüber stand in der Zeitung eine gute Kritik."**

2. When Stefan says, **"Ich hätte ja mal große Lust wieder ins Theater zu gehen,"** the word **hätte** is the subjunctive form of **haben**. The subjunctive is often used in wishes and will be presented in *Kapitel 11*.

3. When Stefan says, **"Ich wäre auch gern dabei gewesen!"** he is using the past subjunctive form of **sein: wäre gewesen**. Stefan would like to have been there but couldn't for the reason he gives.

1. Wo warst du? Ihre Partnerin/Ihr Partner ist gestern Abend ausgegangen. Finden Sie heraus, wo sie/er war und wie der Abend war.

Talking about cultural events

S1:
Wo warst du gestern Abend?

S2:
Im Theater.
In einem Musical.
Im Konzert.
Im Kino.
In der Oper⁺.

Was gab es?

Die Dreigroschenoper
  [The Threepenny Opera].
Goethes *Faust.*
Ende gut, alles gut.
Die Zauberflöte [The Magic Flute].
Fidelio.
Lohengrin.
Beethovens *Neunte.*
Schumanns *Klavierkonzert⁺.*
Das Phantom der Oper.
Der König der Löwen.

2. Wohin möchtest du? Laden Sie Ihre Partnerin/Ihren Partner ein, mit Ihnen zusammen auszugehen. Der Partner/Die Partnerin kann ja oder nein sagen.

Making and responding to an invitation

S1:
Möchtest du in die Oper gehen?
ins | Musical
    | Theater
    | Konzert
    | Popkonzert⁺
    | Open-Air-
    | Konzert⁺
    | Kino

S2:
Ja, gern.
In welche?/In welches?
Oh ja, das interessiert mich sehr.
Wenn du mich einlädst, schon.
Nein, ich habe leider keine Zeit.
Nein, ich hätte wirklich keine Lust.

3. Interview. Fragen Sie Ihre Partnerin/Ihren Partner, was ihr/ihm gefällt. Schreiben Sie die Antworten auf und erzählen Sie den anderen Kursteilnehmerinnen/Kursteilnehmern, was Sie herausgefunden haben.

Asking about cultural interests

Fragen Sie Ihre Partnerin/Ihren Partner,

1. ob sie/er oft ins Theater geht.
2. was für Theaterstücke sie/er gern sieht.
3. ob sie/er lieber ins Kino geht.
4. wie oft sie/er ins Kino geht – einmal in der Woche, zweimal im Monat, usw.°   **und so weiter: etc.**
5. welche neuen Filme sie/er gut findet.
6. ob sie/er manchmal in die Oper geht.
7. welche Opern sie/er kennt.
8. ob sie/er oft ins Konzert geht.
9. was für Musik sie/er gern hört.
10. welche Rockbands sie/er gut findet.
11. welche Fernsehsendungen sie/er gut findet.

Erweiterung des Wortschatzes

1. The suffix -ung

wandern	*to hike*	**die Wanderung, -en**	*hike*
wohnen	*to live*	**die Wohnung, -en**	*dwelling, apartment*

The suffix **-ung** may be added to a verb stem (e.g., **wander-, wohn-**) to form a noun. All nouns ending in **-ung** are feminine.

1. Eine Einladung. Katja erzählt von einer Party bei Rolf Braun. Bilden Sie Substantive mit der Endung **-ung** aus den fett gedruckten Verben und ergänzen Sie die Sätze. (Einige der Substantive sind im Plural und haben die Endung **-ungen.**) Geben Sie dann das englische Äquivalent für die Substantive wieder.

1. Rolf Braun hat mich für Samstagabend **eingeladen.** Habt ihr auch eine

    _____ bekommen?
2. Ja, aber ich habe mich **erkältet** und meine _____ wird einfach nicht besser.
3. Ach, komm' doch. Rolf **wohnt** doch jetzt in Berlin-Mitte. Er will uns sicher

    seine neue _____ zeigen.
4. Hmmm, die interessiert mich ja schon. Aber du weißt doch, Rolf zeigt immer

    seine Camcorderbilder aus seinem letzten Urlaub. Und er **beschreibt** jede

    Szene sehr genau. Solche _____ finde ich immer ein bisschen langweilig.
5. Aber er **erzählt** doch oft auch nette Anekdoten von seinen Reisen. Ich höre

    seine _____ ganz gern.
6. Außerdem **empfiehlt** er oft schöne Urlaubsziele. Seine _____ waren bisher°

    immer gut.
7. **Meinst** du? Da habe ich eigentlich eine andere _____.

°until now

SWR ≫ Studio Tübingen

Aktuelles[1]
Kultur
Sport
Musik
Unterhaltung

SWR ≫ 4

Da sind wir daheim[2].

[1]current events [2]at home

Unterhaltung bedeutet *entertainment.* Nennen *(name)* Sie das entsprechende *(corresponding)* Verb.

Stellen Sie sich vor *(imagine)*, Sie sind die Programmdirektorin/der Programmdirektor des Senders *(TV channel)* SWR und suchen nach interessanten Themen. Suchen Sie für drei der Kategorien ein mögliches Thema aus. (Vergessen Sie nicht auch im Internet zu suchen.) **Beispiel:** *Musik:* Johann Sebastian Bach

Bertolt Brecht

www Go to the *Deutsch heute* website at http://college.hmco.com.

Bertolt Brecht (1898–1956) is one of the most important figures of the twentieth-century theater. His dramatic theories have influenced many playwrights and theater directors throughout the world. As a young playwright during the twenties, Brecht took the German theater by storm with *The Threepenny Opera (Die Dreigroschenoper);* it shocked and fascinated audiences with its depiction of London's criminal underworld and the social and political forces underlying it. Brecht's critical focus on society and his dramatic theories revolutionized the German stage and made him a celebrity.

As an outspoken opponent of National Socialism, however, Bertolt Brecht had to flee Germany in 1933. He lived temporarily in several European countries until he settled down in California. Like many other German emigrants, he found refuge in the United States until the end of World War II and the end of the National Socialist regime. Brecht wrote some of his major plays in exile: *Mutter Courage und ihre Kinder* (1941), *Der gute Mensch von Sezuan* (1942), *Leben des Galilei* (1943).

Bertolt Brecht

Das Berliner Ensemble spielt *Der gute Mensch von Sezuan.* **(Bertolt-Brecht-Platz)**

In 1947, after he had been called before the House Committee on Un-American Activities, he moved back to Europe and eventually chose the German Democratic Republic as his home. With his wife, Helene Weigel, he founded the *Berliner Ensemble,* a theater in former East Berlin that continues to perform Brecht's plays and tries to put his theories into practice.

Diskussion

During the Third Reich many Germans, like Brecht, left Germany. This choice is often called **"äußere Emigration"** in contrast to **"innere Emigration"** which refers to writers, artists, and intellectual figures who remained in Germany but were unable to publish their work during the Third Reich. Imagine that you are a major novelist living in a dictatorship. Which path would you choose? Which factors would you have to consider in making the decision?

2. City names used as adjectives

Na, wie findet ihr das **Berliner** Nachtleben?

Well, how do you like *Berlin* night life?

Gut, aber ich vermisse die **Wiener** Gemütlichkeit.

Fine, but I miss the relaxed *Viennese* atmosphere.

Names of cities used as adjectives end in **-er.** The **-er** ending is never declined; that is, no additional adjective endings are used to indicate gender or case.

7.–9. Juni 2002

Tübinger Bücherfest

Wo findet am 7.–9. Juni ein Bücherfest statt (*take place*)?
Wie heißt ein Bücherfest in Frankfurt? in Hamburg?

Vokabeln 1

Beginning with the **Vokabeln** of *Kapitel 10,* the simple past tense of irregular weak and strong verbs (e.g., **empfahl**) is given.

Substantive

die **Aktivität, -en** activity
die **Bar, -s** bar, pub; nightclub
der **Euro, -** euro, currency of European Union
der/die **Glückliche** *(noun decl. like adj.)* lucky/fortunate one
das **Klavier, -e** piano; das **Klavierkonzert** piano concerto
die **Kritik, -en** criticism; review

die **Lust** desire; pleasure; **Lust haben** (+ **zu** + *infinitive*) to be in the mood, feel like; **ich habe keine Lust das zu tun** I don't feel like doing that
das **Open-Air-Konzert, -e** outdoor concert
die **Oper, -n** opera; **in die Oper gehen** to go to the opera
das **Popkonzert, -e** pop concert
die **Rockband, -s** rock band

Verben

**empfehlen (empfiehlt), empfahl,
  empfohlen**   to recommend
**sich unterhalten (unterhält),
  unterhielt, unterhalten**   to talk;

sich unterhalten über (+ *acc.*)   to
talk about
zeigen   to show

Andere Wörter

absolut   absolutely, completely
dabei   (to be) there, (to be) present
danach   afterwards
prima   fantastic, great (**prima** *takes
  no adj. endings*)

unbedingt   without reservation,
  absolutely
wach   awake

Besondere Ausdrücke

einmal in der Woche   once a week
es stand in der Zeitung   it said in the
newspaper

was gab es?   what was playing? what
was offered?
zweimal im Monat   twice a month

⧫URGTHEATER

SPIELZEIT

PREMIEREN   PLÄNE

**BERLINER
ENSEMBLE**   **Bertolt Brecht
LEBEN DES GALILEI**

Deutschland: 1945 bis heute

Vorbereitung auf das Lesen

▉ Vor dem Lesen

1. Sie lesen hier über Deutschlands Geschichte zwischen 1945 und heute. Was
   wissen Sie schon über diese Zeit?
2. Stellen Sie eine Liste von Daten, Wörtern oder Namen zu den folgenden Themen auf°. Versuchen Sie mindestens° drei Stichwörter° für jeden Punkt°
   aufzuschreiben⁺.
   a. der Zweite Weltkrieg   c. der Kalte Krieg
   b. Berlin   d. die Europäische Union (EU)
3. Berichten Sie einer kleinen Gruppe, was Sie aufgelistet haben.

Stellen auf: set up / at least / key
words / point

■ *Beim Lesen*

events / that

Machen Sie Notizen von allen Ereignissen°, die° mit dem Kalten Krieg zu tun haben.

decades / for all practical purposes

Über vier Jahrzehnte° lang gab es praktisch° zwei deutsche Hauptstädte: Bonn und Ost-Berlin. Theoretisch blieb Berlin jedoch immer die Hauptstadt. Als

allied

1994 die letzten alliierten° Soldaten die Stadt verließen, war Berlin erst seit vier Jahren wieder die offizielle Hauptstadt von Deutschland, aber Bonn war bis

seat

5 Sommer 1999 der Sitz° der Regierung. 1945 hatten die Alliierten die

former / das Dritte Reich: the Third Reich

ehemalige° Hauptstadt des Dritten Reiches° in vier Sektoren aufgeteilt und sie kontrollierten Berlin bis zur Wiedervereinigung. Wenn die Hauptstadt und Deutschland geteilt waren – so argumentierte man – konnte das Land nie wieder stark genug werden, um einen neuen Krieg anzufangen.

10 Europa hatte Angst vor einem starken Deutschland, denn es war im 20. Jahrhundert für zwei Weltkriege verantwortlich gewesen. Deutsche Soldaten hatten zwischen 1938 und 1944 außer der Schweiz alle Nachbarländer zumin-

at least / a while / occupied

dest° eine Zeitlang° besetzt°. Außerdem hatten die Nationalsozialisten nicht nur im eigenen Land, sondern auch in allen besetzten Nachbarländern

Jewish / population / persecuted / concentration camps / Jews

15 systematisch die jüdische° Bevölkerung° verfolgt° und in Konzentrationslager° gebracht. Im Holocaust starben über sechs Millionen Juden°. Außer den Juden

Sinti, Roma: Gypsies / the handicapped / as well as / opponents

verfolgten die Nationalsozialisten auch noch Sinti und Roma°, Behinderte°, Homosexuelle sowie° ihre politischen Gegner° – die Kommunisten, Sozialisten und Sozialdemokraten.

tensions

20 Nach dem Ende des Krieges wurden die Spannungen° zwischen den

victorious powers

Russen und den drei westlichen Siegermächten° (England, Frankreich und den USA) immer stärker. Sie kulminierten schließlich 1948 in der Berliner Blockade. Die Russen wollten die westlichen Soldaten zwingen Berlin zu ver-

leadership

lassen und blockierten die Straßen von und nach Berlin. Unter der Führung°

airlift

25 Amerikas organisierten die westlichen Alliierten die Berliner Luftbrücke°. Ein

provided

Jahr lang versorgten° die Flugzeuge die Stadt mit allem, was die Leute zum Leben brauchten – von Rosinen° bis Kohle°. Und deshalb nannten die Berliner

raisins / coal

die Flugzeuge der Luftbrücke „Rosinenbomber". Doch als die Blockade 1949 zu Ende war, gab es zwei souveräne° deutsche Staaten: die Bundesrepublik

sovereign

August 1961: Bau der Berliner Mauer.

30 Deutschland (BRD) mit der provisorischen° Hauptstadt Bonn und die Deut- — provisional
sche Demokratische Republik (DDR) mit der Hauptstadt Ost-Berlin. Der
Kalte Krieg hatte begonnen. Die neuen Fronten waren der Ostblock und der
Westblock. Die neue Grenze hieß „der Eiserne Vorhang°". Nicht alle Ostdeut- — der Eiserne Vorhang: the Iron Curtain
schen waren für den Kommunismus. Da es dem Westen auch wirtschaftlich
35 besser ging als dem Osten, versuchten viele Ostdeutsche nun ihr Land zu verlassen. Um den Exodus zu beenden baute die DDR-Regierung 1961 die Mauer.
Als John F. Kennedy 1963 die geteilte Stadt besuchte, demonstrierte er mit den
Worten: „Ich bin ein Berliner" die Solidarität des Westens mit den Berlinern.

In dieser Zeit war die Angst vor dem Kommunismus größer als die Angst
40 vor einem starken Deutschland. Ein wirtschaftlich und politisch starkes West-
europa sollte vor dem Kommunismus schützen°. Besonders Westdeutschland — protect
wollte nach dem Krieg wirtschaftlich, politisch und kulturell mit seinen Nachbarn zusammenarbeiten, um wieder ein Teil Europas zu werden. Es wollte seinen Nachbarn zeigen, dass es wirklich für den Frieden war. So entstand° die — was established
45 Europäische Gemeinschaft° (EG) und ihre ersten Mitglieder waren außer — community
Deutschland noch Belgien, Frankreich, Italien, Luxemburg und die Niederlande. In den nächsten Jahrzehnten bekam die EG immer mehr Mitglieder.
Heute heißt die Organisation die Europäische Union (EU) und zu ihr gehören
25 Länder.
50 Ende der 80er Jahre gab es in der wirtschaftlichen Union der Ostblockstaa-
ten (COMECON) wirtschaftliche und politische Reformen. In der DDR, besonders in Leipzig, kam es 1989 zu großen, friedlichen° Demonstrationen. Die — peaceful
Menschen wollten mehr individuelle Freiheit und am 9. November 1989
musste die Regierung der DDR die Mauer öffnen. Endlich war das verhasste° — hated
55 Symbol des Kalten Krieges gefallen.

Seit dem 3. Oktober 1990 sind West- und Ostdeutschland wieder ein Land.
Mit ihren 83 Millionen Einwohnern ist die neue Bundesrepublik jetzt der
größte Staat in der EU. Das vereinte° Berlin ist mit über drei Millionen Ein- — unified
wohnern die größte deutsche Stadt. Der Kalte Krieg war endgültig° vorbei, als — definitely
60 1994, nach 49 Jahren, die Alliierten Berlin offiziell verließen. Doch neben den
großen wirtschaftlichen Aufgaben der Vereinigung zeigte sich nun auch, dass
es große kulturelle Unterschiede zwischen Ost- und Westdeutschen gab. Nun
begann der lange und oft schwierige Prozess des „Zusammenwachsens°, was — growing together
zusammengehört", wie es der westdeutsche Politiker Willy Brandt genannt
65 hatte.

Brauchbares

1. l. 6, **das Dritte Reich:** Hitler declared that he would build a third empire, suc-
cessor to the Holy Roman Empire (962–1806) and the Empire (1871–1918)
established under William I of Prussia. William I was proclaimed Emperor of
Germany in 1871.

2. l. 13, **Nationalsozialisten:** National Socialists (Nazis) were members of the
Nationalsozialistische Deutsche Arbeiterpartei that ruled Germany under
Adolf Hitler from 1933 to 1945. The policies of the party were anti-
democratic, extremely nationalistic, imperialistic, and virulently anti-Semitic.

3. l. 15–19: In 2001 the German government and over 100 companies established
a fund of 4.2 billion euros that has been used for reparations to former victims of the Nazi regime.

Menschen aus Ost und West
sind zum Brandenburger Tor
gekommen, um die Öffnung
der Mauer zu feiern

4. l. 19, **Sozialdemokraten:** Social Democrats were members of the labor-oriented Social Democratic party (**Sozialdemokratische Partei Deutschlands).** The party was outlawed by Hitler.

5. l. 22, **immer stärker** and l. 47, **immer mehr:** For more information on the construction **immer** + comparative, see p. 354.

6. l. 25, **Berliner Luftbrücke:** During the blockade of Berlin (**Berliner Blockade)** the Allies supplied over 2 million West Berliners with food and fuel by a round-the-clock air lift. There were 277,264 flights made at 3.5-minute intervals. By the end of the lift in 1949, 8,000 tons of goods (2/3 of it coal) were flown in daily. A monument commemorating the U.S. and British airmen who died during the airlift stands at Tempelhof Field, the airport in former West Berlin that was the main terminal of the airlift.

7. l. 32, **Ostblock:** The eastern block was made up of nations under communist domination and the influence of the Soviet Union. COMECON (Council for Mutual Economic Assistance) was founded in 1949 but was only active between the years 1956–1991. COMECON was controlled by the heads of state and was a vehicle for organizing industrial production and coordinating economic policy.

8. l. 33, **der Eiserne Vorhang:** The Iron Curtain was the name for the political and ideological barrier that prevented understanding between the Soviet bloc and western Europe after World War II. The expression became current after it was used by Winston Churchill in a speech at Fulton, Missouri, in 1946.

9. l. 38, **Worten:** The German word **Wort** has two plurals. The plural form, **Worte,** is used for words in context. The other plural, **Wörter,** is used for words not in a particular context as in a dictionary or list.

10. l. 64: As Chancellor of the Federal Republic of Germany from 1969–1974, Willy Brandt was largely responsible for bringing about treaties that lessened tension between West and East Germany.

Nach dem Lesen

1. Fragen zum Lesestück

1. Wie viele Jahre gab es zwei deutsche Hauptstädte?
2. Warum teilten die Alliierten Berlin auf?
3. Benutzen Sie eine Landkarte und machen Sie eine Liste von den Ländern, die° Deutschland im Zweiten Weltkrieg besetzt hat.   *which*
4. Die Nazis verfolgten viele Gruppen. Nennen Sie diese Gruppen.
5. Welche Gruppe verfolgten die Nazis am konsequentesten°?   *most persistently*
6. Was ist im Holocaust passiert?
7. Warum blockierten die Russen im Jahre 1948 Berlin?
8. Was nannten die Berliner „Rosinenbomber"? Warum?
9. Zwischen welchen Jahren gab es zwei deutsche Staaten?
10. Was wollte John F. Kennedy zeigen, als er sagte: „Ich bin ein Berliner"?
11. Warum wollte Deutschland Mitglied der Europäischen Gemeinschaft werden?
12. Wer waren die ersten Mitglieder der westlichen Wirtschaftsunion?
13. Warum demonstrierten viele Menschen 1989 in der DDR?
14. Mit welchem Wort beschreibt das Lesestück die Revolution in Leipzig?
15. Bei der Vereinigung der beiden deutschen Staaten gibt es auch heute noch Probleme. Was für Probleme sind das?

2. Der Kalte Krieg

1. Viele Historiker sagen, dass Deutschland ein wichtiger Schauplatz° des Kalten Krieges war. Beim Lesen des Textes haben Sie Notizen zum Thema Kalter Krieg gemacht. Vergleichen Sie Ihre Notizen mit der folgenden Liste. Was haben Sie aufgeschrieben, was nicht auf dieser Liste steht?   *scene*

2. Ordnen Sie die folgenden Ereignisse° chronologisch ein° und geben Sie ein Jahr oder eine Zeit an°.   *events / **ordnen ein:** arrange* / ***geben an:** give*

Chronologie	Jahr	Ereignis	
_____	_____	der Zweite Weltkrieg	
_____	_____	Gründung° der BRD und der DDR	*establishment*
_____	_____	die alliierten Truppen verlassen Berlin	
_____	_____	Bau° der Mauer	*construction*
_____	_____	Aufteilung° Berlins	*division*
_____	_____	Vereinigung Deutschlands	
_____	_____	Fall der Mauer	
_____	_____	die Luftbrücke	
_____	_____	Reformen in den Ostblockländern	
_____	_____	Demonstrationen in Leipzig	
_____	_____	Gründung einer Wirtschaftsunion im Westen	

3. Erzählen wir. Erklären Sie in einfachen Worten die folgenden Ereignisse oder Daten. Ihr Publikum spricht nur wenig Deutsch.

der Holocaust
die Luftbrücke
der 3. Oktober 1990
die EU

4. Hören Sie zu. Hören Sie den kurzen Radiobericht an und geben Sie an, ob die Sätze unten richtig oder falsch sind. Sie hören vier neue Wörter: **der Jahrestag** *(anniversary);* **erinnern sich** *(remember);* **beliebt** *(popular);* **die Solidarität** *(solidarity).*

1. John F. Kennedy besuchte Berlin im Jahr 1963.
2. An der Berliner Mauer sagte er: „Ich bin ein Berliner."
3. Kennedy sagte, dass er dem Osten helfen wollte, weniger kommunistisch zu sein.
4. John F. Kennedy war in Deutschland sehr beliebt. Deshalb gibt es in vielen deutschen Städten Straßen, Plätze und Brücken, die seinen Namen tragen.

Erweiterung des Wortschatzes

1. *Immer* + comparative

Seit dem Krieg ist der Lebensstandard der Deutschen **immer mehr** gestiegen.	Since the war, the living standard of the Germans has risen *more and more.*

The construction **immer** + comparative indicates an increase in the quantity, quality, or degree expressed by the adjective or adverb. In English, the comparative is repeated (e.g., *more and more*).

1. Wie geht es den Deutschen heute? Frau Weiß, die während des Krieges eine junge Frau war, erzählt Ihnen und Ihrem Freund, wie sich das Leben in Deutschland seit dem Ende des Krieges verändert hat. Ihr Freund versteht kein Deutsch, also übersetzen° Sie die Aussagen von Frau Weiß ins Englische.

translate

1. Der Lebensstandard der Deutschen wird immer höher.
2. Die Wohnungen werden immer größer.
3. Sie tragen immer bessere Kleidung.
4. Die Arbeitszeit° wird immer kürzer.

working hours

5. Die Ferien werden immer länger.
6. Immer weniger Leute bleiben während der Ferien zu Hause.
7. Das Leben wird immer schöner.

immigrate

8. Immer mehr Ausländer wollen nach Deutschland einwandern°.

2. Dates

1945 teilten die Alliierten Berlin in vier Sektoren auf.	*In 1945* the Allies divided Berlin into four sectors.
Im Jahre 1963 besuchte Präsident Kennedy Berlin.	*In 1963* President Kennedy visited Berlin.

In dates that contain only the year, German uses either the year by itself (e.g., **1945**) or the phrase **im Jahr(e) 1945**. English uses the phrase *in* + the year (e.g., *in 1945*).

Zwei deutsche Staaten

Two German states existed from 1949–1990. In the later years of the separation, West Germany (The Federal Republic of Germany/**Die Bundesrepublik Deutschland**) referred to this situation as "two states, but one nation" (**zwei Staaten, eine Nation**), and its constitution assumed a future reunification. East Germany (The German Democratic Republic/**Die Deutsche Demokratische Republik**), in contrast, was increasingly dedicated to building an independent, separate country. While West Germany developed a market economy, East Germany followed an economic system of central planning. While the citizens of East Germany liked the fact that there was no unemployment, that government subsidies kept rents and prices of food staples low, and that the government provided health care and a pension system, they found that the political system restricted individual freedom, and the scarcity of non-staple consumer goods was a daily irritant.

The construction of the Berlin Wall (**Mauerbau**) in 1961 was the most dramatic attempt to stop the wave of people leaving East Germany. In addition, the gradual build-up of the border system of fences, dogs, and minefields between the two states had made the border practically impenetrable.

In the early seventies, Willy Brandt, Chancellor of the Federal Republic of Germany, made the first open overtures to East Germany (part of his **Ostpolitik**) and thereby laid the groundwork for cooperation with East Germany. In the course of the years the climate between the two countries improved. At first retirees (**Rentner**) and later others from East Germany were allowed to visit West Germany, permanent representations similar to embassies (**ständige Vertretungen**) were established, and West Germans living in border areas were allowed to travel more freely across the border (**grenznaher Verkehr**).

Mit den Worten „Wir sind ein Volk!" demonstrierten die Ostdeutschen 1989 in Leipzig für ein vereintes Deutschland.

In 1989, the overall political climate in eastern European countries began to change. Hungary was the first to open the Iron Curtain by taking down the barbed wire and letting vacationing East Germans cross into Austria. A democratic movement spread throughout the Warsaw Pact countries, of which East Germany was a member. Throughout East Germany there were large demonstrations and in November 1989, the government opened the Berlin Wall and subsequently resigned. The freedom movement culminated in free elections in March 1990.

Diskussion

In both the East and the West the Germans expressed their feelings about the divided state. During the protests in East Germany, the people marched carrying banners with slogans, while in the West, people had covered the Berlin Wall with graffiti.

Explain the meaning of the following slogans from that time.
1. Wir sind ein Volk°.
2. Auf die Dauer° fällt die Mauer.
3. Wende° ohne Umkehr°.
4. Privilegien° weg! Wir sind das Volk!

people
auf die Dauer: in the long run
change (revolution of 1989) / turning back / perks provided to the functionaries of the ruling party

Von München nach Leipzig. Seit der Wiedervereinigung können Züge wieder ohne Grenzkontrolle von West- nach Ostdeutschland fahren. (Münchner Bahnhof)

Vokabeln 2

Substantive

die **Aufgabe, -n**   task; assignment
die **Brücke, -n**   bridge
die **Bundesrepublik Deutschland**
   Federal Republic of Germany *(the
   name of West Germany from 1949 to
   1990; today the official name for all
   of Germany)*
die **Demonstration, -en**
   demonstration
der **Flughafen, ⁓**   airport
die **Freiheit**   freedom
der **Frieden**   peace
die **Grenze, -n**   border, boundary;
   limit

die **Hausaufgabe, -n**   homework;
   Hausaufgaben machen   to do
   homework
der **Lehrer, -/**die **Lehrerin, -nen**
   teacher
die **Mauer, -n**   wall
der **Politiker, -/**die **Politikerin, -nen**
   politician
der **Punkt, -e**   point; dot; spot; period
die **Regierung, -en**   government
der **Soldat, -en, -en/**die **Soldatin,
   -nen**   soldier
der **Unterschied, -e**   difference
die **Vereinigung**   unification

Verben

**an·fangen (fängt an), fing an,
   angefangen**   to begin
**auf·schreiben, schrieb auf,
   aufgeschrieben**   to write down
bauen   to build
berichten   to report
demonstrieren   to demonstrate
fallen (fällt), fiel, ist gefallen   to fall
nennen, nannte, genannt   to name

öffnen   to open
**sterben (stirbt), starb, ist
   gestorben**   to die
teilen   to divide; **auf·teilen (in +
   acc.)**   to split up (into)
**verlassen (verlässt), verließ,
   verlassen**   to leave, abandon
zwingen, zwang, gezwungen   to
   force, compel

Andere Wörter

eigen   own
politisch   political(ly)
verantwortlich (für)   responsible (for)

vorbei   over; gone
westlich   Western

Besondere Ausdrücke

zu Ende   over, finished

Nach der Vereinigung

When the Berlin Wall fell (9 November 1989), few observers believed that East and West Germany would be unified less than a year later. Unification came about in two major stages. In July 1990, economic union occurred when the **Deutsche Mark** became the common currency of East and West Germany. On 3 October 1990, political unification was completed and the districts of former East Germany were regrouped into five new states (**Länder**), referred to as **FNL (Fünf Neue Länder)**: **Mecklenburg-Vorpommern, Brandenburg, Sachsen-Anhalt, Sachsen,** and **Thüringen.** Berlin also acquired the full status of a **Bundesland.** The first all-German elections followed in December 1990. For the most part, unification meant that West German laws applied in the new states.

Economic unification revealed that the economy of East Germany, the strongest in Eastern Europe and supporting the highest living standard in that area, was by western standards in a shambles. Unemployment grew rapidly. To facilitate the conversion to a market economy, the German government established a trustee agency (**Treuhandanstalt**). It broke up the state-owned combines (**Kombinate**) and helped establish 30,000 private businesses, arranging for new or restructured ownership. West Germans have been paying a surtax to finance these changes. Between the years 1991–2000, support (**Solidarpakt**) for East Germany was over a trillion marks. The contribution between 2002–2010 is estimated to run to 156 billion euros, and further subsidies may continue until 2020.

Unification also called for coordination of social and governmental services in the east and west. Generally, for former East Germans, it meant fewer social benefits and government services than before unification. At the same time consumer prices rose substantially.

In addition to these political and economic considerations, the two parts of Germany were faced with the necessity of adjusting to each other on a personal level. The social division was reflected in the terms **"Ossis"** (eastern Germans) and **"Wessis"** (western Germans). **Wessis** accused the **Ossis** of being lazy while the **Ossis** perceived the **Wessis** as arrogant and unfriendly.

Das Brandenburger Tor wurde zum Symbol für die deutsche Einheit. Statt der Mauer stehen heute moderne Gebäude um das renovierte Tor.

www Go to the *Deutsch heute* website at http://college.hmco.com.

Diskussion

Even many years after unification, one still hears of the **"Mauer im Kopf."** What do you think the **Mauer im Kopf** is? What is your interpretation of this expression?

Grammatik und Übungen

das Präteritum

① The simple past tense° vs. the present perfect tense

The simple past tense, like the present perfect (see *Kapitel 6*), is used to refer to events in the past. However, the simple past and the present perfect are used in different circumstances.

■ Uses of the simple past

Als ich zehn Jahre alt **war, wohnten** wir in Berlin. Da **stand** die Mauer noch. Die Leute aus Ostberlin **konnten** nicht zu uns in den Westen kommen. Das **verstand** ich nicht.	When I *was* ten years old, we *lived* in Berlin. The wall *was* still *standing* then. The people from East Berlin *could*n't come to us in the West. I *didn't understand* that.

The simple past tense (e.g., **wohnten, stand**) is often called the narrative past because it narrates a series of connected events in the past. It is used more frequently in formal writing—literature, newspaper articles, recipes, directions, etc.

■ Uses of the present perfect tense

MONIKA: **Hast** du gestern Abend **ferngesehen?**	*Did* you *watch* TV last night?
DIETER: Nein, ich **habe** ein paar Briefe **geschrieben.**	No, I *wrote* a few letters.

The present perfect tense (e.g., **hat ferngesehen, hat geschrieben**) is also called the conversational past because it is used in conversational contexts and in informal writing such as personal letters, diaries, and notes, all of which are actually a form of written "conversation."

Note that English always uses the simple past (e.g., *did watch, wrote*) when referring to an action completed in the past.

■ Uses of sein, haben, and modals in the simple past

MONIKA: Jürgen **konnte** am Freitag nicht kommen.
DIETER: **War** er krank oder **hatte** er keine Zeit?
MONIKA: Er **war** leider krank.

The simple past tense forms of **sein (war), haben (hatte),** and the modals (e.g., **konnte**) are used more frequently than the present perfect tense, even in conversation.

Das bekannte Museum **Haus der Geschichte** präsentiert deutsche Geschichte von 1945 bis heute in einer Ausstellung *(exhibition)* mit akustischen und optischen Eindrücken *(impressions)*. Denken Sie an das Lesestück auf Seite 350–351 und nennen Sie drei geschichtliche Themen, über die Sie im **Haus der Geschichte** wohl etwas erfahren *(find out)* können.

**Haus der Geschichte
der Bundesrepublik Deutschland**

Dienstag bis Sonntag 9.00 - 19.00 Uhr, Eintritt frei.

Museumsmeile   Willy-Brandt-Allee 14   53113 Bonn
Tel.: 02 28/91 65-0 Fax: 02 28/91 65-3 02 www.hdg.de

2 *Sein* and *haben* in the simple past tense

sein	
ich war	wir war**en**
du war**st**	ihr war**t**
er/es/sie war	sie war**en**
Sie war**en**	

haben	
ich hatte	wir hatt**en**
du hatte**st**	ihr hatte**t**
er/es/sie hatte	sie hatt**en**
Sie hatt**en**	

You learned in *Kapitel 2* that the simple past tense of **sein** is **war.** The simple past tense of **haben** is **hatte.** In the simple past, all forms except the **ich-** and **er/es/sie**-forms add verb endings.

1. Noch einmal. Wiederholen Sie die Kurzgespräche im Präteritum.

→ Wie ist das neue Musical?   *Wie war das neue Musical?*
   —Ach, es ist nichts Besonderes.   *—Ach, es war nichts Besonderes.*

1. Bist du in den Ferien zu Hause?
   —Nein, ich bin bei meinem Onkel.
2. Seid ihr heute in der Bibliothek?
   —Ja, wir sind den ganzen Tag da.
3. Ist das Buch interessant?
   —Nein, es ist furchtbar langweilig.

2. In den Bergen. Erzählen Sie Ihrer Freundin, warum Sie und einige andere Leute nicht zu einem Ausflug° in die Berge mitgekommen sind.   excursion

→ Dennis _____ viel Arbeit.   *Dennis hatte viel Arbeit.*

1. Irma _____ eine Erkältung.
2. Ich _____ eigentlich keine Zeit.
3. Wir _____ Besuch aus England.
4. Simon _____ keine guten Wanderschuhe.
5. Nils und Anke _____ eine Vorlesung.
6. Markus _____ Angst.

3 Modals in the simple past

Infinitive	Past stem	Tense marker	Simple past	English equivalent
dürfen	durf-	-te	**durfte**	was allowed to
können	konn-	-te	**konnte**	was able to
mögen	moch-	-te	**mochte**	liked
müssen	muss-	-te	**musste**	had to
sollen	soll-	-te	**sollte**	was supposed to
wollen	woll-	-te	**wollte**	wanted to

In the simple past tense, most modals undergo a stem change. The past tense marker **-te** is added to the simple past stem. Note that the past stem has no umlaut.

können
ich konnte   wir konnten
du konntest   ihr konntet
er/es/sie konnte   sie konnten
Sie konnten

In the simple past, all forms except the **ich-** and **er/es/sie**-forms add verb endings to the **-te** tense marker.

3. Auf einem Geburtstagsfest. Sie und Ihre Freunde haben ein Fest organisiert. Erzählen Sie, was passierte. Benutzen Sie die Modalverben im Präteritum.

➡ Ich will meine Freunde einladen.
Ich wollte meine Freunde einladen.

1. Klaus kann die CDs nicht mitbringen.
2. Katja muss noch abwaschen.
3. Frank will abtrocknen.
4. Michael soll das Wohnzimmer sauber machen.
5. Die Gäste sollen in zwei Stunden kommen.
6. Wir müssen daher schnell aufräumen.
7. Jens kann leider nicht lange bleiben.

Leipzig und Dresden

Freistaat Sachsen (Free State of Saxony) in eastern Germany is the home of two remarkable cities—Dresden, its capital, and Leipzig. Each city has a population of approximately 500,000 and the two cities comprise an industrial center in Eastern Germany.

Since the fifteenth century, **Leipzig** has been famous as a site for trade fairs, and the tradition continues today. In 2002 more than a million visitors attended fairs and conferences in Leipzig. Many classical authors attended the university in Leipzig, among them Johann Wolfgang von Goethe (1749–1832) who called Leipzig **"ein klein Paris"** in his drama *Faust*. Today, Saxony's universities are among the most diverse in Germany, including one private university, the Leipzig Graduate School of Management.

Music has long played a central role in Leipzig's culture. Johann Sebastian

Bei den Montagsdemonstrationen (September/Oktober 1989) in Leipzig: „Wir wollen Freiheit."

Bach (1685–1750) spent the last 27 years of his life in Leipzig as music director of the St. Thomas church and the music school. Both the world-famous boys' choir, the **Thomanerchor,** and the equally renowned 250-year-old **Gewandhausorchester** are at home in Leipzig. Kurt Masur, the director of the **Gewandhausorchester** (1970–1996) was director of the New York Philharmonic from 1991 to 2002. Both Leipzig and Masur played crucial roles in the days leading up to the fall of the Berlin Wall. In 1989 Leipzig was the center of opposition to the regime in the German Democratic Republic. One hundred thousand people gathered in Leipzig and demonstrated against the East German government. Masur used his stature as one of the most famous people in East Germany to persuade the government not to attack the demonstrators. And thus were created the conditions for the peaceful reunification of Germany in 1990.

Dresden is known as the "Florence of the North" (**Florenz des Nordens**). Before World War II, Dresden was called a baroque pearl on the Elbe and the most beautiful city in Germany. Much of this heritage was destroyed in World War II. Most of the famous buildings were rebuilt before 1990. However, only after unification did the rebuilding of the **Frauenkirche** begin. The ruins of this beautiful church, where Bach once performed, stood as a reminder of the devastation of war. After unification it was decided to rebuild the church, and the restoration should be complete in 2006. Dresden has now regained its position as one of Germany's most beautiful cities and as a center for industry. Siemens and Volkswagen are only two of the major companies with offices in Dresden. Seven million tourists a year come to see the **Zwinger,** probably the most famous baroque palace in Germany that today houses a number of excellent museums, the baroque **Königsstraße,** the opera house (**Semperoper**), and the immeasurable number of treasures in the art museums.

Der Zwinger in Dresden, heute ein weltberühmtes Museum, ist bekannt für seine elegante barocke Architektur.

www **Go to the *Deutsch heute* website at http://college.hmco.com.**

Diskussion

1. Dresden is famous for its baroque architecture. Do some research on the basic characteristics of baroque buildings.
2. Kurt Vonnegut's novel, *Slaughterhouse Five, Or the Children's Crusade* (1969), depicts the bombing of Dresden in February, 1945. Find out what you can about this American novel.

4. Frage-Ecke. Letzte Woche hatten Sie, Ihre Partnerin/Ihr Partner und einige andere Leute viel zu tun. Finden Sie heraus, wer was tun konnte, wollte, sollte und musste. Die Informationen für *S2* finden Sie im Anhang (Appendix B).

S1: Was wollte Adrian tun?
S2: Er wollte mehr Sport treiben.

S1:

	konnte	wollte	sollte	musste
Bettina		mit ihrer Diät beginnen	ein Referat schreiben	
Adrian	seine Arbeit fertig machen			die Garage aufräumen
Frau Müller	sich mit Freunden unterhalten	eine kurze Reise nach Paris machen		
Herr Meier			seinem Sohn bei der Arbeit helfen	sich einen neuen Computer kaufen
ich				
Partnerin/ Partner				

Asking someone about her/his past

5. Meine Kindheit. Vergleichen Sie Ihre Kindheit mit der Kindheit Ihrer Partnerin/Ihres Partners. Beantworten Sie die folgenden Fragen erst für sich selbst. Dann fragen Sie Ihre Partnerin/Ihren Partner. Schließlich erzählen Sie den anderen Kursteilnehmerinnen/Kursteilnehmern von Ihrer eigenen Kindheit und der Ihrer Partnerin/Ihres Partners.

1. Musstest du deinen Eltern viel helfen?
2. Durftest du viel fernsehen?
3. Musstest du sonntags Hausaufgaben machen?
4. Wie lange durftest du abends ausbleiben°?
5. Um wie viel Uhr musstest du ins Bett gehen?
6. Konntest du machen, was du wolltest?
7. Was durftest du nicht machen?
8. Was wolltest du werden, als du ein Kind warst?

stay out

4 Regular weak verbs in the simple past

Infinitive	Stem	Tense marker	Simple past
machen	mach-	-te	machte
sagen	sag-	-te	sagte
reden	red-	-ete	redete
arbeiten	arbeit-	-ete	arbeitete
regnen	regn-	-ete	regnete

In the simple past tense, regular weak verbs add the past-tense marker **-te** to the infinitive stem. Regular weak verbs with a stem ending in **-d** (**reden**) or **-t** (**arbeiten**) and verbs like **regnen** and **öffnen** insert an **-e** before the tense marker. The addition of the **-e** ensures that the **-t,** as a signal of the past, is audible. This is parallel to the insertion of the extra **-e** in the present tense (**er arbeitet;** past tense **er arbeitete**).

machen	
ich machte	wir machten
du machtest	ihr machtet
er/es/sie machte	sie machten
Sie machten	

reden	
ich redete	wir redeten
du redetest	ihr redetet
er/es/sie redete	sie redeten
Sie redeten	

In the simple past, all forms except the **ich** and **er/es/sie**-forms add verb endings to the **-te** tense marker.

6. So war es früher. Erzählen Sie, was Sie und Ihr Freund Michael vor einigen Jahren gemacht haben. Benutzen Sie das Präteritum.

→ Wir arbeiten beide nicht besonders viel für die Schule.
Wir arbeiteten beide nicht besonders viel für die Schule.

1. Nachmittags hören wir meistens stundenlang Rockmusik.
2. Unsere Hausaufgaben machen wir oft nicht.
3. Ich jobbe manchmal in einem Supermarkt.
4. Natürlich verdiene ich dort nicht viel.
5. Michael spielt jeden Tag Basketball.
6. Sein Vater kritisiert° ihn oft wegen seiner schlechten Noten.   criticizes
7. Die beiden reden nicht wirklich miteinander.
8. Dann arbeitet Michael doch mehr.
9. Und bald machen wir beide unser Abitur.

7. Wir fahren zelten. Erzählen Sie im Präteritum, wie Ihr Wochenende auf dem Campingplatz war.

→ Am Samstag regnet es nicht.   *Am Samstag regnete es nicht.*

1. Gerd arbeitet nur bis 12 Uhr.
2. Gerd und Klaus machen eine Wanderung.
3. Sie zelten in den Bergen.
4. Susi und Alex warten am Campingplatz auf ihre Freunde.
5. Alle baden im See°.   lake
6. Am Abend machen Sie ein Feuer und grillen Würstchen.
7. Sie reden über dies und das.
8. Sie machen schon Pläne für die nächste Wanderung.

5 Irregular weak verbs in the simple past

Infinitive	Past stem	Tense marker	Simple past	Examples
bringen	brach-	-te	**brachte**	Peter brachte die Blumen nach Hause.
denken	dach-	-te	**dachte**	Jutta dachte an ihre Arbeit.
kennen	kann-	-te	**kannte**	Wir kannten ihre Chefin.
nennen	nann-	-te	**nannte**	Sie nannten das Kind nach dem Vater.
wissen	wuss-	-te	**wusste**	Du wusstest das schon, nicht?

German has a few weak verbs that have a stem-vowel change in the simple past. (For this reason they are called *irregular* weak verbs.) The verbs **bringen** and **denken** also have a consonant change. The tense marker **-te** is added to the simple past stem. Several of the most common irregular weak verbs are listed in the chart above.

bringen	
ich brachte	wir brachten
du brachtest	ihr brachtet
er/es/sie brachte	sie brachten
Sie brachten	

In the simple past, all forms except the **ich-** and **er/es/sie-**forms add verb endings to the **-te** tense marker.

8. Vor Jahren. So haben viele Leute vor zwanzig Jahren die Rolle der Frauen gesehen. Berichten Sie von den Meinungen im Präteritum.

→ Viele Leute haben wenig über die Emanzipation gewusst.
Viele Leute wussten wenig über die Emanzipation.

1. Sie haben nur typische Rollen von Mann und Frau gekannt.
2. Viele Frauen haben aber anders gedacht.
3. Sie haben andere Ideen gehabt.
4. Die Kinder haben oft so wie ihre Eltern gedacht.
5. Viele Frauen haben nur ihre Hausarbeit gekannt.
6. Vom Berufsleben haben sie nur wenig gewusst.
7. Manche haben berufstätige Frauen „Rabenmütter"° genannt.
8. In vielen anderen Ländern hat man schon mehr über Emanzipation gewusst.

unfit mothers

6 Separable-prefix verbs in the simple past

Present	Simple past
Wolf **kauft** für seine Freunde **ein**.	Wolf **kaufte** für seine Freunde **ein**.
Er **bringt** für alle etwas zu trinken **mit**.	Er **brachte** für alle etwas zu trinken **mit**.

In the simple past, as in the present, the separable prefix is separated from the base form of the verb and is in final position.

9. Eine Party. Erzählen Sie, wie Ihre Freunde eine Party vorbereiteten. Bilden Sie Sätze im Präteritum.

→ Lilo / aufräumen / die Wohnung   *Lilo räumte die Wohnung auf.*

1. Ralf / einkaufen
2. er / mitbringen / vom Markt / Blumen
3. Lilo und Theo / zurückzahlen / ihm / das Geld
4. Theo / vorbereiten / die ganzen Salate
5. dann / sie / anschauen / das Partybuffet

7 Strong verbs in the simple past

Infinitive	Simple past stem	Examples
sprechen	sprach	Adrian sprach mit Bettina.
gehen	ging	Bettina ging ins Theater.

A strong verb undergoes a stem change in the simple past. The tense marker **-te** is not added to a strong verb in the simple past tense.

sprechen	
ich sprach	wir sprachen
du sprachst	ihr spracht
er/es/sie sprach	sie sprachen
Sie sprachen	

In the simple past, all forms except the **ich-** and **er/es/sie**-forms add verb endings to the simple past stem. The stem change of strong verbs cannot always be predicted, but you will probably not have trouble guessing the infinitive form and thus the meaning of most of the verbs. While there are thousands of weak verbs, the number of strong verbs in German is fortunately relatively small. This book uses approximately 60 strong verbs. The list of these verbs is found in the Grammatical Tables in Appendix F. In the vocabularies of this book, the simple past stem is printed after the infinitive, followed by the past participle: **liegen, lag, gelegen.**

10. Alexanders merkwürdiges° Erlebnis°. Lesen Sie die folgende Anekdote und setzen Sie alle fett gedruckten Verben ins Präteritum. Benutzen Sie die folgende Liste mit dem Präteritum der Verben. Achtung! Es gibt hier schwache und starke Verben.   strange / experience

antwortete ■ empfahl ■ gab ■ ging ■ lud ein ■ sagte ■ sah
■ sollte ■ sprach ■ stand ■ trank ■ war ■ wollte ■ wusste

Heute **gehe** ich in der Fußgängerzone einkaufen. Plötzlich° **steht** ein Mann vor mir, **sieht** mir in die Augen und **sagt**: „Hallo, Stefan. Wie geht's denn?"   suddenly
„Na, gut, danke", **antworte** ich und **weiß** nicht, was ich im Moment noch sagen **soll**, denn ich **weiß** seinen Namen nicht. Er **will**, dass wir zusammen

essen gehen, **empfiehlt** ein gutes Restaurant und wir **gehen** hin. Das Essen **ist** gut und wir **trinken** eine Flasche Wein dazu. Beim Essen **spricht** er über dies und das. Ich **sage** sehr wenig. „Du kennst mich nicht mehr", **sagt** er. „Doch", **sage** ich, aber es ist nicht wahr. Nach dem Essen **sagt** er: „Ich rufe dich in einer Woche an. Vielleicht können wir uns wieder treffen." „Das wäre schön", **antworte** ich. Ich **gebe** ihm die Hand und **sage:** „Also, mein Lieber, bis bald." Du, Ute, etwas **verstehe** ich nicht. Warum hat er immer Stefan zu mir gesagt? „Ja, das ist ja wirklich merkwürdig, Alexander", **antwortet** Ute.

Land und Leute

Deutschland:
Die Regierung

www Go to the *Deutsch heute* website at http://college.hmco.com.

In the Federal Republic of Germany each state (**Bundesland**) has a constitution. However, the central government is strong.

National elections to the House of Representatives (**der Bundestag**) take place every four years. All German citizens over 18 have a "first vote" (**Erststimme**) and a "second vote" (**Zweitstimme**), which permits them to vote for a particular candidate as well as for a political party. The representative one votes for need not belong to the party one votes for. The constitution (**Grundgesetz**) of the Federal Republic stipulates that a political party has to have a minimum of 5% of all the votes cast to be represented in the **Bundestag.**

Eröffnungsfeier des Bundestags im Berliner Reichstagsgebäude.

The **Bundestag** is the only federal body elected directly by the people. The Federal Council (**Bundesrat**) represents the federal states (**Bundesländer**) and is made up of members of the state governments or their representatives. The President (**Bundespräsident/ Bundespräsidentin**) is elected by the Federal Convention (comparable to the U.S. Electoral College). The President's tasks are mainly ceremonial in nature.

The head of the government in the Federal Republic of Germany is the Federal Chancellor (**Bundeskanzler/Bundeskanzlerin**), who is nominated by the President and elected by the **Bundestag.**

The major German parties are **SPD (Sozialdemokratische Partei Deutschlands); CDU (Christlich-Demokratische Union); CSU (Christlich-Soziale Union); Grüne (Bündnis 90/Die Grünen); FDP (Freie Demokratische Partei);** and **PDS (Partei des Demokratischen Sozialismus).** 79.1% of eligible voters voted in the elections of 2002. Of the representatives in the new **Bundestag,** 31.5% (190 out of 603) are women. The government is a coalition of **SPD** and **Die Grünen.** Of the parties mentioned above, only the **PDS** did not meet the minimum 5% for a seat in the 2002 **Bundestag.**

Diskussion

Compare the government of Germany to your own. Which institutions are similar to ones in your country, and which aspects are different?

11. Berlin. Lesen Sie die Informationen über die Teilung° und Wiedervereini-
gung° von Berlin (Zeile 1–9, Seite 350). Merken Sie sich° jedes Verb im Präteritum und schreiben Sie auf ein Blatt° Papier das englische Äquivalent. Dann
geben Sie die Infinitivform auf Deutsch.

division / reunification

Merken Sie sich: note down

sheet

▨ *Verbs with past-tense vowel long ā and short ă*

Infinitive	Simple past stem *(ā)*
empfehlen	empfahl
essen	aß
geben	gab
kommen	kam
lesen	las
liegen	lag
nehmen	nahm
sehen	sah
sitzen	saß
sprechen	sprach
treffen	traf
tun	tat

Infinitive	Simple past stem *(ă)*
finden	fand
helfen	half
stehen	stand
trinken	trank

12. Die Sommerarbeit. Peggy, eine Amerikanerin, hat ihrer deutschen Freundin
Marga einen Brief über ihren Sommerjob bei einer deutschen Firma geschrieben.
Lesen Sie den Brief und beantworten Sie die Fragen.

Samstag, den 1. Oktober

Liebe Marga,

du wolltest etwas über meinen Sommerjob wissen. Also, ich kam am 5. Juni in
München an. Viele Menschen waren auf dem Flughafen. Zuerst verstand ich nur
wenig. Aber die Deutschen waren sehr nett, vor allem meine Chefin° Frau Volke.   boss
Sie half mir auch sehr bei der Arbeit. Ich fand die Arbeit dann viel leichter. Am
Anfang gab es nicht viel zu tun. Deshalb machten wir um 10 Uhr morgens immer Pause und tranken Kaffee. Manchmal waren unsere Gespräche so interessant, dass wir nicht pünktlich wieder an die Arbeit gingen. Aber Frau Volke sagte
nichts. Wie du siehst, kann ich jetzt viel mehr Deutsch. Schreib bald.

Herzliche Grüße

deine *Peggy*

1. Wann kam Peggy in München an?
2. Was sah sie auf dem Flughafen?
3. Wer war besonders nett?
4. Warum fand Peggy die Arbeit im Büro leicht?
5. Was machte man um 10 Uhr morgens?
6. Warum ging man manchmal im Büro nicht wieder pünktlich an die Arbeit?

■ *Verbs with past-tense vowel* **ie, u,** *and* **i**

Infinitive	Simple past stem *(ie)*
bleiben	blieb
fallen	fiel
gefallen	gefiel
halten	hielt
laufen	lief
schlafen	schlief
schreiben	schrieb
verlassen	verließ

Infinitive	Simple past stem *(u* or *i)*
fahren	fuhr
tragen	trug
gehen	ging

liest vor: reads aloud

13. Hören Sie zu. Uwe hat seinem Freund Rainer einen Brief über seine Reise nach Frankfurt geschrieben. Der Brief ist zu Hause und Rainers Bruder liest ihm den Brief am Telefon vor°. Hören Sie, was Rainers Bruder liest, und beantworten Sie die Fragen dazu. Sie hören einen neuen Ausdruck: **den ganzen Weg** *(the whole way)*.

1. Wie war das Wetter?
2. Wohin fuhren Uwe und Claudia?
3. Was für Hosen trugen sie?
4. Wo liefen sie ein bisschen herum?
5. Warum blieben sie nur eine halbe Stunde im Kino?
6. Was machten sie nach dem Kino?

return trip

7. Was tat Claudia auf der Rückreise° nach Hause?
8. Was tat Uwe?

14. Eine Nacht im Leben von Herrn Zittermann. Lesen Sie die Anekdote und beantworten Sie die Fragen. Dann schreiben Sie ein Ende für die Geschichte.

suddenly / light / motionless

flashlight / firmly

Herr Zittermann war allein im Haus. Er lag im Bett, aber er schlief noch nicht. Er hatte die Augen offen. Plötzlich° sah er unter der Tür Licht°. Starr° blieb er liegen. Was war los? Er bekam Angst. Er stand auf und nahm seine große Taschenlampe°, die natürlich auf dem Nachttisch lag. Fest° hielt er die Taschenlampe in der Hand. Er ging zur Tür und sah ...

1. Wo lag Herr Zittermann?
2. Wie viele Leute waren im Haus?
3. Schlief Herr Zittermann?
4. Was sah er plötzlich?
5. Was war seine Reaktion?
6. Was lag auf dem Nachttisch?
7. Wohin ging er?

15. Ein Unfall° in der Herzogstraße. Sie sind Journalistin/Journalist und schreiben über einen Unfall. Benutzen Sie die Bilder und Wortverbindungen und schreiben Sie Ihren Artikel. Leider haben Sie nicht alle Informationen und müssen die Geschichte selber zu Ende schreiben.

accident

➡ ein blauer Wagen / schnell um die Ecke / fahren
   Ein blauer Wagen fuhr schnell um die Ecke.

1. eine alte Frau / über die Straße / laufen

2. sie / nicht / das Auto / sehen

3. dann / sie / auf der Straße / liegen

4. ein Fußgänger / zu der Frau / kommen

5. er / die Frau / zu einer Bank° / tragen

bench

6. Wie ging die Geschichte weiter?

■ *Past tense of* **werden**

Infinitive	Simple past stem
werden	wurde

class reunion

16. Das Klassentreffen. Giselas Eltern waren auf einem Schultreffen°. Am Sonntag sitzen sie mit Gisela am Frühstückstisch und erzählen ihrer Tochter, was ihre Klassenkameradinnen und Klassenkameraden von Beruf wurden. Was sagen sie? Benutzen Sie das Präteritum von **werden.**

➡ FRAU RIEDHOLT: Erika / Ingenieurin
Erika wurde Ingenieurin.

1. FRAU RIEDHOLT ZU IHREM MANN: du / Journalist und ich / Lehrerin
2. HERR RIEDHOLT: Ja, und Inge / Geschäftsfrau
3. GISELA: Was / Sebastian ?
4. HERR RIEDHOLT: Sebastian / Apotheker
5. FRAU RIEDHOLT: Steffi und Franziska / Ärztinnen
6. HERR RIEDHOLT: Mein Freund Gerd / Ingenieur
7. FRAU RIEDHOLT: Deine Ex-Freundin Karen / Krankenschwester
8. GISELA: Was / Mamas Ex-Freund?

das Plusquamperfekt

8 Past perfect tense°

Thomas **war** noch nie in Köln **gewesen.**	Thomas *had* never *been* to Cologne.
Er **hatte** noch nie den Rhein **gesehen.**	He *had* never *seen* the Rhine.

The English past perfect tense consists of the auxiliary *had* and the past participle of the verb. The German past perfect tense consists of the simple past of **haben** (e.g., **hatte**) or **sein** (e.g., **war**) and the past participle of the verb. Verbs that use a form of **haben** in the present perfect tense also use a form of **haben** in the past perfect; those that use a form of **sein** in the present perfect also use a form of **sein** in the past perfect.

9 Use of the past perfect tense

Edith konnte am Montag nicht anfangen, weil sie am Sonntag krank **geworden war.**	Edith couldn't begin on Monday, because she *had gotten* sick on Sunday.

The past perfect tense is used to report an event or action that took place before another event or action that was itself in the past. The following time-tense line will help you visualize the sequence of tenses.

2nd point earlier in past	1st point in past time	Present time	Future time
Past perfect	Present perfect or simple past		

17. Der Fall der Mauer. Herr Pabst hat immer in Ostdeutschland gewohnt und spricht über den Fall der Berliner Mauer. Geben Sie das englische Äquivalent seiner Aussagen wieder.

1. Zuerst konnte niemand° glauben, dass die DDR das Reisen nach Westdeutschland erlaubt° hatte.

    no one
    erlauben: to permit

2. Als die Mauer gefallen war, fuhren unglaublich viele DDR-Bürger° in den Westen.

    citizens

3. Nachdem° sie diese Reise gemacht hatten, kamen die meisten wieder nach Hause zurück.

    after

4. Sie hatten ein Stück vom Westen gesehen und wollten dann einfach wieder zu Hause sein.

5. Wer nie selbst in der Bundesrepublik gewesen war, kannte sie doch ein wenig aus dem Fernsehen.

6. Viele gingen aber zurück, weil sie eine andere Idee vom Westen gehabt hatten.

10 Uses of *als, wenn,* and *wann*

Als, wenn, and **wann** are all equivalent to English *when*, but they are not interchangeable in German.

Als Paula gestern in Hamburg war, ging sie ins Theater.	When Paula was in Hamburg yesterday, she went to the theater.
Als Paula ein Teenager war, ging sie gern ins Theater.	When Paula was a teenager, she liked to go to the theater.

Als is used to introduce a clause concerned with a single event in the past or with a block of continuous time in the past.

Wenn Renate in Hamburg ist, geht sie ins Theater.	When Renate is in Hamburg, she goes to the theater.
Wenn Erik in Hamburg war, ging er jeden Tag ins Theater.	When (whenever) Erik was in Hamburg, he went (would go) to the theater every day.

Wenn is used to introduce a clause concerned with events or possibilities in present or future time. **Wenn** is also used to introduce a clause concerned with repeated events *(whenever)* in past time.

An der Universität
Freiburg machen
Studenten eine Pause.

| **Wann** gehen wir ins Kino? | When are we going to the movies? |
| Ich habe keine Ahnung, **wann** wir ins Kino gehen. | I have no idea when we're going to the movies. |

Wann is used only for questions. It is used to introduce both direct and indirect questions.

18. Wann ...? Ein Freund stellt Ihnen viele Fragen, die Sie nicht beantworten können. Antworten Sie mit indirekten Fragen. Benutzen Sie die folgenden Sätze, wenn Sie antworten.

> *Redemittel:* Ich weiß nicht ▪ Ich frage mich auch ▪ Ich möchte auch wissen ▪ Ich habe keine Ahnung

> ➜ Wann schreiben wir die nächste Deutschklausur?
> *Ich weiß nicht, wann wir die nächste Deutschklausur schreiben.*

1. Wann müssen wir die nächste Hausaufgabe abgeben°?
2. Wann macht die Bibliothek am Samstag zu°?
3. Wann kommen unsere Pizzas?
4. Wann ruft Stefan an?
5. Wann können wir Pause machen°?

(margin notes:)
turn in
macht zu: close

Pause machen: take a break

19. Bernd und der Fall der Mauer. Erzählen Sie, was Bernd nach dem Fall der Mauer getan hat. Verbinden Sie die Sätze mit **als, wenn** oder **wann.**

> ➜ Die Mauer stand noch. Bernd wohnte in Dresden.
> *Als die Mauer noch stand, wohnte Bernd in Dresden.*

1. Seine Tante schrieb ihm aus Köln. Er wurde immer ganz traurig.
2. Die Mauer fiel. Ein großes Chaos begann.
3. Die Tante fragte Bernd am Telefon: „Wann kommen die Eltern?"
4. Auch Bernd setzte sich ins Auto. Er hörte die Nachricht°.
5. Er fuhr dann nach Köln. Er war sehr neugierig°.
6. Seine Tante hat ihm gesagt: „Die Eltern kommen in Köln an. Wir haben dann ein großes Fest." (*Do not change the introductory sentence:* Seine Tante hat ihm gesagt.)

(margin notes:)
news
curious

Leserunde

In *Kapitel 4* (see page 158), we saw how Hans Manz used modal auxiliaries and interrogative pronouns to evoke a comment on the everyday event of vacations. In "Fernsehabend," Manz again uses language, in this case everyday expressions, to show the difficulty of achieving genuine communication between human beings.

Fernsehabend

„Vater, Mutter, hallo!"
„Pssst!"
„Ich bin ..."
„Später!"
5 „Also ich wollte nur ..."
„Ruhe[1]!"
„Dann geh ich ..."

„Momentchen. Gleich
haben sie den Mörder[2].
10 So, was wolltest du sagen,
mein Kind? –
Jetzt ist es wieder weg.
Nie kann man in Ruhe reden
mit ihm.“

Hans Manz

[1]**Ruhe!:** *Quiet!*   [2]**Mörder:** *murderer*

Wiederholung

1. Rollenspiel. Sie unterhalten sich mit Ihrer Partnerin/Ihrem Partner über ihre/seine nächste Prüfung. Sie/Er hat große Angst davor und Sie wollen ihr/ihm ein paar Tipps geben. Sie/Er antwortet Ihnen aber mit Ratlosigkeit° darauf.

perplexity, helplessness

Redemittel: Ratlosigkeit ausdrücken *(Expressing perplexity)*

Ich weiß wirklich nicht, was ich machen soll. ■ Ich weiß nicht, wie ich das machen soll. ■ Ich will ja, aber es geht nicht. ■ Ich kann nicht. ■ Es geht nicht. ■ Ich weiß nicht. ■ Keine Ahnung.

---

1. Du musst versuchen, dich ganz auf die Prüfung zu konzentrieren.
2. Du darfst jetzt nicht an andere Dinge denken.
3. Arbeite nicht zu viel!
4. Fünf oder sechs Stunden am Tag sind genug.
5. Mach auch immer mal wieder eine Pause.
6. Versuch es doch mal mit Yoga.
7. Genug schlafen ist natürlich auch wichtig.
8. Du musst fest daran glauben, dass du die Prüfung bestehst°.

pass

9. Denkst du denn nicht, dass du noch genug Zeit hast?

2. Eine Reise nach Paris. Lesen Sie den Bericht von Kristinas Reise nach Paris und beantworten Sie die sechs Fragen.

Kristina wohnte in Leipzig. Sie war Ingenieurin. Sie wollte immer gern Paris sehen. Aber als es noch die Grenze in Deutschland gab, konnte sie natürlich nicht nach Frankreich reisen. Sie fuhr in alle Länder von Osteuropa und kam sogar bis nach China. Doch in Wirklichkeit träumte° sie immer von Paris. Als dann die Grenze fiel, konnte sie es kaum° glauben. Sofort° kaufte sie sich eine Fahrkarte für die Eisenbahn° und machte die lange Reise nach Paris. Die Stadt fand sie ganz toll, aber unglaublich teuer. Solche Preise kannte sie nicht! Da war sie dann ganz froh, dass sie wieder nach Hause fahren konnte. Aber – sie hatte Paris gesehen!

dreamed
hardly / immediately
railroad

1. Was war Kristina von Beruf?
2. Wovon träumte sie immer?

3. In welche Länder konnte sie früher nur reisen?
4. Wohin fuhr sie, als die Grenze fiel?
5. Wie fand sie die Stadt?
6. Warum war sie froh, wieder nach Hause zu fahren?

3. Zwei kurze Gespräche. Ergänzen Sie die Kurzgespräche. Benutzen Sie die richtige Form der Verben aus der Liste in jedem Satz.

aufstehen ▪ stehen ▪ verstehen

MANUEL: Sonntags _____ ich immer sehr spät _____. Meistens _____ dann das Mittagessen schon auf dem Tisch.

STEFFI: Also wirklich, ich kann nicht _____, wie man so lange schlafen kann.

ankommen ▪ bekommen ▪ kommen

ELISABETH: Wann sind Sie denn in München _____?

THERESA: Vor einer Stunde. Ich bin dieses Mal mit dem Zug _____, nicht mit dem Flugzeug.

ELISABETH: Ah, also haben Sie meinen Brief noch früh genug _____.

4. Erzählen Sie von gestern. Was haben Sie gestern Morgen gemacht? Benutzen Sie passende Wörter und Wortverbindungen aus der Liste. Wenn Sie wollen, können Sie auch noch andere Aktivitäten hinzufügen°.

add

aufstehen ▪ baden ▪ sich die Haare kämmen ▪ sich anziehen ▪ Kaffee kochen ▪ ein Stück Toast essen ▪ Kaffee trinken ▪ Zeitung lesen ▪ sich die Zähne putzen ▪ in die Vorlesung gehen

5. Was bedeutet das? Bilden Sie neue Substantive aus den folgenden Wörtern und geben Sie die englischen Äquivalente wieder.

1. die Bilder + das Buch
2. die Farb(e) + der Fernseher
3. die Blumen + das Geschäft
4. die Kinder + der Garten
5. die Geschicht(e) + s + der Professor

6. das Hotel + der Gast
7. der Abend + das Kleid
8. das Haus + das Tier
9. der Brief + der Freund
10. die Sonne + n + die Brille

6. Ferienpläne. Sprechen Sie mit Ihrer Partnerin/Ihrem Partner über Dinge, die Sie in Ihren Ferien machen wollten, und warum. Erklären Sie auch, was Sie machen konnten. Denken Sie daran: In einer Konversation benutzt man das Perfekt, außer für die Verben **sein** und **haben** und Modalverben.

→ *Ich wollte jeden Tag mit Jürgen Tennis spielen.*
Aber er ist selten gekommen, und so habe ich wenig gespielt.

Themen: reisen ▪ [Tennis] spielen ▪ nach [Europa] fliegen ▪ [einem Freund] helfen ▪ eine Arbeit suchen ▪ [Freunde] besuchen ▪ einen Film sehen ▪ [ein Buch] lesen ▪ spät aufstehen ▪ schwimmen ▪ einkaufen gehen

WER BIN ICH? bzw. WER IST DIESE PERSON?

Studenten bekommen alle den Namen einer berühmten Person (tot oder lebendig) auf ihren Rücken geklebt oder ihre Stirn. Sie fragen andere Studenten, wer sie sind. Sie dürfen nur nicht fragen, "Was bin ich von Beruf?" oder nach ihrem Namen. Erst wenn sie ganz sicher sind.

z. B.: StudentIN, die/der "George W. Bush" ist.

"Bin ich ein Mann oder eine Frau?"
"Wo wohne ich?"
"Habe ich eine Familie?"
"Wie groß ist meine Familie?"
"Wo wohnt meine Familie?"

ZIEL: > Bringt die Studenten dazu Fragen zu stellen.

7. Zum Schreiben

Wählen Sie einen Satz, der° mit **als** beginnt, und einen, der mit **wenn** beginnt. Schreiben Sie dann einen kurzen Absatz° zu jedem Satz. Denken Sie daran, dass Sie das Präteritum benutzen müssen, wenn Sie Ihren Absatz mit **als** beginnen.

that

paragraph

- Als ich vier Jahre alt war, ...
- Als ich noch in die Schule ging, ...
- Als ich das letzte Mal auf einem Fest war, ...
- Als ich ...
- Wenn ich [müde/glücklich/deprimiert°/nervös/böse] bin, ...
- Wenn ich Hausarbeit machen muss, ...
- Wenn ich ...

depressed

Hinweise: After you have written your paragraph or story ending, check the following:

- Choice of past tenses
- Form of the past tenses
- Use of **als, wenn, wann**

Grammatik: Zusammenfassung

Sein, haben, and *werden* in the simple past

sein	
ich war	wir waren
du warst	ihr wart
er/es/sie war	sie waren
Sie waren	

haben	
ich hatte	wir hatten
du hattest	ihr hattet
er/es/sie hatte	sie hatten
Sie hatten	

werden	
ich wurde	wir wurden
du wurdest	ihr wurdet
er/es/sie wurde	sie wurden
Sie wurden	

Modals in the simple past

Infinitive	Simple past
dürfen	durfte
können	konnte
mögen	mochte
müssen	musste
sollen	sollte
wollen	wollte

Simple past of regular weak verbs

Infinitive	Stem	Tense marker	Simple past
glauben	glaub-	-te	glaubte
spielen	spiel-	-te	spielte
baden	bad-	-ete	badete
arbeiten	arbeit-	-ete	arbeitete
regnen	regn-	-ete	regnete

Irregular weak verbs in the simple past

Infinitive	Simple past
bringen	brachte
denken	dachte
kennen	kannte

Infinitive	Simple past
nennen	nannte
wissen	wusste

In the simple past tense, modals, weak verbs, and irregular weak verbs have the past-tense marker **-te.** In verbs with a stem ending in **-d** or **-t,** and in some verbs ending in **-n** or **-m,** the tense marker **-te** expands to **-ete.** Like **hatte,** all forms except the **ich-** and **er/es/sie-**forms add endings to the past-tense marker **-te.**

Simple past of strong verbs

Infinitive	Simple past
gehen	ging
sehen	sah
schreiben	schrieb

Strong verbs undergo a stem vowel change in the simple past. Like **sein,** they do not take the past-tense marker **-te.** The **ich-** and **er/es/sie-**forms have no verb endings.

Selected strong verbs

Below is a table of selected strong verbs. For a more complete list see the Grammatical Tables, #24, in Appendix F.

Infinitive	Simple past stem
anfangen	fing an
anziehen	zog an
bleiben	blieb
empfehlen	empfahl
essen	aß
fahren	fuhr
fallen	fiel
finden	fand
geben	gab
gefallen	gefiel
gehen	ging

Infinitive	Simple past stem
halten	hielt
helfen	half
kommen	kam
laufen	lief
lesen	las
liegen	lag
nehmen	nahm
schlafen	schlief
schreiben	schrieb
sehen	sah

Infinitive	Simple past stem
sein	war
sitzen	saß
sprechen	sprach
stehen	stand
tragen	trug
treffen	traf
trinken	trank
tun	tat
verlassen	verließ
werden	wurde

Separable-prefix verbs in the simple past

Present tense	Simple past
Sie **kauft** immer im Supermarkt **ein**.	Sie **kaufte** immer im Supermarkt **ein**.
Er **kommt** immer **mit**.	Er **kam** immer **mit**.

In the simple past tense, as in the present tense, the separable prefix is separated from the base form of the verb and is in final position.

Past perfect tense

Ich **hatte** vor zwei Tagen
  angefangen zu arbeiten.

Gerd **war** am Montag **angekommen**.

I *had started* working two days
  before.

Gerd *had arrived* on Monday.

The German past perfect is a compound tense that consists of the simple past of either **haben** or **sein** plus the past participle of the main verb. It is used to report an event or action that took place before another past event or action.

Uses of *als, wenn,* and *wann* meaning "when"

Als, wenn, wann are used as follows:

1. **als**—a single event in past time

   Als Katrin Dieter gestern sah,
     sprachen sie über Politik.

   When Katrin saw Dieter yesterday,
     they talked about politics.

2. **als**—a block of continuous time in the past

   Als Katrin jung war, sprach sie
     gern über Politik.

   When Katrin was young, she
     liked to talk about politics.

3. **wenn**—repeated events *(whenever)* in past time

   Früher **wenn** sie Dieter sah,
     redete sie immer über
     Politik.

   In the past, *when* (whenever) she used
     to see Dieter, she always spoke
     about politics.

4. **wenn**—present or future time

   Wenn wir in München sind,
     gehen wir ins Konzert.

   When (whenever) we are in Munich,
     we go to a concert.

5. **wann**—introduces direct questions

   Wann beginnt das Konzert?

   When does the concert begin?

6. **wann**—introduces indirect questions

   Ich weiß nicht, **wann** das
     Konzert beginnt.

   I don't know *when* the concert
     begins.

KAPITEL 11

Wirtschaft und Beruf

Die Hypovereinsbank in München. Die Bankindustrie ist ein integraler Teil der Wirtschaft.

LERNZIELE

Sprechintentionen

Presenting oneself for an appointment

Telling about one's qualifications for a job

Talking about future plans

Discussing post-graduation plans

Inquiring about and expressing wishes

Discussing goals

Expressing wishes and hypothetical statements

Lesestück

Die Kündigung, nur noch drei Tage

Land und Leute

Social legislation in Germany

Codetermination in Germany

The European Union

The apprenticeship system in Germany

Vokabeln

Occupations

Suffix -lich

Grammatik

Future time: present tense

Future time: future tense

Subjunctive vs. indicative

The *würde*-construction

Present-time subjunctive of the main verb

Bausteine für Gespräche

Ein Termin

UWE: Guten Tag. Ohrdorf ist mein Name, Uwe Ohrdorf. Ich würde gern Frau
Dr. Ziegler sprechen. Ich habe einen Termin bei ihr.

SEKRETÄRIN: Guten Tag, Herr Ohrdorf. Ja bitte, gehen Sie doch gleich hinein. Sie
erwartet Sie schon.

Ein Ferienjob

PERSONALCHEFIN: Herr Ohrdorf, Sie studieren
jetzt im achten Semester Informatik und
wollen zwei Monate bei uns arbeiten.

UWE: Ja, richtig.

PERSONALCHEFIN: Wie ich sehe, haben Sie
schon als Informatiker gearbeitet.

UWE: Ja, ich habe letztes Jahr auch einen
Ferienjob gehabt und da habe ich ganz
gute praktische Erfahrungen gesammelt.

PERSONALCHEFIN: Und was wollen Sie später damit machen?

UWE: Ich möchte eine Stelle bei einer Bank, eine Aufgabe mit viel Verantwortung, hoffe ich.

Fragen

1. Wen möchte Uwe sprechen?
2. Warum soll er gleich hineingehen?
3. Was studiert Uwe? In welchem Semester?
4. Wie hat ihn der Ferienjob letzten Sommer auf die neue Stelle vorbereitet?
5. Was für eine Stelle möchte Uwe später finden? Wo?

Traumkonzerne[1] der Jungmanager

Deutsche Lieblings-
arbeitgeber: Mercedes,
BMW und Lufthansa

Wo deutsche Hochschulabsolventen am liebsten arbeiten würden

BMW	60%
Mercedes-Benz	59%
The Boston Consulting Group	55%
Lufthansa	52%
McKinsey & Company	52%
Siemens	52%
Bosch	50%
Audi	48%

FOCUS-Magazin

[1]dream companies

Welcher ist der beliebteste *(most popular)*
Konzern für deutsche Jungmanager?
Welche Konzerne haben mit Transport zu tun?
Warum, glauben Sie, ist BMW der beliebteste
Konzern? Welche Gründe könnte es geben?
Für welchen der acht Konzerne würden Sie
am liebsten arbeiten? Warum?

Brauchbares

1. In **Ein Termin** Uwe says, **"Ich würde gern Frau Dr. Ziegler sprechen."** All forms of formal social address begin with **Frau** or **Herr**. Titles such as **Doktor** or **Professor** follow. The family name comes last.

2. Note in the same sentence that to request to speak to someone officially, the construction in German is **sprechen** + direct object. In English one might say *I would like to speak with* or *to Dr. Ziegler.*

meaningful

aids for conversation

1. Rollenspiel: Im Büro. Wählen Sie eine der folgenden Rollen und führen Sie ein sinnvolles° Gespräch. Vergessen Sie nicht, sich zu grüßen. Hier sind einige Sprechhilfen°.

Presenting oneself for an appointment

S1 (Frau/Herr Richter):	**S2 (Sekretärin/Sekretär):**
Ich würde gern Frau/Herrn Dr. Schulze sprechen.	Es tut mir Leid. Sie/Er ist im Moment beschäftigt⁺. Sie/Er telefoniert gerade. Haben Sie einen Termin mit ihr/ihm?
Ich habe einen Termin für ... Uhr.	Um ... Uhr hat sie/er einen Termin. Sind Sie sicher, dass der Termin für heute/... Uhr war?
Ich bin ganz sicher, dass ich den Termin heute habe.	Gehen Sie bitte gleich hinein. Sie/Er erwartet Sie.

conduct

job interview / applicant

think about

2. Eine neue Stelle. Sie und Ihre Partnerin/Ihr Partner führen° ein Vorstellungsgespräch°. Die Bewerberin/der Bewerber° sollte vor dem Interview überlegen°, was sie/er weiß.

Talking about one's qualifications for a job

S1 (Personalchefin/ Personalchef):	**S2 (Bewerberin/ Bewerber):**
Können Sie | mit **dem Computer** arbeiten? | Textverarbeitungsprogrammen⁺	Ja. Sehr gut. Nein, tut mir Leid.
Haben Sie schon praktische Erfahrung als Informatikerin/Informatiker?	Ja, | **ich habe bei einer kleinen Firma gearbeitet.** ich habe letztes Jahr einen Ferienjob gehabt.
Warum wollen Sie die Stelle wechseln⁺?	Ich möchte | **neue Erfahrungen sammeln.** mehr Verantwortung bekommen. mehr verdienen.

outdoors

those

3. Wo möchten Sie lieber arbeiten – in einem Büro oder im Freien°? Beantworten Sie die folgenden Fragen erst selbst und vergleichen Sie dann Ihre Antworten mit denen° der anderen Kursteilnehmer.

1. Was studierst du?
2. Arbeitest du lieber allein oder mit anderen zusammen?
3. Wo möchtest du lieber arbeiten? In einem Büro oder im Freien?
4. Wie sollte die Arbeit sein? Interessant? Leicht? Schwer?

Ärztin in ihrer Praxis in Hannover.

Erweiterung des Wortschatzes

Berufe

der **Lehrer**/die **Lehrerin**

der **Zahnarzt**/die **Zahnärztin**

die **Architektin**/der **Architekt**

der **Rechtsanwalt**/
die **Rechtsanwältin**

der **Musiker**/die **Musikerin**

die **Politikerin**/der **Politiker**

der **Informatiker**/
die **Informatikerin**

die **Journalistin**/
der **Journalist**

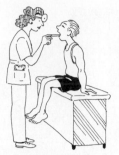

die **Ärztin**/der **Arzt**

die **Geschäftsfrau**/
der **Geschäftsmann**

additional

*Talking about future
goals*

🔄 **1. Berufe.** Fragen Sie vier Kursteilnehmerinnen/Kursteilnehmer über ihre Berufswünsche. Benutzen Sie die Fragen unten. Zusätzliche° Vokabeln zum Thema Berufe finden Sie im Anhang (Appendix C: Supplementary Word Sets).

> *S1:* Was möchtest du werden?
> *S2:* Ich möchte [Ingenieurin/Ingenieur] werden.
> *S1:* Ich [arbeite gern mit Maschinen].

1. Was möchtest du werden? Warum?
2. Wie wichtig ist dir das Geld? Ein sicherer Arbeitsplatz?
3. Kannst du mit dem Computer arbeiten?
4. Mit welchen Textverarbeitungsprogrammen und anderen Computerprogrammen kannst du arbeiten?

job opportunities

2. Stellenangebote°. Sehen Sie die Stellenangebote an und beantworten Sie die Fragen.

1. Welche Stellen sind für eine Studentin/einen Studenten praktisch?
2. Welche Stelle ist nicht in Deutschland?
3. Welche Stellen sind nur für eine Frau? Für eine Frau oder einen Mann? Woher wissen Sie das?+ Was halten Sie davon?

Kindermädchen[1]
f. 3jhr. Zwillingsmädchen[2] von italienischer Familie auf dem Lande gesucht. Separates Zimmer mit Bad. Bewerbung[3] mit Lebenslauf,[4] Foto und Zeugnissen[5] an **G. Vrafino, 10034 Boschetto-Chivasso (Turin)**

Studentenjob
Taxifahrer/in[12] auch als Festfahrer/Aushilfen.[13] Gute Konditionen, Ausbildung[14] im Schnellkurs.[15]
☎ **4484770, 17-19 U.**

Zahnarztpraxis[6] in Köln-Ehrenfeld
sucht nette und dynamische
Zahnarzthelferin[7]
für Teilzeitstelle[8], 20 Stunden pro Woche.
Telefon auch am Wochenende
0221/913678

Wir suchen für unser Fotofachlabor[16] eine/n
Fotolaborant/in[17]
ganz- od. halbtags, auf Wunsch[18]
Schichtdienst.[19] ☎ **47 20 91**

Exportfirma sucht ab sotort[9] eine/n
Sekretär/in
mit Sprachkenntnissen[10] in Italienisch u.
Englisch. Zuschr.[11] u. ✉ ZS9800194

---

[1]*nanny* [2]*twin girls* [3]*application* [4]*short biography in narrative form* [5]*references* [6]*dental practice* [7]*dental assistant* [8]*part-time* [9]**ab sofort:** *beginning immediately* [10]*proficiency in foreign languages* [11]**Zuschr. (= Zuschriften):** *replies* [12]*permanent employee (driver)* [13]*temporary job* [14]*training* [15]*crash course* [16]*photo lab* [17]*photo lab technician* [18]**auf Wunsch:** *if desired* [19]*shift work*

Das soziale Netz

The foundations of German social legislation were laid during the time that Otto von Bismarck (1815–1898) was chancellor. Statutory health insurance (**Kranken-versicherung**), workers' compensation (**Unfall- und Invalidenversicherung**), and retirement benefits (**Rentenversicherung**) were introduced at that time. The costs were to be shared by the employer, the employee, and the state. Retirement age was set at 65.

In Germany today these kinds of insurance are still statutory. All employed people below a certain income must belong to a **Krankenkasse,** which takes care of basic health costs. There is also unemployment insurance (**Arbeitslosenversicherung**) and insurance for long-term nursing care (**Pflegeversicherung**). The entire social "safety net" (**soziales Netz**) includes further benefits such as **Kindergeld,** a monthly payment to parents to offset child-rearing expenses, low-income rent allowances (**Wohngeld**), compensation for the victims of war, financial aid for students, subsidized child care, and others. The state also provides social welfare (**Sozial-hilfe**) for those in need.

Das Arbeitsamt kann helfen, wenn man eine Stelle sucht.

These benefits come at a cost to the employee and add to the labor costs of the employer. In 2002, employee deductions and employer contributions amounted to 41.3% of gross pay, shared equally by the employee and the employer. Retirement cost 19.1%, health insurance 14.0%, long-term care 1.7%, and unemployment insurance 6.5%. The income tax rate varies from a low of 16% to a high of 45%. The combination of fringe benefit deductions and taxes for a German worker is the second highest of western industrial countries. Only Belgium is higher.

www Go to the *Deutsch heute* website at http://college.hmco.com.

Diskussion

Make a list of the social benefits in Germany which have been mentioned in this chapter and in *Kapitel 8* (**Familienpolitik,** p. 291). What are the equivalent benefits in your country?

Kindergeld: Parents receive 154 euros monthly for each of the first three children and 179 euros for the fourth and each additional child. Payments continue until the child has finished school or vocational training, but not beyond the age of 27.

Vokabeln 1

Substantive

die **Bank, -en**   bank
der **Chef, -s**/die **Chefin, -nen**   boss
die **Erfahrung, -en**   experience
die **Geschäftsfrau, -en**
   businesswoman/der
   Geschäftsmann, -leute
   businessman, businesspeople
der **Informatiker, -**/die
   Informatikerin, -nen
   computer specialist
der **Journalist, -en, -en**/die
   Journalistin, -nen   journalist
der **Musiker, -**/die **Musikerin,
   -nen**   musician
der **Personalchef, -s**/die
   Personalchefin, -nen   head of

the human resources (personnel)
department
der **Rechtsanwalt, -anwälte**/die
   Rechtsanwältin, -nen   lawyer,
   attorney
der **Termin, -e**   appointment; **einen
   Termin bei jemandem haben**   to
   have an appointment with someone
das **Textverarbeitungsprogramm,
   -e**   word processing program; **mit
   Textverarbeitungsprogrammen
   arbeiten**   to do word processing
die **Verantwortung, -en**
   responsibility
der **Zahnarzt, ̈-e**/die **Zahnärztin,
   -nen**   dentist

Verben

beschäftigen   to keep a person busy;
   to employ; **beschäftigt sein (mit)**
   busy, occupied (with);   **sich
   beschäftigen (mit)**   to be occupied
   (with)

erwarten   to expect
sammeln   to collect
tippen   to type; **er tippt seine
   Arbeiten**   he types his papers
wechseln   to change

Andere Wörter

hinein   in (*as in* **hineingehen**   to go
   in)

Besondere Ausdrücke

bei einer Firma arbeiten   to work
   for a company; **bei [Siemens]
   arbeiten**   to work for [Siemens]

mit dem Computer arbeiten   to do
   work (on) a computer
Woher wissen Sie das?   How do you
   know that?

Die Kündigung, nur noch drei Tage

Vorbereitung auf das Lesen

Dieser Text kommt aus einem Artikel der *Süddeutschen Zeitung*. Er beschreibt die
Sorgen⁺ eines Angestellten⁺ in der Zeit wirtschaftlicher Probleme.

■ Vor dem Lesen

cues / **kreuzen an:** check off

Lesen Sie die Stichwörter°. Kreuzen Sie die Kategorien an°, mit denen Sie die
Stichwörter assoziieren.

	Wirtschaft allgemein°	Firma	Mitarbeiter
Angst			
Familienprobleme			
Arbeitssuche			
Depression			
mehr Freizeit			
Finanzprobleme			
Profit			
Kündigung°			
Streiks+			
Inflation			
Sorgen			
sinkende Produktion			
Kosten sparen+			
weniger Arbeitsplätze			
teure Rohstoffe			
Konkurrenz°			

in general

dismissal

competition

▨ Beim Lesen

Dieser Text zeigt die Konsequenzen wirtschaftlicher Probleme für das Leben von Mitarbeitern. Was für Probleme haben die Wirtschaft und die Firma? Was für Probleme haben die Mitarbeiter? Beim Lesen machen Sie zwei Listen:

Probleme	
Wirtschaft/Firma	Mitarbeiter

erst einmal: first of all

in between

to get into

affects

changes / affect

rechnen mit: count on

dismissal

um ... gehen: revolve around
money / gone through

the more fortunate one

severance pay

Heute ist Montag und ich bin wieder im Büro. Wie immer, wenn ich weg war,
liegen Berge von Post auf meinem Schreibtisch. Letzte Woche war ich auf einer
Geschäftsreise in San Francisco. Jetzt muss ich erst einmal° alles durcharbeiten.
Dazwischen° klingelt immer wieder das Telefon. Wie soll ich denn da den
5 Postberg nur vom Tisch kriegen? Diesmal ist es das Büro des Personalchefs.
Seine Assistentin fragt: „Herr Gartner, hätten Sie in einer halben Stunde Zeit?
Herr Sundmann möchte Sie sprechen." „Ja, kein Problem, wenn's nicht zu
lange dauert", antworte ich und merke, dass ich blass werde. Schließlich weiß
ich ja, was das heißt. Jetzt bin ich dran. Ich versuche, klar zu denken und nicht
10 in Panik zu geraten°.

Herr Sundmann ist unser Personalchef. Wenn er anruft oder seine
Assistentin, dann weiß jeder in der Firma, was das heißt. In drei Jahren haben
dreihundertfünfzig Mitarbeiter ihre Stelle verloren. Die Büros links and rechts
von mir sind eins nach dem anderen leer geworden. Die Krise betrifft°
15 natürlich nicht nur uns allein. Heute gibt es mehr Streiks als früher. Neue
Technologie und Veränderungen° auf dem Markt betreffen° heute die ganze
deutsche Wirtschaft. Wie die meisten deutschen Firmen, so lebt auch unsere
vom Außenhandel. Deutschland muss viele Rohstoffe importieren. Früher
hatte Deutschland eine niedrige Inflationsrate. Da konnten unsere Kunden mit
20 stabilen Preisen rechnen°. Heute wird jedoch alles immer teurer. Aber jetzt gibt
es auch immer mehr Länder, die die gleichen Waren billiger herstellen. Mit
ihnen kann Deutschland immer weniger konkurrieren. Das haben wir hier in
unserer Firma gemerkt. Also weiß ich, dass der Besuch beim Personalchef in
diesen Tagen Kündigung° bedeutet. Beim Gespräch mit ihm wird es auch vor
25 allem um Geld gehen°. Ich muss mich gut darauf vorbereiten. Susanna, meine
Exkollegin, hat dies alles vor einem halben Jahr durchgemacht°. Sie ist immer
noch arbeitslos und meist zu Hause, wenn ich sie anrufe.

Oh je! Warum muss mir das jetzt passieren? Wenn ich etwas jünger wäre,
dann fände ich sicher leichter eine neue Stelle. Aber mit fünfundvierzig? Es
30 würde mir auch nichts ausmachen, weniger zu verdienen. Wer weiß, vielleicht
bin ich am Ende der Glücklichere°? Vielleicht finde ich schnell eine neue
Stelle, und ich bekomme ja auch meine Abfindung° von der Firma. Da ich
zwölf Jahre lang hier gearbeitet habe, müsste meine Abfindung ein

**Münchner gehen zur
Arbeit.**

Jahresgehalt sein. Aber mein jetziges hohes Gehalt ist bei der Bewerbung° (job) application
35 sicher ein Problem. Und wenn ich in einem Jahr keine neue Stelle finden
kann, muss ich vielleicht meine Wohnung verkaufen. Aber Moment mal! Wäre
es denn wirklich das Ende der Welt? Ich hätte doch auch mehr Zeit für die
Kinder und meine Hobbys! Ich könnte endlich Bücher lesen oder die

Retirement age: Germany: men
63, women 60; Austria: men 65,
women 60; Switzerland: men 65,
women 62.

Wohnung renovieren. Alles Dinge, die ich immer schon machen wollte, für die
40 ich aber früher nie Zeit hatte. Aber würde ich diese Dinge wirklich alle tun?
Hätte ich wirklich Freude daran? Ich glaube nicht, denn ich mache mir jetzt
schon große Sorgen um meine berufliche° Zukunft. Unsichere Zeiten zur
Zeit°!

related to one's job or career
zur Zeit: at the moment

Brauchbares

1. l. 15, **Streiks:** In the over 50 years of its existence the Federal Republic of
   Germany has had relatively few labor strikes. Employer- and union-
   representatives of the major industries usually meet once a year to modify
   existing industry-wide work agreements (**Tarifverträge**). If they cannot agree,
   both parties accept an independent negotiator. It is only in exceptional cases
   that unions organize strikes, for which they need the votes of 75% of their
   members.

2. l. 18, **Außenhandel:** Germany exports one-third of its industrial output. The
   most important German exports are machinery, automobiles, chemical
   products, and electronics. In 2002 Germany reached a record level of exported
   goods with a value of 648.3 billion euros. Worldwide, Germany has for a
   number of years been second in the monetary value of exports; the U.S. is
   first. France, at 69.8 billion euros, is the leading recipient of German exports;
   the U.S. with 66.6 billion is second. In return Germany imported goods with a
   value of 45.5 billion euros from the U.S.

3. l. 21, **Waren billiger herstellen:** In the year 2000, hourly compensation costs
   for production workers in Germany averaged $22.99 (West Germany alone
   $24.01), the highest in the industrial world. Costs for comparison purposes
   show Norway at $22.05, Japan $22.00, Switzerland $21.24, U.S. $19.86, Austria
   $19.46, Canada $16.16, Korea $8.13, and Portugal $4.75.

Nach dem Lesen

1. Fragen zum Lesestück

1. Warum war Herr Gartner in San Francisco?
2. Was liegt auf seinem Schreibtisch?
3. Wer ruft Herrn Gartner an?
4. Warum wird Herr Gartner blass?
5. Wer ist Herr Sundmann?
6. Wie viele Leute haben schon ihre Stelle in der Firma verloren?
7. Wovon lebt die deutsche Wirtschaft?
8. Warum ist die deutsche Wirtschaft in einer Krise? Geben Sie mindestens zwei
   Gründe[+] an.
9. Wie hoch könnte Herrn Gartners Abfindung sein?
10. Was wird das Thema sein, wenn Herr Gartner mit dem Personalchef spricht?
11. Was für Probleme sieht Herr Gartner bei der Bewerbung um eine neue Stelle?
12. Wofür hätte Herr Gartner Zeit, wenn er arbeitslos würde?
13. Wie sieht Herr Gartner seine Zukunft?

Die Mitbestimmung

Democratic codetermination (**Mitbestimmung**) is a right guaranteed by law in Germany. **Mitbestimmung** gives workers the right and the responsibility to participate in important decisions about their company. Employees of the company have representatives on special councils. These councils ensure that wage agreements, laws, and regulations are carried out. They also participate in decisions about work shifts, overtime, personnel changes, continuing education, and other internal policies.

For companies with more than 2,000 employees, the law requires that an equal number of representatives of shareholders and of employees sit on the board of directors (**Aufsichtsrat**). In Austria, the ratio of employees to shareholders on the board is 1:3. Switzerland does not require **Mitbestimmung;** however, some companies have internal councils that function like those in German companies.

Was wollen diese Metallarbeiter?

Diskussion

Group project: Contact your local chamber of commerce or a state or provincial agency and find out if there are any German, Austrian, or Swiss companies in your region.

2. Unsichere Zukunft. In diesem Text gibt es viele Stellen, wo der Mitarbeiter über seine Zukunft nachdenkt°. Suchen Sie fünf Stellen im Text mit den Wörtern: **vielleicht, könnte, müsste, würde.** Benutzen Sie jeden Ausdruck in einem Satz[+].

thinks about

3. Zum Schreiben. Lesen Sie die folgenden Sätze zur Situation der Wirtschaft, der Firma und der Mitarbeiter. Verbinden Sie Sätze der verschiedenen° Gruppen und zeigen Sie Zusammenhänge°. Viele Variationen sind möglich.

various
connections

Konjunktionen: weil ▪ aber ▪ denn ▪ und
Adverbien: deshalb ▪ später ▪ dann ▪ leider ▪ in einem Jahr

➔ *Weil die Inflation höher ist, kann die Firma keine stabilen Preise garantieren.*

Wirtschaft
1. Die Wirtschaft ist in einer Krise.
2. Viele Länder stellen die Waren billiger her.
3. Die Rohstoffe werden teurer.
4. Die Inflation ist höher.
5. Es gibt mehr Streiks.

Firma

1. Die Firma verkauft nicht mehr so viele Waren.
2. Die Firma kann keine stabilen Preise garantieren.
3. Die Firma reduziert ihr Personal.
4. Die Firma muss/will sparen.
5. Die Firma macht weniger Profit.

Mitarbeiter/innen

1. Die Mitarbeiter/innen verlieren ihre Stellen.
2. Die Mitarbeiter/innen haben mehr Zeit für ihre Kinder.
3. Die Mitarbeiter/innen müssen neue Stellen suchen.
4. Die Mitarbeiter/innen haben Angst vor der Zukunft.

4. Erzählen wir. Benutzen Sie die Notizen, die Sie sich beim Lesen gemacht haben, und sprechen Sie über ein Thema:

1. Stellen Sie sich vor°, Sie verlieren vielleicht Ihre Stelle. Was sagen Sie zu Ihrer Familie oder Ihren Freunden? Versuchen Sie eine Minute zu sprechen.   **stellen ... vor:** imagine
2. Sprechen Sie kurz über die deutsche Wirtschaft.

Erweiterung des Wortschatzes

The suffix *-lich*

der Beruf	occupation	**beruflich**	career-related
der Freund	friend	**freundlich**	friendly
fragen	to ask	**fraglich**	questionable
krank	ill, sick	**kränklich**	sickly

German adjectives and adverbs may be formed from some nouns or verbs by adding the suffix **-lich.** The suffix **-lich** may also be added to other adjectives. Some stem vowels are umlauted: **ä, ö,** and **ü.** The English equivalent is often an adjective or adverb ending in *-ly,* e.g., *sick* and *sickly.*

1. Politische Reden°. Gestern Abend hat der Wirtschaftsminister an der Universität eine Rede gehalten. Heute Abend soll die Rede im Fernsehen kommen. Claudia und Uwe sprechen über die Rede. Geben Sie die fett gedruckten Wörter auf Englisch wieder. Welche Verben, Substantive oder Adjektive sind mit den fett gedruckten Wörtern verwandt?   speeches

CLAUDIA: Wie war es gestern Abend?

UWE: Ich fand die Rede inhaltlich° sehr interessant, aber Sarah sagt, der Minister hat über viele politisch unkluge° Dinge gesprochen.   in regard to the content / unwise

CLAUDIA: Dass Sarah das gesagt hat, ist wirklich **unglaublich. Schließlich** ist ihr Vater der Assistent des Ministers. Hat sie das wirklich **öffentlich** gesagt?

UWE: Nein, sie hat mir das privat gesagt. Wusstest du eigentlich, dass Hans-Jürgen gestern Abend schließlich doch noch gekommen ist?

CLAUDIA: Ja, aber es ist **fraglich,** ob er heute Abend kommt. Wir wollten doch nach der Sendung die Rede diskutieren, nicht wahr?

UWE: Ja, und ich freue mich schon darauf. Gestern Abend war jeder so **freundlich.**

CLAUDIA: Das ist **natürlich verständlich.** Die meisten sind Politologiestudenten° und haben die gleichen Interessen.   political science students

Vokabeln 2

Substantive

der/die **Angestellte** (*noun decl. like adj.*)   salaried employee, white-collar worker

der **Außenhandel**   foreign trade

die **Freude, -n**   pleasure, joy; **Freude an** + (*dat.*)   pleasure in; **Freude machen**   to give pleasure

das **Gehalt, ̈er**   salary

das **Gespräch, -e**   conversation; **ein Gespräch führen**   to carry on a conversation

der **Grund, ̈e**   reason

der **Kunde, -n, -n**/die **Kundin, -nen**   customer, client

der **Mitarbeiter, -**/die **Mitarbeiterin, -nen**   employee

die **Post**   mail; post office

der **Preis, -e**   price

der **Satz, ̈e**   sentence

die **Sorge, -n**   care, worry; **sich Sorgen machen (um)**   to worry (about)

der **Streik, -s**   strike

die **Ware, -n**   wares, merchandise, goods

die **Zukunft**   future

Verben

antworten (+ *dat.*)   to answer (*as in* **ich antworte der Frau**); **antworten auf** (+ *acc.*)   to answer (*as in* **ich antworte auf die Frage**)

aus·machen   to matter; **es macht mir nichts aus**   it doesn't matter to me

bedeuten   to mean; **Was bedeutet das?**   What does that mean?

dauern   to last; to require time

finden: fände   would find

her·stellen   to produce; to manufacture

klingeln   to ring

konkurrieren   to compete

können: könnte   would be able to

kriegen   to get

merken   to notice; to realize

müssen: müsste   would have to

sparen   to save

verkaufen   to sell

sich vor·bereiten (**auf** + *acc.*)   to prepare oneself (for)

wollen: wollte   would want

Andere Wörter

arbeitslos   unemployed, out of work

diesmal   this time

leer   empty

links   on/to the left

niedrig   low

rechts   on/to the right

unsicher   insecure; unsafe

Besondere Ausdrücke

das heißt   that means

[ich bin] dran   it is [my] turn

Moment mal!   Just a minute!

wie immer   as always

Die Europäische Union

The European Union (**Europäische Union**) strives for economic and political union of its member countries. Since its beginning as the European Community (**Europäische Gemeinschaft**), it has made considerable progress in creating a single market without internal borders. Goods, services, and capital can move freely without custom regulations within the EU. Citizens of EU countries can, without restrictions, travel, live, and work anywhere within the EU.

The European Union stretches from the Arctic Circle to the island of Malta in the Mediterranean. In 2004, the number of countries in the EU increased from 15 to 25. Over 453 million people now live in the EU. The gross domestic product (**Bruttosozialprodukt**) of the EU and that of the U.S.A. are the two largest in the world.

In spite of its successes, many problems and goals remain. Working hours, wages, and extended benefits are issues that need to be resolved. The goal of a political confederation of states with common foreign and defense policies and common laws seems to be even more difficult to obtain.

Die Flagge der Europäischen Union. Die zwölf Sterne symbolisieren Einheit und Stabilität.

Diskussion

www Go to the *Deutsch heute* website at http://college.hmco.com.

Fifteen members of the EU before 2004: Austria, Belgium, Denmark, Finland, France, Germany, Greece, Ireland, Italy, Luxembourg, Netherlands, Portugal, Spain, Sweden, United Kingdom. Ten members added in 2004: Czech Republic, Cyprus, Estonia, Hungary, Latvia, Lithuania, Malta, Poland, Slovakia, Slovenia.

In 2002, the gross domestic product of the U.S.A. was 10 trillion dollars and that of the EU was 6 trillion dollars.

Citizens of the European Union have certain rights in common. These rights are called single market rights. Often the rights guaranteed by the European Commission in regard to job qualifications or residence conflict with the regulations of an individual member state. One of the most common areas of conflict concerns vehicles. For instance, a problem resolved by the Commission concerned a ban on trailers towed by motorcycles in Denmark. Danish legislation (Traffic Law §70) applied this prohibition to foreign-registered as well as Danish-registered motorcycles. The Commission considered the prohibition incompatible with the principle of free movement of goods in the single market (Article 30 of the EC Treaty). Following the Commission's intervention, the Danish legislation in question has been modified to permit motorcycles in Denmark to tow trailers. The move has been warmly welcomed by motorcycle enthusiasts in both Denmark and other member states.

Do you agree with the way in which the conflict was resolved?

Grammatik und Übungen

1 Future time: present tense

Ich **helfe** dir morgen bestimmt.

> *I'll help* you tomorrow for sure.
> *I'm going to help* you tomorrow
>   for sure.

Arbeitest du heute Abend?

> *Are you working* tonight?
> *Are you going to work* tonight?

German generally uses the present tense (e.g., **ich helfe, arbeitest du?**) to express future time. English expresses future time by the future tense (e.g., *I'll help*), with a form of *go* (e.g., *I'm going to help*), or with the present progressive tense (*are you working?*).

1. Was für Pläne hast du? Michael spricht mit Claudia über ihre Pläne. Bilden Sie Sätze im Präsens, um das Futur auszudrücken°.

to express

1. kommen / du / heute Abend / mit / ins Kino / ?
2. nein, ich / gehen / auf eine Party
3. was / machen / du / morgen / ?
4. die Semesterferien / anfangen / doch / morgen
5. fahren / du / bald / in Urlaub / ?
6. nein, ich / lernen / zuerst / für meine Prüfungen
7. und in ein paar Wochen / ich / besuchen / eine Freundin / in der Schweiz

2 Future time: future tense°

das Futur

Wir **werden** unsere Freunde **einladen.**   We *will invite* our friends.
Jutta **wird** es allein **machen.**   Jutta *will do* it alone.

German, like English, does have a future tense, although in German it is not used as often as the present tense to express future time. The future tense in German may be used to express intention.

Katrin **wird** wohl zu Hause **sein.**   Katrin *is probably* at home.
Das **wird** sicher falsch **sein.**   That's *most likely* wrong.

In addition to expressing intention, the future tense may be used to express an assumption (present probability) when it is used with adverbs such as **wohl, sicher,** or **schon.**

ich **werde** es sicher **finden**	wir **werden** es sicher **finden**
du **wirst** es sicher **finden**	ihr **werdet** es sicher **finden**
er/es/sie **wird** es sicher **finden**	sie **werden** es sicher **finden**
Sie **werden** es sicher **finden**	

In both English and German, the future tense is a compound tense. In English, the future tense is a verb phrase consisting of *will* or *shall* plus the main verb. In German, the future tense is also a verb phrase and consists of a form of **werden** plus an infinitive in final position.

2. Kein Streik. Der Gewerkschaftsführer° erklärt, was die Gewerkschaft mit dem   union leader
Management besprechen wird. Sagen Sie die Sätze noch einmal im Futur.

→ Wir verdienen bestimmt mehr.   *Wir werden bestimmt mehr verdienen.*

1. Wir arbeiten wohl 38 Stunden die Woche.
2. Bei Krankheit zahlt die Firma ja weiter.
3. Wir bekommen ja sechs Wochen bezahlten Urlaub.
4. Der Arbeitstag fängt wohl um halb acht an.
5. Das Arbeitsklima wird doch besser.
6. Wir streiken bestimmt nicht.

Michael weiß nicht, ob Ursel ihn **besuchen wird.**	Michael doesn't know whether Ursel *will visit* him.
Hans sagt, dass sie sicher **kommen wird.**	Hans says she'*ll come* for sure.

The auxiliary **werden** is in final position in a dependent clause because it is the
finite verb. It follows the infinitive.

3. Ein tolles Wochenende. Erik erzählt, was seine Freunde wahrscheinlich
am Wochenende machen werden. Beginnen Sie jeden Satz mit **Erik sagt,
dass _____** .

→ Inge wird wohl mit Gülay Hausaufgaben machen.
Erik sagt, dass Inge wohl mit Gülay Hausaufgaben machen wird.

1. Erkan wird wohl seinem Vater im Geschäft helfen.
2. Am Sonntag werden alle drei wohl aufs Schulfest gehen.
3. In der Schulband wird Erkan wohl Gitarre spielen.
4. Hinterher° werden sie wohl in ein türkisches Lokal° gehen.   afterwards / restaurant
5. Sie werden dort wohl andere Freunde treffen.

4. Was für Pläne hast du für die Zeit nach dem Studium? Bilden Sie
eine kleine Gruppe und fragen Sie die anderen Gruppenmitglieder nach
ihren Plänen nach dem Studium. Benutzen Sie die Sprechhilfen°.   cues

S1: Weißt du schon, was du nach dem Studium machen wirst?
S2: Ich werde wohl bei einer Computer-Firma arbeiten. Und du?   *Discussing post-
graduation plans*

ein Jahr ins Ausland gehen
bei einer [spanischen/deutschen/großen/kleinen/Computer-/Auto-] Firma
   arbeiten
mit meinem italienischen Freund ein Lokal aufmachen°   open up
eine Stelle in [Brüssel/Straßburg/Berlin] suchen
in die Politik gehen
weiterstudieren
in einem Forschungslaboratorium° arbeiten   research lab
erst mal nichts tun

5. Hören Sie zu. Gisela und Alex denken an das Ende ihres Studiums und
sprechen über die Zukunft. Hören Sie zu und beantworten Sie die Fragen. Sie
hören ein neues Wort: **der Traum** (*dream*).

1. Warum wird Alex vielleicht nach seinem Studium in Deutschland ein oder
   zwei Jahre in Amerika studieren?
2. Was glaubt Alex, was er in zehn Jahren haben wird?

3. Wo wird Gisela in zehn Jahren vielleicht wohnen?
4. Was wird sie in zehn Jahren hoffentlich haben?
5. Was wird Alex jetzt machen?

der Konjunktiv

 ### Subjunctive mood° vs. indicative mood

Indicative	Kerstin kommt heute nicht.	*Kerstin is not coming today.*
	Vielleicht kommt sie morgen.	*Perhaps she'll come tomorrow.*

In *Kapitel 1–10* you have primarily been using verbs in sentences that make statements and ask questions dealing with "real" situations. Verb forms of this type are said to be in the indicative mood. The indicative is used in statements that are factual *(Kerstin is not coming today)* or likely *(Perhaps she'll come tomorrow)*.

Subjunctive	Ich **würde** das nicht **tun.** ⎫	*I would not do that.*
	Ich **täte** das nicht. ⎭	

When we talk about "unreal" situations we may use verbs in the subjunctive mood. The subjunctive is used in statements that are hypothetical, potential, unlikely, or contrary to fact. When a speaker says "I wouldn't do that," she/he means "I wouldn't do that if I were you (or she, he, or someone else)," because she/he thinks it is not a good idea. The speaker is postulating a hypothetical situation.

Wishes	Ich **möchte** eine Tasse Kaffee.	*I would like* a cup of coffee.
Polite requests	**Würden** Sie das bitte **tun?**	*Would* you *do* that, please?

The subjunctive is also used to express wishes and polite requests. You have been using **möchte** to express wishes since *Kapitel 3*. **Möchte** *(would like)* is the subjunctive form of **mögen** *(to like)*.

German has two ways to express the subjunctive mood. One way is to use the **würde**-construction (Ich **würde** das nicht **tun**). The other way is to use the subjunctive form of the main verb (Ich **täte** das nicht). The meaning of both ways is the same (I *would* not *do* that). In conversational German the **würde**-construction is used much more frequently than the subjunctive form of main verbs, with the exception of a few verbs that are commonly used in the subjunctive (**hätte, wäre,** and the modals).

Wenn ich nur Zeit **hätte.**   If only I *had* time.

Present-time subjunctive can refer to the future as well as to present time *(if only I had time now or in the future)*.

4 Verb endings in present-time subjunctive°

der Konjunktiv der
Gegenwart

kommen	
ich käme	wir kämen
du kämest	ihr kämet
er/es/sie käme	sie kämen
Sie kämen	

The subjunctive endings above are used for all verbs, strong and weak. Note that the endings are identical to the past-tense endings of weak verbs, minus the **-t** (**ich spielte, du spieltest,** etc.) In colloquial German, the endings **-est** and **-et** often contract to **-st** and **-t** if the form is clearly subjunctive, as indicated by the umlaut in strong verbs, e.g., **kämst, kämt.** (See Section 12 of this chapter.)

5 The *würde*-construction°

die würde-Konstruktion

Ich **würde** das nicht **machen.**	I *would* not *do* that.
Max **würde** uns bestimmt **helfen.**	Max *would* certainly *help* us.

To talk about "unreal" situations in the present, German often uses a **würde**-construction. English uses a *would*-construction.

ich **würde** es **machen**	wir **würden** es **machen**
du **würdest** es **machen**	ihr **würdet** es **machen**
er/es/sie **würde** es **machen**	sie **würden** es **machen**
Sie **würden** es **machen**	

The **würde**-construction consists of a form of **würde** plus an infinitive. **Würde** is the subjunctive form of **werden.** It is formed by adding an umlaut to **wurde,** the simple past of **werden.**

6. Freizeit. Was würden diese Leute tun, wenn sie nächste Woche frei hätten?

→ Jens   sein Referat fertig schreiben   *Jens würde sein Referat fertig schreiben.*

1. Christoph — viel im Internet surfen
2. ich — faulenzen
3. Liane und Ina — jeden Tag ins Kino gehen
4. du — öfter ins Fitnesscenter gehen
5. mein Onkel Mark — inlineskaten lernen
6. meine Eltern — eine kleine Reise machen

6 Uses of the *würde*-construction

Hypothetical statements	Ich **würde** ihm **helfen.**	I *would help* him.
Wishes	Wenn er mir nur **helfen würde.**	If only he *would help* me.
Polite requests	**Würden** Sie mir bitte **helfen?**	*Would* you please *help* me?

The **würde**-construction is used in hypothetical statements, in wishes, and in polite requests.

7. Monika würde das auch gern tun. Was würde Monika auch gern tun? Benutzen Sie die **würde**-Konstruktion und **gern**.

→ Christine arbeitet in einer großen Firma.
  Monika würde auch gern in einer großen Firma arbeiten.

1. Christine verdient viel.
2. Sie macht oft Geschäftsreisen.
3. Sie fährt dreimal im Jahr in Urlaub.
4. Sie kauft sich eine größere Wohnung.
5. Am Wochenende macht sie Fitnesstraining.

Inquiring about someone's wishes

8. Was würden Sie gern machen? Beantworten Sie die folgenden Fragen erst selbst und vergleichen Sie Ihre Antworten dann mit den Antworten von zwei anderen Kursteilnehmerinnen/Kursteilnehmern.

class (session)

→ Was würdest du nach dem Deutschkurs° am liebsten machen?
  Ich würde am liebsten nach Hause gehen/einen Kaffee trinken/schlafen.

1. Was würdest du heute Abend gern machen?
2. Was würdest du am Freitagabend am liebsten machen?
3. Was würdest du im Sommer gern machen?
4. Was würdest du nach dem Studium gern machen?

telephone call

5. Von wem würdest du am liebsten einen Brief, eine E-Mail oder einen Anruf° bekommen?

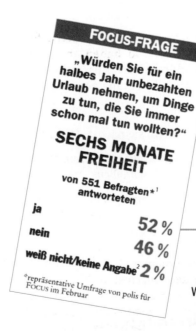

FOCUS-FRAGE

„Würden Sie für ein halbes Jahr unbezahlten Urlaub nehmen, um Dinge zu tun, die Sie immer schon mal tun wollten?"

SECHS MONATE FREIHEIT

von 551 Befragten*[1] antworteten

ja **52 %**

nein **46 %**

weiß nicht/keine Angabe[2] **2 %**

°repräsentative Umfrage von polis für FOCUS im Februar

[1]*those queried* [2]*response*

Wie viel Prozent der befragten (*queried*) Personen würden für ein halbes Jahr Urlaub nehmen? Würden Sie auch gern für sechs Monate unbezahlten Urlaub nehmen? Warum (nicht)?

Present-time subjunctive of the main verb

Wenn Alex besser Golf **spielte,** würden wir mit ihm spielen.	If Alex *played* better golf, we'd play with him.
Wenn ich das **könnte,** würde ich es tun.	If I *could* (do that), I would (do it).
Wenn Claudia nicht müde **wäre,** würde sie heute Golf spielen.	If Claudia *were* (colloquial: *was*) not tired, she would play golf today.

Notice that in English the subjunctive forms of main verbs are often identical with the past tense (e.g., *played, could, were* [colloquial: *was*]). In German the same principle applies. For weak verbs, the present-time subjunctive is identical to the simple past tense (e.g., **spielte**); for modals and strong verbs, the subjunctive is based on the simple-past tense form of the verb (e.g., **konnte > könnte, war > wäre**). German uses the present-time subjunctive to express subjunctive for present and future time.

8 Present-time subjunctive of the main verb vs. the *würde*-construction

Present-time subjunctive	*Würde-construction*
Wenn Alex nur besser **spielte.**	Wenn Alex nur besser **spielen würde.**
Wenn Tanja nur etwas **täte.**	Wenn Tanja nur etwas **tun würde.**
Wenn Kevin nur **ginge.**	Wenn Kevin nur **gehen würde.**

In present time either the **würde**-construction or the subjunctive form of the main verb can be used. However, for the verbs **sein, haben,** and the modals, the present-time subjunctive is generally used instead of the **würde**-construction.

9 Present-time subjunctive of *sein* and *haben*

sein				haben		
ich wäre	wir wären			ich hätte	wir hätten	
du wärest	ihr wäret			du hättest	ihr hättet	
er/es/sie wäre	sie wären			er/es/sie hätte	sie hätten	
Sie wären				Sie hätten		

The verbs **haben** and **sein** are more commonly used in their subjunctive forms, **wäre** and **hätte,** than as part of the **würde**-construction. Notice that the subjunctive form of **sein** is the simple past tense **war** plus umlaut and subjunctive endings (**wäre, wärest,** etc.). The subjunctive of **haben** is the simple past tense form **hatte** plus umlaut and subjunctive endings (**hätte, hättest,** etc.).

9. Wären alle froh darüber? Manche Politiker möchten auf allen Autobahnen ein Tempolimit°. Sagen Sie, was die folgenden Leute davon halten.

speed limit

➔ Robert / sicher froh   *Robert wäre sicher froh.*

1. Christine / unglücklich
2. du / sicher auch unglücklich

3. Corinna und Rafael / dagegen
4. wir / dafür
5. ihr / hoffentlich dafür
6. die Grünen / glücklich
7. ich / sehr froh

> *Eine Million im Lotto - was nun?*
> *CDs für eine Million wäre mein Traum.[1]*
> *(Chrissi, 24)*

[1]dream

Was wäre Chrissis Traum?

10. Was hättest du lieber? Sagen Sie, was für eine Stelle Sie lieber hätten.

➡ Was hättest du lieber? Eine Stelle mit einem guten Gehalt oder viel
Freizeit? *Ich hätte lieber eine Stelle mit viel Freizeit.*

1. mit viel Verantwortung oder wenig Verantwortung?
2. in einer großen Firma oder in einer kleinen Firma?
3. mit netten Kollegen oder mit einem netten Chef?
4. in der Nähe° einer Großstadt oder in einer Kleinstadt?
5. mit vielen Geschäftsreisen oder ohne Geschäftsreisen?

vicinity

der Konditionalsatz

10 Conditional sentences°

A conditional sentence contains two clauses: the condition (**wenn**-clause) and the
conclusion. The **wenn**-clause states the conditions under which some event may
or may not take place.

▪ Conditions of fact

Wenn ich Zeit **habe, komme** ich **mit.**	If I *have* time (maybe I will, maybe I won't), I'll *come* along.

Conditions of fact are conditions that can be fulfilled. Indicative verb forms are
used in conditions of fact.

▪ Conditions contrary to fact

Wenn ich Zeit **hätte, würde** ich **mitkommen.** Wenn ich Zeit **hätte, käme** ich mit.	If I *had* time [but I don't], I *would come along.*

A sentence with a condition contrary to fact indicates a situation that will not
take place. The speaker only speculates on how some things could or would be
under certain conditions (if the speaker had time, for example).

To talk about the present, a speaker uses present-time subjunctive of the main
verb (e.g., **hätte**) in the condition clause (**wenn**-clause) and in the conclusion a
würde-construction (e.g., **würde mitkommen**) or the present-time subjunctive of

the main verb (e.g., **käme**). Formal written German tends to avoid the **würde**-construction in the **wenn**-clause. Subjunctive forms of strong and weak verbs are discussed under headings 12–14 in this section.

11. Hören Sie zu. Hören Sie zu, was Gisela und Alex einer Reporterin sagen. Geben Sie an, ob die Sätze unten richtig oder falsch sind. Sie hören drei neue Wörter: **die Traumreise** *(dream trip)*; **der Lotterieschein** *(lottery ticket)*; **überhaupt** *(absolutely)*.

1. Alex spielt gern Lotto.
2. Gisela spielt fast jede Woche Lotto.
3. Wenn Gisela in der Lotterie gewinnen würde, würde sie sich ein Haus kaufen.
4. Gisela würde ihren Freunden eine Reise nach Hawaii oder Tahiti kaufen.
5. Gisela kann dieses Mal gar nicht im Lotto gewinnen, weil sie keinen Lotterieschein gekauft hat.

12. Frage-Ecke. Fragen Sie Ihre Partnerin/Ihren Partner und finden Sie heraus, was die folgenden Leute tun würden, wenn sie arbeitslos oder krank wären oder wenn sie mehr Zeit und viel Geld hätten. Die Informationen für *S2* finden Sie im Anhang (Appendix B).

> *S1:* Was würde Herr Schäfer machen, wenn er mehr Zeit hätte?
> *S2:* Wenn er mehr Zeit hätte, (dann) würde er seine Freunde besuchen.

S1:

	arbeitslos wäre	krank wäre	mehr Zeit hätte	viel Geld hätte
Frau Müller	Zeitung lesen		öfter Tennis spielen	in die Schweiz reisen
Herr Schäfer		viel schlafen		
Susanne und Moritz	spazieren gehen		Auto fahren	
ich				
Partnerin/Partner				

13. Was wäre, wenn … ? Beantworten Sie die folgenden elf Fragen erst selbst. Fragen Sie dann Ihre Partnerin/Ihren Partner, was sie/er tun würde. Berichten Sie den Kursteilnehmerinnen/Kursteilnehmern, was Sie herausgefunden haben.

> *S1:* Was würdest du tun, wenn du 10 Jahre älter wärest?
> *S2:* Ich würde ein Haus kaufen/ein Buch schreiben/heiraten.

Was würdest du tun, …

1. wenn du 10 Jahre älter wärest?
2. wenn du sehr reich wärest?
3. wenn du Deutschlehrerin/Deutschlehrer wärest?
4. wenn du Präsidentin/Präsident der USA wärest?
5. wenn du kein Geld fürs Studium hättest?

6. wenn deine Freunde keine Zeit für dich hätten?
7. wenn du morgen frei hättest?
8. wenn du kein Auto hättest?
9. wenn dein Fernseher kaputt wäre?
10. wenn du morgen krank wärest?
11. wenn wir morgen 30°C hätten?

Land und Leute

Berufliche Ausbildung

Despite high income-tax rates and high labor costs, Germany has a very productive economy. Experts attribute this in large measure to the fact that Germany has a well-trained labor force.

Most young people who finish the **Hauptschule** (*see* **Das Schulsystem in Deutschland,** p. 143) or have a **Mittlere Reife** enter an apprenticeship (**Ausbildung**) program. There are 357 recognized **Ausbildungsberufe.** An **Ausbildung** generally lasts three years. During this time the trainees (**Auszubildende,** also called **Lehrlinge**) work three to four days a week in a company and attend vocational school (**Berufsschule**) one to two days a week. Large companies have special workshops and staffs for trainees; in small businesses trainees often learn directly from the boss. **Auszubildende** receive benefits and a salary that increases every year. At the end of their **Ausbildung** trainees take exams at both the workplace and the **Berufsschule.** By passing the exam a woman becomes a journeywoman (**Gesellin**) and a man becomes a journeyman (**Geselle**). After five more years of work and additional schooling a **Geselle/Gesellin** may become a **Meister/Meisterin.** People who achieve the status of **Meister/Meisterin** have demonstrated on the basis of rigorous testing that they possess all the knowledge and skills necessary to operate a business. Only people who have passed the **Meisterprüfung** are allowed to train **Auszubildende (Azubis).**

Eine Wissenschaftlerin mit einer Auszubildenden im European Space Operations Center in Darmstadt.

www Go to the *Deutsch heute* website at http://college.hmco.com.

Austria and Switzerland also have extensive apprenticeship programs. In Austria an **Ausbildung** takes 3 years, in Switzerland it may take up to 4 years.

Some monthly wages for selected apprenticeships: **Bankkaufmann** (bank teller) €650; **Hotelfachmann** (hotel manager) €600; **Arzthelfer** (physician's assistant) €550; **Kfz-Mechaniker** (auto mechanic) €470; **Friseur** (hair dresser) €430.

Diskussion

1. Imagine that you would like to open a cabinetry business and perhaps teach young people carpentry. Compare what you would need to do to achieve your goal in Germany with your own country.
2. In Germany one needs apprenticeship training to become a mechanic, a hairdresser or a graphic artist. Compare this situation to that in your own country.

11 Modals in present-time subjunctive

Infinitive		Simple past	Present-time subjunctive
dürfen		durfte	**dürfte**
können		konnte	**könnte**
mögen	er/es/sie	mochte	**möchte**
müssen		musste	**müsste**
sollen		sollte	**sollte**
wollen		wollte	**wollte**

The present-time subjunctive of modals is identical to the simple-past tense except that the modals that have an umlaut in the infinitive also have an umlaut in the subjunctive.

> **Müsstest** du die Arbeit allein machen? *Would* you *have* to do the work alone?

Like **sein (wäre)** and **haben (hätte)**, the modals are generally used in their subjunctive form rather than as infinitives with the **würde-**construction.

> **Dürfte** ich auch mitkommen? *Might* I come along, too?
> **Könntest** du noch etwas bleiben? *Could* you stay a while?
> **Müsste** Monika vor allen Leuten sprechen? *Would* Monika *have to* speak in front of all the people?
> **Möchten** Sie in einer Stunde essen? *Would* you *like to* eat in an hour?
> **Solltet** ihr jetzt nicht gehen? *Should*n't you be going now?

The subjunctive forms of the modals are frequently used to express polite requests or wishes.

> **Ich wollte,** ich hätte Zeit. *I wish* I had time.
> **Ich wollte,** sie käme bald. *I wish* she would come soon.

The expression **ich wollte** is used frequently to introduce wishes. Note that the verb **wollte** is subjunctive. Thus, strictly, **ich wollte** is equivalent to *I would wish.*

14. Etwas höflicher°, bitte! Sie und einige Freunde möchten heute Abend ausgehen. Sie haben einige Fragen. Sie wollen höflich sein und benutzen deshalb den Konjunktiv für die Modalverben.

more politely

→ Können wir das Restaurant allein finden?
  Könnten wir das Restaurant allein finden?

1. Können wir nicht bald gehen?
2. Du musst noch abwaschen.
3. Kann ich dir helfen?
4. Dürfen Susi und Christiane mitkommen?
5. Sollen wir Gerd nicht auch einladen?
6. Darf ich euch alle zu einem Getränk einladen?
7. Kannst du für das Essen zahlen?

Expressing wishes

15. Wenn es nur anders wäre. Sie wünschen sich, dass vieles in Ihrem Studentenheim anders wäre. Erzählen Sie einer Freundin/einem Freund davon.

➡ Klaus kocht immer Spaghetti.
Ich wollte, Klaus würde nicht immer Spaghetti kochen.

➡ Michael macht das Zimmer nicht sauber.
Ich wollte, Michael würde das Zimmer sauber machen.

1. Martin spielt den ganzen Tag Computerspiele.
2. Christoph hört immer Musik.
3. Bernd redet so viel.
4. Wolfgang kommt immer zu spät.
5. Stefan schließt die Tür nicht.

16. Ich wollte, ich könnte ... Ergänzen Sie die Sätze. Finden Sie dann heraus, was Ihre Partnerin/Ihr Partner geschrieben hat und was sie/er gern tun würde.

1. Ich wollte, ich könnte _____ .
2. Wenn ich Zeit hätte, _____ .
3. Wenn meine Eltern viel Geld hätten, _____ .
4. Ich sollte _____ .
5. Ich würde gern _____ .

Discussing goals

17. Was ist dir im Leben am wichtigsten? Finden Sie heraus, was drei bis vier Lebensziele Ihrer Partnerin/Ihres Partners sind.

S1: Was ist dir im Leben wichtig?
S2: Ich möchte vor allem [einen guten Job haben].
Dann möchte ich [einen Sinn° im Leben finden].
Drittens° möchte ich [gesund bleiben].

meaning
thirdly

Lebensziele:
heiraten und Kinder haben
viel Geld verdienen
gesund sein
schöne Dinge haben wie
  ein tolles Auto, teure
  Kleidung
ein schönes/großes Haus
  haben
einen guten Job haben
glücklich sein
Spaß und Freude am
  Leben haben
einen Sinn im Leben
  finden
anderen Menschen
  helfen

¹lonely ²island

Present-time subjunctive of strong verbs

Infinitive			Simple past	+ umlaut for a, o, u	+ subjunctive ending	Present-time subjunctive
finden	er/es/sie	{	fand	fänd	-e	fände
gehen			ging	ging	-e	ginge

finden	
ich fände	wir fänden
du fändest	ihr fändet
er/es/sie fände	sie fänden
Sie fänden	

The present-time subjunctive of strong verbs is formed by adding subjunctive endings to the simple-past stem of the verb. An umlaut is added to the stem vowels **a, o,** or **u.** Although the **würde**-construction and the subjunctive form of the main verb are equivalent in meaning, the **würde**-construction is more common in spoken German.

While all verbs have subjunctive forms (see #24 of the Grammatical Tables in Appendix F), only a few of them are common in informal German. In written German the most common are: **fände (finden), gäbe (geben), ginge (gehen), hielte (halten), hieße (heißen), ließe (lassen), käme (kommen), täte (tun).** Of these verbs **fände, gäbe, ginge,** and **käme** are also common in spoken German.

18. An einem langweiligen Arbeitstag. Hier sind einige Gedanken°, die Frau Müller hat, wenn sie sich im Büro langweilt°. Die Verben in diesen Sätzen sind im Konjunktiv. Suchen Sie den passenden englischen Satz auf der rechten Seite.

thoughts
langweilt sich: is bored

→ Das ginge.   *That would work.*

1. Das täte ich gern.
2. Wir kämen gern zu der Konferenz.
3. Frau Lange ginge sicher mit zum Chef.
4. So etwas gäbe es bei mir nicht.
5. Das wäre ein gutes Geschäft.
6. Und wenn die Sekretärin krank würde?

a. That would be a good deal.
b. Such a thing would never happen with me.
c. And (what) if the secretary got sick?
d. I would do that gladly.
e. We would be glad to come to the conference.
f. Frau Lange would certainly come along to [see] the boss.

19. Die feste° Stelle. Frau Burmann arbeitet als freie° Journalistin, doch nun könnte sie wieder eine feste Stelle bei einer Zeitung bekommen. Sie spricht mit ihrem Mann darüber, ob sie diese Stelle annehmen° soll oder nicht. Setzen Sie jeweils° die Konjunktivform des Verbs in Klammern ein.

permanent / freelance

accept
in each case

HERR BURMANN: Und wie viele Stunden _____ (sein) das pro Tag?

FRAU BURMANN: Ich _____ (gehen) morgens um zehn aus dem Haus und _____ (kommen) abends aber sicher nicht vor acht oder neun Uhr zurück.

HERR BURMANN: Hmmm, wie _____ (gehen) das denn mit den Kindern? Das _____ (geben) doch ein ziemliches Chaos, wenn sie den ganzen Nachmittag allein _____ (sein).

FRAU BURMANN: Wir _____ (müssen) nachmittags so lange einen Babysitter haben, bis du nach Hause _____ (kommen).

HERR BURMANN: Das _____ (können) wir ja schon organisieren. Es _____ (sein) natürlich nicht so einfach, einen guten Babysitter zu finden.

FRAU BURMANN: Ja, aber eigentlich _____ (finden) ich es nicht so gut, wenn ich die Kinder nur noch ein oder zwei Stunden am Tag sehen würde. Wir _____ (haben) ja gar kein Familienleben mehr.

13 Present-time subjunctive of regular weak verbs

Infinitive		Simple past	Present-time subjunctive
spielen		spielte	**spielte**
kaufen	er/es/sie	kaufte	**kaufte**
arbeiten		arbeitete	**arbeitete**
baden		badete	**badete**

The present-time subjunctive forms of regular weak verbs are identical to the simple-past forms. For this reason, the **würde**-construction is frequently used rather than the subjunctive form of regular weak verbs.

Ich **würde** den Computer nicht **kaufen.**

14 Present-time subjunctive of irregular weak verbs

Infinitive		Simple past	Present-time subjunctive
bringen		brachte	brächte
denken	er/es/sie	dachte	dächte
wissen		wusste	wüsste

The present-time subjunctive forms of irregular weak verbs are like the simple-past forms, but with an umlaut added. With the exception of **wüsste,** the subjunctive forms of irregular weak verbs are rarely used. The **würde**-construction is more common in colloquial German.

Würdest du die CDs **mitbringen?**
Ich **wüsste** nicht, ob ich das machen könnte.

Eine Million im Lotto - was nun?
Meine Familie könnte ein Auto gebrauchen. Ich selbst habe keine großen Träume.
(Miroslav, 21)

Frankfurt am Main
ist das deutsche
Bankzentrum.

405

KAPITEL
ELF

20. Ein Picknick. Stefan spricht mit seiner Schwester Monika über seine Pläne für ein Picknick. Übersetzen Sie, was er sagt, ins Englische.

STEFAN: Hättest du Zeit mitzukommen?
MONIKA: Ja, sicher. Ich könnte einen Tag frei nehmen.
STEFAN: Wüsstest du, wen wir sonst einladen sollten?
MONIKA: Vielleicht Onkel Max und Tante Gabi.
STEFAN: Vielleicht könnten wir alle zusammen fahren?
MONIKA: Schön. Das könnten wir.
STEFAN: Wenn ich nur wüsste, wo die beiden sind!
MONIKA: Was meinst du, was Onkel Max mitbringen wird?
STEFAN: Heringe°, natürlich, wie immer. Und ich werde dann viel zu trinken mitbringen.

herring

Leserunde

little bird

Wenn ich ein Vöglein° wär is a well-known German folk song (**Volkslied**). Even though a folk song may have been written by a single person, it becomes a folk song when it is taken over by a group of people (**Volk**). Because folk songs are sung by memory, the lines are short, the meter is musical or rhythmical, the language is simple, and the content is uncomplicated, unsophisticated, and even naive. A frequent theme in German folk songs is unrequited love. Notice the importance of the subjunctive mood here.

Wenn ich ein Vöglein wär

Wenn ich ein Vöglein wär,
Und auch zwei Flügel[1] hätt
Flög ich zu dir.
Weils aber nicht kann sein,
Bleib ich allhier[2].

Dichter unbekannt

[1]wings   [2](obsolete term) *simply here*

Wiederholung

1. Rollenspiel. Sie erzählen Ihrer Partnerin/Ihrem Partner, dass Sie vielleicht gerne für ein Jahr eine Weltreise machen würden. Sie/Er ist gleich sehr interessiert und stellt Ihnen alle möglichen Fragen. Antworten Sie darauf mit hypothetischen Aussagen.

expressing

das ... egal: that would be all the same to me

Redemittel: Wünsche ausdrücken°/Hypothetische Aussagen machen

Das wäre schön. ▪ Wenn ich genug Geld hätte! ▪ Das würde ich (gern) machen. ▪ Das würde Spaß machen. ▪ Dazu hätte ich große/keine Lust. ▪ Ich müsste natürlich viel aufgeben. ▪ Ich würde viel riskieren. ▪ Ich glaube, das wäre mir egal°.

---

1. Und du hast vor deinen Job aufzugeben?
2. Willst du dann alle Kontinente besuchen?
3. Und ein ganzes Jahr lang nur reisen?
4. Hast du vor alleine zu reisen?
5. Musst du dann nicht während der Reise Geld verdienen?
6. Und was passiert mit deinen ganzen Sachen?
7. Glaubst du, dass du danach wieder deinen Job bekommst?
8. Was sagt denn dein Freund/deine Freundin dazu?

unter ... Bedingungen: under certain circumstances

2. Was sagen Sie? Sagen Sie, was Sie unter bestimmten Bedingungen° tun würden. Fragen Sie dann Ihre Partnerin/Ihren Partner.

Was würdest du tun, ...

1. wenn du viel Geld bekämest?
2. wenn heute Sonntag wäre?
3. wenn du heute Geburtstag hättest?
4. wenn du jetzt zwei Wochen Ferien hättest?
5. wenn du das teure Essen im Restaurant nicht bezahlen könntest?
6. wenn Freunde dich zu einem Fest nicht einladen würden?

missing / blanks

3. Meine Freundin Sandra. Erzählen Sie von Ihrer Freundin Sandra und setzen Sie die fehlenden° Präpositionen in die Lücken° ein.

1. Habe ich dir _____ meiner Freundin Sandra erzählt?

2. Mit 19 Jahren hat sie _____ dem Studium angefangen.

3. Jetzt arbeitet sie _____ Siemens.

4. Sie arbeitet den ganzen Tag _____ Computer.

5. Sie und ihre Kollegen bereiten sich _____ eine Konferenz vor.

6. Sie erzählt ihrem Freund _____ ihrer Arbeit.

7. In ihrer Freizeit schreibt sie einen Roman. Sie spricht gern mit Mark _____ ihr Projekt.

4. Was möchten Sie? Erzählen Sie, was Sie möchten. Ergänzen Sie die Sätze mit den Adjektiven in Klammern oder anderen passenden Adjektiven. Achten° Sie auf die richtigen Adjektivendungen.　　　　　　　　　　　　　　　pay attention

1. Wenn ich Geld hätte, würde ich mir ein _____ **Auto** kaufen. (klein, groß, billig, teuer)

2. Ich wollte, man würde mich zu einem _____ **Fest** einladen. (nett, toll, klein, laut, interessant)

3. Ich möchte einen _____ **Pulli** kaufen. (warm, blau, leicht, toll)

4. Ich würde gern mal einen _____ **Film** sehen. (toll, interessant, schön, modern, klassisch, gut)

5. Ich möchte eine _____ **Reise** nach Deutschland machen. (lang, kurz, billig)

6. Ich möchte einen Computer haben, aber es müsste ein _____ **Computer** sein. (billig, teuer, klein, einfach, groß, schnell, anwenderfreundlich°)　　　　user-friendly

5. Wie sagt man das?

1. I have nothing planned for the weekend. (*use* **vorhaben**; for = **am**)
   —Would you like to go hiking?
2. Could it be that Erik is ill?
   —I don't know. You could ask him.
3. Would you like to go for a walk?　*Ich könnte dieses Nachmittag gehen.*
   —Gladly. I could go this afternoon.
4. Could you help me, please?　*Könntest du mir helfen, bitte?*
   —I wish I had (the) time.　*Ich wollte, dass ich die Zeit hätte*
5. Would you like to watch TV?
   —No. I don't feel like it.

6. Deutsch als Berufssprache. Viele Studentinnen/Studenten lernen Deutsch, um bessere Qualifikationen für den Arbeitsmarkt zu haben. Aber es gibt auch andere Gründe Deutsch zu lernen. Hier sind sechs Gründe Deutsch zu lernen. Welcher ist für Sie der wichtigste Grund? Welche anderen Gründe gibt es Deutsch zu lernen? Besprechen Sie Ihre Antworten mit Ihrer Partnerin/Ihrem Partner.

1. *Wichtige Geschäftssprache in Europa und in der Welt.* 100 Millionen Europäer haben Deutsch als Muttersprache. In Osteuropa lernen mehr Schüler Deutsch als Englisch. In Japan lernen 68% der Schüler Deutsch.
2. *Mit Deutschen ins Geschäft kommen.* Deutschland ist der wichtigste Handelspartner° für fast alle europäischen Länder und viele außereuropäische° Länder.　　　　trading partner / non-European
3. *Vorteile° im Tourismus.* Besucher aus deutschsprachigen Ländern sind in vielen Ländern die größte und wichtigste Touristengruppe.　　　　advantages
4. *Kultursprache Deutsch.* Deutsch ist die Sprache Goethes, Nietzsches und Kafkas, von Mozart, Bach und Beethoven, von Freud und Einstein.
5. *Wissenschaftliche Fortschritte°.* Deutschsprachige Publikationen belegen° den zweiten Platz in der Forschung°.　　　　advances / occupy / research
6. *Nobelpreisträger.* Von 1901 bis 2002 haben insgesamt° 109 Männer und Frauen aus Deutschland, Österreich und der Schweiz einen Nobelpreis gewonnen.　　　　altogether

wählen aus: choose

paragraph

guideline

spend time

7. Zum Schreiben. Wählen Sie ein Thema aus° und schreiben Sie einen kurzen Abschnitt°.

1. Schreiben Sie einen Abschnitt auf Deutsch über die wirtschaftlichen Unterschiede zwischen Ihrem Land und Deutschland. Benutzen Sie die Fragen als Hilfestellung°.

   • In welchem Land spielt der Außenhandel eine größere Rolle? Warum?
   • Welches Land hat mehr Rohstoffe?
   • Welche Produkte exportieren diese Länder vor allem?
   • In welchem Land sehen die Chancen für eine gesunde Wirtschaft besser aus? Warum?

2. Wie wäre es, wenn Sie einen Tag mit einer berühmten Person verbringen° könnten? Die Person kann heute leben oder eine historische Persönlichkeit sein. Schreiben Sie einen kurzen Abschnitt über den Tag und benutzen Sie die Fragen als Hilfestellung.

   • Was würden Sie machen?
   • Worüber würden Sie sprechen?
   • Warum möchten Sie den Tag mit diesem Menschen verbringen?

Hinweise:
1. Use the subjunctive when expressing hypothetical statements, suppositions, wishes.
2. In expressing hypothetical situations or giving reasons for your comments, you will be using dependent clauses. Be sure to watch the position of the verbs.

Jack Wohl, USA. © Bulls

[1]*bet*

Grammatik: Zusammenfassung

The future tense

ich **werde** es **machen**	wir **werden** es **machen**
du **wirst** es **machen**	ihr **werdet** es **machen**
er/es/sie **wird** es **machen**	sie **werden** es **machen**
Sie **werden** es **machen**	

The German future tense consists of the auxiliary **werden** plus an infinitive in final position.

> Erika sagt, dass sie es sicher **machen wird.**

In a dependent clause, the auxiliary **werden** is in final position because it is the finite verb.

Future time: present tense

Ich **komme** morgen bestimmt.	I'll come tomorrow for sure.
Fahren Sie nächstes Jahr nach Deutschland?	Are you going to Germany next year?

German uses the future tense less frequently than English. German generally uses the present tense if the context clearly indicates future time.

Uses of the future tense

Future time	Frank **wird** mir **helfen.**	Frank *will help* me.
Intention	Frank **wird** mir **helfen.**	Frank *will (intends to) help* me.

Future tense is used to express intention or future time if the context doesn't make it clear that the events will take place in the future.

Assumption	Anna **wird** uns sicher **glauben.**	Anna *probably believes* us.
	Das **wird** wohl **stimmen.**	That is *probably correct.*

The future tense may also be used to express an assumption (present probability) when it is used with adverbs such as **sicher, schon,** and **wohl.**

Subjunctive mood

Indicative	Ich **komme** nicht zur Party.	I'm not *coming* to the party.
	Kannst du mir **helfen?**	*Can* you *help* me?
Subjunctive	Ich **käme** nicht zur Party.	I *wouldn't come* to the party.
	Könntest du mir **helfen?**	*Could* you *help* me?

In both English and German, the indicative mood is used to talk about "real" conditions or factual situations. The subjunctive mood is used to talk about "unreal," hypothetical, uncertain, or unlikely events as well as to express wishes and polite requests.

Wenn ich heute (oder morgen) nur mehr Zeit **hätte!**	If only I *had* more time today (or tomorrow)!

Present-time subjunctive can refer to the future as well as to the present.

The *würde*-construction

■ *Forms*

ich **würde** es **machen**	wir **würden** es **machen**
du **würdest** es **machen**	ihr **würdet** es **machen**
er/es/sie **würde** es **machen**	sie **würden** es **machen**
	Sie **würden** es **machen**

The **würde**-construction consists of a form of **würde** + infinitive. **Würde** is the subjunctive form of **werden**. It is formed by adding an umlaut to **wurde**, the simple past of **werden**.

■ *Uses*

Hypothetical statement	Ich **würde** das nicht **machen**.	I *would* not *do* that.
Wishes	Wenn er mir nur **helfen würde**.	If only he *would help* me.
Polite requests	**Würdest** du mir bitte **helfen**?	*Would* you please *help* me?

To talk about "unreal" situations or hypothetical statements in the present, to express wishes, and to make polite requests, German may use a **würde**-construction. The **würde**-construction is the most common way to express subjunctive mood in conversational German.

Present-time subjunctive of main verbs

Ich **täte** das nicht.
Ich **würde** das nicht **tun**. } I *would* not *do* that.

The subjunctive form of the main verb (e.g., **täte**) and the **würde**-construction (e.g., **würde tun**) are equivalent in meaning. However, the **würde**-construction is more common in conversation for most verbs.

Subjunctive verb endings

ich **käme**	wir **kämen**
du **kämest**	ihr **kämet**
er/es/sie **käme**	sie **kämen**
	Sie **kämen**

The subjunctive endings above are used for all verbs. The subjunctive verb endings **-est** and **-et** often contract to **-st** and **-t**: kämest > kämst, kämet > kämt.

Present-time subjunctive of *sein* and *haben*

sein			haben		
ich **wäre**		wir **wären**	ich **hätte**		wir **hätten**
du **wärest**		ihr **wäret**	du **hättest**		ihr **hättet**
er/es/sie **wäre**		sie **wären**	er/es/sie **hätte**		sie **hätten**
	Sie **wären**			Sie **hätten**	

The verbs **haben** and **sein** are more commonly used in their subjunctive forms, **wäre** and **hätte,** than in the **würde**-construction.

Modals in present-time subjunctive

Infinitive	Simple past	Present-time subjunctive
dürfen	durfte	**dürfte**
können	konnte	**könnte**
mögen	mochte	**möchte**
müssen	musste	**müsste**
sollen	sollte	**sollte**
wollen	wollte	**wollte**

The modals are generally used in their subjunctive form rather than as infinitives with the **würde**-construction. The present-time subjunctive forms of modals are identical to the simple-past tense forms except that the modals with an umlaut in the infinitive also have an umlaut in the subjunctive.

Present-time subjunctive of strong verbs

Infinitive	Simple past	Present-time subjunctive
finden	fand	**fände**
geben	gab	**gäbe**
gehen	ging	**ginge**
halten	hielt	**hielte**
heißen	hieß	**hieße**
kommen	kam	**käme**
lassen	ließ	**ließe**
tun	tat	**täte**

The present-time subjunctive forms of strong verbs are formed by adding subjunctive endings to the simple-past stem. An umlaut is added to the stem vowels **a, o,** and **u.** The verbs in the list above are common in written German. Of these verbs, **fände, gäbe, ginge,** and **käme** are also common in spoken German.

Present-time subjunctive of regular weak verbs

Infinitive	Simple past	Present-time subjunctive
kaufen	kaufte	**kaufte**
arbeiten	arbeitete	**arbeitete**

The present-time subjunctive forms of weak verbs are identical to the simple-past forms but are usually replaced by the **würde**-construction.

Present-time subjunctive of irregular weak verbs

Infinitive	Simple past	Present-time subjunctive
bringen	brachte	**brächte**
denken	dachte	**dächte**
wissen	wusste	**wüsste**

With the exception of **wüsste,** the subjunctive form of irregular weak verbs is rarely used. The **würde**-construction is more common in colloquial German.

Uses of the *würde*-construction and the subjunctive of the main verb

■ *Hypothetical statements*

Ich **würde** das nicht **tun.**
Ich **täte** das nicht. } *I would* not *do* that [if I were you].

■ *Wishes*

Wenn Inge das nur **tun würde.**
Wenn Inge das nur **täte.** } If only Inge *would* do that.

■ *Polite requests*

Würden Sie das für mich **tun?**
Täten Sie das für mich? } *Would* you *do* that for me?
Könnten Sie das für mich **tun?** *Could* you *do* that for me?

■ *Conditions contrary to fact*

Wenn ich Zeit **hätte, käme** ich.
Wenn ich Zeit **hätte, würde** ich **kommen.** } If I *had* time [but I don't], I *would come.*

Contrary-to-fact sentences consist of two clauses: the condition (**wenn**-clause) and the conclusion. Conditions contrary to fact cannot be fulfilled. Conditions contrary to fact are expressed in the subjunctive mood.

The *würde*-construction vs. present-time subjunctive of the main verb

Wenn Jutta nicht so fleißig **wäre, hätte** sie mehr Freizeit und **könnte** ein Hobby **haben.**

If Jutta *were* not so diligent, she *would have* more time and *could have* a hobby.

In conversational German the **würde**-construction is frequently used instead of the subjunctive of the main verb. However, the subjunctive of the main verb is preferred to the **würde**-construction for **sein (wäre), haben (hätte),** and the modals, e.g., **könnte.**

Wenn Gerd täglich Zeitung **läse,** würde er alles besser verstehen.

If Gerd *read* the newspaper daily, he would understand everything better.

Formal written German tends to avoid the **würde**-construction in the **wenn**-clause.

Die multikulturelle Gesellschaft

Multikulturelles Leben in der Innenstadt von München.

LERNZIELE

Sprechintentionen

Talking about future plans
Talking about cultural events
Making suggestions
Discussing who invented, wrote, or
  discovered something
Indicating that you don't understand
  something

Lesestück

Fremd im eigenen Zuhause

Land und Leute

Other nationalities in Germany

Grammatik

Relative clauses
Relative pronouns
Passive voice
Summary of uses of **werden**

Kurzgeschichten

"Der Verkäufer und der Elch: Eine
  Geschichte mit 128 deutschen
  Wörtern" – Franz Hohler
"Schlittenfahren" – Helga M. Novak

413

Bausteine für Gespräche

Rockfans gegen Ausländerhass

MONIKA: Peter, hast du Lust am Wochenende zu dem Open-Air-Konzert im Tiergarten zu gehen?

PETER: Hmmm, ich weiß nicht. Ich wollte mir eigentlich noch Freiburg ansehen. In zwei Wochen fliege ich doch wieder nach Amerika zurück.

MONIKA: Ach, komm doch. Nach Freiburg kannst du auch noch nächstes Wochenende fahren.

PETER: Aber ich kenne doch nur wenige von den Rockmusikern, die da spielen werden.

MONIKA: Manche sind doch ganz bekannt. Aber es geht ja gar nicht nur um die Musik. Das Motto ist „Rock gegen Rechts". Mit dem Konzert demonstrieren die Musiker gegen Rassismus und Ausländerhass. Und wir zeigen unsere Solidarität, wenn wir hingehen. Das ist doch wichtig.

PETER: Glaubst du denn, dass da viele Leute kommen werden?

MONIKA: Oh ja. Es werden ungefähr 100.000 Leute erwartet.

PETER: Na gut, lass uns hingehen. Es ist ja für eine gute Sache.

Brauchbares

1. **Tiergarten** is a large, picturesque park in Berlin, full of shady paths, lakes, and streams. The three-kilometer long, one-kilometer wide site has 32 kilometers of paths. It was totally destroyed during heavy fighting in World War II, but since then over a million trees and shrubs have been planted.

2. **Freiburg** is a popular tourist town because of its location at the foot of the Black Forest (**Schwarzwald**) mountains. There are numerous ski slopes, mountain trails for hiking, and lakes for boating, windsurfing, and swimming. **Freiburg** has a famous cathedral and an excellent university, which many Americans attend.

3. **Rock gegen Rechts:** In 2000, the German rock singer Udo Lindenberg started the tour **"Rock gegen Rechts,"** an initiative that promotes tolerance and integration of foreigners. Since then other events have been organized, and many German musicians have given benefit concerts. The proceeds are donated to the victims of right-wing violence and to the organization "Exit," whose goal is to encourage young neo-Nazis to leave their right-wing environment and its influence.

4. **Demonstrieren:** Since the 1990s, Germany has been the scene of many events that give people the chance to voice their opposition to the hostility toward foreigners that is expressed by groups such as skinheads. These events have included rock concerts, **Lichterketten** (chains of people holding candles), **Schweigemärsche** (people marching silently), and other demonstrations.

5. **Lass uns:** The phrase **lass uns** is equivalent to English *let's (do something).* The verb **lassen** is like the modals in that it takes an infinitive without **zu: lass uns gehen.**

Fragen

1. Warum wollte Peter zuerst nicht zu dem Open-Air-Konzert gehen?
2. Für Monika geht es nicht um die Musik. Worum geht es ihr?
3. Wie viele Leute erwartet man zu dem Konzert?

1. Nächste Woche. Fragen Sie drei Kursteilnehmerinnen/Kursteilnehmer, was sie nächste Woche machen wollen.

Talking about future plans

S1:
Was machst du nächste Woche?

S2:
Ich fahre nach [Freiburg].
Ich fliege nach [Europa].
Ich fange einen neuen Job an.
Ich bereite ein Referat vor.

2. Kennst du das? Spielen Sie zusammen mit Ihrer Partnerin/Ihrem Partner die Rolle von zwei Personen, die über kulturelle Veranstaltungen° sprechen.

events

Talking about cultural events

S1:
Kennst du | **die Rockband, die heute [in der Stadt] spielt?**
den Film, der diese Woche im [Odeon] spielt?
die Oper, die heute Abend im Fernsehen kommt?
den neuen Roman, den ich lesen sollte?

S2:
Ja, sehr gut sogar.
Ja, aber das interessiert mich nicht.
Nein, leider nicht.
Nein, warum fragst du?

Diese Gymnasiasten diskutieren in ihrer Arbeitsgruppe.

schlägt vor: suggests

3. Lass uns ins Konzert gehen. Sprechen Sie in einer Gruppe darüber, was Sie machen wollen. Jedes Gruppenmitglied schlägt etwas anderes vor°.

→ *Lass uns ...*

Making suggestions

essen gehen ■ unsere Freunde anrufen ■ unseren Freunden helfen
■ Tennis oder Fußball spielen ■ joggen gehen ■ den ganzen Tag faulenzen

decide

4. Hättest du Lust? Entscheiden° Sie erst selbst, was Sie in Ihrer Freizeit machen wollen. Dann fragen Sie drei Kursteilnehmerinnen/Kursteilnehmer, was sie gern machen möchten.

S1:
Hättest du Lust | **inlineskaten zu gehen?**
ins Kino zu gehen?
eine Party zu geben?
eine Radtour zu machen?
Musik zu hören?
ein Video auszuleihen?
Russisch zu lernen?
einkaufen zu gehen?

S2:
Das wäre schön.
Wenn ich nur Geld hätte.
Das würde ich gern
machen.
Das würde Spaß machen.
Wenn ich nur Zeit hätte.
Dazu hätte ich keine Lust.

Vokabeln 1

Substantive

der **Ausländerhass**   xenophobia,
hatred of foreigners
der **Fan, -s**   fan; supporter (sport)
der **Hass**   hate
das **Motto, -s**   motto

der **Rassismus**   racism
der **Rockfan, -s**   rock fan
der **Rockmusiker, -/die
Rockmusikerin, -nen**   rock
musician

Verben

lassen (lässt), ließ, gelassen   to leave
behind; to let, permit; **lass uns
gehen**   let's go

**zurück·fliegen, flog zurück, ist
zurückgeflogen**   to fly back

Besondere Ausdrücke

**es geht nicht nur um [die
Musik]**   it's not just about [the
music]
etwas anderes   something else,
something different

ich sehe es mir an   I'm having a look
at it

fremd im eigenen Zuhause

Vorbereitung auf das Lesen

influence

Sie lesen in diesem Text von Ausländern in Deutschland, ihrem Einfluss° auf die
deutsche Kultur⁺ und ihren Problemen.

■ **Vor dem Lesen**

1. Die Kultur jedes Landes zeigt Elemente von anderen Ländern und Kulturen. Versuchen Sie in Gruppenarbeit die folgende Tabelle zu ergänzen°. Mit welcher Kultur oder welchem Land verbinden° Sie diese Dinge oder Ideen?

    complete

    connect

Idee/Ding	Wo findet man sie/es?	Woher kommt sie/es?
Jeans	fast überall	Amerika
Kartoffeln		
Kaffee		
Football		
Fußball		
Demokratie		
Papier		
Kindergarten		

2. Listen Sie fünf Elemente Ihrer Kultur auf°. Wissen Sie, woher sie kommen?

    listen auf: list

    ➜ Jazz   *Der Jazz kommt aus Amerika.*

3. Sehen Sie sich die Tabelle unten an und schreiben Sie drei Sätze über die Tabelle.

    ➜ *Mehr Ausländer kommen aus Italien als aus Griechenland.*

In 2001 there were also 113,600 Americans in Germany, 115,300 from Great Britain and 2,296,000 from various other countries.

Ausländer in Deutschland	
7.296 Millionen Anfang 2002	
Die zehn größten Nationalitätengruppen sind:	
Türken	1.947.900
Jugoslawen (Serben)	627.500
Italiener	616.300
Griechen	362.700
Polen	310.400
Kroaten°	223.800
Österreicher	188.950
Bosnier und Herzegowiner	159.000
Portugiesen	132.600
Spanier	128.700

    Croatians

4. Was für Probleme könnten Ausländer in einer fremden Kultur haben? Stellen Sie in Gruppenarbeit eine Liste von vier oder mehr Problemen auf.

■ **Beim Lesen**

Geben Sie die Zeilen° an, wo man Informationen über die folgenden Punkte findet.

1. Ausländische Arbeiter kommen nach Deutschland
2. Klein-Istanbul
3. Unterschiede und Erfahrungen von jungen und älteren Ausländern
4. Integration: Rolle der Sprache
5. Türken und Deutsche: Interaktion
6. Religion: offen praktizieren

Peter trifft in der Bibliothek Hakan, der mit ihm die Politikvorlesung besucht. Peter erzählt Hakan, dass er in zwei Wochen nach Amerika zurückfliegt. Spontan lädt Hakan ihn zum Essen ein, und zwar in das türkische Lokal „Bosporus", das seinen Eltern gehört. Peter und Hakan werden von Hakans

married couple

5   Eltern, dem Ehepaar° Gümeshan, begrüßt, und beim Essen unterhalten sie sich.

lentil soup
appetizer

HAKAN: Die Linsensuppe° kann ich nur empfehlen. Die nehme ich als Vorspeise°. Und das Kebab ist auch fantastisch.

PETER: Es ist nett hier. Hmm, ich glaube ich nehme den Kebabteller mit Salat.

10   Seit wann habt ihr denn dieses Restaurant? Schon lange?

HAKAN: Nein, erst seit fünf Jahren. Da hat mein Vater sich entschieden, sein Hobby, das Kochen, zum Beruf zu machen. Davor war er viele Jahre Arbeiter bei Siemens. Ach, er ist schon ewig hier in Deutschland.

PETER: Ja? Wann kam dein Vater denn nach Deutschland?

urgently / workers

15   HAKAN: Ende der sechziger Jahre. Damals brauchte die deutsche Wirtschaft doch dringend° Arbeitskräfte° und im Süden der Türkei, wo wir wohnten, gab es zu wenig Arbeitsplätze. Also ging mein Vater nach Deutschland, um Geld zu verdienen. Meine Mutter und meine Geschwister allerdings° blieben in der Türkei und mein Vater kam einmal im Jahr zu Besuch. Doch natür-

however

kamen nach: joined later

20   lich war das kein Familienleben und 1973 kamen sie dann nach°. Und 1977 bin dann ich hier geboren. Inzwischen habe ich auch die deutsche Staatsbürgerschaft°.

citizenship

PETER: Und du fühlst dich sicher als Deutscher, nicht? Oder stehst du irgendwie zwischen den Kulturen?

Children born in Germany to foreign parents are not automatically given German citizenship.

25   HAKAN: Ich fühle mich schon als Deutscher, aber ich bin in Berlin-Kreuzberg aufgewachsen – das wird auch Klein-Istanbul genannt. Fast ein Drittel der Bewohner in Kreuzberg sind Ausländer und zwar vor allem Türken. Deshalb ist mir die türkische Kultur natürlich sehr nahe. Aber ich denke, meine Eltern fühlen sich auch heute nach über 30 Jahren in Deutschland immer

30   noch ein bisschen fremd. Die Türkei ist einfach ihre Heimat. Meine Mutter war in den ersten Jahren hier ziemlich unglücklich und sie wollte auch gar nicht Deutsch lernen. Erst wir Kinder haben sie davon überzeugt, dass Sprache eine große Rolle spielt, wenn man sich integrieren möchte. Doch was mir manchmal passiert, ist, dass ich gefragt werde, wo ich denn so gut

35   Deutsch gelernt hätte. Da ich türkisch aussehe, finden manche Deutsche es wohl komisch, dass ich perfekt Deutsch spreche. Wenn ich dann antworte „Hier in Berlin, wo ich geboren bin!" sind sie oft perplex. Na ja, aber eigentlich ärgert mich das nicht wirklich, ich finde es eher° ein bisschen zum Lachen°.

rather

laughable

40 PETER: Hast du persönlich denn schon häufig Erfahrungen mit
Ausländerfeindlichkeit° gemacht? Als es Anfang der neunziger Jahre besonders häufig Angriffe° gegen Ausländer gab, hattest du auch Angst?

HAKAN: Angst nicht direkt. Aber es war damals schon schlimm. Und auch
heute noch gibt es Gewalt° gegen Ausländer und Parolen° wie „Ausländer
45 raus°" und „Deutschland den Deutschen". Zum Glück sind diese Menschen,
die so denken, eine Minderheit°. Ich engagiere° mich in verschiedenen Initia-
tiven° gegen Ausländerfeindlichkeit. Und da treffe ich viele Deutsche, die es
toll finden, dass Deutschland endlich auch ein bisschen multikulturell ist.
Doch es gibt auch relativ tolerante Deutsche, die es zum Beispiel nicht gut
50 finden, wenn die Türken ihre Kultur und Religion offen praktizieren. Meine
Schwester zum Beispiel ist überzeugte° Muslimin und sie trägt immer ein
Kopftuch. Doch nun wurde ihr bei der Arbeit gesagt, dass es besser wäre,
wenn sie ihre Religion nicht so offen zeigen würde und ohne Kopftuch
zur Arbeit käme. Das hat sie verletzt und seitdem ist sie natürlich etwas
55 unsicher.

PETER: Hmmm, das kann ich mir vorstellen. Ich weiß gar nicht, wie das in
Amerika wäre. Ich denke, in manchen Firmen könnte das auch problema-
tisch sein. ... Ah, da kommt ja das Essen.

FRAU GÜMESHAN: Na, schon hungrig, ihr beiden? Hier habe ich noch Schafs-
60 käse° und Oliven für euch, frisch aus der Türkei. Ach, wie ich mich freue im
August wieder nach Hause zu fahren. Und Sie, Peter? Sie freuen sich sicher
auch wieder auf die Heimat, nicht?

Glosses (right margin):
- xenophobia
- attacks
- violence / slogans
- out
- minority / involve
- projects
- dedicated
- cheese made from sheep's milk

Brauchbares

1. ll. 3–4, **das Lokal „Bosporus", das Hakans Eltern gehört:** 147,000 foreigners
   are owners of businesses in Germany: **Kaffeehäuser, Computerläden,
   Speditionen** (shipping), **Export- und Importgeschäfte, Imbissbuden** (fast-
   food booths), **Gemüseläden.** They generate a revenue of over 100 billion
   euros a year.

Essen aus vielen Ländern
gibt es auf diesem
internationalen Volksfest
in Berlin.

2. l. 8, **Kebab:** A southeastern European dish of small pieces of grilled meat (usually mutton). **Kebab** is an Arabic/Turkish word.

3. l. 13, **Siemens:** Siemens produces electrical goods and is one of Germany's largest companies. It has branches in many countries, including the U.S.A.

4. l. 16, **Arbeitskräfte:** Between 1955 and 1973, the West German economy needed a larger work force and recruited foreign workers, primarily from Turkey, Italy, Spain, and Greece.

5. l. 22, **Staatsbürgerschaft:** Citizenship requirements for children born to foreigners are discussed in **Ausländische Mitbürger,** pages 422–423.

6. ll. 25 and 26, **Berlin-Kreuzberg/Klein-Istanbul:** Berlin-Kreuzberg is an area of Berlin that is referred to as the "little capital" of Turkey because so many Turks live there.

7. l. 35, **gelernt hätte:** The subjunctive is often used in indirect discourse, that is, repeating indirectly or giving the essence of what someone else has said. Hakan was asked (by someone) where he had learned German. He restates the words in past subjunctive: **hätte gelernt.**

8. ll. 52–54, **besser wäre, zeigen würde, käme:** These subjunctive forms are being used in indirect discourse. Hakan tells what was said to his sister. See #7 above.

Nach dem Lesen

1. Fragen zum Lesestück

1. Wo haben sich Peter und Hakan kennen gelernt?
2. Wohin lädt Hakan Peter zum Essen ein?
3. Warum kam Hakans Vater nach Deutschland?
4. Warum kamen in dieser Zeit viele Ausländer nach Deutschland?
5. Warum wollte Hakans Mutter zuerst nicht Deutsch lernen?
6. Warum fühlt sich Hakan auch in der türkischen Kultur wohl, obwohl er in Berlin geboren wurde?
7. Was passiert Hakan manchmal, was er zum Lachen findet?
8. Was machen einige Deutsche, die gegen Ausländer sind?
9. Wo trifft Hakan viele tolerante Deutsche?
10. Warum ist Hakans Schwester bei ihrer Arbeit unsicher?
11. Was kann man aus Frau Gümeshans Aussage am Ende herauslesen°?

interpret or understand from

2. Einige Themen. Lesen Sie den Text noch einmal⁺. Stellen Sie eine Liste von Stichwörtern zu den folgenden Themen auf.

1. Geschichte eines ausländischen Arbeiters in Deutschland
2. Erfahrungen eines jungen Türken oder einer jungen Türkin in Deutschland
3. Probleme der Ausländer in Deutschland
4. Sprache und Integration in die Gesellschaft

3. Zur Diskussion. Machen Sie eine Liste: Was sollte eine Ausländerin/ein Ausländer von der deutschen Kultur wissen? Was sollte eine Ausländerin/ein Ausländer von Ihrer Kultur wissen?

4. Erzählen wir.

1. Stellen Sie sich vor, dass Sie als Ausländerin/Ausländer in Deutschland leben. Erzählen Sie etwas von sich. Woher kommen Sie? Warum sind Sie nach Deutschland gekommen? Wie gefällt es Ihnen in Deutschland?

2. **Rollenspiel.** Eine Reporterin/Ein Reporter interviewt eine ausländische Mitbürgerin°/einen ausländischen Mitbürger in Ihrem Land.

3. Sie sind Reporter/Reporterin. Sie wollen Hakan oder Hakans Schwester interviewen. Welche Fragen würden Sie stellen?

fellow citizen

Vokabeln 2

Substantive

der **Arbeiter, -**/die **Arbeiterin, -nen** worker
die **Gesellschaft, -en** society; company
die **Heimat** native country
die **Kultur, -en** culture

das **Lokal, -e** restaurant; pub
die **Rolle, -n** role; **eine Rolle spielen** to play a role
der **Teller, -** plate; dish (food)
das **Tuch, -er** cloth; scarf; shawl
das **Zuhause** home

Verben

ärgern to annoy; **sich ärgern** to become annoyed
auf·wachsen (wächst auf), wuchs auf, ist aufgewachsen to grow up
sich entscheiden, entschied, entschieden to decide
geboren: ist geboren was born
lachen to laugh; **zum Lachen** laughable

überzeugen to persuade, convince
sich (dat.) **vorstellen** to imagine; **ich kann es mir vorstellen** I can imagine that
wachsen (wächst), wuchs, ist gewachsen to grow

Andere Wörter

damals then, at that time
erst only, just, not until
fantastisch fantastic
fremd foreign; strange
häufig frequently
hungrig hungry
inzwischen in the meantime
irgendwie somehow
jemand (-en, -em) (can be used with or without endings) someone

komisch strange; funny
kulturell cultural, culturally
multikulturell multiculturally
nahe (+ dat.) near; **mir nahe** close to me
niemand (-en, -em) (can be used with or without endings) no one
seitdem since then
verschieden various

Besondere Ausdrücke

die **(sechziger, neunziger) Jahre** the (1960s, 1990s)
noch einmal once more, again

zu Besuch on a visit
zum Essen for dinner

Land und Leute

Ausländische Mitbürger

www Go to the *Deutsch heute* website at
http://college.hmco.com.

Germany is home to approximately 7.3 million foreigners. Just under 2 million are from Turkey, and hundreds of thousands more have come from countries such as Serbia, Italy, Greece, and Poland.

In diesem Geschäft in Hannover gibt es Spezialitäten aus der Türkei.

Between 1955 and 1973, West Germany sought many "guest workers" (**Gastarbeiter**) to relieve the labor shortage of the postwar economic boom (**Wirtschaftswunder**). The early workers came from Italy, Greece, Spain, and Turkey. In 1961 there were 700,000 foreigners living in Germany; by 1979 there were 2.6 million. Even though many of the foreign workers returned to their home countries, many others have stayed and raised their children in Germany. Approximately 1.5 million of the foreigners in Germany were born in Germany. Until 2000, children born in Germany to foreign-born parents were not given German citizenship. In 2000, however, a new citizenship law took effect that makes it easier to become a German citizen. Children born to foreigners who have lived in Germany for at least eight years automatically have dual citizenship until the age of 23. At that time, they must choose one citizenship. Today foreign workers are still an important factor in the German economy: 30% of all foreigners have lived in Germany 20 years or more, 40% more than 15 years, 55% more than 10 years. Foreigners are eligible to receive all social benefits, and in some cities they have received the right to vote and to run for local office.

Alle Menschen sind Ausländer. Fast überall.

Wo wären Sie Ausländer oder Ausländerin?

In the late 1980s and early 1990s, the number of ethnic German resettlers (**Aussiedler**) coming from the former Soviet Union and Eastern Europe increased dramatically. During the Cold War, the **Aussiedler** were seen as courageous people who had escaped a totalitarian regime. However, in the economic recession following unification in 1990, the **Aussiedler** were seen as competition for jobs, housing, and social benefits. At the same time, a large number of refugees who were fleeing political persecution in their home countries arrived in Germany. Between 1989 and 1992 more than 1 million people applied for asylum. Asylum seekers (**Asylbewerber**) receive financial aid while waiting for their cases to be heard and, if asylum is granted, further benefits to help start a new life in Germany. A 1993 amendment to the asylum law (**Asylgesetz**) reduced the number of people who are granted asylum.

In the first half of the 1990s, radical groups such as the neo-Nazis and skinheads gave vent to virulent xenophobia (**Ausländerhass**) and committed numerous hate crimes against foreigners. A large segment of the public protested against these acts of violence. While xenophobia remains an issue, there has been increasing public debate about how Germany can become a true multicultural society (**multikulturelle Gesellschaft**).

Diskussion

1. The issue of citizenship has been hotly debated in Germany. How does one define a citizen of a country? Should countries acknowledge dual citizenship? What rights and benefits do citizens have that foreigners living in a country usually do not? Discuss your idea of citizenship.
2. To facilitate the entry of foreigners into life in Germany, Germany now requires foreigners who want to stay in Germany to take an **Integrationskurs.** This 15-week course consists of language instruction as well as an introduction to the institutions, customs, and culture of Germany. Topics can range from shopping habits to folklore. Do you think that such a course should be required of immigrants? What topics would you include in a course for foreigners coming to live in your country?

Leserunde

Meltem Ayaz was born in 1956 in Ankara, Turkey, and came to Germany in 1962. She studied medicine at the University of Bonn. She has since returned to Turkey, where she is a member of a medical faculty in Istanbul. In her poem "Ein lachendes – ein weinendes Auge," Ayaz uses a basic formula of poetry, the movement from the specific to the general. Her situation of being a Turk in Germany is a condition shared by many foreigners in an adopted country.

Ein lachendes — ein weinendes Auge

Ob ich hier lebe und mir vorstelle alt zu werden –
oder
ob ich dort lebe und dort alt werde.

Beide Möglichkeiten fasse ich ins Auge[1] –
nur habe ich in jedem Fall ein lachendes und
ein weinendes[2] Auge.

Meltem Ayaz

[1]**fasse ... Auge**: *contemplate*   [2]*weeping*

Grammatik und Übungen

 Relative clauses

Ist das **der Mann, den** Sie meinen?	Is that *the man (whom)* you mean?
Das ist **das Auto, das** du kaufen möchtest.	That's *the car (that)* you'd like to buy.
Wer ist **die Frau, die** gerade hereinkommt?	Who is *the woman (who* is) just coming in?

A relative clause provides additional information about a previously mentioned noun or pronoun. The clause is introduced by a relative pronoun (e.g., **den, das, die**) that refers back to the noun, which is the antecedent (e.g., **Mann, Auto, Frau**). Since a relative clause is a dependent clause, the finite verb (e.g., **meinen, möchtest, hereinkommt**) stands in last position.

In English, the relative pronoun may or may not be stated. In German, the relative pronoun must always be stated. In written German, relative clauses are set off from main clauses by commas.

Wer die Welt verstehen will, der muß sie lesen.

DIE ⊕ WELT

Was ist „Die Welt"?
Was muss eine Person
machen, die die Welt
verstehen will?

das Relativpronomen

2 **Relative pronouns°**

	Masculine	Neuter	Feminine	Plural
Nominative	der	das	die	die
Accusative	den	das	die	die
Dative	dem	dem	der	**denen**
Genitive	**dessen**	**dessen**	**deren**	**deren**

The forms of the relative pronoun are the same as the forms of the definite articles, except for the dative plural and all genitive forms.

Masculine	Das ist der Mann, **der** uns gefragt hat.
Neuter	Das ist das Kind, **das** uns gefragt hat.
Feminine	Das ist die Frau, **die** uns gefragt hat.
Plural	Das sind die Leute, **die** uns gefragt haben.

The *gender* (masculine, neuter, or feminine) of the relative pronoun depends on the gender of the noun to which it refers. In the examples above, **der** is masculine because it refers to **der Mann** and **die** is feminine because it refers to **die Frau**. Whether a pronoun is singular or plural also depends on the noun to which it refers. The pronoun **die** that refers to **die Leute** is plural and therefore requires the plural verb **haben.**

Nominative	Ist das der Mann, **der** hier war?
Accusative	Ist das der Mann, **den** Sie meinen?
Dative	Ist das der Mann, **dem** Sie es gesagt haben?
Genitive	Ist das der Mann, **dessen** Auto Sie gekauft haben?

The *case* (nominative, accusative, dative, or genitive) of a relative pronoun depends on its grammatical function in the relative clause. In the examples above, **der** is nominative because it is the subject of its clause; **den** is accusative because it is the direct object of the verb **meinen** in that clause; **dem** is dative because it is an indirect object in the clause; and **dessen** is genitive because it shows possession.

[1]breathes

Identify, in each of the visuals on this page, the relative pronoun and the antecedent.

Wie heißt die Frau, **für die** Sie arbeiten?	What is the name of the woman *for whom* you work?
Wo ist die Firma, **bei der** Sie arbeiten?	Where is the firm *(that)* you work *for*?

A relative clause can also be introduced by a preposition followed by a relative pronoun. The case of the relative pronoun then depends on what case the preposition takes. In **für die, die** is accusative because of **für;** in **bei der, der** is dative because of **bei.**

In German, whenever a relative pronoun is the object of a preposition, the preposition precedes the pronoun. In colloquial English the preposition is usually in last position [*(that) you work for*].

1. Die deutsche Wirtschaft. Lesen Sie die Sätze über die deutsche Wirtschaft. Identifizieren Sie die Relativpronomen darin und erklären Sie, in welchem Fall° jedes Pronomen ist und worauf es sich bezieht°.

case
bezieht sich: refers to

world trade

→ Die Regierung arbeitet für einen Welthandel°, der wirklich frei ist.
der = nominative, subject, Welthandel

1. Ein Land wie Deutschland, das wenig Rohstoffe hat, lebt vom Handel.
2. Die Produkte, die man produziert, müssen von bester Qualität sein.
3. Denn es gibt mehrere Länder, mit denen Deutschland konkurrieren muss.
4. In der Zukunft ändert sich° wohl der Markt, für den Deutschland produzieren muss.

ändert sich: changes

5. Einige Firmen, die Dinge produzieren, die man nicht mehr kauft, werden Bankrott machen°.

Bankrott machen: go bankrupt

6. Das bedeutet, dass die Arbeiter, deren Firmen bankrott sind, arbeitslos werden.
7. Die Arbeitslosigkeit ist ein Problem, das nur schwer zu lösen° ist.

solve

2. Die sind doch gar nicht kaputt. Ihr Freund repariert gern elektrische Geräte°. Er sagt, welche Geräte er reparieren wird. Sagen Sie ihm, dass die Dinge, die er für Sie reparieren will, gar nicht kaputt sind. Benutzen Sie den Nominativ des Relativpronomens.

appliances, equipment

S2: Ich repariere jetzt diesen Computer, ja?
S1: Das ist doch nicht der Computer, der kaputt ist.

1.

2.

3.

4.

5.*

3. Die Sachen sind toll. Gabi hat neue Kleidung. Fragen Sie Gabi, ob sie die Kleidung zum Geburtstag bekommen hat. Benutzen Sie den Akkusativ der Relativpronomen.

→ Wie gefällt dir diese Jacke?
Toll. Ist das die Jacke, die du zum Geburtstag bekommen hast?

1. Wie gefällt dir diese Hose?
2. Wie gefällt dir dieses Hemd?
3. Wie gefällt dir dieser Rock?
4. Wie gefällt dir dieser Pulli?
5. Wie gefallen dir diese Jeans?
6. Wie gefallen dir diese Schuhe?

4. Peter schreibt über die Ausländer. Peter schreibt seinem Freund Thomas über die Situation der Ausländer in Deutschland. Ergänzen Sie die Sätze mit den passenden Relativpronomen.

1. In dem Brief, _____ Peter an seinen Freund Thomas schreibt, berichtet er über die Ausländer.

2. In Deutschland sind viele Ausländer, _____ in den großen Industriestädten leben.

3. In manchen Vierteln°, in _____ die Ausländer wohnen, wohnen nur wenige Deutsche. quarters, sections (of a city)

4. Dort gibt es Läden, in _____ die Ausländer die Lebensmittel kaufen können, _____ sie von ihrer Heimat her kennen.

5. Es sind meistens die Kinder, _____ es in dem fremden Land ganz gut gefällt.

6. Die Kinder lernen Deutsch, _____ sie dann oft besser sprechen als die Eltern.

7. Die Ausländer, _____ die Deutschen bei der Integration im Allgemeinen° **im Allgemeinen:** in general
wenig helfen, bleiben oft unter sich.

Mein Freund
ist
Ausländer

---

*Note that you need a plural construction: **Das sind doch nicht die …**

5. Wer sind diese Leute? Sie, Ihre Freundin Katie und Ihr Freund Jens sind auf einer Party. Katie kennt niemanden. Jens sagt etwas über die Leute. Da Katie kein Deutsch spricht, übersetzen Sie die Sätze für sie ins Englische.

→ Frau Meier, deren Sohn in Marburg studiert, ist Rechtsanwältin.
Mrs. Meier, whose son is studying in Marburg, is a lawyer.

1. Herr Schnell, dessen Tochter bei Volkswagen arbeitet, fährt einen Golf.
2. Herr und Frau Gescheit, deren Kinder gut Englisch können, haben ein neues großes Haus.
3. Der alte Herr, dessen Sohn arbeitslos ist, hat vor ein paar Wochen Bankrott gemacht.
4. Herr Ettel, dessen Frau Chefärztin ist, studiert noch.
5. Diese junge Frau, deren Vater ein bekannter Rechtsanwalt ist, hat letzte Woche geheiratet.
6. Und dieser junge Mann, dessen Eltern sehr reich sind, ist der Glückliche.

6. Wer ist ... Fragen Sie Ihre Partnerin/Ihren Partner, wer die verschiedenen Leute sind. Ihre Partnerin/Ihr Partner fragt Sie auch. Es ist möglich, dass Sie beide die Leute unterschiedlich° beschreiben.

differently

S1: Wer ist Herr Rot?
S2: Das ist der Journalist, der für die *Times* arbeitet. Und wer ist Frau ... ?
S1: Das ist ...

Frau Blau	der Professor	Sie/Er schreibt an einem Roman.
Herr Klein	die Studentin	Sie/Er trägt immer komische Hüte.
Herr Rot	der Ingenieur	Alle mögen sie/ihn.
Dr. Kühler	der Journalist	Ihr Mann ruft sie jeden Tag an.
Herr Hamburger	die Sekretärin	Ihr/Ihm gefällt es gut hier.
Frau König	der Arzt	Sie/Er arbeitet für die *Times*.
Frau Kaiser	der Musiker	Sie/Ihn sieht man nur mit der
Herr Bass	die Lehrerin	Zeitung unterm Arm.
		Sie/Er lächelt immer so viel.

7. Erzähl mal. Bilden Sie Dreiergruppen° und beenden Sie die Sätze.

groups of three

→ Wien ist eine Stadt, ...   [*die sehr alt ist*].
                          [*die ich besuchen möchte*].
                          [*in der ich leben möchte*].

1. Die Schweiz ist ein Land, ...
2. Österreich ist ein Land, ...
3. Volkswagen ist eine Firma, ...
4. Ich hätte gern eine Präsidentin/einen Präsidenten, ...
5. Ich habe einen Freund, ...
6. Ich habe eine Freundin, ...
7. Ich habe eine Professorin/einen Professor, ...
8. Der Juli ist ein Monat, ...

radio commercial

8. Hören Sie zu. Hören Sie eine Radiowerbung° für ein Restaurant in München-Haidhausen an. Beantworten Sie dann die Fragen. Sie hören drei neue Wörter: **Achtung!** (*Attention!*); **Neueröffnung** (*new opening*); **in der Nähe** (*near*).

1. Was haben die Leute vielleicht gemacht, die in Haidhausen abends noch Hunger haben?

2. Was für ein Restaurant ist das „Restaurant Konya" in der Rablstraße?
3. Wann kann man im „Restaurant Konya" essen?
4. Wie viel kostet das billigste Essen im „Restaurant Konya"?
5. Was gibt es alles im Gasteig, einem Kulturzentrum in München?

3 The passive voice°

das Passiv

| Active voice | **Stefan** fragt mich fast jeden Tag. | *Stefan* asks me almost every day. |
| Passive voice | **Ich** werde fast jeden Tag gefragt. | *I'm asked almost every day.* |

In the active voice, the subject is "active": the subject is the agent that performs the action expressed by the verb. Active voice focuses attention on the agent. The attention in the active sentence above is focused on Stefan, who asks me almost every day.

In the passive voice, the subject is "passive": the subject is acted upon by an expressed or unexpressed agent. Passive voice focuses attention on the receiver of the action. The attention in the passive sentence above is focused on the person (*me*) who is asked almost every day.

The subject (e.g., **ich**) of a passive sentence corresponds to the object of an active sentence (e.g., **mich**).

In everyday conversation, speakers of German use the active voice much more often than the passive voice. The passive is used in instructions, recipes, and technical and scientific manuals, where, just as in English, an impersonal style is preferred.

4 Passive voice: present tense and simple-past tense

| Present | Ich **werde** gefragt. | I *am asked.* |
| Simple past | Ich **wurde** gefragt. | I *was asked.* |

In English, a passive verb phrase consists of a form of the auxiliary verb *to be* and the past participle of the verb (e.g., *asked*). In German, the passive verb phrase consists of a form of the auxiliary **werden** and the past participle of the main verb (e.g., **gefragt**). The tenses you will encounter most frequently in passive voice are the present and simple past.

9. Was wird heute gemacht? Es ist Samstag und es gibt viel zu tun. Sagen sie, was heute alles bei Monika gemacht wird.

→ Brot / kaufen   *Brot wird gekauft.*

1. die Wäsche / waschen
2. das Haus / sauber machen
3. das Auto / waschen
4. die Gartenarbeit / machen
5. das Essen / kochen
6. die Garage / aufräumen

Wie kann man
Fremdenhass heilen?

„FREMDENHASS
IST EINE KRANKHEIT,
DIE DURCH
RESPEKT GEHEILT[1]
WERDEN KANN."

[1]*healed*

5 *Von* **+ agent**

Without agent	Die Gartenarbeit wird gemacht.	The yard work is being done.
With agent	Die Gartenarbeit wird **von meiner Schwester** gemacht.	The yard work is done *by my sister.*

In the passive voice, the agent is often omitted. If the agent (e.g., **Schwester**) is expressed, in most passive sentences it is the object of the preposition **von** and thus in the dative case.

Discussing who invented, wrote, or discovered something

10. Wer war das? Sie und Ihre Partnerin/Ihr Partner fragen einander, was von wem gemacht wurde.* Benutzen Sie die Stichwörter und bilden Sie Sätze im Passiv.

invented

> *S1:* Von wem wurde das Telefon erfunden°?
> *S2:* Das Telefon wurde von Alexander Graham Bell erfunden.

der Film *Titanic*	gebaut	Carl Friedrich Benz
Mickey Mouse	geschrieben	James Cameron
die Brooklyn Bridge	gemacht	Christopher Columbus
Hamlet	entdeckt°	Walt Disney
die Unabhängigkeits erklärung°	erfunden	Alexandre Eiffel
der Eiffelturm		Albert Einstein
die Röntgen-Strahlen°		Thomas Jefferson
Amerika		Robert Koch
der Tuberkelbazillus°		Johann Roebling
das erste deutsche Auto		Wilhelm Conrad Röntgen
die Relativitätstheorie		William Shakespeare

discovered
Declaration of Independence

X-rays

tuberculosis bacillus

[1]**behauptet:** *claimed*   [2]**dummes Gerede:** *idle talk*

*****Antworten:** der Film *Titanic:* James Cameron; Mickey Mouse: Walt Disney; die Brooklyn Bridge: Johann Roebling; *Hamlet:* William Shakespeare; die amerikanische Verfassung: Thomas Jefferson; der Eiffelturm: Alexandre Eiffel: die Röntgen-Strahlen: Wilhelm Conrad Röntgen; Amerika: Christopher Columbus; der Tuberkelbazillus: Robert Koch; das erste deutsche Auto: Carl Friedrich Benz; die Relativitätstheorie: Albert Einstein

11. Ausländer in Deutschland. Der Austauschstudent David spricht mit Gisela über Ausländer in Deutschland. Lesen Sie das Gespräch und beantworten Sie die Fragen.

DAVID: Gisela, ich sehe hier in Deutschland so viele ausländische Geschäfte – türkische, griechische, italienische, spanische.

GISELA: Ja, das stimmt. Es gibt in Deutschland über 7 Millionen Ausländer. Zwischen 1955 und 1973 wurden Arbeiter in Westdeutschland gebraucht. Sie kamen vor allem aus Italien, Griechenland, Spanien und der Türkei.

DAVID: Wurden sie gut akzeptiert?

GISELA: Nicht alle. Wegen der größeren kulturellen Unterschiede wurden zum Beispiel Türken nicht so leicht in die deutsche Gesellschaft integriert wie Italiener.

DAVID: Und heute?

GISELA: In der Zeitung wird oft von Problemen berichtet. Aber in den letzten Jahren wird immer mehr gegen Ausländerhass protestiert.

1. Was für ausländische Geschäfte und Restaurants sieht David in Deutschland?
2. Woher kamen die meisten Arbeiter, die Westdeutschland zwischen 1955 und 1973 brauchte?
3. Warum integrierten sich die Türken nicht so leicht in die deutsche Gesellschaft wie die Italiener?
4. Was passiert in den letzten Jahren immer mehr?

12. Hören Sie zu. David fliegt nächste Woche wieder zurück nach Amerika. Die Studentenzeitung möchte noch ein Interview mit ihm machen, bevor er abreist. Hören Sie das Interview und geben Sie an, ob die folgenden Sätze richtig oder falsch sind. Sie hören drei neue Wörter: **Lederhosen** (*short leather pants*); **Schloss Neuschwanstein** (*castle built by Ludwig II of Bavaria in the nineteenth century, a popular tourist attraction*); **vor kurzem** (*recently*).

1. Die Amerikaner glauben, dass Deutschland ziemlich multikulturell ist.
2. Wurst, schnelle Autos und viele Neonazis sind ein Teil des amerikanischen Deutschlandbildes.
3. Das „Rock gegen Rechts"-Konzert war ein Protestkonzert gegen Ausländer in Deutschland.
4. In Deutschland dauert es manchmal eine Weile, bis man Freunde hat.
5. David hat viele Fotos von stereotypen Deutschen, die Lederhosen tragen.

⑥ Impersonal passive construction

Samstags **wird** schwer **gearbeitet.**	On Saturdays people *work* hard.
Sonntags **wird** nicht **gearbeitet.**	No one *works* on Sundays.

In German it is possible to use passive without having a subject or an agent. Such a construction is called an impersonal passive construction.

Es wird jetzt gearbeitet. { There is work going on now. / People are working now.

The pronoun **es** begins an impersonal passive construction if no other words precede the verb. **Es** is a dummy subject. An English equivalent of the impersonal passive often uses an introductory phrase such as *there is* or *there are*.

13. Was wird hier gemacht? In diesem Wohnhaus ist viel los. Sprechen Sie mit Ihrer Partnerin/Ihrem Partner darüber, was in jeder Wohnung gemacht wird.

> *S1:* Was wird in Wohnung Nummer 2 gemacht?
> *S2:* In Wohnung Nummer 2 wird gespielt. *or* Es wird gespielt.

⑦ Summary of the uses of *werden*

■ *Active voice: main verb*

Herr Heller **wird** alt.	Mr. Heller *is growing* old.
Die Kinder **wurden** müde.	The children *were getting* tired.
Frau Ullmann **ist** Chefin der Firma **geworden.**	Ms. Ullmann *has become* head of the company.

Werden as a main verb is equivalent to English *to grow, get,* or *become.*

■ *Auxiliary verb in future tense*

Matthias **wird** hoffentlich mehr **arbeiten.**	I hope Matthias *will work* more.
Du **wirst** das wohl **wissen.**	You *probably know* that.

Werden is used with a dependent infinitive to form the future tense.

■ *Passive voice: auxiliary verb*

Viele Geschäfte **wurden** von Ausländern **aufgemacht.**	Many businesses *were opened* by foreigners.
Die Gäste **werden** oft von ethnischen Musikgruppen **unterhalten.**	The guests *are* often *entertained* by ethnic music groups.

Werden is used with a past participle to form the passive voice. The passive voice can occur in any tense.

14. Die deutsche Wirtschaft. Eine deutsche Geschäftsfrau spricht mit ausländischen Journalisten über die wirtschaftliche Situation in Deutschland. Stellen° Sie fest, wie **werden** benutzt wird. Dann geben Sie die Sätze auf Englisch wieder. Sagen Sie, ob **werden** (a) Hauptverb im Aktiv ist (geben Sie die Zeit° an), (b) als Futur benutzt wird oder (c) als Passiv-Konstruktion benutzt wird (geben Sie die Zeit an).

stellen fest: determine

tense

→ Viele alte Fabriken werden modernisiert.
***werden modernisiert** / present passive*
Many old factories are being modernized.

1. Hier wird noch viel gemacht.
2. Die Situation wird im nächsten Jahr sicher besser.
3. Der Export wird langsam weniger.
4. Wer wird dem Land helfen?
5. Werden die Waren auf dem Weltmarkt eine Zukunft haben?
6. Man meint, dass das Land immer weniger Rohstoffe haben wird.
7. Das Leben wurde in letzter Zeit teurer.
8. Die Industrie wird sich wohl neue Märkte suchen.
9. Manche Arbeiter wollen einfach nicht arbeiten. Was soll aus ihnen werden?
10. Die Situation wird hoffentlich in den nächsten Jahren besser.

Wiederholung

1. Rollenspiel. Sie machen Urlaub in Deutschland und wollen ein Auto mieten°. Ihre Partnerin/Ihr Partner arbeitet bei der Autovermietung° und kann nur Deutsch. Da sie/er sehr schnell spricht, fragen Sie nach mit Ausdrücken°, die signalisieren, dass Sie nicht verstehen. (Ihre Partnerin/Ihr Partner soll ihre/seine Sätze möglichst schnell und undeutlich° sprechen.)

rent / car rental

expressions

unclearly

Redemittel: Ausdrücke, die Nichtverstehen signalisieren *(Indicating that you don't understand something)*

Bitte? ■ Wie bitte? ■ Entschuldigung, was haben Sie gesagt? ■ Ich verstehe Sie leider nicht. ■ Ich habe Sie leider nicht verstanden. ■ Könnten Sie das bitte wiederholen°? ■ Würden Sie bitte langsamer sprechen? ■ Sie sprechen sehr/zu schnell. ■ Ich kenne das Wort _____ nicht. ■ Was bedeutet denn das Wort _____? ■ Wissen Sie, was _____ auf Englisch heißt?

repeat

Sätze für Ihre Partnerin/Ihren Partner:

1. Wenn Sie das Auto für eine ganze Woche mieten, ist es billiger.
2. Mit dem Auto dürfen Sie weder ost- noch° südeuropäische Länder besuchen.
3. Wenn Sie einen Porsche oder einen Mercedes mieten wollen, müssen Sie aber über 25 Jahre alt sein.
4. Möchte noch eine zweite Person den Wagen fahren?
5. Die Haftpflichtversicherung° beträgt° 12 Euro pro Tag.
6. Sie müssen das Auto wieder mit vollem Tank abgeben°.
7. Der Wagen braucht übrigens° Super Benzin.

weder ... noch: neither ... nor

personal liability insurance / amounts to / return

by the way

2. Über Politik. Gisela erzählt über Professor Lange. Ergänzen Sie ihre Sätze im Passiv mit dem passenden Verb.

besuchen ▪ diskutieren ▪ halten ▪ lesen ▪ schreiben ▪ sprechen

➜ An der Universität _____ oft über Politik _____.
An der Universität wird oft über Politik gesprochen.

1. Die interessantesten Vorlesungen _____ von Professor Lange _____.

2. Diese Vorlesungen _____ von den Studenten gut _____.

3. Sein Buch *Die neue Politik* _____ nicht nur von Studenten _____.

4. Im Fernsehen _____ auch über Politik _____.

5. In der Zeitung _____ darüber _____.

3. Ein Student an der Uni. Bernd möchte wissen, wie es Phillip an der Universität geht. Sagen Sie ihm, dass es nicht so gut geht, aber dass es Phillip nichts auszumachen scheint°. Beenden Sie die Sätze mit den passenden Adjektivendungen, wo sie notwendig° sind. Dann beantworten Sie die Fragen negativ mit Adjektiven aus der Liste von Antonymen.

seems
necessary

alt ▪ dumm ▪ faul ▪ groß ▪ leicht ▪ lustig ▪ schlecht ▪ teuer

➜ Studiert Peter an einer klein_____Universität?
Studiert Peter an einer kleinen Universität? Nein, an einer großen.

1. Ist er ein fleißig_____ Student?

2. Ist er intelligent_____?

3. Liest er gern ernst_____ Geschichten?

4. Wohnt er in einer modern_____ Wohnung?

5. Hat er ein klein_____ Schlafzimmer?

6. Hat er ein schwer_____ Leben?

7. Hat er einen gut_____ Studentenjob?

8. Findet er Wohnen und Essen billig_____?

4. Markus schreibt über Frauen. Ergänzen Sie die Kommentare von Markus über die Situation der Frauen in Deutschland mit den passenden Relativpronomen.

1. Viele Frauen sind mit dem Frauenbild, _____ in vielen Schulbüchern noch zu finden ist, unzufrieden°.

dissatisfied

2. In diesen Büchern ist es immer ein Junge, _____ etwas baut oder Fußball spielt.

3. Und es ist immer ein Mädchen, _____ zusieht° und weniger gefährliche° Sachen macht.

watches / dangerous

4. Die Frauen, _____ Berufe wie Elektrikerin und Mechanikerin gelernt haben, haben es besonders schwer.

5. Man nennt eine Frau, _____ wegen der Arbeit vier Tage von zu Hause weg ist, eine Rabenmutter°.

unfit mother

6. Ein Mann, _____ dieselbe Arbeit macht, ist aber kein Rabenvater°.

unfit father

7. Es gibt also noch traditionelle Rollen, von _____ Männer und Frauen sich emanzipieren müssen.

Die einzige Bank, auf der sie gerne sitzen.

Welcher Fußballer sitzt schon gerne auf der Ersatzbank? Busbänke dagegen sind bei kleinen Kickern beliebt. Denn mit Bussen und Bahnen kommen sie sicher zum Training. Und so ein gutes Stück weiter auf ihrem Weg zum Fußballstar.

BUSSE&BAHNEN
Verband Deutscher Verkehrsunternehmen
Deutsche Bahn AG

Umdenken, einsteigen!

[1]**Ersatzbank:** *bench (where substitute players sit)*

Wenn ein Fußballspieler auf der Bank sitzt, dann darf er nicht Fußball spielen. Warum ist die Bank im Bus eine Bank, auf der ein Fußballspieler gern sitzt?

 5. Ihre Meinung. Beantworten Sie die folgenden Fragen und fragen Sie dann Ihre Partnerin/Ihren Partner, was ihre/seine Meinung ist.

1. Möchten Sie in einem anderen Land studieren? Warum (nicht)?
2. Möchten Sie während des Sommers in einem anderen Land arbeiten? Warum (nicht)?
3. Möchten Sie in einem anderen Land leben? In welchem Land? Warum?
4. Möchten Sie in einem Land leben, dessen Sprache Sie nicht können? Warum (nicht)?
5. Würden Sie in einem anderen Land für weniger Geld als in Amerika arbeiten? Warum (nicht)?

6. Erzählen Sie mal. Diskutieren Sie die folgenden Themen in kleinen Gruppen.

1. Erzählen Sie mal von einem Buch, das Sie gern kaufen würden.
2. Erzählen Sie mal von einer Reise, die Sie gern machen würden.
3. Erzählen Sie mal von Ferien, die Sie gern machen würden.
4. Erzählen Sie mal von Politikern, die Sie gern reden hören würden.
5. Erzählen Sie mal von einem Film, den Sie gern sehen würden.
6. Erzählen Sie mal von einer Rockband, die Sie gern hören würden.

entweder ... oder: either ... or
at least / paragraph

minorities

agree with

stellen vor: present

advantages
agree with

7. Zum Schreiben

1. Beschreiben Sie entweder° was für eine Familie oder was für eine Welt Sie gern hätten. Benutzen Sie mindestens° zwei Relativpronomen in Ihrem Absatz°.

2. Machen Sie eine Liste mit Problemen, die ausländische Arbeitnehmer oder Minderheiten° in einem Land haben können. Diskutieren Sie in kleinen Gruppen über Ihre Listen. Stellen Sie dann eine Liste zusammen, mit der alle übereinstimmen°, und nummerieren Sie die Probleme. Beginnen Sie mit „1" für das wichtigste Problem. Wenn Sie fertig sind, stellen Sie Ihre Liste den Kursteilnehmern vor°.

3. Was meinen Sie zu der folgenden Aussage: „Kinder, die in zwei Sprachen und zwei Kulturen aufwachsen, haben viele Vorteile°"? Schreiben Sie einen kurzen Absatz, in dem Sie der Aussage zustimmen° oder dagegen argumentieren.

Hinweise: In a relative clause the finite verb is in final position. The gender of the relative pronoun depends on the gender of the noun to which it refers. Its case depends on its function in the clause.

Grammatik: Zusammenfassung

Relative clauses

Wie teuer ist **der Fernseher, den** du kaufen willst?	How expensive is *the television (that)* you want to buy?
Wie alt ist **das Auto, das** du verkaufen möchtest?	How old is *the car (that)* you want to sell?
Ist das **die CD, die** du gestern gekauft hast?	Is that *the CD (that)* you bought yesterday?

A relative clause provides additional information about a previously mentioned noun or pronoun. The clause is introduced by a relative pronoun, which refers back to the noun or pronoun (called an antecedent). A relative clause is a dependent clause, and thus the verb is in final position. In written German, relative clauses are set off from main clauses by commas.

Relative pronouns

	Masculine	Neuter	Feminine	Plural
Nominative	der	das	die	die
Accusative	den	das	die	die
Dative	dem	dem	der	**denen**
Genitive	**dessen**	**dessen**	**deren**	**deren**

Nominative	Ist das der Mann, **der** immer so viel fragt?
Accusative	Ist das der Mann, **den** Sie meinen?
	für den Sie arbeiten?
Dative	Ist das der Mann, **dem** Sie oft helfen?
	von dem Sie erzählt haben?
Genitive	Ist das der Mann, **dessen** Auto Sie gekauft haben?

The *gender* (masculine, neuter, or feminine) and *number* (singular or plural) of the relative pronoun are determined by its antecedent, i.e., the noun to which it refers. The *case* (nominative, accusative, dative, or genitive) of the relative pronoun is determined by its function within its clause (subject, direct object, object of a preposition, etc.).

Present and simple past tenses in the passive voice

| Present | Der Brief **wird geschrieben.** | The letter *is being written.* |
| Simple past | Der Brief **wurde geschrieben.** | The letter *was being written.* |

Von + agent

| Das Geld wurde **von den Arbeitern** verdient. | The money was earned *by the workers.* |

In passive voice the agent is the object of the preposition **von** and thus in the dative case. The agent may be omitted. (**Viel Geld wurde verdient.**)

Zwei Kurzgeschichten

*Franz Hohler was born in 1943 in Biel, Switzerland. He is a well-known and popular cabaret artist who appears regularly in one-person shows in Switzerland and Germany. He is also a singer/songwriter (**Liedermacher**) with a number of CD's to his credit and an author of plays for the stage, TV, and radio and of stories for children and adults. The essence of much of his work is satire. A good example of his humor with a serious intent is his story "Der Verkäufer und der Elch" from his work* Kontakt mit der Zeit *(1981).*

    What view of successful merchandising does the factory owner in this story represent?

Der Verkäufer und der Elch

Eine Geschichte mit 128 deutschen Wörtern

Franz Hohler

Kennen Sie das Sprichwort° „Dem Elch° eine Gasmaske verkaufen?" Das sagt man bei uns von jemandem°, der sehr tüchtig° ist, und ich möchte jetzt erzählen, wie es zu diesem Sprichwort gekommen ist.   proverb / moose
           someone / competent

    Es gab einmal einen Verkäufer, der war dafür berühmt, daß er allen alles
5 verkaufen konnte.

    Er hatte schon einem Zahnarzt eine Zahnbürste° verkauft, einem Bäcker ein Brot und einem Blinden einen Fernsehapparat.   toothbrush

„Ein wirklich guter Verkäufer bist du aber erst", sagten seine Freunde zu ihm, „wenn du einem Elch eine Gasmaske verkaufst."

10 Da ging der Verkäufer so weit nach Norden, bis er in einen Wald kam, in dem nur Elche wohnten.

„Guten Tag", sagte er zum ersten Elch, den er traf, „Sie brauchen bestimmt eine Gasmaske."

what for / air — „Wozu°?" fragte der Elch. „Die Luft° ist gut hier."

nowadays — 15 „Alle haben heutzutage° eine Gasmaske", sagte der Verkäufer.

„Es tut mir leid", sagte der Elch, „aber ich brauche keine."

„Warten Sie nur", sagte der Verkäufer, „Sie brauchen schon noch eine."

in the middle — Und wenig später begann er mitten° in dem Wald, in dem nur Elche wohnten, eine Fabrik zu bauen.

crazy — 20 „Bist du wahnsinnig°?" fragten seine Freunde.

rose / poisonous / waste gases / smokestack — „Nein", sagte er, „ich will nur dem Elch eine Gasmaske verkaufen." Als die Fabrik fertig war, stiegen° soviel giftige° Abgase° aus dem Schornstein°, daß der Elch bald zum Verkäufer kam und zu ihm sagte: „Jetzt brauche ich eine Gasmaske."

immediately — 25 „Das habe ich gedacht", sagte der Verkäufer und verkaufte ihm sofort° eine. „Qualitätsware!" sagte er lustig.

polite form — „Die anderen Elche", sagte der Elch, „brauchen jetzt auch Gasmasken. Hast du noch mehr?" (Elche kennen die Höflichkeitsform° mit „Sie" nicht.)

„Da habt ihr Glück", sagte der Verkäufer, „ich habe noch Tausende."

by the way — 30 „Übrigens°", sagte der Elch, „was machst du in deiner Fabrik?"

„Gasmasken", sagte der Verkäufer.

P.S. Ich weiß doch nicht genau, ob es ein schweizerisches oder ein schwedisches Sprichwort ist, aber die beiden Länder werden ja oft

werden verwechselt: are confused — verwechselt°.

Fragen

1. Welche Beispiele zeigen, dass der Verkäufer ein guter Verkäufer ist?
2. Was muss ein „sehr guter" Verkäufer verkaufen können?
3. Warum glaubt der Elch, dass er keine Gasmaske braucht?
4. Warum kann der Verkäufer Gasmasken an alle Elche verkaufen?

Fragen zur Diskussion

1. Glauben Sie, dass die Worte **„Dem Elch eine Gasmaske verkaufen"** wirklich ein Sprichwort sind? Warum (nicht)?

develops / necessity arises / in order that happened — 2. Der Autor entwickelt° eine Situation, in der die Notwendigkeit° eines Produktes entsteht°, damit° Menschen es wollen oder brauchen. An was für Beispiele können Sie aus Ihrem eigenen Leben denken, wo dies geschehen° ist?

3. Wo sehen Sie Beispiele von Ironie in dieser Geschichte?

Helga Novak was born in 1935 in Berlin. She studied philosophy and journalism in Leipzig and worked in various types of places: factories, a laboratory, and a bookstore. In 1961 she moved to Iceland and returned to Germany in 1967 to live in Frankfurt as a writer. In 1980, the New Literary Society in Hamburg gave her an award for her novel Die Eisheiligen, *as the best first novel by a German speaker. Novak is also recognized as an outstanding poet. In 1997 she was awarded the*

*Literary Prize of Brandenburg (**Brandenburgischer Literaturpreis**) for her most recent volume of poems,* Silvatica *(Songs of the Forest).*

In her stories, Helga Novak deals with ordinary people in everyday situations. Through the use of simple sentences and a dry, unemotional style, she suggests much more about human relationships than she actually says. In "Schlittenfahren," taken from her work Geselliges Beisammensein (1968), the father does not communicate with his children but simply leaves his retreat long enough to shout the same sentences in their direction, sentences devoid of meaning for them and him. However, the repetition of "kommt rein" at the end of the story takes on a new and possibly serious dimension and reveals the problem of using language just to be saying something.

In what sense do the private home (**Eigenheim**) and the garden represent two separate and unrelated scenes of activity? What do the father's actions say about his relationship with the children?

Schlittenfahren°

Helga M. Novak

sledding

Das Eigenheim° steht in einem Garten. Der Garten ist groß. Durch den Garten	private home
fließt° ein Bach°. Im Garten stehen zwei Kinder. Das eine der Kinder kann	flows / brook
noch nicht sprechen. Das andere Kind ist größer. Sie sitzen auf einem	
Schlitten°. Das kleinere Kind weint. Das größere sagt, gib den Schlitten her.	sled

5 Das kleinere weint. Es schreit°. — screams

Aus dem Haus tritt° ein Mann. Er sagt, wer brüllt°, kommt rein°. Er geht in — steps / bawls / **rein = herein**: in

das Haus zurück. Die Tür fällt hinter ihm zu°. — **fällt zu**: closes

Das kleinere Kind schreit.

Der Mann erscheint° wieder in der Haustür. Er sagt, komm rein. Na wirds — appears

10 bald°. Du kommst rein. Nix°. Wer brüllt, kommt rein. Komm rein. — **Na ... bald**: hurry up / **Nix = nichts**

Der Mann geht hinein. Die Tür klappt°. — slams

Das kleinere Kind hält die Schnur° des Schlittens fest. Es schluchzt°. — rope / sobs

Der Mann öffnet die Haustür. Er sagt, du darfst Schlitten fahren, aber nicht

brüllen. Wer brüllt, kommt rein. Ja. Ja. Jaaa. Schluß° jetzt. — **Schluß jetzt**: that's enough

15 Das größere Kind sagt, Andreas will immer allein fahren.

Der Mann sagt, wer brüllt, kommt rein. Ob er nun Andreas heißt oder

sonstwie°. — otherwise

Er macht die Tür zu°. — **macht zu**: closes

Das größere Kind nimmt dem kleineren den Schlitten weg. Das kleinere

20 Kind schluchzt, quietscht°, jault°, quengelt°. — squeals / howls / whines

Der Mann tritt aus dem Haus. Das größere Kind gibt dem kleineren den

Schlitten zurück. Das kleinere Kind setzt sich auf den Schlitten. Es rodelt°. — sleds

Der Mann sieht in den Himmel°. Der Himmel ist blau. Die Sonne ist groß — sky

und rot. Es ist kalt.

25 Der Mann pfeift° laut. Er geht wieder ins Haus zurück. Er macht die Tür — whistles

hinter sich zu.

Das größere Kind ruft°, Vati, Vati, Vati, Andreas gibt den Schlitten nicht — calls

mehr her.

Die Haustür geht auf°. Der Mann steckt den Kopf heraus. Er sagt, wer — **geht auf**: opens

30 brüllt, kommt rein. Die Tür geht zu.

Das größere Kind ruft, Vati, Vativativati, Vaaatiii, jetzt ist Andreas in den

Bach gefallen.

Die Haustür öffnet sich einen Spalt° breit°. Eine Männerstimme° ruft, wie — crack / wide / man's voice

oft soll ich das noch sagen, wer brüllt, kommt rein.

Fragen

1. In was für einem Haus wohnt die Familie?
2. Was wissen Sie über den Garten?
3. Was wissen Sie über die Kinder?
4. Warum weint das kleinere Kind?
5. Warum kommt der Mann aus dem Haus? Was sagt er?
6. Wie ist das Wetter?
7. Wer fährt am Ende mit dem Schlitten?
8. Warum ruft das ältere Kind am Ende den Vater?
9. Was antwortet der Vater?

Fragen zur Diskussion

1. Der Mann kommt mehrere Male zur Tür. Welche Sätze beschreiben das? Was sagen diese Sätze über den Mann?

2. Der Mann geht mehrere Male ins Haus. Welche Sätze beschreiben das? Was ist damit gesagt?

3. Welchen Satz sagt der Mann immer wieder? Welchen Effekt hat das auf die Kinder? Auf den Leser?

4. Was wird über Jahreszeit und Wetter gesagt? Welche Rolle spielt das?

5. Warum benutzt die Autorin immer wieder das Wort „der Mann"? Welches andere Wort könnte sie benutzen?

6. Wie meint der Mann den letzten Satz? Wie verstehen Sie ihn?

Reference Section

BAUSTEINE: ENGLISH EQUIVALENTS

Note that the English versions of the dialogues are equivalents rather than literal translations.

Einführung

What is your name?

In front of the bulletin board

ALEX: Hi. My name is Alex. How about you?

GISELA: Hi. My name is Gisela.

ALEX: Are you also planning to go to Florence?

GISELA: Yes.

ALEX: Great. Hey, here is my telephone number: 35 67 81.

GISELA: Thanks—and my telephone number is 79 23 09.

ALEX: I beg your pardon?

GISELA: 79 23 09.

ALEX: OK. Well then, see you later.

GISELA: So long.

What is your name?

In the office

MS. KLUGE: Can I help you? What is your name?

GISELA: Gisela Riedholt.

MS. KLUGE: How do you spell (write) that?

GISELA: R-i-e-d-h-o-l-t.

MS. KLUGE: And your address?

GISELA: My school address or my home address?

MS. KLUGE: Your school address, please.

GISELA: Pfleghofstraße 2, Room 15, 72070 Tübingen.

MS. KLUGE: Thank you, Ms. Riedholt.

GISELA: You're welcome.

Kapitel 1

How are you?

In the library

PROFESSOR LANGE: Good morning, Ms. Riedholt. How are you?

GISELA: Good morning, Professor Lange. Fine, thanks. And you?

PROFESSOR LANGE: Thanks, not bad.

In the lecture hall

ALEX: Hi, Gisela.

GISELA: Hello, Alex. How are you?

ALEX: Oh, not so well.

GISELA: What's wrong? Are you sick?

ALEX: No, I'm just terribly tired.

What are you doing tonight?

MICHAEL: What are you doing tonight?

GISELA: Nothing special. Listening to music or something like that. Maybe I'll go to the movies.

MICHAEL: Hmm. You like to play chess, don't you?

GISELA: Chess? Yes. But [I do] not [play] very well.

MICHAEL: Oh come on, we'll play together, OK?

GISELA: All right. When?

MICHAEL: At seven?

GISELA: OK. See you then.

Kapitel 2

How's the weather?

In the summer

MS. KLUGE: Nice weather, isn't it, Professor Lange? Too nice for the library!

PROFESSOR LANGE: Yes, but it's too hot and too sunny. This evening I'm working in the garden. Everything is quite dry there.

MS. KLUGE: Maybe it'll rain tomorrow after all.

PROFESSOR LANGE: Well, I hope so!

In the fall

GISELA: What weather! The wind is awfully cold. And everything is so gray. I think it's still going to rain today.

MICHAEL: It's almost too cold for rain. It's only one degree. I think maybe it'll snow. On the weekend I'm going hiking. I hope it's dry and not so cold then. And maybe the sun will shine after all.

GISELA: Yes, for sure. Who's coming along?

MICHAEL: My friend Klaus from Hamburg.

GISELA: How nice! Unfortunately I'm staying here and working for the university.

Kapitel 3

Are you going shopping today?

MONIKA: Stefan, aren't you going shopping today?

STEFAN: Yes, I am. What do you need?

MONIKA: We don't have any more coffee. (We're out of coffee.)

STEFAN: One pound is enough, right? Would you like anything else?

MONIKA: Yes, a loaf of bread, please. But buy that at Reinhardt's. It's better there.

STEFAN: We still have enough bread. And after all, this weekend we're at Gisela's in Tübingen.

MONIKA: Oh yes, that's right!

Where is there a pharmacy?

DAVID: Tell me Gisela, where is there a pharmacy (around) here?

GISELA: Why? What do you need?

DAVID: I need something for a headache.

GISELA: I always have aspirin in my backpack. Here, take one.

Kapitel 4

Notes for the test

GISELA: Hi, Michael. Can you please lend me your notes?

MICHAEL: Yes, glad to.

GISELA: That's nice [of you]. I still have to study a lot for this test.

MICHAEL: Of course, here they are. Can you please bring them back tomorrow?

Is that your major?

MICHAEL: Hi there, Melanie! Since when have you been taking a literature course? Aren't you studying history?

MELANIE: No, not any more. I'm taking German now.

MICHAEL: Oh yes? As a minor?

MELANIE: No, as a major.

MICHAEL: Oh, really? Say, would you like to go out for coffee afterwards?

MELANIE: Unfortunately I can't. I still have to read something. Tomorrow I have an oral report and I'm not especially well prepared.

Kapitel 5

Are you driving to the university tomorrow?

UWE: Are you going by car to the university tomorrow?

CLAUDIA: Yes. Why? Do you want to come along?

UWE: Is that OK? I've got so many library books. Can you pick me up maybe?

CLAUDIA: Of course, no problem. I'll come by your place at eight-thirty. Is that OK?

UWE: Yes, eight-thirty is good. I'll be waiting downstairs then.

On vacation

MICHAEL: What are you doing on vacation, Melanie?

MELANIE: I'm going to Austria.

MICHAEL: Are you going alone?

MELANIE: No, I'm going with my friend, Sibylle. She knows Austria rather well.

MICHAEL: Are you going by car?

MELANIE: No, by train. We're staying in Vienna for three days and then we're going hiking.

MICHAEL: And where are you staying?

MELANIE: In Vienna we're sleeping at our friends' house. And otherwise we're camping.

Kapitel 6

What are your plans?

UWE: Say, what are you doing on the weekend?

MELANIE: No idea.

MICHAEL: I've got a rehearsal with the band on Friday. On Saturday we're playing at the Musikfabrik.

UWE: Hey, you know, Melanie, we can go there together, right?

MELANIE: Good idea. That's great. Maybe Alex will go along too?

MICHAEL: He can't. He has to study for his comprehensives.

UWE: All right then, Melanie, I'll pick you up at eight. Is that all right?

I was surfing the internet.

GISELA: Tell me, Alex, who were you on the phone with so long last night? I tried again and again from eight to eleven to call you. The line was always busy.

ALEX: Oh, I was only surfing the Internet a little.

GISELA: What, surfing for three hours?

ALEX: Yes, I was looking for cheap flights to the U.S. Besides, I needed a few additional items of information for my homework. And I wrote you an e-mail. Didn't you get it?

GISELA: Don't know. You know, I don't sit at my computer every day like you do.

Kapitel 7

Munich in the summer

Peter is visiting his friend Christine in Munich.

PETER: What are you doing after the lecture? Do you have to go to the library?

CHRISTINE: No, I have time. Shouldn't we go to a typical Bavarian beer garden today? In this weather, we can sit comfortably outside.

PETER: Oh yes, gladly. In the English Garden?

CHRISTINE: Hmmmm. Naturally there are some beer gardens there, but there are always so many tourists there. Besides it's rather expensive there. I'm somewhat broke at the moment.

PETER: Doesn't matter. I'll treat. As long as I'm in Munich, I would really like to go to the English Garden.

Preparations for a party

MONIKA: Say, don't you finally want to straighten up the living room? Your books are lying around everywhere.

STEFAN: Do I have to?

MONIKA: Of course, we have to prepare the food and set the table. People are coming in an hour.

STEFAN: What? In an hour? Good heavens! And we still have to vacuum, dust, do the dishes, dry them, the kitchen looks like . . .

MONIKA: Now stop talking so much and hurry up. You know I'm going to help you.

Kapitel 8

Want ads

ALEX: Well, what's new in the newspaper?

UWE: I don't know. Up to now I have only looked through the classified ads.

ALEX: Which ones? The ones for marriage partners?

UWE: Nonsense. The want ads! I'm looking for work. I would like an interesting job where you can earn a lot of money.

ALEX: Yes, that would be great. You've been looking a long time already. Lots of luck!

Kapitel 9

Have you caught a cold?

CLAUDIA: Hi, Uwe! What's wrong? You're coughing terribly.

UWE: Yes, I've caught a cold. My throat really hurts.

CLAUDIA: Do you have a fever, too?

UWE: Yes, a little—38 [=100.4°F].

CLAUDIA: You poor guy! You also look pretty pale!

UWE: I do feel really sick. Perhaps I'd better go to the doctor.

CLAUDIA: Well, I would certainly say that, too. Don't forget that beginning Saturday we want to go skiing with Gisela and Alex in Zermatt for a week.

(*Three days later*)

How do you feel today?

CLAUDIA: How do you feel today? Did you go to the doctor yesterday?

UWE: Yes, I was at the university clinic. The doctor prescribed something and I already feel significantly better. The fever is gone.

CLAUDIA: Do you still want to go to Switzerland on Saturday?

UWE: Of course. After all, we've planned this vacation for months.

CLAUDIA: The weather is supposed to be great next week. Don't forget to bring your sunglasses along.

Kapitel 10

How was it?

Gisela and Alex are at Gisela's friends Monika and Stefan's in Berlin for a few days. In the morning at breakfast, they talk over their activities.

STEFAN: Well, what do you think of Berlin nightlife? Where were you last night?

GISELA: Monika went to her volleyball game, of course, but Alex and I were at the Berliner Ensemble.

STEFAN: Oh, what were they playing?

GISELA: They did the Brecht play, *Galileo*. It was very interesting.

STEFAN: Oh yes, there was a good review of it in the newspaper. Did you have good seats?

ALEX: Yes, as a matter of fact we had excellent seats, even though we had student tickets. They cost only 8 euros.

STEFAN: I would love to go to the theater again sometime. Would you recommend the play?

GISELA: Yes, without reservation. At first I didn't want to see it, but then I found it absolutely great.

STEFAN: And what did you do afterwards? You didn't come home until really late.

ALEX: We were at the Wunder-Bar, drank something, and talked for a long time about the play.

STEFAN: Oh, you lucky guys! I would love to have been there too! I was awake until two o'clock too, you know, but I had to study for my test!

Kapitel 11

An appointment

UWE: Hello. My name is Ohrdorf, Uwe Ohrdorf. I would like to speak to Dr. Ziegler. I have an appointment with her.

SECRETARY: Hello, Mr. Ohrdorf. Yes, please go right in. She's expecting you.

A summer job

PERSONNEL DIRECTOR: Mr. Ohrdorf, you're now in your eighth semester of computer science and want to work here for two months.

UWE: Yes, that's right.

PERSONNEL DIRECTOR: From what I can see, you have already worked as a computer specialist.

UWE: Yes, I also had a summer job last year and I got some good practical experience there.

PERSONNEL DIRECTOR: And what do you want to do with it later on?

UWE: I would like a position with a bank, an assignment with lots of responsibility, I hope.

Kapitel 12

Rock fans against xenophobia

MONIKA: Peter, do you feel like going to the outdoor concert in the Tiergarten this weekend?

PETER: Hmmm, I don't know. I actually still wanted to get a look at Freiburg. After all, I'm flying back to America in two weeks.

MONIKA: Ah, come on. You can still go to Freiburg next weekend, too.

PETER: But I know only a few of the rock musicians who'll be playing there.

MONIKA: But some are pretty well-known. However it's not only about the music. The slogan is: "Rock against the right." By means of the concert, the musicians are demonstrating against racism and xenophobia. And we'll be showing our solidarity with them if we go to it. That's important.

PETER: Do you think that many people will come?

MONIKA: Oh yes. About 100,000 people are expected.

PETER: Well OK, let's go. After all, it's for a good cause.

FRAGE-ECKE, S2 INFORMATION

The **Frage-Ecke** charts with the information for *S2* apppear here. The charts for *S1* are found in the chapters themselves on the pages indicated.

Einführung (p. 9)

7. The charts in this **Frage-Ecke** activity show the postal codes of particular sections of cities in Germany, Austria, and Switzerland. Take turns with a partner and find out the postal codes that are missing in your chart.

S1: Wie ist eine Postleitzahl von Zürich?
S2: Eine Postleitzahl von Zürich ist 8000. Wie ist eine Postleitzahl von Berlin?

S2:

_____ Berlin
8000 Zürich
_____ Hamburg
80331 München
_____ Frankfurt
1010 Wien
_____ Salzburg

Einführung (p. 12)

12. You and a partner are talking about Rebecca, Dennis, Sara, and Kevin. Take turns finding out which subjects they study on which days. Note that Germans use the word **am** with days of the week: **am Montag.**

S1: Was hat Dennis am Dienstag und Donnerstag?
S2: Mathe. Was hat Dennis am Montag, Mittwoch und Freitag?
S1: Deutsch. Was hat . . .

S2:

	Montag	Dienstag	Mittwoch	Donnerstag	Freitag
Dennis		Mathe		Mathe	
Rebecca	Englisch		Englisch		Englisch
Sara	Physik		Physik		Physik
Kevin		Philosophie		Philosophie	

Kapitel 1 (pp. 29–30)

4. You and your partner are talking about the characteristics of certain people. Take turns finding out the information that is missing in your own chart.

S1: Was für ein Mensch ist Alex?
S2: Er ist ruhig und freundlich. Was für ein Mensch ist Gisela?

S2:

Gisela		
Alex	ruhig	freundlich
Melanie		
Claudia	praktisch	ruhig
Michael		
Stefan	intelligent	sportlich

Kapitel 1 (p. 32)

8. Some of the clocks in this activity show particular times. Others are blank. Take turns with a partner and find out the times that are missing on your clocks.

S1: Nummer 1. Wie viel Uhr ist es?
S2: Es ist Viertel nach neun. (Es ist neun Uhr fünfzehn.) Und Nummer 2? Wie spät ist es?
S1: Es ist . . .

S2:

1	2	3	4	5	6

Kapitel 1   (p. 52)

7. You and your partner are talking about the activities of certain people. Ask each other questions to find out who does what and at what times. Then fill in the **ich** column of your schedule with your own information and ask your partner about her/his activities.

S1: Was macht Peter heute Morgen?
S2: Er macht heute Morgen Deutsch. Was machen Alex und Gisela am Samstag?
S1: Sie spielen am Samstag Schach.

S2:

	heute Morgen	heute Abend	Samstag	Sonntag
Monika		arbeiten		Karten spielen
Peter	Deutsch machen			Videospiele spielen
Alex und Gisela	Sport treiben			wandern
ich				
Partnerin/ Partner				

Kapitel 2   (pp. 68–69)

3. Find out where the following people are from and where they live now. Obtain the missing information by asking your partner.

S1: Woher kommt Anton?
S2: Er kommt aus Deutschland. Was ist Anton?
S1: Er ist Deutscher. Wo wohnt Anton?
S2: Er wohnt in Hamburg.

S1: Und woher kommst du?
S2: Ich komme aus . . .

S2:

	Woher kommt . . . ?	Was ist . . . ?	Wo wohnt . . . ?
Anton	Deutschland		Hamburg
Anne	Liechtenstein		
Kristina		Deutsche	Leipzig
Herr Heller		Österreicher	
ich			
Partnerin/Partner			

Kapitel 2 (p. 74)

7. Find out how old the following people are, when their birthdays are, and what the typical weather in that month is. Obtain the missing information from your partner.

S1: Wie alt ist Manfred?
S2: Manfred ist 21 Jahre alt. Wann hat er Geburtstag?
S1: Im Januar. Wie ist das Wetter im Januar?
S2: Es ist kalt.

S2:

	Wie alt?	Geburtstag	das Wetter
Manfred	21		kalt
Stefanie		Oktober	
Herr Hofer	45		
Frau Vogel		April	nass und kühl
ich			
Partnerin/Partner			

Kapitel 3 (p. 91)

4. Find out why various people, including your partner, are going to certain places of business.

S1: Warum geht Herr Sommer ins Kaufhaus?
S2: Er braucht ein Radio. Warum gehst du ins Kaufhaus?
S1: Ich brauche ein Heft./Ich gehe doch nicht ins Kaufhaus. Ich brauche nichts.

S2:

	ins Kaufhaus	in die Drogerie	in die Metzgerei	in die Bäckerei	in den Supermarkt
Jochen		Bleistifte		sechs Brötchen	
Monika und Stefan	zwei Kulis		250 Gramm Wurst	Brot	Kaffee
Herr Sommer	ein Radio		Salami		
Partnerin/Partner					

Kapitel 3   (p. 122)

5. Compare the picture of your room with that of your partner.

   S1: Mein Zimmer hat [eine Pflanze]. Hast du auch [eine Pflanze]?
   S2: Ja, ich habe auch [eine Pflanze]./Nein, aber ich habe Blumen.

   S2:

Kapitel 4   (p. 142)

4. Ergänzen Sie die fehlenden Informationen. Fragen Sie Ihre Partnerin/Ihren Partner. (Supply the missing information. Ask your partner.)

   S1: Wie heißt die Mutter von Angelika?
   S2: Sie heißt Kersten Clausen.
   S1: Wie alt ist Angelikas Mutter?
   S2: Sie ist 35 Jahre alt.

S2:

	Vater	Mutter	Tante	Onkel	Großvater	Großmutter
Angelika		Kersten Clausen, 35		Volker Clausen, 43		
Christoph	Volker Clausen, 43		Kersten Clausen, 35		Willi Clausen, 67	Käthe Clausen, 63
ich						
Partnerin/ Partner						

Kapitel 4 (p. 156)

22. Ergänzen Sie die fehlenden Informationen. Fragen Sie Ihre Partnerin/Ihren Partner. (Supply the missing information. Ask your partner.)

S1: Was muss Martina machen?
S2: Sie muss jobben.

S2:

	müssen	dürfen	wollen	sollen	können
Martina	jobben				gut tanzen
Kai und Sabine		Kuchen essen	ins Kino gehen		das Essen bezahlen
Dominik	in die Vorlesung gehen			sein Referat vorbereiten	gut Englisch
Stefans Schwester		Milch trinken		lesen	
ich					
Partnerin/ Partner					

Kapitel 5 (p. 190)

19. Sie und einige Freundinnen und Freunde haben im Lotto° gewonnen°. Mit dem Geld kaufen Sie Ihren Freunden und Familienmitgliedern° schöne Geschenke°. Wer bekommt was?

lottery / won
members of your family
presents

S1: Was schenkt Ralf seinen Eltern?
S2: Er schenkt ihnen zwei Wochen in Wien.

S2:

	Eltern	Schwester	Bruder	Melanie
Karsten			ncuc Skier	einen schönen Ring
Stefanie		einen CD-Player	ein Kassettendeck	
Ralf	zwei Wochen in Wien			eine Uhr
ich				
Partnerin/ Partner				

about

Kapitel 6 (p. 229)

18. Sprechen Sie mit Ihrer Partnerin/Ihrem Partner darüber°, was Evi, Dirk, Stefan, Silke, Sie und Ihre Partnerin/Ihr Partner am Wochenende gemacht haben.

S1: Was hat Evi gemacht?
S2: Evi ist spazieren gegangen und hat einen Roman gelesen.

S2:

	Evi	Dirk	Stefan	Silke	ich	Partnerin/Partner
im Restaurant essen						
spazieren gehen	X					
fernsehen			X			
Rad fahren						
faulenzen						
in die Kneipe gehen			X			
einen Roman lesen	X					
mit Freunden telefonieren			X			

Kapitel 7 (p. 244)

stellen auf: draw up

2. Sie und Ihre Partnerin/Ihr Partner stellen den Plan für die Hausarbeit am Wochenende auf°. Sagen Sie, was Julia, Lukas, Alex, Lena, Sie und Ihre Partnerin/Ihr Partner am Freitag und Samstag machen.

S1: Was macht Julia am Freitag?
S2: Sie kocht das Abendessen.

S2:

	Freitag	Samstag
Julia	das Abendessen kochen	
Lukas		Staub saugen
Alex	das Bad putzen	
Lena		Geschirr spülen
ich		
Partnerin/ Partner		

Kapitel 7 (p. 251)

2. Ihre Partnerin/Ihr Partner und verschiedene andere Leute haben einige neue Möbel und andere neue Sachen in ihren Wohnungen. Finden Sie heraus, was sie haben und in welchen Zimmern die Sachen sind.

S1: Was ist im Wohnzimmer und im Schlafzimmer von Herrn Becker neu?
S2: Im Wohnzimmer ist die Pflanze und im Schlafzimmer ist der Schrank neu.

S2:

	in der Küche	im Wohnzimmer	im Esszimmer	im Schlafzimmer
Herr Becker		Pflanze		Schrank
Frau Hauff	Kühlschrank			Nachttisch
Andrea		Sessel	Teppich	
Jens	Spülmaschine		Bild von den Großeltern	
ich				
Partnerin/ Partner				

Kapitel 8 (p. 295)

14. Sie und Ihre Partnerin/Ihr Partner sprechen über Geburtstagsgeschenke. Finden Sie erst heraus, was Ihre Freunde ihrer Familie und ihren Freunden schenken. Fragen Sie dann Ihre Partnerin/Ihren Partner, was sie/er ihrer/seiner Familie und ihren/seinen Freunden schenken möchte.

S1: Was möchte Susi ihren Eltern schenken?
S2: Sie möchte ihren Eltern einen neuen Computer schenken.

S2:

	Eltern	Schwester	Bruder	Freundin/Freund
Gerhard			ein neuer Krimi	ein schönes Bild
Susi	ein neuer Computer	ein roter Mantel		
Anna	ein guter CD-Player			ein gutes Buch
ich				
Partnerin/ Partner				

Kapitel 10   (p. 362)

4. Letzte Woche hatten Sie, Ihre Partnerin/Ihr Partner und einige andere Leute viel zu tun. Finden Sie heraus, wer was tun konnte, wollte, sollte und musste.

S1: Was wollte Adrian tun?
S2: Er wollte mehr Sport treiben.

S2:

	konnte	wollte	sollte	musste
Bettina	jeden Tag genug schlafen			die Fenster putzen
Adrian		mehr Sport treiben	seine Großeltern besuchen	
Frau Müller			mit ihren Freunden Golf spielen	bei ihrer Tochter Babysitting machen
Herr Meier	jeden Tag spazieren gehen	einen neuen Krimi lesen		
ich				
Partnerin/ Partner				

Kapitel 11   (p. 399)

12. Fragen Sie Ihre Partnerin/Ihren Partner und finden Sie heraus, was die folgenden Leute tun würden, wenn sie arbeitslos oder krank wären oder wenn sie mehr Zeit und viel Geld hätten.

S1: Was würde Herr Schäfer machen, wenn er mehr Zeit hätte?
S2: Wenn er mehr Zeit hätte, (dann) würde er seine Freunde besuchen.

S2:

	arbeitslos wäre	krank wäre	mehr Zeit hätte	viel Geld hätte
Frau Müller		zum Arzt gehen		
Herr Schäfer	eine neue Stelle suchen		seine Freunde besuchen	ein neues Auto kaufen
Susanne und Moritz		nichts essen		ihr Haus renovieren
ich				
Partnerin/Partner				

Appendix C

SUPPLEMENTARY WORD SETS

The following word lists will help you to increase the number of things you can say and write.

Audiovisual equipment

die **Boxen** (*pl.*)   speakers
die **Compact Disk**   compact disk
der **DVD-Recorder**   DVD recorder
der **Farbfernseher**   color television
der **Kassettenrecorder**   cassette recorder
der **Kopfhörer**   headphone
der **Lautsprecher**   loudspeaker
das **Mikrofon**   microphone
der **Plattenspieler**   record player
der **Radiorecorder**   cassette radio
der **Schwarzweißfernseher**   black-and-white
   television
die **Stereoanlage**   stereo system
das **Tonband, das Band**   tape
das **Tonbandgerät**   (reel-to-reel) tape recorder
der **Tuner**   tuner
der **Verstärker**   amplifier
der **Videorecorder**   video recorder (VCR)

Body care and hygiene

die **Haarbürste**   hair brush
der **Haartrockner, der Föhn**   hair dryer
das **Handtuch**   hand towel
das **Make-up**   makeup
der **Rasierapparat**   razor
die **Schere**   scissors
die **Seife**   soap
der **Spiegel**   mirror
das **Taschentuch**   handkerchief
der **Waschlappen**   washcloth
die **(elektrische) Zahnbürste**   (electric) toothbrush
die **Zahnpasta**   toothpaste

Buildings and other landmarks

die **Autobahnauffahrt (-ausfahrt)**   expressway
   on-ramp (off-ramp)
die **Bahnlinie**   railroad line
der **Bauernhof**   farm
die **Brücke**   bridge
die **Bundesstraße**   federal highway
die **Burg**   fortress
das **Denkmal**   monument
die **Fabrik**   factory

der **Fernsehturm**   TV tower
der **Friedhof**   cemetery
der **Funkturm**   radio and TV tower
der **Fußweg**   footpath
die **Kapelle**   chapel
die **Kirche**/der **Dom**/das **Münster**   church/cathedral
das **Kloster**   monastery
die **Mühle**   mill
das **Museum**   museum
das **Parkhaus**   parking garage
die **Polizei**   police
die **Post**   post office
die **Ruine**   ruin
das **Schloss**   castle
die **Tiefgarage**   underground garage
der **Tunnel**   tunnel

Chores

(das) **Abendessen vorbereiten, machen**   to prepare
   supper
Fenster putzen   to clean windows
den **Hund**/die **Katze füttern**   to feed the dog/cat
(die) **Wäsche bügeln**   to iron the wash, laundry
Wäsche, Kleider flicken   to mend clothes

(die) **Bäume beschneiden/pflanzen/fällen**   to
   prune/to plant/to cut down trees
das **Haus**/den **Zaun**/das **Boot streichen**   to paint the
   house/the fence/the boat
die **Hecke schneiden**   to trim the hedge
(das) **Holz sägen/spalten/hacken**   to saw/to split/to
   chop wood
das **Laub harken**   to rake leaves
(den) **Rasen mähen**   to mow the lawn
(den) **Schnee fegen, kehren/schippen**   to sweep/to
   shovel snow
(das) **Unkraut jäten**   to pull out weeds

Classroom objects

der **Filzstift**   felt-tip pen
die **Folie**   transparency
das **Klassenzimmer**   classroom
die **Kreide**   chalk
die **Landkarte;** die **Wandkarte**   map; wall map

der **Overheadprojektor** overhead projector
der **Papierkorb** wastebasket
das **Ringbuch** loose-leaf binder
der **Schwamm** sponge
das **Sprachlabor** language lab
die **Videokassette** videocassette
der **Videorecorder** video recorder (VCR)
die **(Wand)tafel** chalkboard

Clothing

das **Abendkleid** evening dress/gown
der **Anorak** jacket with hood, parka
der **Blazer** blazer
das/der **Blouson** lightweight men's jacket
    (windbreaker); lightweight women's blouse
die **Daunenjacke** down jacket
die **Kniestrümpfe** (*pl.*) knee socks
das **Kostüm** woman's suit
die **Latzhose** bib overalls
der **Mantel** coat
der **Overall** jumpsuit
der **Parka** parka
das **Polohemd** polo shirt
der **Regenmantel** raincoat
der **Rollkragenpullover** turtleneck
die **Sandalen** (*pl.*) sandals
der **Schal** scarf
der **Schlafanzug** pajamas
die **Sportschuhe** (*pl.*) athletic shoes
die **Stiefel** (*pl.*) boots
die **Strickjacke** (cardigan) sweater
das **Sweatshirt** sweatshirt
der **Trainingsanzug** sweat suit
die **Turnschuhe** (*pl.*) fitness/workout shoes
die **Weste** vest
der **Wintermantel** winter coat

Collectibles

sammeln to collect
alte Flaschen old bottles
der **Bierdeckel** beer coaster
Briefmarken stamps
Glas glass
das **Kuscheltier** stuffed animal
Münzen coins
Pflanzen (getrocknet) plants (dried)
Puppen dolls
Silber silver
Streichholzschachteln matchboxes
Zinn pewter

College majors

Amerikanistik American studies
Anglistik English language and literature

Betriebswirtschaft business administration
Biologie biology
Chemie chemistry
Chinesisch Chinese
Englisch English
Französisch French
Germanistik German language and literature
Informatik computer science
Ingenieurwesen engineering
Italienisch Italian
Japanisch Japanese
Jura law
Kommunikationswissenschaft communications
Kunstgeschichte art history
Marketing marketing
Medizin medicine
Pädagogik/Erziehungswissenschaften education
Philosophie philosophy
Physik physics
Politik political science
Psychologie psychology
Publizistik journalism
Rechnungswesen accounting
Religionswissenschaft/Theologie religion
Romanistik Romance languages and literature
Russisch Russian
Sozialkunde social studies
Sozialwissenschaften/Soziologie sociology
Spanisch Spanish
Sprachwissenschaft/Linguistik linguistics
Theaterwissenschaft theater studies
Volkswirtschaft economics

Colors

dunkel[blau] dark [blue]
hell[blau] light [blue]
lila lilac
orange orange
purpur purple
rosa pink

Computer terminology

der **Bildschirm** screen
der **Browser** browser
die **CD-ROM** CD-ROM
der **Cursor** cursor
die **Datei, -en** file
das **Diskettenlaufwerk** disk drive
downloaden/herunterladen to download
der **(Farb)Drucker** (color) printer
die **E-Mail** e-mail; **eine E-Mail schicken/senden** to
    send e-mail; **mailen** to e-mail
faxen to send a fax
die **Festplatte** hard drive

die **Floppy-Disk**   floppy disk
ein **Gbyte(GB)-Speicher**   a gigabyte memory
die **Homepage**   homepage
das **Internet**   Internet
klicken   to click (on)
kopieren   to copy
laden   to load
der **Laptop**   laptop computer
der **Laserdrucker**   laser printer
die **Mailbox**   mailbox
mit dem Computer arbeiten   to work on the
  computer
der **Monitor**   monitor
das **Netz**   network
das **Newsboard**   bulletin board
online   online
das **Passwort**   password
der **Personalcomputer, PC**   personal computer
scannen   to scan
die **Software; das Softwarepaket**   software; software
  package
speichern to store; **auf Diskette speichern**   to store
  on disk
die **Tastatur**   keyboard
die **Taste; die Funktionstaste**   key; function key
das **Textverarbeitungsprogramm**   word processing
  program
der **Tintenstrahldrucker**   inkjet printer
die **Website**   website

Directions

Asking directions

Wo ist [der Bahnhof]?   Where is the [train station]?
Wie weit ist es [zum Bahnhof]?   How far is it [to the
  train station]?
Wie komme ich am schnellsten [zum Bahnhof]?
  What is the quickest way [to the train station]?
Wo ist hier in der Nähe [ein Café]?   Is there [a café]
  around here?
Wissen Sie den Weg nach [Obersdorf]?   Do you
  know the way to [Obersdorf]?
**Wir wollen nach [Stuttgart]. Wie fahren wir am
  besten?**   We're going to [Stuttgart]. What is the
  best route?

Giving directions

Da fahren Sie am besten mit [der U-Bahn].   It's best
  if you go by [subway].
**Fahren Sie mit dem [Dreier]; Nehmen Sie den
  [Dreier].**   Take number [3] [bus].
Fahren Sie mit der [Drei]; Nehmen Sie die [Drei].
  Take number [3] [subway or streetcar].
**[Dort/An der Ecke/An der Kreuzung] ist die
  Haltestelle.**   [Over there/on the corner/at the
  intersection] is the [bus]stop.

An der [ersten] Kreuzung gehen Sie [rechts].   At the
  [first] intersection turn [right].
Gehen Sie die [erste] Straße [links].   Take the [first]
  street [to the left].
Gehen Sie geradeaus.   Go straight ahead.
Bei der Ampel biegen Sie [rechts] ab.   At the traffic
  light turn [right].

Family

der **Enkel**   grandson
die **Enkelin**   granddaughter
das **Enkelkind**   grandchild
der **Halbbruder**   half brother
die **Halbschwester**   half sister
die **Schwiegermutter**   mother-in-law
der **Schwiegervater**   father-in-law
der **Schwager**   brother-in-law
die **Schwägerin**   sister-in-law
Stief- (e.g., der **Stiefvater**)   step-

alleinerziehend   rearing alone (single parent)
alleinstehend   single
geschieden   divorced
ledig   single
verheiratet   married

Farewells and greetings

Ade.   'Bye. (*used in southern Germany and Austria*)
Auf Wiederhören.   Good-bye. (*on the telephone*)
Bis dann!   See you later.
Ciao.   So long.
Grüezi.   Hello. (*used in Switzerland*)
Grüß Gott.   Good-bye. Hello. (*used in southern
  Germany and Austria*)
Mach's gut.   Take it easy.
Servus.   Good-bye! Hello! (*used in southern Germany
  and Austria among friends*)

Film

der **Abenteuerfilm**   adventure movie
der **Actionfilm**   action movie
der **Horrorfilm**   horror film
der **Liebesfilm**   romance
der **Science-Fiction-Film**   science fiction movie

die **Außenaufnahme**   location shot
das **Drehbuch**   (film) script
der **Filmemacher/die Filmemacherin**   filmmaker
die **Filmfestspiele**(*pl.*)   film festival
die **Filmkomödie**   comedy film
die **Filmkritik**   movie criticism
die **(Film)leinwand**   (movie) screen
der **(Film)schauspieler/die (Film)schauspielerin**
  movie actor/actress

die **(Film)szene** (movie) scene
das **(Film)studio** (movie) studio
der **Kameramann**/die **Kamerafrau**
  cameraman/camerawoman
der **Produzent**/die **Produzentin** producer
der **Regisseur**/die **Regisseurin** director

Foods

Breakfast

das **Ei (weich gekocht)** egg (soft-boiled)
das **Graubrot** light rye bread
der **Honig** honey
der **Jogurt** yogurt
der **Kakao** cocoa
die **Marmelade** jam, marmalade
der **Pumpernickel** pumpernickel bread
die **Schokolade** hot chocolate
das **Schwarzbrot** dark rye break
der **Tomatensaft** tomato juice
das **Vollkornbrot** coarse, whole-grain bread
das **Weißbrot** white bread

Main meal

die **Suppe** soup

der **gemischte Salat** vegetable salad plate
der **grüne Salat** tossed (green) salad

der **Braten** roast
das **Kalbfleisch** veal
das **Kotelett** chop
das **Rindfleisch** beef
die **Roulade** roulade
das **Schnitzel** cutlet
das **Schweinefleisch** pork
der **Speck** bacon
der **Truthahn** turkey

die **Bohnen** (*pl.*) beans
der **Champignon** mushroom
die **Erbsen** (*pl.*) peas
die **Karotten, gelbe Rüben** (*pl.*) carrots
der **Kohl** cabbage
der **Mais** corn
die **(gefüllte) Paprikaschote** (stuffed) pepper
die **Pilze** (*pl.*) mushrooms
der **Reis** rice
das **Sauerkraut** sauerkraut
der **Spargel** asparagus
die **Zwiebel** onion

das **Gewürz, -e** spices
der **Pfeffer** pepper
das **Salz** salt
der **Zucker** sugar

Lunch/supper

die **(saure) Gurke** (half-sour) pickle
das **Spiegelei** fried egg
der **Tunfisch** tuna fish
die **Wurst**/der **Aufschnitt** sausage/cold cuts

Desserts and fruit

das **Eis** ice cream
der **Karamelpudding** caramel custard
das **Kompott** stewed fruit
die **Schokoladencreme** chocolate mousse
der **Vanillepudding** vanilla pudding

die **Sahne** cream
die **Schlagsahne** whipped cream

die **Ananas** pineapple
die **Erdbeeren** (*pl.*) strawberries
die **Himbeeren** (*pl.*) raspberries
die **Orange, Apfelsine** orange
der **Pfirsich** peach
die **Pflaume** plum
der **Rhabarber** rhubarb
die **Zitrone** lemon
die **Zwetsch(g)e** plum

Food preparation

backen to bake
braten to fry; to roast
grillen to grill
kochen to cook

Free time

angeln to fish
ausgehen to go out
basteln do-it-yourself projects
Blumen (z.B. Rosen, Dahlien, Lilien, Nelken) flowers
  (e.g., roses, dahlias, lilies, carnations)
campen to go camping
fotografieren to photograph
Freunde treffen to meet friends
die **Gartenarbeit** gardening
im Internet surfen to surf the Internet
Konzerte/Theater besuchen to attend concerts/plays
malen to paint
pflücken to pick (flowers)
reisen to travel
schreiben (Gedichte, Geschichten, Romane, Dramen)
  to write (poems, stories, novels, plays)
Video-, Computerspiele video/computer games
Videofilme ansehen to watch videotapes
zeichnen to draw
züchten to cultivate (plants)
zum Fitnesstraining gehen to go for a workout

Geographic terms

die **Anhöhe;** der **Hügel**   hill
der **Atlantik**   Atlantic (Ocean)
der **Bach**   brook
das **(Bundes)land**   (federal) state in Germany and Austria
der **(Bundes)staat**   (federal) state in the U.S.A.
die **Ebbe/**die **Flut**   low tide/high tide
der **Fluss**   river
das **Gebirge**   mountain range
die **Gezeiten** (*pl.*)   tides
der **Gipfel**   peak
der **Gletscher**   glacier
die **Insel**   island
der **Kanal**   canal; channel
der **Kanton**   canton (*Switzerland*)
die **Küste**   coast
das **Meer**   sea
der **Pazifik**   Pacific (Ocean)
der **See**   lake
die **See**   sea
der **Strand**   beach
das **Tal**   valley
der **Teich**   pond
das **Ufer**   shore
der **Wald**   woods
die **Wiese**   meadow
die **Wüste**   desert

Household

der **Backofen**   oven
die **Badewanne**   bathtub
die **Dusche**   shower
die **Mikrowelle**   microwave
das **Spülbecken/**die **Spüle**   kitchen sink
der **Trockner/**der **Wäschetrockner**   clothes dryer
das **Waschbecken**   washbasin

Jewelry

das **Armband**   bracelet
die **Halskette**   necklace
die **Kette**   chain
die **Ohrringe** (*pl.*)   earrings
der **Ring**   ring

Literature

die **Anthologie**   anthology
das **Drama**   drama, play
das **Gedicht**   poem
die **Illustrierte**   illustrated magazine
die **Kurzgeschichte**   short story
der **Roman**   novel
die **Zeitschrift**   magazine

der **Autor/**die **Autorin**   author
der **Dichter/**die **Dichterin**   poet
der **Dramatiker/**die **Dramatikerin**   dramatist
der **Schriftsteller/**die **Schriftstellerin**   writer

Music and theater

das **Musical**   musical comedy
die **Oper**   opera
die **Operette**   operetta
das **Theaterstück;** die **Tragödie;** die **Komödie;** der **Einakter**   play; tragedy; comedy; one-act play

der **Dirigent/**die **Dirigentin**   conductor
der **Regisseur/**die **Regisseurin**   director
der **Sänger/**die **Sängerin**   singer
der **Schauspieler/**die **Schauspielerin**   actor/actress
der **Zuschauer/**die **Zuschauerin**   spectator

der **Beifall,** der **Applaus**   applause
die **Bühne**   stage
das **Foyer**   hallway, lobby
die **Inszenierung**   mounting of a production
das **Orchester**   orchestra
die **Pause**   intermission
das **Programmheft**   program
die **Vorstellung**   performance

dirigieren   to conduct
proben   to rehearse
singen   to sing
üben   to practice

Musical instruments

das **Akkordeon**   accordion
die **Blockflöte**   recorder
die **Bratsche**   viola
das **Cello**   cello
das **Fagott**   bassoon
die **Flöte**   flute
die **Geige, Violine**   violin
die **Gitarre**   guitar
die **Harfe**   harp
die **Klarinette**   clarinet
das **Klavier**   piano
der **Kontrabass**   double bass
die **Oboe**   oboe
die **Orgel**   organ
die **Pauke**   kettle drum
die **Posaune** (**+ blasen**)   trombone (to play)
das **Saxophon**   saxophone
das **Schlagzeug**   percussion (instrument)

die **Trommel** drum
die **Trompete (+ blasen)** trumpet (to play)
die **Tuba (+ blasen)** tuba (to play)
das **(Wald)horn (+ blasen)** French horn (to play)

Personal qualities and characteristics

Adjectives for mood or personality

ausgezeichnet excellent
elend miserable
erstklassig first-rate
fantastisch fantastic
furchtbar horrible
kaputt worn out, tired
klasse terrific
miserabel miserable
nervös nervous
prima excellent
schrecklich dreadful
toll great
traurig sad

Adjectives for personality

fies disgusting; unfair
klug smart
lahm slow, sluggish
langsam slow
praktisch practical
schlau clever, smart
verrückt crazy

Physical description of people

blond blond
dick fat
dunkel brunette
fett fat
gut aussehend handsome
hässlich ugly
hübsch pretty
mager thin, skinny
normal normal
schwach weak
stark strong
vollschlank full-figured

Professions

ein **Angestellter**/eine **Angestellte** white-collar worker
der **Apotheker**/die **Apothekerin** pharmacist
der **Arzt**/die **Ärztin** physician
der **Betriebswirt**/die **Betriebswirtin** manager
der **Dolmetscher**/die **Dolmetscherin** interpreter
der **Elektriker**/die **Elektrikerin** electrician
der **Flugbegleiter**/die **Flugbegleiterin** flight attendant
der **Hochschullehrer**/die **Hochschullehrerin** college/university professor

der **Ingenieur**/die **Ingenieurin** engineer
der **Journalist**/die **Journalistin** journalist
der **Krankenpfleger**/die **Krankenschwester** nurse
der **Lehrer**/die **Lehrerin** teacher
der **Mechaniker**/die **Mechanikerin** mechanic
der **Musiker**/die **Musikerin** musician
der **Pfarrer**/die **Pfarrerin** clergyperson
der **Physiotherapeut**/die **Physiotherapeutin** physical therapist
der **Rechtsanwalt**/die **Rechtsanwältin** lawyer
der **Sekretär**/die **Sekretärin** secretary
der **Sozialarbeiter**/die **Sozialarbeiterin** social worker
der **Sozialpädagoge**/die **Sozialpädagogin** social worker (with college degree)
der **Tierarzt**/die **Tierärztin** veterinarian
der **Verkäufer**/die **Verkäuferin** salesperson
der **Volkswirt**/die **Volkswirtin** economist
der **Wissenschaftler**/die **Wissenschaftlerin** scientist
der **Zahnarzt**/die **Zahnärztin** dentist

Specialty shops

das **Blumengeschäft** florist shop
die **chemische Reinigung** dry cleaning shop
das **Eisenwarengeschäft** hardware store
das **Elektrogeschäft** appliance store
das **Feinkostgeschäft** delicatessen
das **Fotogeschäft** camera store
der **Juwelier** jeweler's; jewelry store
der **Kiosk** kiosk, stand
der **Klempner** plumber's shop
die **Konditorei** coffee and pastry shop
das **Möbelgeschäft** furniture store
der **Optiker** optician's shop
das **Schreibwarengeschäft** stationery store
das **Schuhgeschäft** shoe store
der **Schuhmacher;** der **Schuster** shoe repair (shop)
das **Sportgeschäft;** die **Sportausrüstungen** sporting goods store; sporting goods
der **Waschsalon** laundromat

Sports and games

das **Ballonfahren** ballooning
das **Billard** billiards
das **Bodybuilding** bodybuilding
die **Dame** checkers
das **Drachenfliegen** hang gliding
das **Eishockey** hockey
das **Fallschirmspringen** parachute jumping
der **Federball** badminton
das **Fitnesstraining** working out
der **Flipper** pinball machine; **ich flippere** I play the pinball machine
die **Gymnastik** calisthenics
der **Handball, Hallenhandball** handball

das **Hockey**   field hockey
auf dem **Hometrainer/Heimtrainer fahren**   to ride an exercise bike
das **Inlineskating**   inline skating
das **Krafttraining**   power training
die **Leichtathletik**   track and field
das **Mountainbiking**   mountain biking
der **Radsport,** das **Radfahren**   bicycling
das **Rollschuhlaufen**   roller skating
das **Schlittschuhlaufen**   ice skating
das **Segelfliegen**   glider flying
das **Skateboardfahren**   skateboarding
der **Skilanglauf**   cross-country skiing
das **Snowboarding**   snowboarding
das **Turnen**   gymnastics
der **Wasserball**   water polo
das **Windsurfen**   windsurfing

boxen   to box
fechten   to fence
jagen   to hunt
kegeln   to bowl
ringen   to wrestle
rudern   to row
schießen   to shoot
(hart) trainieren   to have a (good) workout

Table setting

die **Butterdose**   butter dish
der **Eierbecher**   egg cup
der **Esslöffel**   tablespoon
das **Gedeck**   table setting
das **Gericht**   dish (food)
die **Kaffeekanne**/die **Teekanne**   coffeepot/teapot
das **Milchkännchen**   creamer (small pitcher for cream or milk)
die **Schüssel**   bowl
die **Serviette**   napkin
die **Speise**   dish (food)
der **Teelöffel**   teaspoon
der **Teller**   plate
die **Untertasse**   saucer
die **Zuckerdose**   sugar bowl

Transportation

der **Anhänger**   trailer
der **Campingwagen,** der **Wohnwagen**   camper (pulled by a car)
der **Caravan**   camper (recreational vehicle)
der **Combi**   station wagon
die **Kutsche**   carriage
der **LKW (= Lastkraftwagen)**/der **Laster**   truck
der **Pferdewagen**   horse-drawn wagon
der **PKW (= Personenkraftwagen)**   passenger car

die **Bergbahn**   mountain railway; cable car
die **Eisenbahn**   train, railway
der **Güterzug**   freight train

das **Boot**   boat
das **Containerschiff**   container ship
die **Fähre**   ferry
der **Frachter**   freighter
das **Kanu**   canoe
das **Motorboot**   motorboat
der **Passagierdampfer**   passenger ship
das **Ruderboot**   rowboat
das **Segelboot**   sailboat
das **Segelschiff**   sailing ship
der **Tanker**   tanker

der **Hubschrauber**   helicopter
der **Jet**   jet
der **Jumbojet**   jumbo jet
das **(Propeller)flugzeug**   propeller plane
das **Raumschiff**   spaceship
das **Segelflugzeug**   glider; sailplane

TV programs

das **Familiendrama**   soap opera
die **Fernsehkomödie**   sitcom (situation comedy)
die **Fernsehserie**   series
die **Fernsehshow,** die **Unterhaltungsshow**   game show
der **Krimi**   detective or crime drama
die **Nachrichten** (*pl.*)   news
die **Quizsendung,** das **Fernsehquiz**   quiz show
die **Seifenoper**   soap opera
der **Spielfilm**   feature (film)
die **Sportschau**   sports program
der **Zeichentrickfilm**   cartoon

Weather expressions

der **Blitz**   lightning
Celsius   centigrade
der **Donner**   thunder
das **Gewitter**   thunderstorm
der **Hagel**   hail
das **Hoch**   high-pressure system
die **Kaltfront**   cold front
der **Luftdruck**   air pressure
der **Nebel**   fog
der **Niederschlag**   precipitation
der **Nieselregen**   drizzle
der **Schauer**   shower
der **Schneefall**   snowfall
der **Sprühregen**   drizzle
der **Tau**   dew

die **Temperatur**   temperature
das **Tief**   low-pressure system
die **Warmfront**   warm front
der **Wetterbericht**   weather report; **Was steht im Wetterbericht?**   What's the weather report?
die **Wettervorhersage**   weather forecast
die **Windrichtung**   wind direction

bedeckt   overcast
bewölkt   cloudy; **stark bewölkt**   very cloudy
eisig   icy cold

heiter   fair
klar   clear, cloudless
neb(e)lig   foggy
schwül   humid
stürmisch   stormy
wolkenlos   cloudless
wolkig   cloudy

Es gießt (in Strömen).   It's pouring.
Es regnet Bindfäden.   It's raining cats and dogs.
Es ist nasskalt.   It's damp and cold.

Appendix D

SUPPLEMENTARY EXPRESSIONS

1. Expressing skepticism

Ist das dein Ernst?   Are you serious?
Meinst/Denkst/Glaubst/Findest du? Wirklich? Meinst du das wirklich?   Do you think so? Really? Do you really mean that?
Das ist ja komisch/eigenartig/merkwürdig.   That's funny/strange.
Irgendetwas stimmt hier nicht.   Something's wrong here.
Ist das wahr?   Is that true?
Woher weißt du das? Wo/Von wem hast du das gehört?   How do you know that? Where/From whom did you hear that?
Hoffentlich.   I hope so.
Vielleicht.   Maybe.

2. Expressing insecurity or doubt

Das ist unwahrscheinlich.   That's unlikely.
Das glaub' ich nicht.   I don't believe that.
Das ist zweifelhaft.   That's doubtful.
Das kann nicht sein.   That can't be.

3. Expressing annoyance

Quatsch! / Unsinn! / Blödsinn!   Nonsense!
Hör mal.   Listen.
Geh.   Go on.
(Das ist doch) nicht zu glauben.   (That is) not to be believed.
(Das ist) unerhört/unglaublich.   (That is) unheard of/unbelievable.
Das tut/sagt man nicht.   One doesn't do/say such a thing.
Das kannst du doch nicht machen/sagen.   You can't do/say that.
Frechheit!   The nerve!; She's/He's/You've got some nerve!
Also komm.   Come on.

4. Expressing perplexity or helplessness

Ich weiß wirklich nicht, was ich machen soll/kann.   I really don't know what I should/can do.
Ich will ja, aber es geht nicht.   I want to but it won't work.
Ich kann nicht.   I can't.
Ich weiß nicht.   I don't know.
Keine Ahnung.   No idea.

5. Stalling for time

Also./Na ja./Ja nun.   Well./Well, of course./Well, now.
hmmmmmmmmmm   hmmmmmmmmmm
Lass mich mal nachdenken.   Let me think about it.
Das kann ich so (auch) nicht sagen.   I can't say that (either).
Da muss ich erst mal überlegen.   Let me think.

6. Being noncommital

(Das ist ja) interessant.   (That is) interesting.
hmmmmmmmmmm   hmmmmmmmmmm
Wirklich?   Really?
Ach ja?   Oh really?
So so.   Oh yes, I see.

7. Expressing good wishes

Gesundheit!   Bless you!
Guten Appetit.   Enjoy your meal.
Prost! / Auf Ihr Wohl! / Zum Wohl!   Cheers! / To your health!
Herzlichen Glückwunsch!   Congratulations!
Herzlichen Glückwunsch zum Geburtstag!   Happy birthday!
Gute Besserung.   Get well soon.
Viel Glück!   Good luck!
Viel Vergnügen/Spaß!   Have fun!
Alles Gute!   All the best! Best wishes!

8. Courtesy expressions

Bitte (sehr/schön).   Please.
Danke (sehr/schön).   Thanks (very much).
Keine Ursache.   Don't mention it.

9. Saying "you're welcome"

Bitte (sehr/schön).   You're (very) welcome.
Gern geschehen.   Glad to do it.
Nichts zu danken.   Don't mention it.

10. Expressing surprise

Ach nein!   Oh no!
(Wie) ist das (nur) möglich!   (How) is that possible?
Das hätte ich nicht gedacht.   I wouldn't have thought that.
Das ist ja prima/toll/klasse/stark/Wahnsinn!   That's great/fantastic/terrific, etc.!

(Das ist ja) nicht zu glauben! (That's) unbelievable!
Kaum zu glauben. Hard to believe.
Um Himmels willen! For heaven's sake!
Sag' bloß. You don't say.

11. Inquiring about an opinion

Wie findest du das? / Was hältst du davon? What do
you think of that?
Wie siehst du das? How do you see that?
Bist du dafür oder dagegen? Are you for it or against
it?
Findest du es gut (nicht gut), dass... Do you find it
good (bad), that . . .

12. Expressing agreement (and disagreement)

Natürlich (nicht)! / Selbstverständlich (nicht)!
Naturally, of course (not)!
Klar. Sure.
Ja, gern. Yes, gladly.
Na gut. Well, OK.
Warum denn nicht? Why not?
Das kann (nicht) sein. That can(not) be.
(Das) stimmt (nicht). (That's) (not) right.
Richtig. / Falsch. Right. / Wrong.
Kein Problem. No problem.
Ich glaube ja (nicht). I (don't) think so.
Es geht. It'll work.
Ich sehe das ganz anders. I see it differently.
Das finde ich auch/nicht. I think so, too./I don't
think so.
Genau. / Eben. Exactly. / That's right.
Du hast Recht. You're right.

13. Responding to requests

Bitte. / Selbstverständlich. / Natürlich. / Klar. Glad
to. / Of course. / Naturally.
Gern. / Machen wir. / Mit Vergnügen. Glad to. /
We'll do it. / With pleasure.
(Es tut mir Leid, aber) das geht nicht. (I'm sorry
but) that won't work.
Kein Problem. No problem.
Sicher. Sure.

14. Expressing regret

(Das) tut mir Leid. I'm sorry.
(Es) tut mir Leid, dass [ich nicht kommen kann].
I'm sorry [I can't come].
Leider [kann ich morgen nicht]. Unfortunately [I
can't tomorrow].
(Es) geht leider nicht. That won't work,
unfortunately.
Schade. That's a shame. / Too bad.
(So ein) Pech. That's tough luck.

15. Excusing oneself

Bitte entschuldigen Sie mich. Please excuse me. / I
beg your pardon.
Entschuldigung. / Verzeihung. / Entschuldigen Sie.
Excuse (pardon) me.
Es tut mir Leid, aber... I'm sorry, but . . .
Das habe ich nicht so gemeint. I didn't mean it that
way.
Das wollte ich nicht. I didn't intend that.

16. Expressing indifference

(Das) ist mir egal. That's all the same to me.
Das macht mir nichts aus. It doesn't matter to me.
Das ist nicht meine Sorge. That's not my problem.
Macht nichts. Doesn't matter.
Das ist mir Wurscht. I couldn't care less.
Ich habe nichts dagegen. / Meinetwegen. I have
nothing against it.

17. Expressing admiration

Ach, wie schön! / Klasse! Oh, how nice! / Great! /
Terrific!
**Fantastisch! / Toll! / Super! / Stark! / Irre! / Einsame
Spitze!** Fantastic! / Great! / Super! / Incredible! /
Really great!, etc.
Erstklassig! / Ausgezeichnet! First-rate! / Excellent!
Das ist aber nett [von Ihnen/dir]. That's really nice
[of you].

18. Expressing rejection

(Das ist) schrecklich! (That is) awful!
Das ärgert mich. That annoys me.
Der/Das/Die gefällt mir (gar) nicht. I don't like
him/that/her (at all).
Ich mag sie/ihn nicht. I don't like her/him.
Ich kann sie/ihn nicht leiden. I don't like her/him.
Ich finde das schlecht/langweilig. I think that is
bad/boring.
Ich finde sie/ihn nicht sympathisch/nett. I don't
find her/him likeable/nice.

19. Expressing joy and pleasure

Wir freuen uns auf [seinen Besuch/die Ferien].
We're looking forward to [his visit/our vacation].
Wir sind froh (darüber), dass [er wieder arbeitet].
We're happy (about the fact) that [he's working
again].
Es freut mich, dass [sie gekommen ist]. I'm happy
that [she has come].
Das tun/kochen/essen wir gern. We like to
do/cook/eat that.
Das macht mir/uns Spaß. I/We enjoy that. / That's
fun.

20. Expressing sadness

Ach (nein)! Oh (no)!
Wie schrecklich! How awful/horrible.
Mein Gott! / O je! My God!
Ich bin sehr traurig darüber. I am very unhappy about that.
Ich bin deprimiert/frustriert. I am depressed/frustrated.

21. Expressing sympathy

Schade. Too bad.
du Armer / du Arme you poor thing
Das ist ja dumm/blöd/ärgerlich/schade. That's dumb/stupid/annoying/too bad.
Was hast du denn? What's the matter? What's wrong (with you)?
Das verstehe ich nicht. I don't understand that.
Das tut mir aber Leid für dich. I am sorry for you.
Dass dir das passieren muss! How awful for you!

22. Making requests

Hättest du/Hätten Sie Lust [mitzukommen]? Would you like [to come along]?
Hättest du/Hätten Sie Zeit [uns zu besuchen]? Would you have time [to come see us]?
Ich hätte gern [ein Pfund Äpfel]. I'd like [a pound of apples].
Könntest du/Könnten Sie [mein Auto reparieren]? Could you [repair my car]?
Würdest du/Würden Sie mir bitte helfen? Would you please help me?
Hättest du/Hätten Sie etwas dagegen? Would you mind?
Dürfte ich [ein Stück Kuchen haben]? May I/Is it OK if I [have a piece of cake]?
Macht es dir/Ihnen etwas aus? Do you mind?
Sei/Seien Sie so gut. Be so kind.
Ist es dir/Ihnen recht? Is it OK with you?

23. Asking for favors

Könntest du/Könnten Sie mir einen Gefallen tun und [mich mitnehmen]? Could you do me a favor and [take me along]?
Ich hätte eine Bitte: könntest/würdest du (könnten/würden Sie) [mich mitnehmen]? I have a request: could/would you [take me along]?

24. Making surmises

Ich glaube schon. / Ich denke ja. I think so.
Das dürfte/könnte wahr/richtig sein. That might/could be true/right.
Wahrscheinlich [stimmt das]. Probably [that's right].
Ich bin ziemlich sicher, dass [er das gesagt hat]. I'm quite sure that [he said that].
Ich nehme an, dass [das stimmt]. I assume that [that's right].
Das scheint [nicht zu stimmen]. That appears [not to be right].

25. Expressing expectation

Hoffentlich. / Hoffentlich [kommt sie]. I hope. / I hope [she comes].
Ich hoffe (es) (sehr). I hope (so) (very much).
Ich freue mich auf [die Ferien]. I'm looking forward to [my vacation].
Ich kann es kaum erwarten. I can hardly wait.

26. Expressing fears

Ich befürchte/Ich fürchte, dass [sie nicht kommt]. I'm afraid [she's not coming].
Ich habe Angst [nach Hause zu gehen]. I'm afraid [to go home].
Ich habe Angst vor [dem Hund]. I'm afraid of [the dog].
Das ist mir unheimlich. It scares me.

27. Giving advice

Ich schlage vor, dass [wir um acht anfangen]. I suggest that [we begin at eight].
Das würde ich dir/Ihnen (nicht) raten. I would (not) advise that.
Das würde ich (nicht) machen/sagen. I would (not) do/say that.
An [deiner/ihrer/seiner] Stelle würde ich [zu Hause bleiben]. If I were [you/her/him], I'd [stay home].

28. Correcting misunderstandings

Das habe ich nicht so gemeint. I didn't mean it that way.
Das habe ich nur aus Spaß gesagt. I only said that in fun/jest. I was only kidding.
Das habe ich nicht ernst/im Ernst gemeint. I wasn't serious.

Appendix E

PRONUNCIATION AND WRITING GUIDE

The best way to learn to pronounce German is to imitate speakers of German, as completely and accurately as you can. Some of the sounds of German are just like those of English and will cause you no trouble. Others may sound strange to you at first and be more difficult for you to pronounce. With practice, you will be able to master the unfamiliar sounds as well as the familiar ones.

Though imitation is the one indispensable way of learning to pronounce any language, there are two things that should help you in your practice. First, you should learn how to manipulate your vocal organs so as to produce distinctly different sounds. Second, you should learn to distinguish German sounds from the English sounds that you might be tempted to substitute for them.

As you learn to pronounce German, you will also start to read and write it. Here a word of caution is in order. The writing system of German (or any language) was designed for people who already know the language. No ordinary writing system was ever designed to meet the needs of people who are learning a language. Writing is a method of reminding us on paper of things that we already know how to say; it is not a set of directions telling us how a language should be pronounced.

This Pronunciation and Writing Guide will give you some help with the German sound system. Further practice with specific sounds will be given in the Lab Manual section of the *Arbeitsheft.*

Stress

Nearly all native German words are stressed on the "stem syllable," that is, the first syllable of the word, or the first syllable that follows an unstressed prefix.

Without prefix		With unstressed prefix	
den′ken	to think	**beden′ken**	to think over
kom′men	to come	**entkom′men**	to escape

In the end vocabulary of this book, words that are not stressed on the first syllable are marked. A stress mark follows the stressed syllable.

German Vowels

German has short vowels, long vowels, and diphthongs. The short vowels are clipped, and are never "drawled" as they often are in English. The long vowels are monophthongs ("steady-state" vowels) and not diphthongs (vowels that "glide" from one vowel sound toward another). The diphthongs are similar to English diphthongs except that they, like short vowels, are never drawled. Compare the English and German vowels in the words below.

English (with off-glide)	German (without off-glide)
bait	**Beet**
vein	**wen**
tone	**Ton**
boat	**Boot**

Spelling as a reminder of vowel length

By and large, the German spelling system clearly indicates the difference between long and short vowels. German uses the following types of signals:

1. A vowel is long if it is followed by an **h** (unpronounced): **ihn, stahlen, Wahn.**
2. A vowel is long if it is double: **Beet, Saat, Boot.**
3. A vowel is generally long if it is followed by one consonant: **den, kam, Ofen, Hut.**
4. A vowel is generally short if it is followed by two or more consonants: **denn, Sack, offen, Busch, dick.**

Pronunciation of vowels

Long and short a

Long [ā] = aa, ah, a (**Saat, Bahn, kam, Haken**): like English *a* in *spa,* but with wide-open mouth and no off-glide.

Short [a] = a (**satt, Bann, Kamm, Hacken**): between English *o* in *hot* and *u* in *hut.*

Long and short e

Long [ē] = e, ee, eh, ä, äh (**wen, Beet, fehlen, gähnt**): like *ay* in English *say,* but with exaggeratedly spread lips and no off-glide.

Short [e] = e, ä (**wenn, Bett, fällen, Gent**): Like *e* in English *bet,* but more clipped.

Unstressed [ə] *and* [ər]

Unstressed [ə] = e (**bitte, endet, gegessen**): like English *e* in *begin, pocket.*

Unstressed [ər] = er (**bitter, ändert, vergessen**): When the sequence [ər] stands at the end of a word, before a consonant, or in an unstressed prefix, it sounds much like the final *-a* in English *sofa;* the **-r** is not pronounced.

Long and short i

Long [ī] = ih, ie (**ihn, Miete, liest**): like *ee* in *see,* but with exaggeratedly spread lips and no off-glide.

Short [i] = (**in, Mitte, List**): like *i* in *mitt,* but more clipped.

Long and short o

Long [ō] = oh, o, oo (**Sohne, Ofen, Tone, Moos**): like English *o* in *so,* but with exaggeratedly rounded lips and no off-glide.

Short [o] = o (**Most, Tonne, offen, Sonne**): like English *o* often heard in the word *gonna.*

Long and short u

Long [ū] = uh, u (**Huhne, schuf, Buße, Mus**): like English *oo* in *too,* but with more lip rounding and no off-glide.

Short [u] = u (**Hunne, Schuft, Busse, muss**): like English *u* in *bush,* but more clipped.

Diphthongs

[ai] = ei, ai, ay (**nein, Kaiser, Meyer, Bayern**): like English *ai* in *aisle,* but clipped and not drawled.

[oi] = eu, äu (**neun, Häuser**): like English *oi* in *coin,* but clipped and not drawled.

[au] = au (**laut, Bauer**): like English *ou* in *house,* but clipped and not drawled.

Long and short ü

Long [ü] = üh, ü (**Bühne, kühl, lügen**): To pronounce long [ü], keep your tongue in the same position as for long [ī], but round your lips as for long [ū].

Short [ü] = ü (**Küste, müssen, Bünde**): To pronounce short [ü], keep your tongue in the same position as for short [i], but round your lips as for short [u].

Long and short ö

Long [ö] = ö, öh (**Höfe, Löhne, Flöhe**): To pronounce long [ö], keep your tongue in the same position as for long [ē], but round your lips as for long [ō].

Short [ö] = ö (**gönnt, Hölle, Knöpfe**): To pronounce short [ö], keep your tongue in the same position as for short [e], but round your lips as for short [o].

Consonants

Most of the German consonant sounds are similar to English consonant sounds. There are four major differences.

1. German has two consonant sounds without an English equivalent: [x] and [ç]. Both are spelled **ch**.
2. The German pronunciation of [l] and [r] differs from the English pronunciation.
3. German uses sounds familiar to English speakers in unfamiliar combinations, such as [ts] in an initial position: **zu**.
4. German uses unfamiliar spellings of familiar sounds.

The letters b, d, *and* g

The letters **b**, **d**, and **g** generally represent the same consonant sounds as in English. German **g** is usually pronounced like English *g* in *go*. When the letters **b**, **d**, and **g** occur at the end of a syllable, or before an **s** or **t**, they are pronounced like [p], [t], and [k] respectively.

b = [b] (**Diebe, gaben**)
b = [p] (**Dieb, Diebs, gab, gabt**)

d = [d] (**Lieder, laden**)
d = [t] (**Lied, Lieds, lud, lädt**)

g = [g] (**Tage, sagen**)
g = [k] (**Tag, Tags, sag, sagt**)

The letter j

The letter **j** (**ja, jung**) represents the sound *y* as in English *yes.*

The letter l

English [l] typically has a "hollow" sound to it. When an American pronounces [l], the tongue is usually "spoon-shaped": It is high at the front (with the tongue tip pressed against the gum ridge above the upper teeth), hollowed out in the middle, and high again at the back. German [l] (**viel, Bild, laut**) never has the "hollow" quality. It is pronounced with the tongue tip against the gum ridge, as in English, but with the tongue kept flat from front to back. Many Americans use this "flat" [l] in such words as *million, billion,* and *William.*

The letter r

German [r] can be pronounced in two different ways. Some German speakers use a "tongue-trilled [r]," in which the tip of the tongue vibrates against

Appendix E

the gum ridge above the upper teeth—like the *rrr* that children often use in imitation of a telephone bell or police whistle. Most German speakers, however, use a "uvular [r]," in which the back of the tongue is raised toward the uvula, the little droplet of skin hanging down in the back of the mouth.

You will probably find it easiest to pronounce the uvular [r] if you make a gargling sound before the sound [a]: ra. Keep the tip of your tongue down and out of the way; the tip of the tongue plays no role in the pronunciation of the gargled German [r].

r = [r] + vowel (**Preis, Jahre, Rose**): When German [r] is followed by a vowel, it has the full "gargled" sound.

r = vocalized [r] (**Tier, Uhr, Tür**): When German [r] follows a vowel, it tends to become "vocalized," that is, pronounced like the vowel-like glide found in the final syllable of British English *hee-uh* (here), *thay-uh* (there).

The letters s, ss, ß

s = [s] (**sehen, lesen, Gänse**): Before a vowel, the letter **s** represents the sound [s], like English *z* in *zoo*.

s = [s] (**das, Hals, fast**): In most other positions, the letter **s** represents the sound [s], like English [s] in *so*.

[s] = **ss, ß** (**wissen, Flüsse, weiß, beißen, Füße**): The letters **ss** and **ß** (called **ess-tsett**) are both pronounced [s]. The double letters **ss** signal the fact that the preceding vowel is short, and the single letter **ß** signals the fact that the preceding vowel is long (or a diphthong).

The letter v

v = [f] (**Vater, viel**): The letter **v** is generally pronounced like English [f] as in *father*.

v = [v] (**Vase, November**): In words of foreign origin, the letter **v** is pronounced [v].

The letter w

w = [v] (**Wein, Wagen, wann**): Many centuries ago, German **w** (as in **Wein**) represented the sound [w], like English *w* in *wine*. Over the centuries, German **w** gradually changed from [w] to [v], so that today the **w** of German **Wein** represents the sound [v], like the *v* of English *vine*. German no longer has the sound [w]. The letter **w** always represents the sound [v].

The letter z

z = final and initial [ts] (**Kranz, Salz, Zahn, zu**): The letter **z** is pronounced [ts], as in English *rats*.

In English, the [ts] sound occurs only at the end of a syllable; in German, [ts] occurs at the beginning as well as at the end of a syllable.

The consonant clusters gn, kn, pf, qu

To pronounce the consonant clusters **gn, kn, pf, qu** correctly, you need to use familiar sounds in unfamiliar ways.

gn: pronunciation is [gn]
kn: pronunciation is [kn]

pf: pronunciation is [pf]
qu: pronunciation is [kv]

gn = [gn-] (**Gnade, Gnom**)
kn = [kn-] (**Knie, Knoten**)
pf = [pf-] (**Pfanne, Pflanze**)
qu = [kv-] (**quälen, Quarz, quitt**)

The combination ng

ng = [ŋ] (**Finger, Sänger, Ding**): The combination **ng** is pronounced [ŋ], as in English *singer*. It does not contain the sound [g] that is used in English *finger*.

The combinations sch, sp, and st

sch = [š] (**Schiff, waschen, Fisch**)
sp = [šp] (**Spaten, spinnen, Sport**)
st = [št] (**Stein, Start, stehlen**)

Many centuries ago, both German and English had the combinations **sp, st, sk,** pronounced [sp], [st], [sk]. Then two changes took place. First, in both languages, [sk] changed to [š], as in English *ship, fish,* and German **Schiff, Fisch.**

Second, in German only, word-initial [sp-] and [st-] changed to [šp-] and [št-]. The *sp* in English *spin* is pronounced [sp-], but in German **spinnen** it is pronounced [šp-]. The *st* in English *still* is pronounced [st-], but in German **still** it is pronounced [št-]. Today, German **sch** always represents [š] (like English *sh*, but with more rounded lips); **sp-** and **st-** at the beginning of German words or word stems represent [šp-] and [št-].

The letters ch

The letters **ch** are usually pronounced either [x] or [ç]. The [x] sound is made in the back of the mouth where [k] is produced.

If you have ever heard a Scotsman talk about "Lo*ch* Lomond," you have heard the sound [x]. The sound [x] is produced by forcing air through a narrow opening between the back of the tongue and the back of the roof of the mouth (the soft palate). Notice the difference between [k], where the breath stream is stopped in this position and [x], where the breath stream is forced through a narrow opening in this position.

To practice the [x] sound, keep the tongue below the lower front teeth and produce a gentle gargling sound, without moving the tongue or lips. Be careful not to substitute the [k] sound for the [x] sound.

ck, k = [k] (**Sack, pauken, Pocken, buk**)
ch = [x] (**Sache, hauchen, pochen, Buch**)

The [ç] sound is similar to that used by many Americans for the *h* in such words as *hue, huge, human.* It is produced by forcing air through a narrow opening between the front of the tongue and the front of the roof of the mouth (the hard palate). Notice the difference between [š], where the breath stream is forced through a wide opening in this position and the lips are rounded, and [ç], where the breath stream is forced through a narrow opening in this position and the lips are spread.

To practice the [ç] sound, round your lips for [š], then use a slit-shaped opening and spread your lips. Be careful not to substitute the [š] sound for [ç].

sch = [š] (**misch, fischt, Kirsche, Welsch, Menschen**)
ch = [ç] (**mich, ficht, Kirche, welch, München**)

Note two additional points about the pronunciation of **ch**:
1. **ch** = [x] occurs only after the vowels **a, o, u, au.**
2. **ch** = [ç] occurs only after the other vowels and **n, l,** and **r.**

The combination **chs**
chs = [ks] (**sechs, Fuchs, Weichsel**)
chs = [xs] or [çs] (**des Brauchs, du rauchst, des Teichs**)

The fixed combination **chs** is pronounced [ks] in words such as **sechs, Fuchs,** and **Ochse.** Today, **chs** is pronounced [xs] or [çs] only when the **s** is an ending or part of an ending (**ich rauche, du rauchst; der Teich, des Teichs**).

The suffix **-ig**
-ig = [iç] (**Pfennig, König, schuldig**): In final position, the suffix **-ig** is pronounced [iç] as in German **ich.**

-ig = [ig] (**Pfennige, Könige, schuldige**): In all other positions, the **g** in **-ig** has the sound [g] as in English *go.*

The glottal stop

English uses the glottal stop as a device to avoid running together words and parts of words; it occurs only before vowels. Compare the pairs of words below. The glottal stop is indicated with an *.

an *ice man	a nice man
not *at *all	not a tall
an *ape	a nape

German also uses the glottal stop before vowels to avoid running together words and parts of words.

Wie *alt *ist *er?
be*antworten

The glottal stop is produced by closing the glottis (the space between the vocal cords), letting air pressure build up from below, and then suddenly opening the glottis, resulting in a slight explosion of air. Say the word *uh-uh*, and you will notice a glottal stop between the first and second *uh.*

The Writing System

German punctuation

Punctuation marks in German are generally used as in English. Note the following major differences.

1. In German, dependent clauses are set off by commas.
   German   Der Mann, der hier wohnt, ist alt.
   English   The man who lives here is old.

2. In German, independent clauses, with two exceptions, are set off by commas. Clauses joined by **und** (*and*) or **oder** (*or*) need not be set off by commas, unless the writer so chooses for the sake of clarity.
   German   Robert singt und Karin tanzt. *or*
              Robert singt, und Karin tanzt.
   English   Robert is singing and Karin is dancing.

3. In German, a comma is not used in front of **und** in a series as is often done in English.
   German   Robert, Ilse und Karin singen.
   English   Robert, Ilse, and Karin are singing.

4. In German, opening quotation marks are placed below the line.

German Er fragte: „Wie heißt du?"

English He asked, "What is your name?"

Note that a colon is used in German before a direct quotation.

5. In German, commas stand outside of quotation marks.

German „Meyer", antwortete sie.

English "Meyer," she answered.

German capitalization

1. In German, all nouns are capitalized.

German Wie alt ist der Mann?

English How old is the man?

2. Adjectives are not capitalized, even if they denote nationality.

German Ist das ein amerikanisches Auto?

English Is that an American car?

3. The pronoun **ich** is not capitalized, unlike its English counterpart *I*.

German Morgen spiele ich um zwei Uhr Tennis.

English Tomorrow I am playing tennis at two o'clock.

Appendix F

GRAMMATICAL TABLES

1. Personal pronouns

Nominative	ich	du	er	es	sie	wir	ihr	sic	Sie
Accusative	mich	dich	ihn	es	sie	uns	euch	sie	Sie
Dative	mir	dir	ihm	ihm	ihr	uns	euch	ihnen	ihnen

2. Reflexive pronouns

	ich	du	er/es/sie	wir	ihr	sie	Sie
Accusative	mich	dich	sich	uns	euch	sich	sich
Dative	mir	dir	sich	uns	euch	sich	sich

3. Interrogative pronouns

Nominative	wer	was
Accusative	wen	was
Dative	wem	
Genitive	wessen	

4. Relative and demonstrative pronouns

	Masculine	Neuter	Feminine	Plural
Nominative	der	das	die	die
Accusative	den	das	die	die
Dative	dem	dem	der	denen
Genitive	dessen	dessen	deren	deren

5. Definite articles

	Masculine	Neuter	Feminine	Plural
Nominative	der	das	die	die
Accusative	den	das	die	die
Dative	dem	dem	der	den
Genitive	des	des	der	der

6. *Der*-words

	Masculine	Neuter	Feminine	Plural
Nominative	dieser	dieses	diese	diese
Accusative	diesen	dieses	diese	diese
Dative	diesem	diesem	dieser	diesen
Genitive	dieses	dieses	dieser	dieser

Common **der**-words are **dieser, jeder, mancher, solcher,** and **welcher.**

7. Indefinite articles and *ein*-words

	Masculine	Neuter	Feminine	Plural
Nominative	ein	ein	eine	keine
Accusative	einen	ein	eine	keine
Dative	einem	einem	einer	keinen
Genitive	eines	eines	einer	keiner

The **ein**-words include **kein** and the possessive adjectives: **mein, dein, sein, ihr, unser, euer, ihr,** and **Ihr.**

8. Plural of nouns

Type	Plural signal	Singular	Plural	Notes
1	ø (no change)	das Zimmer	**die Zimmer**	Masculine and neuter nouns
	⁝ (umlaut)	der Garten	**die Gärten**	ending in **el, -en, -er**
2	-e	der Tisch	**die Tische**	
	⁝e	der Stuhl	**die Stühle**	
3	-er	das Bild	**die Bilder**	Stem vowel **e** or **i** cannot take umlaut
	⁝er	das Buch	**die Bücher**	Stem vowel **a, o, u,** takes umlaut
4	-en	die Uhr	**die Uhren**	
	-n	die Lampe	**die Lampen**	
	-nen	die Freundin	**die Freundinnen**	
5	-s	das Radio	**die Radios**	Mostly foreign words

9. Masculine *N*-nouns

	Singular	Plural
Nominative	der Herr	die Herren
Accusative	den Herrn	die Herren
Dative	dem Herrn	den Herren
Genitive	des Herrn	der Herren

Some other masculine N-nouns are **der Journalist, der Junge, der Komponist, der Kollege, der Mensch, der Nachbar, der Pilot, der Präsident, der Soldat, der Student, der Tourist.**

A few masculine N-nouns add **-ns** in the genitive; **der Name → des Namens.**

10. Preceded adjectives

	Masculine	Neuter	Feminine	Plural
Nom.	der **alte** Tisch ein **alter** Tisch	das **alte** Buch ein **altes** Buch	die **alte** Uhr eine **alte** Uhr	die **alten** Bilder keine **alten** Bilder
Acc.	den **alten** Tisch einen **alten** Tisch	das **alte** Buch ein **altes** Buch	die **alte** Uhr eine **alte** Uhr	die **alten** Bilder keine **alten** Bilder
Dat.	dem **alten** Tisch einem **alten** Tisch	dem **alten** Buch einem **alten** Buch	der **alten** Uhr einer **alten** Uhr	den **alten** Bildern keinen **alten** Bildern
Gen.	des **alten** Tisches eines **alten** Tisches	des **alten** Buches eines **alten** Buches	der **alten** Uhr einer **alten** Uhr	der **alten** Bilder keiner **alten** Bilder

11. Unpreceded adjectives

	Masculine	Neuter	Feminine	Plural
Nominative	kalter Wein	kaltes Bier	kalte Milch	alte Leute
Accusative	kalten Wein	kaltes Bier	kalte Milch	alte Leute
Dative	kaltem Wein	kaltem Bier	kalter Milch	alten Leuten
Genitive	kalten Weines	kalten Bieres	kalter Milch	alter Leute

12. Nouns declined like adjectives

◼ *Nouns preceded by definite articles or* **der**-*words*

	Masculine	Neuter	Feminine	Plural
Nominative	der Deutsche	das Gute	die Deutsche	die Deutschen
Accusative	den Deutschen	das Gute	die Deutsche	die Deutschen
Dative	dem Deutschen	dem Guten	der Deutschen	den Deutschen
Genitive	des Deutschen	des Guten	der Deutschen	der Deutschen

◼ *Nouns preceded by indefinite articles or* **ein**-*words*

	Masculine	Neuter	Feminine	Plural
Nominative	ein Deutscher	ein Gutes	eine Deutsche	keine Deutschen
Accusative	einen Deutschen	ein Gutes	eine Deutsche	keine Deutschen
Dative	einem Deutschen	einem Guten	einer Deutschen	keinen Deutschen
Genitive	eines Deutschen	—	einer Deutschen	keiner Deutschen

Other nouns declined like adjectives are **der/die Bekannte, Erwachsene, Fremde, Jugendliche, Verwandte.**

13. Irregular comparatives and superlatives

Base form	bald	gern	gut	hoch	nah	viel
Comparative	eher	lieber	besser	höher	näher	mehr
Superlative	ehest-	liebst-	best-	höchst-	nächst-	meist-

14. Adjectives and adverbs taking umlaut in the comparative and superlative

alt	jung	oft
arm	kalt	rot
blass (blasser *or* blässer)	krank	schwach
dumm	kurz	schwarz
gesund (gesünder *or* gesunder)	lang	stark
groß	nass (nässer *or* nasser)	warm

15. Prepositions

With accusative	With dative	With either accusative or dative	With genitive
bis	aus	an	(an)statt
durch	außer	auf	trotz
für	bei	hinter	während
gegen	mit	in	wegen
ohne	nach	neben	
um	seit	über	
	von	unter	
	zu	vor	
		zwischen	

16. Verbs and prepositions with special meanings

anfangen mit	lächeln über (+ *acc.*)
anrufen bei	lachen über (+ *acc.*)
antworten auf (+ *acc.*)	nachdenken über (+ *acc.*)
arbeiten bei (*at a company*)	reden über (+ *acc.*) *or* von
aufhören mit	riechen nach
beginnen mit	schreiben an (+ *acc.*)
sich beschäftigen mit	schreiben über (+ *acc.*)
danken für	sprechen über (+ *acc.*), von, *or* mit
denken an (+ *acc.*)	sterben an (+ *dat.*)
sich erinnern an (+ *acc.*)	studieren an *or* auf (+ *dat.*)
erzählen von	suchen nach
fahren mit (*by a vehicle*)	teilen durch
fragen nach	telefonieren mit
sich freuen auf (+ *acc.*)	sich unterhalten über (+ *acc.*)
sich freuen über (+ *acc.*)	sich vorbereiten auf (+ *acc.*)
sich fürchten vor (+ *dat.*)	warten auf (+ *acc.*)
halten von	wissen über (+ *acc.*) *or* von
helfen bei	wohnen bei
hoffen auf (+ *acc.*)	zeigen auf (+ *acc.*)
sich interessieren für	

17. Dative verbs

antworten	helfen
danken	Leid tun
fehlen	passen
folgen	passieren
gefallen	schaden
gehören	schmecken
glauben (*dat.* of person)	weh·tun
gratulieren	

The verb **glauben** may take an impersonal accusative object: **ich glaube es.**

18. Guidelines for the position of <u>nicht</u>

1. **Nicht** always *follows* the finite verb.
   Kevin **arbeitet nicht.**
   Anne **kann nicht** gehen.

2. **Nicht** always *follows:*
   a. noun objects
      Ich glaube Kevin nicht.
   b. pronouns used as objects
      Ich glaube **es nicht.**
   c. specific adverbs of time
      Anne geht **heute nicht** mit.

3. **Nicht** *precedes* most other elements:
   a. predicate adjectives
      Dieter ist **nicht freundlich.**
   b. predicate nouns
      Dieter ist **nicht mein Freund.**
   c. adverbs
      Katrin spielt **nicht gern** Tennis.
   d. adverbs of general time
      Katrin spielt **nicht oft** Tennis.
   e. prepositional phrases
      Oliver geht **nicht ins Kino.**

4. If several of the elements that are preceded by **nicht** occur in a sentence, **nicht** usually *precedes* the first one.
   Ich gehe **nicht oft** ins Kino.

19. Present tense

		lernen[1]	arbeiten[2]	tanzen[3]	geben[4]	lesen[5]	fahren[6]	laufen[7]	auf·stehen[8]
	ich	lerne	arbeite	tanze	gebe	lese	fahre	laufe	stehe … auf
	du	lernst	arbeitest	tanzt	gibst	liest	fährst	läufst	stehst … auf
er/es/sie		lernt	arbeitet	tanzt	gibt	liest	fährt	läuft	steht … auf
	wir	lernen	arbeiten	tanzen	geben	lesen	fahren	laufen	stehen … auf
	ihr	lernt	arbeitet	tanzt	gebt	lest	fahrt	lauft	steht … auf
	sie	lernen	arbeiten	tanzen	geben	lesen	fahren	laufen	stehen … auf
	Sie	lernen	arbeiten	tanzen	geben	lesen	fahren	laufen	stehen … auf
Imper. sg.		lern(e)	arbeite	tanz(e)	gib	lies	fahr(e)	lauf(e)	steh(e) … auf

1. The endings are used for all verbs except the modals, **wissen, werden,** and **sein.**
2. A verb with a stem ending in **-d** or **-t** has an **e** before the **-st** and **-t** endings. A verb with a stem ending in **-m** or **-n** preceded by another consonant has an **e** before the **-st** and **-t** endings, e.g., **atmen** > **du atmest, er/es/sie atmet; regnen** > **es regnet.** Exception: If the stem of the verb ends in **-m** or **-n** preceded by **-l** or **-r,** the **-st** and **-t** do not expand, e.g., **lernen** > **du lernst, er/es/sie lernt.**
3. The **-st** ending of the **du**-form contracts to **-t** when the verb stem ends in a sibilant (**-s, -ss, -ß, -z,** or **-tz**). Thus the **du**- and **er/es/sie**-forms are identical.
4. Some strong verbs have a stem-vowel change **e** > **i** in the **du**- and **er/es/sie**-forms and the imperative singular.
5. Some strong verbs have a stem-vowel change **e** > **ie** in the **du**- and **er/es/sie**-forms and the imperative singular. The strong verbs **gehen** and **stehen** do not change their stem vowel.
6. Some strong verbs have a stem-vowel change **a** > **ä** in the **du**- and **er/es/sie**-forms.
7. Some strong verbs have a stem-vowel change **au** > **äu** in the **du**- and **er/es/sie**-forms.
8. In the present tense, separable prefixes are separated from the verbs and are in last position.

20. Simple past tense

		Weak verbs		Strong verbs
		lernen[1]	arbeiten[2]	geben[3]
	ich	lernte	arbeitete	gab
	du	lerntest	arbeitetest	gabst
er/es/sie		lernte	arbeitete	gab
	wir	lernten	arbeiteten	gaben
	ihr	lerntet	arbeitetet	gabt
	sie	lernten	arbeiteten	gaben
	Sie	lernten	arbeiteten	gaben

1. Weak verbs have a past-tense marker **-te** + endings.
2. A weak verb with a stem ending in **-d** or **-t** has a past-tense marker **-ete** + endings. A weak verb with a stem ending in **-m** or **-n** preceded by another

consonant has a past-stem marker **-ete** plus endings, e.g., **er/es/sie atmete; es regnete.** Exception: If the stem of the verb ends in **-m** or **-n** preceded by **-l** or **-r**, the **-te** past-tense marker does not expand, e.g., **lernte.**
3. Strong verbs have a stem-vowel change + endings.

21. Auxiliaries *haben, sein, werden*

ich	habe	bin	werde
du	hast	bist	wirst
er/es/sie	hat	ist	wird
wir	haben	sind	werden
ihr	habt	seid	werdet
sie	haben	sind	werden
Sie	haben	sind	werden

22. Modal auxiliaries: present, simple past, and past participle

	dürfen	können	müssen	sollen	wollen	mögen	(möchte)
ich	darf	kann	muss	soll	will	mag	(möchte)
du	darfst	kannst	musst	sollst	willst	magst	(möchtest)
er/es/sie	darf	kann	muss	soll	will	mag	(möchte)
wir	dürfen	können	müssen	sollen	wollen	mögen	(möchten)
ihr	dürft	könnt	müsst	sollt	wollt	mögt	(möchtet)
sie	dürfen	können	müssen	sollen	wollen	mögen	(möchten)
Sie	dürfen	können	müssen	sollen	wollen	mögen	(möchten)
Simple past	durfte	konnte	musste	sollte	wollte	mochte	
Past participle	gedurft	gekonnt	gemusst	gesollt	gewollt	gemocht	

23. Verb conjugations: strong verbs *sehen* and *gehen*

■ *Indicative*

	Present		Simple past	
ich	sehe	gehe	sah	ging
du	siehst	gehst	sahst	gingst
er/es/sie	sieht	geht	sah	ging
wir	sehen	gehen	sahen	gingen
ihr	seht	geht	saht	gingt
sie	sehen	gehen	sahen	gingen
Sie	sehen	gehen	sahen	gingen

	Present perfect				Past perfect			
ich	habe		bin		hatte		war	
du	hast		bist		hattest		warst	
er/es/sie	hat		ist		hatte		war	
wir	haben	gesehen	sind	gegangen	hatten	gesehen	waren	gegangen
ihr	habt		seid		hattet		wart	
sie	haben		sind		hatten		waren	
Sie	haben		sind		hatten		waren	

■ *Indicative (continued)*

Future				
ich	werde		werde	
du	wirst		wirst	
er/es/sie	wird		wird	
wir	werden	sehen	werden	gehen
ihr	werdet		werdet	
sie	werden		werden	
Sie	werden		werden	

■ *Imperative*

Imperative		
Familiar singular	sieh	geh(e)
Familiar plural	seht	geht
Formal	sehen Sie	gehen Sie

■ *Subjunctive*

Present-time subjunctive		
ich	sähe	ginge
du	sähest	gingest
er/es/sie	sähe	ginge
wir	sähen	gingen
ihr	sähet	ginget
sie	sähen	gingen
Sie	sähen	gingen

■ *Passive voice*

	Present passive		Past passive	
ich	werde		wurde	
du	wirst		wurdest	
er/es/sie	wird		wurde	
wir	werden	gesehen	wurden	gesehen
ihr	werdet		wurdet	
sie	werden		wurden	
Sie	werden		wurden	

24. Principal parts of strong and irregular weak verbs

The following list includes all the strong and irregular verbs from the **Vokabeln** lists. Compounds verbs like **herumliegen** and **hinausgehen** are not included, since the principal parts of compound verbs are identical to the basic forms: **liegen** and **gehen.** Separable-prefix verbs like **einladen** are included only when the basic verb (**laden**) is not listed elsewhere in the table. Basic English meanings are given for all verbs in this list. For additional meanings, consult the German-English vocabulary on pages R-41 to R-59. The number indicates the chapter in which the verb was introduced.

Infinitive	Present-tense vowel change	Simple past	Past participle	Subjunctive	Meaning
anfangen	fängt an	fing an	angefangen	finge an	to begin 10
anrufen		rief an	angerufen	riefe an	to telephone 6
sich anziehen		zog an	angezogen	zöge an	to get dressed 9
sich ausziehen		zog aus	ausgezogen	zöge aus	to get undressed 9
beginnen		begann	begonnen	begönne or begänne	to begin 9
bleiben		blieb	ist geblieben	bliebe	to stay 2
bringen		brachte	gebracht	brächte	to bring 4
denken		dachte	gedacht	dächte	to think 2
einladen	lädt ein	lud ein	eingeladen	lüde ein	to invite; to treat 6
empfehlen	empfiehlt	empfahl	empfohlen	empföhle	to recommend 10
entscheiden		entschied	entschieden	entschiede	to decide 12
erziehen		erzog	erzogen	erzöge	to rear; to educate 8
essen	isst	aß	gegessen	äße	to eat 3
fahren	fährt	fuhr	ist gefahren	führe	to drive, travel 5
fallen	fällt	fiel	ist gefallen	fiele	to fall 10
finden		fand	gefunden	fände	to find 2
fliegen		flog	ist geflogen	flöge	to fly 5
geben	gibt	gab	gegeben	gäbe	to give 3
gefallen	gefällt	gefiel	gefallen	gefiele	to please 5
gehen		ging	ist gegangen	ginge	to go 1
gewinnen		gewann	gewonnen	gewönne or gewänne	to win 5
haben	hat	hatte	gehabt	hätte	to have 2
halten	hält	hielt	gehalten	hielte	to hold; to stop 6
hängen		hing	gehangen	hinge	to be hanging 7
heben		hob	gehoben	höbe or hübe	to lift 1
heißen		hieß	geheißen	hieße	to be called, named E
helfen	hilft	half	geholfen	hülfe or hälfe	to help 7
kennen		kannte	gekannt	kennte	to know 3
kommen		kam	ist gekommen	käme	to come 1
lassen	lässt	ließ	gelassen	ließe	to let, allow 12
laufen	läuft	lief	ist gelaufen	liefe	to run 5
leiden		litt	gelitten	litte	to suffer 8
leihen		lieh	geliehen	liehe	to lend 4
lesen	liest	las	gelesen	läse	to read 4
liegen		lag	gelegen	läge	to lie 2
nehmen	nimmt	nahm	genommen	nähme	to take 3
nennen		nannte	genannt	nennte	to name 8
riechen		roch	gerochen	röche	to smell 3
rufen		rief	gerufen	riefe	to call 3
scheinen		schien	geschienen	schiene	to shine; to seem 2
schlafen	schläft	schlief	geschlafen	schliefe	to sleep 5
schließen		schloss	geschlossen	schlösse	to close 3
schreiben		schrieb	geschrieben	schriebe	to write E
schwimmen		schwamm	ist geschwommen	schwömme or schwämme	to swim 1
sehen	sieht	sah	gesehen	sähe	to see 4
sein	ist	war	ist gewesen	wäre	to be 1
sitzen		saß	gesessen	säße	to sit 5
sprechen	spricht	sprach	gesprochen	spräche	to speak 5
stehen		stand	gestanden	stände or stünde	to stand 7
sterben	stirbt	starb	ist gestorben	stürbe	to die 10

Infinitive	Present-tense vowel change	Simple past	Past participle	Subjunctive	Meaning
tragen	trägt	trug	getragen	trüge	*to wear; to carry* 6
treffen	trifft	traf	getroffen	träfe	*to meet; to hit* 5
treiben		trieb	getrieben	triebe	*to engage in* 1
trinken		trank	getrunken	tränke	*to drink* 3
tun		tat	getan	täte	*to do* 6
vergessen	vergisst	vergaß	vergessen	vergäße	*to forget* 5
verlieren		verlor	verloren	verlöre	*to lose* 11
wachsen	wächst	wuchs	ist gewachsen	wüchse	*to grow* 12
waschen	wäscht	wusch	gewaschen	wüsche	*to wash* 7
werden	wird	wurde	ist geworden	würde	*to become* 4
wissen	weiß	wusste	gewusst	wüsste	*to know* 4
zwingen		zwang	gezwungen	zwänge	*to compel* 10

German-English Vocabulary

This vocabulary includes all the words used in **Deutsch heute** except numbers. The definitions given are generally limited to the context in which the words are used in this book. Chapter numbers are given for all words and expressions occurring in the chapter vocabularies and in the *Erweiterung des Wortschatzes* sections to indicate where a word or expression is first used. Recognition vocabulary does not have a chapter reference. The symbol ~ indicates repetition of the key word (minus the definite article, if any).

Nouns are listed with their plural forms: **der Abend, -e.** No plural entry is given if the plural is rarely used or nonexistent. If two entries follow a noun, the first one indicates the genitive and the second one indicates the plural: **der Herr, -n, -en.**

Strong and irregular weak verbs are listed with their principal parts. Vowel changes in the present tense are noted in parentheses, followed by simple-past and past-participle forms. All verbs take **haben** in the past participle unless indicated with **sein.** For example: **fahren (ä), fuhr, ist gefahren.** Separable-prefix verbs are indicated with a raised dot: **auf·stehen.**

Adjectives and adverbs that require an umlaut in the comparative and superlative forms are noted as follows: **warm (ä).** Stress marks are given for all words that are not accented on the first syllable. The stress mark follows the accented syllable: **Amerika′ner.** In some words, either of the two syllables may be stressed.

The following abbreviations are used:

abbr.	abbreviation	*dat.*	dative	*p.p.*	past participle
acc.	accusative	*decl.*	declined	*part.*	participle
adj.	adjective	*f.*	feminine	*pl.*	plural
adv.	adverb	*fam.*	familiar	*sg.*	singular
colloq.	colloquial	*gen.*	genitive	*sub.*	subordinate
comp.	comparative	*m.*	masculine	*subj.*	subjunctive
conj.	conjunction	*n.*	neuter	*sup.*	superlative

A

ab (*prep.* + *dat.*) after, from a certain point on; away 9; ~ **heute** from today on 9; ~ **und zu** now and then

der **Abend, -e** evening 1; **gestern** ~ last night 6; **Guten** ~! Good evening. 1; **heute** ~ tonight, this evening 6; **zu** ~ **essen** to have (eat) dinner/supper

das **Abendessen, -** dinner, supper 3; **zum** ~ for dinner 3; **Was gibt's zum** ~? What's for dinner? 3

abends evenings, in the evening 3

aber (*conj.*) but 1

ab·fahren (fährt ab), fuhr ab, ist abgefahren to depart (by vehicle) 7

ab·holen to pick up 5

das **Abitur′** diploma from college-track high school (**Gymnasium**) 4

der **Absatz, ̈e** paragraph

der **Abschnitt, -e** passage; paragraph

absolut′ absolutely, completely 10

ab·trocknen to dry dishes; to wipe dry 7

ab·waschen (wäscht ab), wusch ab, abgewaschen to do dishes 7

ach oh E

achten to pay attention

Achtung! (*exclamation*) Pay attention!; Look out!

die **Adres′se, -n** address E; **Wie ist deine/Ihre** ~? What is your address? E

das **Aero′bic** aerobics 1; ~ **machen** to do aerobics 1

ähnlich similar

die **Ahnung, -en** hunch, idea 6; **Keine** ~! No idea! 6

die **Aktivität′, -en** activity 10

aktuell′ current, up to date

akzeptie′ren to accept

alle all 1

allein′ alone 5

allein′stehend single

allem: vor ~ above all 9

allerdings of course

alles everything 2; all; **Alles Gute.** Best wishes

allgemein′ general; **im Allgemeinen** in general

die **Alliier′ten** (*pl.*) Allies (WW II)

der **Alltag** everyday life

die **Alpen** (*pl.*) Alps 5

als (*after a comp.*) than 2; as; (*sub. conj.*) when 8

also well E; therefore, so 3

alt (ä) old E; **Wie** ~ **bist du/sind Sie?** How old are you? E; **Ich bin [19] Jahre** ~. I'm [19] years old. E

das **Alter** age

am: ~ **Freitag/Montag** on Friday/Monday E

(das) **Ame′rika** America 2

der **Amerika′ner, -/die Amerika′nerin, -nen** American person 2

amerika′nisch American (*adj.*) 4

an (+ *acc./dat.*) at; to 4; on 7

andere other 2

(sich) ändern to change; to alter

anders different(ly) 2

der Anfang, ⁼e beginning 8; am ~ in the beginning 8

an·fangen (fängt an), fing an, angefangen to begin 10; mit [der Arbeit] ~ to begin [the work]

an·geben (gibt an), gab an, angegeben to give; name, cite

der/die Angestellte (noun decl. like adj.) salaried employee, white-collar worker 11

die Anglis′tik English studies (language and literature) 4

die Angst, ⁼e fear 7; ~ haben (vor + dat.) to be afraid (of) 7

der Anhang, ⁼e appendix, reference section

an·kommen, kam an, ist angekommen (in + dat.) to arrive (in) 7

an·kreuzen to check off

an·rufen, rief an, angerufen to phone 6; bei [dir] ~ to call [you] at home 6

an·schauen to look at; to watch 7

(sich) (dat.) an·sehen (sieht an), sah an, angesehen to look at 6; Ich sehe es mir an. I'm having a look at it. 12

(an)statt′ (+ gen.) instead of 8; ~ zu (+ inf.) instead of

die Antwort, -en answer 6

antworten (+ dat.) to answer (as in Ich antworte der Frau. I answer the woman.) 11; ~ auf (+ acc.) to answer (as in Ich antworte auf die Frage. I answer the question.) 11

die Anzeige, -n announcement; ad 8

sich (acc.) an·ziehen, zog an, angezogen to get dressed 9; Ich ziehe mich an. I get dressed 9; sich (dat.) an·ziehen to put on 9; Ich ziehe [mir die Schuhe] an. I put on [my shoes].

der Anzug, ⁼e man's suit 6

der Apfel, ⁼ apple 3

der Apfelsaft apple juice 3

die Apothe′ke, -n pharmacy 3; in die ~ to the pharmacy 3

der Apothe′ker, -/die Apothe′kerin, -nen pharmacist

der Apparat′, -e apparatus, appliance 9

der Appetit′ appetite; Guten ~! Enjoy your meal.

der April′ April 2

das Äquivalent′, -e equivalent

die Arbeit work; die Arbeit, -en (school or academic) paper; piece of work 4

arbeiten to work; to study 1; am Computer ~ to work at the computer 6; bei einer [Firma] ~ to work at a [company] 11; mit dem Computer ~ to do work on a computer 11; mit Textverarbeitungsprogrammen ~ to do word processing 11

der Arbeiter, -/die Arbeiterin, -nen worker 12

der Arbeitgeber, -/die Arbeitgeberin, -nen employer

der Arbeitnehmer, -/die Arbeitnehmerin, -nen employee, worker

die Arbeitsgruppe, -n study group

die Arbeitskraft, ⁼e employee

arbeitslos unemployed, out of work 11

die Arbeitslosigkeit unemployment

der Arbeitsplatz, ⁼e job, position; workplace 8

die Arbeitssuche job search

die Arbeitszeit, -en working hours

der Architekt′, -en, -en/die Architek′tin, -nen architect 8

die Architektur′ architecture

ärgerlich angry, annoyed, irritated

(sich) ärgern to be or feel angry (or annoyed) 12

argumentie′ren to argue

arm (ä) poor 9; Du Armer. Poor fellow/guy/thing. 9

der Arm, -e arm 9

die Armbanduhr, -en wristwatch

die Art, -en type, kind; manner; auf diese ~ und Weise in this way

der Arti′kel, - article 4

der Arzt, ⁼e/die Ärztin, -nen (medical) doctor, physician 6

das Aspirin′ aspirin 3

der Assistent′, -en, -en/die Assisten′tin, -nen assistant, aid

assoziie′ren to associate

atmen to breathe

auch also E

auf (+ acc./dat.) on top of; to; on 7; up; open; awake; ~ dem Weg on the way, ~ den Markt to the market 3; ~ [Deutsch] in [German] 9; ~ Wiedersehen. Good-bye. 1

die Aufgabe, -n assignment; task, set of duties 10; die Hausaufgabe, -n homework 10; Hausaufgaben machen to do homework 10

auf·geben (gibt auf), gab auf, aufgegeben to give up 8

auf·hören to stop (an activity); mit der Arbeit ~ to stop work

auf·listen to list

auf·machen to open

auf·passen to watch out; ~ auf (+ acc.) to take care of

auf·räumen to straighten up (a room) 7

auf·schreiben, schrieb auf, aufgeschrieben to write down 10

auf·stehen, stand auf, ist aufgestanden to get up; to stand up 6

auf·stellen to set up (a list)

auf·teilen (in + acc.) to split up (into) 10

auf·wachsen (wächst auf), wuchs auf, ist aufgewachsen to grow up 12

das Auge, -n eye 9

der August′ August 2

aus (+ dat.) out of 5; to come/be from (be a native of) 2; Ich komme ~ [Kanada]. I come from [Canada]. 2

der Ausdruck, ⁼e expression

aus·drücken to express

auseinan′der apart, away from each other

aus·gehen, ging aus, ist ausgegangen to go out 6

das Ausland (no pl.) foreign countries 7; im ~ abroad 7

der Ausländer, -/die Ausländerin, -nen foreigner 4

die Ausländerfeindlichkeit hostility toward foreigners

der Ausländerhass xenophobia 12

ausländisch foreign

aus·leihen, lieh aus, ausgeliehen to rent (video); to check out (book) 4; to lend out 4

aus·machen to matter 11; Es macht [mir] nichts aus. It doesn't matter to [me]. 11

aus·räumen to empty the [dishwasher] 7

die Aussage, -n statement

aus·sagen to state, assert

aus·sehen (sieht aus), sah aus, ausgesehen to appear, look like, seem 6

das Aussehen appearance

der Außenhandel foreign trade 11

außer (+ dat.) besides; except for 5

außerdem besides, in addition, as well

aus·suchen to select, choose

der **Austauschstudent, -en, -en**/die
Austauschstudentin, -nen
exchange student 7
aus·wählen to choose, select
aus·wandern, ist ausgewandert to
emigrate 9
sich (*acc.*) **aus·ziehen, zog aus,
ausgezogen** to get undressed 9; **Ich
ziehe mich aus.** I get undressed. 9;
sich (*dat.*) **aus·ziehen** to take off;
Ich ziehe [mir die Schuhe] aus. I
take off [my shoes]. 9
der/die **Auszubildende** (*noun decl. like
adj.*) trainee, apprentice
das **Auto, -s** automobile, car 5
die **Autobahn, -en** freeway,
expressway 7
autonom autonomous
der **Autor,** *pl.* **Auto'ren**/die **Auto'rin,
-nen** author

B

backen (ä), backte, gebacken to bake
der **Bäcker, -**/die **Bäckerin, -nen** baker
3; **beim ~** at the baker's/bakery 3;
zum ~ to the baker's/bakery 3
die **Bäckerei', -en** bakery 3
das **Bad, ⸚er** bath; bathroom 7
der **Badeanzug, ⸚e** swimming suit 6
die **Badehose, -n** swimming trunks 6
baden to bathe 9; to swim
das **Badezimmer, -** bathroom
das **BAföG (= das Bundesausbil-
dungsfördcrungsgesetz)** national
law that mandates financial support
for students
die **Bahn, -en** train; railroad 5
der **Bahnhof, ⸚e** train station 7
bald soon 2; **Bis ~.** See you later. E
der **Balkon, -s** *or* **-e** balcony
die **Bana'ne, -n** banana 3
die **Band, -s** band (musical) 6
die **Bank, ⸚e** bench
die **Bank, -en** bank 11
die **Bar, -s** bar, pub, nightclub 10
der **Basketball** basketball 1
der **Bau** construction
der **Bauch,** *pl.* **Bäuche** abdomen;
belly 9
bauen to build 10
der **Bauer, -n, -n**/die **Bäuerin, -nen**
farmer
der **Baum, ⸚e** tree
der **Baustein, -e** building block
bay(e)risch Bavarian 7
beant'worten to answer (a question,
a letter) 5

bedeu'ten to mean 11; **Was bedeutet
das?** What does that mean? 11
die **Bedeu'tung, -en** significance;
meaning
beein'flussen to influence 2
been'den to finish, complete
begin'nen, begann, begonnen to begin
9; **mit [der Arbeit] ~** to begin
[(the) work]
begrü'ßen to greet; to welcome
behaup'tcn to claim
der/die **Behin'derte** (*noun decl. like
adj.*) handicapped person
bei (+ *dat.*) at 3; at a place of; near; in
the proximity of 5; while, during
(*indicates a situation*); **~ Gisela** at
Gisela's 3; **beim Bäcker** at the
baker's/bakery 3; **~der Uni** near the
university 5; **~ [dir]** at [your]
place/house/home 5; **~ [mir]
vorbeikommen** to stop by [my]
place 5; **beim Chatten** while
chatting 6; **~ einer Firma arbeiten**
to work at a company/firm 11;
beim Fernsehen while watching
TV; **~ uns** at our house; in our
country
beide both 1
das **Bein, -e** leg 9
das **Beispiel, -e** example 4; **zum
Beispiel** (*abbrev.* **z.B.**) for
example 4
bekannt' known, famous 5; **Das ist
mir ~.** I'm familiar with that.
der/die **Bekann'te** (*noun declined like
adj.*) acquaintance 9
bekom'men, bekam, bekommen to
receive 3; **Kinder ~** to have
children
beliebt' popular, favorite
bemer'ken to notice; to remark
die **Bemer'kung, -en** remark;
observation
benut'zen to use 7
das **Benzin'** gasoline
beob'achten to observe 7
bequem' comfortable
bereit' ready; prepared; willing 5
der **Berg, -e** mountain 5; **in die Berge
fahren** to go to the mountains
der **Bericht', -e** report
berich'ten to report 10
Berli'ner Berliner (*adj.*); **Berliner
Zeitung** Berlin newspaper 10
der **Beruf', -e** profession, occupation 8;
Was ist er von Beruf? What is his
profession?
beruf'lich career related; professional

berufs'tätig working; gainfully
employed 8
berühmt' famous 5
beschäf'tigen to occupy, keep busy 11;
sich ~ (mit) to be occupied
(with) 11; **beschäftigt sein** to be
busy 11
**beschrei' ben, beschrieb,
beschrieben** to describe 6
die **Beschrei'bung, -en** description
beset'zen to occupy
besetzt' occupied; engaged; busy
(telephone line) 6
der **Besit'zer, -**/die **Besit'zerin, -nen**
owner
beson'der- special; **(nichts)
Besonderes** (nothing) special 1;
besonders especially, particularly 4
besprech'en (i), besprach, besprochen
to discuss
besser (*comp. of* **gut**) better 3
best- (-cr, -es, -e) best 9
bestel'len to order
bestimmt' certain(ly), for sure 2
der **Besuch', -e** visit 3; **~ haben** to
have company 3; **zu ~** for a visit 12
besu'chen to visit 3; to attend (e.g., a
lecture) 5
der **Besu'cher, -**/die **Besu'cherin, -nen**
visitor
beto'nen to emphasize
das **Bett, -en** bed E; **zu (ins) ~ gehen**
to go to bed
die **Bettdecke, -n** blanket 7
die **Bevöl'kerung, -en** population
bevor' (*sub. conj.*) before 5
die **Bewer'bung, -en** application
der **Bewoh'ner, -**/die **Bewoh'nerin,
nen** inhabitant
bezah'len to pay (for) 3; **das Essen
~** to pay for the meal 3
die **Bibliothek', -en** library 1; **in
der ~** in/at the library 1
das **Bier, -e** beer 3
der **Biergarten, ⸚** beer garden 7
das **Bild, -er** picture; photograph E;
image
bilden to form
das **Bilderbuch, ⸚er** picture book
die **Bildgeschichte, -n** picture story
billig cheap 3
bin am E
die **Biografie', -n** (*also* **Biographie**)
biography 4
die **Biologie'** biology 4
bis (+ *acc.*) until, til 1; **~ auf** (+ *acc.*)
except for; **~ bald.** See you later. E
~ dann. See you then. 1

bisher' until now, so far

bisschen: ein ~ a little 1

bitte (*after* **danke**) You're welcome. E; please E; **~?** May I help you? E; **~ schön.** You're welcome.; **~ sehr.** (*said when handing someone something*) Here you are.; **Wie ~?** (I beg your) pardon? E

bitten, bat, gebeten (**um** + *acc.*) to request, ask (for) something

blass pale 9

blau blue E

bleiben, blieb, ist geblieben to stay, to remain 2

der **Bleistift, -e** pencil E

der **Blick, -e** view

blockie'ren to blockade, block

blond blond 9

die **Blume, -n** flower 3

der **Blumenstand, ¨e** flower stand 3

die **Bluse, -n** blouse 6

der **Boden, ¨** floor 7; ground

das **Boot, -e** boat

böse (**auf** + *acc.*) angry (at) 7; bad, mean; **Sei [mir] nicht ~.** Don't be mad at [me]. 7

brauchbar usable; **Brauchbares** something usable

brauchen to need 3

braun brown E; **hell~** light brown 9

das **Brett, -er** board; shelf; das **schwarze ~** bulletin board

der **Brief, -e** letter 5

der **Brieffreund, -e**/die **Brieffreundin, -nen** pen pal 9

die **Brille, -n** eyeglasses 6; **Tragen Sie eine ~?** Do you wear glasses? 6

bringen, brachte, gebracht to bring 4

das **Brot, -e** bread; sandwich 3

das **Brötchen, -** bread roll 3

die **Brücke, -n** bridge 10

der **Bruder, ¨** brother 4

das **Buch, ¨er** book E

das **Bücherregal, -e** bookcase E

die **Büchertasche, -n** book bag

die **Buchhandlung, -en** bookstore 3

der **Buchladen, ¨** bookstore

buchstabie'ren to spell

das **Bundesland, ¨er** federal state

die **Bundesrepublik Deutschland (BRD)** Federal Republic of Germany (FRG) (*the official name of Germany*) 10

der **Bundesstaat, -en** federal state (in the U.S.A.)

der **Bundestag** lower house of the German parliament

der **Bürger, -**/die **Bürgerin, -nen** citizen

das **Büro', -s** office 8

der **Bus, -se** bus 5

die **Butter** butter 3

C

das **Café, -s** café 5

der **Camcorder, -** camcorder

der **Campingplatz, ¨e** campsite

der **CD-Player, -** (*also* der **CD-Spieler, -**) CD player E

der **Chatroom** (*also* **Chat-Room**)**, -s** (online) chat room 6

chatten to chat (online) 6; **beim Chatten** while chatting 6

der **Chef, -s**/die **Chefin, -nen** boss 11

die **Chemie'** chemistry 4

circa (*abbr.* **ca.**) approximately

der **Club, -s** club; dance club 6

die **Cola, -s** cola drink 7

die **Comics** (*pl.*) comics 8

der **Compu'ter, -** computer E; **am ~ arbeiten** to work at the computer 6; **mit dem ~ arbeiten** to do work on the computer 11

das **Compu'terspiel, -e** computer game 1

der **Couchtisch, -e** coffee table 7

der **Cousin', -s** cousin (*m.*) (*pronounced* **kuzē'**)

D

da there E; here; then; (*sub. conj.*) since, because 8

dabei' and yet, with it; here (with me) 10; **dabei sein** to be there, be present 10

dage'gen against it; on the other hand

daher therefore, for that reason 4

das **da-Kompositum** da-compound

damals at that time 12

die **Dame, -n** lady 5

danach' after it; afterwards 10

der **Dank** thanks 5; **Vielen ~.** Many thanks. 5

danke Thanks E; **~ sehr; ~ schön.** Thank you very much. 1

danken (+ *dat.*) to thank 5; **~ für** to thank for

dann then E; **Bis ~.** See you then. 1

das the (*n.*); that E

dass (*sub. conj.*) that 5

das **Datum,** *pl.* **Daten** date

dauern to last; to require time 11

dazu' to it, to that; in addition 7

decken to cover 7; **den Tisch ~** to set the table 7

dein(e) your (*fam. sg.*) E

die **Demokratie', -n** democracy

die **Demonstration', -en** demonstration 10

demonstrie'ren to demonstrate 10

denen (*dat. pl. of demonstrative and relative pronoun*) them; which 12

denken, dachte, gedacht to think, believe 2; **~ an** (+ *acc.*) to think of/ about 7; **~ daran** to think about it

denn (*conj.*) because, for 4; (*flavoring particle adding emphasis to questions*) 3

deprimiert' depressed

der the (*m.*) E

dersel'be, dassel'be, diesel'be the same

deshalb therefore, for that reason 4

deswegen therefore, for this reason 9

deutsch German (*adj.*) 2

(das) **Deutsch** German class E; German (language) 1; **~ machen** to do German (homework) 4; **auf ~** in German 9

der/die **Deutsche** (*noun decl. like adj.*) German person 2

die **Deutsche Demokra'tische Republik' (DDR)** German Democratic Republic (GDR)

der **Deutschkurs, -e** German class or course

(das) **Deutschland** Germany 2

deutschsprachig German-speaking

der **Dezem'ber** December 2

der **Dialekt', -e** dialect 9

der **Dialog', -e** dialogue

der **Dichter, -**/die **Dichterin, -nen** poet

dick fat; thick 9

die the (*f.*) E

der **Dienstag** Tuesday E

dies (**-er, -es, -e**) this, these 4

diesmal this time 11

die **Digital'kamera, -s** digital camera 9

das **Ding, -e** thing 8

dir (*dat.*) (to or for) you 5; **und ~?** And you? (How about you?) (*as part of response to* **Wie geht's?**) 1

die **Disco, -s** (*also* **Disko**) dance club 6

die **Disket'te, -n** disk, diskette 4

die **Diskussion', -en** discussion; debate

diskutie'ren to discuss

doch (*flavoring particle*) really, after all, indeed 3; Yes, of course; on the contrary (*response to negative statement or question*) 3; but still, nevertheless, however, yet 3; **Geh ~ zum ...** Well then, go to . . . 3

die **Donau** Danube

der **Döner, -** (*short for* **Dönerkebab**) Arabic/Turkish dish of grilled meat and spices

der **Donnerstag** Thursday E

dort there 2

dorthin′ (to) there

die **Dose, -n** can, tin; box

dran: ich bin ~ it's my turn 11

draußen outside 7

dritt- (**-er, -es, -e**) third 8

das **Drittel, -** third

die **Drogerie′, -n** drugstore 3

der **Drogerie′markt, ¨e** self-service drugstore

drucken to print

du you (*fam. sg.*) E; **~!** Hey! E; **~ Armer/ ~ Arme** you poor fellow/guy/thing 9; **~ meine Güte!** My heavens! 7

dumm (ü) dumb, stupid 9

dunkel dark 9

dunkelhaarig dark-haired

dünn thin 9

durch (+ *acc.*) through 3; divided by E; by (means of which)

durch·arbeiten to work through; to study 4

durch·machen to work/go through

durch·sehen (sieht durch), sah durch, durchgesehen to look through; to glance over; to examine 8

dürfen (darf), durfte, gedurft to be permitted, be allowed to; may 4

der **Durst** thirst 3; **~ haben** to be thirsty 3

(sich) duschen to shower 9

duzen to address someone with the familiar **du**-form

die **DVD′ -s** DVD 4

der **DVD-Player, -** (der **DVD-Spieler, -**) DVD player E

E

eben just, simply 7; even, smooth; (*flavoring particle*) used to support a previous statement, express agreement; made as a final statement it implies the speaker has no desire to discuss a point further

echt genuine; **~?** (*slang*) Really?

die **Ecke, -n** corner 7

egal′ same; **das ist mir ~** it's all the same to me, I don't care

egois′tisch egocentric 1

die **Ehe, -n** marriage 8

die **Ehefrau, -en** wife

der **Ehemann, ¨er** husband

das **Ehepaar, -e** married couple 8

ehrlich honest; frank 6

das **Ei, -er** egg 3; **Rühr~** scrambled egg; **Spiegel~** fried egg; **weich gekochtes ~** soft-boiled egg

die **Eidgenossenschaft, -en** confederation

eigen own 10

eigentlich actually 3

ein(e) a, an E; **ein paar** a couple 6

einan′der one another, each other 6; **mit~** with each other 6

der **Eindruck, ¨e** impression

einfach simple; simply 2

das **Einfami′lienhaus, ¨er** single-family house

der **Einfluss,** *pl.* **Einflüsse** influence

die **Einführung, -en** introduction

die **Einheit** unity; **Der Tag der deutschen ~** The Day of German Unity (*celebrated on October* 3)

einige some, several 5; **einiges** something

ein·kaufen to shop 3; **~ gehen** to go shopping 3

die **Einkaufstasche, -n** shopping bag 3

ein·laden (lädt ein), lud ein, eingeladen to invite 6; to treat (pay for someone) 7

die **Einladung, -en** invitation

einmal once, one time 6; **~ in der Woche** once a week 10; **noch ~** again, once more 12

ein·räumen to place or put in; to load the dishwasher 7; **Geschirr in die Spülmaschine ~** to put dishes into the [dishwasher]

ein·setzen to insert, fill in

der **Einwohner, -/die Einwohnerin, -nen** inhabitant 2

einzeln single, singly, individual(ly)

einzig- (**-er, -es, -e**) only, sole

das **Eis** ice; ice cream 3

die **Eisenbahn, -en** railroad

eisern iron; **der Eiserne Vorhang** Iron Curtain

elegant′ elegant

die **Eltern** (*pl.*) parents 4

der **Elternteil** parent

die **E-Mail, -s** e-mail 6

empfeh·len (ie), empfahl, empfohlen to recommend 10

die **Empfeh′lung, -en** recommendation

das **Ende, -n** end, conclusion 4; **am ~** (in) the end 4; **zu ~** over, finished 10

endgültig final; definite

endlich finally 7

die **Energie′** energy

(das) **Englisch** English (language); (academic subject) 1; **auf Englisch** in English

der **Enkel, -/die Enkelin, -nen** grandson/granddaughter

das **Enkelkind, -er** grandchild

enorm′ enormously

entde′cken to discover

(sich) entschei′den, entschied, entschieden to decide 12

(sich) entschul′digen to excuse (oneself); **Entschuldigen Sie!** Excuse me!

die **Entschul′digung, -en** apology

entweder ... oder (*conj.*) either . . . or

er he, it E

das **Erd′geschoss** the ground floor of a building

das **Ereig′nis, -se** occasion, event

erfah′ren (ä), erfuhr, erfahren to come to know, learn

die **Erfah′rung, -en** experience 11

erfin′den, erfand, erfunden to invent

die **Erfin′dung, -en** invention

der **Erfolg′, -e** success

ergän′zen to complete

sich erin′nern (an + *acc.*) to remember

sich erkäl′ten to catch a cold 9; **erkältet: ich bin ~** I have a cold 9

die **Erkäl′tung, -en** cold (illness) 9; **Was macht deine ~?** How's your cold? 9

erklä′ren to explain 4

erle′ben to experience

ernst serious 1

erschei′nen, erschien, ist erschienen to appear, seem

erst (*adj.*) first 9; (*adv.*) not until, only, just 12; **~ einmal** first of all

erstaunt′ to be astonished, astounded

erstens first of all

der/die **Erwach′sene** (*noun decl. like adj.*) adult

erwäh′nen to mention

erwar′ten to expect 11

die **Erwei′terung, -en** expansion, extension

erzäh′len (über + *acc.*/**von**) to tell (about) 4

die **Erzäh′lung, -en** account; story

erzie′hen, erzog, erzogen to bring up, rear; to educate 8

der **Erzie′her, -/die Erzie′herin, -nen** teacher, educator

die **Erzie′hung** bringing up, rearing; education 8

der **Erzie′hungsurlaub** leave of absence for child rearing

es it E; **~ gibt** (+ *acc.*) there is, there are 3

das **Essen, -** meal; prepared food, 3; **zum ~** for a meal 12

essen (isst), aß, gegessen to eat 3; **zu Abend ~** to have (eat) dinner 6

das **Esszimmer, -** dining room 7

etwa approximately, about 2

etwas something 1; some, somewhat 1; **noch ~** something else (in addition) 4; **~ anderes** something else 12

die **EU: Europä′ische Union′** EU, European Union

euch: bei~ in your country

euer your (*pl. fam.*) 2

der **Euro, -** euro (*EU currency*)

(das) **Euro′pa** Europe 2

europä′isch European

die **Europä′ische Union′** (EU) European Union

ewig forever, eternally 6

das **Exa′men, -** comprehensive exam, finals 4; **~ machen** to graduate from the university 4

exportie′ren to export

F

die **Fabrik′, -en** factory

das **Fach, ¨er** (academic) subject; field 4

fahren (ä), fuhr, ist gefahren to drive; to travel 5; **mit [dem Auto] ~** to go by [car] 5

die **Fahrkarte, -n** ticket

das **Fahrrad, ¨er** bicycle 5

die **Fahrschule, -n** driving school

die **Fahrt, -en** drive, ride, trip

der **Fall, ¨e** case, situation; fall, demise

fallen (ä), fiel, ist gefallen to fall 10

falsch wrong, false E

die **Fami′lie, -n** family 4; das **Fami′lienleben** family life

der **Fan, -s** fan; supporter (sports) 12

fände (*subj. of* **finden**) would find 11

fantas′tisch fantastic 3

die **Farbe, -n** color E; **Welche ~ hat ... ?** What color is . . . ? E

das **Farbfernsehen** color TV

fast almost 2

faul lazy 1

faulenzen to lounge around, be idle 6

der **Februar** February 2

fehlen (+ *dat.*) to be lacking, missing

fehlend missing

feiern to celebrate 6

der **Feiertag, -e** holiday

das **Fenster, -** window E

die **Ferien** (*pl.*) vacation 4; **in den ~** on/during vacation 4; **in die ~ gehen/fahren** to go on vacation; **Semes′terferien** semester break 4

die **Ferienreise, -n** vacation trip 7

das **Fernsehen** television (the industry) 4

fern·sehen (sieht fern), sah fern, ferngesehen to watch TV 4

der **Fernseher, -** television set E

das **Fernsehprogramm′, -e** TV channel, TV program 6

die **Fernsehsendung, -en** television program 6

die **Fernsehserie, -n** TV series

fertig finished; ready 4

fest firm(ly)

das **Fest, -e** party; celebration; feast 5; **auf dem ~** at the party 7; **ein ~ geben** to give a party 7

fett gedruckt in boldface

das **Feuer, -** fire

das **Fieber** fever 9

der **Film, -e** film 4

finanziell′ financial

finden, fand, gefunden to find; to think 2; **Sie finden die Brötchen gut.** They like the rolls. 3; **Wie findest du das?** What do you think of that?

der **Finger, -** finger 9

die **Firma,** *pl.* **Firmen** company 5; **bei einer ~ arbeiten** to work for a company 11

der **Fisch, -e** fish 3

der **Fischmann, ¨er**/die **Fischfrau, -en** fishmonger

fit fit

das **Fitnesstraining** fitness training, workout 1; **~ machen** to work out

die **Flasche, -n** bottle; **eine ~ Mineral′wasser** a bottle of mineral water 7

das **Fleisch** meat 3

fleißig industrious, hard-working 1

fliegen, flog, ist geflogen to fly 5

der **Flug, ¨e** flight 6

der **Flughafen, ¨** airport 10

das **Flugzeug, -e** airplane 5

der **Fluss, ¨e** river

föhnen to blow-dry; **ich föhne mir die Haare** I blow-dry my hair

folgen, ist gefolgt (+ *dat.*) to follow

folgend following

formell′ formal

das **Foto, -s** photo

der **Fotograf′, -en, -en**/die **Fotogra′fin, -nen** photographer

die **Fotografie′, -n** photograph; photography

fotografie′ren to photograph 6

die **Frage, -n** question 1; **eine ~ stellen** to ask a question; **eine ~ an** (+ *acc.*) **stellen** to ask someone a question 9; **Sie stellt eine Frage an ihn.** She asks him a question; *also* (+ *dat.*) **Sie stellt ihm eine Frage.** She asks him a question. 9

fragen to ask, to question 3; **~ nach** to inquire about

fraglich questionable

der **Franken** frank; **Schweizer Franken (sFr.)** Swiss unit of currency

(das) **Frankreich** France

der **Franzo′se, -n, -n**/die **Französin, -nen** French person

franzö′sisch French (*adj.*)

(das) **Franzö′sisch** French (language)

die **Frau, -en** woman; wife E; **Frau ...** Mrs. . . . ; Ms. . . . (*term of address for all adult women*) E

frei free 4; **~ haben** to be off work 6; **~ sein** to be unoccupied 6; **~ nehmen** to take time off

die **Freiheit, -en** freedom 10

der **Freitag** Friday E; **am ~** on Friday E

die **Freizeit** free time 6

die **Freizeitbeschäftigung, -en** leisure activity

fremd foreign; strange 12

der **Fremdenhass** xenophobia

die **Freude, -n** pleasure, joy 11; **~ machen** to give pleasure 11; **~ an** (+ *dat.*) pleasure in 11

sich freuen (auf + *acc.*) to look forward (to) 9; **~ (über** + *acc.*) to be pleased (about/with) 9

der **Freund, -e**/die **Freundin, -nen** friend 1; boyfriend/girlfriend

freundlich friendly 1

die **Freundlichkeit** friendliness

der **Frieden** peace 10

friedlich peaceful

frisch fresh 3

froh happy 1

früh early 6

der **Frühling** spring 2

das **Frühstück, -e** breakfast 3; **zum ~** for breakfast 3

frühstücken to eat breakfast

die **FU (Freie Universität′ Berlin′)** Free University of Berlin

sich fühlen to feel (ill, well, etc.) 9
führen to lead; carry in stock, have for sale; **ein Gespräch ~** to conduct a conversation
der **Führerschein, -e** driver's license 6
funktionie'ren to function, work
für (+ *acc.*) for 2
furchtbar terrible, horrible; very 1
fürchten to fear; **sich ~ (vor + *dat.*)** to fear, be afraid (of)
fürchterlich horrible, horribly 9
der **Fuß, ̈e** foot 5; **zu ~** on foot 5
der **Fußball** soccer 1
der **Fußgänger, -/die Fußgängerin, -nen** pedestrian
die **Fußgängerzone, -n** pedestrian zone 7

G

die **Gabel, -n** fork 7
ganz complete(ly), whole; very 1; **~ gut** not bad, OK 1; **~ schön** really quite 9; **~ schön [blass]** pretty [pale] 9; **im Ganzen** altogether
gar: ~ nicht not at all 6; **~ nichts** nothing at all 6
der **Garten, ̈** garden E
der **Gast, ̈e** guest 5
das **Gebäu'de, -** building
geben (gibt), gab, gegeben to give 3; **es gibt** (+ *acc.*) there is, there are 3; **Was gibt's zum [Abendessen]?** What's for [dinner]? 3; **Was gibt's/gab es?** What is/was playing? 10; **Was gibt's Neues?** What's new? 8
das **Gebir'ge, -** mountain range; (*pl.*) mountains
gebo'ren, ist geboren born 12
gebrau'chen to use
die **Geburt', -en** birth 8
der **Geburts'tag, -e** birthday 2; **Ich habe im [Mai] ~.** My birthday is in [May]. 2; **Wann hast du ~?** When is your birthday? 2; **zum ~** for one's birthday; **Alles Gute zum ~.** Happy birthday.
das **Gedicht', -e** poem
die **Gefahr', -en** danger
gefähr'lich dangerous
gefal'len (gefällt), gefiel, gefallen (+ *dat.*) to please, be pleasing (to) 5; **Es gefällt [mir].** [I] like it. 5
das **Gefühl', -e** feeling 8
gegen (+ *acc.*) against 3; **~ [sechs] Uhr** around/about [six] o'clock

die **Gegend, -en** region; area
gegenü'ber (+ *dat.*) opposite; across from there; toward
der **Gegner, -/die Gegnerin, -nen** opponent
das **Gehalt', ̈er** salary 11
gehen, ging, ist gegangen to go 1; **~ wir!** Let's go!; **Es geht (nicht).** It will (won't) do./It's (not) OK/It's (not) possible. 1; **Es geht nicht nur um [die Musik].** It's not just about [the music]. 12; **Geht das?** Is that OK? 5; **Mir geht es gut.** I'm fine 9; **Wie geht es Ihnen?** How are you? (*formal*) 1; **Wie geht's?** How are you? (*informal*) 1; **zu Fuß ~** to walk 5
gehö'ren (+ *dat.*) to belong to 5
gelb yellow E
das **Geld** money 3
das **Gemü'se, -** vegetable 3
gemüt'lich comfortable, informal 5
genau' exact(ly) 7; **Genau!** That's right! 7
die **Genau'igkeit** exactness
genau'so exactly the same 7
genug' enough 3
geöf'fnet open
gera'de just; straight 9
das **Gerät', -e** apparatus; tool; instrument
gera'ten, geriet, ist geraten get into a state; **in eine [Panik]~** to get in a [panic]
die **Germanis'tik** German studies (language and literature) 4
gern gladly, willingly; *used with verbs to indicate liking, as in* **Ich spiele gern Tennis.** I like to play tennis. 1; **~ haben** to be fond of (*with people only*), *as in* **Ich habe Anne ~.** I am fond of Anne.
das **Geschäft', -e** store; business 3
die **Geschäfts'frau, -en** businesswoman 11
der **Geschäfts'mann, - leute** businessman 11
die **Geschäfts'zeit, -en** business hours
das **Geschenk', -e** present, gift
die **Geschich'te, -n** story; history 4
das **Geschirr'** dishes 7; **~ spülen** to wash dishes 7
der **Geschirr'spüler** dishwasher
die **Geschwis'ter** (*pl.*) siblings 4
die **Gesell'schaft, -en** society; company 12
das **Gesetz', -e** law
das **Gesicht', -er** face 9

das **Gespräch', -e** conversation 11; **ein ~ führen** to carry on a conversation 11
gestern yesterday 2; **~ Abend** last night 6
gestresst' stressed 8
gesund' (ü) healthy 6
die **Gesund'heit** health
geteilt' durch divided by (*in math*) E
das **Getränk', -e** beverage 3
die **Gewalt'** violence
die **Gewerk'schaft, -en** labor union
die **Gewich'te** (*pl.*) weights; **~ heben** to lift weights 1
das **Gewicht'heben** weightlifting 1
gewin'nen, gewann, gewonnen to win 5
gewöhn'lich common; general; usual
die **Gitar're, -n** guitar E
das **Glas, ̈er** glass 3
glauben (+ *dat. when used with a person*) to believe 1; **Ich glaube, ja.** I think so. 1; **Ich glaube nicht.** I don't think so. 1
gleich immediately; in a minute; same; similar; simultaneously 7
gleichberechtigt entitled to equal rights
die **Gleichberechtigung, -en** equal rights
die **Gleichheit** sameness; equality
gleichzeitig at the same time
das **Glück** luck; happiness 8; **Viel ~!** Good luck! 8; **zum ~** fortunately
glücklich happy; lucky 1
der/die **Glückliche** (*noun decl. like adj.*) lucky/fortunate one 10
Glückwunsch: Herzlichen ~ (zum Geburtstag)! Happy birthday!
das **Golf** golf 1
der **Grad** degree 2; **Es sind minus [10] ~.** It's minus [10] degrees. 2; **Wie viel ~ sind es?** What's the temperature? 2
das **Gramm** (*abbr.* **g**) gram (1 ounce = 28.35g) 3
grau gray E
die **Grenze, -n** border, boundary; limit 10
(das) **Griechenland** Greece
das **Grillfest, -e** barbecue party
groß (ö) large, big; tall (people) E
(das) **Großbritan'nien** Great Britain
die **Größe, -n** size
die **Großeltern** (*pl.*) grandparents 4
die **Großmutter, ̈** grandmother 4
die **Großstadt, ̈e** city 8
der **Großvater, ̈** grandfather 4
grün green E
der **Grund, ̈e** reason 11

das **Grundgesetz** constitution of Germany

die **Grünen** (*pl.*) environmentalist political party

die **Gruppe, -n** group

der **Gruß, ⸚e** greeting 9; (*closing of a letter*) **viele Grüße** best regards 1; (*closing of a letter*) **liebe/herzliche Grüße** best regards 9

grüßen to greet; **Grüß dich!** (*fam.*) Hi! E

die **Gurke, -n** cucumber; die **saure ~** pickle 3

gut good, well; fine 1; **Mir geht es ~.** I'm fine. 9; **Na ~!** All right. 1

Güte: Du meine ~! Good heavens! 7

das **Gymna'sium,** *pl.* **Gymnasien** college-track secondary school 4

H

das **Haar, -e** hair 9

haben (hat), hatte, gehabt to have 2; **Angst ~ vor** (+ *dat.*) to be afraid of 7; **Besuch ~** to have company 3; **Was hast du?** What is wrong with you?, What's the matter? 9

das **Hähnchen, -** chicken 3

halb half 1; **~ [zwei]** half past [one] 1; **~ so groß** half as large 2

der **Halbbruder, ⸚** half brother

die **Halbschwester, -n** half sister

halbtags half days, part-time

Hallo! Hello., Hi; Hey! E

der **Hals, ⸚e** throat, neck 9

halten (hält), hielt, gehalten to hold; to keep 6; **~ von** to think of, have an opinion about 6; **eine Vorlesung ~** to give a lecture

die **Hand, ⸚e** hand 9

der **Handel** trade

der **Handschuh, -e** glove 6

die **Handtasche, -n** handbag, purse 6

das **Handy, -s** cellular phone E

hängen, hängte, gehängt to hang something, put 7

hängen, hing, gehangen to be hanging, be suspended 7

hart (ä) hard; difficult

der **Hass** hatred 12

hässlich ugly; hideous

hast has E

hat has E

hätte (*subj. of* **haben**) would have 8

häufig often, frequently 12

der **Hauptbahnhof** main train station

das **Hauptfach, ⸚er** major (subject) 4

die **Hauptstadt, ⸚e** capital 2

das **Hauptverb, -en** main verb

das **Haus,** *pl.* **Häuser** house 3; **nach Hause** (to go) home 3; **zu Hause** (to be) at home 5

die **Hausarbeit** homework 6; housework 7; chore 7

die **Hausaufgabe, -n** homework 10; **Hausaufgaben machen** to do homework 10

die **Hausfrau, -en** housewife

der **Haushalt** household; **den ~ machen** to take care of the house; to do the chores

der **Hausmann, ⸚er** househusband

das **Haustier, -e** domestic animal

He! Hey!

heben, hob, gehoben to lift; **Gewichte ~** to lift weights 1

das **Heft, -e** notebook E

die **Heimat** native country 12

die **Heimatadresse, -n** home address E

die **Heirat** marriage 8

heiraten to marry, to get married 8

die **Heiratsanzeige, -n** ad for marriage partner

heiß hot 2

heißen, hieß, geheißen to be named, be called E; **Wie heißt du?** What is your name? (*informal*); **Wie heißen Sie?** What is your name? (*formal*) E; **Du heißt [Mark], nicht?** Your name is [Mark], isn't it? E; **das heißt (d. h.)** that means, that is (i.e.) 11; **es heißt** it says

helfen (i), half, geholfen (+ *dat.*) to help 7; **~ bei** to help with 7; **Hilfe!** Help!

hell light; bright 9; **~braun** light brown 9

das **Hemd, -en** shirt 6

her (*prefix*) (*indicates motion toward speaker*) 7

herauf' up here

heraus' out

heraus'·finden, fand heraus, herausgefunden to find out

der **Herbst** autumn, fall 2; **im ~** in the fall 2

der **Herd, -e** cooking range 7

herein' in

der **Herr, -n, -en** gentleman E; **Herr ...** Mr. ... (*term of address*) E; **~ Ober** (*term of address for a waiter*)

her·stellen to produce; to manufacture 11

herum' around 7

herum'·liegen, lag herum, herumgelegen to lie around 7

das **Herz, -ens, -en** heart 9

herzlich cordial; **herzliche Grüße** best regards

heute today E; **~ Abend** this evening 1; **~ Morgen** this morning 1; **~ Nachmittag** this afternoon 1

heutzutage nowadays

hier here 2

die **Hilfe** help

hin (*prefix*) (*indicates motion away from speaker*) 7

hinein' into, in 11

hinein'·gehen, ging hinein, hineingegangen to go in 11

hin·gehen, ging hin, ist hingegangen to go there 6

hinter (+ *acc./dat.*) behind, in back of 7

hinterher' afterwards

der **Hinweis, -e** tip, hint

hm hm 2

das **Hobby, -s** hobby 6

hoch (höher, höchst-) high 4; **hoch-** *before nouns, as in* **ein hoher Lebensstandard** a high standard of living

das **Hochdeutsch** High German, standard German

die **Hochschule, -n** institution of higher education (e.g., university)

der **Hochschullehrer, -/**die **Hochschullehrerin, -nen** teacher at a university or college

hoffen to hope 5; **~ auf** (+ *acc.*) to hope for

hoffentlich (*colloq.*) hopefully; I hope so. 2

höflich polite

hoh- (-er, -es, -e) high (*the form of* **hoch** *used before nouns, as in* **hohe Berge** high mountains) 5

hören to hear; to listen to 1; **Musik ~** listening to music 1

der **Hörsaal, -säle** lecture hall

die **Hose, -n** pants, trousers 6; **ein Paar Hosen** a pair of pants; **die kurzen Hosen** shorts 6

der **Hund, -e** dog 7

der **Hunger** hunger 3; **~ haben** to be hungry 3; **Riesenhunger haben** to be very hungry

hungrig hungry 12

husten to cough 9

der **Hut, ⸚e** hat 6

I

ich I E; **~ auch** me, too

die **Idee', -n** idea 6

identifizie′ren to identify

Ihnen (*dat. of* **Sie**) (to) you; **Und Ihnen?** And you? (*as part of response to* **Wie geht es Ihnen?**) 1

ihr (*pron.*) you (*familiar pl.*) 1; (*poss. adj.*) her, their 2

Ihr (*poss. adj.*) your (*formal*) E

illustrie′ren to illustrate

immer always 3; ~ **mehr** more and more 8; ~ **noch** still 9; **noch** ~ still; **wie** ~ as always 11; ~ **wieder** again and again 5

importie′ren to import

in (+ *acc./dat.*) in 2; into; to 3

individuell′ individual(ly)

die **Industrie′, -n** industry

die **Informa′tik** computer science 4

der **Informa′tiker, -/**die **Informa′tikerin, -nen** computer scientist 11

die **Information′, -en** information 4

der **Ingenieur′, -e/**die **Ingenieu′rin, -nen** engineer 4

inlineskaten to go in-line skating 1

der **Inlineskater, -/**die **Inlineskaterin, -nen** in-line skater

das **Inlineskating** in-line skating 1

das **Instrument′, -e** instrument 9

integrie′ren to integrate

intelligent′ intelligent, smart 1

interessant′ interesting 3

das **Interes′se, -n** interest

interessie′ren to interest 6; **sich interessieren (für)** to be interested (in) 9

interessiert′ sein (**an** + *dat.*) to be interested (in)

international′ international

das **Internet** Internet 4; **im** ~ on the Internet 4; **im** ~ **surfen** to surf the Internet 4; **übers** ~ **kaufen** to buy on the Internet 6

das **Internetcafé, -s** cybercafe 6

das **Interview, -s** interview 6

interviewen to interview

die **Intoleranz′** intolerance

inzwi′schen in the meantime 12

irgendwann′ sometime, at some point

irgendwie′ somehow 12

isoliert′ isolated

ist is E

(das) **Ita′lien** Italy

italie′nisch Italian (*adj.*)

J

ja yes E; (*flavoring particle*) indeed, of course 2; **na** ~ well now

die **Jacke, -n** jacket 6

das **Jackett′, -s** (*pronounced* /zhakĕt′/) a man's suit jacket; sport coat 6

das **Jahr, -e** year E; **Ich bin [19] Jahre alt** I'm [19] years old. E; **die [sechziger/achtziger] Jahre** the [1960s/1980s] 12; **vor [10] Jahren** [10] years ago

die **Jahreszeit, -en** season 2

das **Jahrhun′dert, -e** century 9

-jährig . . . years old

das **Jahrzehnt′, -e** decade

der **Januar** January 2

je ... desto ... the . . . the . . . (*with comp.*); **je größer desto besser** the bigger the better

die **Jeans** (*sg. and pl.*) jeans 6

jed- (**-er, -es, -e**) each, every 4; **jeder** everyone 4

jedenfalls at any rate

jedoch′ (*conj. or adv.*) however, nonetheless 9

jemand (**-en, -em**) (*endings are optional*) someone 12

jetzt now 2

jetzig of the present time; current

der **Job, -s** job 4

jobben to have a temporary job (e.g., a summer job) (*colloq.*) 4

joggen to jog 1

das **Jogging** jogging 1; ~ **gehen** to go jogging 1

der **Journalist′, -en, -en/**die **Journalis′tin, -nen** journalist 11

der **Jude, -n, -n/**die **Jüdin, -nen** Jew

jüdisch Jewish

die **Jugendherberge, -n** youth hostel

der/die **Jugendliche** (*noun decl. like adj.*) young person

der **Juli** July 3

jung (**ü**) young 4

der **Junge, -n, -n** boy E

der **Juni** June 2

das **Jura** law studies

K

der **Kaffee** coffee 3

das **Kaffee′haus, -häuser** café (in Austria); coffeehouse

der **Kalen′der, -** calendar

kalt (**ä**) cold 2; **es wird** ~ it is getting cold 6

die **Kamera, -s** camera 9

der **Kamm, ̈-e** comb 3

(**sich**) **kämmen** to comb 9; **Ich kämme mich./Ich kämme mir die Haare.** I comb my hair. 9

(das) **Kanada** Canada 2

der **Kana′dier, -/**die **Kana′dierin, -nen** Canadian (person) 2

kana′disch Canadian (*adj.*) 4

der **Kanton′, -e** canton (a Swiss state)

kaputt′ broken; exhausted (*slang*) 5

die **Karot′te, -n** carrot 3

die **Karrie′re, -n** career

die **Karte, -n** card; postcard 1; ticket 1; die **Karten** (*pl.*) playing cards 1

die **Kartof′fel, -n** potato 3

der **Käse** cheese 3

das **Käsebrot, -e** cheese sandwich

die **Kasset′te, -n** cassette

das **Kasset′tendeck, -s** cassette deck E

die **Kategorie′, -n** category

die **Katze, -n** cat 7

kaufen to buy 3

das **Kaufhaus, -häuser** department store 3

kaum hardly

kein not a, not any 3; ~ **... mehr** no more . . . 3

kennen, kannte, gekannt to know, be acquainted with [people, places, or things] 3; ~ **lernen** to get to know; to make the acquaintance of 6

das **Kilo(gramm)** (*abbr.* **kg**) kilo(gram) (= 2.2 pounds) 3

der **Kilometer, -** (*abbr.* **km**) kilometer (= .062 miles) 2

das **Kind, -er** child E

der **Kindergarten, ̈** nursery school; kindergarten 8

das **Kindermädchen, -** nanny

die **Kindheit** childhood

das **Kinn, -e** chin 9

das **Kino, -s** movie theater 1; **ins** ~ **gehen** to go to the movies 1

die **Kirche, -n** church

das **Kissen, -** pillow 7

klagen to complain 8

die **Klammer, -n** parenthesis

klar clear; (*interj.*) of course, naturally 4

die **Klasse, -n** class 4; die **erste** ~ first grade; **Klasse!** Great!

der **Klassenkamerad, -en, -en/**die **Klassenkameradin, -nen** classmate

klassisch classic(al)

die **Klausur′, -en** test 4; **eine** ~ **schreiben** to take a test 4

das **Klavier′, -e** piano 10; das **~konzert** piano concerto; piano concert 10

das **Kleid, -er** dress 6

die **Kleidung** clothing 6; das **Kleidungsstück, -e** article of clothing

klein small; short (*of people*) E

das Klima climate 2

klingeln to ring 11

die Klinik, -en clinic 9

das Klischee', -s cliché 5

die Kneipe, -n bar, pub 6

das Knie, - (*pl. pronounced* /Kni ə/) knee 9

der Koch, ⁻e/die Köchin, -nen cook

kochen to cook 6

der Kolle'ge, -n, -n/die Kolle'gin, -nen colleague 8

Köln Cologne

komisch funny; strange 12

kommen, kam, ist gekommen to come 1; **aus ... ~** to be from . . . ; **Woher kommst du?** Where are you from?/Where do you come from? 2; **Ich komme aus ...** I come/am from . . . 2

der Kommentar', -e comment; commentary

der Kommilito'ne, -n, -n/die Kommilito'nin, -nen fellow student

die Kommo'de, -n chest of drawers 7

der Kommunis'mus communism

kommunizie'ren to communicate

kompliziert' complicated

der Komponist', -en, -en/die Komponis'tin, -nen composer 5

die Konditorei', -en pastry shop

die Konjunktion', -en conjunction

die Konkurrenz', -en competition

konkurrie'ren to compete 11

können (kann), konnte, gekonnt to be able to; can 4; **Deutsch ~** to know German

könnte (*subj. of* **können**) would be able to 11

sich konzentrie'ren to concentrate

das Konzert', -e concert 6; **ins ~ gehen** to go to a concert 6

der Kopf, ⁻e head 9

die Kopfschmerzen (*pl.*) headache 3

das Kopftuch, ⁻er headscarf

der Körper, - body 9

korrigie'ren to correct

kosten to cost 4

das Kostüm', -e costume; ladies' suit

krank sick, ill 1

das Krankenhaus, -häuser hospital 6

die Krankenkasse health insurance

der Krankenpfleger, -/die Kranken-pflegerin, -nen nurse

die Krankenschwester, -n female nurse 7

die Krankheit, -en illness 9

die Krawat'te, -n necktie 6

kreativ' creative 1

die Kredit'karte, -n credit card 9

der Krieg, -e war 5

kriegen to get 11

der Krimi, -s mystery (novel or film) 4

die Krise, -n crisis

die Kritik' criticism; review 10

kritisch critical 1

die Küche, -n kitchen 7

der Kuchen, - cake 3

das Küchengerät, -e kitchen appliance

der Kugelschreiber, - ballpoint pen E

kühl cool 2

der Kühlschrank, ⁻e refrigerator 7

der Kuli, -s (*colloq. for* **Kugelschreiber**) ballpoint pen E

kulminie'ren to culminate

die Kultur', -en culture 12

kulturell' culture, culturally 12

der Kunde, -n, -n/die Kundin, -nen customer, client 11

die Kündigung, -en dismissal

die Kunst, ⁻e art; skill

die Kunstgeschichte art history 4

der Künstler, -/die Künstlerin, -nen artist 5

der Kurs, -e course, class 4

der Kursteilnehmer, -/die Kursteilnehmerin, -nen member of a class or course

kurz short, brief 5; **die kurzen Hosen** shorts 6

die Kurzgeschichte, -n short story

die Kusi'ne, -n cousin (*f.*) 4

küssen to kiss

L

lächeln to smile 7; **~ über** (+ *acc.*) to smile about

lachen to laugh 12; **~ über** (+ *acc.*) to laugh about; **zum Lachen** laughable 12

der Laden, ⁻ store 3

die Lampe, -n lamp E

das Land, ⁻er country, land 2; **aufs ~ fahren** to go to the country

die Landkarte, -n map 5

lang (ä) long 4

lange (*adv.*) for a long time 3

langsam slow(ly) 9

sich langweilen to feel bored

langweilig boring

lassen (lässt), ließ, gelassen to leave; to let, permit; to have something done 12; **Lass uns gehen.** Let's go. 12

laufen (läuft), lief, ist gelaufen to run; to go on foot, to walk 5

laut (*adj.*) loud; noisy 1; (*prep. + gen. or dat.*) according to

das Leben life 7

leben to live 5

die Lebensmittel (*pl.*) food; groceries 3

der Lebensstandard standard of living 9

die Lederjacke, -n leather jacket

leer empty 11

legen to lay or put something in a horizontal position 7

lehren to teach

der Lehrer, -/die Lehrerin, -nen teacher 10

leicht light; easy 8

Leid: Es tut mir ~. I'm sorry. 4

leiden, litt, gelitten to suffer; to tolerate; to endure 8

leider unfortunately 2

leihen, lieh, geliehen to lend; to borrow 4

lernen to learn; to study 4

lesen (ie), las, gelesen to read 4

das Lesestück, ⁻e reading selection

letzt last 5

die Leute (*pl.*) people 2

das Licht, -er light

lieb (*adj.*) dear; **Liebe [Barbara], Lieber [Paul] ...** Dear [Barbara], Dear [Paul] . . . (*used at the beginning of a letter*) 1

die Liebe love 4

lieben to love

lieber (*comp. of* **gern**) preferably, rather 9

der Liebesroman, -e romance (novel) 4

der Liebling, -e favorite 3; darling; **Lieblings-** (*prefix*) favorite: **das Lieblingsgetränk** favorite drink 3

liebsten: am ~ best liked; most of all 9

liegen, lag, gelegen to lie; to be situated, be located 2

lila lavender, lilac

die Limona'de soft drink; lemonade 3

links on/to the left 11

die Lippe, -n lip 9

die Liste, -n list; **eine ~ auf-stellen/machen** to make a list

der Liter,- (*abbr.* l) liter (= 1.056 U.S. quarts) 3

die Literatur' literature 4

der Löffel, - spoon 7

logisch logical

das Lokal', -e restaurant; bar 12

los loose; **Was ist ~?** What's the matter? What's going on? What's up? 1; **Los!** Let's go!; **es ist nicht viel ~** there's not much going on 6

lösen to solve

die **Luft** air
die **Luftbrücke** airlift
die **Lust** desire; enjoyment 10; ~ **haben** (+ **zu** + *inf.*) to be in the mood, to feel like doing something 10
lustig funny; merry; cheerful 1
die **Lustigkeit** merriment; fun

M

machen to do; to make 1; **Mach's gut!** Take it easy. 1; **Deutsch ~** to do/study German (homework) 1; **Examen ~** to graduate from the university 4; **(Es) macht nichts.** (It) doesn't matter. 7; **Mach schnell!** Hurry up! 7
das **Mädchen,** - girl E
der **Magen,** - stomach 9; die **~schmerzen** (*pl.*) stomachache 9
der **Mai** May 2
mal time; times (in multiplication) E; **drei~** three times; **mal** (= **einmal**) once; sometime; (*flavoring particle that softens a command and leaves the time indefinite*) **Sag ~ ...** Tell me ... 3; **Moment ~!** Just a minute! 11
das **Mal, -e** time
die **Mama** mom 4
man one, people, (*impersonal*) you E
manch (-er, -es, -e) many a (*sg.*); some (*pl.*) 4
manchmal sometimes 2
der **Mann, ¨er** man E; husband
der **Mantel, ¨** outer coat 6
die **Margari'ne** margarine 3
markie'ren to check
der **Markt, ¨e** market 3; **auf den ~** to the market 3
die **Marmela'de** marmalade, jam 3
der **März** March 2
die **Maschi'ne, -n** machine 9
die **Mathe** (*short for* **Mathematik**) math 4
die **Mathematik'** mathematics 4
die **Mauer, -n** (exterior) wall 10
der **Mecha'niker,** -/die **Mecha'nikerin, -nen** mechanic
mehr (*comp. of* **viel**) more 2; **immer ~** more and more 8; **~ oder weniger** more or less; **kein ... ~** no more ... 3; **nicht ~** no longer, not anymore 4
mehrere several; various 8
die **Mehrheit** majority
mein(e) my E

meinen to mean; to think, have an opinion 7; **Was meinst du?** What do you think?
die **Meinung, -en** opinion; **meiner ~ nach** in my opinion
meist (*superlative of* **viel**) most 4; die **meisten (Leute)** most of (the people) 4
meistens most of the time, mostly 5
die **Mensa, -s** university cafeteria
der **Mensch, -en, -en** person, human being 1; **~!** Man!/Wow!
merken to notice; to realize 11; **sich** (*dat.*) **~** to note down
das **Messer,** - knife 7
der **Meter,** -(*abbr.* **m**) meter (= 39.37 inches)
der **Metzger,** - butcher 3; **beim ~** at the butcher's 3; **zum ~** to the butcher's 3
die **Metzgerei', -en** butcher shop, meat market 3
mieten to rent
der **Mikrowelle, -n** microwave (oven)
die **Milch** milk 3
die **Million', -en** million 2
die **Minderheit, -en** minority
mindestens at least
das **Mineral'wasser** mineral water 3
minus minus E
die **Minu'te, -n** minute 1
mit (+ *dat.*) with 3; **~ dem [Auto] fahren** to go by [car] 5
der **Mitarbeiter,** -/die **Mitarbeiterin, -nen** employee 11
der **Mitbewohner,** -/die **Mitbewohnerin, -nen** roommate
mit·bringen, brachte mit, mitgebracht to bring along 4
der **Mitbürger,** -/die **Mitbürgerin, -nen** fellow citizen
miteinan'der with each other 6
mit·fahren (fährt mit), fuhr mit, ist mitgefahren to drive/ride along 5
mit·gehen, ging mit, ist mitgegangen to go along 6
das **Mitglied, -er** member 9
mit·kommen, kam mit, ist mitgekommen to come along 2; **Wer kommt mit?** Who's coming along? **Kommst du mit ins Kino?** Are you coming along to the movie?
mit·nehmen (nimmt mit), nahm mit, mitgenommen to take along
der **Mittag, -e** noon 8

das **Mittagessen** midday meal 3; **zum ~** for the midday meal, for lunch 3
mittags at noon
die **Mitte** middle
mitten: ~ in ... in the middle of ...
der **Mittwoch** Wednesday E
die **Möbel** (*pl.*) furniture 7
das **Möbelstück, ¨e** piece of furniture 7
möchte (*subj. of* **mögen**) would like 3
modern' modern 4
mögen (mag), mochte, gemocht to like 4
möglich possible 6
die **Möglichkeit, -en** possibility
moin moin hello (*North German greeting*)
der **Moment', -e** moment 7; **im ~** at the moment 7; **~ mal!** Just a minute! 11
der **Monat, -e** month 2; **einmal im ~** once a month
der **Montag** Monday E; **am ~** on Monday E; **~ in acht Tagen** a week from Monday
morgen tomorrow 2; **~ früh** tomorrow morning
der **Morgen** morning 1; **Guten ~.** Good morning 1
morgens mornings, every morning 3
das **Motorrad, ¨er** motorcycle 5
das **Motto, -s** motto 12
das **Mountainbike, -s** mountain bike
müde tired 1
multikulturell' multicultural 12
der **Mund, ¨er** mouth 9
das **Muse'um,** *pl.* **Muse'en** museum
das **Musical, -s** musical 6
die **Musik'** music 1; **~ hören** listening to music 1
musika'lisch musical 1
der **Mu'siker,** -/die **Mu'sikerin, -nen** musician 11
der **Muslim, -e**/die **Musli'min, -nen** Muslim
müssen (muss), musste, gemusst to have to; must 4
müsste (*subj. of* **müssen**) would have to 11
die **Mutter, ¨** mother 4
die **Muttersprache, -n** native language
die **Mutti, -s** mom 4
die **Mütze, -n** cap 6

N

na well 2; **~ gut!** All right. 1; well (*interjection*); **naja** oh well; well now

nach (+ *dat.*) after 1; to (*with cities and countries used without an article, e.g.,* **nach Berlin; nach Deutschland**) 2; ~ **Hause** (to go) home 3; **fragen** ~ to ask about

der **Nachbar, -n, -n**/die **Nachbarin, -nen** neighbor 1

das **Nachbarland, ̈er** neighboring country 2

nachdem' (*conj.*) after

nach·denken, dachte nach, nachgedacht (**über**) (+ *acc.*) to think (about), reflect (on)

nachher afterwards 4

der **Nachmittag, -e** afternoon 1

der **Nachname, -ns, -n** last name

die **Nachricht, -en** message; **Nachrichten** (*pl.*) newscast

nach·schlagen (**schlägt nach**), **schlug nach, nachgeschlagen** to look up

nach·sehen (**sieht nach**), **sah nach, nachgesehen** to look up

die **Nachspeise, -n** dessert

nächst next 7

die **Nacht, ̈e** night 1; **Gute ~.** Good night. 1; das **Nachtleben** nightlife

der **Nachtisch, -e** dessert

der **Nachttisch, -e** bedside table 7

nahe (+ *dat.*) near 12; **mir ~** close to me 12

die **Nähe** nearness, proximity; vicinity; **in der ~** near at hand

der **Name, -ns, -n** name 7

nämlich after all; that is (to say); you know; you see 7

die **Nase, -n** nose 9

nass (**nasser** *or* **nässer**) wet 2

die **Nationalität', -en** nationality

der **National'rat** National Council (*Switzerland*)

die **Natur'** nature

natür'lich natural 1; naturally 3; of course

die **Natür'lichkeit** naturalness

der **Natur'wissenschaftler, -/**die **Natur'wissenschaftlerin, -nen** (natural) scientist

neben (+ *acc./dat.*) beside, next to, besides 7

das **Nebenfach, ̈er** minor (subject) 4

nee (*colloq.*) no, nope

der **Neffe, -n -n** nephew 4

negativ negative

nehmen (**nimmt**), **nahm, genommen** to take 3

nein no E

nennen, nannte, genannt to name 10

nervös' nervous

nett nice 1

neu new E; **Was gibt's Neues?** What's new? 8

neugierig curious

neutral' neutral 9

die **Neutralität'** neutrality

nicht not E; **~?** (*tag question*) don't you?; isn't it? 1; **Bettina ist sehr ernst, ~?** Bettina is very serious, isn't she? 1; **~ mehr** no longer, not anymore 3; **~ nur ... sondern auch** not only . . . but also 5; **~ so** [**heiß**] not as [hot] 2; **~ wahr?** isn't that so? 2; **noch ~** not yet 2

die **Nichte, -n** niece 4

nichts nothing 1; **~ Beson'deres** nothing special 1; **(Es) macht ~!** (It) doesn't matter. 7

nie never 8

(die) **Niederlande** (*pl.*) the Netherlands

niedrig low 11

niemand (**-en, -em**) (*endings are optional*) no one 12

noch still; in addition 2; **~ ein ...** another . . . 3; **~ einmal** again, once more 12; **~ etwas** something else 4; **~ immer** still; **~ mehr** even more; **~ nicht** not yet 3; **immer ~** still 9; **Sonst ~ einen Wunsch?** Anything else? 3; **sonst ~ etwas** something else 3; **was ~?** what else? 7

der **Norden** north 2

nördlich to the north 2

(das) **Norwegen** Norway

die **Note, -n** grade; note 4

(**sich**) **notie'ren** to make a note of

die **Notiz', -en** note 4

der **Novem'ber** November 2

die **Nudeln** (*pl.*) noodles 3

der **Numerus clausus** limited number of university positions for study in certain subjects

die **Nummer, -n** number E

nummerie'ren to number

nun now, at present 7

nur only 1

O

ob (*sub. conj.*) whether, if 7

oben above

der **Ober, -** waiter

oberflächlich superficial 7

das **Obst** fruit 3

obwohl' (*sub. conj.*) although 5

oder or 1; **~?** Or don't you agree? 6; **Du kommst doch, ~?** You're coming, aren't you?

offen open 3; frank 6

öffentlich public(ly) 7

offiziell' official

öffnen to open 10

oft often 1

oh je oh dear 3

ohne (+ *acc.*) without 3; **~ . . .** (+ *inf.*) without

das **Ohr, -en** ear 9

okay' okay, OK E

der **Okto'ber** October 2

die **Oli've, -n** olive

die **Oma, -s** grandma 4

der **Onkel, -** uncle 4

der **Opa, -s** grandpa 4

das **Open-Air-Konzert** outdoor concert 10

die **Oper, -n** opera 10; **in die ~ gehen** to go to the opera 10

optimis'tisch optimistic

die **Oran'ge, -n** orange 3

der **Oran'gensaft** orange juice 3

die **Ordnung** order; **in ~** that is all right, OK 6

organisato'risch organizational

organisie'ren to organize

der **Ort, -e** place (geographical) 9

der **Ostblock** the eastern block

der **Osten** east 2

(das) **Österreich** Austria 2

der **Österreicher, -/**die **Österreicherin, -nen** Austrian person 2

österreichisch Austrian (*adj.*) 5

östlich eastern

der **Ozean, -e** ocean 2

P

das **Paar, -e** pair; couple 8

paar; ein ~ a few 6; **alle ~ Minuten** every few minutes

der **Papa, -s** dad 4

das **Papier', -e** paper E

der **Park, -s** park 7

parken to park

der **Partner, -/**die **Partnerin, -nen** partner

die **Partnerschaft, -en** partnership

die **Party, -s** party 4; **auf eine ~** to a party; **auf einer ~** at a party

passen (**passt**) (+ *dat.*) to fit; to be appropriate

passend appropriate; suitable

passie'ren, ist passiert (+ *dat.*) to happen 7; **Was ist dir passiert?** What happened to you? 7

passiv passive(ly) 6

die **Pause, -n** break, rest; intermission

die **Person′**, -en person

der **Personal′chef**, -s/die **Personal′chefin**, -nen head of the human resources (personnel) department 11

persön′lich personal(ly) 3

die **Persön′lichkeit**, -en personality; personage

die **Pflanze**, -n plant E

pflanzen to plant

das **Pfund**, -e (*abbrev.* **Pfd.**) pound (= 1.1 U.S. pounds) 3

die **Philosophie′** philosophy 4

die **Physik′** physics 4

der **Phy′siker**, -/die **Phy′sikerin**, -nen physicist

der **Physiotherapeut′**, -en, -en/die **Physiotherapeu′tin**, -nen physical therapist

das **Picknick**, -s picnic; ~ **machen** to have a picnic

die **Pizza**, -s, also **Pizzen** pizza

plädie′ren to plead

der **Plan**, ̈e plan 5; schedule

planen to plan 9

der **Platz**, ̈e place; seat; space; square 4; ~ **nehmen** to take a seat

pleite broke, out of money 7

plötzlich suddenly

die **Politik′** politics; political science 8

der **Poli′tiker**, -/die **Poli′tikerin**, -nen politician 10

poli′tisch political(ly) 10

die **Polizei′** police

das **Polohemd**, -en polo shirt 6

die **Pommes frites** (*pl.*) French fries

das **Popkonzert**, -e pop concert 10

das **Porträt**, -s portrait 5

positiv positive

die **Post** mail; post office 11

das *or* der **Poster**, - poster E

die **Postleitzahl**, -en postal code

praktisch practical(ly); for all practical purposes 1

praktizie′ren to practice (medicine, law)

der **Präsident′**, -en, -en/die **Präsiden′tin**, -nen president

präzis′ precise(ly)

der **Preis**, -e price 11

prima fantastic, great (**prima** *takes no adj. endings*) 10

privat′ private 4

privilegiert′ privileged

pro per 8

die **Probe**, -n rehearsal 6

proben to rehearse

probie′ren to try; to (put to the) test; (*food*) to taste

das **Problem′**, -e problem 5

das **Produkt′**, -e product 5

produzie′ren to produce

der **Profes′sor**, *pl.* **Professo′ren**/die **Professo′rin**, -nen professor E

protestie′ren to protest

proviso′risch provisionally

das **Prozent′** percent 4

die **Prüfung**, -en test, examination 4

die **Psychologie′** psychology 4

das **Publikum** public

der **Pulli**, -s sweater 6

der **Punkt**, -e dot, spot, point; period 10

pünktlich punctual 7

putzen to clean 7; **Ich putze mir die Zähne** I'm brushing my teeth 9

Q

die **Qualität′**, -en quality 9

der **Quatsch** nonsense 8; ~! Nonsense! 8

R

das **Rad**, ̈er (*short for* **Fahrrad**) bike, bicycle 5; wheel; **Rad fahren (fährt Rad)**, **fuhr Rad**, **ist Rad gefahren** to (ride a) bicycle, to bike 5

das **Radio**, -s radio E

die **Radtour**, -en bicycle trip

(sich) rasie′ren to shave 9

der **Rassis′mus** racism 12

raten (ä), **riet**, **geraten** to guess

der **Rauch** smoke

rauchen to smoke

der **Raum**, ̈e room; space

raus (*contraction of* **heraus**) out

reagie′ren (auf + *acc.*) to react (to)

das **Recht**, -e right; law 8; ~ **auf** + *acc.* right to 8; **Recht haben** to be right 7; **Du hast Recht.** You're right. 7

rechts on/to the right 11

der **Rechtsanwalt**, -anwälte/die **Rechtsanwältin**, -nen lawyer 11

die **Rede**, -n speech; **eine ~ halten** to give a speech

reden (über + *acc.*) to talk/speak (about) 2

das **Redemittel**, - speech act

reduzie′ren to reduce, diminish

das **Referat′**, -e report; seminar paper 4

die **Regelstudienzeit** limit on time to complete university studies

der **Regen** rain 2

der **Regenmantel**, ̈ raincoat 6

der **Regenschirm**, -e umbrella 5

die **Regie′rung**, -en government 10

regnen to rain 2; **es regnet** it's raining 2

reich rich 5

reif ripe

rein (*contraction of* **herein**) in

die **Reise**, -n trip, journey 7; **Gute ~!** Have a good trip!

das **Reisebüro**, -s travel agency

reisen, ist gereist to travel

relativ′ relative; relatively 1

renovie′ren to renovate

repariе′ren to repair

der **Repor′ter**, -/die **Repor′terin**, -nen reporter 6

das **Restaurant′** -s restaurant 7

richtig correct, right; proper 6

die **Richtigkeit** correctness; accuracy

riechen, roch, gerochen to smell 3; ~ **nach** to smell of

der **Rinderbraten** roast beef 3

riskie′ren to risk

der **Rock**, ̈e skirt 6

die **Rockband**, -s rock band 10

der **Rockfan**, -s rock fan 12

die **Rockmusik** rock (music) 6

der **Rockmusiker**, -/die **Rockmusikerin**, -nen rock musician 12

der **Rohstoff**, -e raw material 9

die **Rolle**, -n role; **eine ~ spielen** to play a role 12

das **Rollenspiel**, -e role play

der **Roman′**, -e novel 4

die **Rose**, -n rose

die **Rosi′ne**, -n raisin

rot red E

der **Rotwein**, -e red wine 3

der **Rücken**, - back 9; die **Rückenschmerzen** (*pl.*) backache 9

die **Rückreise**, -n return trip

der **Rucksack**, -säcke backpack E

rufen, rief, gerufen to call 3

die **Ruhe** rest; peace and quiet

ruhig calm, easygoing; quiet 1

das **Rührei**, -er scrambled egg

der **Russe**, -n, -n/die **Russin**, -nen Russian person

(das) **Russland** Russia

S

die **Sache**, -n thing 6; affair, concern; (*pl.*) clothes 6

der **Saft**, ̈e juice 3

sagen to say; tell 2; **sag mal** tell me 3

der **Salat′**, -e lettuce; salad 3

sammeln to collect 11

der **Samstag** (*in southern Germany*) Saturday E

samstags Saturdays, every Saturday 3
sanft gentle; soft
der **Sänger, -**/die **Sängerin, -nen** singer
der **Satz, ⸚e** sentence 11
sauber clean 7
sauber machen to clean 7
sauer sour; cross, morose
saugen to suck; **Staub ~** (*also* **staubsaugen, gestaubsaugt**) to vacuum 7
das **Schach** chess 1
schade that's too bad, a pity, a shame
schaden (+ *dat.*) to harm
die **Schallplatte, -n** (phonograph) record
schauen to see; to look
der **Schein, -e** glow; (*type of official document*) der **Geldschein** bill; der **Seminarschein** certificate of attendance for one semester of a course
scheinen, schien, geschienen to shine 2; to appear, seem
schenken to give (as a gift) 5
schick chic
schicken to send
das **Schiff, -e** ship 5
der **Schinken, -** ham 3
der **Schirm, -e** umbrella 6
schlafen (ä), schlief, geschlafen to sleep 5; **bei jemandem ~** to sleep at someone's house
das **Schlafzimmer, -** bedroom 7
schlagen (ä), schlug, geschlagen to hit, beat; to whip
die **Schlagsahne** whipped cream
schlank slender 9
schlecht bad, badly 1; **Mir ist ~.** I feel nauseated. 9
schließen, schloss, geschlossen to close 3
schließlich finally, after all 9
schlimm bad, serious, severe 8
schmecken (+ *dat.*) to taste 6; **Es schmeckt [mir].** It tastes good to [me]. 6; **Hat es geschmeckt?** Did it taste good? 6
der **Schmerz, -en** pain 9
(sich) schminken to put on makeup 9; **ich schminke mich** I put on makeup 9; **Ich schminke mir die Augen.** I put on eye makeup. 9
schmutzig dirty
der **Schnee** snow 2
schneien to snow 2; **es schneit** it's snowing 2
schnell fast, quickly 3; **Mach ~!** Hurry up! 7

die **Schokola′de** chocolate; das **Schokola′deneis** chocolate ice cream
schon already 3
schön nice, beautiful 2; **~ warm** nice and warm 2; **schönes Wetter** nice weather 2; **ganz ~** really quite 9
die **Schönheit** beauty
der **Schrank, ⸚e** wardrobe 7
schreiben, schrieb, geschrieben to write E; **~ an** (+ *acc.*) to write to 9; **~ über** (+ *acc.*) to write about 7; **~ von** (+ *dat.*) to write about; **Wie schreibt man das?** How do you spell that? E
der **Schreibtisch, -e** desk 7
der **Schriftsteller, -**/die **Schriftstellerin, -nen** writer 5
der **Schritt, -e** step 8
schüchtern shy
der **Schuh, -e** shoe 6
die **Schule, -n** school 4
schützen to protect
schwach (ä) weak 9
schwarz black E
(das) **Schweden** Sweden
die **Schweiz** Switzerland 2
der **Schweizer, -**/die **Schweizerin, -nen** Swiss person 2
Schweizer Swiss (*adj.*) 9
(das) **Schweizerdeutsch** Swiss German
schwer hard, difficult; heavy 4
die **Schwester, -n** sister 4
Schwieger- (*prefix meaning* in-law); **~tochter** daughter-in-law
schwierig difficult 8
die **Schwierigkeit, -en** difficulty
schwimmen, schwamm, ist geschwommen to swim 1
schwül humid 2
der **Science-Fic′tion-Film, -e** science fiction film
der **See, -n** lake
die **See, -n** sea
segeln to sail
sehen (ie), sah, gesehen to see 4
sehr very (much) 1
sei (**du**-*imperative of* **sein**) 3; **~ [mir] nicht böse.** Don't be mad [at me]. 7
die **Seife** soap
die **Seifenoper, -n** soap opera
sein his; its 1
sein (ist), war, ist gewesen to be 1
seit (+ *dat.*) since (*time or date*) 4; for (*time period*) 4; **~ wann** since when, (for) how long 4; **~ kurzer Zeit** recently

seitdem′ since then 12
die **Seite, -n** side; page 9
der **Sekretär′, -e**/die **Sekretä′rin, -nen** secretary
selber oneself, myself, itself, etc.
selbst oneself, myself, itself, etc. 7; even
selbstständig independent, self-reliant
selbstverständlich of course, it goes without saying
selten seldom 9
das **Semes′ter, -** semester 4
die **Semes′teradresse, -n** school address E
die **Semes′terferien** (*pl.*) semester break 4
das **Seminar′, -e** seminar 4
die **Seminar′arbeit, -en** seminar paper 4
der **Seminar′schein, -e** certificate of attendance for one semester of a course
die **Sendung, -en** TV or radio program 6
der **Septem′ber** September 2
die **Serie, -n** series
servie′ren to serve
der **Sessel, -** easy chair 7
setzen to set or put something down 7; **sich setzen** to take/have a seat 9
das **Shampoo′, -s** shampoo
die **Shorts** (*pl.*) shorts 6
sicher safe; secure; certain(ly) 8
die **Sicherheit** safety, security
sicherlich surely, certainly
sie she, it E; they 1
Sie you (*formal*) E
silber (*adj.*) silver
sind are E
der **Sinn** meaning, purpose
die **Situation′, -en** situation
der **Sitz, -e** headquarters, seat
sitzen, saß, gesessen to sit 5
der **Ski, -er** (**Ski** *is pronounced* **Schi**) ski 5; **Ski laufen** (*also* **Ski fahren**) to ski 5; **zum Skilaufen gehen** to go skiing
der **Skiläufer, -**/die **Skiläuferin, -nen** skier 5
das **Snowboard, -e** snowboard 5
snowboarden to snowboard 5
so so, thus; this way E, **so genannt** so-called, **~ ... wie** as . . . as 2; **~?** Is that so? Really? 4; **~ ein** such a 4
sobald′ (*sub. conj.*) as soon as
die **Socke, -n** sock 6
das **Sofa, -s** sofa 7
sofort′ immediately
sogar′ even 8
der **Sohn, ⸚e** son 4

solch (-er, -es, -e) such a (*sg.*); such (*pl.*) 4

der **Soldat'**, -en, -en/die **Solda'tin**, -nen soldier 10

sollen (soll), sollte, gesollt to be supposed to; to be said to 4

der **Sommer** summer 2

sondern (*conj.*) but, on the contrary 5; **nicht nur ... ~ auch** not only . . . but also 5

der **Sonnabend** (*in northern Germany*) Saturday E

die **Sonne** sun 2

die **Sonnenbrille**, -n sunglasses 6

sonnig sunny 2

der **Sonntag** Sunday E

sonntags (on) Sundays

sonst otherwise 3; **~ noch etwas?** Anything else? 3; **~ noch einen Wunsch?** Would you like anything else? 3

die **Sorge**, -n care, worry 11; **sich Sorgen machen (um)** to worry (about) 11

die **Sorte**, -n type, kind

sowie' (*conj.*) as well as

sowieso in any case

die **Spaghet'ti** *pl.* spaghetti 3

(das) **Spanien** Spain

spanisch Spanish (*adj.*)

sparen to save (e.g., money, time) 11

der **Spaß** enjoyment; fun 8; **Es/Das macht ~.** It/That is fun. 8; **an der Arbeit ~ haben** to enjoy one's work; **Viel ~.** Have fun; der **Spaß**, **¨e** joke; **Er hat nur ~ gemacht.** He was only joking.

spät late 1; **Wie ~ ist es?** What time is it? 1; **später** later 1

spazie'ren fahren (ä), **fuhr spazieren, ist spazieren gefahren** to go for a drive 6

spazie'ren gehen, ging spazieren, ist spazieren gegangen to go for a walk 1

der **Spazier'gang**, -gänge walk, stroll

der **Spiegel**, - mirror 7

das **Spiegelei**, -er fried egg

das **Spiel**, -e game 1

spielen to play 1

der **Spielfilm**, -e feature film

spontan' spontaneously

der **Sport** sport(s) 1; **~ treiben** to engage in sports 1

sportlich athletic 1

der **Sportverein**, -e sports club

die **Sprache**, -n language 9

sprechen (i), **sprach, gesprochen** to speak 5; **~ mit** to speak to/with (someone); **~ über** (+ *acc.*) to speak about 7; **~ von** (+*dat.*) to speak about/of 7

spülen to rinse; to wash 7; **Geschirr ~** to wash dishes 7

die **Spülmaschine**, -n dishwasher 7

der **Staat**, -en state; country 4

staatlich (*abbrev.* **staatl.**) public, government-owned 4

der **Staatsbürger**, -/die **Staatsbürgerin**, -nen citizen

das **Stadion**, *pl.* **Stadien** stadium

die **Stadt**, ¨e city 2; das **~viertel** city district

der **Stammbaum**, -bäume family tree

stark (ä) (*adj.*) strong 8; (*adv.*) greatly, very much 8

statt (+ *gen.*) instead of 9; **~ ...** (+ *inf.*) instead of

statt'finden, fand statt, stattgefunden to take place

der **Staub** dust 7; **~ wischen** to dust 7; **ich wische ~** I'm dusting; **~ saugen** to vacuum 7

das **Steak**, -s steak

stecken to stick, put or insert something into something else 7

stehen, stand, gestanden to stand 3; to be located 7; **es steht in der Zeitung ...** it says in the newspaper . . . 10; **stehen bleiben, blieb stehen, ist stehen geblieben** to stop

steigen, stieg, ist gestiegen to rise, climb

die **Stelle**, -n job; position; place, spot 8

stellen to stand, place, put something (upright) 7; **eine Frage ~** + *dat.* to ask someone a question 9; **eine Frage an** + *acc.* **~** to ask someone a question 9

das **Stellenangebot**, -e job offer (ad)

die **Stellenanzeige**, -n want ad

sterben (i), **starb, ist gestorben** to die 10; **~ an** (+ *dat.*) to die of

die **Stereoanlage**, -n stereo system

stereotyp' stereotypical

das **Stichwort**, ¨er key word, cue

der **Stiefel**, - boot 6

die **Stiefmutter**, ¨ stepmother 4

der **Stiefvater**, ¨ stepfather 4

stimmen to be correct 3; **Das stimmt.** That's right. 3

das **Stipen'dium**, *pl.* **Stipendien** scholarship, grant 4

stolz (**auf** + *acc.*) proud (of) 8

die **Straße**, -n street E

die **Straßenbahn**, -en streetcar 5

der **Streik**, -s strike 11

streiken to strike

der **Stress** stress

stressen to stress; **gestresst** stressed

stressfrei free of stress

die **Strumpfhose**, -n pantyhose 6

das **Stück**, -e piece 3; piece (of music); play (theater) 6

der **Student'**, -en, -en/die **Studen'tin**, -nen student E

das **Studen'tenheim**, -e dormitory 4

das **Studienfach**, ¨er college major

die **Studiengebühren** (*pl.*) administrative fees at the university; tuition

der **Studienplatz**, ¨e opening for student in a particular course of study at a university

studie'ren to study; to go to college 1; **~ an/auf** (+ *dat.*) to study at (a college) 7

das **Studium** studies 4

der **Stuhl**, ¨e chair E

die **Stunde**, -n hour 6; lesson; class; die **Klavier~** piano lesson

stundenlang for hours

das **Substantiv**, -e noun

suchen to look for 3; **~ nach** to look for 6

der **Süden** south 2

südlich to the south 2

super super, great 6

der **Supermarkt**, ¨e supermarket 3; **in den ~** to the supermarket 3

surfen to surf 4

süß sweet; nice

das **Sweatshirt**, -s sweatshirt

sympa'thisch likeable, agreeable 1; **er ist mir ~** I like him

systema'tisch systematic(ally)

die **Szene**, -n scene

T

die **Tabel'le**, -n chart; table

die **Tablet'te**, -n tablet, pill 3

der **Tag**, -e day E; **Guten ~./~.** Hello.; Hi. 1; **eines Tages** one day; **[Montag] in acht Tagen** a week from (Monday)

das **Tagebuch**, ¨er diary

der **Tagesplan**, ¨e daily schedule

die **Tagesreise** a day's journey

täglich daily

die **Tante**, -n aunt 4

der **Tante-Emma-Laden,** ⸚ mom-and-pop store

tanzen to dance 1

die **Tasche, -n** bag; pocket 3; handbag, purse 6

das **Taschenbuch,** ⸚er paperback book 5

die **Tasse, -n** cup 3

die **Technologie', -n** technology

der **Tee** tea 3

der **Teil, -e** part 9; **zum ~** partly; **zum größten ~** for the most part

teilen to divide (up) 10; (*math*) **~ durch** to divide by

die **Teilzeitarbeit** part-time work 8

die **Teilzeitbeschäftigung, -en** part-time work

das **Telefon', -e** telephone E

telefonie'ren (mit jemandem) to telephone (someone) 6

die **Telefon'nummer, -n** telephone number E; **Wie ist deine/Ihre ~?** What's your telephone number? E; **Wie ist die ~ von...?** What is the telephone number of . . . ? E

die **Telefon'zelle, -n** telephone booth

der **Teller, -** plate; dish 12

die **Temperatur', -en** temperature 2

das **Tempolimit** speed limit

das **Tennis** tennis 1

der **Teppich, -e** rug, carpet 7

der **Termin', -e** appointment 11; **einen ~ bei jemandem haben** to have an appointment with someone 11

der **Termin'kalender, -** appointment calendar

teuer expensive 3

das **Textverarbeitungsprogramm, -e** word processing program 11; **mit Textverarbeitungsprogrammen arbeiten** to do word processing 11

das **Thea'ter, -** theater 6; **ins ~ gehen** to go to the theater 6; **die ~karte, -n** theater ticket 6; **das ~stück** play 6

das **Thema,** *pl.* **Themen** theme, topic

tippen to type 11

der **Tisch, -e** table E; **den ~ decken** to set the table 7

das **Tischtennis** table tennis, Ping-Pong 1

die **Tochter,** ⸚ daughter 4

tolerant' tolerant 1

toll great, fantastic E; **das wäre ~** that would be great 8

die **Toma'te, -n** tomato 3; **die Tomatensoße** tomato sauce

die **Torte, -n** layered cake with a cream or fruit filling 3

der **Tourist', -en, -en/die Touris'tin, -nen** tourist 7

die **Tradition', -en** tradition

tragen (ä), trug, getragen to carry; to wear 6

die **Traube, -n** grape 3

der **Traum,** *pl.* **Träume** dream

träumen (+ von) to dream (of)

traurig sad 1

(sich) treffen (i), traf, getroffen to meet 5; **Ich treffe mich mit Freunden,** I'm meeting friends.

treiben, trieb, getrieben to drive; to engage in 1; **Sport ~** to engage in sports 1

trinken, trank, getrunken to drink 3

trocken dry 2

die **Trockenheit** dryness

trotz (+ *gen.*) in spite of 8

trotzdem nevertheless

tschüs so long, good-bye (*informal*) E

das **T-Shirt, -s** T-shirt 6

das **Tuch,** ⸚er cloth; scarf 12

tun, tat, getan to do 6; **Es tut mir Leid** I'm sorry 4

die **Tür, -en** door E

der **Türke, -n, -n/die Türkin, -nen** Turk

die **Türkei'** Turkey

türkisch Turkish

typisch typical 7

U

die **U-Bahn, -en** (*abbr. for* **Untergrundbahn**) subway 5

üben to practice

über (+ *acc./dat.*) about 3; over, above 3; across 7

überall everywhere 5

überein'·stimmen to agree

überfüllt' overfilled

überglücklich ecstatic

überhaupt' generally (speaking); actually, altogether; **~ nicht** not at all 7

übernach'ten to spend the night, to stay (in hotel or with friends) 5

überset'zen to translate

überzeu'gen to convince 12

übrigens by the way

die **Uhr, -en** clock E; **Wie viel ~ ist es?** What time is it? 1; **um [zehn] ~** at [ten] o'clock 1; **Um wie viel ~?** At what time? 1

um (+ *acc.*) at 1; around 3; **~ [zehn] Uhr** at [ten] o'clock 1; **~ wie viel Uhr?** At what time? 1; **Er ging ~ die Ecke.** He went around the corner.; **~ . . . zu** (+ *inf.*) (in order) to 9; **Es geht nicht nur ~ [die Musik].** It's not just about [the music]. 12

die **Umfrage, -n** opinion poll, survey

unbedingt without reservation, absolutely 10

und and E; plus (*in addition*) E; **~ dir/Ihnen?** And you? (How about you?) 1

der **Unfall,** ⸚e accident

unfreundlich unfriendly 1

ungarisch Hungarian

(das) **Ungarn** Hungary

ungefähr approximately 5

ungewöhnlich unusual, uncommon

unglaub'lich unbelievable, unbelievably 7

unglücklich unhappy 1

die **Uni, -s** (*colloq. for* Universität) 1

die **Universität', -en** university 1

unmöglich impossible

unmusikalisch unmusical 1

unpersönlich impersonal 3

uns us 3

unser our 2

unsicher insecure; unsafe 11

unsympathisch unpleasant, unappealing, disagreeable 1

unten downstairs; below 5

unter (+ *acc./dat.*) under, beneath; among 7; **~ sich** among themselves

unterhal'ten (unterhält), unterhielt, unterhalten to entertain; **sich unterhalten** to converse 10; **~ über** (+ *acc.*) to converse about 10

die **Unterhal'tung, -en** entertainment; conversation

der **Unterschied, -e** difference 10

unzufrieden dissatisfied

die **Urgroßeltern** (*pl.*) great-grandparents

der **Urlaub** vacation 8; **~ machen** to go on vacation 8; **in** *or* **im** *or* **auf ~ sein** to be on vacation 8; **in ~ fahren** to go on vacation 8

die **USA** (*pl.*) U.S.A. 2

usw. (= **und so weiter**) and so forth

V

die **Vase, -n** vase 7

der **Vater,** ⸚ father 4

der **Vati, -s** dad 4

sich verab′reden to make an appointment/date

(sich) verän′dern to change

die Verän′derung, -en change

verant′wortlich (für) responsible (for) 10

die Verant′wortung, -en responsibility 11

das Verb, -en verb

verbin′den, verband, verbunden to combine

verbrin′gen, verbrachte, verbracht to spend (time)

verdie′nen to earn 4

der Verein′, -e club

die Verei′nigung unification 10

die Verein′ten Natio′nen (pl.) United Nations

die Verfas′sung, -en constitution

verfol′gen to pursue; to follow; to persecute

verges′sen (vergisst), vergaß, vergessen to forget 5

verglei′chen, verglich, verglichen to compare

verhasst′ hated

verhei′ratet married 8

verkau′fen to sell 11

der Verkäu′fer, -/die Verkäu′ferin, -nen salesperson

der Verkehr′ traffic; transportation

das Verkehrs′mittel, - means of transportation 7

verlas′sen (verlässt), verließ, verlassen to leave, abandon 10

verlet′zen to injure, hurt 9; Ich habe mir den Arm verletzt. I've hurt my arm. 9; Ich habe mich verletzt. I hurt myself. 9

verlie′ren, verlor, verloren to lose 8

vermis′sen to miss someone or something; to regret

verschie′den various 12

verschrei′ben, verschrieb, verschrieben to prescribe 9

verständ′lich understandable

versteh′en, verstand, verstanden to understand 9

versu′chen to try 5

verwandt′ related

der/die Verwand′te (noun decl. like adj.) relative 9

die Verzei′hung pardon; ~! I beg your pardon.

der Vetter, -n cousin (m.) 4

das Video, -s video 4

der Videorecorder, - VCR, video cassette recorder E

das Videospiel, -e video game 1

viel (mehr, meist-) much 1; viele many 3; Viel Glück! Good luck! 11; viele Grüße (closing in a personal letter) regards 1

vieles much

vielleicht′ maybe, perhaps 1

das Viertel, - a fourth, quarter 1; district of a city; ~ vor [zwei] quarter to [two]; ~ nach [zwei] quarter past [two] 1

die Vitamin′tablette, -n vitamin pill

die Voka′bel, -n vocabulary word

das Volk, ¨er people; nation

voll full

der Volleyball volleyball 1

von (+ dat.) of E; from 2; by [the person doing something]

vor (+ acc./dat.) before 1; in front of 7; ~ allem above all 9; ~ zwei Wochen two weeks ago 6

vorbei′ over; gone 10

vorbei′·kommen, kam vorbei, ist vorbeigekommen to come by 5; bei [mir] ~ to come by [my] place 5

vor·bereiten to prepare 4; sich ~ (auf + acc.) to prepare oneself (for) 11

vorbereitet prepared; Ich bin (nicht) gut vorbereitet. I'm (not) well prepared. 4

die Vorbereitung, -en preparation 7

vor·haben to intend, have in mind 6

vorher previously; beforehand

vorig last, previous; voriges Jahr last year

die Vorlesung, -en lecture 4; eine ~ halten to give a lecture; eine ~ besuchen to attend a lecture

der Vorname, -ns, -n first name 7

der Vorschlag, ¨e suggestion

vor·schlagen (ä), schlug vor, vorgeschlagen to suggest

sich (dat.) vor·stellen to imagine 12; Ich kann es mir vorstellen. I can imagine that. 12

das Vorurteil, -e prejudice

die Vorwahl, -en area code

W

wach awake 10

wachsen (ä), wuchs, ist gewachsen to grow 12

der Wagen, - car; wagon 5

wählen to choose; to elect

wahr true 5; nicht ~? isn't that so? 5

während (prep.) (+ gen.) during 8; (conj.) while

die Wahrheit, -en truth

wahrschein′lich (adj.) probable; (adv.) probably 5

der Wald, ¨er forest

die Wand, ¨e (interior) wall E

der Wanderer, -/die Wanderin, -nen hiker

wandern, ist gewandert to hike; ~ gehen to go walking/hiking 1

die Wanderung, -en hike; eine ~ machen to go on a hike

der Wanderweg, -e hiking path

wann when E; seit ~ since when, (for) how long 4

war (past tense of sein) was 2

die Ware, -n wares, merchandise, goods 11

wäre (subj. of sein) would be 8; das ~ toll that would be great 8

das Warenhaus, ¨er department store

warm warm 2; schön ~ nice and warm 2

warten (auf + acc.) to wait (for) 5

warum′ why 1

was what 1; ~ für (ein) ... what kind of (a) ... 1; ~ für ein Wetter! Such weather! 2; ~ gab es? What was playing? 10; ~ gibt's Neues? What's new? 11; ~ gibt's zum [Abendessen]? What's for [dinner]? 3; ~ hast du? What's wrong? 9; ~ ist los? What's wrong? 1; ~ noch? What else? 7

die Wäsche laundry 7; ~ waschen to do the laundry

waschen (ä), wusch, gewaschen to wash 7; sich ~ to wash oneself 9; Ich wasche [mir] die Hände. I'm washing [my] hands. 9

die Waschmaschine, -n washing machine

das Wasser water 3; ein ~ a bottle/glass of mineral water 6

der Wasserski, -er water ski 5; Wasserski fahren to waterski 5

die Webseite, -n website

wechseln to change 11

weder ... noch neither ... nor

weg away; off; gone 2

der Weg, -e way; auf dem ~ on the way

wegen (+ gen.) on account of, because of 8

weg·fahren (fährt), fuhr weg, ist weggefahren to drive away; to leave

weh·tun (+ dat.) to hurt 9; Die Füße tun mir weh. My feet hurt. 9

weil (*sub. conj.*) because 5

die **Weile** while; **eine ganze ~** a long time 8

der **Wein, -e** wine 3

weiß white E

der **Weißwein, -e** white wine 3

weit far 2

weiter farther, further 2; additional

welch (-er, -es, e) which E; **Welche Farbe hat . . . ?** What color is . . . ? E; **Welcher Tag ist heute?** What day is today? E

die **Welt, -en** world 5

der **Weltkrieg, -e** world war 5

wem (*dat. of* **wer**) (to or for) whom 5

wen (*acc. of* **wer**) whom 3

wenig little 4; **ein ~** a little 4; **wenige** few 4

weniger minus (*in subtraction*) E; less

wenigstens at least

wenn (*sub. conj.*) when, whenever 4; if 4

wer who 1

werden (wird), wurde, ist geworden to become 4; will (*auxiliary verb of the fut. tense*): **Das wird sie sicher finden.** She will certainly find it.

werfen (i), warf, geworfen to throw

wesentlich essential; substantial; in the main 9

wessen (*gen. of* **wer**) whose 8

der **Westen** west 2

westlich western 10

das **Wetter** weather 2; **Was für ein ~!** Such weather! 2; **Wie ist das ~?** How's the weather? 2

wichtig important 2

die **Wichtigkeit** importance

wie how E; as 2; **~ alt bist du?** How old are you? E; **~ bitte?** I beg your pardon? E; **~ geht es Ihnen?** How are you? 1; **~ geht's?** How are you? 1; **~ immer** as always 11; **~ ist das Wetter?** How is the weather? 2; **~ ist deine Telefonnummer?** What is your telephone number? E; **~ lange** for how long; **~ schreibt man das?** How do you spell that? E; **~ spät ist es?** What time is it? 1; **~ viel** how much E; **~ viel Grad sind es?** What's the temperature? 2; **~ viel macht das?** How much/What does that come to? **~ viele** how many? E **~ wär's mit ... ?** How about . . . ?

wieder again 4; **immer ~** again and again 5

wieder·geben (gibt), gab wieder, wiedergegeben to reproduce, render

wiederho'len to repeat

die **Wiederho'lung, -en** review; repetition

Wiedersehen: Auf ~. Good-bye. 1

wiederum in turn; on the other hand

die **Wiedervereinigung** reunification

Wien Vienna

wie viel' how much E; **~ Grad ist es?** What's the temperature? 2; **~ macht das?** How much/What does that come to? **wie viele** how many? E

der **Wind** wind 2

windig windy 2

windsurfen to windsurf; **~ gehen** to go windsurfing 6

der **Winter** winter 2

wir we 1

wirklich really 2

die **Wirklichkeit** reality

die **Wirtschaft** economy 5

wirtschaftlich economically 5

der **Wirtschaftsminister, -/die Wirtschaftsministerin, -nen** minister for economic affairs

wissen (weiß), wusste, gewusst to know (a fact) 4; **~ über** (+ *acc.*)/ **~ von** to know about; **Woher weißt du das?** How do you know that? 11

die **Wissenschaft, -en** science

der **Wissenschaftler, -/die Wissenschaftlerin, -nen** scientist 5

wissenschaftlich scientific

wo where 2

die **Woche, -n** week E; **einmal in der ~** once a week

das **Wochenende, -n** weekend 1; **am ~** on the weekend 1; **Schönes ~!** Have a nice weekend!

woher where from 2; **~ kommst du?** Where are you from? 2; **~ weißt du das?** How do you know that? 11

wohin where (to) 5

wohl probably; indeed; well 9

wohnen to live, reside 2; **bei jemandem ~** to live at someone else's residence

das **Wohnhaus, -häuser** residential building; apartment building

die **Wohnung,-en** dwelling; apartment 7

das **Wohnzimmer, -** living room 7

wolkig cloudy 2

wollen (will), wollte, gewollt to want to; intend to 4

wollte (*subj. of* **wollen**) would want 11

das **Wort, -er** word 2; **Worte** words (in context)

die **Wortverbindung, -en** phrase; expression

der **Wortschatz** vocabulary

wozu' what for, to what purpose, why

das **Wunder, -** miracle; wonder 8; **kein ~** no wonder

wunderbar wonderful

der **Wunsch, -e** wish 3; **Sonst noch einen ~?** Anything else? 3

wünschen to wish 9; **Was wünschst du dir?** What do you wish for? 9

würde (*subj. of* **werden**) would 9; **Ich ~ das auch sagen** I would also say that 9

die **Wurst, -e** sausage 3; lunch meat

das **Wurstbrot, -e** cold meat sandwich

das **Würstchen, -** frankfurter 3

Z

z.B. (*abbr. for* **zum Beispiel**) e.g. (for example) 4

die **Zahl, -en** number, numeral E

zahlen to pay 4; **~, bitte.** I'd like to pay, please (*in a restaurant*).

der **Zahn, -e** tooth 9; **Ich putze mir die Zähne** I'm brushing my teeth

der **Zahnarzt, -e/die Zahnärztin, -nen** dentist 11

die **Zahnbürste, -n** toothbrush

die **Zahnpaste/Zahnpasta** toothpaste

die **Zahnschmerzen** (*pl.*) toothache 9

zeigen to show 10; **~ auf** (+ *acc.*) to point to

die **Zeile, -n** line

die **Zeit, -en** time 4; **zur ~** at the moment

die **Zeitschrift, -en** magazine; journal

die **Zeitung, -en** newpaper 4; **Es steht in der ~.** It says in the newspaper. 10

das **Zelt, -e** tent

zelten to camp in a tent 5

das **Zentrum, (*pl.*) Zentren** center

zerstö'ren to destroy

der **Zettel, -** note; slip of paper

ziehen, zog, ist gezogen to move

das **Ziel, -e** goal 9

ziemlich quite, rather, fairly 2

das **Zimmer, -** room E

zu (+ *dat.*) (*prep.*) to (*with people and some places*) 3; shut, closed; **~ Besuch** for a visit; **~ Ende** over, finished 10; **~ Fuß gehen** to walk, 5; **~ Hause** (to be) at home 5; **um ... ~** (+ *inf.*) (in order) to 9; **zum Essen** for dinner 12; **zur Zeit** at the moment

zu too 2; **zu viel'** too much 4

der **Zucker** sugar

zueinan′der to each other
zuerst′ first of all; at first 6
zufrie′den satisfied, content
der **Zug, ⸚e** train 5
das **Zuhau′se** home 12
zu·hören to listen to
die **Zukunft** future 11
zum (*contraction of* **zu dem**) to or for the

zu·machen to close
zumin′dest at least
zurück′ back, in return 4
zurück′·bringen, brachte zurück, zurückgebracht to bring back
zurück′·fliegen, flog zurück, ist zurückgeflogen to fly back 12
zurück′·zahlen to pay back 4
zusam′men together 1

der **Zusam′menhang, ⸚e** connection
zwar to be sure, it's true, indeed 7
zweimal twice, two times 10; **~ im Monat** two times a month
zweit- second 8
zwingen, zwang, gezwungen to force, compel 10
zwischen (+ *acc./dat.*) between, among 7

The English-German end vocabulary contains the words included in the active vocabulary lists and the *Erweiterung des Wortschatzes* section of the chapters. Not included from the active lists are numbers, articles and pronouns. The plural forms of nouns are given. Strong and irregular weak verbs are indicated with a raised degree mark (°). Their principal parts can be found in Appendix F. Separable-prefix verbs are indicated with a raised dot: **mit·bringen.**

A

abandon verlassen°
abdomen der Bauch, ⁼e
able: to be ~ to können°
about über (*prep.*); etwa (*adv.*)
above all vor allem
abroad im Ausland
absolute(ly) absolut; unbedingt; ~ **great** ganz/wirklich toll
account: on ~ of wegen
acquaintance der/die Bekannte (*noun decl. like adj.*); **to make the ~ of** kennen lernen
activity die Aktivität, -en
actually eigentlich; überhaupt
addition: in ~ noch, dazu; außerdem
address die Adresse, -n; **home ~** die Heimatadresse; **school ~** die Semesteradresse; **What is your ~?** Wie ist deine/Ihre Adresse?
advertisement die Anzeige, -n
aerobics das Aerobic; **to do ~** Aerobic machen
afraid: to be ~ (of) Angst haben (vor + *dat.*), (sich) fürchten (vor + *dat.*)
after nach (*prep.*); nachdem (*conj.*); ~ **all** schließlich
afternoon der Nachmittag, -e; **this ~** heute Nachmittag
afternoons nachmittags
afterwards nachher; danach
again wieder; noch einmal
against gegen
ago: [ten years] ~ vor [zehn Jahren]
agree: Or don't you ~? Oder?
agreeable sympathisch
airplane das Flugzeug, -e
airport der Flughafen, ⁼
all alle; alles; **at ~** überhaupt; ~ **day** den ganzen Tag
allowed: to be ~ to dürfen°

all right in Ordnung; **It's ~.** Es geht.
almost fast
alone allein
Alps die Alpen (*pl.*)
already schon
also auch
although obwohl
always immer
America (das) Amerika
American (*adj.*) amerikanisch; ~ **(person)** der Amerikaner, -/die Amerikanerin, -nen
among unter
and und; ~ **so on** und so weiter
angry böse; **Don't be ~ with me.** Sei mir nicht böse; **to feel ~** sich ärgern
announcement die Anzeige, -n
annoy ärgern
annoyed: to become annoyed sich ärgern
another noch ein
answer die Antwort, -en; **to ~ [the woman]** [der Frau] antworten; **to ~ the question** auf die Frage antworten, die Frage beantworten
any einige; etwas; **I don't have any ...** Ich habe kein ...
anyone jemand
anything: ~ else? Sonst noch etwas?
apartment die Wohnung, -en
apology die Entschuldigung, -en
apparatus der Apparat, -e
appear scheinen°; erscheinen°
apple der Apfel, ⁼; ~ **juice** der Apfelsaft
appliance das Gerät, -e
appointment der Termin, -e
approximately ungefähr
April der April
architect der Architekt, -en, -en/die Architektin, -nen
arm der Arm, -e

around herum
arrive an·kommen°
art die Kunst, ⁼e; ~ **history** die Kunstgeschichte
article der Artikel, -
artist der Künstler, -/die Künstlerin, -nen
as als; wie; ~ ... ~ so ... wie; ~ **always** wie immer
ask fragen; ~ **for** bitten° um; **to ~ him a question** ihm/an ihn eine Frage stellen
aspirin das Aspirin
assignment die Aufgabe, -n
at an; auf; ~ **(a place)** bei; ~ **[seven]** um [sieben]; ~ **once** gleich
athletic sportlich
attend (a lecture, school) besuchen; ~ **college** studieren
attorney der Rechtsanwalt, ⁼e/die Rechtsanwältin, -nen
August der August
aunt die Tante, -n
Austria (das) Österreich
Austrian österreichisch (*adj.*); ~ **(person)** der Österreicher, -/die Österreicherin, -nen
automobile das Auto, -s
autumn der Herbst
awake wach
away weg; ab

B

back (*adv.*) zurück; (*n.*) der Rücken, -; **~ache** die Rückenschmerzen (*pl.*)
backpack der Rucksack, ⁼e
bad schlecht; schlimm; böse; **not ~** ganz gut; **too ~** schade
badly schlecht
bag die Tasche, -n
bake backen°
baker der Bäcker, -/die Bäckerin, -nen

bakery die Bäckerei, -en; **at the ~** beim Bäcker; **to the ~** zum Bäcker
balcony der Balkon, -s
ballpoint pen der Kugelschreiber, - [der Kuli, -s (*colloq.*)]
banana die Banane, -n
band die Band, -s
bank die Bank, -en
bar die Bar, -s; die Kneipe, -n
basketball der Basketball
bath das Bad, ̈-er
bathe baden
bathing: ~ suit der Badeanzug, ̈-e; **~ trunks** die Badehose, -n
bathroom das Bad, ̈-er; die Toilette, -n
Bavarian bay(e)risch
be sein°; **~ so kind.** Sei/Seien Sie so gut.; **~ there** dabeisein
beautiful schön
because weil; denn; da; **~ of** wegen
become werden°
bed das Bett, -en; **to make the ~** das Bett machen
bedroom das Schlafzimmer, -
beef roast der Rinderbraten
beer das Bier; **~ garden** der Biergarten, ̈-
before vor; vorher; bevor
begin an·fangen°; beginnen°; **~ the work** mit der Arbeit anfangen
beginning der Anfang, ̈-e; **in the ~** am Anfang
behind hinter
believe glauben; **I ~ so.** Ich glaube schon/ja.
belong to gehören
below unten
beside bei; neben; außer
besides außerdem; außer
best best; **~ of all** am besten
better besser
between zwischen
beverage das Getränk, -e
bicycle das Fahrrad, ̈-er; **to ride a ~** mit dem Fahrrad fahren; Rad fahren
big groß
bike das Rad, ̈-er; **~ trip** die Radtour, -en
biology die Biologie
birth die Geburt, -en
birthday der Geburtstag, -e; **When is your ~?** Wann hast du Geburtstag?; **for one's ~** zum Geburtstag
black schwarz
blanket die Bettdecke, -n
blond blond

blouse die Bluse, -n
blue blau
body der Körper, -
book das Buch, ̈-er
bookcase das Bücherregal, -e
bookstore die Buchhandlung, -en
boot der Stiefel, -
border die Grenze, -n
boring langweilig
born geboren, **I was born in 1987.** Ich bin 1987 geboren.
borrow leihen°
boss der Chef, -s/die Chefin, -nen
both beide; beides
bottle die Flasche, -n
boy der Junge, -n, -n; **~friend** der Freund, -e
bread das Brot, -e
breakfast das Frühstück; **for ~** zum Frühstück; **to eat ~** frühstücken
bridge die Brücke, -n
bright hell
bring bringen°; **~ along** mit·bringen°
broke (out of money) pleite
broken: ~ down kaputt
brother der Bruder, ̈-; **brothers and sisters** die Geschwister (*pl.*)
brown braun
brush: to ~ [my] teeth [mir] die Zähne putzen
build bauen
bus der Bus, -se
business das Geschäft, -e
businessman der Geschäftsmann, *pl.* Geschäftsleute
businesspeople die Geschäftsleute
businesswoman die Geschäftsfrau, -en
busy: to be ~ beschäftigt sein; **to keep ~** (sich) beschäftigen; **(line is) ~** besetzt
but aber; sondern
butcher der Metzger, -/die Metzgerin, -nen
butcher shop die Metzgerei, -en; **at the ~** beim Metzger; **to the ~** zum Metzger
butter die Butter
buy kaufen
by (close to) bei, an (*+ dat.*), neben (*+ dat.*); **~ [car]** mit [dem Auto]

C

café das Café, -s
cafeteria (university) die Mensa, -s *or* Mensen
cake der Kuchen, -; die Torte, -n

call nennen°; rufen°; an·rufen°; **to ~ [your] home** bei [dir] anrufen
called: it's ~ (es) heißt
calm ruhig
camera der Fotoapparat, -e; die Kamera, -s
camp campen; **to ~ in a tent** zelten
can (*v.*) können°
can (*n.*) die Dose, -n
Canada (das) Kanada
Canadian (*adj.*) kanadisch; **~ (person)** der Kanadier, -/die Kanadierin, -nen
cap die Mütze, -n
capital die Hauptstadt, ̈-e
car das Auto, -s; der Wagen, -
card die Karte, -n; **(playing) cards** die Karten (*pl.*)
care die Sorge, -n; **to ~ for** sorgen für
carpet der Teppich, -e
carrot die Karotte, -n
carry tragen°
cassette die Kassette, -n
cassette deck das Kassettendeck, -s
cat die Katze, -n
CD player der CD-Player, -; der CD-Spieler, -
celebrate feiern
celebration die Feier, -n; das Fest, -e
cell phone das Handy, -s
century das Jahrhundert, -e
certain(ly) bestimmt; sicher
chair der Stuhl, ̈-e; **easy ~** der Sessel, -
change wechseln
chat (on the Internet) chatten
chat room der Chatroom, -s (*also* Chat-Room, -s)
cheap billig
check out (book from library) aus·leihen°
cheerful lustig
cheese der Käse
chemistry die Chemie
chess das Schach; **~ game** das Schachspiel
chest of drawers die Kommode, -n
chicken das Hähnchen, -
child das Kind, -er
chin das Kinn
chocolate die Schokolade, -n; **~ ice cream** das Schokoladeneis
chore: household chores die Hausarbeit; **to do the chores** den Haushalt machen
Christmas das Weihnachten; **Merry ~!** Frohe *or* Fröhliche Weihnachten!
church die Kirche, -n
city die Stadt, ̈-e; **~ hall** das Rathaus, ̈-er

class die Klasse, -n; **German ~** die Deutschstunde
classical klassisch
clean sauber; **to ~** putzen; auf·raumen; sauber machen
clear klar
cliché das Klischee, -s
client der Kunde, -n, n/die Kundin, -nen
climate das Klima
clinic die Klinik, -en
clock die Uhr, -en
close: to ~ schließen°; zu·machen
cloth das Tuch, ¨er
clothing die Kleidung, die Sachen (*pl.*); **article of ~** das Kleidungsstück, -e
cloudy wolkig
coat der Mantel, ¨; **sport ~** das Jackett, -s; der Sakko, -s
coffee der Kaffee; **for (afternoon) ~** zum Kaffee; **to go for ~** Kaffee trinken gehen; **~house** das Kaffeehaus, ¨er; **~ table** der Couchtisch, -e
cola drink die Cola
cold kalt; die Erkältung, -en; **to catch a ~** sich erkälten
colleague der Kollege, -n, -n/die Kollegin, -nen
collect sammeln
college: to go to ~ studieren; auf/an die Universität gehen
color die Farbe, -n; **What ~ is . . . ?** Welche Farbe hat ... ?
comb der Kamm, ¨e; **to ~ (one's hair)** (sich) kämmen
come kommen°; **to ~ along** mit·kommen°; **to ~ by** vorbei·kommen°
comfortable gemütlich
comics die Comics (*pl.*)
compact disc die Compact Disc, -s; die CD, -s
company die Gesellschaft, -en; die Firma, *pl.* Firmen; **to have ~** Besuch haben
compel zwingen°
compete konkurrieren
complain klagen
complete(ly) ganz; voll; absolut
composer der Komponist, -en, -en/die Komponistin, -nen
computer der Computer, -; **~ game** das Computerspiel, -e; **~ science** die Informatik; **~ specialist** der Informatiker, -/die Informatikerin, -nen; **to work at a ~** mit dem Computer arbeiten

concept die Vorstellung, -en
concert das Konzert, -e; **to go to a ~** ins Konzert gehen
contrary: on the ~ sondern; doch
conversation das Gespräch, -e; **to conduct a ~** ein Gespräch führen
convince überzeugen
cook kochen
cool kühl
corner die Ecke, -n
correct richtig; **That's ~.** Das stimmt.
cost kosten
cough husten
could könnte
country das Land, ¨er; der Staat; **in our ~** bei uns; **in the ~** auf dem Land(e); **out into the ~** ins Grüne; **to the ~** aufs Land
couple das Paar, -e
course der Kurs, -e; die Vorlesung, -en
course: of ~ bestimmt; natürlich; klar; sicher
cousin (*female*) die Kusine, -n; **~** (*male*) der Vetter, -n
cover decken
cozy gemütlich
creative kreativ
credit card die Kreditkarte, -n
criticism die Kritik, -en
cucumber die Gurke, -n
cultural(ly) kulturell
culture die Kultur, -en
cup die Tasse, -n
customer der Kunde, -n, -n/die Kundin, -nen
cyber café das Internetcafé, -s

D

dad der Vati, -s
dance (*v.*) tanzen
dance club die Disco, -s
dancing: I'm going ~. Ich gehe tanzen.
dark dunkel; **~haired** dunkelhaarig
date das Datum; **What's the ~ today?** Den Wievielten haben wir heute?; Der Wievielte ist heute?
daughter die Tochter, ¨
day der Tag, -e; **one/some ~** eines Tages; **all ~** den ganzen Tag; **days of the week** die Wochentage (*pl.*); **every ~** jeden Tag; **What ~ is today?** Welcher Tag ist heute?
dear lieb (-er, -e, -es)
December der Dezember
decide (sich) entscheiden°
deed die Tat, -en
degree der Grad

demonstrate demonstrieren
demonstration die Demonstration, -en
dentist der Zahnarzt, ¨e/die Zahnärztin, -nen
depart ab·fahren°
department store das Kaufhaus, -häuser
describe beschreiben°
desire die Lust
desk der Schreibtisch, -e
dessert der Nachtisch, -e
dialect der Dialekt, -e
die sterben°
difference der Unterschied, -e
different verschieden; anders; **something ~** (et)was anderes
difficult schwer; schwierig
digital camera die Digitalkamera, -s
dining room das Esszimmer, -
dinner das Abendessen, -; **for ~** zum Abendessen; **to eat ~** zu Abend essen
diploma (from high school) das Abitur
dish (for food) der Teller, -
dishes das Geschirr; **to do/wash ~** abwaschen°; Geschirr spülen
dishwasher die Spülmaschine, -n; der Geschirrspüler, -; **to empty the ~** die Spülmaschine ausräumen; **to load the ~** die Spülmaschine einräumen
diskette die Diskette, -n
divide teilen; auf·teilen (in + *acc.*)
divided by [in mathematics] geteilt durch
do machen; tun°
doctor der Arzt, ¨e/die Ärztin, -nen; **to go to the ~** zum Arzt gehen
doesn't he (she) nicht? nicht wahr?
dog der Hund, -e
done fertig
door die Tür, -en
dormitory das Studentenheim, -e
downstairs unten
dress das Kleid, -er; **to ~** (sich) an·ziehen°; **I get dressed.** Ich ziehe mich an.
drink das Getränk, -e; **to ~** trinken°
drive fahren°; **to ~ along** mit·fahren; **to ~ away** weg·fahren°; **to go for a ~** spazieren fahren°
driver der Fahrer, -/die Fahrerin, -nen
driver's license der Führerschein, -e
drugstore die Drogerie, -n, die Apotheke, -n
dry trocken; **to ~ (dishes)** ab·trocknen

dumb dumm
during während
dust der Staub; **to ~** Staub wischen
DVD die DVD, -s
dwelling die Wohnung, -en

E

each jed- (-er, -es, -e)
each other einander; **with ~** miteinander
ear das Ohr, -en
early früh
earn verdienen
east der Osten
easy leicht; **Take it ~.** Mach's gut.
easygoing ruhig
eat essen°
economic wirtschaftlich
economy die Wirtschaft
educate aus·bilden; erziehen°
education die Erziehung; die Ausbildung
egg das Ei, -er
else: what ~? was noch?; **something ~?** sonst noch etwas?
employ beschäftigen
employed berufstätig
employee der Arbeitnehmer, -/die Arbeitnehmerin, -nen; der Mitarbeiter, -/die Mitarbeiterin, -nen; der/die Angestellte (*noun. decl. like adj.*)
employer der Arbeitgeber, -/die Arbeitgeberin, -nen
empty leer
end das Ende, -n; **in/at the ~** am Ende
endure leiden°
engage: to ~ in sports Sport treiben
engineer der Ingenieur, -e/die Ingenieurin, -nen
England (das) England
English (*adj.*) englisch; **~ (language)** (das) Englisch; **~ studies** die Anglistik
enjoy: to ~ something Spaß an einer Sache haben
enjoyment die Lust; der Spaß
enough genug
especially besonders
essential wesentlich
etc. usw.
eternal(ly) ewig
euro der Euro, -
Europe das Europa
even sogar; **~ if** auch wenn
evening der Abend, -e; **Good ~.** Guten Abend.; **this ~** heute Abend

evenings abends
every jed- (-er, -es, -e); **~ day** jeden Tag
everyone jeder
everything alles
everywhere überall
exactly genau; **~ the same** genauso
exam die Klausur, -en
examination die Klausur, -en; die Prüfung, -en; **comprehensive ~** das Examen, -; **to take an ~** eine Klausur schreiben
examine durch·sehen°; prüfen
example das Beispiel, -e; **for ~** zum Beispiel (z.B.)
except außer
exchange student der Austauschstudent, -en, -en/die Austauschstudentin, -nen
excuse die Entschuldigung, -en; **~ me!** Entschuldigung!
exhausted (*slang*) kaputt
expect erwarten
expensive teuer
experience die Erfahrung, -en
explain erklären
expressway die Autobahn, -en
eye das Auge, -n

F

face das Gesicht, -er
factory die Fabrik, -en
fairly ganz; ziemlich
fall der Herbst; **to ~** fallen°
false falsch
familiar bekannt
family die Familie, -n
famous bekannt; berühmt
fan (team supporter) der Fan, -s
fantastic fantastisch; toll; prima
far weit
farther weiter
fast schnell
fat dick
father der Vater, ¨
favorite Lieblings-; **~ (program)** (die) Lieblings(sendung)
fear die Angst, ¨e, **to ~** sich fürchten (vor + *dat.*); **to ~ for** Angst haben um
February der Februar
Federal Republic of Germany die Bundesrepublik Deutschland (BRD)
feel sich fühlen; **to ~ like** Lust haben; **I don't ~ like working.** Ich habe keine Lust zu arbeiten.; **I don't ~ like it.** Dazu habe ich keine Lust.

feeling das Gefühl, -e
festival das Fest, -e
fever das Fieber
few wenig(e); **a ~** ein paar
film der Film, -e
finally endlich, schließlich
finals das Examen, -
find finden°
fine fein; gut; **I'm ~.** Es geht mir gut.
finger der Finger, -
finished fertig; zu Ende
first erst; **at ~** zuerst; **~ of all** erst einmal, erstens
first name der Vorname, -ns, -n
fish der Fisch, -e
fit passen
flight der Flug, ¨e
floor der Boden, ¨
flower die Blume, -n
fly fliegen°
food das Essen; die Lebensmittel (*pl.*)
foot der Fuß, ¨e; **to go on ~** zu Fuß gehen°; laufen°
for für (*prep.*); denn (*conj.*); (**time**) seit; **~ a year** seit einem Jahr
force zwingen°
foreign fremd; **~ country** das Ausland; **~ trade** der Außenhandel
foreigner der Ausländer, -/die Ausländerin, -nen
forest der Wald, ¨er
forever ewig
forget vergessen°
fork die Gabel, -n
formerly früher
fortunately zum Glück
fourth das Viertel, -
France (das) Frankreich
frank(ly) offen
free frei; **~ time** die Freizeit; **for ~** umsonst, gratis
freedom die Freiheit, -en
freeway die Autobahn, -en
freezer der Gefrierschrank, ¨e
French (*adj.*) französisch; **~ (language)** (das) Französisch
French fries die Pommes frites (*pl.*)
fresh frisch
frequent(ly) häufig
Friday der Freitag
friend der Freund, -e/die Freundin, -nen
friendly freundlich
from von; **~ (native of)** aus; **~ a certain point on** ab; **Where do you come ~?** Woher kommst du?
fruit das Obst
full voll

fun der Spaß; **That's ~.** Es macht Spaß.; **to have lots of ~** viel Spaß haben
funny lustig; komisch
furnished möbliert
furniture die Möbel (*pl.*); **piece of ~** das Möbelstück, -e
further weiter
future die Zukunft

G

game das Spiel, -e
garage die Garage, -n
garden der Garten, ¨
gasoline das Benzin
general: in ~ überhaupt; im Allgemeinen
gentleman der Herr, -n, -en
German (*adj.*) deutsch; **~ (person)** der/die Deutsche (*noun decl. like adj.*); **~ (language)** (das) Deutsch; **to do ~ (homework)** Deutsch machen; **I'm doing ~.** Ich mache Deutsch; **~ studies (language and literature)** die Germanistik
German Democratic Republic die Deutsche Demokratische Republik (DDR)
Germany (das) Deutschland
get bekommen°; kriegen; holen; **to ~ up** auf·stehen°; **to ~ together** sich treffen°
girl das Mädchen, -; **~friend** die Freundin, -nen
give geben°; **to ~ (as a gift)** schenken; **to ~ up** auf·geben°
glad froh; **~ to** gern
gladly gern
glass das Glas, ¨er
glove der Handschuh, -e
go gehen°; **to ~ along** mit·gehen; **to ~ by [car]** mit [dem Auto] fahren°; **to ~ for coffee** Kaffee trinken gehen; **to ~ in** hinein·gehen°; **to ~ out** aus·gehen°; **to ~ there** hin·gehen°
goal das Ziel, -e
going on: What's ~? Was ist los?; **There's not much ~** Es ist nicht viel los.
golf das Golf
gone weg; vorbei
good gut; **~ Gracious/Heavens!** Du meine Güte!
good-bye Auf Wiedersehen.; Tschüs. (*colloq.*)
goods die Ware, -n
government die Regierung, -en

grade die Note, -n; **[seventh] ~** [die siebte] Klasse
graduate (from the university) (*v.*) Examen machen
gram das Gramm, -
grandfather der Großvater, ¨
grandma die Oma, -s
grandmother die Großmutter, ¨
grandpa der Opa, -s
grandparents die Großeltern (*pl.*)
grape die Traube, -n
gray grau
great toll, super, prima; **absolutely ~** ganz/wirklich toll
green grün
greeting der Gruß, ¨e
groceries die Lebensmittel (*pl.*)
group die Gruppe, -n
grow wachsen°; **~ up** auf·wachsen°
guest der Gast, ¨e; **to have a ~** Besuch haben
guitar die Gitarre, -n

H

hair das Haar, -e
half die Hälfte, -n; halb
ham der Schinken, -
hand die Hand, ¨e
handbag die (Hand)tasche, -n
hang hängen°
happen passieren° (+ *dat.*); **What happened to you?** Was ist dir passiert?
happy froh, glücklich
hard hart; schwer
hardly kaum
hard-working fleißig
has hat
hat der Hut, ¨e
hatred der Hass; **~ of foreigners** der Ausländerhass
have haben°; **to ~ to** müssen°; **to ~ in mind** vor·haben°; **~ some cake.** Nehmen Sie etwas Kuchen.
head der Kopf, ¨e
headache die Kopfschmerzen (*pl.*)
headscarf das Kopftuch, ¨er
healthy gesund
hear hören
heavy schwer
hello Guten Tag.; Grüß dich.; Hallo (*informal*)
help helfen°, **to ~ with [work]** bei [der Arbeit] helfen
here hier, da; **~ [toward the speaker]** her; **~ you are** bitte sehr
Hey! Du!; He!

Hi! Tag! Hallo! Grüß dich! Hi!
high hoch
high school (college track) das Gymnasium, *pl.* Gymnasien
hike die Wanderung, -en; **to ~** wandern
history die Geschichte
hobby das Hobby, -s
hold halten°
holiday der Feiertag, -e
home: at ~ zu Hause; **(to go) ~** nach Hause; **at the ~ of** bei
homeland die Heimat
homework die Hausaufgaben (*pl.*); **to do ~** die Hausaufgaben machen
honest ehrlich
hope die Hoffnung, -en; **to ~** hoffen; **to ~ for** hoffen auf (+ *acc.*); **I ~** hoffentlich
horrible furchtbar; fürchterlich
horribly furchtbar; fürchterlich
hospital das Krankenhaus, ¨er
hot heiß
hot dog das Würstchen, -
hour die Stunde, -n
house das Haus, ¨er
housework die Hausarbeit
how wie; **~ are you?** Wie geht es Ihnen?/Wie geht's?; **~ do you know that?** Woher weißt du das?
however aber; doch; jedoch
human being der Mensch, -en, -en
humid schwül
hunch die Ahnung, -en
hunger der Hunger
hungry hungrig; **to be ~** Hunger haben; **to get ~** Hunger bekommen/kriegen
Hurry up. Mach schnell.
hurt weh·tun°, verletzen
husband der (Ehe)mann, ¨er

I

ice das Eis
ice cream das Eis
idea die Idee, -n; die Ahnung; **No ~!** Keine Ahnung!
idle: be ~ faulenzen
if wenn; ob; **even ~** wenn auch
ill krank
illness die Krankheit, -en
image das Bild, -er
imagine sich (*dat.*) vor·stellen; **~ that!** Stell dir das vor!
immediately gleich
important wichtig; **to be ~** eine Rolle spielen
in(to) in; hinein

indeed zwar
individual einzeln
industrious fleißig
influence beeinflussen°
information die Information, -en
inhabitant der Einwohner, -/die Einwohnerin, -nen
injure verletzen
in-line skating das Inlineskating; inlineskaten; **to go ~** inlineskaten gehen
in order to um ... zu
insecure unsicher
insert stecken
in spite of trotz
instead of (an)statt
instrument das Instrument, -e
intelligent intelligent
intend to vor·haben°; wollen
interested: to be ~ (in) (sich) interessieren (für)
interesting interessant
Internet das Internet; **to surf the ~** im Internet surfen; **to buy on the ~** übers Internet kaufen; **~ café** das Internetcafé, -s
interview das Interview, o
invite ein·laden°
is ist; **isn't it?** nicht?; nicht wahr? (*tag question*); **Your name is [Sandra], isn't it?** Du heißt [Sandra], nicht?

J

jacket die Jacke, n
jam die Marmelade
January der Januar
jeans die Jeans (*sg. and pl.*)
job der Beruf, -e; der Job, -s; die Stelle, -n; **to have a ~** berufstätig sein; **to have a temporary ~** jobben
jog joggen
jogging das Jogging
journalist der Journalist, -en, -en/die Journalistin, -nen
journey die Reise, -n
juice der Saft, ⸚e
July der Juli
June der Juni
just eben; erst; gerade

K

kilogram das Kilo(gramm)
kilometer der Kilometer, -
kind gut, nett; **be so ~** sei/seien Sie so gut/nett; **what ~ of person** was für ein Mensch

kindergarten der Kindergarten
kitchen die Küche, -n; **~ appliance** das Küchengerät, -e; **~ range** der Herd, -e
knee das Knie, -
knife das Messer, -
know (a fact) wissen°; **to ~ (be acquainted)** kennen°; **to get to ~** kennen lernen; **to ~ [German]** (Deutsch) können
known bekannt

L

lack fehlen
lady die Dame, -n; die Frau, -en
lake der See, -n
lamp die Lampe, -n
land das Land, ⸚er
language die Sprache, -n
large groß
last letzt; **~ night** gestern Abend; **to ~** dauern
late spät
later später; **until -/see you ~** bis später, tschüs, bis dann, bis bald
laugh lachen
laughable zum Lachen
laundry die Wäsche
law das Gesetz, -e; das Recht; **~ (field of study)** Jura (*no article*)
lawyer der Rechtsanwalt, ⸚e/die Rechtsanwältin, -nen
lay legen
lazy faul
lead führen
learn lernen
least: at ~ wenigstens
leave lassen°; weg·fahren°; ab·fahren°; verlassen°
lecture die Vorlesung, -en
left: on/to the ~ links
leg das Bein, -e
leisure time die Freizeit
lend leihen°
lesson die Stunde, -n; **piano ~** die Klavierstunde, -n
let lassen°
letter der Brief, -e
lettuce der (Kopf)salat, -e
library die Bibliothek, -en
lie liegen°; **to ~ around** herum·liegen°
life das Leben, -
lift heben°; **to ~ weights** Gewichte heben°
light (*adj.*) leicht; **~ (in color)** hell
like: would ~ to möchte; **to ~** gern haben; mögen; gefallen°; **What do**

you ~ to do? Was machst du gern?; **I ~ to swim.** Ich schwimme gern.; **How do you ~ the cheese?** Wie findest du den Käse?; **would you ~ to** hättest du Lust
likeable sympathisch
likewise ebenso; auch
limit die Grenze, -n
lip die Lippe, -n
listen: to ~ to music Musik hören
liter der Liter, -
literature die Literatur
little klein; wenig; **a ~** ein bisschen, ein wenig
live leben; wohnen
living room das Wohnzimmer, -
load: to ~ the dishwasher die Spülmaschine einräumen
located: to be ~ liegen°
long lang; lange; **a ~ time** lange; **how ~** seit wann
longer: no ~ nicht mehr
look: to ~ at an·sehen°, an·schauen; **to ~ like . . .** wie ... aus·sehen°; **to ~ for** suchen; **to ~ forward to** sich freuen auf (+ *acc.*); **to ~ through** durch·sehen°
lose verlieren°
lot: a ~ viel
lots of viel
loud laut
lounge around faulenzen
love die Liebe; **to ~** lieben
low niedrig
luck das Glück; **Good ~!** Viel Glück!; **to be lucky** Glück haben
lucky person der/die Glückliche (*noun decl. like adj.*)
lunch das Mittagessen; **for ~** zum Mittagessen; **to have ~** zu Mittag essen°
lunch meat die Wurst, ⸚e

M

machine die Maschine, -n
magazine die Zeitschrift, -en
major subject das Hauptfach, ⸚er
mail die Post
main Haupt-; **~ train station** der Hauptbahnhof, ⸚e
make machen
makeup: to put on ~ (sich) schminken
mama die Mama
man der Mann, ⸚er; **~!** Mensch!
manufacture her·stellen
many viele; **how ~** wie viele; **too ~** zu viele; **~ a** manch (-er, -es, -e)

map die Landkarte, -n
March der März
margarine die Margarine
market der Markt, ⁝e
marmalade die Marmelade
marriage die Heirat, -en; die Ehe, -n
married verheiratet; ~ **couple** das Ehepaar, -e
marry heiraten
math die Mathe
mathematics die Mathematik
matter aus·machen; **it doesn't ~** (es) macht nichts; **it doesn't ~ to [me]** es macht [mir] nichts aus; **What's the ~?** Was ist los?; Was hast du denn?
May der Mai
may dürfen°; **that ~ well be** das mag wohl sein; **~ I help you?** Bitte?
maybe vielleicht
meal das Essen
mean meinen; bedeuten; **What does that ~?** Was bedeutet das?; **that means** das heißt
meantime: in the ~ inzwischen
meanwhile inzwischen
meat das Fleisch
meat market die Metzgerei, -en
meet (sich) treffen°; kennen lernen; **I'm meeting friends.** Ich treffe mich mit Freunden.
member das Mitglied, -er
merchandise die Ware, -n
merry lustig
microwave oven der Mikrowelle, -n
milk die Milch
million die Million, -en
mind: to have in ~ vor·haben°
mineral water das Mineralwasser
minor subject das Nebenfach, ⁝er
minus (in subtraction) minus
minute die Minute, -n; **Just a ~, please!** Einen Moment, bitte!; Moment mal.
mirror der Spiegel, -
missing: to be ~ fehlen
modern modern
mom die Mutti, -s; die Mama
moment der Moment, -e; **at the ~** im Moment, zur Zeit
Monday der Montag
money das Geld; **out of ~** pleite
month der Monat, -e; **a ~ ago** vor einem Monat; **every ~** jeden Monat
mood: to be in the ~ Lust haben
more mehr; **no ~ . . .** kein ... mehr; **~ and ~** immer mehr; **~ or less**

mehr oder weniger; **not any ~** nicht mehr
morning der Morgen; **Good ~.** Guten Morgen.; **this ~** heute Morgen
mornings morgens
most meist; **~ of the people** die meisten Leute; **~ of the time** meistens
mostly meistens
mother die Mutter, ⁝
motorcycle das Motorrad, ⁝er
motto das Motto, -s
mountain der Berg, -e
mouth der Mund, ⁝er
movie der Film, -e; **~ theater** das Kino, -s
movies das Kino, -s; **to the ~** ins Kino
Mr. Herr
Mrs. Frau
Ms. Frau
much viel, **how ~** wie viel; **too ~** zu viel
multicultural(ly) multikulturell
music die Musik
musical das Musical, -s; (*adj.*) musikalisch
musician der Musiker, -/die Musikerin, -nen
must müssen°
mystery (novel or film) der Krimi, -s

N

name der Name, -ns, -n; **first ~** der Vorname, -ns, -n; **last ~** der Nachname, -ns, -n; **What is your ~?** Wie heißen Sie?; **to ~** nennen°; **Your ~ is [Mark], isn't it?** Du heißt [Mark], nicht?
named: to be ~ heißen°
narrate erzählen
native country die Heimat
natural(ly) klar; natürlich
nauseated: I feel ~. Mir ist schlecht.
near bei; **~by** in der Nähe, nah(e)
neck der Hals, ⁝e
need brauchen
neighbor der Nachbar, -n, -n/die Nachbarin, -nen
neighboring country das Nachbarland, ⁝er
nephew der Neffe, -n, -n
nervous nervös
neutral neutral
never nie
nevertheless trotzdem; doch
new neu; **What's ~?** Was gibt's Neues?
newspaper die Zeitung, -en

next nächst
nice nett; schön; **~ and warm** schön warm
niece die Nichte, -n
night die Nacht, ⁝e, **last ~** gestern Abend; **Good ~.** Gute Nacht.
nightclub das Nachtlokal, -e
night table der Nachttisch, -e
no nein; kein; nicht; **~ longer** nicht mehr; **~ more . . .** kein ... mehr
noisy laut
nonetheless jedoch
nonsense der Quatsch
noodles die Nudeln (*pl.*)
noon der Mittag, -e
no one niemand
north der Norden; **to the ~** nördlich
nose die Nase, -n
not nicht; **isn't that so?** nicht?; **~ at all** gar nicht; **~ any, no** kein; **~ bad** ganz gut; Es geht.; **~ only . . . but also . . .** nicht nur ... sondern auch ...
note die Notiz, -en; die Note, -n
notebook das Heft, -e
nothing nichts; **~ special** nichts Besonderes
notice bemerken, merken
novel der Roman, -e
November der November
now jetzt; nun; **~ and then** ab und zu
number die Zahl, -en; die Nummer, -n; **phone ~** die Telefonnummer
numeral die Zahl, -en
nurse der Krankenpfleger, -/die Krankenpflegerin, -nen; **~ (female only)** die Krankenschwester, -n
nursery school der Kindergarten, ⁝

O

obtain bekommen°; kriegen
occupation der Beruf, -e
occupied: to be ~ beschäftigt sein
occupy beschäftigen
ocean der Ozean, -e
October der Oktober
of von
off weg
office das Büro, -s
often oft
oh ach, ah; **~ I see** ach so; **~ my** o je; **~ well** na ja
OK okay (O.K.); ganz gut; **It's (not) ~.** Es geht (nicht).
old alt; **I'm [19] years ~.** Ich bin [19] Jahre alt. **How ~ are you?** Wie alt bist du?

on an; auf; ~ **account of** wegen
once einmal; mal; ~ **more** noch einmal; ~ **a week** einmal in der Woche
one (*pronoun*) man; ~ **another** einander; ~ **time** einmal
oneself selbst, selber
only nur; erst
open offen, geöffnet; **to** ~ auf·machen; öffnen
opera die Oper, -n
opinion die Meinung, -en; **What's your ~?** Was hältst du davon?; Was meinst du?
or oder
orange die Orange, -n; ~ **juice** der Orangensaft
order die Ordnung; **in** ~ in Ordnung; **to** ~ bestellen
other ander- (-er, -es, -e)
otherwise sonst; anders
out of aus
outside draußen; ~ **of** außerhalb (+ *gen.*)
over (**time**) vorbei; zu Ende; ~ (**task**) fertig; ~ (**position**) über
own (*adj.*) eigen

P

page die Seite, -n
pain der Schmerz, -en
pair das Paar, -e
pale blass
pants die Hose, -n
pantyhose die Strumpfhose, -n
papa der Papa
paper das Papier, - (**theme, essay**) die Arbeit, -en
paperback das Taschenbuch, ̈er
pardon: I beg your ~? Wie bitte?
parents die Eltern (*pl.*)
park der Park, -s
part der Teil, -e; **to play a ~** eine Rolle spielen
particular besonder-
particularly besonders
part-time work die Teilzeitarbeit
party die Party, -s; die Feier, -n; das Fest, -e; die Fete, -n; **at a ~** auf einem Fest; **to give a ~** ein Fest geben; **to go to a ~** auf ein Fest gehen
passive passiv
pay: to ~ for bezahlen; zahlen; **to ~ back** zurück·zahlen
peace der Frieden
pedestrian der Fußgänger, -/die Fußgängerin, -nen; ~ **zone** die Fußgängerzone, -n

pen der Kugelschreiber, - [der Kuli, -s (*colloq.*)]
pencil der Bleistift, -e
pen pal der Brieffreund, -e/die Brieffreundin, -nen
people die Leute (*pl.*); die Menschen (*pl.*); man
per pro
percent das Prozent
perhaps vielleicht
period der Punkt, -e
permit lassen°
permitted: to be ~ dürfen°
person der Mensch, -en, -en; die Person, -en
personal persönlich
persuade überzeugen
pharmacy die Apotheke, -n; **to the ~** in die Apotheke
philosophy die Philosophie
phone das Telefon, -e; ~ **number** die Telefonnummer, -n; **to ~** an·rufen
photo das Bild, -er; das Foto, -s
photograph das Bild, -er; das Foto, -s; **to ~** fotografieren
physics die Physik
piano das Klavier, -e; ~ **lesson** die Klavierstunde, -n; ~ **concerto** das Klavierkonzert, -e
pickle die saure Gurke, -n
pick up ab·holen
picnic das Picknick, -s
picture das Bild, -er
piece das Stück, -e
pill die Tablette, -n; die Pille, -n
pillow das Kissen, -
Ping-Pong das Tischtennis
pity: what a ~ schade
place der Platz, ̈e; die Stelle, -n; der Ort, -e; **to my ~** zu mir; **at my ~** bei mir
plan der Plan, ̈e; **to ~** vor·haben°; planen
plant die Pflanze, -n
plate der Teller, -
play das Theaterstück, -e; **to ~** spielen
please bitte; **to ~** gefallen°
pleased: to be ~ (**about**) sich freuen (über + *acc.*)
pleasure die Freude, -n; die Lust
plus (**in addition**) und
pocket die Tasche, -n
point der Punkt, -e
political(**ly**) politisch
political science die Politik(wissenschaft)
politician der Politiker, -/die Politikerin, -nen

politics die Politik
polo shirt das Polohemd, -e
poor arm; **You ~ thing!** Du Armer!/Du Arme!
pop concert das Popkonzert, -e
portion der Teil -e
portrait das Porträt, -s
position die Stelle, -n; der Arbeitsplatz, ̈e
possible möglich; **It's (not) ~.** Es geht (nicht).; **That would (not) be ~.** Das ginge (nicht).
postal code die Postleitzahl, -en
postcard die Postkarte, -n
poster das/der Poster, -
post office die Post; **to go to the ~** auf die *or* zur Post gehen
potato die Kartoffel, -n
pound das Pfund, -e
practical(**ly**) praktisch
prefer: I ~ to work. Ich arbeite lieber.
preparation die Vorbereitung, -en
prepare (**for**) (sich) vor·bereiten (auf + *acc.*)
prepared bereit; vorbereitet
prescribe verschreiben°
present das Geschenk, -e
pretty schön; ~ **pale** ganz schön blass
price der Preis, -e
private(**ly**) privat
probably wahrscheinlich
problem das Problem, -e
produce her·stellen, produzieren
product das Produkt, -e
profession der Beruf, -e
professor der Professor, -en/die Professorin, -nen
program das Programm, -e; **TV** *or* **radio ~** die Sendung, -en
proper richtig
proud(**ly**) stolz
psychology die Psychologie
pub die Bar, -s; die Kneipe, -n; die Gaststätte, -n; das Lokal, -e; die Wirtschaft; -en
public öffentlich; staatlich
pullover der Pulli, -s; der Pullover, -
punctual(**ly**) pünktlich
purse die Handtasche, -n
put legen; stellen; stecken; setzen; hängen

Q

quarter das Viertel, -; ~ **after one** Viertel nach eins; ~ **to two** Viertel vor zwei
question die Frage, -n

quick schnell
quiet ruhig; still; **Be ~!** Sei ruhig!
quite ziemlich; ganz

R

racism der Rassismus
radio das Radio, -s
railroad die Bahn, -en
rain der Regen; **to ~** regnen
raincoat der Regenmantel, ¨
range (kitchen) der Herd, -e
rare(ly) selten
rather ziemlich; **~ than** lieber als
raw material der Rohstoff, -e
read lesen°
ready fertig; bereit
realize merken
really wirklich; richtig; eigentlich
rear (*v.*) erziehen°
rearing die Erziehung
reason der Grund, ¨e; **for that ~**
    daher; darum; deshalb; deswegen;
    aus diesem Grund
receive bekommen°
recommend empfehlen°
red rot
refrigerator der Kühlschrank, ¨e
regards (closing in a letter) Herzliche
    Grüße, Viele Grüße
rehearsal die Probe, -n
relative der/die Verwandte (*noun decl.
    like adj.*)
remain bleiben°
remember (someone/something) sich
    erinnern (an + jemand/etwas)
rent die Miete, -n; **to ~** mieten;
    vermieten; aus·leihen°
repair reparieren
report der Bericht, -e; das Referat, -e;
    to ~ berichten
reporter der Reporter, -/die
    Reporterin, -nen
reservation: without ~ unbedingt
responsibility die Verantwortung, -en
responsible verantwortlich
restaurant das Restaurant, -s; die
    Gaststätte, -n; das Lokal, -e
return zurück·fahren°; zurück·gehen°;
    zurück·kommen°; **to ~ (something)**
    (etwas) zurück·geben
review die Kritik; **to ~ (schoolwork,
    etc.)** wiederholen
rich reich
ride: to ~ a bike mit dem Fahrrad
    fahren°, Rad fahren°
right das Recht, -e; **Is it all ~ with
    you?** Ist es dir recht?; **to be ~**

Recht haben; **you're ~** du hast
    Recht; **All ~!** Na, gut!; **that's ~**
    genau; richtig; **~ to** Recht (auf +
    acc.); **on/to the ~** rechts
ring klingeln
rinse spülen
river der Fluss, ¨e
roast beef der Rinderbraten
rock: ~ band die Rockband, -s;
    ~ music die Rockmusik;
    ~ musician der Rockmusiker,
    -/die Rockmusikerin, -nen
role die Rolle, -n
roll das Brötchen, -
Rollerblading das Rollerblading; **to
    go ~** Rollerblading gehen
romance (novel) der Liebesroman, -e
room das Zimmer, -
rug der Teppich, -e
run laufen°
running das Jogging

S

sad traurig
safe sicher
salad der Salat
salary das Gehalt, ¨er
same gleich; **It's all the ~ to me.** Das
    ist mir egal.
sandwich das [Wurst]Brot, -e
satisfied zufrieden
Saturday der Samstag; der Sonnabend;
    on ~ am Samstag
sausage die Wurst, ¨e
save (time, money, etc.) sparen
say sagen
scarf (for neck) das Halstuch, ¨er
scholarship das Stipendium, *pl.*
    Stipendien
school die Schule, -n
science die Wissenschaft, -en; die
    Naturwissenschaft, -en
scientist der Wissenschaftler, -/die
    Wissenschaftlerin, -nen
season die Jahreszeit, -en
seat der Platz, ¨e; **to ~ oneself** sich
    setzen°
secretary der Sekretär, -e/die
    Sekretärin, -nen
secure sicher
see sehen°; **~ you then/soon.** Bis
    dann/bald.
seem scheinen°
seldom selten
self: oneself, myself, itself, etc. selbst,
    selber
sell verkaufen

semester das Semester, -; **~ break** die
    Semesterferien (*pl.*)
seminar das Seminar, -e; **~ room** das
    Seminar, -e; **~ report/paper** die
    Seminararbeit, -en
send schicken
sentence der Satz, ¨e
September der September
serious ernst; schlimm; **Are you ~?** Ist
    das dein Ernst?
set setzen; **to ~ the table** den Tisch
    decken
several einige; mehrere
severe schlimm
shave (sich) rasieren
shine scheinen°
ship das Schiff, -e
shirt das Hemd, -en
shoe der Schuh, -e
shop das Geschäft, -e; der Laden, ¨;
    to ~ ein·kaufen
shopping: to go ~ ein·kaufen gehen
shopping bag die Einkaufstasche, -n
short kurz; **~ (people)** klein
shorts die Shorts (*pl.*), die kurzen
    Hosen
show zeigen
shower die Dusche, -n; **to ~** (sich)
    duschen
siblings die Geschwister (*pl.*)
sick krank
side die Seite, -n
similar ähnlich; gleich
simple einfach
simply einfach; eben
simultaneous(ly) gleich
since seit (*prep.*); da (*conj.* = **because**);
    ~ when seit wann; **~ then** seitdem
sing singen°
single einzeln
sister die Schwester, -n
sit sitzen°; **to ~ down** sich setzen
situated: to be ~ liegen°
ski der Ski, -er; **to ~** Ski laufen°, Ski
    fahren°
skier der Skiläufer, -/die Skiläuferin,
    -nen
skirt der Rock, ¨e
sleep schlafen°; **to ~ at [a friend's]
    house** bei [einem Freund] schlafen
slender schlank
slow(ly) langsam
small klein
smart intelligent
smell riechen°
smile (about) lächeln (über + acc.)
smoke der Rauch; **to ~** rauchen
snow der Schnee; **to ~** schneien

so so; also; **Isn't that ~?** Nicht?; **~ that** damit; **~ long.** Tschüs; **I believe ~.** Ich glaube schon/ja.

soccer der Fußball

society die Gesellschaft, -en

sock die Socke, -n

sofa das Sofa, -s

soft drink die Limonade, -n

soldier der Soldat, -en, -en/die Soldatin, -nen

some etwas; einige; manch (-er, -es, -e)

somehow irgendwie

someone jemand

something etwas/was; **~ like that** so was; **~ different/else** etwas anderes

sometimes manchmal

somewhat etwas

son der Sohn, ˍe

soon bald; **as ~ as** sobald

sorry: I'm ~ (es) tut mir Leid

south der Süden; **to the ~** südlich

space der Platz, ˍe

spaghetti die Spaghetti (*pl.*)

speak sprechen°; reden

spell buchstabieren; **How do you ~ that?** Wie schreibt man das?

spend (money) aus·geben°; **to ~ (time)** verbringen°; **to ~ the night** übernachten

spite: in ~ of trotz

split up auf·teilen

spoon der Löffel, -

sport der Sport; **to engage in sports** Sport treiben°

spot die Stelle, -n; der Punkt, -e

spring der Frühling

stand stehen°; **to ~ up** auf·stehen°; **to ~/put upright** stellen

standard German (das) Hochdeutsch

standard of living der Lebensstandard

state (in Germany) das Land, ˍer; **~ (in the U.S.A.)** der Staat, -en

state-owned staatlich

stay bleiben°; **to ~ at a hotel** im Hotel übernachten

steak das Steak, -s

step der Schritt, -e; die Stufe, -n

stepfather der Stiefvater, ˍ

stepmother die Stiefmutter, ˍ

stick (*v.*) stecken

still noch; immer noch; noch immer; doch

stomach der Magen

stomachache die Magenschmerzen (*pl.*)

store das Geschäft, -e; der Laden, ˍ

story die Geschichte, -n

stove (kitchen) der Herd, -e

straight gerade

straighten up auf·räumen

strange komisch; fremd

street die Straße, -n; **~car** die Straßenbahn, -en

stress der Stress

stressed gestresst

strike der Streik, -s; **to ~** streiken

stroll spazieren gehen

strong stark

student der Student, -en, -en/die Studentin, -nen

studies das Studium

study studieren; lernen; arbeiten; durch·arbeiten; **to ~ for a test** für eine Klausur lernen

stupid dumm

subject (academic) das Fach, ˍer

substantial wesentlich

subway die U-Bahn

such solch (-er, -es, -e); **~ a** so ein

suddenly plötzlich

suffer leiden°

suit (man's) der Anzug, ˍe; **(woman's) ~** das Kostüm, -e; **to ~** passen

summer der Sommer

sun die Sonne, -n

sunglasses die Sonnenbrille, -n

Sunday der Sonntag

sunny sonnig

super super

superficial oberflächlich

supermarket der Supermarkt, ˍe **to the ~** in den Supermarkt; **at the ~** im Supermarkt

supper das Abendessen; **for ~** zum Abendessen; **to have ~** zu Abend essen

supporter (of a team) der Fan, -s

supposed: to be ~ to sollen°

sure sicher; bestimmt; **(agreement) ~!** Natürlich!

surf surfen

sweater der Pulli, -s; der Pullover, -

swim schwimmen°

swimming: to go ~ schwimmen gehen°; **~ suit** der Badeanzug, ˍe; **~ trunks** die Badehose, -n

Swiss (*adj.*) Schweizer; **~ (person)** der Schweizer, -/die Schweizerin, -nen

Switzerland die Schweiz

T

table der Tisch, -e; **bedside/night ~** der Nachttisch, -e

tablet die Tablette, -n

table tennis das Tischtennis

take nehmen°; **~ along** mit·nehmen°

take off sich (*dat.*) [etwas] aus·ziehen°; **I take off my shoes** Ich ziehe mir die Schuhe aus.

talk sich unterhalten°; **to ~ (about)** reden (über); sprechen° (über + *acc.*/von)

tall (people) groß

task die Aufgabe, -n

taste schmecken; probieren

tea der Tee

teacher der Lehrer, -/die Lehrerin, -nen

telephone das Telefon, -e; **to ~** telefonieren; an·rufen°

telephone number die Telefonnummer, -n; **What is your ~?** Wie ist deine/Ihre Telefonnummer?

television das Fernsehen; **~ set** der Fernseher, -; **color ~** der Farbfernseher; **~ program** die Fernsehsendung, -en; **to watch ~** fern·sehen°

tell sagen; erzählen; **to ~ (about)** erzählen (über + *acc.*/von)

temperature die Temperatur, -en

tennis das Tennis

terrible schlimm; furchtbar; schrecklich

terrific toll; prima

test die Klausur, -en; die Prüfung, -en; **to take a ~** eine Klausur schreiben°; **to study for a ~** für eine Klausur lernen

than als (*after a comparison*)

thank danken; **~ you very much** danke sehr/schön

thanks danke; der Dank; **~ a lot, many ~** vielen Dank

that dass; jen- (er, -es, -e)

theater das Theater, -; **to go to the ~** ins Theater gehen; **~ play** das Theaterstück, -e; **movie ~** das Kino, -s

then dann; da; damals

there da; dort; dahin; **~ is/are** es gibt

therefore also; deshalb; daher; darum; deswegen

these diese

thin dünn, schlank

thing das Ding, -e; die Sache, -n

think denken°; meinen; **What do you ~?** Was meinst du? **What do you ~ of the cake?** Was hältst du von dem Kuchen?; **I don't ~ so.** Ich glaube nicht.

third das Drittel, -

thirst der Durst

thirsty: to be ~ Durst haben°
this dies (-er, -es, -e); **~ afternoon** heute Nachmittag
throat der Hals, ⸚e
Thursday der Donnerstag
thus also
ticket die Karte -n; **entrance ~** die Eintrittskarte; **train/bus ~** die Fahrkarte
tie: neck~ die Krawatte, -n
till bis
time die Zeit, -en; das Mal, -e; mal; **at that ~** damals; **at the same ~** zur gleichen Zeit; **for a long ~** lange; eine ganze Weile; **a short ~ ago** vor kurzem, neulich; **free ~** die Freizeit; **this ~** diesmal; **What ~ is it?** Wie viel Uhr ist es?/Wie spat ist es?; **At what ~?**; Um wie viel Uhr?; **Have a good ~!** Viel Spaß!
times mal; **[three] ~** [drei]mal
tired müde; kaputt (*colloq.*)
to an; auf, in; nach; zu
today heute; **What day is it ~?** Welcher Tag ist heute?
together zusammen
tolerant tolerant
tolerate leiden°
tomato die Tomate, -n
tomorrow morgen
tonight heute Abend
too zu; **me ~** ich auch; **~ little** zu wenig; **~ much** zu viel
tooth der Zahn, ⸚e; **to brush [my] teeth** [mir] die Zähne putzen
toothache die Zahnschmerzen (*pl.*)
tourist der Tourist, -en, -en/die Touristin, -nen
trade der Handel; **foreign ~** der Außenhandel
traffic der Verkehr
train der Zug, ⸚e; die Bahn; **~ station** der Bahnhof, ⸚e; **to go by ~** mit dem Zug/der Bahn fahren
transportation: means of ~ das Verkehrsmittel, -
travel fahren°; reisen; **to ~ by train** mit dem Zug fahren
tree der Baum, ⸚e
treat (to pay for someone) ein·laden°
trip die Reise, -n, die Fahrt, -en; die Tour, -en; **bike ~** die Radtour, -en
trousers die Hose, -n
true wahr
try versuchen; probieren
T-shirt das T-Shirt, -s
Tuesday der Dienstag
Tuesdays dienstags

turn: to have one's ~ dran sein; **it's your ~** du bist dran
TV das Fernsehen; **~ set** der Fernseher, -; **~ program** die Fernsehsendung, -en; **to watch ~** fern·sehen°
twice zweimal; **~ a month** zweimal im Monat
type: to ~ tippen
typical typisch

U

umbrella der Regenschirm, -e; der Schirm, -e
unappealing unsympathisch
unbelievable unglaublich
uncle der Onkel, -
under unter
understand verstehen°
undress (sich) aus·ziehen°; **I get undressed.** Ich ziehe mich aus.
unemployed arbeitslos
unfortunately leider
unfriendly unfreundlich
unification die Vereinigung
union die Gewerkschaft, -en
university die Universität, -en; die Uni, -s; **to attend a ~** an die Universität gehen; **at the ~** an der Universität
unmusical unmusikalisch
unpleasant unsympathisch
unsafe unsicher
until bis; **~ now** bisher; **~ later** bis später; tschüs; bis dann; bis bald
up: What's ~? Was ist los?
U.S.A. die USA (*pl.*); **to the ~** in die USA
use benutzen; gebrauchen

V

vacation der Urlaub; die Ferien (*pl.*); **~ trip** die Ferienreise, -n; **on/during ~** in Urlaub/in den Ferien; **to go on ~** in Urlaub/in die Ferien fahren°; **to be on ~** in Urlaub/in den Ferien sein°
vacuum der Staubsauger, -; **to ~** Staub saugen
various mehrere; verschieden
vase die Vase, -n
VCR der Videorecorder, -
vegetable das Gemüse, -
very sehr; ganz
video das Video, -s
video game das Videospiel, -e
video recorder der Videorecorder, -

visit der Besuch; **on a ~** zu Besuch; **to ~** besuchen
volleyball der Volleyball

W

wait (for) warten (auf)
walk der Spaziergang, ⸚e; **to take a ~** einen Spaziergang machen; **to go for a ~** spazieren gehen°
walking: to go ~ wandern/spazieren gehen°
wall die Wand, ⸚e; die Mauer, -n
want (to) wollen°
war der Krieg, -e; **world ~** der Weltkrieg, -e
wardrobe (closet) der Schrank, ⸚e
ware die Ware, -n
warm warm
was war
wash die Wäsche; **to ~** (sich) waschen°; **to ~ dishes** ab·waschen°; Geschirr spülen
watch die (Armband)uhr, -en; **to ~** an·sehen°; **to ~ TV** fern·sehen°
water das Wasser
water ski der Wasserki, -er; **to ~** Wasserski fahren°
way der Weg, -e; **on the ~** auf dem Weg; die Art
weak schwach
wear tragen°
weather das Wetter; **~ report** der Wetterbericht, -e; **What ~!** Was für ein Wetter!
Wednesday der Mittwoch
week die Woche, -n; **a ~ from [Monday]** [Montag] in acht Tagen; **a ~ ago** vor einer Woche
weekend das Wochenende; **on the ~** am Wochenende; **over the ~** übers Wochenende
weightlifting das Gewichtheben
weights die Gewichte (*pl.*); **to lift ~** Gewichte heben°
welcome: you're ~ bitte (sehr)
well also; gut; wohl; **I'm not ~.** Mir geht's schlecht; **~ (interjection)** na!, nun!; **~ now, oh ~** na
well known bekannt
west der Westen
western westlich
wet nass
what was; **~ kind (of), ~ a** was für (ein)
when wann; wenn; als
whenever wenn
where wo; **~ (to)** wohin; **~ do you come from?** Woher kommst du?

whether ob

which welch (-er, -es, -e)

while während; die Weile; **~ chatting** beim Chatten

white weiß

white-collar worker der/die Angestellte (*noun decl. like adj.*)

who wer

whole ganz

whom wen (*acc. of* wer); wem (*dat. of* wer)

whose wessen

why warum

willingly gern

win gewinnen°

wind der Wind

window das Fenster, -

windsurfing: to go ~ windsurfen gehen°

windy windig

wine der Wein, -e; **red ~** der Rotwein; **white ~** der Weißwein

winter der Winter

wish der Wunsch, ⸚e; **to ~** wünschen; **I ~ I had . . .** Ich wollte, ich hätte ...

with mit, **~ it** damit, **~ me** mit mir, **to live ~ a family** bei einer Familie wohnen

woman die Frau, -en

wonder das Wunder; **no ~** kein Wunder

woods der Wald, ⸚er

word das Wort, ⸚er

word processing die Textverarbeitung; **~ program** das Textverarbeitungsprogramm; **to do ~** mit Textverarbeitungsprogrammen arbeiten

work die Arbeit; **to do the ~** die Arbeit machen; arbeiten; **to ~ through** durch·arbeiten; **It doesn't ~.** Es geht nicht.; **to be off from ~** frei haben; **It works.** Es geht.

worker der Arbeiter, -/die Arbeiterin, -nen; der Arbeitnehmer, -/die Arbeitnehmerin, -nen

working (gainfully employed) berufstätig

workout das Fitnesstraining; **to work out** Fitnesstraining machen

workplace der Arbeitsplatz, ⸚e

world die Welt, -en; **~ war** der Weltkrieg, -e

worry die Sorge, n; **to ~ about** sich Sorgen machen (um)

would würde; **~ like** möchte; **How ~ it be?** Wie wär's?; **~ you like to**
hättest du Lust; **~ have** hätte; **~ be able to** könnte

write schreiben°; **to ~ to someone** jemandem/an jemanden schreiben; **to ~ down** auf·schreiben

writer der Schriftsteller, -/die Schriftstellerin, -nen

wrong falsch; **What's ~?** Was ist los?; **What is ~ with you?** Was hast du?

X

xenophobia der Ausländerhass

Y

year das Jahr, -e; **a ~ ago** vor einem Jahr

yellow gelb

yes ja

yesterday gestern

yet noch; schon; **not ~** noch nicht

young jung

Z

Zip code die Postleitzahl, -en

Index

Permissions and Credits

Projekt Stuttgart; p. 289: Steinsieker; p. 295: Berliner Universitätsbuchhandlung; p. 298: Ristorante Pizzeria Molino; p. 307: courtesy EMS; p. 312: Schweizer Bankverein/Swiss Bank Corporation, Basel; p. 316: Heimet-Chörli Basel; p. 321: Gernots; p. 324: Sportpark am Kreuzeck; p. 335: Gasthof zum goldenen Sternen; p. 336: Blick; p. 346: SWR Studio Tübingen; p. 348: Universität Tübingen; p. 349: Burgtheater; p. 349: Berliner Ensemble; p. 358: Haus der Geschichte; p. 379: Focus 2/1998, Quelle: DataConcept; p. 396: Focus 10/2000; p. 398: Hörzu, 7/8/98; p. 402: Beck für Die Zeit; p. 408: Jack Wohl, USA. © Bulls; p. 424: Die Welt; p. 425: Geox; p. 425: ecco; p. 425: Die Welt; p. 429: HYPERLINK "www.strellson. com" www.strellson.com ; p. 430: © Manfred Papen; p. 434: courtesy Foyer; p. 435: Deutsche Bahn AG.

Photos

Page 1: David R. Frazier Photolibray; p. 5: David R. Frazier Photolibray; p. 8: Gianni Dagli Orti/Corbis; p. 8: Beryl Goldberg; p. 8: Ulrike Welsch; p. 10: Stuart Cohen; p. 10: David R. Frazier Photolibrary; p. 13: David R. Frazier Photolibrary; p. 23: David R. Frazier Photolibrary; p. 25: David R. Frazier Photolibrary; p. 30: Beryl Goldberg; p. 34: © 2003 H. Mark Weidman; p. 41: Ulrike Welsch; p. 42: Ulrike Welsch; p. 42: Ulrike Welsch; p. 42: Ulrike Welsch; p. 42: Ulrike Welsch; p. 47: Stuart Cohen; p. 51: David R. Frazier Photolibrary; p. 56: David R. Frazier Photolibrary; p. 65: Stuart Cohen; p. 73: Ulrike Welsch; p. 78: Bildarchiv Foto Marburg/Art Resource; p. 88: Robert van der Hilst/Corbis; p. 94: David R. Frazier Photolibrary; p. 98: David R. Frazier Photolibrary; p. 101: David R. Frazier Photolibrary; p. 101: Ulrike Weslch; p. 103: Beryl Goldberg; p. 106: Ulrike Welsch; p. 108: David R. Frazier Photolibrary; p. 113: David R. Frazier Photolibrary; p. 127: Beryl Goldberg; p. 129: David R. Frazier Photolibrary; p. 131: Ulrike Welsch; p. 133: Ulrike Welsch; p. 137: Kathy Squires; p. 139: Ulrike Welsch; p. 145: Ulrike Welsch; p. 145: Ulrike Welsch; p. 161: Beryl Goldberg; p. 164: Neil Beer/Corbis; p. 166: Kathy Squires; p. 168: David R. Frazier Photolibrary; p. 170: David R. Frazier Photolibrary; p. 172: Kathy Squires; p. 178: David R. Frazier Photolibrary; p. 193: David R. Frazier Photolibrary; p. 198: Stuart Cohen; p. 201: Beryl Goldberg; p. 204: Beryl Goldberg; p. 207: Beryl Goldberg; p. 210: David R. Frazier Photolibrary; p. 213: David R. Frazier Photolibrary; p. 218: Beryl Goldberg; p. 222: Bildarchiv Huber; p. 234: Beryl Goldberg; p. 237: Kathy Squires; p. 231: Kobal Collection; p. 239: Beryl Goldberg; p. 241: David R. Frazier Photolibrary; p. 244: Ulrike Welsch; p. 247: David R. Frazier Photolibrary; p. 249: Beryl Goldberg; p. 251: Ulrike Welsch; p. 253: Beryl Goldberg; p. 255: Beryl Goldberg; p. 261: Ulrike Welsch; p. 265: David R. Frazier Photolibrary; p. 268: Balch Institute; p. 277: Beryl Goldberg; p. 287: Beryl Goldberg; p. 291: David R. Frazier Photolibrary; p. 292: Ulrike Welsch; p. 306: Beryl Goldberg; p. 308: Roger Antrobus/Corbis; p. 315: Steven Saks/Index Stock; p. 316: Weltrekords/Hans Schneeberger/Bern; p. 320: G. Anderson/Corbis; p. 323: Robin Prange/Corbis; p. 326: Keystone Press AG Archiv; p. 331: Lindsay Hebberd/Corbis; p. 343: Beryl Goldberg; p. 347: German Information Center; p. 347: Kathy Squires; p. 350: Sipa Press; p. 352: Nelly Rau-Haring/Ipol, Inc.; p. 355: Deutsches Historisches Museum, Berlin; p. 356: Beryl Goldberg; p. 357: Jon Hicks/Corbis; p. 360: dpa/Ipol, Inc.; p. 361: Wolfgang Kaehler/Corbis; p. 366: dpa/Ipol, Inc.; p. 371: Beryl Goldberg; p. 378: Beryl Goldberg; p. 381: Kathy Squires; p. 383: Ulrike Welsch; p. 386: Stuart Cohen; p. 388: dpa/Ipol, Inc.; p. 391: Corbis; p. 400: Ulrike Welsch; p. 405: David R. Frazier Photolibrary; p. 413: Ulrike Welsch; p. 415: Ulrike Welsch; p. 419: Beryl Goldberg; p. 422: Ulrike Welsch.

Illustrations

Anna Veltfort